Southern Baptist Preaching Yesterday

SOUTHERN BAPTIST PREACHING YESTERDAY

COMPILERS

R. EARL ALLEN &
JOEL GREGORY

BROADMAN PRESS
NASHVILLE, TENNESSEE

Unless otherwise stated, all Scripture quotations are from the *King James Version of the Bible*.

Scripture quotations marked RSV are from the *Revised Standard Version of the Bible*, copyrighted 1946, 1952, © 1971, 1973.

Scripture quotations marked ASV are from the *American Standard Version of the Bible*.

Scripture quotations marked Phillips are from *The New Testament in Modern English* by J. B. Phillips, reprinted with permission of Macmillan Publishing Co., Inc. © 1958, 1960, 1972.

Scripture quotations marked Williams are from the *Williams New Testament, the New Testament in the Language of the People,* by Charles B. Williams. Copyright © 1937, 1966, 1986 by Holman Bible Publishers. Used by permission.

Library of Congress Cataloging-in-Publication Data

Southern Baptist preaching yesterday / R. Earl Allen and Joel Gregory, compilers.
     p.   cm.
   Includes bibliographical references.
   ISBN 0-8054-5738-0
   1. Southern Baptist Convention—Sermons.   2. Baptists—Sermons.
3. Sermons, American.   I. Allen, R. Earl.   II. Gregory, Joel C.,
1948-
BX6333.S596S67   1991
252'.06132—dc20   90-28704
                                                                CIP

To the Earl Allen Family
Lovers of God
Servants of Christ
Friends to Preachers

R. EARL ALLEN
1922-1990
"He being dead yet speaketh."

Preface

Southern Baptist Preaching Yesterday and its earlier counterpart, Southern Baptist Preaching Today (1987) were born in the heart of R. Earl Allen at least a decade ago. I am grateful that he invited me to join in these ventures. As I write this Preface by myself, I am saddened and gladdened, saddened that Earl is gone but gladdened about where he has gone—to be with his Lord. While this book was being completed, he was called to his eternal home (September 11, 1990).

R. Earl Allen was a pastor-preacher-writer-teacher with few peers. For thirty-four years he pastored the Rosen Heights Baptist Church, Fort Worth, Texas, and wrote close to thirty published books. He was a master at preparing convicting, forceful sermons. He was an adjunct professor at Southwestern Baptist Theological Seminary, where he influenced many preachers toward pulpit excellence.

He and I, along with the staff of Broadman Press, and the counsel of professors of preaching from our Southern Baptist seminaries, had selected fifty-nine choice preachers—all deceased. I included Earl after his departure because his preaching merits his being in these pages.

This "roll call of the saints" encompasses pastors, evangelists, seminary and college presidents, denominational executives, Southern Baptist Convention presidents, a congressman of the United States, a governor of Texas, and a corporation president.

The late H. C. Brown, Jr., wrote in 1959:

> From great preachers of the past I sought illustrations to share with my students. In searching for materials I made the sad discovery that many capable men had failed to leave adequate information concerning their homiletic methods. Perhaps if someone had encouraged them, they would have left valuable data for future generations.[1]

Earl Allen and I encountered the same dilemma in compiling this volume. Many of these preachers left a book or books—or at least available transcripts of their sermons. A number had biographies written about them, usually after their deaths, and a certain amount of information was recorded about their ministries. But, by and large, there is a dearth of data as to how they prepared and preached.

Dr. Allen (I would rather call him Earl) and I made every possible effort to gather material on their methods of preparation and pulpit presentation. We found innumerable books praising certain preachers for their Christian influence, their particular specialties in ministry—whether preaching, teaching, organizing, and related skills—but we were able to put together articles concerning their methodology on only about two-thirds of these preachers. The majority have not written down their *modus operandi* for posterity.

Many readers may ask, "Why didn't you include so and so?" From hundreds of preachers, whom do you include? In one volume you cannot do justice.

These men and their preaching need to be preserved for Southern Baptist and evangelical enlightenment. As we Southern Baptists better understand our roots, perhaps we can carry out the Great Commission and our own Bold Mission Thrust.

Being a Baptist—and even more so a Southern Baptist—carries a heritage for which a host of men and women have been willing to die. May these preachers remind us of the high calling, now forsaken and spurned by many. May they cause us to recall the admonition of Charles Haddon Spurgeon, "If God calls you to preach, do not deign to be a king."

Every preacher in this book—whether Truett, Robertson, Havner, Sampey, Scarborough, Latimer, Boyce, Hays, Webb, you name them—has a major factor in common. They are remembered for preaching Jesus Christ and Him crucified, buried, risen, ascended, and coming again. Yes, their methods were diversified. All were doing their best as God gifted them.

I quote H. C. Brown once again:

> Three major purposes have inspired the preparation of this work. One has been to record for future generations the personal homiletic methods of outstanding contemporary men [in our case, men of the past]. A second has been to inspire young ministerial students to find the best qualities in these men and to seek to develop like qualities in themselves. A third pur-

pose has been to encourage mature ministers to test themselves in comparison with these twenty-two men [in our present work, sixty].[2]

As you read and study these sermons, you will sit in heavenly places with Christ Jesus. May this book motivate you all the more to:

Preach the Word!

NOTES

1. H. C. Brown, Jr., Compiler, *Southern Baptist Preaching* (Nashville: Broadman Press, 1959), viii.
2. Ibid., ix.

Acknowledgments

Our debt is immense. We have endeavored in every instance to give proper credit where it is due. In the section on "How They Prepared and Preached," some information was input by the compilers and editors from personal knowledge. We have striven to document credit even where public domain material is used. In several cases, we could not contact publishing companies mainly because they have not existed for years.

In addition, the source for every sermon is included. We are deeply indebted to the staff of the Historical Commission of the Southern Baptist Convention, Nashville, for its invaluable assistance, especially Dr. Lynn May, Executive Director, Bill Sumners, Director of the Southern Baptist Historical Library and Archives, and Mrs. Pat Brown, Librarian. We cannot sufficiently thank the Dargan Research Library personnel of the Baptist Sunday School Board, Nashville, particularly Howard Gallimore, Manager, Pat Huddleston, Research Librarian, and Ray Minardi, Archivist.

When we were deciding on the preachers to include here, we asked the opinions of some preaching professors of our seminaries, who also suggested certain professors late of their ranks. We thank all of our seminaries, and we are grateful to Baptist state papers from which we have quoted.

I could not release this book without thanking my secretary at Travis Avenue Baptist Church, Fort Worth, Mrs. Jo Ann Morgan, and my research assistant, Steve Harmon, a doctoral student at Southwestern and member of the Travis Avenue staff. The Allen family, especially his widow Joyce, thank Dr. Allen's secretary of thirty-two years, Mrs. Barbara Brian.

We also acknowledge the encouragement and help of the editors and staff of Broadman Press of the Baptist Sunday School Board, Nashville,

Johnnie C. Godwin, Vice-president of General Publishing. A number of these sermons and materials are from Broadman books (or the Sunday School Board before Broadman's inception in 1934). Let me note that the sermons are printed exactly as they appeared originally from the standpoint of style. Until recent years, for instance, the Sunday School Board did not cap the pronouns of Deity in keeping with the King James Version. Double thanks.

We offer our thanks to the following doctoral theses:

E. E. Lacy, "A History of Representative Southern Baptist Preaching from 1895 to the First World War," Th.D., 1960, Southwestern Baptist Theological Seminary;

J. Dee Cates, "B. H. Carroll: The Man and His Ethics," Th.D., 1962, Southwestern Baptist Theological Seminary;

Austin B. Tucker, "Monroe Elmon Dodd and His Preaching," Th.D., 1971, Southwestern Baptist Theological Seminary;

C. Ferris Jordan, "Thomas Treadwell Eaton: Pastor, Editor, Controversialist," Th.D., 1965, New Orleans Baptist Theological Seminary;

George Alexander Jones, "Richard Fuller and His Preaching," Ph.D., 1953, The Southern Baptist Theological Seminary.

John M. Langlois, "A Study of Roland Q. Leavell's Concept of Evangelism," Th.D., 1972, New Orleans Baptist Theological Seminary.

Following are the sources of the sermons themselves:

ADAMS, THEODORE F., "The Home of Tomorrow"—from John L. Hill, Comp., *Faith of Our Fathers* (Nashville, TN: Broadman Press, 1942), 35-45 (originally preached on "The Baptist Hour"). ALLEN, R. EARL, "Blessed Bequests"—from unpublished sermon donated by Mrs. R. Earl (Joyce) Allen. ANGELL, C. ROY, "The Interrupted Sermon"—from Angell, *Baskets of Silver* (Broadman, 1955), 118-128. BASSETT, WALLACE, "A Star at Midnight"—from Bassett, *A Star at Midnight* (Broadman, 1942), 117-122 (sermon preached the Sunday after Bassett experienced "a great sorrow"). BOYCE, JAMES PETIGRU, "Christ Receiving and Eating with Sinners"—from Timothy George, Comp., *James Petigru Boyce: Selected Writings* (Nashville: Broadman, 1989), 77-84. BROADUS, JOHN A., "Preachers and Preaching"—from Broadus, *"Follow Thou Me"* (Broadman, 1919), 229-241 (preached to a group of pastors at the First Baptist Church, Nashville). BROWN, FRED FERNANDO, "Her Central Message"—from Hill, Ed., *Faith of Our Fathers*, 71-78 (originally preached on "The Baptist Hour"). BROWN, H. C., JR., "The Walk of the Pharisee"—from Brown, Comp., *Southwestern Sermons* (Broadman, 1960), 36-42.

CAMPBELL, R. C., "Baptists and the Bible"—from Campbell, *Keeping the Foundation* (Broadman, 1946), 158-174. CARROLL, B. H., "Pressing Toward the Mark"—from Carroll, *The River of Life* (Nashville: The Sunday School Board of the Southern Baptist Convention, 1928), 54-66 (preached at Cleburne, TX, "on the occasion of a rally in the interest of Christian education"). CAUTHEN, BAKER JAMES, "Rejoice"—from Cauthen, *Beyond Call* (Broadman, 1973), 59-61. CLINARD, H. GORDON, "Planting Trees You Will Never Sit Under"—from Clinard, *Planting Trees You Will Never Sit Under* (Abilene, TX: Hardin Simmons U., 1977), 93-100. Used by permission. COOPER, OWEN, "A Call for a Theology of Non-ordained"—edited text of a message delivered to the 1983 Louisiana State Evangelism Conference (appeared in the *Baptist Message*, February 10, 1983). Used by permission. CRAIG, W. MARSHALL, "This I Do for Christ's Sake"—from an unpublished sermon courtesy of R. Earl Allen. CRANFILL, J. B., "A Man in Hell"—from J. F. Lowe, Ed., *The Southern Baptist Pulpit* (Philadelphia: The American Baptist Publication Society, 1895), 281-293. DARGAN, EDWIN CHARLES, "Watchman, What of the Night?"—from Dargan, *The Changeless Christ* (Sunday School Board, 1918), 46-61. DIXON, A. C., "Hallelujah"—from Dixon, *Through Night to Morning* (Grand Rapids, MI: Baker Book House, 1969), 207-216. Used by permission. DODD, M. E., "Democracy of the Saints"—booklet of sermon preached at the First Baptist Church, Shreveport, LA. Used by permission. DRUMWRIGHT, HUBER L., JR., "An Unexpected Conversion"—from H. C. Brown, Comp., *Southwestern Sermons* (Broadman, 1960), 66-71. EATON, T. T., "Conscience in Missions"—Eaton, *Conscience in Missions* (Louisville, KY: Baptist Book Concern, 1893), 1-26. FORD, W. HERSCHEL, "Sanctification, the Most Misunderstood Doctrine in the Bible"—from Ford, *Simple Sermons on the Great Christian Doctrines* (Broadman, 1951), 79-89. FULLER, RICHARD, "Personal Religion, Its Aids and Hindrances"—from Fuller, *Personal Religion, Its Aids and Hindrances* (Baltimore, MD: Innes & Co., Book Printers, 1873), 1-16. GAMBRELL, J. B., "Three Steps Up"—from Lowe, Ed., *The Southern Baptist Pulpit,* 180-190 (preached in Trinity M. E. Church, Washington, D. C., during the Jubilee Session of the Southern Baptist Convention, 1895). GIDEON, VIRTUS E., "The Infinity of Little"—from Brown, *Southwestern Sermons,* 101-106. GREY, J. D., "A Christian in Spite of Everything"—from H. C. Brown, Jr., Comp., *Southern Baptist Preaching* (Broadman, 1959), 77-82. HAVNER, VANCE, "Look Who's Here!"—from Havner, *Playing Marbles with Diamonds* (Grand Rapids, MI: Baker Book House, 1985), 43-50. Used by permission. HAYS, BROOKS, untitled President's message at the Southern Baptist Convention, Houston, May 20, 1958, courtesy of SBC Executive

Committee. HUDGINS, W. DOUGLAS, "Look to the Rock"—from booklet published by First Baptist Church, Jackson, MS, 1963. Used by permission. JAMES, E. S., "The Invincible Gospel"—from booklet published by First Baptist Church, Vernon, TX, courtesy of the James family. JOHNSON, C. OSCAR, "A Light in the Valley"—from Brown, *Southern Baptist Preaching*, 106-111. LATIMER, LEON MOBLEY, "Divinely Commissioned"—from sermon delivered at the Georgia Baptist Convention, Augusta, GA, December 6, 1927, courtesy of Loulie Latimer Owens. LAWRENCE, J. B., "The Secret of Christian Living"—Lawrence, *The Peril of Bread* (Broadman, 1945), 143-157. LEAVELL, ROLAND Q., "Evangelism Is Essential in Kingdom Building and Christian Living"—from Leavell, *Evangelism: Christ's Imperative Commission* (Broadman, 1951), 22-34. LEE, ROBERT G., "The Constant Call of Christ's Cross"—from Lee, *Pulpit Pleadings* (Broadman, 1945), 82-98. MATTHEWS, C. E., "Heaven"—from Matthews, *Life's Supreme Decision*, (Zondervan, 1942), 119-127. Used by permission. McDANIEL, GEORGE W., "An Analogy of Prayer"—from *Seeing the Best* (New York: Doran, 1923), 103-113. MEIGS, PAUL A., "The Object of a New Testament Church"—from John Bisagno, Kenneth Chafin, and others, Comps., *How to Win Them* (Broadman, 1970), 101-110. MOORE, H. GUY, "Intruder in the Heavens"—from Brown, *Southern Baptist Preaching*, 141-149. MOORE, WALTER L., "What I Have I Give"—H. C. Brown, Jr., *More Southern Baptist Preaching* (Nashville: Broadman, 1963), 72-76. MULLINS, EDGAR YOUNG, "The Irreducible Christ: In Christian History"—from Mullins, *Christianity at the Cross Roads* (Sunday School Board, 1924), 263-276. NEFF, PAT M., "Christian Education"—from Hill, *Faith of Our Fathers*, 46-54 (originally preached on "The Baptist Hour"). NEWTON, LOUIE D., "Southern Baptists—Yesterday, Today, and Tomorrow"—from Presidential address at SBC, St. Louis, May 7, 1947, courtesy of Executive Committee, SBC. PEARCE, J. WINSTON, "We Do Well to Conform"—from Pearce, *Seven First Words of Jesus* (Broadman, 1966), 29-44. PETTIGREW, W. R., "The Rending of the Veil"—from the Convention Sermon at the SBC, 1948, courtesy of Executive Committee, SBC. POLLARD, RAMSEY, "Undivided Heart"—from *Stoop and Drink* (Fort Worth, TX: Radio and Television Commission, SBC, 1955), 34-42 (originally preached on "The Baptist Hour"). POWELL, W. F., "Love Is the Answer"—from "The Baptist Hour," Radio Committee of the SBC, Atlanta, GA, 1944. ROBERTS, RAY E., "The Unpaid Debt of Southern Baptists"—from Porter Routh, *Waiting in the Wings* (Broadman, 1978), 83-89. ROBERTSON, A. T., "Good Out of Ill"—from Robertson, *Paul's Joy in Christ* (Broadman, 1959), 40-50. SAMPEY, JOHN R., "Where Are the Righteous Dead?"—from Sampey, *Ten*

Vital Messages (Nashville: Broadman, 1946), 101-110. SCAR-BOROUGH, L. R., "The Tears of Jesus"—from *The Tears of Jesus* (New York: Doran, 1922), 13-24. SEGLER, FRANKLIN M., "Grace Abounding"—from Brown, *Southwestern Sermons,* 178-183. STORER, JAMES WILSON, "A New Heaven and a New Earth"—from H. C. Brown, Jr., *More Southern Baptist Preaching* (Broadman, 1964), 115-120. THORN, F. B., "True Greatness"—from Thorn, *The Higher Path* (Grand Rapids, MI: Zondervan, 1937), 125-134. Used by permission. TRUETT, GEORGE W., "Baptists and Religious Liberty"—from Powhatan W. James, Comp., *Truett Memorial Series: The Inspiration of Ideals* (Sunday School Board, 1928), 85-111 (preached from the steps of the Capitol, Washington, D.C., May, 1920). VAUGHT, W. O., JR., "Passing Through the Midst of Them"—from Brown, *More Southern Baptist Preaching,* 121-131. WEBB, PERRY F., SR.—from Webb, *Doves in the Dust* (Broadman, 1953), 47-55. WHITE, K. OWEN, "The Great Door and the Many Adversaries"—from booklet published by Metropolitan Baptist Church, Washington, D.C. Used by permission. WHITE, W. R., "Around the Corner"—from White, *The Royal Road to Life* (Broadman, 1938), 31-39. WILLIAMS, J. HOWARD, "Love in Action"—from Brown, *Southern Baptist Preaching,* 221-227. YATES, KYLE M., "From Doubt to Certainty"—from Yates, *Preaching from the Psalms* (Broadman, 1948), 24-33.

Contents

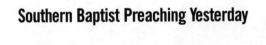

Southern Baptist Preaching Yesterday

PART I
The Sermons

Theodore F. Adams
The Home of Tomorrow

Matthew 7:24-25

As we come to the last of our three talks together about the home, I must thank you again for all your messages of appreciation and interest. The home is so basic in life. It is one enterprise in which we must succeed, and with Christ's help, we can.

The other day I watched a mason from my study window as he began building a house next to mine. He took several hours and infinite pains to get the corner started right. Every line had to be true and he painstakingly tested every angle with square and level. It took time, but that foundation was essential if the rest of the house was to be right.

In the building of a life or a home, we think of Christ as "The chief corner stone" on which every part must be "fitly framed together." The writer of Proverbs says, "The house of the righteous shall stand," and we share his faith as we build our home on Christ. "Other foundation can no man lay," that will be adequate for these testing times.

You remember the parable with which Jesus closed the Sermon on the Mount. He describes the house of the wise man and says, "The rain descended, and the floods came, . . . and beat upon that house; and it fell not: for it was founded upon a rock." So our homes, if they are to endure, must be founded upon the rock of faith. John Oxenham puts this thought into verse.

> The cornerstone in truth is laid,
> The guardian walls of honor made,
> The rock of faith is built above,
> The fire upon the hearth is love,

25

> Though rains descend and loud winds call,
> This happy home shall never fall.

The homes of tomorrow are in the making today. This fact is vital, both to the church and to the state. You will be reminded of this as you listen to the other speakers in future "Baptist Hour" broadcasts. Was it not former President Garfield who said, "The sanctity of marriage and the family relations are the foundation of American life"?

None of us can evade our share of responsibility for the homes of tomorrow. You young people listening in may not be married as yet, but your future husbands and wives are living now, waiting for you. Perhaps you have already met, perhaps not, but the very fact challenges you to live a life worthy of the love and home that someday will be yours.

You who are already married—what is your home to be in the days to come? The ideals and attitudes you cherish now will have much to do with that. Are you making Christ the cornerstone of your home, the guide in your life together, the Lord of your own life? With a future so unknown, how dare you go on without him? Can you and your life partner say together with all your hearts—

> In hope that sends a shining ray
> Far down the future's broad'ning way,
> In peace that only thou canst give,
> With thee, O Master, let me live.

Parents—what of you? So much depends on you as you rear your children and prepare them for homes of their own. What contribution are you making through your children to the homes of tomorrow? Dr. Carey Myers emphasizes your importance when he says that in your hands rests the married happiness of the next generation. You largely determine the child's attitudes, habits, ideals, and expectations. You are the ones who, with the help of the church, and the school, must develop in the next generation such qualities as integrity, restraint, honor, concern for others, a sense of fair play, the ability to face one's difficulties with a smile, getting one's way by fair means, tolerance, and good-will. All of these qualities are needed in the homes of tomorrow, and they must be taught and caught in the homes of today.

Who of us is great enough alone for such a responsibility! Those who bear it best are those who take God's help in it all. One of the leading ministers of our day bears this testimony to what his home gave to him.

He says, "The things that make for happiness in the home are the things that make for happiness everywhere. Only more so, because the home is the most profound of all human relationships. There . . . we give and forgive, bear and forbear, and so learn the fine art of living together. It is in the home we are emotionally conditioned—and that decides what we are to be, whether we are to live by faith or by fear. If I am a minister of religion, it is because my mother was not only a fine scholar, but one who lived by faith and prayer. My earliest memory of her is hearing her pray—hearing my name in her prayer—when she did not know I heard. She lifted my little life on the wings of prayer and gave it to God—and that consecration abides."

What are you parents giving your children for their tomorrow? What are you building into their lives that will endure? What memories are you giving them that will guide their lives, come what may? Dare you give them less than the highest? Give them, above all else, love at its best, your own love, the love of Christ, the love of God, and all that is good.

Recent studies help in predicting the success two young people can expect in the building of a home. Professors Burgess and Cottrell of the University of Chicago in their book, *Predicting Success and Failure in Marriage,* combine their own studies with those of a number of others in a very interesting table of factors that have been found in actual experience to contribute to success in marriage. Let me give you a number of them—and remember these are sociologists, not ministers, speaking.

1. Length of acquaintance—two or more years.
2. Age at marriage—husband twenty-two and over, wife twenty and over.
3. Close attachment and lack of conflict with parents.
4. Church attendance two to four times a month.
5. Engagement of six months or more.
6. Similar family background.
7. Happiness in childhood.
8. Good health.
9. A religious marriage service.
10. Parents happily married.
11. Religious training at home.
12. Adequate sex instruction.
13. Many friends before marriage.
14. Sunday School attendance after eighteen years of age.

Parents and children alike will do well to consider these important factors as a guide in choosing and being a life partner.

After the home is established, other problems must be faced. Let me give you a number of suggestions. We might call them Practical Rules for Success in Marriage:

1. Maintain your personal attractiveness. This is important for both husband and wife.

2. Eliminate needless irritants and sources of antagonism. Stop the little annoying things that get on each other's nerves, and also the habit of criticizing or joking about each other in public in such a way as to embarrass or make one feel inferior.

3. Do not cherish feelings of resentment. Forgive and forget. Don't keep bringing up past troubles that have been settled once.

4. Keep looking for joyful ways to do things together. Keep the spirit of courtship and romance. Don't neglect each other because children come. Your ties will last long after they have left home.

5. Be loyal. Don't talk about faults or troubles to oursiders. If you need help, talk to your pastor or doctor or some trusted friend or adviser.

6. Let neither try to dominate the other. Respect each other's personality, convictions, and sincerity.

7. Remember the importance of the little courtesies of life.

8. Don't keep wondering what would have happened if you had married someone else. Such daydreams do no good.

9. Be partners in every sense of the word. Cultivate common interests and share all your joys and problems. Always put the other's happiness first.

10. Don't both get mad at the same time. Learn to talk things over at the right time and place. Expect to disagree sometimes, but resolve to love always. Learn to give in and to admit when you are wrong. The first one to do this usually wins in the end, anyway.

11. Don't try to get your way by unfair means, such as getting mad, crying, sulking, and other childish tricks. The right way out is a "reconciliation in which both gain, rather than a mere compromise in which both feel they have lost."

12. Remember the impulse to criticize others often comes from dissatisfaction with yourself. Make it your business always to be your own best self.

13. Keep your sense of humor.

14. Put your partner first in your life and be sure he or she knows it. This is basic in dealing with the "in-laws" and with many other problems.

15. Make the best of whatever life brings. You and God together can meet any problem life presents.

16. Plan your finances together. Remember you both earn the money, no matter who gets the paychecks. God should be a partner in your finances, too. Try tithing and see what a difference it makes.

17. Don't neglect your health. Your body is the temple of the Spirit of God. Respect it.

18. Cultivate your own spiritual life. Take time for prayer and meditation. Talk daily with God and give Him a chance to talk to you.

Many other suggestions, of course, might be given if there were time, but one other important factor must be stressed. In these days and especially in a time of war, temptations increase and it is easier to "let down the bars" and yield to bad habits. Gambling, extravagance, immorality, drunkenness—all these and other evils threaten the family. The home has no greater enemy than liquor in all its forms. As Mrs. Grace Sloan Overton rightly says, "You can repeal the Eighteenth Amendment, but you can't repeal the chemistry of alcohol." It is as ruinous as ever. Keep it out of your life and out of your home. It is an insidious foe that you trifle with at your peril. Home, job, ideals, self-respect, purity, and honor all may be the price you and your loved ones pay. To be sure, not all who drink end as drunkards, but you do not know when you start to use alcohol, or introduce it into your home, who the victims will be or the price you and your loved ones eventually may have to pay. Week after week men and women come to me, as they do to every minister, asking in desperation, what they can do about the problem of drink that is ruining some life or home. There is only one safe way to handle it. Leave it alone.

On the day long ago at Gettysburg, when Pickett's men were waiting word from Longstreet to begin the fatal charge, the gallant Pickett had written a letter to his fiancee in Richmond. When the word was finally given to move forward, he wrote in pencil on the envelope, "If old Peter's nod means death—good-bye, and God bless you, little one."

As he rode to his place, a fellow officer said, "Pickett, take a drink with me. In an hour you'll be in hell or glory."

Pickett refused and said, "I promised the little girl who is waiting and praying for me down in Virginia that I would keep fresh upon my lips, until we should meet again, the breath of the violets she gave me when we parted. Whatever my fate, I shall try to do my duty like a man, and I hope that, by that little girl's prayer, I shall today reach glory or glory."

Such men, such girls, and such ideals are our hope for better homes tomorrow.

We must remember, however, that ours are not to be the only homes tomorrow. We shall not be true to our Christian faith and duty if we are concerned only about our own homes and our own loved ones. We are all "bound in the bundle of life," and have been told, "Bear ye one another's burdens, and so fulfill the law of Christ." We must be as concerned for the homes and lives and happiness of all God's children as for our own.

We must think then of the attitudes and ideals we are to pass on to the next generation and of the kind of world in which tomorrow's homes are to be built. We are but a part of the family of God on the earth. Did not the Master say, "This is my commandment, That ye love one another as I have loved you"?

Is it not time for us Christians to strike at old prejudices that have counted others of God's children as inferior and beneath us, forgetting that, "He hath made of one blood, all nations . . . to dwell on all the face of the earth"? Recognizing the differences of color and tongue and culture, let us teach our children to respect all other races and nations for what they are. Let us seek to substitute knowledge for ignorance, understanding for prejudice, love for hate, brotherhood for strife, justice for injustice. "He . . . hath broken down the middle wall of partition" between us. God forbid that man-made barriers should bar Christian fellowship and goodwill between all those for whom Christ died.

Poverty, insecurity, insufficient food and clothing, inadequate shelter and education everywhere must be our concern as Christians. We dare not seek in God's name any blessings for our own lives and homes that we do not seek for others. Jesus said, "Inasmuch as ye have done it unto the least of these my brethren, ye have done it unto me." His universal love and concern for His brethren must be ours. Only then is there hope that all the homes of tomorrow can be His.

War and hate challenge the very existence of our homes today. As we do our utmost as citizens to win the war, let us remember that in our homes today we are rearing the generation that in time must win the

...paper that should be put away carefully, remembered, and
...d upon often.

...I was holding a revival meeting in Burlington, Maine, and we had
...the last Sunday. In the morning service the minister announced,
...ining Union time, we will have the head of the department of
...from the state school come and talk to us on comparative reli-

...at afternoon, I asked him about the young man, who he was and
...he was. My host replied, "I do not know. He is brilliant and young—
...han thirty years old—and has his Ph.D. He is married to an Oriental
..., they have never been to church. I know nothing about him."
...s I tried to preach that night on heaven, I wondered what would be
...young man's attitude toward my message. (I have been asked, "Do
...ever wonder how people receive you?" Yes, of course!)
...When the young Ph.D. came into the evening worship service, I made
...a matter of prayer. I prayed for him and that God would use me in this
...articular message on John 14.

Afterward, the church was having a fellowship time for me. The young
...man came to me and said, "When you get through, I want to talk to you a
...minute."

I thought perhaps he wanted an argument, but as we sat down, he
began, "I want to thank you for what you did for me tonight."

He continued, "I was saved as a boy in North Carolina. Then my father
died, and my mother moved, taking my brother and me to California to
be with her family. She blamed God for my father's death. I don't think
we went to Sunday School a single time in California.

"But when you started talking about heaven, it warmed my soul. I
recognized it as a message I had heard when I first believed." He added,
"I must go back to my Buddhist wife and try to tell her about Jesus."

In verses 2 and 3, Jesus promised us *a prepared place*. He has a special place for all His followers, to all who belonged to Him from that time
on. He will prepare a place for us. We often think of these words as being
only for a funeral. Not so! In reality, Jesus gave them to His disciples for
courage to face life. Yet a short time later the disciples's world caved in.
What then?

John Mott, whose son was killed and the murderer never found, was
preaching at a missions conference. He seemed to approach this passage

peace. We must give to them Jesus' ideals of world redemption and
world brotherhood. The Christian homes of today are our hope for a
better tomorrow. Someone has said of the mother of John and Charles
Wesley that, as she taught her children in that home in England so long
ago, she was really a "pioneer electrical engineer." Hers was the gift and
privilege of developing and guiding the energy of that nursery until, one
day, under God, it should send messengers of light around the world,
making lives that had been dull and cold, glow with a new fire. Such is
the radiance all our homes must shed abroad as a light of hope in a dark
world.

You and I will never do this alone. Each of our homes must be rein-
forced by a church home—a church home where our children will be
taught the Word of God and given a faith in God that will fit them for the
coming days. "The Christian church," someone has truly said, "is always
within one generation of extinction." It must win the next generation. Are
you and your home helping Christ and His church do that?

Make religion natural in your home. Prayers at bedtime, the blessing at
the table, some form of devotion and Bible reading should have a place in
the daily program. Lead the children naturally to the day when they
make their own decision for Christ and the church. What folly it is to
neglect all this, saying that you will wait and let them decide for themselves about their religion. The ultimate choice, of course, is theirs. No
one can choose Christ as Lord for someone else, but yours is the responsibility for giving them the religious training and atmosphere that ultimately lead to that all-important decision.

A recent writer says that in all modern arguments about religion, he
cannot forget seeing his father kneel to pray at night before he went to
bed, "My father prayed." What a help that is in guiding a life. Yet thousands of children today have never seen nor heard their father pray.
What about your home?

This matter of a family faith and a church home is perhaps more important than you realize. Dr. Henry C. Link, eminent psychologist, states
in his book *The Return to Religion* that he found himself telling so many
other people to go back to church, he finally decided he needed it himself. He tells how his decision brought him genuine satisfaction and then
goes on to point out that the two most effective things in producing fine
personalities in children are (1) that the children attend Sunday School,

and, (2) that the parents go to church. In such homes he says children are more likely to have fine personalities and grow to be poised and self-reliant leaders in society.

Have you a church home to help you live today and do better tomorrow? You endanger your happiness and strike at the heart of marriage when you neglect the nurture of faith and hope and love.

> Live not without your God! However low or high,
> In every house should be a window to the sky.

This leads us to one last word. What about your home for the eternal tomorrow? Through faith in the living Christ we know we have "an house not made with hands, eternal in the heavens." That home is in the making now, too. Are you preparing for it and living worthily of it? Let Christ help you so to live that someday you can take your place in that eternal home with those whom "we have loved long since and lost awhile."

In his beautiful story of his father's life, *One Foot in Heaven,* Hartzell Spence tells of the last time he saw his father alive. The old minister had served his Lord well, but now was at the end of life's journey below. The son must leave at once to accept a new job and he and the father both know they will never see each other again. The minister takes the boy's hands and says, "Son, I am very happy over your promotion. I like to be proud of my sons. You are going far away. When you return, I probably will not be here. But don't worry about me. We are both moving up to new jobs. You know you are going to New York, and just as surely, I know where I am going. You know what to expect when you get there; so, too, do I." He looks at him steadily for a moment and says, "God bless you, son. Good-bye."

What a faith to have, and to give! Is it yours? You can have it, through Christ, and your love and your home can be all God meant them to be. "The house of the righteous shall stand," and when life's journey here is ended, we do have "an house not made with hands, eternal in the heavens" (Prov. 12:7).

R. Earl A[...]
Blessed Beque[...]

John 14

John 14 probably has comforted more bewildered an[...] tians than any other chapter of the Bible. An elderly pa[...] he let the Bibles of his older people fall open, usually it [...] chapter. I hasten to add that this comfort is not merely for[...] for believers of all ages.

One scholar wrote with a clear mind and a warm hear[...] "Your people may feel you should be quiet here and let Chri[...] there is one passage more sacred than others to many, this is [...] it! All of us, regardless of age, origin, and background, need tr[...] reassurance today and even more for tomorrow, the comfort whi[...] promised here.

Why do many people turn to religion? Statistics show that most[...] do for one or more of three reasons:

1. They seek *light* (truth).
2. They seek *comfort* (help).
3. They look for *immortality.*

Come quietly with me, if you will, to the Upper Room with Jesus. H[...] disciples were distraught and distracted. Judas had deserted. Now Jesu[...] predicted He was leaving them as well. However, He promised they [...] would see Him again and spoke of an untroubled heart: "Let not your [...] heart be troubled; ye believe in God, believe also in me" (v. 1). Indeed, this is a "cover verse" for the entire chapter.

Quaint old Matthew Henry said in his *Commentary* (written over 250 years ago), "In John 14, Jesus is making His last will and testament to His followers. It is a legacy of Christ prepared for believers." It is like an impor-

as if it startled him. Pointing, he declared, "If the world collapses, if the world crumbles in, what then?"

His friend sitting behind him on the platform reported that the veins on his neck popped out, but he composed himself and continued. "What shall the righteous do? The Word says, 'Go on being righteous!' That's what we should do!" That is our option. Go on believing Jesus! Don't be distressed. Have a quiet heart.

The psalmist sang, "I would have fainted unless I had believed to see the goodness of the Lord in the land of the living" (Ps. 27:13). Jesus taught, "Ye believe in God, believe also in me!" (verse 1*b*). Stake your life on Jesus!

There were three troubles the disciples were already beginning to experience: (1) the loss of Jesus' presence, (2) no earthly kingdom as James and John had hoped there would be, and (3) persecution that was beginning to overtake them.

Jesus urged them to look beyond the difficulties of this world to a wonderful reunion. "In my Father's house there are many rooms," Jesus assured them. Heaven is a prepared place for a prepared people. That may sound trite, but the nearer you come to the rolling Jordan, the more blessed it is. We have treasures stored up in heaven.

Heaven is more than a state of mind, more than simply an air castle. It has to be a place. Jesus stressed, "Lay up treasures in this one place." His blessed children will not be cut out. God's blessed Son had no room on earth, but we will have confirmation of our reservations in heaven.

Heaven may seem vague to many people, those whose heart strings have never been cut by death. But heaven is real if you have loved ones over there.

An evangelist of another generation, T. T. Martin, testified that the first time he heard someone preach about heaven, he was, in winter time, a barefoot boy trying to warm himself by a pot-bellied stove in an old wooden church.

He heard the preacher ask, "What is your concept of heaven? What do you think about when you think of heaven?" Martin said, "I am ashamed of it now, what my thoughts of heaven were that day: 'Thank God, I won't have to pick cotton anymore, or be barefoot on a frosty morning.'"

That was inadequate, but I suspect that most of our concepts of heaven are childish. Jesus knows all about it. He was the Carpenter, building heaven by His Father's plans.

We are far too involved in the world; we have two cars and a mortgage that we think we will pay off, and everything will be all right. We are "this worldish" rather than looking at the world to come. "Eye hath not seen, nor ear heard, neither has entered into the heart of man the things which God hath prepared for those who love him" (1 Cor. 2:9).

The apostle Paul wrote (about fourteen years after the fact) that "he knew a man" who "was caught up into paradise," and who had heard "unspeakable words, which it is not lawful for a man to utter" (2 Cor. 12:2,3).

John Jasper, a remarkable old slave preacher of Richmond, Virginia, of a bygone generation, said, "People are always asking me if we will know each other in heaven. What I would ask them is, 'Will you know Jesus in heaven?' How real is Jesus with you?" He said, "I will come again . . . that where I am, there ye may be also" (v. 3).

Dr. R. W. Dale preached, *"That steadies me!"*

G. Campbell Morgan, one of the greatest Bible expositors, assured us, "You have the word of a gentleman."

Jesus bequeathed to us *a provided path:* "I am the way, the truth, and the life; no man cometh unto the Father, but by me" (v. 6).

Occasionally I hear a person remark, "You take the high road, and I'll take the low road," implying that we will all get to heaven together. That is all right if you are going to Scotland, but it is not all right if you are going to heaven. There is only one way—the Jesus way!

Jesus is the only way of forgiveness. There is no other provision. Jesus expressed it, "He that entereth not by the door into the sheepfold, but climbeth up some other way, the same is a thief and a robber" (John 10:1).

A man was in the Alps trying to hire a guide. In a small inn he found the guides huddled around the stove. He said, "I want to be taken over to a certain village."

One answered, "I haven't been there, but I know about where it is. I believe I can take you."

The man answered, "That won't do."

Another came back, "I haven't been there, but I have been to the village next to it."

The man said, "That won't do."

One held up his hand and asserted, "I will take you. It is home country for me."

That's what Jesus said: "I came down from the Father, and I will go back to the Father." Heaven is "home country" for Jesus. And we "won't have to cross Jordan alone." He comes for us and receives us Himself.

As a ship reaches a harbor, a ferry boat comes out with a pilot to guide the ship into the harbor, because it is familiar territory to him.

It is usually a servant who prepares for his master to come, but in this case it is the Master getting ready for His servants to come. We are God's people; we are God's servants. One day Jesus will certainly come for us; and He is, in the meantime, readying a place for us.

Jesus left us *a personal portrait* of God. Isaiah, 700 years before Jesus' incarnation, turned his sanctified lens toward heaven and prophesied the Messiah would be born of a virgin. He told us the coming King would be a lamb without spot or blemish, describing to us what Jesus would be like.

A little girl commented that "Jesus is the best picture of God that has ever been took."

Think that over. Jesus is the best picture we have of God. From Him, we may learn all we need to know about the Father.

Philip went in over his head with his question of verse 8: "Shew us the Father." It demonstrated Philip's lack of faith. He realized that and cried out, "Help my unbelief!" Jesus showed His disciples the Father in words and deeds: in healing, in the transfiguration, on the cross, and in the power of His resurrection!

"The Father and I are one," Jesus stressed. "Philip, have I been such a long time with you, and yet you have not known the Father? He that hath seen me hath seen the Father. Believest thou not that I am in the Father, and the Father in me? (vv. 9-10).

A class of students graduating from Yale University promised each other than in twenty-five years they would return for a reunion. Twenty-five years later, they began to gather and greet one another. Sometimes they did not remember one another immediately. Then a man entered who seemed nearer to sixty than fifty years old. Life obviously had not been easy on him: he was arthritic, bent over; he had a difficult problem walking. His face was drawn with pain. No one could remember him or place him.

Finally, they began to ask him, "Who are you? What is your name?"

"I will do better than that," he answered, "I will call in my son."

From outside the door his son, age about twenty-two, came in. They looked at the boy and began to say, "I know who you are." Then they called him by his correct name, because the son was the image of the father as they had known him.

Jesus said, "I am the image of my Father. The Father and I are one." Jesus is the living picture of God.

You may not understand all about the mysteries of God, but when you know Jesus you can affirm, "I recognize God."

The world is saying to the church, "Show us your Father." The request is worldwide; "Show us God." I believe with all my soul that the world is still hungry to know about God.

If we could persuade our church, who are God's people, to become hungry for the things of God, we would have no problem persuading prospects to come. If it were noised about that God was in this place, they would show up. People want to know about God and see Him work. But God doesn't have a chance to work if He can't work through His people; that's all He has!

There's a hue and cry in your town, in your church, in each of our souls, for a fresh concept and image of God, for a new outpouring from God. Are not the peoples of the world crying to us, out of their own dead lives, "Show us your Christ in your lives—and we will be satisfied!"?

Thomas Carlyle, a well-known atheist, was strolling the streets of Paris one day and passed a store window where he saw a crucifix exhibited. He remarked to his companion, "Aye, poor fellow, you have had your day!" But Carlyle didn't know it all.

Don't paint Jesus' portrait on the cross—dead. Paint the cross empty because He is alive! He will come again one day and receive us unto Himself. Paint Him alive, for there is a great day coming!

Then remember, Jesus sent us *a perfect Paraclete.*

Napoleon once boasted to his father, "When I am dead, I will come back and throb in countless revolutions." But when Napoleon died, he was gone from this world forever, as other people are. He left widespread influence, but he never came back.

Jesus said, "When I go away, I will send you another Comforter, and when He is come . . ." When He comes what a difference that will be! The Holy Spirit is called a "paraclete," an advocate and comforter. "Paraclete," I think, is the better word: the "helper." He came to teach us. What we want to know about God, we can ask the Holy Spirit to teach us. He is our living Companion; He is other-worldly. This world neither sees Him nor knows Him.

The Holy Spirit's work among unbelievers is to *convict;* in the believers it is to give *courage.* The Holy Spirit comes to encourage desolate soldiers. We grow weary in battle and exhausted in spirit, and we fall out by the way. We ask God to revive us again and give us a sense of victory. The Spirit comes to do that.

He comes to us as a lawyer, a friend at court. He stands by us at the judgment bar of God and says, "This person is mine! He is covered under the blood of forgiveness."

Barclay noted that the paraclete was "called in to cope with things."

A young fellow in my church received too many traffic tickets and his license to drive was about to be revoked. His father was in Greenland. He came to me after church at night and asked, "Preacher, would you go with me to the court house in the morning?"

"Yes, I'll go with you," I explained, "but let me tell you, so you don't misunderstand, that I don't have any standing in your court. All I can do is go with you as a friend and as your pastor to let you know I love you and am praying for you. Even though you have made some mistakes, when you come before the judge you will have to stand by yourself— unless you ask the Lord to stand with you."

There are limitations to what we can do for one another, but there are no limitations on what God can do for us. The Holy Spirit is among us to convict a world of sin, of righteousness, and of judgment. The Holy Spirit is among us to give courage to Christians.

This chapter is what Kyle Yates, Sr., called "solid comfort."

Jesus Christ's supreme legacy to us is a personal, a present, and *a permanent peace.* Jesus emphasized that He came into the world to bring peace.

One historian many years ago observed, "We do not have peace in this world today; we have a cease-fire." In the years since he made that statement, we have had 197 known conflicts.

Jesus said, "I will give you permanent peace." Then He qualified it: "not as the world giveth, give I unto you." That is, "I don't simply give you a tranquilizer. I give you an inward peace, a 'peace that passeth all understanding.'"

Some people make false claims about peace. They spout ". . . Peace, peace; when there is no peace" (Jer. 8:11).

The world's only offer of peace is *avoiding trouble:* "Play it safe," they insist. Jesus' prescription for peace is not avoiding trouble, but controlling circumstances. The world being as it is, without Christ, we *cannot* hold our peace!

Hurricane specialists indicate that there is a core of absolute quietness in the center of a hurricane. To chart the velocity of a hurricane, an airplane flies into the center of it to measure its width and dangers.

Jesus, to the Christians, is the very center of life. When He is in control, there is perfect peace and quietness. Matters are all right in the hands of God.

If you have been to Washington, D.C., you may have watched a silent sentry as he walked in front of the Tomb of the Unknown Soldier. So does the Holy Spirit keep watch over us.

We lost our little ten-year-old girl, Norma Aline, in a car wreck on the way to Sunday School one morning. The hardest chore we had afterward was trying to change her room. She had a room all by herself, full of all the things that a ten-year-old would have. We left it for a while. Then we realized we could not leave it as a shrine; we had to change it.

We did not want to give the clothes to the children in the town where we lived; we sent them to Buckner's, the Southern Baptist child-care center in Texas. We had a long day of packing clothes. Finally, when we unloaded the dresser, we found her Bible.

I have always encouraged my people to mark their Bibles. She had not been a Christian for long, but in a childish scrawl, in the 27th verse of this 14th chapter of John, she had underlined, "My peace I leave with you; my peace I give unto you."

God comforts His people in many ways and under many circumstances. They argue there is not a will a lawyer can't make or can't break—but not this one! Jesus arose to execute it Himself.

Keep in mind all that Jesus willed to others. He gave the responsibility of His mother to John, His body to Joseph of Arimathea. His Spirit went back to His Father, the God of the universe. His clothes went to the executioners. There was no money left: Judas had seen to that. There was nothing left but peace, and He bestowed that upon us.

More people seek peace of mind and peace of soul than any other earthly treasure.

The apostle Paul wrote, "And the peace of God, which passeth all understanding, shall keep your hearts and minds through Christ Jesus" (Phil. 4:7). Paul and Silas demonstrated this in the Philippian jail. Their faith and their peace burst out in a song—a faith that sings!

The experience of personal peace falls into two categories: living peace and dying peace. A song writer exulted, "It will do when I'm dying!" If it won't do when you're dying, it won't do while you live. It is no good to you. The Greeks had a saying, "Call no man happy until the day of his death."

Then, in the Upper Room, Jesus spoke these words: "Let us rise and go hence." If we have His peace, then we are equipped to follow Him without question.

C. Roy Angell
The Interrupted Sermon

And he preached the word unto them (Mark 2:2).

The president of the seminary that I attended once said to all of us assembled in chapel, "Young men, when you get into the pastorate and someone asks you where they should start reading the Bible, tell them to start with the Gospel of Mark, because the very first chapters of the Gospel of Mark present the finest picture of the strong Son of God to be found anywhere in the world." This incident of the interrupted sermon is a vital part of the grand picture of the strong Son of God.

Jesus had been preaching and teaching and healing in the towns and villages not far from Capernaum. The whole country was in such an uproar that people were flocking to him from every quarter. They came in such crowds that he "could not openly enter in the city but was without in desert places." After a time he did enter Capernaum, and when it was noised that he was in a certain house, the crowd gathered immediately. They packed the house and the yard to hear Jesus preach.

Suddenly the sermon was interrupted by a thud of falling mud and drifting thatch which dropped to the floor in front of him. Of course, everybody's eyes went to the ceiling. They saw a hole, and some men were making the hole bigger. When it was large enough, the men took off their sashes and tied them to the four corners of a litter. Then they carefully lowered a man down to the feet of Jesus. I imagine that the men lay on their faces and looked down through the hole to see what would happen. They had done all they could. They had brought their friend to the feet of the Master. They hadn't been able to get in the house; so they had used the outside steps and had gone up on the flat roof. Now they waited expectantly. Jesus looked on the sick man and used a most endearing word and followed it with a startling statement, "Son, thy sins be forgiven thee." The crowd of church men and religious leaders sitting around re-acted instantly. I am sure indignation and anger were written all over their faces. You can almost see them nudge each other and shake their heads in negation. They were thinking, "This man blasphemes. Nobody but God can forgive sins. Anyhow, those men didn't bring him here to have his sins forgiven. They brought him here to have him healed of the palsy." Jesus listening with his mind heard what their minds said and answered them audibly, "[Is] it easier to say Thy sins be forgiven thee; or to say, Arise, and walk? But that ye may know that the Son of man hath power on earth to forgive sins, (then saith he to the sick of the palsy) Arise, take up thy bed, and go unto thine house." The man arose and took up his bed, and the sermon was over, and the preaching service was broken up. Everything was in turmoil and confusion, but it was a wonderful hour, and the story has many beautiful lessons in it. Let me point out three of them.

I have an idea that it would be very pleasing to God if one of our formal services was interrupted by four men who were so dead in earnest to have one man made whole spiritually that they couldn't wait till the ser-mon was over. I am thinking of an experience that Dwight L. Moody had. He said, "I was preaching in a revival one evening when a baby on the fourth bench in front of me suddenly cried out in a clear, strong voice. Then the mother was able to quiet it for a few minutes, and I preached along until it cried out again. When this had happened several times, everybody around that baby stopped looking at me, and with frowning faces they stirred nervously in their seats and looked at the mother, al-most wondering out loud why she didn't take it outside instead of letting it disturb the whole service.

"I am sure God inspired me to stop preaching and say to them, 'I wish you people wouldn't pay any attention to that baby. It isn't bothering me. I can talk louder than any baby can cry, and you are embarrassing the little mother. Maybe she couldn't come to church except she bring the baby. Let's not worry about it any more.'

"I turned to the little mother and said, 'Are you a Christian, Mother?'" She shook her head.

"I said to those people, 'There, she isn't a Christian, and she has come to church to hear the gospel. It seems to me—' I didn't get any further with what I was going to say. They were ahead of me. A dozen mothers were converging on that spot, every one of them reaching for that baby. They took it over to another room and took care of it.

"I forgot what I was preaching about, but it didn't matter. I said to them, 'This is what pleases God and will please God more than anything else in the world—that a dozen people would want to make it possible that one single unsaved person might have a chance to get forgiveness for sin.' It was one of those services that God just took over. I didn't need to preach another word. I talked on for a few minutes and gave an invitation. People crowded each other to accept it."

I think it would please God today if we wouldn't think of church and church services and sermons the way we do. I am sure there are many people who come up to the hour of worship with the thought that the church service is something that they will *endure* because it's the proper thing for them to do. It will be a grand day in the kingdom of God when people get so concerned over the spiritual lameness of others that four of them will go after one lost soul.

What a refreshing thing it would be to a minister if the thing that happened to Mr. Finney would happen to one of us. A Supreme Court Judge walked up to the platform where Mr. Finney was preaching and stopped him in the middle of his sermon to say, "I want to be a Christian *now*. I want to make my profession of faith, and I don't want to wait any longer." I wonder if we preachers of today lack the fervor of Moody and Finney and so are going to miss having a sermon interrupted by someone who wants the salvation that we have and want to offer to others.

Here is Jesus' own explanation of why some miracles were performed by him. There are no Sunday school teachers and preachers who haven't been asked the question, "Why don't we have miracles today like those in the New Testament?"

And most of us have answered, "We do have miracles today. Many of them more wonderful than those in the New Testament. To be sure, they are not the same kind of miracles. In Christ's own words the reason for the miracles of healing is plainly stated, 'That ye may know that the Son of man hath power on earth to forgive sins . . . I say to thee Arise.'" Isn't Jesus saying that these miracles were necessary to launch the kingdom, that they were necessary to convince people that he was really the Son of God, that they were necessary to persuade people that he had the power to forgive sins, that they were necessary to show his gentleness and compassion?

Now, beloved, far more miracles are performed today in the spiritual kingdom than those we read about in the New Testament. Let me illustrate. One year when Dr. Truett was on a world tour of missions, Dr. Ernest Thorne and I were doing our best to fill his preaching engagement at the Cowboy Encampment at Paisano, Texas. One afternoon, Ernest said something like this to me: "I was listening to you preach the other night and decided to tell you the most dramatic thing that ever happened to me at a church service. I was holding a revival in a schoolhouse at the foot of a mountain. The people had no church and no preacher, but some Christians in the neighborhood had asked me to come for a week and help them organize a church.

"On the third night of the meeting one of the men was waiting for me at the schoolhouse at the foot of a mountain. The people had no church and no preacher, but some Christians in the neighborhood had asked me to come for a week and help them organize a church.

"On the third night of the meeting one of the men was waiting for me at the schoolhouse door. He was very excited when he spoke.

"'Dr. Thorne, we've got trouble. Over by that tree is a group of men who have terrorized this whole country for a long time. They are all moonshiners, and they don't want a church here. They came down tonight to break up the meeting; so I guess this is the end of it.'

"I gathered the little group of Christians together, and we talked and prayed inside of the schoolhouse for a few minutes. I felt God with me as I walked over to the group under the trees and asked if their leader, calling him by name, was there.

"A man stood up and came over to me, and I said to him, smiling as I said it, 'Could I talk to you alone for a minute or two?'

"He answered, 'Sure.'

"We walked a little way from the group, and I quietly said to him, 'I understand you came down to break up the revival.'

"He nodded his head as he answered, 'That's right.'

"'I want to make you a proposition,' I continued. 'I usually preach half an hour. It's about time to start the service. Won't you come on in the schoolhouse, all of you, and let me preach half of the sermon—fifteen minutes—and then I'll stop. If you still want to break up the meeting, you certainly can, for we can't stop you. There is nothing in the world that we can do, but I thought maybe you'd be a good sport and give me a chance.'

"The man stood there a minute or two, shifted from one foot to the other, and then said, 'Come on over and talk to the boys about that. Let's see what they say.'

"I went over, still smiling, and made my little speech to the boys. I said, 'There are sixteen or eighteen of you, and everybody is afraid of you. I guess you could do anything you wanted to do to me, but I still would like to preach one half of the sermon. Then I'll stop. Just don't hurt anybody. Tell us to get out, if you want to, and we'll adjourn.' They thought it over for a minute or two, and then took a vote. All were in favor, and they filed into the church.

"I walked up on the platform and told the congregation. 'Nothing is going to happen the first fifteen minutes of my sermon. Then I will stop, and that may be the end of the revival.'

Ernest said to me, "Roy, I never prayed so earnestly nor preached with such power as I did those first fifteen minutes. Then I stopped and held my watch up and said to the gang of men down in front of me, 'Well, that's half of it. What do you want me to do?' They looked at each other and shifted around a little, and then I said to them, 'I wish you would let me finish it. How many of you are willing for me to go on and finish the sermon? Put up your hands.' Every hand in the gang went up. Oh, how I preached after that!

"When the sermon was over, we bowed our heads in prayer. I said, 'If there are any of you people here tonight who would like to raise your hand and say to God, "I am not happy with my life. I would like to have my sins forgiven," would you just raise your hands now?' The leader of that gang put his hand up just as high as he could reach. A few of the others followed him.

"After the service was over that leader and four or five others sat down in the corner of the schoolhouse. The leader's question was this, 'Dr. Thorne, would God forgive a man who had killed another man?'

"I answered, 'Yes, God will forgive a man who has killed another man.'

"Earnestly he looked at me, 'Dr. Thorne, don't fool me. Tell me the truth. I have been sorry ever since I killed him.' He put his hands over his face and wept."

Then Ernest said, "Roy, the best revival service I ever had in my life I had right there."

To me that is the greater miracle that Jesus was talking about—far greater than the miracle of healing the man with the palsy—the miracle of healing a man of soul sickness.

God uses the interruptions of life just as Jesus used this unusual one. Interruptions that come in our own lives are often opportunities for God to bless us in a special way, just as he blessed in Mr. Moody's sermon and Dr. Thorne's revival. I am sure that we often take the wrong attitude toward the upsets that come to us in life. We think of them as imposters. We are very much like the people who wanted Isaiah to "speak unto us smooth things," whereas the thing that we often need most is an interruption. Someone has said, "Interruptions are normal, just as change is normal, and we ought to look for the hand of God in life's severest disappointments."

Dr. J. Wallace Hamilton, in his book *Ride the Wild Horses*, expresses it this way: "Look again at the interruptions of Jesus, even the minor ones. He didn't merely endure them; He employed them, and used every one of them to promote the purposes of God. When the man out of the crowd broke in on His teaching, He used the interruption to heighten His teaching. When the Pharisees broke in with their ugly criticism of His morals—eating, as they said, with publicans and sinners—He did not merely endure their criticism, He employed it; He took their nasty insinuations, which were meant to discredit Him, and made them the sounding board for the loveliest story in all literature—the story of the Prodigal Son. 'The Son of Man is come to seek and to save that which was lost.' Every interruption He accepted as a divine opportunity; every ugly thing He transformed into something beautiful. Even the Cross, which was the utmost interruption meant to destroy Him and His purpose forever, provided Him with a force by which He lifted men to the very heights of God."

I remember hearing a university president at Ridgecrest talking to the students about the life of Joseph. In substance he said, "We often think of Joseph as a great hero, and we are forever admiring the beautiful thing that he did for his brethren, his forgiveness, and his tolerant treatment of them. We forget so easily that Joseph was not always like that.

"In his boyhood days Joseph was a spoiled brat. Remember the morning he got up and told his brothers that he had had a dream last night and very arrogantly he told them that he saw all of them bow down and touch the ground in front of him and that he waved a wand above them and they all obeyed him. He seemed to think it was perfectly natural for him to be a ruler over them. Certainly his father coddled him, gave him a coat of many colors, never sent him into the field to tend the cattle or the horses. It is no wonder that his brethren were jealous of him, and it should not surprise us in the least that when they saw at a long distance this beautiful coat of many colors, so different from their sweat-stained clothes, that they decided they would do something about it. Their resentment was keen, and wrath and anger filled them completely. The answer was, 'Put him to death or sell him as a slave.'

"Look at him as he is in his boyhood days and as someone has well said, 'I cannot see a Prime Minister in him. There is nothing of the Secretary of State in his personality. But when I look at him a few years later after this shocking interruption of life has come to him and he is a steward in Potiphar's home, the makings of a Prime Minister are written all over him, and as he stands that day and looks at his brethren in Egypt he is a different man.'" What happened to bring about this change? One word will express it, the word *interruption*.

When some calamity befalls us and some disappointment or frustration breaks our hearts, when circumstances throw a roadblock before us, or when we run into a dead-end street or a blind alley, wouldn't it be well for us to look up? Maybe this is an occasion for a particular blessing from God. The day may come when our prayers will be filled with gratitude for this interruption.

Wallace Bassett
A Star at Midnight

Love . . . hopeth all things (1 Cor. 13:7).

Man lives in two worlds, an outside world and an inside world. He sees the outside world and feels the inside world, and what he sees in the outside world depends on what he feels in the inside world. If he feels the inside world triumphantly, it is because he sees a star—even at midnight—that star is the star of hope. That which God gives that enables him to feel triumphantly is hope. Faith has to do with the past and the present growing out of the past. Hope has to do with the present and the future growing out of the present. Hope is the temper of faith and the highest expression of love. Hope brings the future into the present. What wings are to the bird, hope is to life. It is the recognition of the good, desire for the good, and expectancy of the good. Man is the child of hope when at his best.

While hope is a human trait and is partly due to temperament and environment, yet it is, in its highest sense, a Christian virtue. God is spoken of as the God of all hope, and it is said in one place, "If we are without God, we are without hope." Mark Rutherford calls hope a forefancying. You remember reading, when a child, of Pandora opening the lid of the tantalizing box which had been forbidden. As a result, out flew all the troubles which have since distressed mankind. Last came out hope with rainbow-tinted wings to make amends for all the mischief caused by the other creatures. Pandora's forehead was stung by one of the pests, and straightway the hurt was kissed away by hope.

I

The Christian hope is life's sustaining power. It is called the anchor of the soul both sure and steadfast. The figure of an anchor is said to be

49

carved all over the catacombs of Rome, where early Christians fled for worship during times of great persecution. What the rainbow was to Noah, during a flood which covered the earth, so hope is to us when the world is flooded with a deluge of sorrow. It becomes at such times the sunny side of patience. To some people religion is just a fair-weather affair, but Christ did not often live in fair weather. His religion was a house built on a rock that stood firm during a storm.

Christ in the soul does not mean ease, but it means a hope that forms a last defense against despair and defeat. Mrs. Nansen spent thirty months in anxiety and despair, when, in flew a carrier pigeon with a note from her husband in the faraway north. So to you, who know what it means to have only an emptiness when once you had a home, I want to fly out of the darkness with a message. I know now what Ezekiel meant when he said, "So I spake unto the people in the morning: and at even my wife died." My message to you as I fly out of the darkness is, "Hope thou in God." John Vance Cheney expresses my message:

> Not in times of pleasure
>   Hope doth set her bow;
> But in the sky of sorrow,
>   Over the vale of woe.
> Through gloom and shadow look we
>   On beyond the years
> The soul would have no rainbow
>   Had the eyes no tears.

II

Christian hope is life's transforming power. Phillips Brooks said to a group of young preachers, that tendency was the great fact of the world. "It does not yet appear what we shall be, but he that hath a hope within purifieth himself as Christ is pure." Tendency to a man with hope is always forward, and this hope positionizes one and leaves him facing the future. It gives an urge to life. Transformation is impossible without ambition, and ambition is impossible without hope. Just as a returning spring transforms a landscape, so hope transforms our lives into a rejuvenated earth.

III

Christian hope is an energizing power. If we study the life of our Lord, we see that his first step in helping a man was to awaken hope. He created hope in the dying thief, in the man with the withered hand, the man at the Pool of Bethesda, and the man with the palsy. Before Peter and John healed the lame man at the gate of the Temple, they asked the man to look on them. Thus they awakened hope in the man they would help. In this way they were following the pattern of the Master. The Lord fed Elijah and awakened hope before he took him out from under the juniper tree. So, if we would have the energy of God upon us, we must have hope within us.

IV

Our great need today is hope. We need it for this troubled, distressed world, where we find war, rumors of war, and hunger—so much unnecessary suffering. Lord Morley said that hope burned like a pillar of fire in Cromwell after it had gone out in all others. So it was with Moses journeying toward a promised land. Paul said, "We are saved by hope." Note that he said it just as he was saying that the whole creation groaneth and travaileth in pain. The world today is a groaning travailing world, and God wants us to hope for its redemption.

We need it for the church. Through the trying centuries the church has hit on many distressful days. But our Saviour said that the gates of hell should not prevail against it. Never man spake like he spake, for never man hoped like he hoped.

We need it for our characters. While we have much to do in the world, yet our first great task is to be the kind of men and women we ought to be. This cannot be without realizing that "love . . . hopeth all things."

In the famous and familiar picture, *The Doctor,* we see an intelligent, anxious face of a doctor watching a dying child. Behind them stands the young father with his hand on the shoulder of his wife, whose face is covered as she weeps. A doctor, Sir Luke Fieldes, criticized the picture, saying that no one ever saw a mother with covered face so long as a sick child was still living.

We need it when we think of the other world. Jesus awakened hope in Jairus, and then raised up the little twelve-year-old girl. We all have interests in the other world, and it draws nearer to us when we hope. When we are very young, heaven is a vague and nebulous and shadowy place. But later, as loved ones go over, it gains body and vividness and becomes more homelike. Where the treasure is, there is the heart. When children we sang, "There is a happy land far, far away." But it is not far away; it is quite near.

Adoniram Judson buried his wife under a tree in Burmah, and often said that the name of the tree had great significance to him. Edwin Markham speaks in verse of bridging the Niagara by first flying a kite over the cataract with a small string attached and then a larger one until the strong cable held a bridge. So our loved ones, one by one, cross over and build the bridge between us and the other world until it is very near to us.

I got my subject from a skeptic's words, Ingersoll, when he said at his brother's grave, "In the night of death hope sees a star, and listening love can hear the rustle of a wing." There is a star in the night, and that star is hope.

Where do we get this hope? It is not an accident. It comes from Christ. Paul speaks of Christ being in us the hope of glory. Those who once sat in darkness saw a great light, and that was the light of Christ's birth. Though you sit in darkness, if Christ be in you, you, too, see a great light.

The ship *Glenco* lay in New York harbor, submerged beneath the waters. Mechanical means were ineffectual to raise her. Then airtight bags were placed inside and pumped full of air, and up she came. That within brought her up. "Is Christ within?" is life's most important question to every man on earth.

James Petigru Boyce
Christ Receiving and Eating with Sinners

And the Pharisees and scribes murmured, saying, This man receiveth sinners, and eateth with them (Luke 15:2).

This man was Jesus. The meaning of His name is Jehovah Savior. The angel Gabriel commanded His mother so to call Him because He should save His people from their sins.

His name was, therefore, an index of His character and work. He came to seek and to save that which was lost. He came to call, not the righteous but sinners to repentance. In His more especial work He was declared by His forerunner to be the Lamb of God which taketh away (or beareth away) the sin of the world. It was by His sacrifice for sin that He made atonement for our sins and met all the demands of the law for our condemnation. It is in the furtherance of this work that as our High Priest He is ever interceding for us with God, praying for us as sinners that God will pardon our sins and remove afar from us our transgressions. It is into our sinful hearts that He sends His Holy Spirit, to change them, to convict of sin, to lead us as sinners to look unto Him for salvation, to teach us that there is nothing in us, but everything in Christ, to enable us to cast away all confidence in our own works or merit as fitness, to rely alone upon Christ's work and His promises, and to trust our whole salvation, beginning and middle and end, entirely into His hands.

Christ deals with us as sinners utterly lost and already condemned and becomes to us a complete Savior in every respect. He is the Jehovah Savior of His sinful people.

But there is a wide step between this position, itself so gracious, and merciful, and that in which our text presents him.

We have not here the mere Savior of sinners but their companion. He is not here exhibited only as dying for man but living with him. The picture presented is not that of the Lamb bearing away the sin of the world, but of the Holy One of God holding fellowship with the worst classes of mankind.

Even our text as translated does not present to us the whole truth. The pious Bonar says with reference to its teaching,

> The word "receiveth" is in the original singularly expressive. It means waiteth, watcheth, looks out for, lies in wait. It occurs fourteen times in the New Testament, and in all other places it is translated in some such way: as in Mark 15:43—"who waited for the kingdom of God"; Luke 2:25—"waiting for the consolation of Israel"; Luke 2:3—"looked for redemption in Jerusalem"; Luke 12:30—"men that wait for their Lord"; Acts 23:21—"looking for a promise from thee"; Titus 2:13—"looking for that blessed hope"; Jude 21—"looking for the mercy of our Lord Jesus Christ."

Our text, then, if it presents Christ in His true aspect shows Him to us, as waiting for sinners, looking out for them, longing for them, having that expectation of their coming of which hope is a decided element. And then when these hopes have been fulfilled and they have come to Him, or been found of Him, He is said to take them into intimate fellowship and friendship. "This man receiveth sinners, and eateth with them."

But is this statement of the text correct? It is not Christ that says it. It is not one of his disciples. It is not even the language of the ordinary multitude which surrounded him.

It is an accusation against Him made by the Pharisees. We know that their statements cannot be relied upon.

They hated Jesus and were always on the look out for something wherewith to accuse him. The gospel records evince that they were constant spies upon Him and sought continually to mislead the people about Him. They saw Him cast out devils and said, "He casteth out devils through the prince of the devils." When a man with a withered hand was present they asked Him, "Is it lawful to heal on the sabbath days? that they might accuse him." Luke 6:7 says they "watched him . . . that they might find an accusation against him." When He said to the sick of the palsy, "Thy sins are forgiven thee," they began to reason, saying, "Who is this which speaketh blasphemies?" When He went on the sabbath day to eat bread in the house of one of the chief Pharisees, they watched Him to see if he would heal the man with the dropsy. When He opened the eyes of the man blind from his birth, some of them said, "This man is not of

God, because he keepeth not the sabbath day." Thus did they hate and slander Him, and their accusation in the text might have been the result of this hatred.

The whole information we have from the Gospels teaches us to beware how we receive as true the accusations of the Pharisees. And our text is one of these accusations. The Pharisees and scribes murmured and said, "This man receiveth sinners, and eateth with them."

The charge which they made against Jesus was an extraordinary one. His alleged conduct seems greatly to have astonished them. We live at too great a distance of time and under too different circumstances to judge of it. But it was such action as must greatly have perplexed the pious people among the Jews. Here was a religious teacher, one who was declared to be the Messiah, one whose personal purity and sinlessness were asserted by Himself and by His disciples, and whom does He make His companions? The men of authority and position in the nation? The men who were of special purity of life? The Pharisees who were especially the national purists? The scribes who were so intimately associated with the Scriptures of God? No, none of these—not even the men of ordinary purity and morality. But men who were especially recognized as sinners, who were so known as such as to be marked as a special class. And, then, not only these, but even the publicans, the oppressive tax-gatherers, who had sold themselves to the Roman nation and who were enriching themselves by their extortions upon the Jews. These were they whom Jesus is said to have sought after, waited for, expected and longed for as guests, and chosen to sit with Him at table.

Hence the Pharisees immediately seize upon it as a ground of accusation. They show their malice and mischief-making spirit by immediate murmurs. "See what he is doing, this teacher of morals, this Messiah of the Jews, this pretended pure and Holy One. Men are known by the company they keep. See his companions, his chosen ones, whom he delights to honor, whom he eats and drinks with—see him—Why, this man receiveth sinners, and eateth with them."

Is their charge correct?

We look to the record, and we see that the charge is true in all its fullness. At the feast of Matthew, himself a publican, though called as one of the twelve, we are told that "many publicans and sinners came and sat down with him and his disciples." When Christ entered Jericho, He offered Himself as a guest to Zaccheus the chief of the publicans. Indeed, the very occasion of the murmuring of the Pharisees in our text was that all the publicans and sinners draw near unto Christ to hear him, and doubtless the very manner of His reception of them justifies the peculiar word of the accusation which charged Christ as expectantly awaiting them.

At the feast of Matthew, Christ Himself acknowledged that the accusation made at that feast was true and assigned the reason for His conduct. But on that occasion He seems simply to have admitted these sinners as companions. His answer was that He had come to call not the righteous but sinners to repentance. It was, therefore, natural that He should consort with those He came to save. The more wicked they were, the more they needed His salvation. The more steeped in sin, the more call was there for His influence to draw them from it. The more guilty they were, the more did they need encouragement to come to Him. The announcement of the nature of His work was, therefore, an assignment of sufficient reason for His stooping to the very depths of human sin to lift out of its toils and from their own defilement the men who were most deeply stained and most inextricably entangled.

In the light of Christ's life and work as we now see it, we can comprehend the fullness of His mercy and the appropriateness of His action.

He who brings bread to the hungry will seek first those who are ready to perish. Though all may need his help, yet must these first be relieved who otherwise may die before their turn may come.

Such, therefore, was Christ's true and justifying answer to the charge at Matthew's feast that He was consorting with sinners. But, as we have seen, the accusation in our text is stronger. It is not merely companionship where men had come in as these did and sat down at the feast with Him and His disciples. It is more than this that is here implied. It is that Christ was waiting, watching, looking out for, hoping to receive, and expecting with earnest desire that these sinners should come to Him.

And Christ makes to this charge a most remarkable answer, one which shows that we may give to this word "receiveth" all the fullness of meaning which may at any time be ascribed to it.

His answer is contained in three of the most remarkable parables to be found in all His sayings. In them He shows that this is His true attitude, nay, that the word of the accusation does not go far enough. It does not express the full truth. There is much more than any could have imagined from His conduct.

Thus replying, too, He shows us unmistakably that the disposition toward sinners He then sets forth is not that of a transient occasion but the pervading and ruling spirit of His life. Nay, that thus is set forth the grand truth in His spiritual kingdom of the deep yearning which He feels that every sinner, a single sinner though but one, any sinner the more vile he be the more is it true, should find in Him salvation and restoration to the failed relationship of God.

The first parable by which He teaches this is that of the shepherd of an hundred sheep leaving the ninety and nine safe within the fold while he goes forth into the wilderness to seek the one that is lost. How strongly and yet how sweetly does the familiar illustration come home to the hearts of all. The anxiety of the shepherd, the danger of the sheep, his going forth with longing heart into the pathless wilderness to seek the sheep, straying perhaps in indifference, in ignorance of danger, perhaps in joy of forbidden pastures, and the speed which the shepherd makes lest the darkness should overtake him and his search be vain or the cold of the night benumb the straying lamb until it perish or the wolf come and devour it when there is no protector by, and when he finds, how tenderly does he deal with it, not chiding nor chastising, not roughly driving it before him nor even leading it back again over the rough roads, but laying it upon his shoulders, bearing for it all the pain and toil of the return and gladly bearing it because of the joy which he feels that he has recovered his sheep. As we recall the emotions natural to the shepherd, we can imagine that joy with which he makes his voice to ring, over hill and dale, calling out to his friends and neighbors, "I have found my sheep, I have found my sheep! Rejoice with me! I have found my sheep!"

Is it true that Jesus thus yearns over every lost sinner and thus longs to find him and to bring him back into his fold? He tells us so. It is thus that He answers the accusation of the Pharisees that He was an expectant looker-out for sinners, eagerly desires to receive and entertain them. Yes, and He adds that as He thus brings each one by persistence and faith into His kingdom, He shouts out His triumph throughout the realms of heaven, and the angelic hosts rejoice at the salvation of a single man.

> There are ninety and nine that safely lay
> In the shelter of the fold,
> But one had wandered far away
> In the desert so lone and cold

Away in the mountains wild and bare,
Away from the Shepherd's tender care.

Shepherd! hast thou not here thy ninety and nine?
Are they not enough for thee?
But the Shepherd replied "This one of mine
has wandered away from me;
The way may be wild and rough and steep;
I go to the desert to find my sheep."

But none of the ransomed ever knew
How deep were the waters crossed;
Nor how dark was the night the Lord passed thro'
Ere he found the sheep that was lost.
Away in the desert he heard its cry
So feeble and helpless and ready to die.

Shepherd; whence are those blood drops all the way
Up the mountain's rugged track?
They were shed for the one who had gone astray.
Ere the shepherd could bring him back.
Lord, why are thy hands so rent and torn?
For him they were pierced with many a thorn.

And afar up the mountain thunder riven
And along the rocky steep
There arose the glad song of joy to heaven
Rejoice, I have found my sheep.
And the angels echoed around the throne
Rejoice, for the Lord brings back His own.

This first parable in which He thus replies mingles the idea of compassion for the sheep with that of the loss of something which is owned. Our Lord, therefore, proceeds one step further in the next by the exclusion of the possible suffering of that which was lost. He thus sets before us the fact that His yearning is not simply compassion, but earnest desire to regain a lost possession. It is the parable of the woman who has lost one out of ten pieces of silver. The lost piece cannot suffer. It cannot be destroyed. It will remain as valuable in itself as ever. If found by another, it will be as useful as ever. But it is a lost piece of property. And the woman begins for it a diligent search. Can we not see her as she looks in one possible place and then another? "Where can I have put it?" she exclaims. "Could I have mislaid it, or have I dropped it?" And as she thinks of this possibility, she lights a candle and sweeps the house and seeks diligently until she finds it.

Is this descriptive of Christ? He says it is. He says it to the Pharisees, who have despised Him for His intercourse with sinners. And, thus, He declares to them these sinners are mine. Each one of them is mine. You say that I am waiting for them. I am doing more than this. Your word waiting does not express the idea. I have lost my property, which I would regain for my happiness and joy, and I am searching for it.

How blessed the language, how deeply should it impress every heart: Christ is searching after sinners. He has lighted His candle. He is sweeping the floor. He is determined to find that poor sinner if possible. Who is it that He thus seeks? It is every sinner. It is any sinner. It is the sinner that is most utterly lost. It is the sinner who cannot even move to come unto Him, but upon whom He will throw the light of His candle, and by the reflection of His light from the lost one will recover His own, and replace him in His treasury.

Here again, the joy He asserts as His in such finding. Imagine the woman's exultation after her long and diligent search. She calls to all her friends. "I have found it, I have found it!" And so Christ also has His joy as He sees of the travail of His soul and the angels who strengthened Him in Gethsemane proclaim to the heavenly host the new cause of rejoicing— "Another soul of man is saved. Another penitent is found!"

Ah, but our hearts respond "there is no sin there, no sin in the coin, none even in the sheep even if willfully it had strayed." Doubtless the Pharisees were ready to say the same thing with a sneer. Why talk of such loss and finding in connection with such sinners?

But Christ stopped the sneer of the Pharisees by His third and last parable, that inimitable one of the Prodigal Son. Here there was sin. It was a willful son, one not content with his father's house and love, one anxious to shake off dependence upon that father's authority, one bent upon the free use of all he might call his own, going forth—and that not to a wise but a foolish and sinful use of his opportunities, spending his whole substance in riotous living, brought to a sense of his sinful rebellious and wasted life only by his condition of starvation and servitude, and thus returning. And to such as one how does the father, who here stands for Jesus, appear? As one stern and unbending and unforgiving, turning away in wrath from his spendthrift son and looking with disgust upon his tattered rags? Nay, it is the father who has never forgotten the absent one, who has ever yearned over him, who now sees him while yet afar off, and recognizes him even in his beggary and rags, and who waits not for words of penitence, but filled with compassion runs and falls upon his neck and kisses him, owns him as his son, clothes him with the best robe, putting the ring upon his finger and shoes upon his feet, and kills the fatted calf in honor of his return.

No question here of sinfulness, nor of abundant provocation to anger. But still less question of earnest love and vehement desire to get back the lost one. The parable appeals to every child, and especially to every parent. Can there be such love, such forgiveness, such indestructible compassion? Our hearts say, "yes, yes." They yearn for our own children. We would do all this for them. No joy could exceed the joy which would fill a father's heart at this the safe return of one long mourned as lost.

Christ says, as are your hearts so is mine. It is on this account and with these feelings that I seek after sinners. Each of them is as dear to Me as such a son to you. As you feel more tenderly even to the undeserving when lost, than to the dutiful who have never strayed, so do I feel towards My poor lost ones. The more they have strayed, the more do I yearn. The greater the sinner, the more anxious My heart. My love has never failed. I have never forgotten one. And I stand as did the father of the prodigal looking out even into the far distance that I may see the penitent return.

Such then is Christ's answer to the charge of the Pharisees. He uses all three of these parables to explain it. No one of them is sufficient. They must be continued together to teach the whole truth. His enemies said, "He receiveth sinners," He waits for them, watches for them, is expecting them, takes delight in their coming. This was their reproach.

Christ says to them, You have but a part of the truth. I do not only wait, I go and seek the lost, I am filled with anxiety to find my sheep. I search for my treasure as with lighted candle and sweeping broom. My heart yearns for the wanderer, I look eagerly for him, my spirit within cries out in weariness at his delay. I am ready to welcome him with unequalled honors. It is not pleasure only that I take in the society of these sinners. My soul cries out with joy. I cannot contain my feelings. To all my servants around as each returns I impart my rapture, and the heavens ring with joyful exclamation as a single sinner comes back to God.

Do you believe Jesus, my hearers? Has He spoken here the truth concerning Himself? Is it, can it be, true that Jesus thus yearns over each one here? That He thus earnestly desires the salvation of each soul?

Too long have you lingered in the ways of sin and folly. Too long have you stood and trembled and doubted what might be His feelings toward you.

Hearken today to the message of His yearning love by which he would win you.

It tells you of sinners waited for, longed for with deep desire.

It tells you of the yearnings of your Jehovah Savior who cannot afford to lose you. It tells you of His earnest seeking, by which He would take you wounded and sore and unable to return and bear you back upon His shoulders to the fold.

Can you resist these pleadings? Can you reject such love? Can you disappoint such earnest longings and desires?

Will you not welcome to your heart your blessed Lord, your glorious Savior, who thus seeks you that He may regain His wandering sheep, His lost treasure, His prodigal child, that He may once more number you among His own.

Suffer this day the word of exhortation. Would that I could utter such words as would make you hesitate no longer.

Where shall I find them? Isaiah 55:1, "Ho, every one that thirsteth, come ye to the waters, and he that hath no money; come ye, buy, and eat; yea, come, buy wine and milk without money and without price."

John A. Broadus
Preachers and Preaching

Brother Chairman and Fellow Preachers:

The many courtesies and privileges that have been mine, in connection with this week's visit to Nashville, have very deeply touched my heart, but none more so than this privilege of "breaking bread" with you, my honored fellow preachers. Closer and dearer to me than any other group of workers in all the world are my brother preachers.

No formal address would I attempt to bring you, as we sit together about these tables. With a painful sense of my unworthiness do I now respond to your request. Let me talk with you, quite informally, just as my heart shall constrain me. I would hasten to offer you my most cordial congratulations that you are privileged to be Christ's preachers. Yours is the most worth while work beneath the stars. I feel about it as the great-souled Phillips Brooks felt, when he laughingly told a large gathering of business men in Boston, at a noonday luncheon: "I am sorry for all you fellows who are not parsons." A modern writer who seems to have a penchant for cheapening preachers, and for deriding churches and all the activities of organized Christianity, said recently in a widely circulated journal that he could not for the life of him understand why any red-blooded man could give his life to the business of being a preacher. I suppose that he is utterly unable to understand it! But you understand it, and I understand it, and each of us would whole-heartedly exclaim with Paul: "I thank Christ Jesus our Lord, who hath enabled me, for that he counted me faithful, putting me into the ministry." If I may speak quite personally for a moment, I would say that it was the consuming ambition of my heart from my earliest recollection to be a lawyer, but that noble calling was not Christ's appointed calling for me. Now, for a generation, I have given my humble testimony, as a preacher of his glorious gospel. If he should give me a thousand lives, today, and ask me to choose what calling I would have them follow, I would not hesitate one moment, to choose that every one of the thousand lives should be a preacher for him.

> "Happy if with my latest breath,
> I may but speak His name;
> Preach Him to all, and gasp in death,
> Behold, behold the Lamb!"

You would very earnestly agree that nothing can take the place of the Christian ministry. The triumphs of the press and of the schools; the marvelous advances in the realm of science; none of these, nor all combined, can take the place of Christ's preacher. "For after that in the wisdom of God, the world by wisdom knew not God, it pleased God by the foolishness of preaching to save them that believe."

Nor will history let us forget that the halcyon days of Christianity have always been the days of great preaching. It was so in the days of Tertullian, was so in the days of Luther and Calvin and Latimer and Knox. It was so in the days of Whitefield and Wesley and Robert Hall and Jonathan Edwards. It was so in the days of Spurgeon and Maclaren and Beecher and Joseph Parker. It was so in the days of Phillips Brooks and John A. Broadus and B. H. Carroll and Charles B. Galloway. Triumph goes ever with true preaching, and defeat goes ever with false preaching. An ignorant, ineffective, unworthy pulpit is the supreme handicap to the furtherance of Christ's cause throughout the earth. The moral safety of the nation and of the world is largely in the keeping of the Christian pulpit.

God's Word has much to say to preachers, personally, as well as to give them solemn admonitions concerning their all-important message. Paul's ringing admonition to Timothy is to be faithfully taken to heart by every preacher: "Take heed to thyself, and to thy teaching; for in doing this, thou shalt both save thyself and them that hear thee." And also Paul's word to Titus comes with great force to every preacher: "Let no man despise thee." Let us mark well the expression. Paul does not say: "Let no man hate thee," but "Let no man despise thee." Paul exhorts us so to live that our character and conduct shall not be despicable. True manhood is to be exalted in the preacher's calling, to the highest degree. One can be easily assured that John the Baptist was a true man, and so was Paul. Terrible is it beyond all words for Christ's preacher to be the wrong kind of a man. The Christian ministry is not for prigs and fops and charlatans. It is the most masculine, virile, heroic calling on this earth. Often are we correctly reminded that knowledge is power, but character is far more so. What a man is, in himself, counts far more than what he says with his lips or works with his hands. If the preacher be lacking in fundamental integrity, then, his life is a ghastly, living lie. The men of the world will bear with our crotchets, as preachers, if we so live as to convince them that we are true, genuine, sincere men. Every preacher ought to be such a sincere and unselfish man that his community would be willing to trust its life into his hands.

So immeasurably important is this great matter that you will at once agree that it behooves us, as preachers, to watch with all diligence and conscientiousness against every wrong habit and motive. The preacher is perhaps more sorely tempted than is any other man. Satan's chief grudge is doubtless against the true preacher. Therefore, the preacher is ever to watch most faithfully against every wrong habit and motive. For one thing, the preacher is to set himself resolutely against idleness. By all means, he is to learn the value of time. Quaint old Ben Franklin's word should never be forgotten: "Value time, for time is the stuff of which life is made." Over the gateway of many a man who has failed, might be written the secret of his failure in these two words: "He dawdled." The preacher is to be the busiest man in the community, and he is to be busy with the right things. He is never to lose the sense of proper perspective and proportion in his matchless work. He will be tempted constantly to give his time and energy to the smaller things. The story is widely told of a preacher who spent nearly all of his time in going from one business house to another in his town, writing promiscuous letters, wherever he paused, and then hurrying to the depot to mail them, when he heard the sound of the coming train. One day, this same preacher declaimed loudly against the indifference of his people, vehemently asking them: "What more can I do, in this town, than I am doing?" To which question, one of the men present made the blunt reply: "Nothing more, unless you meet all the freight trains too!" The preacher is never to be a trifler for one hour with his incomparable task. He is to be the most indefatigable toiler in his community. It is said that Whitefield preached eighteen thousand times, ere he reached the age of fity-six. Certainly, the preacher is one man who should be utterly unwilling to eat the bread of idleness.

He should also watch most conscientiously against the love of ease, even as one should watch against some fatal infection. Ease is the bane of mankind. It undoes nations and organizations and families and individuals. God's Word sounds a woe for them who are at ease in Zion. Paul's exhortation to Timothy is to be heeded by every preacher: "Thou therefore endure as a good soldier of Jesus Christ." Certain it is that if a preacher is hankering for some easy job in the ministry, he is already on the toboggan; and unless his spirit shall be radically changed, he is traveling rapidly to a humiliating defeat. If men in Christ's work would save their lives, they must lose them for Christ and his gospel. Emerson's essay pictures the selfish striving of many for fame, while here and there an unselfish worker forgets himself into immortality. Jowett's great word is for preachers: "When we cease to bleed, we cease to bless." So was Mazzini's word with which he challenged the youth of Italy: "Come and suffer." So was Carlyle's last word, whispered to a friend: "Give yourself royally."

The preacher is to watch against impatience. "Patient continuance in well doing" is to be the rule of our lives. Paul thus speaks to us: "And let us not be weary in well doing; for in due season, we shall reap, if we faint not." And again: "Therefore, my beloved brethren, be ye steadfast, unmovable, always abounding in the work of the Lord, forasmuch as ye know that your labor is not in vain in the Lord." I am a believer in the long pastorate, both for the sake of the preacher, and for the cause for which he lives. The frequently changing pastorates may well give us deep concern. They may well revive the old question asked by Jeremiah: "Why gaddest thou about so much to change thy way?" Or the statement, made in the eleventh chapter of Hebrews: "They declare plainly that they seek a country."

The preacher is to guard against professionalism. Just here is a very serious snare for the preacher. If a preacher preaches just to preach, he is indeed in a wretched plight, and the people who hear him are in a still more wretched plight. The fires of zeal and passion are to be kept blazing in a preacher's life, even at white heat if possible. If preaching becomes insipid and stale to the preacher, if it does not taste good to him, let him betake himself to the quiet place, and so wait on God, by prayer and by meditation on his word, that his preacher heart will again be ablaze with interest and compassion for the souls of the people. Professional preaching is abominable both in the sight of God and of serious men.

The preacher is unceasingly to guard against every unworthy habit and motive. How wretched a sight for a preacher to be a coward, or a blustering braggart! How terrible a thing for him to be jealous and envious, on any pretext, against his fellow preacher! Envy is as rottenness in a man's bones. Well does the Bible ask: "Who can stand before envy?" The prophet of God, the shepherd of souls, the ambassador of Christ, is to be the right kind of a man. He is to be gladly willing to pay the price, whatever it costs and wherever it leads, for spiritual power. He is ever to tread the blood-sprinkled way of the cross. Paul paid the price for spiritual power. Let us ponder long and deeply his pungent words: "But what things were gain to me, those I counted loss for Christ. Yea, doubtless, and I count all things but loss for the excellency of the knowledge of Christ Jesus my Lord: for whom I have suffered the loss of all things, and do count them but refuse, that I may win Christ." Verily, the most epic, heroic, important business in all this earth calls for the right kind of men.

Let me hurry on for some words about the preacher's message. He is divinely commanded ever to see faithfully to his message. It is to be God's message. In season and out of season, the preacher is unwaveringly to declare the whole counsel of God. He is to magnify biblical preaching. He is to remember that his pulpit is his supreme throne of power and responsibility. The Thermopylae of Christianity is the pulpit. Surely, the preacher must realize that he must needs be a constant, earnest student, and supremely a student of God's holy Word. If the preacher does not study, he will become an echo, instead of a voice. Christ would have his preachers to be voices and not echoes. "Study to show thyself approved unto God, a workman that needeth not to be ashamed, rightly dividing the word of truth." It will mark the beginning of a preacher's certain decline, when he ceases to be an earnest student. Just here is a matter calling for the most frequent and conscientious self-examination at the hands of every preacher. To be careless here is indeed a tragedy.

Let me frankly express my humble, personal conviction that very few preachers preach often enough. I do not now speak of the regulation sermon—"firstly, secondly, thirdly, and finally, brethren"—but I speak of the preacher's wayside ministry. His opportunities to witness for Christ are constant and endless. He is to seek to make faithful use of them all. In doing so, he will be walking in the steps of Jesus, the one perfect Preacher. Jesus gave his vast message on the new birth to just one man, and his far-reaching message on life spiritual and eternal to just one woman. Has the preacher one soul for an audience? Then let him there give his most faithful testimony for Christ, for issues are bound up with the preacher's audience and message, both for time and for eternity. Let Jesus teach us all by his suggestive, unceasing, wayside ministry.

You will fully agree, I am happy to believe, that the preacher is to keep to the great central themes of God's Word. The false prophet is not only the one who denies and perverts the truth, but he is also a false prophet whose chief emphasis is given to minor and secondary contentions. Misplaced emphasis explains the pitiful defeat of preachers again and again. Sometimes one's heart is pierced with grave concern for the pulpit, as he reads the printed list of subjects to be discussed from the pulpit. It is easy for a preacher to catch the cheap cheer, but such behavior presages a cheap man. The itch for notoriety is indeed a deadly microbe. We do not go forth on our God-appointed mission as preachers, to be ranters and lambasters and snickering caterers, with an endless succession of grotesque, spectacular, bizarre, barn-storming methods; but we are to go as true prophets of God, as faithful, compassionate shepherds of souls, hiding ourselves ever behind the cross of Christ. Thus does Paul put it: "We preach not ourselves, but Christ Jesus the Lord, and ourselves as your servants for Jesus' sake." Both our message and our method as preachers are to be such that the sinning, needy people to whom we preach, shall see Jesus only.

Certainly, the preacher is forever to sound the positive and not the negative note. The pulpit is no place for a religious stammerer. It is conviction that convinces. "For if the trumpet give an uncertain sound, who shall prepare himself to the battle?" Let us hark back to the preachers of the New Testament, and mark their positive note. Listen to Peter and John: "Whether it be right in the sight of God, to hearken unto you more than unto God, judge ye. For we cannot but speak the things which we have seen and heard." And to these words from Paul: "Wherefore I take you to record this day, that I am pure from the blood of all men. For I have not shunned to declare unto you all the counsel of God." And again, let us listen to this positive word from Paul—a word that has reassured myriads, both in life and in death: "For I know whom I have believed, and am persuaded that he is able to keep that which I have committed unto him, against that day."

Again, the preacher is to preach with the conquering note of hopefulness. The preacher is not to be a whining blubberer. He is not to mistake hysterics for piety. He is not to be a wailing pessimist, but he is ever to be a Christian optimist. He is to assure the people that God's grace and promises are adequate for every possible test and experience that can come to mankind. Somebody has given us this definition both of the pessimist and of the optimist: "A pessimist is one who sees a difficulty in every opportunity, and an optimist is one who sees an opportunity in every difficulty." The preacher is to show the people the way of certain triumph in Christ. The preacher can surely do better than to give his emphasis to the sounding of dirges and of lamentations, and to the teasing of a burdened people with hopeless jeremiads. A little boy who was made to sit under such a pulpit, protestingly asked: "Mother, will his fusser never get tired?" Surely, surely, the preacher is not to degenerate into an old scold. Paul's expression: "Neither murmur ye," is ever a timely word for preachers. Paul always sounded the conquering note, whether in jail or out of it. "Rejoice," "rejoice evermore," "rejoice in the Lord, always." Paul was an invincible Christian optimist, as ought every preacher to be, and all because of Christ.

Once more, you will earnestly agree that the seeking note for the salvation of the people is ever to be the regnant note in the pulpit. It is always to be the primary and crowning note in the message of Christ's preacher. Our Saviour and Master will not let us forget that his commission for his preachers today is the same as that which he gave to the mighty Paul: "I send thee to open their eyes, to turn them from darkness to light, and from the power of Satan unto God, that they may receive forgiveness of sins, and an inheritance among them that are sanctified, by the faith that is in me." Let us listen to the same mighty Paul as he tells us of his God-given ministry: "And hath given to us the ministry of reconciliation; to wit, that God was in Christ, reconciling the world unto himself, not imputing their trespasses unto them; and hath committed unto us the word of reconciliation. Now then we are ambassadors for Christ, as though God did beseech you by us: we pray you in Christ's stead, be ye reconciled to God." The seeking note for lost souls is forever to be regnant in every pulpit and also in every church. What better would our churches be than ethical clubs, if such note should be absent from them? Christ's preachers are to watch for souls, as men who must give a most solemn account to God. May we so faithfully watch that we may give such account with joy and not with grief! Let us unceasingly paraphrase the cry of Rutherford of Anwoth:

"Oh, if these souls about me,
  Would meet me at God's right hand,
My heaven would be two heavens,
  In Immanuel's Land!"

Far too long have I detained you, but your patient and sympathetic attention has constrained me to keep on talking. From my deepest heart I thank you for this courtesy at your hands, and I thank God for you and your incomparably blessed work. One of the mightiest preachers of earth, in the generation just gone, was Dr. B. H. Carroll of Texas. He was pre-eminently a preacher to preachers. In one of his messages to preachers, on the text, "I magnify mine office," he closed his message with this expression, which I trust, all of us as preachers will joyfully adopt as our individual confession, today and forever: "I magnify my office, O my God, as I get nearer home. I can say more truthfully every year, I thank God that he put me in this office; I thank him that he would not let me have any other; that he shut me up to this glorious work. And when I get home among the blessed on the bank of everlasting deliverance, and look back toward time and all of its clouds, and sorrows, and pains and privations, I expect to stand up and shout for joy, that down there in the fog and mists, down there in the dust and in the struggle, God let me be a preacher. I magnify my office in life; I magnify it in death; I magnify it in heaven; I magnify it, whether poor or rich, whether sick or well, whether strong or weak, anywhere, everywhere, among all people. Lord God, I am glad that I am a preacher, that I am a preacher of the glorious gospel of Jesus Christ."

Fred F. Brown
Her Central Message

It was my privilege to be in the Army of Occupation for a while after the signing of the Armistice in 1918. One Sunday morning I had a call from an American officer asking if I would come to a little village some thirty kilometers away and speak at the noon hour. I demurred because there were four other engagements for the day, but he insisted, and after telling me that his was an isolated outfit without a chaplain, he added, "If you will come, the service will be held in a Protestant church building." That interested me because for eleven months I had held services in all kinds of places—on ship deck, in hotel lobbies, in barns, in barrack rooms, sometimes out in the open, but I had not been in a church since leaving America, so I went. In the center of the little village that nestled there in the Moselle Mountains, I found a small stone church that was older than our Western civilization. An American lady played a crude pipe organ and I sat on the front seat in such deep meditation that time and place were forgotten until the officer plucked my sleeve and said, "It's time for you to speak." I stood and with the open Bible in my hand turned to face those American soldiers. They were in the Army of Occupation—all of them were men who had seen action. Their courage had been tested on the battlefields of northern France. Something strange had taken place as we sat there. When I arose I was unable to read until I had brushed away the mist that dimmed my eyes and had gained control of my emotions. Tears, of which they were frankly unashamed, were flowing down the cheeks of those strong men. I did not understand then what had happened, but later I knew. We were home again! Back in America! It was Sunday morning, and we had gathered for worship. We were looking across the aisles into the faces of parents, wives, sweethearts, and friends. The pastor was before us with the open Bible. The unbidden tears were our silent tribute to our home churches—to the teachings and influence of those churches that had followed us through the years.

May we not now, without the unusual circumstances, gather in thought in our accustomed places of worship. God help us to see something of the transcendent glory of what transpires in the church from Sunday to Sunday. What are the central elements of her message?

The church of Jesus Christ is telling people how to be saved. Many of us are identified with other groups—cultural, civic, and fraternal groups. I have no light word to speak of these organizations. Most of them are making wholesome, constructive contributions to society. In this meditation, however, I want us to see our churches as they stand apart and above all other organizations and institutions in the world bringing to lost men and women the story of a Saviour who died for our sin.

If we can but realize something of the significance of this message which the church is speaking from Sunday to Sunday, year in and year out, I believe that we will give her first place in our thought and affections—first place in our life loyalties.

The Bible has no misleading, superficial word to say about humanity. It is said that rugged old Cromwell remarked to an artist who was making his picture: "Paint me warts and all." The Bible paints us "warts and all." Listen: "All have sinned and come short of the glory of God." "All we like sheep have gone astray, we have turned every one to his own way." I realize that very few people are alarmed about sin today. Proud of our achievements and triumphs in the natural world, flattered by the teachings and emphasis of humanism, lulled into a sense of false security by the siren voice of sin itself, we are perhaps a little exasperated with one who would use the old fashioned word "sin." We have dabbled with sin and fondled sin until her ugly face has been transformed.

> Vice is a monster of so frightful mien,
> As to be hated needs but to be seen;
> Yet seen too oft, familiar with her face,
> We first endure, then pity, then embrace.

And yet those three letters, s-i-n, spell the tragedy of the universe. We may hear the word with an impatient shrug of the shoulders, we may try to dismiss the subject as unpleasant and irrelevant, we may wash our hands with easy going excuses and try to chloroform our souls but the fact of sin—personal sin, remains. The fact of guilt—personal guilt—remains. The fact of responsibility—personal responsibility—remains. The fact of consequences—sure and unalterable—remains. The Bible keeps before us the reality and issue of sin. The Bible begins with us at the beginning. Thorough diagnosis always precedes intelligent prescription.

> He reads each wound, each meaning clear—
> He puts his hand upon the place,
> And says thou ailest here, and here.

Having brought the Bible's message about sin the church brings the message about the Saviour. Earnestly, yearningly, and continuously she points to Calvary's cross and says: "Behold the lamb of God, which taketh away the sin of the world," "Believe on the Lord Jesus Christ, and thou shalt be saved," "Christ died for our sins according to the scriptures."

The church leads the lost person into the presence of a wondrous Saviour—the Saviour who said: "I am come to seek and to save that which was lost," the Saviour who said: "Come unto me, all ye that labour and are heavy laden, and I will give you rest," and "Him that cometh unto me, I will in no wise cast out." The church pleads with the lost person to hear the gracious, golden invitation and exhortation of the Bible, to accept Christ. She lingers with the last invitation in the Bible, where the Saviour seems to lean out of heaven, touch John on the shoulder, and say: "Give them one more opportunity. Before you close the Book—before the curse is pronounced on any who shall add to or take from the message of the Bible—tell them once more to come—make the invitation cordial as the heart of God—make it universal—gather into this final appeal all the voices that speak to the human soul:" "And the Spirit and the bride say, Come. And let him that heareth say, Come. And let him that is athirst come. And whosoever will, let him take the water of life freely."

The church sees the "radium in the rubbish," "the angel in the ashes," the God-like in broken sinful man. The church reminds people that they are lost without Christ, and assures them that they can be saved by the atoning blood of Christ.

Years ago I read the story of the husband and wife, neither of them Christian, who decided to read the Bible through. Beginning at the first they read on, and on, and on. After several evenings the husband said: "Wife, if this book is true we are lost." They read on, and on, and on, until at last they were at Calvary's cross. Then the man said: "Wife, if this Bible is true we can be saved." That is the message of the church. That is the message which will be proclaimed from thousands of pulpits in America today. It is the message which I am trying to send out to any unsaved man or woman who may be listening to this broadcast. Whoever you are, wherever you are—in your home, in your car, in camp, on ship, wherever you are—I point to the Christ of Calvary who said: "And I, if I be lifted up from the earth, will draw all men unto me," to the one who said: "For God so loved the world, that he gave his only begotten Son, that whosoever believeth in him should not perish, but have everlasting life." I am urging you now to stand face to face with Jesus Christ the only Saviour from sin, "Neither is there salvation in any other: for there is none other name under heaven given among men, whereby we must be saved."

>Who will open mercy's door?
>Jesus will! Jesus will!
>As for pardon I implore?
>Jesus, blessed Jesus will!
>
>Who can take away my sin?
>Jesus will! Jesus will!
>Make me pure, without, within?
>Jesus, Blessed Jesus will!

This is an old, old message, but it is the message of the Bible. And I repeat, the church is the only institution in the world speaking this message to humanity. The church is the only institution in the world singing:

>There is a fountain filled with blood,
>Drawn from Immanuel's veins
>And sinners plunged beneath that flood
>Lose all their guilty stains.

Then, too, the church is telling people how to live after they are saved. Christianity is not only the way of salvation, Christianity is a way of life—the way to live. We are thinking now about character—the old fashioned, rugged virtues of honesty, sobriety, truthfulness, purity, kindness, unselfishness, love.

Some things do not change. Air, sunlight, and water have not changed since the creation of the universe. The great verities of character do not change. There can be no permanent progress and prosperity, no stability and security for the individual, the home, the school, the business enterprise, or the nation that is not undergirded by enduring moral and spiritual values. We may forget, we may neglect, we may deny, we may deceive ourselves and try various substitutes, but sooner or later we come to know that we cannot manage life without character.

The church of Jesus Christ continuously teaches that character is basic and indispensable. There are lapses, failures, and breakdowns among her members, but the church continues to challenge every life she touches to follow Christ's way. She points to the great abiding principles of character exemplified in the person and underscored in the teachings of her Lord and says: "This is the way, walk ye in it."

The presumption is not that there is no character outside of the church. There is. I know people of high ideals, unquestioned honor and integrity who do not belong to any church. As a matter of fact, some of them are hostile to the church. As I think of that group, however, I am unable to recall a single one of them who does not have a Christian background—a Christian home, parents who were followers of Christ and members of the church. It has always seemed to me that these fine people are like trees growing by a stream which feeds, nurtures, and keeps them alive while they are unconscious of their source of life and strength.

As the church moves on with her appeal for righteousness, rightness, as a way of life she is not in competition with other institutions that are trying to build a better world. She is far out ahead. She believes that one right who said: "The soul of reform is the reform of the soul." She believes that redeemed personality expressing itself in a Christian life is "the light of the world," "the salt of the earth."

Surely we may agree that this message of the church on how to live—the appeal for character—is timely, pertinent, and urgent.

I quote from some laymen: In 1929 Mr. Thomas A. Edison was in his laboratory in Fort Myers, Florida, and Mr. Roger Babson visiting him asked: "What do you visualize as the next great invention for America and the world?" Mr. Edison replied, "Babson, I have never posed as a preacher, but I say this to you, if there be a God, He will not permit us to advance a single step materially until we catch up spiritually. I say to you as a scientist that there is a fundamental law that there must be a balance of forces in this world, and when anybody or any force goes off on a tangent there is a crash. This applies to America as it has to every nation before it."

Giving the same emphasis the philosopher Bergson has said: "Man never had such a body as he now has. Science has elongated man's arm until he can strike an enemy miles away from him; has increased the power of his vision until he can see stars and worlds hitherto invisible; has improved the range of speech and hearing until he can send and receive messages to and from the ends of the earth; has accelerated the speed of his feet until he hurries across the earth faster than the twelve league booted one of ancient fable. But the greater spirits to handle these greater bodies, there's the problem."

On October 26, 1931, Mr. Roger Babson wrote in his Special Letter: "In these days of economic earthquakes, words fail me to emphasize sufficiently the great importance of this economic principle! *Character is the real security* and the basis of all permanent progress. Capitalism, Socialism, Communism, Fascism and all other 'isms' are mere tools. Any one of these systems operated in 'Jesus' way,' would be an improvement over present conditions. On the other hand, any one of these systems of itself, without the spirit of Jesus, is bound to fail. The history of Babylon, Persia, Egypt, Greece, Rome, Spain and other formerly great and prosperous nations proves this.

"To those militarists who are depending for protection upon armaments: to those employers who are depending for protection upon *money;* and to those wage workers who are depending for their protection upon *unions* . . . my closing word is:—*Remember the Chinese Wall.* The Chinese Wall was the greatest piece of construction work ever attempted. It was started in 214 B.C. under the Emperor Shi Hwang-ti to keep out the Mongol Tartars, and it took generations to build. It was 1200 miles long stretching across the entire frontier of China. It was the most carefully planned and gigantically constructed protective measure ever conceived. But did this wall keep the Mongols out? Surely no. They finally bribed a gate keeper and walked through the gate! Once again I say that the only security is character and the only progress comes through its development."

In these statements the scientist, the philosopher, and the economist are emphasizing the message which an aged preacher in the long ago sent to a group of people in a little city called Philippi. He said: "Whatsoever things are true, whatsoever things are honest, whatsoever things are just, whatsoever things are pure, whatsoever things are lovely, whatsoever things are of good report: if there be any virtue, and if there be any praise think on these things."

Jesus calls us; o'er the tumult
Of our life's wild, restless sea,
Day by day His sweet voice soundeth,
Saying, "Christian, follow Me."

Jesus calls us from the worship
Of the vain world's golden store,
From each idol that would keep us,
Saying "Christian, love Me more."

Jesus calls us: by Thy mercies,
Savior, may we hear Thy call,
Give our hearts to Thy obedience,
Serve and love Thee best of all.

H. C. Brown, Jr.
The Walk of the Pharisee

Matthew 23:1-36

Two blindfolded soldiers who were part of an experiment designed to determine directional accuracy without physical sight were led to the edge of a runway. The two men were equipped with special metal containers, filled with lime, to spray white streams to mark their routes as they marched across the field. Within a few minutes after the soldiers started walking it was evident that they were unable to walk a straight line without physical vision. When the accompanying attendants stopped them, both men were hundreds of feet from their assigned targets. Even though they tried to walk straight courses, they both failed.

We have recorded in the Bible, and in other sources, the story of a group of people who intended to walk straight for God but whose spiritual judgment proved to be faulty. Around 200 B.C. these people separated themselves from heathenism and diluted Judaism for the purpose of doing the will of Jehovah. They were called the "separated" or the "Pharisees." Their motive was exalted; they were counted among the best people God had.

Between the time of their noble dedication and the time that Jesus preached something happened. Matthew's Gospel, in chapter 23, verses 1-36, sets forth a graphic picture of the Pharisees in Jesus' day. This chapter shows that a dreadful change had come to the exalted purpose of the Pharisees. The origin of the pharisaical group was pleasing in God's sight, but the conclusion was abominable.

It is important that we see the Pharisees as Christ saw them for the purpose of avoiding the walk of the Pharisee. In the New Testament the term "walk" is used as a designation for a course of action or a course of life. Thus the subject is "The Walk of the Pharisee."

The person most likely to be a Pharisee in the biblical sense is the person who tries to please God but fails. The title "Pharisee" will never be given to a drunkard, an athiest, or an ungodly person in revolt against the Lord. Rather, it is to be given to the person who loses his way in God's service. He it is who is most likely to be a modern Pharisee.

The Pharisee conceitedly craves personal prominence. He seeks to be seen of men as he serves God. "But all their works they do for to be seen of men: they make broad their phylacteries, and enlarge the borders of their garments" (v. 5).

Phylacteries were small leather boxes, strapped to the forehead or to the left arm near the heart, containing Scripture verses written on parchment. The size of the phylacteries gave an indication of the zeal for God's Word on the part of those wearing them. It was easy to enlarge those phylacteries and to allow that visual mechanical display of obedience to God to take the place of true obedience.

The borders of garments referred to in the text were the borders of prescribed clothes that the Jews wore in recognition of obedience to the laws of Jehovah. In order to demonstrate that they were wearing the proper clothes with the prescribed borders, some Pharisees deliberately enlarged those borders for all people to see.

Christ placed his finger upon a problem that is very real to a religious person. This delicate problem is to know the difference between service for God and service which sinfully and shamefully displays self. If an individual serves God, he must be active, and to be active means to be seen of men. The pressures that would drive a person to a sinful desire to be seen of men are insidious and terrifying. In the desire to solve this dilemma some individuals resort to sub-Christian levels of conduct. When the Pharisee does engage in service for God, he does so for the purpose of having people notice that he is serving the Lord. The person with the pharisaical mind has an insatiable appetite for prominence, and he feeds that appetite by constantly pushing self to the center of the stage.

The Pharisee seeks to be honored by men as a reward for his service to God. They "love the uppermost rooms at feasts, and the chief seats in the synagogues" (v. 6).

When does a simple desire to have one's work recognized become a sinful craving for praise and honor? The problem is in knowing the difference between serving God for the glory of God and serving God for the purpose of being honored by men. There is a dividing line between these extremes, and a dedicated individual who deserves to serve God must know where the point of division is. To cross that invisible line and to court honor and glory from doting parents and admiring friends because of service for God is to walk like a Pharisee.

Christ gave a remarkable answer to this perplexing problem when he said, "But he that is greatest among you shall be your servant. And whosoever shall exalt himself shall be abased; and he that shall humble himself shall be exalted" (vv. 11-12).

The Pharisee tragically endangers the eternal destiny of men. He refuses the kingdom of God. "But woe unto you, scribes and Pharisees, hypocrites! for ye shut up the kingdom of heaven against men: for ye neither go in yourselves" (v. 13).

Christ presented a paradox. Though the Pharisees thought that they, as religious people, were within the kingdom of God, the judgment of Jesus was that they were not. Because of their training, the Pharisees should have been the first to accept Jesus Christ as the Messiah, but because of their spiritual blindness they rejected Him. How pitiful and tragic was the example set by the Pharisees!

Within the doors of many churches there are, no doubt, individuals who are just as lost to the kingdom of God as were the Pharisees. Because these individuals are active in church affairs and are honored by fellow church members, they suppose that they are in the kingdom. As modern men who walk like Pharisees, they, too, stand outside the kingdom of God.

The present-day Pharisee tries to prevent seeking sinners from entering the kingdom. "But woe unto you, scribes and Pharisees, hypocrites! for ye shut up the kingdom of heaven against men: . . . neither suffer ye them that are entering to go in" (v. 13).

The Pharisees tried to prevent seeking sinners from entering the kingdom by closing the door to the kingdom. They denied that the kingdom was at hand; they spread false teachings about the kingdom of God and about Jesus Christ; and seeking sinners were turned away from the door of eternal life. The Pharisees tried to prevent seeking sinners from entering the kingdom by proselyting those sinners to themselves and to their cause. "Woe unto you, scribes and Pharisees, hypocrites! for ye compass sea and land to make one proselyte, and when he is made, ye make him twofold more the child of hell than yourselves" (v. 15). The tragic truth is that when the Pharisees won other individuals to their cause, the disciples were more perverted than their teachers. The Pharisees went to fantastic extremes to win individuals to their position without any regard as to the consequences to those persons.

A preacher who resorts to high-pressure tactics, whether in revival or in personal visitation, to cause a person to join a church is in danger of adding one to the church but not to the kingdom of God. The church member who is more concerned with numbers on the Sunday School record book than with eternal life for the Sunday School pupils is in danger of pushing people into the church apart from conversion. It is absolutely necessary that a person be converted before he be counted.

The Pharisees deliberately deceived others with a double standard of speech. "Woe unto you, ye blind guides, which say, Whosoever shall swear by the temple, it is nothing; but whosoever shall swear by the gold of the temple, he is a debtor!" (v. 16).

The religious leaders of Jesus' day practiced trickery in speech in regard to the use of promises and oaths. The Pharisees could make vows and seal those vows with oaths to the temple. Then if they desired to do so, they could break those vows because, they said, general oaths to the temple did not bind them. But if they had sealed their promises with oaths to the gold on the temple, they were obligated to keep those vows because, they said, oaths to the gold on the temple were specific and binding. All of this was a system of duplicity and trickery which allowed religious leaders to be liars and to be honorable at the same time.

The modern Pharisee also uses a double standard of speech. In each situation he is able to say the correct words and to win admiration and approval for his conduct because he is a master of duplicity. He agrees verbally with the position of his church that drinking alcohol is immoral, but he sips cocktails with his friends. He loudly praises on Sunday integrity in business, but he sells shoddy shoes on Monday morning. He condemns unclean speech at prayer meeting, but he tells filthy yarns at the Thursday morning coffee break. There is an inconsistence here.

The Pharisee blindly deceives himself with his double standard of speech. "Ye fools and blind: for whether is greater, the gold, or the temple that sanctifieth the gold?" (v. 17).

Christ called the Pharisees blind fools for their stupid use of oaths. The

Pharisees tried to make the gold on the temple of more importance than the temple and used this incorrect logic as their basis for their nefarious system of vows. Christ bluntly told them that their logic was false because their temple was more valuable than the gold which adorned it. The Pharisees thus found themselves under condemnation from the Lord because of their insincerity in speech.

Christ demands from His disciples not professions of orthodoxy of speech but simple, sincere speech which matches a pure and good life. Jesus taught that it is necessary to exemplify words as well as to speak them.

The Pharisee proudly majors on the mechanics of religion. He is scrupulously careful about money matters. "Woe unto you, scribes and Pharisees, hypocrites! for ye pay tithe of mint and anise and cummin, and have omitted the weightier matters of the law, justice, mercy, and faith. . . . Ye blind guides, which strain at a gnat, and swallow a camel" (vv. 23-24).

Christ was not critical of the Pharisees because of their minute attention to money matters. Rather, he commanded them to have financial fidelity to God. The point of the criticism was that the external, material, and mechanical features of religion were of more importance to the Pharisees than the internal, spiritual, and moral aspects of religion. Our Lord did not hesitate to press upon the Pharisees the importance of having a passion for justice, mercy, and faith.

As a person gives scrupulous attention to the material aspect of God's kingdom, he is to recognize that this physical aspect is not of paramount importance. Those distinct elements of religion commanded by Christ—justice, mercy, and faith—speak of righteous conduct in relation to God and man. Because these relate to God and to man, they are the vital elements of religion.

Jesus pointed out that the Pharisees, who were diligent about material matters but who failed to be just, merciful, and faithful, were like the Jew who strained a gnat out of his glass of wine and then swallowed from the same glass a dusty, dirty, smelly camel. If this were not so tragic, it would be laughable, would it not?

The Pharisee is scrupulously careful about form in religion. "Woe unto you, scribes and Pharisees, hypocrites! for ye make clean the outside of the cup and of the platter, but within they are full of extortion and excess" (v. 25).

A cup and a platter—bright and beautiful on the outside, but dirty and filthy on the inside—were the object lessons Christ used as He criticized the Pharisees because they were more concerned with a formal faith than they were with an ethical faith. The Pharisees were largely concerned with proper dress, with endless rules for dealing with sinners, with hundreds of laws for sabbath conduct, and with requirements dealing with feasts, food, and fasting. These formal elements of religion surpassed their concern for ethical righteousness.

The descendants of the first-century Pharisees live yet in the twentieth century, do they not? The modern Pharisee is primarily concerned with proper clothes, dignified personal bearing, social respectability, a stately edifice for worship, an elaborate ritual, a famous preacher, and other niceties of a formal religion. These are the supreme values of a person walking like a Pharisee.

The Pharisee piously practices hypocrisy. He falsely displays righteousness. "Woe unto you scribes and Pharisees, hypocrites! for ye are like unto whited sepulchers" (v. 27).

A revolting contrast was presented by Jesus. Outside, the tombs were clean, whitewashed, and attractive, but inside the tombs were dirty and full of corruption. So, said Christ, the Pharisees had external characters which were godly and righteous, while they had internal characters which were ungodly and corrupt. The Pharisees, Jesus said, knew that they were not righteous. Their pretense of piety earned for them the name "hypocrites."

The graveyard simile commands attention because it is dramatic, graphic, and revolting. It strikes the conscience because it deals with a constant and critical problem. When an individual wants to be righteous before God and man, the task is difficult. It costs much to avoid sham and pretense and hypocrisy; and it costs sacrificially to practice right action in religious affairs, family activities, business dealings, and personal matters.

The Pharisee falsely proclaims reverence for tradition. "Woe unto you, scribes and Pharisees, hypocrites! because ye build the tombs of the prophets, and garnish the sepulchers of the righteous" (v. 29).

With great earnestness the Pharisees professed reverence for the sacred heritage of their faith. Christ said they lied because they professed one thing and prepared to do another. Christ said, in effect, "You hypocrites have not listened to me, and you are preparing to murder me. You thereby demonstrate that you are exactly like your fathers."

How many people today profess a reverence for the noble heritage of the faith and then deny that profession by pharisaical deeds? Many, no doubt. It is commonplace to note that people piously affirm their belief in great traditions such as freedom of the pulpit, Christlike conduct in race relations, and the authority of the Word of God as an adequate guide for personal living. But they pay only lip service to these lofty ideals. The modern Pharisee professes to honor the magnificent principles of our faith, but he proves by his hypocritical deeds that he is a true descendant of the biblical Pharisee.

An embarrassing name, vicious enough to cause the chords of terror to ring in the heart, is the name "Pharisee." The connotations of this name are so ugly that no one who is even remotely acquainted with the thundering denunciations of Jesus against the Pharisees could possibly want to be a Pharisee.

Every Christian should examine his heart critically to determine if there are evidences of a pharisaical walk. The Pharisee conceitedly craves personal prominence; he tragically endangers the eternal destiny of men; he deceivingly professes sincerity of speech; he proudly majors on the mechanics of religion; and he piously practices hypocrisy.

The supreme purpose for this message has been that you and I will avoid that walk of the Pharisee by walking as Jesus walked. As John said, "He that saith that he abideth in him ought himself also so to walk, even as he walked" (1 John 2:6).

R. C. Campbell

Baptists and the Bible

All scripture is given by inspiration of God, and is profitable for doctrine, for reproof, for correction, for instruction in righteousness (2 Tim. 3:16).

Baptists have no creed but the Bible. They follow no man-made book. The Bible is the guide of their faith. It is their one guide.

God's Word rings with authority, has God's stamp upon it, the compulsion of Christ blazing in it, and the burden of a lost world motivating its purposes. Its message has echoed through the halls of time, and will resound in eternity. It has spanned the valleys of centuries, scaled the loftiest heights of human aspirations, plumbed the darkest depth of human needs. Its message will be sung in eternity. The Bible expresses the infinite purpose of God. It has weathered the storms and stress, ridicule and rebuffs, sarcasm and scorn, trouble and tribulations, critics and infidels, fire and sword, spear and bayonet, fagots and frivolities, ignorance and learning, poverty and riches, cynicism and every other ism of the long ages. It brings conviction and gives courage; instills hope and gives happiness; offers liberation and furnishes freedom, joy, and gladness, light and life, songs and sunshine to all earth's population.

Our thoughts are to center around three propositions: Why we believe the Bible; why we preach the Bible; why we love the Bible.

I. Why We Believe the Bible

1. We believe the Bible because it is inspired of God. "All scripture is given by inspiration of God." No one except God could give a book the message of which is adapted to all races of mankind. It is adapted to the passionate Arabian, to the sluggish Hottentot, to the high-bred Chinese, to the polite Frenchman, to the thoughtful Englishman, to the enterprising American, to the keen-witted Japanese. It has an ageless message, a

worldwide appeal, an age-long command, and a universal remedy. It is applicable to all classes, races, conditions, needs, climes, and ages of men. Well has it been said: "Only the Creator of man could be the creator of such a book." Superlatives are needed in our efforts to describe it. Its theme is the broadest, its purpose the noblest, its scope the vastest, its congregation the largest, its stream of influence the most inexhaustible, its lights the most illuminating, its song the most musical, its ideal the most heavenly, and its voice the most vibrant. Truly, "The Bible is not such a book as man would have written, if he could, or could have written if he would."

Give up the inspiration of the Scriptures and you dynamite the foundation on which the Christian system rests; you demolish its pillars; you wreck its superstructure. The only churches that are vigorous and aggressive against sin, mighty in conquest for righteousness, savingly effective as soul-winning agencies are those that believe, preach, and live the Bible. Any other "would-be bible" is weak, effeminate, dumb, and helpless before a world steeped in sin, and crying for help.

The authorship of the Bible is unique. It contains words written by kings, emperors, princes, poets, sages, philosophers, fishermen, statesmen. It was written by men in exile, in deserts, in tents, "by green pastures," and "still waters." Its authors are composed of fishermen, tax collectors, herdsmen, poor men, rich men, statesmen, prophets, exiles, captains, legislators, judges, men who were learned, trained by the best educators. There is no other book in existence comparable to it. The writing of it covered a period of fifteen hundred years. The writers, most of them, did not know one another. They wrote independently and produced this incomparable Book. It has never and shall never be out of date. Only God could give such a book.

Think! It is older than the church, "truer than tradition," more learned than the greatest university, more authentic than tribunals, more infallible than prophets, more orthodox than the truest creed. It is the world's first wonder, and Heaven's light for man's pathway.

It has been reviled, but never refuted; assailed, but never dented. Caesar's empire has passed away; the "Eternal City" of Rome is but a shadow; the strident march of Napoleon has forever ceased; the pyramids of the Pharaohs daily sink into the desert sand; Tyre is but a memory, but God's Word survives. Man's achievements are temporary; God's works are permanent. "Tradition has dug for it many a grave, intolerance has lighted for it many a fagot; many a Judas has betrayed it with a kiss; many a Peter has denied it with an oath; many a Demas has forsaken it, but the Word of God still endures."

2. We believe the Bible because it inspires men. Men are inspired by its wonders. No finite man can fathom its infinite mysteries. The mystery of creation, of death, of immortality, of the universe, of life, of redemption, of revelation are awe-inspiring to men. These mysteries do not lead us to discard the Bible, but to seek to discover more of its truths. There are mysteries everywhere: light, eating, breathing, electricity, the radio, nature—are all filled with mystery. The Bible holds the mysteries of God. It also holds the revelations of God.

Men are inspired by the simplicities of the Bible. Notwithstanding its mysteries, it contains a message so simple that, "The wayfaring men, though fools, shall not err therein." The Golden Rule, the prodigal son, the fourteenth chapter of John, the lost sheep, the good Samaritan—are all easily understood.

Its revelations inspire men. It reveals God to men, and men to themselves. Science, important and outstanding as are its discoveries, has not given us our greatest revelations. Did Science kindle in Luther the fires of the Reformation? Did Science inspire Livingstone to plant his life in Africa? Did Science inspire Columbus to discover America? Did Science inspire McAuley in his missionary work among the down-and-outs? No! the Bible inspired them.

It has inspired men when sin-blackened principalities and world powers and its foes seemed insurmountable. It has inspired them in the face of bitter opposition, appalling indifference, frigid coldness, glaring human weakness, bloody wars, morbid blackness, moral degeneracy, limitless depravity, sickening lukewarmness, hottest fires of destruction, floods of cynicism. It has inspired them to face lions' dens, to brave fiery furnaces, to suffer martyrdom, to face death councils, to expose themselves to disease and death. It has inspired them to seek salvation, cheered them in despair, resurrected their hopes, given happy homes, sent them, a band of singing pilgrims, rejoicing on their way, and declaring: "We seek another country that is a heavenly. We seek a city whose Builder and Maker is God." Thus they have pushed out and on, conquering nations, crossing oceans, traversing deserts, invading strongholds of wickedness.

Said one student to another, after a class period where the teacher had discussed the various versions of the Bible. "I think I prefer the King James Version for my part, although, of course, the Revised Version is more scholarly." His friend smiled and said: "I prefer my mother's translation of the Bible myself to any other version." "Your mother's?" cried the first young man. "Why, what do you mean, Fred?" "I mean that my mother has translated the Bible into the language of daily life for me since I was old enough to understand it. She translates it straight, too, and gives it full meaning. There has never been any obscurity about her version. Whatever printed version of the Bible I may study, my mother's is always the one that clears up my difficulties."

3. We believe the Bible because it involves human destiny. The Bible tells us plainly that those on the right hand will inherit the kingdom of God, while those on the left hand will go away into eternal punishment. According to the Bible, men go to one of two places—heaven or hell. Their acceptance or rejection of its message determines which. It is a signboard on life's highway, pointing men to the "Lamb of God, which taketh away the sin of the world." If we reject him, we are lost. Therefore, it is our most priceless possession. It offers lost mankind the way out of the labyrinthine roads of confusion, light for his dark night, bread for his hunger, water for his thirst, salvation for his lost condition.

Men who neglect it when things go well often cling to it in hours of dire need, all because they know their destiny hinges upon it.

A soldier tells of seeing a line a men several hundred feet in length outside a certain "Y" hut in France. "It looked like a lineup for the World Series in New York City," he said. "What do you think they are waiting for," asked the secretary. "Chocolate or cigarettes," he answered. "No, you will be surprised when I tell you. They are here because I announced that we are to have a new bunch of Testaments. The crowd is going into the trenches tomorrow."

Men in the trenches, facing death, read their Bibles not only unashamed, but with pride and joy. The need is so great that there are not enough Bibles to supply the demand.

II. Why We Preach the Bible

1. It acclaims the Messiah. The Bible centers in Christ, and Christ is central in the Bible. The Old Testament points to his coming. The New Testament is a record of the fact of his coming, the work that he did, the miracles that he wrought, the victories that he won. He was born of the

Virgin Mary, lived among men, wrought righteousness, and died on Calvary for the sins of the world; then ascended back to the Father.

Christ, the Messiah, was sent from God. He bore the image of God. He is God. He is the Anointed of God! Christ is the most powerful single influence in all human history. He transforms life. He replaces hate with love, despair with hope, lust with purity, filth with fineness, cynicism with optimism. He converted Saul into Paul, Cephas into a Peter, a monk into a Luther, a baseball player into a far-famed evangelist. He transforms wavering weaklings into spiritual giants, hopeless vagabonds into kings, slaves into servants of the Most High God. He gives robes for rags, victories for defeat, riches for poverty, salvation for damnation, heaven for hell.

His name is above every name. "His name shall be called Wonderful, Counsellor, The Mighty God, The Everlasting Father, The Prince of Peace." His name is peerless. He is the "Rose of Sharon," a "Fountain in a desert," "The Lily of the Valley," "The Fairest Among Ten Thousand." He is the Mighty One beyond all comprehension of the finite mind. He is the strongest, the mightiest, the loveliest.

> Sweetest note in seraph song,
> Sweetest name on mortal tongue;
> Sweetest carol ever sung,
> Jesus, blessed Jesus.

He has dried away more tears, calmed more restless spirits, driven away more sorrows, sweetened more lives, liberated more captives, inspired more songs and singing, lifted more burdens, bound up more broken hearts, healed more soul wounds, blessed more homes, radiated more sunshine, driven away more clouds, extracted more thorns from dying pillows, planted more hope, and given more assurance to souls than any and all forces in the world.

2. We preach the Bible because it proclaims God's Message. What a message! How saving, how life-giving it is! How needed! How sufficient! It is a needed, dynamic, imperial, indispensable message. About the only possession Southern Baptists had one hundred years ago was their message. Then they had but few organizations and institutions, but they had a God-given message, and proclaimed it in bugle tones and with dying earnestness. We have grown rich, our numbers are vast, our organizations prolific, our churches gladden the view from every summit, but

what will all this amount to if we fail to cling to and proclaim the message of God? The propagation of God's message is our hope for growth and progress.

One hundred years ago our people walked by faith. Today we are seeking to walk by sight. Then we launched our institutions, agencies, and boards without money. Now we talk about reserve funds. Then we preached and depended upon God. Now we must see where every dollar is coming from before we launch an enterprise. Then we were sacrificial. Now we are inclined to be selfish. We are lounging on beds of ease purchased by our forefathers on crosses of sacrifice. We are losing the pioneer spirit. We are failing to lengthen our cords and strengthen our stakes, when every surrounding fact tells us that we should expand and go forward. What would those who sent Carey out to the far-flung mission field think of us now? God's message is our most priceless possession. It is the most powerful, vital, saving, lifting, needed, longed for message on mortal tongue. It contains the pulsebeats and heartthrobs of the Son of God. No wonder it has blazoned its way through the dark wilderness of nations and continents! It reaches down to the abysmal depths of the vilest of the vile. It lifts up to the very mercy seat. It sounds out to the remotest reaches of the earth, with an invitation for all to come. The Word finds its way inward to touch and give direction to the finest fibers of the soul.

It contains the greatest events which adorn history's pages. It pulsates with life, and radiates light. Its events are epochal in the march of the centuries. There is Bethlehem—the Morning Star of hope for a lost world. There stands Calvary—"Grand old Calvary." It is the heart of Christianity. Think of the resurrection! It is the hope of Christianity. Pentecost is there, with its tongues of fire, and dimensions of power. What a message! This message lays hold upon the soiled children of men and washes them white in the blood of the Lamb. It blends life's discords into hymns of praise. It softens life's sobs into melodious music. It rekindles fading hopes into fadeless glory. This is our priceless gift, our glorious message to proclaim to a lost world. It is imperial, imperative, living, throbbing, life-giving, burning. It is amply sufficient for the world's needs.

The message of this Book associates itself with our joys and sorrows, with births, marriages, and burials. It gives us strength in life, and consolation in death.

3. We preach the Bible because it reclaims lost souls. It lifts from servi-

tude to service. It goes beyond feeding the poor, comforting the widow, clothing the orphan, protecting the defenseless. It goes to the root that causes these conditions, and gives pardoning mercy and saving grace to the sinner. It blots out our iniquities, dries away our tears, binds up our broken hearts, and gives assurance in death. "In every land where its tale has been told, and with every new sun that dawns, drunkards may be found whom it has made sober, thieves whom it has taught to be honest, harlots whom it has lifted up to chastity."

The Word of God offers salvation, not sociology; evangelization, not economics; redemption, not reform; conversion, not culture; power, not progress; the new birth, not a new social order; regeneration, not evolution; revitalization, not renovation; resurrection, not resuscitation; a new creation, not a new organization; the gospel, not democracy; Christ, not civilization.

III. Why We Love the Bible

1. We love the Bible because it is the Foundation of our faith. The Word of our God shall stand forever (1 Pet. 1:23). The Bible is our basic foundation. Christianity is not built upon a sandbank. It is built upon the granite rock of God's eternal Word. This foundation is not superficial; it is solid. It is not transitory; it is eternal. It is unshakable. Like the Rock of Gibraltar, it has stood the tests of time and the tides of the centuries; the wars of time, the fickleness of human nature, the storms and stress of generations, the rise and fall of nations, the crumbling of empires, the tottering of thrones, and the tread of dictators. Do not molest it. This foundation is as eternal as God is eternal. "Blessed be the Lord God of Israel from everlasting to everlasting: and let all the people say, Amen. Praise ye the Lord."

> How firm a foundation, ye saints of the Lord,
> Is laid for your faith in His excellent Word!
> What more can He say than to you He hath said,
> You who unto Jesus for refuge have fled?

Its foundations are too deep to be shaken by any crises, catastrophes, or cataclysms. We rest not upon crutches men have made; we rest securely upon God's eternal Word.

The foundation of God's Word is a basis upon which we may firmly plant our feet. On such a foundation, faith will warm, with iridescent fires, the winter's bitter winds caused by sin, will bedeck our midnights with stars of hope, and will ignite a blaze of light which will penetrate the darkness of death; splendor our future with glowing radiance, enrich and ennoble life with its melody of song, guide us onward and upward in sunshine and shadows, in sickness and health, in hopeful days and fearful nights.

An Irishman built his fence three feet high and four feet wide. When asked why, his answer was: "So that if anyone kicks it over, it will be higher than it was in the first place." The Bible has been kicked about, but this has resulted in it rising higher and higher in the estimation of the people.

John Wanamaker, who made vast purchases for the Government and for himself, ranging high into the millions, said that the purchase of a little red-letter Bible, about eight inches long and six inches wide, at a cost of $2.75, which he paid for in installments, was the biggest purchase he ever made. That little red-letter Bible was the foundation on which his life was built, and it made possible all the vast service that he rendered during his life. He said, "Every other investment of my life seemed to me, after mature years, only secondary."

"In this little book," said Ewald to Dean Stanley, holding up his Greek Testament, "is contained all the wisdom of the world."

> A glory gilds the sacred page,
> Majestic like the sun;
> It gives a light to ev'ry age,
> It gives but borrows none.

2. We love the Bible because it is the fountain of life. The psalmist said: "For with thee is the fountain of life: in thy light shall we see light" (Ps. 36:9).

It is said that when Columbus discovered the Oronoco River, someone said he had found an island. He replied: "No such river as that flows from an island. The mighty torrent must drain the waters of a continent." So the fountain which flows from God's Word is not finite, but infinite. It springs from the depths of divine wisdom, love, grace, and is but a hint of the power and love that lie back of it.

A. McAuslane said: "If the Bible were to be as totally eclipsed as the sun has sometimes been, . . . The world mind would be what Greece was when Homer sang, Demosthenes spoke, and Plato taught, ignorant of

God, of the nature and destiny of man, and groping its way like a bewildered, yea, blind traveler, towards the unknown land."

We are told that England, in the days of Elizabeth, became the people of a Book, and that book was the Bible. Its literary and social effects were marked, but the effect of the Bible upon the character of the people at large was revolutionary. "The whole temper of the nation felt the change." One wrote: "A new conception of life, a new moral and religious pulse, spread through every class."

From this fountain has flowed all the institutions of mercy, all the agencies of goodwill, all the boards for the world's evangelization, all the high hopes for life, and confidence for death and eternity. It furnished the water of life for George Peabody, Florence Nightingale, John Howard. This fountain changes the thistle into a rose, deserts into flower gardens, icicles into calm south winds, poison into honey.

Dr. Hight C Moore says: "The Bible is the Water of Life. Don't sweeten it. Don't poison it. Don't divert it. Don't stop it. Don't try to purify it. Don't try to analyze it. Pour it out and pass it on." Well may we study its contents, practice its precepts and examples, proclaim its message, glory in its triumphs, and magnify its Master.

3. We love the Bible because it is the fulfilment of hope. The Bible tells us how to live and how to die. It guides us in the fulfilment of our hopes here and hereafter. "Now we see through a glass, darkly; but then face to face: now I know in part; but then shall I know even as also I am known." "It doth not yet appear what we shall be."

> Lead on, O king Eternal,
> The day of march has come;
> . . . .
> Lead on, O King eternal!
> 'Til sin's fierce war shall cease.

In February, 1925, in a hospital in Shelby, North Carolina, my old pastor, my first pastor, my father in the ministry, Rev. A. C. Irwin, died. The hour was about three o'clock in the morning. He was more than fourscore years old. He had been preaching for fifty years or more. During the evening hours he had chanted the old hymns of Zion—hymns he had sung and heard well-nigh a century. Then in that still, quiet, noiseless morning hour, as death tightened its grip, and as angels came down to bear his sainted spirit home, he sang with his weakened voice, "O bear me away on your snowy wings, to my immortal home," and the music echoed down the corridors of the hospital. Soon he was being carried by the angels into the New Jerusalem. I imagine that as he crossed the river of death thus singing, the river of death was transformed into a crystal sea on whose banks the redeemed of God sat and sang for him a new song, as they welcomed him home, and on through all time, he will sing "the song of Moses . . . and the song of the Lamb."

The Bible meets every condition and need of men. Open its pages and you stand in the library of the greatest subjects, the laboratory of the most meaningful discoveries, the art gallery of the greatest heroes and heroines, the flower garden of the greatest florist, the observatory of the most discerning astronomer, the studio of the sweetest musician, the pages of the profoundest philosophy, the archives of the most treasured documents. Here you find the Christian's Magna Charta, the world's supreme personality, the emblem of the greatest glory, the message of the farthest reach, the subject of profoundest moment.

In this Book you hear the charming eloquence of God's voice. The eruption of volcanoes, the sweep of tornadoes, the thunder of cataracts, the wail of Egypt's darkest night, the triumphal song of the Promised Land, the breaking of the hammers of man on the anvils of God, the thunderclap of the ages. You hear heaven's grand opera, the first music from the thousand-stringed harp, the first Hallelujah Chorus, the first paean of victory, the first mention of the Golden Rule, the Good Samaritan, and the Twenty-third Psalm; and over all the hush of God's stillness.

In this Book you see the first dawn of time, the first billows break, the light of the first day, the first sunrise in its splendor, the first sunset glow, the first star twinkle, the first flower blossom, the first mountain grandeur, the first ocean race and rage, the first lightning flash, the first glimpse of the flower-embroidered garments of the far-flung universe, the first mother's smile, the first ray of hope. You see here the first emigrant, and hear the first footfalls made in the overland march of empires. In this Book is the first mention of the church, the first ray of hope for men, the only authentic promise of salvation, the one source of consolation. It points the way out and up for man, dispels his darkness, dissolves his doubts, drives away his fear, and gives him the deepest sense of security.

B. H. Carroll
Pressing Toward the Mark

Brethren, I count not myself to have apprehended; but this one thing I do, forgetting those things which are behind, and reaching forth unto those things which are before, I press toward the mark for the prize of the high calling of God in Christ Jesus (Phil. 3:13-14).

I am to preach this night from the theme: "Forgetting the things behind and reaching forth to the things before, I press on toward the mark for the prize of the high calling of God in Christ Jesus." As an introduction to this service I have read with earnestness, and I trust you have heard with solemn attention, the following scripture lessons: Romans 8:28-30, inclusive; Ephesians 1:15-23, inclusive; 1 Thessalonians 5:23, and Philippians 3:7-14.

From these declarations of God's Word it is evident that the average Christian has only a faint conception of the sublimity and glory of his destiny under grace. We are accustomed ordinarily to content ourselves in stopping short of God's appointments in our behalf. It is my purpose, God's Spirit assisting, to lead you this night to lift up your eyes to greater things that you may be uplifted by them and drawn toward them by all the attractive power of the gospel.

Before the foundations of the world were laid God fore-knew every Christian in this house; before the morning stars sang together God, according to his fore-knowledge, chose every Christian in this house; before he said, "Let there be light," God predestined every Christian in this house, according to that election and according to that fore-knowledge, to be conformed to the image of Jesus Christ, but fore-knowledge, election and predestination were thousands of years of time in the divine mind only.

In time, and in your own case, nearly six thousand years after this prevenient exercise of the divine mind and heart, God called you. The call was according to the predestination before the world was; the predestination was according to the election before the morning stars sang; the election was according to the fore-knowledge before the foundations of the world were laid.

One might naturally infer that a purpose so anciently carried in the mind of God, and for so many ages, looked to a corresponding consummation. If he called me according to his fore-knowledge and election and predestination, and treasured his purpose to call me through such a period of time, surely he did not mean to call me to an ignoble destiny. The calling must be something infinitely high; hence, our text speaks of the high calling of God; that is, a calling from on high, or a heavenly calling. Heaven does not trifle as earth trifles. He calls us to something higher than any earthly good, higher than the mountains, higher than the clouds that wreathe their base in garments of mist, higher than the stars which illumine their crests, high above all principalities and powers in heavenly places—even as high as the throne and glory of God himself.

Our text declares that this high calling holds out before our eyes a prize to be won; toward that prize, it beckons and incites and stimulates. How important then the calling! What is the prize of the high calling of God? Is it earthly fame, or wealth, or political power, or fading pleasure, or any of the objects toward which the thoughts and aspirations of men on earth are usually turned? May we know definitely what this prize is?

The prize is something to be won. The context tells us just what it was that Paul desired to win. He says: "I have suffered the loss of all things, and do count them refuse, that I may win Christ." What is to be won is the prize, and Christ is to be won. If Paul had not won Christ at the time of this statement we may be sure that no Christian here has won him. In the sense of this text, you did not win Christ when you were converted; you did not win Christ in your richest, sweetest, and highest revival experiences. That is an attainment for the future. Evidently, therefore, it does not mean Christ in the flesh, not Christ in the manger, nor in the Temple disputing with the doctors, nor as a healer and teacher in the cities of Judea and Israel, not Christ working mighty miracles, not Christ in Gethsemane; yea, not even Christ on the cross, nor in the grave, but Christ in glory.

To win Christ in glory is to actually reach him where he is, and to possess him there, to claim him as ours, though he be invested with the sovereignty of the universe, and sitteth on the right hand of the throne of God, reigning as King of kings and Lord of lords.

To win Christ then is not to know him, and hear him and see him as John the Apostle did by the Sea of Galilee, but to enter into an inheritance with him as John saw him in the book of Revelation; that Son of man clothed with a garment down to the foot, and girt about the paps with a golden girdle, with head and hair white like wool, as white as snow, and his eyes as a flame of fire, and his feet like unto fine brass, as if they burned in a furnace, and whose voice was as the sound of many waters. The Christ holding in his hands the angels of the churches, and having at his girdle the keys of death and hell; the Christ that once lived and was dead, but now, behold, is alive forever.

That we may understand better the value of winning Christ, as set forth in the text, let us consider the other thoughts concerning him thus won, as set forth by the apostle in our context. He says: "That I may win Christ and be found in him." Found in him when? Evidently at the judgment day when the searchlight of divine justice discovers the location of every man; to be found in him at that great day of assize; the day of the White Throne; the day when good and bad are separated and assigned to everlasting destinies. When we win him then will we be found in him by the discriminating eye of infinite justice.

This further appears from the additional thought, "Not having my own righteousness, which is of the law, but that which is through the faith of Christ, the righteousness which is of God by faith." The reference is evidently to the time of the revelation of the righteous judgment of God. When indeed we win him then we will be found in him, and being found in him will stand not in our law righteousness but in the righteousness which is through faith. The thought continues: "That I may know him." This is not a knowledge of Christ in the flesh. He seeks to know him as he is in glory. That knowledge follows his winning him. If Christ is his prize, Christ is also his righteousness and his hiding place, and the knowledge of him there is unlike the knowledge of him here. Here we see through a glass darkly; then, face to face; here, we know in part; then, we shall know as we are known.

Such being the prize, evidently there must be some last attainment which precedes the winning and enjoyment of the prize. This leads us to consider next the expression, "the mark for the prize of the high calling of God in Christ Jesus." What is that mark? It is the standard, the measure, the limitation which designates the end of all Christian striving. Sometimes we call it a goal, as in the foot race of the ancient Greeks the goal marked the termination of the race. When one reached the goal he might claim the prize, but he could not lay his hands upon it, nor receive it from the judge until this goal was touched. It is of much importance to us therefore to understand just what is that Ultima Thule of Christian effort and growth.

It will count nothing for us so far as the attainment of the prize is concerned if we stop short of this goal, if on a last analysis we are not up to the mark. The pertinent question, therefore, is, Has God placed this mark anywhere in our earthly life? or, Is death this goal?

Paul surely did not count it as placed anywhere in his earthly life, and just as surely disclaims finding it in the hour and article of death. In the fourth chapter of his letter to Timothy he declares that the time of his departure is at hand, and says: "Henceforth, there is laid up for me a crown of righteousness which the Lord, the righteous Judge, shall give me at that day." He did not obtain the crown when he died. It was laid up for him. There was a day appointed upon which he would receive it. He would receive it by the verdict of a righteous Judge when he reached the goal.

I repeat, death is not that goal. True, at death the spirit is perfect; so he tells us in the letter to the Hebrews: "Ye are come unto Mount Zion and unto the city of the living God, the heavenly Jerusalem, and to an innumerable company of angels, to the general assembly and church of the First Born, who are written in heaven and to God, the Judge of all, and to the spirits of just men made perfect."

Here we find the perfected spirit. When the spirit reaches Mount Zion, when it attains to the heavenly Jerusalem, when it enters the company of the angels, when it joins the general assembly and church of the First Born, when it comes to God, the Judge, then is the spirit made perfect, but even the perfection of the spirit, following upon the dissolution of the body, though like Stephen, we have said: "Lord Jesus, receive my spirit," though like the spirit of Lazarus when he died, which the angels carried to the bosom of Abraham, yet the goal is not there because the whole man is not there. Complete salvation has not been attained.

In the book of Revelation John saw the souls of the martyrs under the altar crying out unto God for something not yet obtained. With greater emphasis then, the question recurs: What is the mark for the prize of the high calling of God in Christ Jesus?

The mark or goal is the last end which we reach. Our context tells us distinctly what it is. Let us listen to Paul's explanation of it: "If by any means I might attain unto the resurrection of the dead"; and again he says, "That I may know him and the power of his resurrection." When that day comes appointed of God for the judgment of the world, the dead will be raised and the judgment will be rendered. The estate of the resurrection from the dead is therefore the completed state of the saved man. This is in accord with one of the scriptures read to you as an introduction. I quote it again from the Revised Version: "And the God of Peace, himself, sanctify you wholly, and may your spirit and soul and body be preserved entire, without blame, at the coming of our Lord Jesus Christ." Mark the date—at the coming of our Lord Jesus Christ.

Now, when he comes, he comes to raise the dead and judge the world. The supreme destiny of the saved man, in all its sublimity and glory, is involved in the meaning of the conditions of the resurrection. Concerning this, Paul says in our context: "Not as though I had already attained, either were already perfect." Nothing but attainment and perfection could satisfy him. Until he reached the estate of the resurrection of the dead and was clothed with its glory he did not believe that he had laid hold upon all of the things for which Christ laid hold of him.

You remember when and how Jesus called him. It was on the way to Damascus. He was going as a persecutor of the faith which he afterwards preached, but about midday Jesus met him; not Jesus in the flesh, but Jesus in glory. Jesus called him: "Saul, Saul, why persecutest thou me? Rise and stand upon thy feet. Thou art a chosen vessel unto me. I will make thee a minister and a witness, not only in the things which thou hath seen, but in those which shall hereafter be revealed unto thee."

It was a high calling. It had a glorious prize, but the mark which measured the limit of upward movement was Paul's resurrection from the dead.

If today one of us were permitted to walk through the treasury house of heaven we might see one crown shining brighter than the stars of the firmament. The question would be asked, "Whose crown is this?" "That is Paul's crown." "Does he wear it now?" "No, though two thousand years have passed away since he took his departure from this world by the way of martyrdom, it is still held in reservation because Paul has not yet reached the mark."

On this point David speaks. He speaks concerning his aspirations and cravings. He declares just when he will be satisfied. His language is: "Then shall I be satisfied when I awake in thy likeness."

In determining what this mark is, we have gained much touching another point. It surely shows us that none of us here has as yet attained, or are already perfect; that we have reached no stopping place; that we should not be content with the present degree of our piety; that we should not yet lay aside our armor; that we not yet have been transferred from the militant force of Jesus Christ to the crowned and glorified throng that will be found in him at that day.

There is but little hope of usefulness for any Christian who is satisfied with his attainments, who counts himself as perfect, who thinks that he has already learned whatever is to be known, who assumes himself to be even now a graduate in the school of God's discipline.

This leads us to the consideration of three things upon which our entire attention should be fastened; three things binding us by imperative obligation. What are these three things? Our text tells us plainly.

First, Something to Remember. When we are enjoined to forget only a certain class of things, that limitation implies an obligation to remember the things not specified. What then are the things that we are to remember? We are to remember that we are not yet up to the mark; that we have not yet attained; that we have not yet laid hold upon all of the things for which Jesus Christ laid hold of us. By day and by night this remembrance should be with us. Caesar once said: "Count nothing done while anything remains to be done." So we should relax no effort until we reach the mark.

One expression, therefore, I trust will ring in your minds like the sound of an alarm bell when you go away from this service: I AM NOT UP TO THE MARK. May each individual Christian here look to mountain heights of endeavor yet to be scaled, may he expect to behold his horizon widening as he ascends.

Excelsior! Let that be his watchword and his motto. Not even your church, Brother Pastor, as a congregation, has attained, is already perfect. For each visible church of Jesus Christ on earth is a type of the general assembly that shall make up the final temple of God. If your church thinks that it has done its full duty, that it has excelled in all Christian training, that there remains for it no more growth and no more work, then it is needful to state for your benefit what Paul calls a perfect church.

"Christ also loved the church and gave himself for it that he might sanctify and cleanse it with the washing of water by the Word, that he might present it to himself a glorious church, not having spot, wrinkle, or any such thing, but that it should be holy and without blemish."

I doubt not you, Brother Pastor, are conscious of some blemish, some unholiness, some wrinkle, some spot that prevents this church from being a church of glory. When we thoroughly understand our deficiencies, our faults, and when we have a clear conception of all the requirements of the standard which God has appointed to measure perfect obedience, we cannot, unless in a greatly backslidden state, rest content. A woe is on us if we remain at ease when we should be up and doing. The mission of a church of Jesus Christ is the highest mission on this earth. God intended that the church should be an instructor—that it should teach the angels of heaven. Such is Paul's expression: "To the intent that now unto the principalities and powers in heavenly places might be made known by the church the manifold wisdom of God."

Some churches seem to consider that God's wisdom has only one fold, and that when they have unfolded that to the angels their work is ended: that if they can unfold the wisdom of God in baptism they have attained to the highest excellency, but the scripture cited speaks of the manifold wisdom of God. His wisdom is not all expressed in one doctrine, but all the doctrines of his symmetrical system of truth, seeing that every one of the scriptures is inspired of God and is profitable that the man of God may be furnished unto every good work. Why stop then at one?

Some churches conceive it to be their duty to get the gospel to the people around their homes; others enlarge this somewhat, and are willing to contribute to mission work in their association, and yet others who are willing to include state missions and some national missions, but God's wisdom in the salvation of man has more folds than that, and the church is to make known to his angels his manifold wisdom, his wisdom of salvation concerning not only our own people, but every race and tribe, and every tongue and kindred in the world.

In other words, we are to be ready as a church for every good work. We are not yet up to the mark. We should not exclude from our attention, from our sympathy, from our help, any department of the work of Jesus Christ.

For this reason I venture to state, Brother Pastor, that you doubtless were conscious that your church as an organization is not a perfect church—has not yet reached the mark for the prize of the high calling of God in Jesus Christ. This, then, is the thing to remember: I am not up to the mark.

Something to Forget—Second our text says: "Forgetting the things which are behind." Yes, there are some things that ought to be forgotten. We should not live in the past. We should not stand like Chinamen with our backs to the present and the future, and facing the past, worship our ancestors. In this connection we should forget the times that are past. "Thou saith not well who saith that the former times were better than these." These are good times in which we live. We live in an age on ages telling. We are not up to the mark when we contrast unfavorably the present with the former times, and spend our time in lamentations over the long time ago. We should forget the men of the past. Quite willing am I to admit that there were giants in that day, but there are giants now, and we should not lose sight of our present giants in order to waste all of our admiration upon the Samsons and Jepthas, or to stir our hearts to fear by the remembrance only of the sons of Anak, and of Og, king of Bashan. There are giant enemies today.

In the days of the Texas Republic there were great men—Houston and Rusk and Travis and Bowie and Crockett, immortal names that were not born to die. And those were good old times in which they lived. Great were the opportunities and responsibilities of that day, but I venture to say that the next twenty-five years is pregnant with more potentialities and more and mightier opportunities for good or evil than any one hundred years of the past. And there are men and women now, God-fearing men and faithful women, worthy to be classed with the ancient heroes and heroines of civil and religious history.

Let us forget the victories of the past. By this is meant that our time should not be taken up in feelings of complacency over the triumphs that have been won. Gates remembered Saratoga. His mind dwelt so much on Saratoga and Burgoyne that he paid not due attention to Camden and Cornwallis, and so withered his former laurels.

Let us forget the defeats of the past. To be defeated in a given instance is not an irreparable disaster unless we allow ourselves to be completely whipped inside. Who lives on past glories never survives defeat. General Gates, at Camden, is an illustration. When the militia of the American Army fled at the first sight of the red British line, without firing a gun and Gates fled with them, their defeat was utter, not only for the hour but for all time. Those who ran then kept running. There is a tradition that after running ten miles from the battlefield of Camden, they halted from sheer exhaustion, and while lying by the roadside panting, an innocent cow entangled in the rear guard came clattering down the road. The fear of the beaten army transmuted her clattering hoofs into the thundering chase of Tarleton's legion; so they fled again, and scattered as they went. Ten miles further on they halted again to catch their breath. This time a harmless countryman chanced to fire his rifle at a squirrel. The crack of that rifle to their affrighted ears was like the sound of Gabriel's trumpet; it was as a volley from the British grenadiers, and so they fled again and never stopped until they were eighty miles from that battlefield, and for all I know some of them may be running yet.

In his first battle Frederick the Great ran at the first firing like the veriest coward, and remained in the fog for a week. His generals whipped the fight and Frederick emerged—only temporarily a coward; but his greatest defeat was at the battle of Kunersdorf. There he broke the storming columns of his entire army all to pieces, endeavoring to batter down the iron phalanx of Russia. The defeat was extreme. No Prussian army was ever seen in such a state. For a short time only was the soul of Frederick overwhelmed. He did not run in this defeat, as in the first. He was the last to quit the ground and the first to recover hope. This made him great. In later victories he forgot the disastrous overthrow at Kunersdorf.

To forget a victory then means not to be always complacent concerning the triumph, not to count our glory complete. To forget a defeat is not to stay whipped, but courageously emerge from the disaster with an unbroken spirit to face new conflicts.

Among the notable things behind us to be forgotten are Texas Baptist strifes. Very sad they have been, every way full of disaster. In their path lie wrecks of men, and hopes and institutions. To remember them always is to believe in the heart that no good can come out of Texas. To forget them is to lay aside all bitterness, all desire for vengeance, fly the flag of healing and seek for the things which make for future peace.

We are not up to the mark when on account of past strifes we sulk like Achilles in the tent, or like Coriolanus we join the enemy and seek to destroy our own people and institutions, or when we seek to rob God of the prerogative of vengeance, and carry a hidden knife with which to smite under the fifth rib some one who we are disposed to think has affronted our dignity. For the cause's sake, let the dead bury the dead.

Let us sponge out the past shame of our great state. Let us demonstrate that we are a lasting band of brothers.

Something to Do—There remains something more to do than the exercise of the mind in remembrance or forgetfulness. If indeed we are not up to the mark, if we have not attained, if we have not laid hold of all for which the Lord laid hold of us, then something should be done. The forgetting the things which are behind and remembering our lack of attainment are but the two wings of the central thought: SOMETHING TO DO. Here we approach the heart of the matter. Paul says: "One thing I do. I press on toward the mark for the prize of the high calling of God in Jesus Christ."

Let the pilgrim pick up his staff and resume his journey; let the soldier strike his tent and take up the line of march; let the warrior brace himself for new and greater conflicts; let the heart turn from doleful recollections of the past to bright anticipations of the future; let us fix our eyes upon the goal, the mark—the estate of the resurrection of the dead, and let us by waiting on the Lord renew our strength; then can we run and not be wearied, walk and not faint, yea! mount up on eagles' wings.

No more profitable meditation can there be for God's people than upon the things that yet need to be done, the attainment yet to be reached, the spirit of piety yet to be cultivated. We must move forward or recede. When a tree ceases to grow it begins to die; when a fountain ceases to flow it stagnates and becomes slime-covered, and breeds malaria and loathsome reptiles; when the flower ceases to bloom it is a herald of winter and its chilly snow; to cease rowing when our destiny is up stream is not merely to stand still, but to be carried down with the current.

Notable victories have been won in our denominational work in the last few years under wise and brave leadership, but greater victories await us all along the line. Individuals, churches, associations and conventions should endeavor to move up to the high standard appointed of God. Let our song be:

> "My soul, be on thy guard;
> Ten thousand foes arise;
> The hosts of sin are pressing hard
> To draw thee from the skies.

> "O watch and fight and pray;
> The battle ne'er give o'er;

Renew it boldly every day,
And help divine implore.

"Ne'er think the victory won,
Nor lay thine armor down;
Thy arduous work will not be done
Till thou obtain thy crown."

Much remains to be done to complete the unification of Texas Baptists, much to bring our mission work up to the proper standard, and great continents of difficulties remain to be subdued before our educational work is commensurate with the necessities of the hour and with our ability. I hail the gathering of these workers from different parts of the state as an omen of good in our educational work. These are no cowards who hear me this night. They have met with reverses; the scars of conflict are on them, and some of them halt from unhealed wounds but their courage survives, their faith in God abides, their hope in God has no broken wing, the eagle can yet soar, their love for God and his people has not been quenched nor waxed cold because of the strifes of the past.

Baker James Cauthen
Rejoice

Rejoice in the Lord always; again I say, Rejoice (Phil. 4:4).

These words came from Paul in prison. Having found God's will for your life, you, like him, have peace and assurance. Rejoice in your calling; rejoice that the Lord God inclined your heart to know him and to sense that in him you are a part of his redemptive purpose in a needy world.

Rejoice in the promises that undergird you in every experience. Your own strength is totally insufficient. You are moving out into deep water, getting beyond your depth. God's promises are so steady, strong, and dependable that you can build your life on them. You will find your peace in his promises, not in your circumstances. If your optimism depends upon your being able to total up your visible assets and liabilities and come out favorably, you may have times of very great disappointment. If your optimism and confidence are based upon the promises of God, you are in for a great and glorious sense of fulfilment.

Rejoice in the wisdom that guides the providences of your life. Some of these providences will be sweet and pleasant. The mission field is not all grim, but abounds with joy, fulfilment, friendship, opportunity, and fruitfulness. The providences you face will sometimes bring a cloudy sky. There is winter as well as summer and spring in the Christian experience. The unbelieving heart where you will serve is as hard as the unbelieving heart in your home neighborhood. Human frailty is just as real in one place as the other. Ingratitude on the part of people to whom you will give yourself is as real as ingratitude you may have known before.

You will find that providences will sometimes be strange, and you may not understand them. Being in the will of God does not mean that you and your family will be immune to sickness, danger, and all the experiences that are the human lot. God does not let his servants walk through this world as people who cannot share the common lot of humanity. He lets them share that common lot of human suffering, disappointment, and failure in order to show the world how those things can be faced when people know God.

When providences come, whether they wear a smiling countenance or a frown, rejoice in the wisdom that guides them. Did not Jesus say the very hairs of your head are all numbered? Did he not say that not a sparrow falls without the Father's will? Did he not say, "Seek first his kingdom and his righteousness, and all these things shall be yours as well"? You do not have to understand the providences, but you do have to trust. You have to believe in the love, goodness, wisdom, power, fatherly quality, and redemptive purpose of the Lord who laid hold upon you and made you one of his light-bearers in a dark world. Trust him who sends you out to show what he sends you to do.

God has his purpose for you. In those providences, whatever they are, just rely upon his wisdom, love, and grace. Rejoice in the absolute victory into which he has called you. Rejoice that when you follow his guidance, you will say at the end, "If I could live my life over again, and it pleased God to use me, I would again seek his will and do it."

"Rejoice in the Lord always; again I say, Rejoice."

H. Gordon Clinard
Planting Trees You Will
Never Sit Under

1 Chronicles 22:1-16

There are many ways to measure the greatness of men. Men can be called great because of their talents, their possessions, their buildings, their service. But the philosopher A. N. Whitehead had a standard of greatness which reflection will confirm as most worthy of all: "The great man is he who plants shade trees he will never sit under."

Immediately you know what he means. Such a man is unselfish, visionary, dedicated. Whether we recognize it or not, we are all planting these trees. What we do today is going to affect those who walk after us. They will inherit both our folly and our wisdom. Next Sunday will be Father's Day. Although apart from the tie salesman the day may not have great significance, it will at least furnish a good opportunity for both fathers and mothers to remember that for better or for worse we are planting trees we shall not sit under but under which our children will sit, to praise us or to blame.

A late issue of *Home Life* tells of the little girl whose mother could not decide whether she should attend her father's funeral or not. They had been quite close, and all their friends knew that it would just be too much for her. But it was the little girl who surprised and gave stability to the whole family. When they went to the funeral home, it was she who talked of the beautiful flowers and it was she who said, "A lot of people loved my Daddy, didn't they?" It was she who was the most sensible when they saw the body for the first time. "That isn't my father," she said. "That's just the place where he lived awhile." She was the most calm at the funeral. She lifted the faith of all the others and reminded them again and again with quiet confidence that her daddy was happy in heaven. It did not happen by accident. Because he and his daughter were so close, he had talked to her a lot about God and about death and about what happens to those who love the Lord. He had planted a tree he would never sit under.

How tragic that not all our plantings are that good. It is inescapable that our sins and our negligence afflict those who come after us. It would be honest of us to admit that the influence of David, the hero of this sermon, was not always for good. The trees of idleness, pride, passion, and forgetfulness of God cast their shade over his children long after he had passed beyond them. Whoever called parents to more sober thought about our responsibility to live so as to influence others for good than he who wrote about the "bridge builder"? Indifference and selfish living which smack of a careless existentialism find no greater challenge than in the poet's simple lines:

> The builder lifted his old gray head,
> "Good friend, in the path I have come," he said,
> "There followeth after me today
> A youth whose feet must pass this way;
> This chasm that has been naught to me,
> To that fair haired youth may a pit-fall be.
> He, too, must cross in the twilight dim,
> Good friend, I am building the bridge for him."

Whether we know it or not, we are all planting trees we shall never sit under. But the truly great man is he who deliberately sets out to make something possible which he will never enjoy, to give of himself and the best he has so that others who walk after him may achieve noble goals.

In an age which generally lives for the moment and which is enamored with building its own monuments, like the men of Babel's tower, such greatness is a worthy goal. We need a revival of men in churches and in homes and in the nation who will plant vineyards for others. To do so deliberately requires certain qualities of life which we must seek.

To Plant Trees You Will Never Sit Under Requires a Great Dream

David had a dream of building a great house for God. It was to be a magnificent house. The reason for his high resolve was clear. For one thing, the people of God under his most successful reign had prospered.

They lived in their cedar houses and enjoyed a high standard of living. To David it was inconsistent that God should have no house when His people were so magnificently affluent. For too long the Ark of the Covenant had known no settled resting place. It was time, the king thought, to do something magnificent for God.

Just by way of passing, let me observe that God must still look with disfavor upon a people who spend their best on their own comfort while bringing their second best to God.

David's other motivation was more personal. It was God's goodness to him that prompted a worthy dream of honoring the Lord; but particularly fresh in his mind was his pride, because David wished to "number" the people. He wanted a census from Dan to Beersheba so that he could brag on his own greatness. The numbers game is pretty old, you see. It was not pleasing to God, and the nation suffered under God's judgment for a ruler's arrogance. But as pestilence fell on the people, David built an altar to God and in repentance called on Him to stay His hand. God heard the prayer. It was on that very spot that David wanted the temple of which he had dreamed to stand. Here the highest purpose of his life was to be fulfilled. A great man wanted to do a great thing for a great God.

The problem with many of us is that we have stopped dreaming of great things. We are so cowed by the rush and apparent frenzy of our lives that the dream has died. We are trapped by the possible, the feasible, and the practical. You may laugh at Utopia if you wish, but I shall stand with him who said, "It is the Utopias that make this world tolerable to us. The cities and mansions that people dream of are the very ones in which they or those whom they love will finally live."

What a shame that so many of us have lost the capacity for fantasy and dreaming, and never can escape the present! This limits human planning and is the ideology of the inert society. It is the opposite of biblical faith. Biblical religion is no sedative that lulls men into accepting the status quo. It is the faith which dreams of the future. In the Old Testament they dreamed of a Messianic Age. In the New they looked forward to the coming of the Lord, and without fear they marched out to conquer. David dreamed of building a house. You too must dream in order to plant any trees you know you will never sit under.

We desperately need to get off the treadmill of the present and dream about some tomorrows. The man who will make a contribution in our time, either to God or to man, is he who never looks back with reminiscence, nor around with cynicism or surrender, but ahead with expectancy. It was George Bernard Shaw who said, "Some men see things as they are and say, why? I dream things that never were and say, why not?"

And the dream ought to be of a great thing. Those who think our dreams of technology are enough to assure a great future need to recall Henry Thoreau who watched men put up something they called telegraph wires. When he asked what they were for, he was told they would make it possible for people in Maine to talk with people in Texas. Thoreau's famous observation was: "But what if the people in Maine have nothing to say to the people in Texas, and the people in Texas have nothing to answer to the people in Maine?" We can still have some tremendous means for some awfully small ends.

Many of our big plans are like the city slicker lawyer in the hands of the wily old farmer. The lawyer wanted to buy a saddle horse. The farmer agreed to sell one to him if he could catch him. The lawyer brought his sons and together they chased the horse for three hours. Finally they caught him. The sincerity and the sweat brought out a measure of honesty in the old farmer. He said, "I'll still take your money for this horse, but before I do I want to tell you two things about him. First, he's awful hard to ketch. The second thing is, he aint worth a durn when you ketch him."

The dream ought to be of something only God can do. The cause has to be great for a man to plant trees he will never sit under.

To Plant Trees You Will Never Sit Under Requires Sensible Humility

There are limits to what any one of us can do. God said to David, "You are not the one to build a Temple unto the name of the Lord, for you have made great wars and shed blood abundantly. Your son, who will be a man of peace, will build this house." David's wars, no matter how honorable and just, made him unfit for this kind of work. God's house is not built by hands reddened by blood. This is a thought so far in advance of David's time that it could have only come to him by revelation. The work of the God of peace does not move forward through a man with a sword in one hand and a trowel in the other. Who built the true and only Temple? The Prince of Peace. And God's work never goes forward where there is division and strife. Some things disqualify us for building for God.

But it is not always a matter of disqualification by our failure to have the character it takes to build, for we are all limited in talents and opportunity. The man who is interested only in what he is capable of doing is limited indeed in the good he will achieve.

How much better to know that we are all wrapped up in the common lot of humanity. If anything great is to be done, we must do it together. I depend on you and you depend on me and together we build for God. A lot of us would be healthier and more Christian if we could get over our sense of being indispensable, if we could learn to share. The man who responded to his friend's question, "How are you?" with the answer, "I am fine; I have resigned as President of the Universe and the resignation has been accepted," understood this.

Paul had the right idea. He was never jealous that the churches he built be limited to what he could do, not even when Christians were divided over him and other preachers. Rather, he said, "I planted. Apollos watered. But God was causing the increase." The change in verb tense shows what he meant. I planted, Apollos watered. Both did their work once and for all. But God keeps giving the increase.

It is amazing what one man can do who does not care who gets the credit for it. We are all limited by talent, by circumstance, by opportunity. But if we are willing to do our part and humbly leave the rest for others—if we are willing to plant trees we shall never sit under—there is no limit to what we can mean to God.

The secret to this is in the last thing I want to say.

To Plant Trees You Will Never Sit Under Requires a Sense of Priority

The thing that is important is the cause. That cause must be big enough for me to want to go forward, far beyond my credit or my days. David was interested in a House for God. On the very spot where God heard his prayer and turned away pestilence from the people, David wanted to build it. The end of his life was not far away. In perfect submission to the will of God, he gave up all thought of building and set himself to preparation for something another would finish. He gave his energy to the cause. He set his servants to work cutting stones. He prepared the nails for the doors of the gates. He brought brass in abundance. He provided cedar trees in abundance. He collected the most unbelievable amount of silver and of gold.

And after his hands could do no more, and after his body was cold, the cause came to fruition. The Temple rose to the glory of God. The world has not yet surpassed it in its magnificence. The stones were brought from Lebanon. They were hewn in quarries, conveyed on rafts, and placed with humble silence on one another, a fitting exaltation to the glory of God: "No hammers fell, no ponderous axes rung; / Like some tall palm the mystic fabric sprung."

The cedars of Lebanon were mixed with the gold and silver. The tapestries were unbelievably beautiful. The building was magnificent indeed. And Solomon dedicated it with the commitment, "I have built Thee a house of habitation, a place for Thee to dwell in forever." And the Shekinah cloud of God's glory entered and filled the place.

David had built a house he never entered. But he entered a better one, one not made with hands, eternal in the heavens. David had *planted a tree he never sat under,* but he found the shade of a better one, the tree of God's good pleasure. The cause was first. And he did an incomparable work for God.

The application of this sermon must by now be apparent. For example, we have our youth. Who is willing to do something great with them, to make a contribution you will never live to see brought to fruition? Who will give to the cause he will never personally benefit from? Here is the work of our Lord. Who will fit himself into his place, by commitment, by self-forgetfulness, by investment beyond his years, in the sure confidence that nothing done for our Lord is ever finally lost?

I think it will take a Christian to plant trees you will never sit under. It is the spirit of Christ. It is He who is the *cause*.

Owen Cooper
A Call for a Theology of Non-ordained

*F*ellow Ministers:

It may be strange to some of you that I, as one unordained, should address you as fellow ministers. I do it with a feeling of some uneasiness because it is not traditional; I do it with a feeling of uneasiness because it may be misunderstood; but I do it with a feeling of hope for the burden of my discussion will be that all Christians should be ministers, that God called all Christians to service or ministries, that God gives each of us a gift, and that the hope of the future for Christianity lies in the involvement of all the people of God, the Laos, in carrying out the Great Commission.

It is a distinct honor to join other past-presidents of the Southern Baptist Convention in speaking to the Louisiana Baptist Evangelism Conference.

My appearance is distinctive in that I am the only living non-ordained person who has served as president of the Southern Baptist Convention and only the third such who has served in the last 70 years.

Two Great Needs

There are two great needs for an accelerated growth of the Christian church and revival in America. The first is a "spiritual awakening." I am altogether inadequate to speak about an awakening. I shall leave further comment on this subject to those more knowledgeable and learned.

It is my plan to speak very frankly with you about some matters that are a burden to my heart. I ask that you hear me with patience and understanding. If, in fulfilling the commission to which you have been called,

113

the program for which Christ died, and the reason that your church (part of the Body of Christ) has been established my words cause you to re-think the ministry of the unordained, my purpose shall have been ac-complished.

Most people, in considering the composition of this program, would refer to the fact that eight former presidents of the Southern Baptist Con-vention, seven ministers and one layman, appeared. I seriously object to such a classification. I believe this classification and its full implication throughout the Southern Baptist Convention is the greatest heresy in our midst.

Greatest Heresy

I believe the greatest heresy among Southern Baptists is that we have divided the people of God into two groups: the pastors, the teachers, the missionaries and others in Christian work being one; and the other group is denominated as lay persons and most commonly as laymen.

I find no basis in the scripture for this division, there seems to be no theological justification for it and it has resulted in irreparable losses to the Kingdom of God.

I looked up the word "layman" and "laity" in a dictionary. Here are the most common definitions:

Layman: (1) a person who is not a clergyman.
           (2) a person who does not belong to a particular profession or who is not expert in some field.
Laity: (1) the people of a religious faith as distinguished from its clergy.
          (2) the mass of the people as distinguished from those of a partic-ular profession or those specially skilled.

This implies two classes of Christians—first and second class.

Sometime ago I was asked to speak to a group and make a statement that would catch the attention on the subject of the role of the laity. I began with the following statement:

I am not a layman, I am not an amateur, I am not a novice, I am not a second class citizen in the Kingdom of God, and I do not want to be called by any of these names according to the current practice and meaning of these terms among Southern Baptists. Call me a sinner, call me a saved sinner, call me a slave, call me a servant, call me a minister, call me a co-laborer, call me a yoke-fellow, call me a sojourner, call me a follower of the way, call me a child of God, call me a member of the Laos, call me a saint, or call me any other biblical term but do not call me a non-biblical term.

This statement was not made altogether with tongue and cheek but it did achieve the desired results of capturing the attention of those in attendance to the panel discussion that followed.

In the Old Testament it was easy to determine who were the priests. The sons of Levi were the priests. If you were not a son of Levi you were not a priest. It was simply that.

Impossible to Make Distinction

It is very difficult in the New Testament to draw a line of distinction between the priests or pastors, and those who are not. In fact, I think it is impossible. I find nothing in the New Testament that says that you, in response to your calling, should live a different life style, should be under different obligations to God, should have a different obligation to obedience, should have a greater commitment to fulfill the Great Commission, should be more obligated to support the church with your material possessions, than I have in my calling.

Jesus did not recruit His disciples from the Sanhedrin or the School of the Prophets, though He utilized a brilliant theologian and highly trained individual to contribute immeasurably to the spread of the gospel.

You will recall when the great persecution arose in Jerusalem that the people were scattered everywhere "except for the pastors." For some reason, unknown to me, they stayed in Jerusalem. The other members of the Laos were scattered abroad. They went everywhere preaching the word and many were saved. I would remind you that the preaching was not by the pastors but by other members of the Laos.

It was such a group of the Laos, not pastors, that went to Cyprus, Cyrene and Antioch and other places spreading the gospel.

Don't misunderstand me, I am not trying to downplay the role of the pastor. As never before we need strong, well-trained, Bible-believing evangelistic, mission-minded, dynamic pastors. We need the same as teachers in our seminaries and colleges, as missionaries at home and abroad, as servants in our various associations, state and SBC offices and agencies, and in other positions. But we need to remind ourselves that these simply cannot do the job alone.

The burden of what I am saying is that we are not receiving help from most of the laos, they are not being told they have a ministry, they are not trained for the ministry, and we have developed an unholy contentment with the average member of the laos sitting in the pew Sunday morning, making a reasonable contribution to support the program and work of the church, contributing to special offerings, helping build a new building or purchase a new organ, attending Sunday School and not becoming an irritant in the church.

This is the great heresy I am talking about.

Theology of the Unordained

One of the great needs of the day is to develop an adequate and satisfactory "theology for the ministry of the unordained." We do not have this in Southern Baptist life. We do not have it generally in Christianity. Unfortunately, I do not come to you with a "theology of the unordained."

I ask only for serious contemplation on your part that the greatest unused resource available for evangelism be understood, be recognized and be provided with an adequate theological base so that they too may feel comfortable in walking worthy in the vocation wherein they were called.

It may not be popular now to use an analogy involving the army. I will do it and do so comfortably because such an analogy is used frequently throughout the Bible.

The army of God, under the name of the Southern Baptist Convention, is the only one I know where anybody at age seven or above can join simply by presenting themselves to the church answering some questions and saying, "I believe and I want to be a member." It's the only army I know where training is entirely voluntary, there is no discipline, there is no requirement for involvement, and most of the recruits are seemingly unaware of the battle being waged, uncommitted toward achieving victory and are willing to sit as spectators on the sideline and passively cheer those who are charging the ramparts.

It is the only army I know where the officers get 95% of the training, where the officers are expected to do battle without the support of the foot soldiers, the officers are expected to live by one standard and the recruits another, where many officers feel that the battle can be won by excellent, well-prepared pronouncements issued from their command post.

Unfortunately, this is not true. It is much less true than it was in yester-years. It is interesting to note that someone has said that 80% of the proclamation is done by 90% of the proclaimers to 10% of the people. I have often asked myself the question—how many times do I want the message proclaimed over and over again to me before it is first proclaimed to someone who has never heard the message before?

About 90% of the officers are proclaiming their message and doing battle in areas already possessed while only 10% of the officers are available to do battle in the unconquered areas.

In the meantime the generals of the army are neglecting the overall strategy of world conquest, as announced by the Commander in Chief, while they argue about insignificant strategies such as the tunes that will be played, the colors of the uniform to be worn, and many other matters that divide their followers, lowering morale, dampening enthusiasm and raising questions as to the validity of the entire strategy.

Many of these generals use 50 to 70 percent of their resources building facilities to seat the increasing number of foot soldiers; places in which they may enjoy recreation, food and fellowship; yet neglecting to become meaningfully involved in the task of worldwide conquest.

Now I do not want to appear negative. I am not negative by nature. I am positive by nature, so here are some suggestions that I would like to make to erase a barrier between the pulpit and the pew, to eliminate the concept of two classes, obligations and responsibilities of Christians; and to get all people to recognize that they are members of the Laos, the people of God, with a corresponding commitment that inevitably follows becoming a child of God.

Positive Suggestions

At the outset we should seriously consider altering the standard for recruiting. If our standard is recruiting people to become members of a large congregation so that a large church can be built and more people become members to provide more money to build a larger church that is the type of people we will get.

> If we recruit numbers we will get numbers. I know of no organization easier to join, easier to maintain membership, easier to fulfill minimum membership requirements, than a Southern Baptist church.
> If we recruit more ministers we will get more ministers.

If we recruit with the idea that everybody should witness, we would
get more witnesses.
If we recruit with the concept that everyone is a missionary, we will
get more missionaries.

The story of Gideon shakes me up. I am not wise enough to apply it to
Southern Baptists; perhaps many of you are; anyway, it's worth thinking
about.

Maybe it isn't how many but how much; not how large but how strong;
not how big but how committed.

Pastor Is Player/Coach

Elton Trueblood likens the clergyman to a coach of a football team.
The coach instructs, teaches, motivates and helps direct the play, but the
team (un-ordained) has the major role in actually playing the game.

It came to me as a surprise many years ago when I discovered that
when Peter wrote his first letter and said, "You are a chosen generation"
that he was not referring to the Jews but the Christians. When he wrote,
"You are a royal priesthood," that he was not writing to the sons of Levi,
he was writing to me: that when he addressed certain people in his letter
as "saints" he was not referring to the venerable and noble old people
who had achieved some degree of spiritual adoration but he was talking
to me. If I have been chosen by God, if I have been denominated as a
priest or minister, and if I am numbered among the saints, that makes me
something special. It makes every Christian something special.

Motivation of High Expectations

Motivators tell us there is something within that responds to the challenge of high expectations. Southern Baptists have a very low level of
expectation from those who occupy the pew. Christ said that unto him
"that much was given, much was expected." Can we as Southern Baptists have a level of expectation so low that it does not challenge the two,
five or ten talent bench-warmer? And, could this be the reason so many
of them become heavily involved with their time, energy, mental ability
and finances with other para-church religious related, service, or civic
activities?

All are called to serve Christ. Doctors, farmers, lawyers, mechanics, homemakers, politicians, secretaries, coal miners, construction workers, engineers and on and on.

I grew up on a farm, studied agriculture in college, taught agriculture, and have spent my life working in the area of agriculture. It has always seemed rather strange to me that if I had decided to utilize my knowledge in agriculture in a foreign country and be paid by the Foreign Mission Board that God might have a "call" for me to do this. If, however, I remained in the United States and followed a career in agriculture, and had the same degree of commitment as if I had gone to the foreign mission field, there would, however, be no call from God for me.

This theology is inadequate for me and I think is entirely inadequate for the average person. I need a theology that will help me validate my call to serve where I am and to challenge me to the same degree of commitment for Christian ministries as the person who is ordained.

Dr. Drummond makes further comments in this area in stating: "It is regrettable that in these early years of church history clericalism began to develop. More and more, as the clergy assumed command of the church's mission, the lay person was slowly squeezed out. The clergy began to dominate the laity. Through the centuries this attitude hardened until in the course of time the English word 'lay' became a synonym for 'amateur' as over against 'professional'; or 'unqualified' as opposed to 'expert.'" How often we hear today, "I am just a layman." This can usually be taken as an apology for not being able to do something very well. Of course, some church members have not objected too vigorously to this development. More than a few have acquired something of a "spectator mentality." What so many church members seem to want, as Sir John Lawrence states, is "A building which looks like a church; a clergyman dressed in the way he approves, services the kind he has been accustomed to, and to be left alone. Such laymen have little if any real interest in church ministry, let alone actively engaging in the task themselves."

This does not mean that dedicated paid professionals are not necessary, including pastors, missionaries and others. The point I am trying to make is that our present method of depending on "paid workers" to usher in the Kingdom or to win the world to Christ or achieve the purposes of Bold Mission Thrust is not viable. The next great upsurge of Christianity awaits the involvement of the "Laos"—all the people of God.

Last year Southern Baptists took in over THREE BILLION DOLLARS from all sources. This is an astounding sum of money. (Incidentally, Southern Baptists spent more of this money on buildings, debt service, building maintenance and operation than on any other one thing. We must continually remind ourselves that buildings will not usher in the Kingdom of God any more than the cathedrals of the Middle Ages did. Buildings are necessary as a tool, but only as a tool.)

Last year Southern Baptists baptized 316,000 people in the United States. Through the Foreign Mission Board there were an additional 127,000 people baptized. This is a total of 443,000 people. It is interesting to note that this is equal to the number of babies born in the world in 32 hours. This also means that Southern Baptists spent 7,200 DOLLARS for ALL PURPOSES for each ONE PERSON baptized.

In 1982 the Foreign Mission Board budget was approximately a HUNDRED MILLION DOLLARS. On the foreign mission fields there were 127,000 baptisms. At this rate of expenditure for baptisms it would take a Foreign Mission budget of EIGHT HUNDRED EIGHTY-FIVE MILLION DOLLARS to baptize 1% of the people in the world.

Please don't misunderstand me. The Foreign Mission Board needs more money, not less. Our Convention needs more money, not less. The point I am trying to make is that our present method of using funds and relying principally on the people that are paid with these funds to evangelize the world is not getting the job done. We need to get multitude millions of Christians throughout the world recognizing that they too have a Christian ministry, that they too are responsible for ushering in the Kingdom of God and that as they are going they should preach and teach and make disciples.

W. Marshall Craig
This I Do for Christ's Sake

1 Corinthians 9

I'm asking that you think with me, if you please, for a little while, on the text found in 1 Corinthians the ninth chapter and a part of the twenty-third verse. "This I do for the gospel's sake." "This I do for the gospel's sake."

I think motives are always interesting. You and I do not want to question individual's motives, even though sometimes we may question their opinions, or their judgment. But, we always give them the benefit of the doubt, feeling in our hearts that their motives are sincere and that they are indeed genuine. But, we are not drawing upon our imagination at all when we look into the very heart of the great apostle Paul to see what his motive really was.

At all times and under all conditions of life that motive was in the forefront. To him there was a great principle involved and he was ready to give himself and to give all that he possessed into the great service of our Lord and Savior. He was governed by great principles, and any life that's projected in the world on the basis of great principles is a life that's bound to tell for God and for humanity. The apostle Paul lived such a life as that. Mr. Henry Ward Beecher said a rather significant thing. He said, "Expediences are but for an hour but principles are for the ages." That's one of the most striking sentences that I have ever read. We may do things sometimes as a matter of expediency, but Mr. Beecher reminds us that expediences are but for an hour. They are some of the passing things. They are here today and gone tomorrow and maybe we do something else as a matter of expediency, but principles are for the ages. And so the great apostle plighted his life on great principles, what had taken place in his own life and what he was ready to testify before the world. And in this particular passage this morning we read with great interest some of his statements. He says "To the weak, I became as weak that I might gain the weak. I am made all things to all men that I might, by all means, save some," a principle in his life, which revealed in part the secret of Paul's success. He could speak to the Athenians as a philosopher, and he could speak to the Jews as a Jew. He could speak to the Romans as a Roman citizen. He could speak to the slaves as a slave of Jesus Christ. He could speak to the free man as Christ's free man. To the wise he pointed them to Christ in whom are hid all the treasures of wisdom and knowledge. To the ignorant he could say God hath chosen the foolish things to confound the wise. And to the poor he declared, Christ became poor that we through His poverty might be made rich. And to the rich he spoke of the unsearchable riches of Jesus Christ. He was "made all things to all men." Why was that? Why was that?

And I reply secondly, not just to be agreeable, not simply to yield to the whims and fancies of those about him, but because it was a great principle in his life, it was the dominating motive and purpose that actuated him in his glorious ministry for Jesus. And he says that I may, by all means, save some. I do all of these things "that I might by all means save some." Save them by bringing them to a knowledge of Jesus Christ as Lord and as Savior.

As one writer has pointed out, the word *some* is very significant for the apostle Paul realized that he couldn't win them all, but "by all means to save some." Wasn't that a great principle, that he was willing to become all things to all men, with one dominating purpose, and that was to win some to the saving knowledge of Jesus Christ? Now he says in connection with all of this, "This I do for the gospel's sake," because of what the gospel had done for him. That gospel that was and is Christ centered. That gospel that he magnified, that he proclaimed and that he lived. I do all of this for the sake of the gospel that is Christ centered.

There are so many things, my dear friends, that we do for the sake of ourselves. There is a certain selfishness, I suppose, about us all and we go around doing this and doing that for the sake of ourselves. Some of those acts are very unselfish because we want to make our lives count a little more. Why get an education? Simply to be called an educated man or woman? Why, certainly not, but in order that that education might somehow be used for the glory of God.

Some of us were unable to attend the great meeting in Waco yesterday, as Baylor University launched that mighty campaign for 50 million dollars. Did you and I ever dream that we would live in such a day when one of our great institutions would be launching a campaign for 50 million dollars? And for all of these various schools under Baylor University here in Dallas and in Waco and in Houston that they might go on. Why raise 50 million dollars? Simply to have more in college or university or in training? No, but that through all of Baylor University there might be better equipped men and women who will honor God with their service and if not, why a great sum of money like that?

We do much for the sake of ourselves and for our institutions that they might go on for the glory of Christ. We do much for the sake of our homes. I would to God that we would do more that our homes might be more Christlike and that there might be more homes in our land that are really honoring God by serving Him. What's the hope of America? It's not primarily in human leadership, though we pray God's gracious blessings upon these who have been chosen by the American people to lead us in these years ahead. They will need our prayers and our support in order that America might be a better place in which to live. But, oh how much we need not primarily great human leadership as necessary as that is, but we need the wisdom and the very power of God in our lives, that our homes might be more Christlike, that we might have more family altars, that we might give ourselves humbly repenting of our sins and come to God that we might be able to say and to sing, "God Bless America." But if God is to bless America, then Americans must get closer to God. That's the great call in my humble judgment in this hour. We do much for the sake of our country for the great cause of freedom. Yonder in Korea sacrifices are being made in order that there might be greater freedom among the people of the earth.

We do much for conscience sake, and thank God we do. There are individuals still left in the world who will not violate conscience. But conscience somehow standing out so prominently, certain decisions must be made in keeping with a good conscience. Some things must be done that will devour the conscience of an individual. Here's the great apostle, he's ready for conscientiousness, and he's ready for all these institutions that everything might be for advancement, but he says I do all of this for the sake of the gospel.

Ah, my dear friends, that means something to us today because the gospel is the primary need in the world. The gospel that is Christ-centered. Someone has written that we have been custodians of the gospel for nearly two thousand years. We have spread it, but not widely enough. We have preached it, but not consistently enough. We have loved it, but not fervently enough. That's the great trouble. Yes, indeed. We have spread it, but not widely enough. And we have preached it, but not consistently enough, and we have loved it, but not fervently enough so that the great gospel of Christ might encircle the earth. That is, of course, very costly.

Peter, on one occasion talking with the Lord, said "why cannot I follow thee now?" That was a great question and then he continued. "I will lay down my life for thy sake." I turn to the thirteenth chapter of John and I read that again and I said, "Oh, Peter that's a wonderful statement" (v. 37). He said unto the Lord "why cannot I follow thee now? I will lay down my life for thy sake." I believe at that very moment the apostle Peter was absolutely sincere in the very presence of the Son of God. I believe he felt ready to do that. But, oh the human weakness of individuals. And Jesus said to him that "The cock shall not crow, till thou hast denied me thrice." And you know the great word that came concerning that. And then there came the glorious change in the apostle's life and he was ready to do exactly what he said he would do. But, oh, the great price that he eventually paid.

"I will lay down my life for thy sake." Do we not need individuals that are willing to be exactly that out in the world, not thinking primarily of the sacrifice but thinking of propagating the gospel of Christ whatever the cost may be. Mr. George Owens, a great writer, has given us a sentence which I think is very arresting. He said, "The world has many religions, it has but one gospel." The world has many religions, it has but one gospel. That's all. And that's the gospel that's Christ centered. It has many religions, but only one gospel to proclaim to the earth. The great apostle had somehow found that in that gospel there was everything for which his heart really sighed.

An unknown preacher gives to us this striking sentence. He said that Christianity is the religion of the superlative. As Christianity it is the religion of the superlative. It's the very end, it's the last. There isn't anything to be added to it. There isn't any new religion in the modern age to supplant Christianity. Here it stands as the superlative coming out of the very heart and mind of Almighty God and put in the very body and purpose of Jesus Christ as He walked the earth as the Savior of the world.

A great preacher in the years ago rose before his congregation and he asked a very pointed question. That question was this, "Is your religion worth propagating?" Is your religion worth propagating? I propound that question anew today and I ask myself as I ask you, "Is our religion worth propagating? Is the gospel of the Son of God worth propagating in the world?" If it isn't, we ought to join our lines and close up shop. But if it is, then we ought to be willing to make the supreme sacrifice. The great things that we cannot do and the small things that we will not do carry the danger for us all that we shall do nothing about it. How many followers of the Lord Jesus preserve the rancor that between the great faith we cannot do and the small things we will not do, there is the danger that we shall do nothing!

Looking through the Bible of Brother John H. Cullum there were many things that interested me. How that grand servant of the Lord lived so wonderfully for our Christ. Such a blessing to our church. I went through that Bible with the dear family, pencil mark after pencil mark, and then there was one outstanding verse to which he clung. "Whatsoever thy hand findeth to do, do it with all thy might." That was the guiding principle for Brother John H. Cullum. That life so faithfully lived and so magnificently served in his day and generation that "Whatsoever thy hand findeth to do, do it with all thy might." Put your whole heart into it. Put your every talent, put your material possessions, put it all into the great cause of propagating the gospel of Christ.

Is it worth propagating? If it is, then you and I ought to be ready whatever the cost may be. That means a great deal of faith for us in such a day as this. But after all says one, a man's faith sets the boundaries of his work. Our work will not be any larger than our faith. If our faith sets the boundaries of our work and our faith sets the boundaries of our church, if our faith is not big enough then our programs will not be big enough. In the light of the great needs of the world in this day our church, my dear friends, certainly in this hour ought to rise to its fullest measure of possibilities so that we may be in service for Christ as never before.

Tomorrow I am due to speak three times in Fort Worth, the Lord willing. One at the great district meeting at noon when they shall come together for a wonderful evangelistic hour. I have been asked to speak in a moment like this challenging us in the months ahead that we might give ourselves as churches, as pastors, as deacons, as teachers, as leaders in various fields of our church life, that we might give ourselves to the supreme faith, and that is soul winning. Every church today ought to set its boundaries far in soul winning. The great apostle said I do all of these things for the sake of the gospel and that I might win some, that's all, might win some. You and I can somehow project our lives in a day like this. We can also project our material substance. Your dollar will go a long way.

Dr. J. D. Grey has a wonderful logic on your missionary dollar. It will do just as much now, just as much. With all of the change in our monetary value that missionary dollar still does good and it has value today, with these individuals who are preaching and teaching and helping to carry forward the work of Christ. Mr. Babson has said that I fear that our prosperity may make us less dependent upon God. I fear that our prosperity may make us less dependent upon God, that there will be a self-sufficiency in our possessions. What we have will make us less dependent upon God. It doesn't matter how much we have or how little we have, we are dependent upon God. God that gives to us His matchless blessings. The great word still comes—"Why call ye me Lord, Lord, and do not the things which I say?" Then that further word, "what do ye more than others?" What are we doing more than those out yonder when we have the great opportunity? Jesus said "I must be about my Father's business" and "As my Father hath sent me [into the world], even so send I you [into the world]." And "we are laborers together with [Him]," not laboring by ourselves, or in our own strength, or in the things that we possess, we are laborers together with Him.

Beautiful song, wasn't it? "My God and I." My God and I. You and I can do anything with God. Anything as we serve Him as God takes possession of our lives that when Christ comes into our lives you can go out and do the things that seem to be impossible. I do all these things for the sake of the gospel of Christ because of what the Christ-centered gospel has done for you, has done for me and for the world.

Last Wednesday night at prayer meeting I told them of a visit that I made in the afternoon of that day in response to a phone call from a very dear man who asked me to come to the home. There we talked for a little while; then he handed me an envelope. He said "We heard your sermon regarding the great needs of our missionary program. Heard your sermon the other Sunday, said we wanted to have a part in it for we believe in tithing." He said "Here's an envelope for you." I carried the envelope on my way after we had talked and prayed together. I didn't know what was in it. But, when I looked in it later there was a wonderful check for $1,650.00. I said "Would you mind if we put that in the Lottie Moon Offering? Would you mind that at Christmastime we might put that in the Lottie Moon Offering to help take care of this great missionary program?" And I said "Yes, for the gospel's sake whatever the amount may be, big or little, to send out the glow of good news of Jesus and His power, to save unto the uttermost all who will come unto God by Him."

J. B. Cranfill
A Man in Hell

The rich man also died, and was buried; and in hell he lifted up his eyes, being in torment (Luke 16:22-23).

It is well from time to time in this short journey of our lives to stop and take our bearings, not only as regards this world, but as regards eternity. This is a very busy life we are living; there is a great rush, great excitement, great and powerful movements, with a broad sweep of power; and in the whirl and excitement we sometimes are prone to forget that after a while this fitful fever shall end; that after a little these that abide with us now shall have gone, and after a little while we shall have taken up our abode eternally in heaven or in hell. There are but two places of abode for the spirits of men after death. One of these places is heaven. God, Jesus on the throne, the angels and spirits of just men made perfect are there. That is heaven. In hell are the devil, the devil's angels, and the spirits of evil men who have passed into that nether world.

The text before us, or rather the entire lesson—for I wish to speak about the entire lesson rather than the few words announced as a text—begins by saying that there was a certain rich man. It does not give his name. It does not matter what his name was—a certain rich man. It is not a crime to be a rich man. There is many a poor man that is rich in a certain sense. He is rich in evil; rich in bad deeds; rich in evil associations; rich in his scorn of God. Riches in themselves are not criminal. There is many a rich man, as we count riches, whose heart is tender, and who is really rich toward God; and who is touched with a feeling of the infirmities of every poor beggar under the shining stars. It is not a crime then to be rich; and I have never had any sympathy with the great cry of people against the rich. It is a great temptation to be rich. I never shall forget the prayer recorded in the Old Testament, "Give me neither poverty nor

128

riches." I have thought sometimes I would like to be rich. I fear it comes to us all in some time of special temptation, of special allurement by the world. We wish we could be rich; but when we come to think about it soberly, we had better not be really rich in this world's goods, because there come great temptations with riches. But as I said before, I have no sympathy with the idea that is getting deeper and broader in our country, that to be rich is evil in itself, and that riches must be pounced upon and destroyed and divided out among tramps and anarchists. All such doctrine comes from the devil. Neither is it a crime to be poor. The really poor can be rich toward God. Look at this man's name now. The poor man had a name. There was a certain rich man, and then there was a certain beggar named Lazarus. You know Lazarus' name meant "helped of God." That is the interpretation of his name.

And now let us go and see the picture. See the mansion with its broad spacious grounds, the blooming flowers, and the fruits in the fields; and then see down at the gate a poor man with a crutch. There he was, laid at the gate, full of sores. Lazarus had very likely been a very prosperous workingman. It is quite likely that at one time he had wrought mightily with his hands and made his daily bread and looked up to nobody except to God. But oh, the great misfortune of a poor man when he is sick. I tell you it is an awful thing to be sick at all, but it is transcendently awful to be sick when you are poor, when you cannot make the daily two dollars. Not long ago it came very close to me. A man in my employ, and as kingly a man as ever wore the crown of honest labor, got sick, and I could see the pain written all over his face when he failed to earn his two dollars a day. It was dreadful. And the fact that Lazarus was a beggar was no disgrace to him, because he was sick. He was not a beggar by choice. He was not a tramp. He did not go around, a healthy and stalwart man, and go to the back kitchen door and say, "I wish you would give me some bread." I have no respect for a tramp—I mean a well tramp. A man in this country who would go out begging for a cup of coffee, who has two good strong arms on him and health flushing his face: shame on him! Lazarus was a beggar because he was sick, and here he was at the rich man's gate. You look at these plain statements of fact. Most of the commentaries say that this was a parable. It may have been a parable, but I don't believe it was a parable. In another place where Jesus mentions a rich man the Scripture says, "He spoke a parable unto them." In this case there is no parable in it, but a plain statement of plain everyday facts. This plain statement was not a parable, as I understand it, but Jesus Christ rent the veil and made that recital of an everyday occurrence in every age. He simply raised the curtain and said, "And Lazarus died."

Let us now think about the rich man a moment. He was having a good time; he fared sumptuously every day. He went and took a box at the theatre and saw the play with opera glasses. He played his game of social cards, and bet a little. He was not really a bad gambler, or else he would not have been rich. And he attended the "german," went down to the saloon on Sunday and drank his wines and whiskies. He was probably a member of the local political executive committee and had influence in the community; a man who thought about everything except God and heaven and eternity; grasping his money, despising God's homeless poor that came to his gate and begged: "Oh, mister, just let me come after dinner is over and eat the crumbs that fall from the table!" He took a stick and drove him away from the gate.

"There was a certain beggar." I have thought about that beggar many a time. I do not think I will ever again let any beggar pass me by without giving him something. I do not mean tramps. As I before stated, I have no respect for tramps; and I wish you would never have any respect for tramps. But I talk about beggars, people who are really in distress, who have sadness written on their faces and poverty marked all over them. It was only the other day in the city of New York, a poor beggar on Broadway came up to me and said, "Oh, give me money; help me." You could see poverty all over him; see that hope had left his heart and despair had come to live with him. I make a plea here to-day, whether you have much or little, that you remember the homeless poor, and help them. The day will come when it will have been more to you to have invested money in a really deserving poor man than to have had a million dollars stock in the Bank of England.

But see the change of scene. Look how sublimely our Saviour goes right on with the story. He does not stop to explain anything about the difference between time and eternity. That is not his purpose just now; but he is depicting the lives of these two men. And he says: "The rich man also died and was buried." See the contrast between the statement made just before about Lazarus: "And . . . the beggar died and was carried by the angels." He did not stop to say whether he was buried or not. The chances are that he was not buried. Probably he dragged himself into some lonely, sequestered spot, and there died. Jesus did not say that he was buried, but the rich man died and was buried. See the funeral procession. Maybe no real mourners even then. He had five brothers, but they were probably glad he was dead. They will get his money now and have a good time over it. But here is the long funeral procession following the man out to the grave, with all the trappings of funerals. On this point I wish to say a word in passing. The saddest thing to me, sadder than the funeral itself, is to see the great pomp and circumstance of some funerals. Oh, the money that is wasted, literally wasted, burying men. Some of the rich pay out thousands of dollars for funerals, and on every side God's cause lifts up its empty hands and the hungry and poor and thinly clad are dying for the very bread of life. Lazarus died and was carried by the angels. The rich man died and, in hell he lifted up his eyes—in hell.

Now this brings us to the subject of our sermon, "A Man in Hell." Stop a moment. Is this an idle picture? The worst and most malignant enemies that Jesus Christ ever had never accused him of telling a lie. You take all the literature written against him to prove that he was not divine, and with one consensus of opinion, one acclaim, one voice, all literature says, "Jesus Christ was totally true." And here he says that this man lifted up his eyes in hell. The curtain is raised. There is the man in hell. Time to him is dead. Opportunity to him is gone forever. He has passed from life's arena. There was sunshine yesterday; the funeral to-day; hell to-day. Eternity, eternity, eternity, has come and the man is in hell. See him. He prays—the first time perhaps in all his life that he had ever prayed, and he says, "Oh, Father Abraham!" Repentance has come.

Did you ever visit a jail? The most humble lot of repentant sinners on earth are in jail. I have talked to men, I have preached to men in jail. They will all give their hand; they all want to be saved. Why? Because they are caught. Not because they committed a crime, but because the sleuth-hound of the law has tracked them down, and now they find themselves incarcerated and the bolts and bars shut them in and there is no hope of escape. They are all humble, all penitent. All of them say, "I wish I was out again. If I were I would be a better man." Turn one out and he would steal a horse to-morrow night.

A man in hell! There was a quaint, strange book anonymously written in England entitled, "Letters from Hell." I wish all sinners might read those letters, though they are imaginary. But, oh, hear the cold, solemn words of Jesus. They are not imaginary. Don't they cause the cold chills to run over you to-day as you hear the words of our Saviour, awful in their terror and truthfulness? "In hell he lifted up his eyes." I don't suppose he believed in hell at all while he lived. I suppose he had argued many a time to prove that there was no hereafter at all, and he had said, "Oh, this nonsense that these people talk about. There is no such place. Get the thing out of my mind, I don't want to hear about it." But hear me to-day, fellow-traveler to the grave: shutting one's eyes does not put out the fire. You may hear the crackling of the flames and the jingle of the firemen's bell, and the shout of the firemen's captain. You may hear the word, "Fire!" And yet you shut your eyes and say, "I don't see any fire; I don't believe there is any fire." But the fire rages still, and block after block of buildings is consumed and crashes in. Oh, vain man, to-day I thunder in your ears, warranted by the word of God and by the burning sentences of Jesus of Nazareth—there is a hell! And every unrepentant man, when the gate of death confronts him and opens wide its portals for him to pass in, will go down into that darkness—into that darkness from which no traveler has ever returned, and in the gloom of whose surroundings no prayer has ever been answered. Hear him pray, "Oh, Father Abraham." Here is prayer to-day. I talked to a man once who said he never had prayed in his life, and didn't believe in prayer. But hear me to-day: The man that dies without believing and praying, wakes up in hell with prayer on his tongue and says, "Oh, Father Abraham." Here is realization at last.

We have often seen men building sidewalks of cement. When the cement was first put down they put planks over it. Why? It was soft. They are to protect it. Once in a while a dog will get on anyhow, and there is his track on the cement sidewalk. Now the cement is as hard as adamant. Nothing could make a track on it now. Its days of softness are gone. It has become fixed, and no imprint can be made on it now. Once a little, tiny bird, singing in the trees beside it, could have lighted on it and left its little footprints there. It was soft. Once upon a time the man who is in hell to-day was a little boy playing at his mother's knee, and he had a tender heart in those childhood days, and oftentimes he wept. There were times when he looked up into his mother's face and asked her about God, and there were other times when he knelt down beside his little baby bed and said his childish prayer. That was a time of innocence, a time when there was a heart to feel and an ear to hear, but those times are gone forever. A hell, a real, eternal, irrevocable hell, awaits the impenitent man or the impenitent woman.

And look at what Abraham said to him, "Son." And the very next word he said was, remember—"Son, remember." Oh, memory, art thou living yet? Quickened indeed by the very impulse of the burning flame, memory revives and takes the back track of the man's life and goes back into those days of innocence and love, goes back and feels the kiss of mother once again, goes back and hears the sermon in the old church, goes back to the very day when the preacher talked about hell and the man believed it not; goes back to opportunity and sunshine and light again. Oh, memory, memory, memory! Oh, if a man could go to hell and leave his memory behind him it would not be hell. After all, hell is memory and memory is hell. Take the debauchee. How does he feel this morning? Ah, if he had no memory! But before he can get up and set his blood on fire again with the hellish liquor, he begins to think and think and think, to think of his little wife at home, his ragged children, and his wrecked manhood; think of the strewn pathway of his life, beset all the way with thorns and tossed about with tempests. Memory! Brother, hear me now. Draw a line fifty years from now and we will all be in heaven or in hell—everyone in this house, certainly every adult in this house; just fifty short years and there will come to the sinner in this house to-day the memory of that quiet summer Sunday, when the preacher in the best way he knew, talked about hell, and the man in hell, and he will say, "Oh, give me back the life of that Sunday," but it will be too late. Oh, may things terrestrial be made luminous with the light of eternity to-day, that men may see where they stand in the sight of Almighty God. May there come from the very throne of God a flash of supernal light, sped by his Spirit, that will seek the hearts of sinners in this house and cause them to fall down and say, "Oh, let me escape from the wrath to come!"

Out of the very fullness of my heart I plead with you to-day. Do not go with Dives into hell. Take your mother's hand, lean on the Saviour, and to-day plead for mercy from the throne of God; for there is mercy to-day, and there is love to-day, and there are blessing and salvation to-day. But in hell, no answer to the prayer. There is something sad, oh, awfully sad, when you think about what this rich man said to Abraham. He thought somewhat about himself and said, "I am in torment here and I wish you would just let Lazarus come and give me a little sympathy, for I am tormented in these flames." But he did not stop there. He said, "Oh, Abraham, Abraham, send Lazarus back to the world again. I have one, two, three, four, five brothers, and they are just as I was. They heard the gospel and slighted it just as I did. And I led them into a thousand wrongs. I said to them, There is no hereafter. I said to them, There is no eternity. And, O God, I am in hell, and they are still unrepentant. And though I know that I cannot escape it, oh, send Lazarus down there to preach to them." Oh, memory, memory, memory! Light it up with a flash of eternity. But the man became a missionary just a day too late. Just a day too late he thought about the awfulness of the fact that his five brethren were not saved. Solemnly, earnestly, prayerfully, I press this scene on your hearts this morning: A lost man. Time is over. Riches all gone. They are of no use now. Once he could have bought a whole county; he cannot buy a drop of water now. Once men followed him; now he is beset about with the evil men of all ages, and he wails out: "Here they are with me. Once I had opportunity. Once I had a mother's love. Once the Spirit of God came and moved my heart and said, 'After all, it is true. After all, you had better be a Christian. After all, you had better give your heart to God.' And I said, 'No, I will just close it up. I won't hear any of it.'" All the wealth of the Indies and the gold of Ophir could not buy for him a single mercy now, because the end has come.

And even poor Lazarus, oh, think about it! Lazarus was God's missionary to that man. Do you know what that poor fellow would have done if the rich man had just opened his gate that day and said: "Come in, poor fellow. You can have more than the crumbs. You can have a seat at the table. Just come in and we will help you. And now bring him something to eat." Do you know, if he had gone and lingered by his side and bound up his wounds, Lazarus would have told him about God, and Lazarus would have been there in that house a very electric current between that home and God, and the wires would have flashed with prayer and the rich man need never have been in hell at all. And he remembered that, and so he wanted the very beggar that he had cast off and scorned, to go back to his brethren and say to them, "Oh, don't you go where your brother has gone!" It seems to me that the saddest thing, when all the sum of our life shall have been cast up and the end shall have come—that the saddest thing of all will be the separation between loved ones. At the gate of death the unrepentant goes into hell to take up his abode with devils, and the penitent goes into the glory world to be with Jesus forever. There will be the separation of fathers and sons there. There will be the separation of wives and husbands. There will be families torn asunder. O God, may all in this house of every family be united in heaven. May every sinner in this house to-day flee from the wrath to come, for I tell you, dear friends, that it is true, every word of it is true, every word.

Now the last thought in this sermon. Why have I preached it? Why preach such a sermon? Why talk to men about a subject as harrowing as this? Why remove the veil and lift up the covering from the seething mouth of hell that we may gaze into it for a moment? I will tell you why. Why is it that when yellow fever comes it is flashed on the wires into a million homes in an hour? Why is it that when contagion makes its home among us that the news passes from lip to lip? It is done that we may escape it. Why is it that men were each other against the blight and deadliness of temporal destruction? Why is it? It is to save them. And so I have come to-day to preach this sermon, because I know—and I realize it more and more as I grow older and come nearer to the end of my own life—I know that very soon the sums of your lives will have been made out forever and for eternity.

A word to the Christians just here. Why don't you talk more to sinners? Why don't you warn men? I tell you there is reality in it all; that there is a real, literal hell; and that the broad sweep of its eternity on the one hand is just as long as heaven on the other.

You say—and that is what this man thought—even in hell he thought that if somebody would just rise from the dead and go down there and tell those five brethren, they would all believe it. That is a great fallacy. Do you know that if a man were to die here in this house today, and stay dead a day, and after he had been dead a day should come back to life again and stand in this pulpit where I am standing, and talk to you and say: "I have been in heaven; I have seen Jesus; I have heard the angels sing; I have clasped hands with Abraham and Elijah and Moses, and men, it is all true; and I looked over that great gulf and I saw into hell, and lost men are there, and they are to-day raising their fruitless cries to heaven"; if he should come and stand here, you would say the man never was dead, and you would not believe him. You would say, "It is all a fraud, that fellow was never dead; he is lying." I tell you, brethren, if men hear not Moses and the prophets; if they hear not this book, these burning truths of the word of God, they would not hear if the whole graveyard should rise from the dead and come and proclaim the gospel with the cerements of the grave around them. If men cannot be convinced by the fact that Jesus Christ rose from the dead, by the militant tread of God's army for two thousand years, and by the testimony of a million men who, on the border line of death, have said, "I see heaven, and I hear the angels, and I know that heaven is real," nothing would convince them. I never shall forget how old Brother Watson died—a man whom some of you knew. When the last hour of his life came and he had no more sight in his eyes, except as he saw into eternity, he called his daughter to him and said, "I see Kitty." That was his wife who had gone to God. Was it a lie? Was it a lie that the old and venerable man of God told when the death-damp was on his brow? Oh, no! And I remember how M. V. Smith died, that consecrated man whom so many loved. In the very last moment almost of his kingly life, he said, "Safe in my Saviour's arms at last." Was it a lie? Blessed be God, it was true. There is salvation to-day and life eternal to-day, and there is hope to-day for every sinner.

One of the saddest things about hell is that there is no hope in hell. And men have committed suicide to get away from a hopeless world and gone straight to a hopeless hell. I point you to-day, dear sinner friend, to light and live and hope. I point you to Jesus Christ on the cross, the living Saviour. But for his mercy you would be in hell to-day. He has been very good to you. He has been very kind to you. He has given you health and prosperity and he has made you glad many a time because life has been so pleasant; and he gave you a Christian home and a Christian mother. Through his mercy you have heard the gospel many a time, and is only through his mercy that we are here to-day. And in his name I plead with you to-day to come and forsake your sins; come and forsake your skepticism if you have it. Come and with humble spirit fall at the feet of Jesus and say, "O Jesus, here I am, an undone sinner with only a few years to live. Take me as I am and give me life eternal to-day." Is there one to-day in all this audience who wants to escape from the wrath to come? Faster than the breath of any cyclone, speedier than the flash of any lightning, deadlier than the embrace of any anaconda, is coming the last day, the last death, the unutterable and eternal death to sinful men. With all the power of my heart to-day, let me impress the transcendent truth of this text, "In hell he lifted up his eyes." And this gleam of hope: "God so loved the world that he gave his only begotten Son, that whosoever believeth on him should not perish, but have eternal life." Will you take him to-day? Take him as your Saviour. Take him for now, for to-morrow, and forever.

Edwin Charles Dargan
Watchman, What of the Night?

The burden of Dumah. He calleth to me out of Seir, Watchman, what of the night? Watchman, what of the night? The watchman said, The morning cometh, and also the night: if ye will enquire, enquire ye: return, come (Isa. 21:11-12).

This is one of those obscure, yet striking passages of Scripture which awaken our curiosity and interest without entirely satisfying them. The meaning is not perfectly clear, and yet it is enough so to bring a valuable lesson to one who attentively considers the words. There is no fully satisfactory explanation. The passage is very brief, abrupt, and without logical connection with what precedes or follows. It is simply one among several brief prophecies, without date, and without logical order, which are grouped here in the book of Isaiah. We do not know what time or occasion brought forth the prophecy. We do not know where Isaiah was, nor who the enquirer was, nor why the divine answer came in this form. Like many other dark passages of Scripture, its very obscurity awakens interest, and suggests a teaching of value. Dark Scriptures and dark providences alike, often bring us important and helpful lessons, even when we cannot penetrate their meaning or see plainly God's purpose in them. Yet this abrupt and obscure prophecy, when carefully studied, may yield us some lessons of hope and help as we trace its meaning. Let us observe the enquiry, the answer, and the admonition.

I. The Enquiry

The title is, "The burden of Dumah." The word "burden" as employed by the prophet signifies the message which God sends. It is equivalent to oracle, as employed in the ancient mythology, being the answer of the deity. But the word burden itself carries the thought of judgment, of punishment sometimes. It is the doom, as well as the revelation, sent of God

137

through the prophet. This last shade of meaning probably does not appear here. It is simply the revelation of God to the prophet concerning Dumah. The word Dumah signifies silence, and is a poetic name for Edom, later known as Idumea. It was the wild country to the South of Judea, inhabited by the descendants of Esau. The feud between the twin brothers had become historic in their descendants. There were frequent wars and there was much hatred, yet there were intervals of peace and many lines of intercourse between the two peoples. Dumah stands for heathenism, for hostility to Israel and to the God of Israel. It represents a proud, irreligious, cruel enemy to the Israel of God. Yet from such a source there comes a call to the prophet. "He calleth to me out of Seir." From the rocky fortress of Edom there rings out a cry to the prophet of God. From Dumah the silence is broken, and out of the dark there rings a cry of distress. The night has long settled down upon the people of Edom; gloom was about them. Their present was dark, and their future darker. The listening prophet, like a watchman waiting for the dawn, hears across the wilderness the call of neighboring heathendom as it rings in his ears, "Watchman, what of the night?" Perhaps the words, according to the late G. A. Smith, may be better rendered "what off of the night?" That is, how much night remains? How long before day comes? When will better times of spiritual as well as temporal blessings come to us? Shall we be always enveloped in the cloud and darkness of irreligion and despair? Canst thou, O prophet, as the spokesman of the living God, give us a word of hope or of help in our long night? Something like this seems to be the meaning of this strange enquirer. Some, even in Edom, were looking for the day, and longing for it to come.

Is it so in our time, that in once far-off lands which now have been brought nigh through the wondrous development of transportation and trade there are some even in heathen darkness who are looking for the light? Through the lengthening years of missionary activity, amid all nations of the earth, frequent voices, like that of the unknown soul that calls from Seir, are heard. To alert and watchful Christian leaders the yearning cry of nonChristian nations has often made itself heard. Is our night to be forever? Is there not in your Christian truth some message of help and hope for us? Many instances have come from various ages and lands through mission workers to show that time and again the yearning of the so-called heathen peoples has reached out toward the light of Christian truth. Sometimes the missionary and his people have been rebuked for their tardiness in bringing the gospel message. Time and again some weary and longing soul has said to the watchman, "Why did you tarry so long? If you had this message, why did you not bring it before? How long will it be until others come among our benighted people to bring the gospel message?" Even now, today, such cries go up from yearning spirits in those countries which have long been the scene of modern missionary endeavor. Word comes of multitudes in the far East, Japan, Korea, China, India, who are yearning for the light; who are asking, "Watchman, what of the night," or, "How much off of the night? How long until day dawns, and the light of the world shall illumine our land?"

We must not direct our thoughts to far off lands alone, but think of the heathen that are near us, nay, that are even among us. Dumah adjoined Judah. Edom was akin to Israel. The great worldly world around us is of our own kind. The hopeless heart is found in the midst of modern civilization, and the yearning soul, unsatisfied with the things of earth, often cries out in its night and lonesomeness, "Watchman, what of the night?" This pleasure-crazed world, frivolous, self-gratifying, heartless, has in its throng sometimes a longing soul who cries out to some watchman for God, "How much off the night?" This materialistic, wealth-sodden world, groaning under its self-imposed burdens of business care, cannot always suppress its own groanings, and asks some watchman on the height of Christian hope and faith, "Watchman, how much off the night?" Is there not something better than to be busy for the accumulation of wealth? In the tangled web of our modern life, godless, gay, greedy, in the night of our hoplessness, our strain, our carking care, is there not some yearning cry to the enlightened soul who knows better? Is there not some voice of appeal to the watchful Christian spirit for a message of help and hope in the Dumah of the world's spiritual silence and darkness? Yes, we hear such voices now and then, and may be able to say with the prophet, "He calleth to me out of Seir, Watchman, what of the night?" What answer shall we bring? Let us turn to our obscure prophecy again and find it.

II. The Answer

It seems strange, obscure, unsatisfactory, a double answer. It is incomplete. It does not bring all that was wanted, and yet it is an answer. The watchman said, "The morning cometh and also the night." Yes, the morning cometh. There is hope of a better day. The night will not endure forever. The coming glories of Messiah's reign in Zion may shine also upon Mount Seir. The spiritual blessings promised to ancient Israel may include Israel's neighboring foe, and bless even the vindictive and hostile tribe of her historic enemy. Even from Mount Seir one shall not call in vain. Hated Esau may become beloved, and the blessing denied to the ancestors may come upon his remote descendants. "The morning cometh." Even the Edomite may not despair. If he were in earnest, and sought the God of Israel, he should not seek in vain. This much the prophet watchman could assuredly say. So also in our modern conditions the like promise may be cherished for the heathen abroad and the heathen at home. The Christian watchman may confidently say, "The morning cometh." A better day lies before us. There is hope of an obedient and prosperous church, glowing with spiritual life and rejoicing in fulfilled blessed hopes. There is hope of an evangelized world. Nearer than ever before in the history of Christianity is this an accomplished fact. Every nation and kindred and people is having the offer of redemption in Christ Jesus. The missionaries of the cross have gone into every land and laid down their lives among every people to make known the unsearchable riches of Christ. Christianity of the purest type has blossomed where foul orgies were practiced in the name of false religion. Idols have been thrown to the owls and the bats, and the cross of Christ has been raised up. Deserted temples in places have given way to Christian chapels, where crowding worshippers have come, and are coming in greater throngs, to hear the message of salvation. In many a place long closed to gospel light, the morning cometh.

Can we say that this is true in the worldly world about us? Just now the ruin of war wastes the fairest parts of Europe. The storm and night lower above lands where the noblest institutions of Christianity have long flourished. It seems as if unbridled heathenism had broken loose in a world that ought to be Christian and at peace. Yet as there are voices to cry for help, there are also indications that the cry is heard. "The morning cometh." The unsatisfied heart of man calls out, and calls not in vain. We are told that in many of the lands afflicted by war there is a great turning toward God. There is recognition of a higher power than that of our vaunted civilization. There is a feeling of fault. There is a yearning for a restraining hand, a guiding wisdom, a purifying and uplifting presence. So may our twentieth century, still in its youth, see the turn toward a brighter day, and those who watch the signs of the times be able to assure the faint-hearted with the prophetic word, "The morning cometh."

Yet we know it is not all bright. The response of the watchman was, "Also the night." He must check undue confidence. From his post of observation he must know that the forces of evil were not to be overcome in a day, nor could the best hopes of the best souls expect to find fruition in a night. If the morning is near there will be a short day and the night will come again. As night follows day, so trouble follows joy; so ignorance succeeds to enlightenment; so wickedness takes its turn with righteousness. No moral or spiritual victory is ever complete in this world. The shades must come along with the shines; the bitterness must be mingled with the sweets; "also the night." By such a figure the existence of both evil and good must necessarily be represented as alternating, but we know that they co-exist. The evil is along with the good. A little boy, bright with the hopes of youth, and beginning to look out upon life with some degree of thoughtfulness, was driving along the road with his father one day, a wise and good servant of God. The lad said, "Father, there is so much good in the world—I know there is bad too. Is it not true that for every bad thing there is also some good thing?" The more experienced father smiled rather sadly, and said to the boy, "Yes, but the evil preponderates." The lad fell silent and pondered over the long word, whose meaning he did not exactly catch, and yet instinctively knew. So to all observers of the slow progress, at home and abroad, of Christian light and life and love, there must come the check even to their most ardent hopes of that word which says "also the night." It will not be full day for our poor, sinful world until he shall come whose right it is to rule, and to whom the sovereignty of the earth belongs. What shall be our attitude of mind and heart in view of the double certainty of morning and of night; of progress and yet of retard; of growing power, and yet of hindering weakness; of victorious truth, and yet of persistent error? If both morning and light are still to be our portion while we wait, in what spirit shall we abide? Let us go back again to our passage, and find our lesson.

III. The Admonition

More obscure yet seems the answer of the watchman. It seems even to bring a rebuke. To those who call of Seir he answers, "If ye will enquire, enquire ye: return, come." What does he mean? Only that his message is not final; that day and night still must be. No final day has yet arrived. Meantime the enquiring soul should not stifle its enquiries. The longing heart should not sink back into despair. The obscure and unsatisfactory answer of the watchman is meant to encourage the one who calls. It says, "Keep on asking. I may have a better message for you later. Come again. My answer is confessedly incomplete, but it is not final." Edom may have hopes along with the certainty of continued trouble, but it is her privilege to keep on asking if the night will not soon pass.

And this must also be the answer of the modern watchman. He must say to the voices which come from the heathen world around him, "If you will enquire keep on enquiring. I have a message for you. I cannot say everything will be bright all at once, but I can say it is worth your while to pursue your enquires. You are directing your request in the right direction. If you wish to keep on asking, keep on." Here is your hope of an answer. God is not unmindful of your cry. From the holy hill of Zion there comes a word of reassurance to harsh and heathenish Seir. From the church of the living God in this modern age, with all her faults and failures, there must come to the sinful world which envelops her the watchman's answer. If you wish your answer upon the dark problems of sin, enquire of me. The enlightened Christian, not by any ambition or assumption of his own, but through the call of God and his enlightening grace, is still the waiting watchman to ring out the world's best hope. The church must purify herself and strengthen herself and devote herself yet more and more that she may be able, with serene confidence, to answer back to an enquiring world, "If ye will enquire, enquire ye." Before the problem the proper state of mind is not surrender, but continued enquiry. Before the problems of the ages, before the failures even of the best, the right attitude of soul for a world that needs help and hope is not one of abandonment, but one of continued effort to know. Through the historic channels of her knowledge of God, the church must still pour the refreshing waters of God's grace and knowledge upon a parched and weary world. Ezekiel's vision of the river that flowed from under Mount Zion and brought life wherever it came is still apt for the needy world of today. The gospel of our Lord Jesus Christ is still the hope of mankind, and they who are seeking for the higher light must be pointed to him who is "the Lamb of God, that taketh away the sin of the world." We Christians still have a message. We must say to enquirers from all quarters, "If ye will enquire, enquire ye." Our light is not full, but we have it. Our problems are not all solved, but we have faith to wait, encouraged. With us you will find the best light and the best help. If you want knowledge of God and hope of eternal life, come, ask us.

And so the counsel grows emphatic. The watchman multiplies his words—"Return, come." There is an imperative that comes from possession of assured hope. There is an imperative that comes from the experience of a satisfied mind. He who can say "I know whom I have believed" can urge those who do not know to come and stand by him. The realization of a divine life in the heart is itself a plea to those who have it not.

So catching our inspiration from the ancient prophet, in his dealings with the world of sin and doubt, and yet of yearning, that lay before him, let us ring out our answer, obscure and partial though it be; let us say to enquiring souls, whether in far distant lands, or nearer to us in the godless world that lies about us, If you wish the way of life, if you long for the hope of glory, if you are weary of the darkness and are yearning for the light, come to us. We have been appointed of God to direct wanderers to him. Not through any merit or worthiness of our own, but through God's grace upon us, we have been placed as watchmen to answer the calls of a needy world. Our message is one of hope. We can say to everyone who calls out of Seir, "The morning cometh," and though the night also must come, do not lose hope nor faith. Press your enquiries. A better day and its fuller answer will surely come. And so together let us watch and wait until the day dawn, and the daystar arise in our hearts.

Watchman, tell us of the night,
  What its signs of promise are.
Trav'ler o'er yon mountain's height,
  See that glory beaming star.

Watchman, does its beauteous ray
  Aught of hope or joy fore-tell?
Trav'ler, yes; it brings the day,
  Promised day of Israel.

Watchman, tell us of the night;
  Higher yet that star ascends.
Trav'ler, blessedness and light,
  Peace and truth, its course portends.
Watchman, will its beams alone
  Gild the spot that gave them birth?

Trav'ler, ages are its own;
   See! it bursts o'er all the earth.

Watchman, tell us of the night,
   For the morning seems to dawn.
Trav'ler, darkness takes its flight,
   Doubt and terror are with-drawn.
Watchman, let thy wand'rings cease;
   Hie thee to thy quiet home.
Trav'ler, lo! the Prince of peace,
   Lo! the Son of God is come.

A. C. Dixon
Hallelujah

Praise ye the Lord (Ps. 146:1).

The word "Hallelujah," which is translated "Praise ye the Lord," occurs, as I have counted, twenty-four times in the Book of Psalms, and four times in the nineteenth chapter of Revelation, making twenty-eight times altogether in the Bible. In the Psalms it is Hallelujah of earth, and in Revelation it is the Hallelujah of heaven. It is a word which cannot be translated by one word into any other language, and is, therefore, transferred. It is about the same in Greek, Latin, German, French, Italian, Dutch and English. It looks as if all nations were practising for the Hallelujah chorus of heaven.

There are six Hallelujahs. Let us pass them in review.

I. The Hallelujah of Nature

The first use of the word is at the close of Psalm 104. This Psalm is a fine poem on nature. It begins by calling on the soul to bless God, and then ascribes to God the greatness, honour and majesty which a study of nature suggests to a religious mind. The light is God's garment. The heaven is the canopy which He has spread, and the foundations of the ocean were laid by Him. He makes the clouds His chariot and rides upon the wings of the wind. The thunder is His voice. He makes the springs which water bird and beast. The grass for the cattle, the trees for the nesting birds, the hills for the wild goats and the rocks for the conies are the expressions of His love and wisdom. He made the laws which govern the sun and moon. Even the darkness serves a benevolent purpose. In the midst of this beautiful scene man "goeth forth to his labour until the evening."

145

Then the Psalmist poet turns to the ocean, "this great and wide sea, wherein are things creeping innumerable," with the ships on its surface and the monsters playing in its depths. God gives life and sustenance to all these.

The study of nature fills the Psalmist with praise to God. He says, "My meditation of Him shall be sweet. I will be glad in the Lord." There is no conflict between the two books God has written for us, the Book of Nature and the Book of Revelation. God reveals Himself in both. The naturalist who does not see God in His works simply shuts his eyes and refuses to see. An agnostic is one who chooses blindness rather than sight. Everything in earth and sea and sky proclaims a God. Over the door of the great museum of McGill University in Montreal Sir William Dawson wrote the twenty-fourth verse of this Psalm, "O Lord, how manifold are thy works: In wisdom hast Thou made them all." Sir William was a scientist, but he did not allow scientific prejudice to blind the eyes of his soul.

II. The Hallelujah of Providence

The 105th Psalm, which also closes with "Hallelujah," deals with the history of Israel, and the Psalmist sees the footprints of God in history as well as in nature. It was God Who covenanted with Abraham, "made oath unto Isaac," and "confirmed the same to Jacob." It was God Who protected His people when they "were but few in number." It was God Who "called for a famine upon the land" when prosperity had caused them to forget His laws. It was God Who sent Joseph into Egypt, and then Moses as the deliverer of His people. It was God Who sent the darkness and turned their water into blood. It was God Who spread a cloud over them for a covering and gave them "fire to give light in the night." It was God Who "opened the rock" and quenched their thirst. The Psalmist closes this review of God's providential dealings with a "Hallelujah."

With some it is easier to see God in nature than in providence. Jacob could praise God for grass and trees and stars, but when Joseph was taken he said, "All these things are against me." On another occasion the Psalmist did not feel like praising and he refused to shout "Hallelujah" with his lips when his heart did not prompt it. "Why art thou cast down, O my soul," he exclaims, "and why art thou disquieted within me? Hope thou in God; for I will yet praise Him." I do not feel like praising now, but I will hope for the time to come when I will praise Him. Indeed I will praise God that I will yet praise Him.

There is no kind of experience in which a Christian has a right to refuse to praise God, for "all things work together for good to them that love God." Praise God in the dark, for He maketh the light to shine out of darkness. Praise God for sorrow, for Jesus said, "Your sorrow shall be turned into joy." Praise God for clouds, for it is upon the clouds that God shows His rainbow of love. Praise God for the furnace, for it is in the fire that the Son of man delights to walk with you, and when you come out you will find that only your bonds have been burned. He who obeys the command, "Rejoice in the Lord," has a Hallelujah in his soul every minute of the day and night.

III. The Hallelujah of Grace

The 106th Psalm begins and closes with "Hallelujah," and the key-note of its contents is in the first verse, "Give thanks unto the Lord, for His mercy endureth for ever." He prays, "O visit me with Thy salvation," and he makes confession of sin: "We have sinned with our fathers; we have committed iniquity, we have done wickedly." Then follows a recountal of God's merciful dealings with His people in spite of their sins. "He remembered for them His covenant and repented according to the multitude of His mercies."

The saved sinner can sing this "Hallelujah" of mercy more loudly and sweetly than any other. And God's mercy fills him with song because His justice has been satisfied in Jesus Christ. Mercy can now rejoice against judgment because judgment has been met and mercy made possible through the atoning sacrifice of Christ. "Hallelujah for the cross" is the song of the redeemed. It comes to us from heaven and will return with us to heaven.

IV. The Hallelujah of Praise

The hallelujahs of nature, providence and grace continue to the end, but the works of God recede while God Himself is more clearly seen. After "Hallelujah" in Psalm 3 come the words, "I will praise the Lord with my whole heart." After "Hallelujah" in Psalm 112: "Blessed is the man that feareth the Lord." After "Hallelujah" in Psalm 113: "Praise, O ye servants of the Lord, praise the name of the Lord." And as the Hallelujahs increase toward the end of the book God alone is the object of praise. In Psalm 146, "Hallelujah, Praise the Lord, O my soul." In Psalm 147: "Hallelujah, for it is good to sing praises unto our God." In Psalm 148: "Hallelujah, Praise ye the Lord from the heavens." And the Psalmist calls the roll of the Hallelujah choir consisting of angels, sun, moon and stars, the heavens, "the dragons and all deeps," fire and hail, snow and vapours, strong wind, mountain and hills, trees, beasts and cattle, creeping things and flying fowl, men and maidens, old men and children. "Let them praise the name of the Lord, for His name alone is excellent."

In Psalm 149: "Hallelujah: Sing unto the Lord a new song," as if thought and words were failing him to express his praise to God. And the climax comes in the last verse of the last Psalm, "Let everything that hath breath praise the Lord. Hallelujah." God is greater and more worthy of praise than are His works in nature, providence and grace.

V. The Hallelujah of Judgment

This appears in Revelation 19:1-2, "Hallelujah. Salvation and honour and power unto the Lord our God, for true and righteous are His judgments; for He hath judged the great harlot, which did corrupt the earth with her fornication. And again they said Hallelujah. And her smoke rose up forever and ever." The Hallelujah of judgment seems to shock sentimental natures who cannot endure the thought that God could allow any one to go to hell. And yet any one with a spark of nobility of character must rejoice over the apprehension and punishment of certain criminals. When the papers published the fact that a young man entered a large room in Buffalo, New York, and stood in line with those who were receiving the greetings of President McKinley, that he might murder the man who was ready to greet him with kindness, some theologians in New England, who had been preaching that there was no hell, were frank enough to confess that there ought to be a hell for at least one man, for McKinley and his murderer ought not to be together in the same place. For such men to escape hell unless they repent, would be cause for everlasting regret. The smoke of their torment satisfies the sense of justice which every righteous soul has. For them to escape punishment would make a discordant note in God's universe. The Hallelujah of judgment is the response of noble natures to the justice of the retribution which comes upon those who wreck the character and destroy the happiness of others.

VI. The Hallelujah of Sovereignty

Hallelujah, for the Lord our God reigneth (Rev 19:6).

> "Truth forever on the scaffold, wrong forever on
>   the throne,
> Yet the scaffold sways the future, and behind
>   the dim unknown
> Standeth God within the shadow, keeping watch
>   above His own."

God seems to be dethroned, but He is not. The fact that He does not strike monsters of iniquity in human shape dead is proof that He is merciful. When, therefore, I read in the press of the orgies of those who lie in wait for the innocent and seek their destruction, I say, "Hallelujah! God is merciful." And when I read that some monster has been overtaken by retribution, I say with equal emphasis, "Hallelujah, God is just." When I hear a blasphemer revile God and the Bible, I say, "Hallelujah, God is merciful or he would be smitten dumb"; and when I hear the same man, yet not the same, because he has been transformed by grace, praising God for redemption through the blood of Christ, I say, "Hallelujah! Hallelujah, for the Lord God Omnipotent reigneth."

M. E. Dodd
Democracy of the Saints: The Method

Matthew 16:18: "Upon this rock I will build my church and the gates of hell shall not prevail against it."

Christ's church is a spiritual democracy. Christ, himself, organized the first Christian church out of the spiritual material which John the Baptist had prepared. This first church in Jerusalem was to be the mother church of all the churches of Christ which should come afterwards.

In the text there are three statements concerning the church:

1. The church would have a great foundation, "upon this rock."
2. The church would have great growth, "I will build."
3. The church would have great conflict, "the gates of hell shall not prevail."

The church was to be built upon a great foundation, "this rock."

When Christ said this he may have had in mind the massive rock on Mount Moriah, where Abraham had offered Isaac. Upon that rock had been built Solomon's Temple, the most glorious house of worship the world ever saw. After its destruction a pagan temple was built. Following its destruction a temple was erected in which Christians gathered for worship. Upon its downfall a Mohammedan mosque, known as Omar, was erected there. This, too, must fall some day.

Seeing these successive temples rise and fall upon the sacred rock of Moriah, Christ gave to his disciples the assuring promise, "Here is another rock more sacred and safe and upon it I will build my church and the gates of hell shall not prevail against it."

What did he mean when he said, "this rock"? There have been many and varied interpretations of this expression. Some say he meant Peter;

M. E. Dodd **151**

others, that he meant Peter's confession; and yet others, that he meant himself.

If he meant to say that he would build his church upon Peter, he certainly did not mean Peter, the man. It is true that the church is built upon the foundation of the apostles (Eph. 2:20). But of all the unstable stones of that foundation, Peter was the poorest, because he was a vacillating, impulsive, high-tempered, shiftless, unreliable sort of personality, notwithstanding his big heart, generous motives and strong declaration of devotion.

If Christ did mean Peter, he meant Peter, the regenerated, reborn, remade personality as a type of the kind of material out of which the church should be established. It is true that Peter, the vacillating, did become, by Christ's power and the Holy Spirit's presence, Peter, the stable; that Peter, the unreliable, did become Peter, the dependable. But Christ surely never meant to commit his church and its sole support and supreme authority to any one man. Peter, himself, disclaimed this. In after years when there were those who would have bowed down to worship him, he said, "Stand up; I myself also am a man." What Peter was by nature would be a sorry foundation for any sort of institution. But such as Peter was by grace should become the chief characteristic of the church throughout all ages.

If Christ meant by "this rock," Peter's confession, he must have had in mind the full meaning of that good confession which Peter had just made, which accepted fully the revelation of the Old Testament Scriptures as the Word of God and the fulfillment of their meaning in Christ as the very Son of God, "Thou art the Christ, the Son of the living God." To this good confession Christ's reply, "Blessed art thou, Simon Bar-Jona, flesh and blood hath not revealed this unto thee, but my Father which is in heaven." This word of God had not come out of man's wisdom, but holy men of God had written it as they were moved by the Holy Ghost. Neither was Jesus of man or by man, but conceived of the Holy Ghost, born of the Virgin Mary, he was very God of very God.

This double confession of Peter, which included the fullness, inerrancy, all sufficiency and authority of the Scriptures and the essential deity of the Lord Jesus Christ, would indeed constitute a substantial foundation upon which to build a church, against which the gates of hell should not prevail.

It is more probable, however, that the third interpretation of the meaning of the expression of "this rock," which refers it to Christ, himself, is the true meaning. Christ is referred to many times in the Scriptures as "a rock." The most notable reference is 1 Corinthians 10:4: "They drank of that spiritual rock that followed them and that rock was Christ." The rock and the temple were constantly associated in the mind of Christ. He remembered how Solomon's temple had been destroyed on that rock. He knew that the temple of his own body would be destroyed, and would so tell his disciples afterward. But his enemies could not destroy the rock nor could they destroy the spiritual temple which he would build on that rock.

Christ was "this rock" for "other foundation can no man lay than that is laid which is Christ Jesus." The deity of Jesus, his virgin birth, his vicarious atonement, his bodily resurrection and his second coming are the component parts of this foundation. Christ said, "Thou are Petros," and pointed at Peter when he said this, but "upon this rock," turning his finger toward his own heart, "I will build my church." Christ, himself, being the rock upon which his church was built, assures us that the church has a sure foundation, a safe foundation, a solid foundation, an enduring foundation, an eternal foundation.

According to this statement of Christ, the church was also to have a great growth. He said: "I will build my church." Christ was a builder. He had built many good and useful things in his carpenter shop at Nazareth. He was now to begin the building of the world's supreme edifice. He would continue this building process until the last spiritual stone at the very pinnacle of the temple should be built in. What he "*began* both to do and teach" (Acts 1:1), he would continue throughout the ages until its completion.

Christ was constructive in his thinking, in his planning and in his working. He would *build* his church, not tear it down. Whatever would contribute to this building process he would approve. Whatever hinders this building process he would disapprove.

Christ meant to say that he would build his church numerically, financially and positionally.

He would build it numerically. He started with himself. Then he chose four and built them into the church, and then eight more and built them into the church, and then seventy. And when he went away he had built in 120 redeemed souls. Soon after his departure, 3,000 were added to the church in one day. A short while afterwards the report in Acts says there were 5,000. And then the statisticians could not count them and wrote it down that "great multitudes were added to the Lord."

The 3,000 who were built into the church at Pentecost were from three continents and fifteen nations. When they went back to their homes; their communities, countries and continents soon felt the power of their renewed lives. They were telling everywhere of the new life, the new power, the new hopes and the new joys, which they had found in Christ, and everywhere churches began springing up.

By A.D. 45, it has been estimated, that, under the preaching of Philip, Peter and Paul and the disciples who were scattered abroad, there were no fewer than 100,000 who had been built into the church. In less than 100 years after the crucifixion of Christ, there were more than 2,000,000, and by A.D. 200 there were 4,000,000 and by A.D. 300, one-tenth of the Roman Empire or more than 10,000,000 souls constituted the churches of Christ. On and on the spiritual tides have swept, the risen and living Christ has moved, and the regenerating spirit of God has worked, until to-day there are 600,000,000 souls in the world who name the name of Jesus. Some of these, no doubt, have but dim visions of him and poor conceptions of what he means as Priest, Prophet and King. And many millions of them are not in his churches but they, nevertheless, more numerous than any other body of religionists on the globe, are named by the name of Jesus. His work of building still goes on.

He will build his church financially. Looking about in his day he could say, "the birds of the air have nests and the foxes have holes, but the Son of man hath not where to lay his head." The disciples he called to follow him were, for the most part, without property. Peter did venture to mention one day, "Master, we have left all and followed thee." But this is quite a ludicrous picture, for all that this barefooted, crusty-toed, hatless-headed fisherman had left was a bundle of old, rotten, torn fishing nets. He, like everybody else, had gotten a great deal more by following Christ than he had given up. The duties of the treasurer of this company were not very large. They were poor men, but Christ began among them a building process. And this constructive program has added more wealth to the world through the spiritual forces of this church than has been produced by all other agencies and institutions combined.

At the present time, American church property alone exceeds the stupendous figure of $2,000,000,000, and American churches expend annually upon their work over $350,000,000. This is American churches alone, to say nothing of the vast property throughout the world held in the name of Christ. And these figures, stupendous as they are, are not a drop in the bucket to the still vaster and incomprehensible sums which are held in trust and controlled by individual men and women who name the name of Christ. The richest man in the world is a Christian. The wealth of the world is in Christian hands. Christ has fulfilled his promise and has built his church financially.

He meant also that he would build his church positionally. The first church in Jerusalem was not conspicuous for its personal influence in the world. Its members were not very highly regarded.

Even in more recent years there have been times when the members of Christ's churches were looked upon more or less contemptuously. In the English House of Commons in December, 1799, there was a heated debate precipitated by the opposition of the East India Company to the Baptist missionaries. Laws were passed forbidding their landing on the mission fields. This aroused Christian sentiment throughout the Empire and the question was constantly recurring in Parliament. In debating the issue, Mr. Pendergast said, "But now India is overspreading with Baptist missionaries, Arminian missionaries, Calvinistic missionaries; I do not know who these Baptist missionaries are, exactly, but they are the most ignorant and bigoted of men. Their head is a Mr. Wm. Carey. It is time to put a complete end to this interference with the interests of the government."

Sir Henry Montgomery, a most influential member of Parliament, also expressed himself as follows: "The sending out of missionaries is the maddest, most extravagant, most costly, most indefensible project which has ever been suggested by a moonstruck fanatic.

"The voice I hear (referring to the petitions from thousands of Christian people) is the voice of fanaticism, I submit if the time has come that every inspired cobbler or fanatical tailor who feels an inward call has a kind of apostolic right to assist in laying siege to the Edifice of the Hindu Economy, then the rule of Great Britain in India is doomed.

"Shall we let loose men like these missionaries upon a helpless and innocent people? I cannot hear without horror of sending our Baptist tinkers and cobblers to convert a noble and virtuous race. If these men had belonged to the Church of England, one might have borne with them; but to think of tolerating Baptists, that may not be borne."

Contrast this with the recent deference shown by diplomats, ambassadors, kings and heads of governments, to Baptists preachers who have appealed to them upon one issue or another.

Contrast this also with the prominence into which our Baptist name has been brought recently by the acquisition to positions of prominence of such men as Professor Mysearick, David Lloyd George, President Harding, and Secretary of State Hughes.

Surely Christ has most graciously fulfilled his promise to build his church numerically, financially and positionally. That little seed of truth which at first was no more than a mustard seed, has grown a great tree, in whose branches the birds sing their songs of freedom, and under whose shady boughs distressed and oppressed humanity may rest from the heat of persecution.

A third promise in this text is that the church should engage in a great conflict and with the assurance of ultimate victory. "And the gates of hell shall not prevail against it."

From the beginning until now, the church has had to fight. She has had to fight for her principles, for her rights, for her existence. Conflict has been the law of her life. The blood of the martyr has been the seed of the church. Whenever she became passive and quiescent, she began to die. The church, as the individual, has found her greatest danger when all men speak well of her. Her conflicts have brought out the love and loyalty of her people. Her triumphs have brought forth the admiration of her enemies. Her turbulent waters have been purified by confusion. Her life has been sanctified by antagonisms. Her character has been chastened and refined by the fires of persecution. It was not meant that the church should sail home on flowery beds of ease. Like a great emperor, who once said, "Conquest has made me what I am and conquest must sustain me," so must the church say.

Christ meant that the church should be aggressive in these conflicts. The old interpretations of this text pictured the church buttressed in her bulwark, fighting a defensive warfare. But this is not a true picture. The gates of hades are the stationary objects. It is sin that is standing in the fortress behind the strong gates. Christ means here that the church shall attack these gates and that in the attack of the church the gates will not be able to stand.

The church has had several successive conflicts. There were the religious conflict of the first century, the political conflict of the fifth century, the social conflicts of the later centuries, and the intellectual conflict of the present day.

The church was established by Christ as a spiritual democracy. It was bound together as a brotherhood. Its worship was very simple and democratic. Its symbolical services, baptism and the Lord's Supper, were very simple and understandable. Thus the church found itself at once in conflict with the established religion of the time and at death grips with the religious ceremonialism and formalism which had held sway through the centuries. One of the climaxes of these conflicts is described in the account of the church conference in Jerusalem over the question of circumcision. In every place where a new church was planted, this contest would arise. We see signs of it throughout all the Pauline Epistles. The Book of Galatians is especially vivid in its description of raging battles between these two ideas. The church everywhere prevailed and Jewish altars, with their bleeding victims and smoking sacrifices, passed forever from the face of the earth. Phariseeism and Sadduceeism dashed themselves to pieces upon the rock on which Christ built his church.

In the political conflict the church seemed less successful at the beginning. This was due to the unholy alliance which the enemy of the true church succeeded in establishing with the civil powers. Wherever the church becomes willing for some other institution or power to share her responsibilities and burdens, then she loses ground. This was the case in the political conflict. But here, there and yonder in the mountains, dens and caves of the earth, there remained churches of the Lord Jesus, loyal to their primitive New Testament ideas, which kept the soul fires burning and, in due process of time, flared forth in the reformation, to again enlighten the world.

The social gates of hades, which have been attacked and overcome by the church, have been many. Most prominent among them have been human slavery, the white slave traffic, the opium traffic and the legalized saloon. Whenever the church has attacked these gates of hades with united and vigorous forces, they have crumbled and melted away under the blistering white heat of her judgments.

In this latter day, the loyal churches of Christ find themselves in conflict with materialism and rationalism in the intellectual realm. There is no real conflict between the fundamental truths, to which the churches of Christ hold, and real science. God's word and God's work cannot be in conflict the one with the other. The 19th Psalm is the marriage ceremony under which God, himself, united forever in blissful harmony, his words and his works, his book, the Bible, and his book of Nature.

The church has nothing to fear from any genuine scientific discovery, from any real fact or from any ultimate truth. Whenever science reaches an ultimate conclusion and comes to a definite finality on any fact or truth, it will find that the churches, which look to the Bible and the Bible alone as the ultimate truth of God, will have no word of condemnation.

But the many vagaries, theories and pseudo-scientific philosophies, which, while admitting their progressiveness, the renunciation of their own theories of yesterday and the possibility of renouncing tomorrow the theories of to-day, yet claiming for themselves absolute authority in the realm of truth and prating of being out of harmony with the church, must find themselves the objects of the churches' attack and ultimately the victims of the churches' triumphs.

Whenever one, be he ignoramus or university professor, announces that he cannot stand for the church because the church is out of harmony with scientific discoveries, he proclaims at once his ignorance of what the Bible teaches, his ignorance of real science, or, perhaps, his ignorance of both.

The intellectual conflict goes beyond the halls of educational institutions and finds itself raging in the literary field and in the entertainment field.

Any man who speaks with a fluent flow of words can go on the platform or into the pulpit with carping criticism of the church, get a large hearing, some following and plenty of pay for his pains. Any literary genius, who wields a trenchant pen and will do so in the interest of the maligners of the church, can find ready sale for his wit and cynicism in most any popular magazine.

In the field of entertainment, most notably among the commercialized picture show business, there is a constant stream of ridicule, sarcasm and criticism against gospel preachers and their churches. It impresses one that there may be some foundation in fact for the charge that there is a highly organized, strongly financed movement of propaganda against the churches.

These intellectual gates of hell are more dangerous than others with which the church has formerly dealt, because they are more insidious and the fruits of their work are not so immediately apparent.

But the church of the present day must attack with all the spirit and confident hope of success, which have characterized her conflicts in the past centuries. Will these gates of hell to-day be able to prevail? There still standeth the assuring promise of the ever-present Christ, "they shall not prevail."

> "Zion stands with hills surrounded,
>   Zion, kept by power divine,
> All her foes shall be confounded,
>   Though the world in arms combine;
> Happy Zion,
>   What a favored lot is thine!
>
> "In the furnace God may prove thee,
>   Thence to bring thee forth more bright,
> But can never cease to love thee;
>   Thou art precious in His sight;
> God is with thee,
>   God, thine everlasting light."

Ambassador Harvey is quoted as having said recently in a London club:

"The real strength of a country is not measured by armies and navies. A schoolhouse at the cross roads is more potent ultimately than a dreadnaught on the sea. One church on a hill is worth a score of regiments. All mankind will some day realize that there is more power and glory in 'Lead Kindly Light' than in all the fighting anthems in the world."

Roger W. Babson, the great political economist and statistician, says:

"Religion is both the anchor and the rudder of prosperity. The real security of the nation is not its militia, but its religion. The real protectors of our homes are not the policemen, but rather the preachers. Only as religion saves the world, can we save ourselves. A religious spirit makes better employers, better workers, and a better public spirit with which to deal. Furthermore, without such a religious spirit, all legislation, co-operation and other plans are of no avail. Religion is to the world what the spring is to a watch, and the sooner it is generally recognized the more people will be healthy, happy and prosperous."

The church of Christ, founded upon a rock, gloriously growing and fearlessly fighting, is the earth's highest and best institution and should call forth the most loving and loyal support of all who love God and desire the highest interest of humanity.

The church of God is the only institution in the world established by divine authority. It is the only institution in the world which has a divinely appointed mission. It is the only institution in the world which can claim a direct divine promise.

The church of God has a three-fold glory which no other institution in the world can claim:

1. The glory of a divine origin. "I will build my church," said Jesus.

2. The glory of a divine infilling. "Know ye not that ye are the temple of the Holy Ghost?"

3. The glory of a divine protection. Providentially kept by the power of God the Father.

The church instituted by God the Son, infilled and energized by God the Holy Spirit, protected and kept by God the Father, stands supreme in this three-fold character among all other institutions of the world.

The church of God has a three-fold mission which no other institution in the world can claim.

Jesus Christ healed, fed and comforted suffering human bodies; he instructed ignorant human minds; and he saved soiled, human souls.

This three-fold ministry he committed to his church:

1. The benevolent ministry of kindness to sick men and women, to hungry orphans and to suffering saints.

2. The educational ministry of enlightenment.

3. The evangelistic ministry of soul winning.

No other institution in the world can carry out this three-fold ministry. Athletic clubs or hospitals may minister to the bodies of men. State schools may minister to the minds of the young. Individuals may do personal soul winning.

But only a church of Jesus Christ can minister truly and fully to body, mind and soul.

No other institution in the world is as broad and unlimited in its service as is a church of Christ.

Boy Scout service is limited to boys only.

The Y.M.C.A. serves only young men. The Y.W.C.A. serves only young women.

The Red Cross serves only suffering bodies.

The schools serve only the minds of the young.

These services are all gracious and beautiful and worthy, but necessarily limited. It is so with all earthly institutions.

It is not so with a church of Christ. The church serves the old and young, the black and white, the sick and poor, the ignorant and the learned. It serves the bodies, minds and souls of men without being limited as to time, place, character, condition, age, sex or circumstance.

The church enjoys a three-fold promise which no other institution in the world can claim:

1. The promise of power. "Ye shall receive power." This is the promise of the departing Saviour.

2. The promise of perpetuity. "The gates of hell shall not prevail against it." It is not a question of "Apostolic Succession." The chief question is church perpetuity. And this is not a question of historical proof but of evangelical faith. Jesus Christ said the gates of hell should not prevail. That is either true or untrue. If Jesus can be trusted, it is true. There has never been a time since Jesus organized his church that there was not one.

3. The promise of his presence. "And lo I am with you always, even unto the end of the age."

For these reasons we sing:

> "I love Thy Church, oh God!
>   Her walls before Thee stand,
> Dear as the apple of Thine eye,
>   And graven on Thy hand.
>
> "For her my tears shall fall;
>   For her my prayers ascend;
> To her my cares and toils be given,
>   Till toils and cares shall end.
>
> "Sure as Thy truth shall last,
>   To Zion shall be given
> The brightest glories earth can yield,
>   And brighter bliss of Heav'n."

Time used, talent invested and money given in service in the church, go farther, spread wider, count for more, exalt Christ higher and glorify God better than when put anywhere else on earth.

Huber L. Drumwright, Jr.
An Unexpected Conversion

Acts 16:10-34, Williams

The structure of the book of Acts is interesting from many points of view. One matter of interest apparent to one who examines the book is an occasional interspersion of a significant conversion. The account of the conversion of the Ethiopian God-fearer is in the eighth chapter; in the ninth chapter there is the conversion of Saul, the persecutor; in the tenth chapter there is the conversion of the Roman centurion. The sixteenth chapter contains the wondrously thrilling account of the conversion of the Philippian jailer.

I have asked myself a question many times: "Why, when there were thousands who turned to Jesus in those days, were these particular experiences selected, and why were the details of the conversion of each included?" Though it would be interesting to examine all such records in Acts, attention is to be given only to the conversion of the Philippian jailer. To be sure, this event came at the beginning of a new work, but such does not explain its place in the book. Paul and Silas had gone to Philippi because they were led of the Holy Spirit to take the gospel to that area of the world. However, this man was not the first person led to faith in Europe, even by Paul. Lydia had already been converted, with her household. Thus the jailer was not the first person on European soil to respond to the message of the apostle Paul, and such consideration could not explain the account. In answer to the question of why this record of the Philippian jailer was included, I would answer that it was because of the unexpectedness of his conversion.

Had I been in Philippi the night that Paul and Silas were in jail there, I suppose I would have been rather despondent for the cause of Christ. I

161

surely would have been downcast. Paul and Silas had been beaten and were in prison; there was no longer any opportunity to preach publicly. It would have seemed that an opportunity for any working of God in Philippi that night was exceedingly remote. Who would have thought that the preachers' jailer would have been saved that night in his own jail? It seemed impossible.

There were difficulties surrounding the conversion of this man. First, he was a Roman. When the charges were brought against Paul and Silas by the citizens of Philippi who had Roman citizenship (because Philippi was a colony), they said, "These men being Jews do teach customs that are not lawful for us, being Romans, to observe." There is in this charge recognition of the great breach that existed between the Romans and the Jews. In fact, there was no group of people in the world so despised by the Romans—the proud, haughty conquerors of the world—as much as the lowly Jews. It may have been that the edict of the Emperor Claudius by which the Jews were driven out of the imperial city and no longer allowed to live there had already gone forth. The Jews' standing in the Roman Empire varied from ruler to ruler, but it was never anything of which to boast. Here was a Roman, and he was the one who needed Christ. And here was a Jew, and he was the one who could tell about Christ. It simply wouldn't be expected in Philippi that night that a proud Roman would go down on his knees in front of a despised Jew.

Something else that is unusual about the conversion of this man has already been suggested. He was converted in spite of the fact that he was the jailer and the preacher was his prisoner. I have spent time in jail. Once in a while I do not explain such a remark and regret that I do not. When I was wrestling with that which I believed to be the call of God to my heart to preach the gospel, there was not an overwhelming demand for my preaching. Because I felt called to preach and had few invitations, I took a literally captive audience. In the Dallas County jail every other Sunday afternoon I preached to those poor souls who could not help themselves. This was my practice for nearly three years. In consequence, I have an acquaintance with jails; and one thing I know is this: one doesn't see a jailer down on his knees in front of his prisoners asking religious advice! It isn't to be expected. It simply does not happen. But before the night was out, the chief jailer in Philippi was down on his knees in front of his prisoners, crying out, "Sirs, what must I do to be saved?"

This man was converted in spite of the fact that there had been no conditioning for Christianity. He had not been reared in an atmosphere where the religion of the Old Testament had had much impact. This particular Roman colony did not have enough Jews to even possess a synagogue. The few God-fearers in the city met outside the city by the river. Even the religion of the Old Testament had been missed in the experience of this man. He was the product of a pagan environment. He knew only the pagan gods and superstitions. This man was totally unconditioned for Christianity.

Furthermore, he was a soldier. His ancient city had been populated very largely by Roman soldiers. Two great battles had been fought outside the walls of Philippi; many Roman veterans had settled in this city. This man may have served in the Roman legions; he was certainly a Roman officer. His dedication was to his emperor. His service was dedicated to the Empire. Here was a man who knew the meaning of commitment to a cause, and he was committed and was charged with heavy responsibilities in that commitment. He was the chief jailer in the Roman colony of Philippi. The dedication of his life was set against his conversion to Christ.

As impossible as it seems, it is to be noted that there were men in Philippi that night who were in the will of God. Paul and Silas had come to Philippi, not because it was their own choice, but because of an impression from God, given through the vision, "Come over to Macedonia and help us." In fact, they had assayed to go to another place, but the Holy Spirit had not permitted them. They were men led by the Spirit of God when they came to Philippi. They were men under divine orders. They were men who had moved to Philippi in obedience to divine command. The fact that there were people in Philippi under divine orders concerning the preaching of the gospel of Jesus Christ was to contribute mightily to the realization of the impossible. Such a fact always makes a difference.

Then it is to be noted that these men who were in Philippi under divine orders were men of prayer and praise. Do not underestimate the importance of their prayer and praise. Although these men had been beaten and could have moaned, though these men had been beaten and could have sobbed, though these men had been beaten and could have despaired, they were praying and praising God. They were praising God and praying to him in the depth of a jail. I am sure the jail at Philippi had never seen anything like it. Never underestimate the power of God's people when they earnestly pray.

A revival meeting in west Texas gives an illustration of this truth. When the evangelist arrived, the pastor told him of a man unusually hard. It was hoped that he could be converted, but he had resisted every effort to reach him. He ran away, as many men do. If the word was abroad that there was to be a meeting at the church, he would plan to be out of town or on his ranch. He would go away and literally hide in the back part of his ranch. It was almost impossible to have a word with him about Jesus. Toward the end of the revival, very unexpectedly this lost man came into the church after an evening service had begun and seated himself in the last pew. Not many knew of his presence in the service, but those who did were greatly taken by surprise. Why had he come? Word was given to the evangelist concerning the man's presence, and the preacher preached with a prayer in his heart that God would speak to this man, prominent and successful in the community, who stood in need of God's grace. The invitation was given, and on the very first note of the first hymn that man walked down the aisle.

The heart of the preacher melted at the response, but the best was yet to come. A little, elderly woman who walked with a cane was seated near the front of the church. When she saw this man walking down the aisle, she fell out into the aisle and into his arms. It was then that a mother's cry was heard; a mother sobbed out her heart to her son. She said, "Oh, Son, the people said that you were too hard to be saved. The people said you would go to hell in your sin. The people said you would never be saved. But, Son, for over sixty years Mother has prayed for and believed in this hour." Here was the explanation. A mother had prayed. Yes, there is victory in the prayer of God's people.

Paul and Silas had come to Philippi to win souls, and no doubt, this was the burden of their prayers in the jail. God's people prayed, and the earthquake came and broke the bonds loose and opened the jail doors. The jailer, being awakened out of his sleep, rushed out and, seeing the doors open, thought that surely all the prisoners were gone. He took a sword and was ready to kill himself. Then there came the voice from within the jail, "Do thyself no harm, for we are all here." There were people in Philippi that night who were ready to pay the price for souls. One might smile at it, but I have thought about it many times. If I had been in jail that night, and the earthquake had come, and all the bonds had been striken from my limbs, and the doors opened wide, I would probably have concluded immediately that God had answered prayer. Out I would have gone, taking it as an answer to prayer. Not so the apostle Paul. He had come to Philippi to win souls. There were souls in the jail to be won, souls that had been so captivated by the preaching and personality of this man that even the other prisoners did not flee. They were not held by bonds any longer, but by the strange attraction of the gospel of Jesus Christ. Here were men held by the apostle Paul with bonds that were unseen, but strong and sure. Because there were Christians who were ready to pay the price for souls, some were born anew that night. Even though the chains be returned, though the doors be fastened again, there were souls in that jail who must hear about Jesus.

The jailer, when he came into the jail, fell down and cried, "Sirs, what must I do to be saved?" Why did he say "saved"? Some commentators suggest that the jailer talked about being saved because he was afraid that he would forfeit his life through failure to keep his prisoners. Surely this is incorrect; his prisoners were all there. Some find a background for his question in the mystery religions, a nebulous doctrine phrased with the words in a later Christian vocabulary. Why did this man speak of being saved? It was because he had heard the message of salvation from Paul and Silas. Remember the charge brought against Paul: "These men are preaching a way of salvation," cried the hysterical girl whom Paul healed. "They are preaching to you a way of salvation," she cried. Why did the Philippian jailer single out Paul? Why not some other prisoner in order to talk about salvation? Why was he down on his knees in front of Paul and Silas, asking, "Sirs, what must I do to be saved?" It was thus because Christians had evidenced that they knew the meaning of salvation. What they had shown and preached was so winsome and wonderful that the proud Roman jailer went down to his knees and cried, "Sirs, what must I do to be saved?"

It was not so remarkable or so unusual after all that the man was saved because the gospel of Jesus Christ had been preached. Perhaps the jailer had eavesdropped. Those strange activities in the jail that night had not escaped his attention. Perhaps he had examined the specifications and charges brought against the prisoners committed to his care, and perhaps he had talked with the prisoners themselves. He had heard the message of salvation, and it had won his heart. The gospel brought him to his knees. Whenever the gospel is preached faithfully, in the power of the

Spirit, there are always mighty things to be seen. It was preached with power in Philippi that night.

This then is the record of the salvation of a man who would never have been counted under the circumstances a good prospect for conversion. It explains the beginning of a revival, for his entire family was won to faith, also. Although totally unexpected from the human point of view, the explanation is found in the wondrous circumstances of God's working in Philippi that night.

T. T. Eaton
Conscience in Missions

One hundred years of mission work have passed, as you have heard till the hearing has become a weariness, since the "consecrated cobbler" went out to preach the gospel to the heathen, expecting great things from God and attempting great things for God. Carey put God first. He cared for the glory of God more than he cared for the whole human race. Giving God thus His rightful place, Carey gave his fellowmen their rightful place and longed, as a weaker man could not have done, for their salvation. Of the temporal ills, of the poverty, the suffering and the woes of the heathen, he thought little; it was their guilt toward God and the awful doom that awaited them which fired his great soul with zeal. But above and beyond all was the thought that God would be glorified by their salvation, and Christ would see of the travail of His soul and be satisfied.

Brethren, I have never been one, and God forbid I should be one, to disparage our Baptist fathers. It is a species of Pharisaism that thanks God for our superiority to the saints who have gone to glory, and which tells with complacency how much greater our achievements have been than theirs. We can rightly thank God for the grace given unto us, whereby we have been able to do what we have done, and we can confess not only our own short-comings but those of our fathers. When Daniel made his great confession in that beautiful prayer of his, he said: "We and our fathers have sinned." Only after we have confessed our own sins may we confess the sins of our fathers. It is a more wholesome exercise of mind and heart to consider the nobleness of the sainted dead and how

167

we can most faithfully carry out the trust they have committed to us, under God.

Let us not harshly blame our fathers because no missionaries went from among them to the heathen. Looking over the world they saw no land unpolluted by the persecution of their brethren, no river unstained by their martyrs' blood; they remembered that through the centuries it had required their utmost exertions to keep their own people supplied with preaching, as they trembled in the catacombs of Rome or lay hid in the forests among wild beasts, kinder than their fellowmen; when crossing the ocean to a land where freedom reigned in the boastful words of its people, they found to their sorrow no freedom for them. Those who claimed freedom for themselves drove Baptists, maimed, beaten, and bleeding, into the wilderness. Think you a government which imprisoned John Bunyan in Bedford jail, whipped Obadiah Holmes on Boston Common and incarcerated James Ireland in Culpeper, Va., would have allowed Baptists to organize to send the gospel to the heathen? Let us remember there was less than a century from the cessation of persecution, so that Baptist missionary organizations became possible, till Carey arose. When I think of all that Baptists have suffered, I do not wonder that when for the first time in 1700 years the woman in the wilderness found a resting place for her weary feet, and gathered her true hearted sons about her with none to molest or to make them afraid, she was content simply to rest "the world forgetting, by the world forgot."

Experience throws light upon the words of Scripture and brings out their beauty and their force. And experience in raising money for missionary work has shown the great force and fitness of Paul's words urging Timothy to be "a good soldier of Jesus Christ." For the appeal to the soldier is to duty. "England expects every man to do his duty" were words to nerve the arms of every Englishman going into the battle of Trafalgar. Duty is a cold, hard word—the sentimentalists sigh: why not appeal to the emotions? Well, stones are cold, hard things, but they make strong foundations for all edifices which men wish to endure. Men cannot found nor build important enterprises on such thistledowns dancing before the wind as human emotions. Pathos is an admirable thing in its place; but the emotion it arouses cannot be a substitute for firm principle: Duty, the sense of responsibility to God, is the thing which abides. Whatever work must be done steadily, ceaselessly, while life continues, must be placed on this one foundation.

An appeal to the emotions will produce a larger immediate result than an appeal to the conscience. If a collection for missions is to be taken, and you can rouse the congregation to enthusiasm by eloquent descriptions of what Baptists have done, or if you can move them to tears by pathetic stories, you will receive more money than if you laid before them their duty to do all in their power to advance God's glory in the salvation of souls. And you will receive more praise for your great eloquence. But the next time you speak to that congregation, you must use more glowing descriptions and tell more harrowing stories in order to move them. And the time will come—it has come to many—when the most eloquent tributes and the most pathetic anecdotes will be a weariness. Whereas, if you make your plea in the first place to the sense of duty to God, you will, indeed, not receive so much money; but the second appeal need not be so strong, provided it be along the same lines, and the result will be greater. And every time it will require less and less effort to bring men to their duty, and thus you will build up a structure of Christian character which will abide. For as the conscience thus is taught to act, the action becomes easier. Appeal to the emotions and your appeals must grow frantic, and at the same time you will get less and less result. But speak plainly and in a straightforward way to the conscience and your appeals can grow less while the results increase.

Men are tired of appeals to their emotions in behalf of missions. It is increasingly difficult to get them to listen. This was shown in an unmistakable way at the Centennial meeting held in Philadelphia in March. There are seventy Baptist churches in that city from which to draw a congregation. An admirable programme was prepared. We have no abler men nor finer speakers than those who were announced to speak. Yet they spoke to mortifying small assemblies. The day for that sort of thing is passing away. Men care for facts rather than phrases, and in this they are not to blame. Missionary work was something of a experiment, but a good deal has been learned in a hundred years and the experimental stage is over.

It is the duty of Christians to support the preaching of the gospel in this and other lands. The duty is the same; the missionary stands on the same footing as the pastor. The arguments for supporting both are the same; and what is trifling in the one case is trifling in the other.

The ideal state of things is that every man should put into the church treasury every week one-tenth of his income for that week, and to do this as a matter of course, without any thought of his giving anything to any body or of his having done a praiseworthy thing, any more than if he paid a grocery bill. Let the church take these tithes and use them for God's work, paying its own expenses, paying fitting amounts to mission boards, and to other objects of benevolence, making the division in the fear of God, after earnest prayer for divine guidance. This should be a simple matter of course; and over and above this, those whom God has blessed in basket and store, or who have had special blessings, should make free-will offerings in various ways. I do not believe there ever has been a time, or ever will be, when, if all the members of the churches thus paid their tithes into the treasury, it would not be as much as could be wisely used in supporting the preaching of the gospel at home and abroad. The gross income of the Evangelical church members in the United States is not less than $6,000,000,000 a year. One-tenth of this is $600,000,000. At an average salary of $1,200 a year, and that is a large average, this amount would support 500,000 preachers of the gospel of Christ. This is more than five times as many as the Evangelical denominations of the land now have, the present number being 94,000, including all not in the active ministry. Allotting 200,000 to this country for pastors and missionaries, we would be able to send abroad 300,000 more. That would give one missionary to every four thousand souls in Pagan, Papal and Mohammedan lands, whereas now, all Evangelical denominations taken together, we have but one missionary for every 167,000. How easy would the evangelization of the world become if only professing Christians had religion!

But the day has not yet come when the consciences of all church members are so enlightened that they will bring their tithes thus, as a matter of justice to God. Some give less, a very few give more, and many give nothing. But all can be taught to see that the support of the missionary is exactly as binding as the support of the pastor, and therefore should be provided for in the same straightforward business way. And the time will come—it is almost in sight now—when it will seem as much out of place to hold big meetings to urge churches to support the missionaries as it would seem now to hold such meetings to urge the churches to support their pastors. The Baptists of Philadelphia—as grand a body of people as can be found on earth—showed that they have almost reached that time. Who would have expected them to attend that big meeting, had the object been to urge them to support their pastors?

The time will come when a missionary society in a church, however helpful now, will be as great an anomaly as a pastor-paying society. There will still be calls for missionaries to go; the baptisms, churches organized and progress made on the foreign fields will be reported as such things are now reported on the home field; but the money will be raised and the missionary literature circulated in a straightforward business way, without frantic appeals and without hysterics. There will be no more appeals then for supporting pastors, and the same solid methods will be used.

Time was when the support of pastors was left to uncertain, spasmodic action—such action as results from appeals to the feelings. When they paid their subscriptions the members felt they were making presents to the pastor. They were influenced to give more or less according as the appeals represented the needs of the pastor and his family as more or less urgent. The emptiness of his larder, the shabbiness of his clothes, the destitution of his wife and children—all these things were urged. In a cowardly way the men often shirked their duty upon the shoulders of the willing, warm-hearted sisters, who did their best to eke out the pastor's meagre support. They gave donation parties, had fairs, suppers, tableaux, and in many ways sought to make outsiders do the neglected duty of the church members.

Yet the brethren and sisters of that day were not avaricious above what is seen to-day, nor were they lacking in piety. The trouble was that the appeals were made to their feelings rather than to their conscience; and taught thus to give from impulse they would not give unless their emotions were stirred. More and more they were told it was right to support their pastor, and wrong to neglect it. It was a duty they owed to God, to the pastor, and to themselves. Thus the appeals came to be made to their sense of duty, and they quit the haphazard way of paying their pastors. They ceased also to believe that what they paid was a gift to the preacher. They saw it was a debt, first to God and then to the under-shepherd God had set over them. Justice required that the pastor be supported, not according to his necessities, but according to the ability of the church. Thus paying the pastor's salary was put upon a manly business footing. The result is known to all. The pastors are not yet paid as they should be in all churches, but they are far better paid and with far less friction than a generation ago. And the salaries are much more easily raised, though they are larger; and what is also a great thing, the preachers know what they can depend upon. A little which is sure, can be made to do more than a larger amount which is uncertain.

We need that our people shall wake up to the truth that mission giving is a regular duty, which must go on till the end, and must be conducted in a manly, business way. There will always be abundant occasion for fervid appeals and for impulsive action, in addition to the regular systematic giving, in order to meet emergencies which arise in the providence of God, from floods, drouths, financial stringency, pestilence and such things as church building and as this Centennial of Missions.

A plan whose merits have commended it to many churches, is to distribute mission subscription cards among the members, calling upon each one to mark the amount he will give weekly to missions, leaving, of course, the right for the contributor to designate his offering, if he so desires. It is insisted that each member shall return this card with some amount named. He may write one cent, but he must write *something* and sign his name. These cards are given in charge of a mission committee who inform the Boards how much may be expected during the year from that church. Were this method generally adopted, the Boards would know what they could depend on and could lay out their work accordingly, and nothing would be heard of mission debts or of interest paid for borrowed money.

Will any one say there is no enthusiasm about such a plan as this? Enthusiasm is a good thing for emergencies, but it is a poor wheel horse for steady pulling. Such a plan gives little opportunity for flaming speeches and high-sounding eloquence, and if that be the object in view this plan will be rejected; but if the object be to get mission work done in the fear of the Lord and with an eye single to His glory, something along this line must be done. Many current devices for raising money must go to the limbo where donation parties have gone, and as few tears will be shed over them. The time for playing at missions and orating about raising money for missions is past. We need action rather than eloquence. The time to put mission work on the solid ground of Christian conscience, under God, has come. It is a good rule to do nothing and say nothing in raising missionary money which would be incongruous in raising the pastor's salary.

Many things will come to pass when the sentimental era of missions ends and the conscientious era begins. Once put the missionaries on the same footing as the pastors, and inevitable changes will result. Churches do not support physicians among their own members, and no more missionary physicians would be appointed. The churches will confine their support to those who preach the gospel abroad, as they do at home. Pious physicians, pious teachers, pious mechanics will go to heathen lands and support themselves there, as foreigners come and support themselves here. Only those who preach the gospel shall live of the gospel. Wicked men go from this country to Africa and China and exhibit to the natives examples of American ungodliness; and why may not Christian laymen go in like manner, and show the natives examples of American piety?

All over the land Christians are waking up to the fact that the era of sentiment has passed and the era of duty has come, in mission work. Our brethren in Ohio have been considering how they can work in a business-like way, depending, under God, upon the consciences of the church members. The *Standard* of Chicago well said: "Yet we are impressed with this fact—that missionary management is becoming more and more a matter of skillful business guidance and impulsion, and less and less one of occasion for eloquent argument and appeal. Is it not, now, really the fact that what is needed is just that same conviction of a thing to do and a way to do it which we act upon in conducting the affairs of a church, and supporting its pastor? Churches need no eloquent urgency in sermon or address in this regard. Why should they need it in that which has come to be just as much a matter of course in practical Christianity as the calling of a pastor or the paying of his salary?

"It is very true that in any such change as we here hint at a very essential thing will be that the churches take in hand the cause of foreign missions as a thing to be done, quite as much as the support of a pastor, or sustaining the appointments of a church from week to week. But why should not that very thing be now attainable? Do we not rather cultivate the impression among our churches that this matter of missions is something exceptional; that it lies outside of what belongs to us as church-members, a something to be brought home to us in some exceptional way, and our interest in it to be measured by the eloquence or tact of the person who tries to interest us in its behalf? Are we not proceeding too much upon the idea that the old-time method of rousing missionary interest is still the necessary one; and do we not undervalue the readiness of brethren in our churches to meet us when we come to them with the proposition that they take hold of missions as they take hold of everything else? Do not pastors themselves often undervalue the readiness of their brethren to put these matters of missionary support fairly alongside whatever else they feel bound to do, and attend to it at the fit times, just as they attend upon worship or pay the salary?"

Similar words have come from many quarters. It is time and more than time for systematic, thorough-going work, leaving to special occasions and needs the arousing of special enthusiasm.

Let us then begin this new century of missions learning wisdom from experience and resolved to follow more closely than ever the command of God and the example of the great first Baptist missionary. He was the greatest man the human race has ever produced; he was infallibly inspired in his words and guided in his movements by the Holy Spirit. Let us keep close to the example thus set us—everything must be made according to the pattern shown on the mount. Other things may seem to us expedient—new brooms have a reputation for sweeping clean—but no created being can tell what is expedient, particularly in matters of religion. The fate of those who have tried what they regarded expedient, instead of what God commanded, is a warning to us. Nadab and Abihu, Uzzah and the rest should not be forgotten. In a certain narrow but true sense they died that we might live, or rather their deaths are recorded that we may live. No man can tell what is expedient; but any man who sincerely desires it, may know what is right and well pleasing to God. And to please God is the highest aim of His children. "This is my beloved Son, in whom I am well pleased" was the voice from Heaven to our Elder Brother; it is written of Enoch, "he had this testimony that he pleased God," and the great, all absorbing purpose of Paul was "to please God." We must not grow impatient because the results of doing God's way seem small and meagre. Results are God's business while obedience is ours. We may be sure we will accomplish no real good trying any other plan but God's. We should study the past century of missions in the light of Scripture to see how God works, that we may be workers together with Him. When He would arouse His children to give the gospel to the heathen, God converted a run away scapegrace in the African slave trade, and sent John Newton home a saved man. Newton preached a sermon God blessed to the conversion of William Carey. Newton preached again and Claudius Buchanan was converted. Buchanan wrote the *Star in the East,* and reading it fired Adoniram Judson with zeal for souls, and thus two continents have been filled with missionary fervor. Truly God's ways are not as our ways, neither are our ways His ways.

The motive is the important thing in giving, as in all else; and here comes a danger in raising money for missions. Those interested fix their eyes on the amount needed, as they think, just as the apostles worried over the amount of bread needed to feed the five thousand. One dollar given from love is more powerful in the kingdom of God than millions given from wrong motives. The greatest gift of history was the two mites given by the poor widow. Let us set out upon this new century then resolved by the Spirit's help to follow Paul's methods, trusting in Paul's God. Let us labor to bring the churches up to the point, where every member will put every week one-tenth of his gross income into the treasury, to be divided out by the church among the different departments of the great work of saving the world, while the free-will offerings will provide for all emergencies. That this glad day may come, we must resolutely begin now to put the missionary giving upon the solid basis of duty to God. When that day comes, thought and time needed for the salvation of souls will not be consumed on finances.

Brethren, we have brought the tables of the money changers into the temples as truly though not so guiltily as did the high priests of old. This talk of money, money, money, in our churches and in our associations and conventions is a repetition of the old filling of the courts of the temple. We say it is necessary—so did the money changers and the sellers of sheep and doves—but the indignant Lord of the Temple made short work of the necessity. Because we fail to give the Lord a tenth as a matter of course, all this talk about money takes up the time of our gatherings. Yet the challenge of God stands: "Bring ye all the tithes into the store-house and prove me herewith, saith the Lord of hosts, if I will not open you the windows of heaven, and pour you out a blessing, that there shall not be room enough to receive it." This means spiritual blessings, the conversion of sinners and the growth in grace of our own souls. When we grieve over our own backslidings and the hardness of men's hearts; when the tides of vice and worldliness seem to sweep everything before them, let us remember this challenge of the Almighty to His people. Every man is to bring his own tithe, he is not to keep his tithe and try to make the Philistines furnish the amount.

There is this difference between the pastor's salary and the missionary money. The pastor's salary remains nearly the same, while the mission fund needs to go on increasing. Therefore the subscriptions to missions should grow every year, with the growth of our people in numbers and in grace.

This then is the conclusion of the whole matter. Put God first. Make the appeals to men's consciences. Follow Paul's plan both for giving and working, put the missionaries and the pastors upon the same footing; and bring the church members to give a tenth of their incomes as a matter of justice to God and not as a charity to man. All this cannot be done at once; the world cannot be saved by passing resolutions; but what ever is right can be done; but it can be done only by faithfully following this way without turning aside to try other devices because they seem expedient. Let us keep this end steadily in view and the second century of modern missions will see such a blessing poured from the opened windows of Heaven as it has not entered into the heart of man to conceive, and the vision of the prophet will be fulfilled.

W. Herschel Ford

Sanctification: The Most Misunderstood Doctrine in the Bible

And the very God of peace sanctify you wholly; and I pray God your whole spirit and soul and body be preserved blameless unto the coming of our Lord Jesus Christ (1 Thess. 5:23).

What is the most misunderstood doctrine in the Bible? It is not baptism, although there is much misunderstanding of this doctrine. Some think that baptism has some saving power, but it has absolutely none. It is an act of obedience. Baptism is an outward thing; salvation is an inward thing. Baptism presents a picture of Christ's experience—his death, burial, and resurrection. It presents a picture of the Christian's experience—his death to sin, the burial of "the old man" and of his being raised to "walk in newness of life."

The Lord's Supper is not the most misunderstood doctrine in the Bible. There are some who think that there is saving grace in the Lord's Supper, but it is another outward thing. A man can partake of this Supper every Sunday and still be far away from God. It is not even a time for fellowship and communion with others; it is a memorial meal given us by Christ to remind us of what he did on Calvary for us.

The divinity of Christ is not the most misunderstood doctrine in the Bible. The Bible teaches that Christ is the divine Son of God. If we believe the Bible at all, we must believe in the divinity of Christ. Atonement through the blood is not the most misunderstood doctrine in the Bible. One great preacher said, "There is no more power in the blood of Christ than in the blood of a chicken." But we believe that, because of his death upon the cross and the shedding of his blood, he made peace with God for us and purchased our eternal salvation. It is true that

There is a fountain filled with blood
Drawn from Immanuel's veins;

177

And sinners, plunged beneath that flood,
Lose all their guilty stains.

The second coming of Christ is not the most misunderstood doctrine in the Bible. However, it is the most ignored doctrine. When you read the Bible in the light of the blessed hope, it will become a great truth shining upon your pathway like a beacon light.

Sanctification is the most misunderstood doctrine in the Bible. The term has been used so loosely by some people as to cause others to shy away from it. Someone says, "I am sanctified." He means that he has had an experience which has made him perfect. But the world looks upon him and knows that he is not perfect. The term "sanctification" has often been connected with those people who boast of their holiness—who claim they are perfect—who talk in unknown tongues and who roll upon the floor. No wonder it has been misunderstood by sincere Christian people.

Some people hold to the idea of holy perfection. They say that since their conversion they have had an experience called "the second blessing." They say that the old nature was taken away and they can never sin again. There is no basis for such an idea in the Word of God. In Romans 7:24, Paul cried out, "Who shall deliver me from the body of this death?" He was simply using an old-time illustration to say that we carry around with us our rotten, carnal natures just as long as we live, and that we will be free from them only when we go home to be with Christ.

Romans 7:15: "For that which I do I allow not: for what I would, that do I not; but what I hate, that do I."

Romans 7:22-23: "For I delight in the law of God after the inward man: but I see another law in my members, warring against the law of my mind, and bringing me into captivity to the law of sin which is in my members."

Philippians 3:12: "Not as though I had already attained, either were already perfect: but I follow after, if that I may apprehend that for which also I am apprehended of Christ Jesus." No there isn't a perfect human being in all the world, but the sincere humble Christian keeps reaching outward and upward and onward to Christ.

Sanctification is threefold. Let us study these three aspects of the subject.

I. Sanctification Is the Act of Setting Someone or Something Apart for God's Use

Jeremiah 1:5: "Before I formed thee in the belly I knew thee; and before thou camest forth out of the womb I sanctified thee, and I ordained thee a prophet unto the nations."

Leviticus 8:10: "And Moses took the anointing oil, and anointed the tabernacle and all that was therein, and sanctified them." These two passages illustrate how both a person and an object were sanctified or set apart for God's use. Now the thing in which we are most interested is personal sanctification. Every Christian is immediately sanctified or set apart at the time of his conversion. He is set apart for God's use. There are many who do not yield to God's touch and therefore they cannot be used, but it is God's purpose to use them just the same.

When America entered World War II, her great automobile plants were changed from peacetime production to wartime production. Instead of making automobiles, they began to make planes and tanks. In other words, they were set apart for a new type of work; the entire purpose of their machines was changed. And so it is that when a man is saved, the purpose of his life is changed, and no longer is he to serve sin. He has been set aside to serve God.

Here is a man who works in an office. During the war he receives a letter from the President which begins with the one word, "Greetings." He answers this call of his country and is soon inducted into the army. His old life is suddenly changed; he has different clothes and different companions. No longer does he live in the bosom of his family; he is living among a group of total strangers. No longer is he sitting at a desk; he is out lugging his gun under the hot sun. He has been changed altogether; his life has been set apart for a new purpose.

So it is when a man is saved and sanctified—he, too, is changed altogether. God sends his greetings of love and mercy, calling him out of the world and setting him aside for a new purpose.

For many years the scientists were studying the matter of splitting the atom. They knew that there was power in the atom if they could just loose it and harness it. One day they found the secret, and now we have the atom bomb, the greatest exhibition of power in the world.

So it is that the Christian is possessed with the power of God. God has set him aside for his own use, and when he realizes his position and surrenders to the Lord and enters into the divine plan, this is the first meaning of sanctification. It is God's instantaneous act of setting one aside for his own use.

II. Sanctification Is a Progressive Work of Growth in Grace

Second Peter 3:18: "But grow in grace, and in the knowledge of our Lord and Saviour Jesus Christ. To him be glory both now and for ever."

Second Corinthians 3:18: "But we all, with open face beholding as in a glass the glory of the Lord, are changed into the same image from glory to glory, even as by the Spirit of the Lord."

Paul pictures the Christian as a child and Jesus as a full-grown man. The child looks upon the man. He begins to grow as he looks, and some day he becomes like the grown man. This is the progressive idea of sanctification—the idea of growing in grace. Now just as certain things cause a child to grow, so there are certain means of spiritual growth.

1. The Study of God's Word Is a Means of Spiritual Growth

The Bible is a mirror. A woman looks into the mirror and sees her wrinkles, and she immediately sets about to correct the situation. We look in the Bible and see our sins. We find that we come short of the glory of God, and we set about to correct our lives. The Bible is a map. It is a lamp unto our feet. Some time ago a travel agency sent me a map on which they had outlined a trip for me from Florida to Canada. They had marked with red ink the road upon which I should travel. The Bible is also marked with a red line—with the red line of Christ's blood, showing us the way from sin to glory. The Bible is our food. You feed a baby properly and you have joy in watching him grow. And so it is if we feed on the Bible, we grow in grace.

A woman one day was dusting her books, one of which was her Bible. The little girl said, "Mother, is that God's Book?" The mother answered, "Yes." "Well," said the little girl, "why don't we send it back to God: we never do use it." No, we will never grow in grace unless we use the Bible.

2. Prayer Is a Means of Spiritual Growth

Prayer isn't so much asking things for ourselves as it is getting ourselves in a right attitude toward God and man. Prayer helps us to get sin out of our lives. When you pray, you look into the face of Christ. You thank him for his blessings, and you confess your sins. You want him to use you, and you ask him to make you usable.

One day you are invited to a meal in a friend's home. You sit down and look at the snowy white linen and the fine silver. You know that the food will be tasty and well-prepared, and you look forward to your meal. Then you look down at your plate and you find that it is filthy—it is covered with the remains of the former meal. Your appetite is soon gone and you do not want any of the food served to you. Well, lost souls are hungry for the Bread of life. They are looking to us for it, and if our lives are unclean, if there are wrong things in them, the world wants none of that thing which we call Christianity. Now, prayer helps us to keep our lives clean and promotes growth in grace.

3. Faithfulness to Duty Is a Means of Spiritual Growth

There is a technique in building a skyscraper or an airplane or a ship. There is also a technique in building a Christian character, and faithfulness is a big part of the technique. We ought to be faithful in church attendance. I challenge you to show me a person who has grown in grace if he has not been faithful in attending his church. The preacher is hurt when his people absent themselves from God's house, because he knows that they are missing a great aid to spiritual growth. We ought to be faithful in our stewardship. Our time, our talents, and our tithe belong to God and we will never grow in grace unless we give them to him in full measure.

Robert E. Lee said that "duty is the sublimest word in the English language." You cannot turn your back upon what you know to be your duty without bringing some harm to your spiritual life. If you see a thing that you ought to do—a thing which you know is of God—and if you refuse to do that thing, something dies within you. "To him that knoweth to do good, and doeth it not, to him it is sin."

You stand by a blind man upon the curb of the street. It is your duty to lead the man through the traffic and across the street. You fail to do this, and immediately you have killed something good within yourself. A warm glow fills your heart if you do that which is your duty. So it is, if you do your duty as a Christian, you bring something good into your own life. Tithing is a part of your duty to God. What is more destructive to good character than dishonesty? Surely if a man steals from God, he will never grow in grace.

4. Looking Up to Jesus Is Another Means of Spiritual Growth

Dr. E. C. Sheridan tells an interesting story about Dr. John Roach Straton, former pastor of the Calvary Baptist Church, of New York City. When Straton was a little boy, he and his brothers decided to have some fun at the expense of Aunt Millie, their faithful old Negro mammy. One night they secured a pumpkin, hollowed it out, cut holes in it for eyes, and formed a mouth with jagged teeth. In the darkness they went down to Aunt Millie's cabin, put the pumpkin upon a post, lighted the candle within it and wrapped a bed sheet around the post. They then slipped to the cabin window and started to rap upon the shutter. They were going to enjoy Aunt Millie's fright when she saw the "ghost" in her yard. But they heard a voice inside the cabin and looked through the crack to see who was there with Aunt Millie. Instead of seeing someone else, they saw Aunt Millie down on her knees in prayer. The light of the moon was shining upon her big black face as it was lifted heavenward. They heard her pray for the "Missus" who was sick in the big house. They heard her call every boy by name as she prayed to God for them. They remembered then how she had cared for them all their lives—how she had comforted them when they had had trouble with their father. They remembered how she had watched over their mother day and night while she was sick, sleeping through many nights on the floor right by her bed. The boys did not scare Aunt Millie that night. They slipped away from the cabin, taking the pumpkin and the bed sheet with them, went to their rooms and fell upon their knees in prayer. Soon they were in bed, sobbing themselves to sleep. John became a great preacher, but he said that he never was able to get away from this picture of devotion, and that every time he thought of Aunt Millie and her prayers it made him a better man.

Oh, let me tell you something greater! If we look into the face of the Lord Jesus Christ, we are moved and inspired to become more like him. Yes, growth in grace is another part of sanctification.

III. Sanctification Reaches Its Final Stage at Christ's Second Coming

First John 3:2 "Beloved, now we are the sons of God, and it doth not yet appear what we shall be: but we know that, when he shall appear we shall be like him; for we shall see him as he is." First Corinthians 15:52: "In a moment, in the twinkling of an eye, at the last trump: for the trumpet shall sound, and the dead shall be raised incorruptible, and we shall be changed." First Corinthians 15:49: "And as we have borne the image of the earthy, we shall also bear the image of the heavenly." Philippians 1:6: "Being confident of this very thing, that he which hath begun a good work in you will perform it until the day of Jesus Christ."

When we are saved, we are sanctified: we are set aside for God's use. If we grow in grace, the process of sanctification is going on within us. But when Jesus comes again, our sanctification will be complete and we shall be perfect, for we shall be like him. Oh, what a change will come to us when Jesus comes again! Some Christians will be in their graves, and some will be living in this old cruel world, but the heavens will open, the Lord will descend with a shout, with the voice of the archangel and with the trump of God, and we shall then go up to meet him, and in the twinkling of an eye we shall be completely changed. If he did not change us, we would all be out of place in God's perfect home.

First, it will be a physical change. We will have a new body, and all the aches and pains will be gone. Then it will be a mental change—all God's mysteries will be as clear as light. "Now we see through a glass darkly; but then face to face: now I know in part; but then I shall know even as also I am known." It will be a spiritual change—we will be absolutely perfect in every way. This is God's ultimate salvation. It is not complete when we are saved nor when we die, but when Jesus comes again. Romans 8:29-30: "For whom he did foreknow, he also did predestinate to be conformed to the image of his Son, that he might be the firstborn among many brethren. Moreover whom he did predestinate, them he also called: and whom he called, them he also justified: and whom he justified, them he also glorified."

All the way from ages past through the ages to come, on into eternity, God plans and labors to save and to sanctify us and to make us over into his likeness and to take us to his spiritual home. In Adam paradise was lost—in Christ paradise is forever regained.

A young man lay upon a hospital bed. He had been hurt in an accident. He wasn't a Christian. He did not know how serious his injury was, but he knew he was in very great pain. Suddenly everything was changed. A nurse came quickly into the ward and put a screen around his bed. He knew what that meant—they expected him to die. His whole world began to collapse around him. He heard the clock chime. He told himself that he would probably be dead before it chimed again. His life began to pass before his eyes. He had lived without God, and now the crushing weight of his sin settled upon him. He trembled as he thought of meeting God. His eyes wandered above the screen, and there upon the opposite wall suddenly the answer came to him, for on that wall was a Scripture motto which said, "Come unto me, all ye that labour and are heavy laden, and I will give you rest."

That was it—these were the words of Jesus. Somehow he remembered that a fellow could be saved if he came to Christ. He remembered the pictures that he had seen of Christ with outstretched arms inviting sinners to come to him. He knew that Jesus had a pardon waiting for all those who accepted his invitation. He read the Scripture passage over several times, and then, with deep emotion, he said from the depths of his heart: "I will come! I do come! I do come to thee! Is it too late?" The man in the next bed heard him and said, "Poor fellow, he is delirious." The man behind the screen was smiling now. He was happy—he had a Saviour, and he was ready to die. He only wished that he could live a little longer in order that he might tell his brothers and his friends about Christ. Then the nurse came back and removed the screen. "I am sorry, sir," she said, "there has been a mistake. I put the screen around the wrong bed. I am very, very sorry, sir." But to her great astonishment the patient sat up in the bed and cried out: "Sorry! Why, that is the greatest thing that ever happened to me!"

Oh, friend, come to Jesus, and it will be the greatest thing that has ever happened to you. He will save you and sanctify you and satisfy you, and some day he will glorify you. Hallelujah, what a Saviour!

Richard Fuller

Personal Religion: Its Aids and Hindrances

He who would drive a boat forward by rowing must use both oars; if he employ only one, his little bark will go round and round, will be a prey to every vagrant current until it is dashed on the rocks or carried out to sea. And it is just so with regard to human and divine agency in the matter of salvation. "For my part," says the hyper-Calvinist, "I do not believe that man's will or efforts have anything to do with his salvation. From first to last it is God's fixed decree." But what does God say? "Work out your own salvation with fear and trembling." "Exactly so," exclaims the Arminian, "that is my doctrine. All depends upon our faithfulness, vigilance, self-denying exertions." But what does the Bible declare? "It is God that worketh in you, both to will and to do of his own good pleasure." If, then, there be a will to live for heaven, it has been wrought in us by God's sovereign grace. And if this volition perish not, if it acquires "the name of action," it is wholly through the efficacy of prevenient, sovereign grace and mercy. If we reject the doctrine of human agency, we sink into all the indolence and impiety of the Antinomian. If we discard the great truth of God's free, sovereign, indispensable grace, we will gradually find all our praying and toiling only so much hopeless drudgery, and will be tempted to give up in despair.

I do not design, however, to enter into this question, nor to show that the life of faith requires of us the compound attitude of one who works as if all depended on himself; and who prays, lives hourly as if everything— will, power, victory, salvation—must be the donation of God's free mercy, the operation of that adorable Spirit without whose immediate influences the holiest man would certainly be lost. My wish is, to submit some serious reflections upon the most important subject that can engage our minds, some thoughts which deeply concern our peace, holiness, preparation for death and eternity.

Religion (from *Re Ligo*) means the reattachment to God of the soul which had estranged itself from him. By the very force of the term we are reminded of our dismal apostasy and of that amazing anomaly in the divine jurisprudence, by which guilt is pardoned, the pinings of despoiled humanity for reconciliation with "the Father" are satisfied, and our entire nature—senses, intellect, conscience, passions—is readjusted.

The subject assigned me is Personal Religion: Its Aids and Hindrances; nor was there ever a period when this topic claimed more serious and prayerful contemplation; for while in theory all admit that there can be no substitute for holiness, yet in reality specious counterfeits and nostrums are on every side corrupting and superseding the doctrines of the Cross.

There is, for example, an artificial orthodoxy, a dry light in the mind, which sheds no influence on the life. D'Aubigne tells us that after hearing Haldane reason upon human depravity, he said to him, "Now I see that doctrine in the Bible." "Yes," replied the Scottish divine, "but do you see it in your heart?" It was this artless, yet profound question which led to the conversion of the great historian; and this is now the inquiry to be pressed, as to all evangelical truth. Do we see it, feel it in our hearts? "I am the way and the truth and the life." It is one thing to admit this imperial self-assertion of our Lord, and a very different thing to realize it; but nothing is saving faith which stops short of a full, controlling reception of it; a reception that thrones Jesus personally over the mind, the heart, the life. This is the religion of the gospel. It is as simple as it is severe and sublime. There is, however, too much reason to fear that for this *personal* following Christ and adhering to him, multitudes adopt a loyalty to creeds, confessions, systems; faith in which is important, but faith in which (yea, a general faith in the written word) may be fatally mistaken for faith in that personal Saviour, whose life, example, death, resurrection are, objectively and subjectively, the grand, informing, controlling rule of faith to his disciples." "Follow me!" When Jesus was upon earth this was the abridgement of all his doctrines, the epitome of all his sermons, his whole body of divinity; and this is still his strict demand, refusing to obey when we "lack one thing," and are fatally defective in everything. "Follow me;" me, not a religion; Jesus came not to teach, but to be our religion. Me; not a dogma. Me; not a doctrine. Me; not linen decencies, apocryphal successions, mystical, cabalistic virtues. Me; not a creed nor a confession. Me; not even faith in the Bible. Me; Me; come follow me; that is what the Saviour requires of all, and he who neglects to comply takes up the whole matter amiss; he misunderstands or neglects the very gospel by which he hopes to be saved.

Then again, instead of personal consecration, we detect all around us the religion of imposing formalisms, of fascinating ritualisms, of externalisms which may be as graceful as the exquisite statuary in the Greek temples, but are just as destitute of real life; which lull the conscience, regale the taste and fancy, but leave the heart unchanged. We are surprised that in the midst of the noontide illumination of the gospel, men can still be bewitched by the superstitions, impostures and pageantry of the church of Rome. We forget two things; first, that in our fallen condition imagination is stronger than reason. We see this in our child. You take your little boy into a toy shop and purchase an ugly mask. He knows you are his father and the mask nothing but a piece of painted pasteboard; yet when you put on the hideous false face he is terrified. How do you explain this? It is a proof that in the child imagination is stronger than reason. Nor is it otherwise with children of a larger growth. A lady weeps over "The Sorrows of Werther," or some other sentimental novel. Does she believe it to be true? Does she not know that it is a pure fiction? A man of sense enters the theatre. The play is Hamlet. Does he really suppose he is in Denmark? Is he not certain that the actor in sables, with such a rueful countenance is, not the Prince of Denmark, but Mr. Jones, whom he met the night before in a drinking saloon? And the lady—with her disheveled air and picturesque miseries—does she think that she is really the love-lorn Ophelia? Does she not know that she is only Jones' wife? Yet she sits there bathed in tears. And what is the solution of all this? We have already given it. In the lady and in the man—as in the little boy—imagination is stonger than reason. And now apply this important moral principle to the matter in hand, and we will understand why the mummeries of Rome exert such a magical spell over people in their senses. The secret is an open secret. It is that spectacles, rites, festivals, processions, robes, censers, relics, choristers, priests and altars, all appeal directly to the imagination.

And we overlook another fact. We forget that these ceremonies are the most subtile form of self-righteousness. They are pleasing to the unrenewed heart because they are performed to merit God's favor, and they thus offer the most grateful incense to the self-complacency of our unregenerate nature. Nor is it only in Popery—the master-piece of human craft—that religion thus crystalizes into seductive forms, that materiolatries are a counterfeit for piety. The bitter hostility of the Pharisees was inflamed against Jesus, because they perceived that he was abrogating the gorgeous machinery of the temple by which their spiritual pride was intensely flattered, and was requiring purity of heart and life. And still, at this day, the cross of Christ, the obedience, the self-renunciation, the holiness of the gospel stir up the enmity of multitudes because they assail the traditions of their fathers and abolish those old hereditary sanctities which, under the insidious garb of religion, flatter their pride, quiet their consciences, and are clung to as sacred heir-looms, transmitted through a long line of honored ancestors.

I mention only one other substitute for personal piety. This we may designate as a sort of corporate religion, a devotedness to some church by which we become, not Christians, but churchmen; and the impositions which men and women practise upon themselves under this delusion are almost incredible. Never, perhaps, did any body of soldiers regard themselves as enlisted in such a high and holy enterprise as those who rallied under the banner of the Crusaders; yet never was there an army more depraved and dissolute. And a self-deception, every whit as infatuated, is witnessed now in thousands who are the bigoted advocates of some ecclesiastical organization, who contribute their wealth and would pour out their blood for some church, the tenets of which they neither understand nor believe, and the morality of which they treat with undisguised contempt.

Unquestionably, the very mission of the gospel, all its aims and appointments, suppose and require the existence of churches; nor do the Scriptures recognize as a Christian any one who refuses to identify himself publicly with that empire which Jesus has set up on the earth. But few heresies have been so degrading to the religion of Jesus as that which exalts faith in sacramentalism, in a priesthood, in church, above sanctity of heart and life. Surely if union with any peculiar society were essential to salvation, Jesus would have clearly defined that society. But neither in the judicature of his kingdom published in the sermon on the mount, nor in his programme of the last judgment, does he utter a single word about church. Nor can this surprise us; for visible churches are only aids, their ordinances and ministries are valuable only as they promote personal holiness. No error of the church of Rome is more fatal than that which teaches that a church can do something mechanically to save us. And all churches practise the same impostures which get rid of religion by something that seems to be religious; which overlook the great truth that every man must be his own priest; which, instead of seeking to awaken and nourish the spirit of faith, pentinence, sanctity, by their prayers, hymns, lessons, sermons, services, invest these performances with a superstitious virtue; and thus satisfy the conscience with something short of holiness, and fix the heart on some sanctimonious machinery instead of Christ.

I have thus indicated some of the dangers which, at this day, urgently admonish us to insist upon the great duty of cultivating true, personal piety. What, however, do we mean by personal piety? This is a question of eternal moment. I therefore, give the answer, seeking in this, as in all I utter, to ascertain "the mind of the Spirit."

By personal piety I mean, first, a principle, a new, gracious principle; not a succession of good deeds, but a spiritual principle of which such good deeds are the fruits and evidences.

By personal piety I mean an internal life; not outward activities but an inward power, an instinct of devotion, of faith, prayer, self-immolation, habitual communion with God, which is incorporated among the very elements of our being. One of the most remarkable features of our age is the energy with which men combine their efforts in every sort of enterprise. In the church, as in the world, whatever people wish to do they form a society to do it with; and, therefore, in the church as in the world, one of our perils is a religion which is from without, not from within, the mistaking what we *do* for what we *are*, and consequently the neglect of our own spiritual health and prosperity, while we engage in the diversified systems of concerted movements which incessantly claim our attention.

By personal piety, I mean a vitalizing principle; a principle the vitality of which—like all real life—is attested by continual growth. If there be spiritual life, there will be a progressive enlargement of the mind and expansion of the soul; we will "grow in grace," and this development will be "according to the proportion of faith"—the harmony and symmetry of the gospel.

In a word, the personal piety defined by the Scriptures is not any emotional impulse; it is a real, deep, practical force which deriving its strength from God, raises the soul above the senses and passions, inbreeds in it temperance, chastity, self-control, cherishes in it that abiding consciousness of the presence and power of Jesus which will cause it to be always perfecting its heavenly faculties, having "its fruit unto holiness and the end everlasting life."

Religion. Personal piety. The very purpose for which Christ "bore our sins in his own body on the tree" was "that we, being dead to sin, should live unto righteousness," and if we are Christians, the subject now in hand must be profoundly interesting to us. For if we are Christians, if we have passed from death unto life, then there has been not merely a change, but a spiritual resurrection, a transition, not only into the peace and privileges of a new forensic relation to God, but into a new character, the very first conscious ingredient of which is an instinctive, irrepressible longing and yearning after perfect holiness. Yet how far are we from that holiness. Happy the man whose good desires ripen into fruits, whose evil thoughts perish in the blossom. But, alas, too often the reverse of this is our mournful experience. We—even we who are the teachers and examples for others—would we be always willing to let them look into our hearts? Woe unto us, how ineffectual are our clearest convictions, our most solemn resolutions; so that at times it really seems as if the gospel cannot accomplish in us what it promises, as if remaining sin were too much for God. Not one of us but, again and again, with bitter weeping, has exclaimed, "We are tied and bound by the chains of our own sins; but do thou, O Lord, of the pitifulness of thy great mercy, loose us;" yet even our prayers have been unavailing. And now why is this so? In answer to this inquiry, it is generally said, that we are fallen, and the taint and pollution of sin still adhere to us. But this is no answer; for the gospel is the divine remedy for this very evil. It is a melancholy fact that we have all been sadly disappointed in the hopes which inspired our hearts when we were first converted to God. Having tasted the love of Jesus, rejoicing in him with a joy unspeakable and full of glory, we believed that we were forever delivered from the solicitations of sin. But too soon this joy withered away from us, too soon the truth broke in bitterly upon us that we were not wholly sanctified, too soon we were amazed and humbled by the consciousness of remaining corruptions. Is this, however, to be forever the Christian's experience? Must the prodigal, even after his return, still be continually grieving his father? Must God be always thus dishonored by the motions of sin in his own children? Is it necessary that a cloud should *ever* separate between Jesus and the soul he has redeemed? We can scarcely adopt a system which so mocks the highest, holiest aspirations of the "new creature." Surely God has not quickened in us a hungering and thirsting after holiness which is not to be filled. *The water that I shall give him shall be in him a well of water springing up into everlasting life.* This cannot mean that there is to be in us a fountain forever sending up impure and poisonous waters. No, and again no. Let us not be calculating accurately how much a Christian must sin. Let us not be examining carefully how much sinning is indispensable to true orthodoxy. Let us not vacate the exceeding great and precious promises of the Bible, and limit the Holy Spirit by whom we are sanctified, and depreciate the efficacy of that faith which "purifies the heart," of that hope which engages us to be "pure as Christ is pure," and thus deduct from the virtue of that atonement the effect of which should be that we walk in the security of an imputed and in the joy of an imparted righteousness.

Nor will it avail much for our growth in personal holiness, that we specify the besetting sin and peculiar hindrances with which each Christian has to contend;—some of which are in the body, others in the mind, others in the heart, the most formidable in the imagination. Nor will a cure be made by prescribing the usual antidotes and precautions—such as fasting, and prayer, and meditation, and reading the word of God. Me, pondering for years this eternally momentous subject, with much prayer, many tears and after most mortifying experiences, one great truth now possesses with all the certainty of perfect conviction. It is that, with the children of God, the chief cause of such deplorable deficiency in holiness is the defect in our conceptions as to the way of holiness revealed in the gospel. Enlightened as to a free, full, present forgiveness through faith in Jesus, the error of those who go to the law, to their own efforts for absolution from the penalty of sin, seems to us the strangest blindness; but we forget that salvation from the power and corruption of sin, from sin itself, must be in the same way.

After all the controversies waged and waging, it appears to me quite incontestable that in the seventh chapter of Romans the apostle is describing the painful conflicts and defeats of a child of God, who is seeking to perfect holiness by the deeds of the law. That was the very "falling from grace," *from the gracious provisions of the gospel,* which he deplored in the Galatians. *This only would I learn of you, Received ye the Spirit by the works of the law, or by the hearing of faith? Are ye so foolish? Having begun in the Spirit, are ye now made perfect by the flesh?* And I may appeal to every Christian and ask whether this same error and its lamentable consequences have not entered into his own experience. Coming to Jesus, casting your soul with all its interests upon him you received all you came for; you experienced the peace and blessedness of pardon; and such was the gratitude and love glowing in your bosom, that "being made free from sin, you became the servants of righteousness."

But did this deadness to sin continue? Did the expulsive potency of this new affection permanently dislodge the evil propensities of your nature? On the contrary, no mortification can be more substantial than that you have felt at the revival of the life and power of sin within you. And now why this? Why but that you sought holiness by the law and not by faith. Nothing could be more sincere than your resolutions, promises and efforts; but the humbling sense of their utter insufficiency caused you in anguish to exclaim, "O wretched man that I am, who shall deliver me from the body of this death?" Nor did you find relief, peace, strength, victory over your corruptions until you repaired to the fountain open for sin and uncleanness, until, looking to Jesus, casting your soul upon him for sanctification just as you did at first for pardon, you uttered that exulting shout, "I thank God through Jesus Christ our Lord."

The one great aid, then, to personal piety, the one essential resource comprehending and giving efficacy to all others, is faith in Jesus, in him who was "called Jesus because he would save his people from their sins;" not only from the guilt of sin, but from sin itself. If we are to "lay aside every weight and the sin which doth so easily beset us," there is but a single way, it is "looking unto Jesus." If we are to have our fruit unto holiness, there is but one way. "Abide in me," says Jesus. "In me;" not in a church. "In me;" not in your own works. Of course the life of every true disciple of the Redeemer will be a life of daily self-denial. Every evangelical grace supposes and requires daily self-denial. Nor only so. The sins most fatal to Christians require and suppose daily self-denial; for it is not through insincerity, or evil intentions, but through indolence, effeminacy, excess in lawful things that those who are really converted so often dishonor the holy name they bear, and pierce themselves through with many sorrows. Yet for all this, it is true that in subduing our depravities one act of *faith* is worth a whole life of attempted *faithfulness*. As the smallest skiff, if sound, will bear a passenger to a richly furnished ship, so the feeblest act of faith, if it be genuine, will unite the soul to Him in whom dwelleth all the treasures of grace and strength, and who "of God is made unto us wisdom and righteousness and sanctification and redemption."

In drawing these observations to a close I would remark that, while we are all familiar with the subject discussed, none of us are familiar with its greatness and its importance. No one can glance at the present state of the world without feeling that Jesus is taking to himself his great name and asserting his imperial supremacy. My soul stands erect and exults as I survey the rapidly extending conquests of that adorable Being who never contemplated for his empire any sphere narrower than the whole earth; whom three continents now worship; whose victories are the standing miracle of the universe; whose word has, for nearly nineteen centuries, been the law of laws to all civilized nations; who, "the holiest among the mighty, and the mightiest among the holy has, with his pierced hand, lifted empires off their hinges, has turned the stream of centuries out of its channel, and is still governing the ages"; who is presiding in senates, ruling tribunals of justice, controlling kings and cabinets, framing and shaping the growing stature of the world, blessing it with good governments, with the highest knowledges, with the fairest humanities, with the noblest powers, with the dearest amenities and charities, with "whatsoever things are just, whatsoever things are true, whatsoever things are lovely and of good report."

But let us not be imposed upon by these external triumphs. The true kingdom of Jesus is spiritual and interior. It is the empire of truth over the mind, of holiness over the heart and the life. Inward sanctity, pure, constraining love to God and man, sincere obedience—where Jesus reigns these are the elements of his sovereignty, and without these, no outward homage can make us his real disciples.

If we are to be useful in winning souls, in advancing the true interests of the Redeemer, the secret is, not genius nor learning; it is, as David declares, "a clean heart," the constant presence and power of the Holy Spirit.

If we are to enjoy spiritual happiness, if the joy of the Lord is to be our strength, the conscience must be purified from the stain of sin, and we must live every day in the consciousness of entire consecration to Jesus. "The kingdom of God," the reign of Christ "is righteousness, peace, and joy in the Holy Ghost." It is first holiness, then peace and blessedness.

Lastly, our salvation. "Without holiness no man shall see the Lord."

Every human being has at some time felt that the one great message of God to him is, "Be thou holy for I am holy;" and again and again—in the most awful terms and by every diversity of emphatic admonition—Jesus warns us of the terrible disappointment which at the judgment shall overwhelm those who forget that repentance is not the utterance of the lips, but the change of the heart; who, living in self-indulgence and sin, stupefy their consciences by that most unsearchable flattery of having "prophesied in his name and in his name done many wonderful works."

Let us enter into these thoughts. Let us begin to "cleanse ourselves from all filthiness of the flesh and spirit, perfecting holiness in the fear of God." And let us enter upon this life now. To-morrow may be too late. Ready or not ready, death is stealing on with silent steps. The summons may be sudden; or if you pass into eternity by a protracted sickness, need I tell you what death-bed conversions are really worth? Believing that one of two brothers who had long been at enmity was about to die, a minister of Jesus was exceedingly anxious to effect a reconciliation between them. The sick man had been the more violent in his feelings; but now he acquiesced in the proposed interview. They met and, after prayer by the pastor, each held the hand of the other and professed sorrow for the past. As his brother was leaving the chamber, however, the patient called him back and said, "James, I have made it up because I think I am going to die; but remember if I get well, it will be just as it was before." This scene was real, and it illustrates the nature of professed changes of heart in a dying hour. All is penitence and tears in prospect of eternity; but let health return, and with it comes the resurrection of the man's passions. If he gets well, it is with his sins just as it was before.

May God in mercy save us from this and from all delusions in a matter of such infinite moment. Let each of us so pass each day as to say, *To me to live is Christ;* remembering it is only then we can add, *And to die is gain.*

Personal piety, growing sanctification of heart and life. Without this, all our hopes are fatal self-deceptions. Talents, erudition, wealth, influence, life—may we dedicate all these to our Lord, and thus be faithful in these stewardships which have been confided to us. But let us ever remember those words so full of solemn significancy, "Not yours, but you;" and, while devoting our zeal and energies to the cause and glory of our common Redeemer, let us "hold a good conscience" as well as "the faith," let us be ever exercising that self-mastery without which, after having preached to others, we ourselves shall be castaways, ever cultivating that all-pervading sanctity which is strength, victory, joy now, and the foretaste and earnest of a blessed immortality.

O Jesus, vouchsafe us this inestimable blessing.

> As thou didst give no law for me,
> But that of perfect liberty,
> Which neither tires nor doth corrode,
> Which is a pillow, not a load.
> Teach both my eyes and hands to move
> Within those bounds set by thy love.
> Grant I May pure and lowly be,
> And live my life, O Christ to Thee.

Now the God of peace that brought again from the dead our Lord Jesus, that great Shepherd of the sheep, through the blood of the everlasting covenant, make you perfect in every good work to do his will, working in you that which is well pleasing in his sight through Jesus Christ; to whom be glory forever and ever, Amen.

J. B. Gambrell
Three Steps Up

And this I pray, that your love may abound yet more and more in knowledge and in all judgment; that ye may approve things that are excellent; that ye may be sincere and without offense till the day of Christ; being filled with the fruits of righteousness, which are by Jesus Christ, unto the glory and praise of God (Phil. 1:9-11).

That is a wonderful prayer, isn't it? The prayer sprang out of the apostle's heart, as he exclaims above, in behalf of the church which he evidently loved very much—one of the churches to which he wrote against which he could lodge no complaint at all. This letter to the Philippians is a beautiful love letter—warm, sweet; ranging from beginning to end on a high plane of thought and feeling. And yet, as good a church as this one was, it was capable of being a better church. The apostle wanted them to get up higher, to see things from a higher standpoint; in other words, to grow in grace, that growing in grace they might burst out like the full sap in the trees, into buds, and flowers, and fruits.

There is a suggestion in the very way in which the apostle comes to the matter of getting this church on the up-grade. He laid the foundation of his whole effort in his prayer for them—an excellent lesson for us. Our brethren pain us often. Some of them are perverse; some of them are so narrow; some of them are so weak. They vex us, and we fret, scold, and talk; they get worse and we get worse. The suggestion of the apostle's method is this: When our brethren are weak, are in any way short of what they ought to be; if they are living on a lower plane than they ought to live on, we should put under them the arms of our prayers and lift them up. I have in my thought at this moment a sister who had been in a great deal of trouble over a succession of inefficient pastors; and after a while one worse than all the others came. She betook herself to earnest prayer for the weak man in the pulpit. Her account of it was that she had never seen any one improve as he did, and I doubt not that she was wonderfully improved herself by her own prayers.

Brethren, let us approach the initial thought—the uplifting power of prayer in the life of a church and in the life of an individual. Might I not say with propriety that what we really need in these troublesome times is a great, swelling undercurrent of prayer in all our work to lift us up? We have great trouble in our Christian work, and a great many of our enterprises are like vessels on the Mississippi River; when the water gets low they go on the sand-banks, and can't be gotten off until the water rises. We want a great rising tide of heartfelt prayer to God throughout the land.

The apostle gives us three distinct stages in this upgrade movement. And they are logically connected; very plain, very simple, they come to my experience and to yours. In the first part of this prayer the burden of the supplication is that the love of these brethren might abound more and more. Our religion, brethren and sisters, is a religion of love. It is no use talking about doing things religiously in cold blood. Love is the manifestation of the divine life in us. It all began in love—"God so loved the world." Christ loved us and gave himself for us; and if we do not love Christ we have missed the whole secret and the whole power of the Christian life. We must put away the idea that people can live a Christian life and not have a Christian life to live; unless we have the life in us we cannot live it out. But some of us who began to love the Lord years ago— and I am satisfied we love him this morning—do not love him as we started out to love him. Might not some of us be compelled to own that some of the old love has gone? We must get the idea of growing in love, not simply the idea of growing in the efficiency of doing things, but primarily of growing in love. I think it ought to be like the love that married people have for each other—the well-married. How fresh, how exuberant is the love of a newly married couple! How sentimental! People laugh at it. Yet it is very beautiful to think on. I am sure that no two people who have ever walked through life in this relation to the end have ever loved each other too much. It is a pity that they sometimes grow cold in love. You know our Lord speaks of our relations to him under the form of marriage; and it is a good figure, a good illustration. People who are just married think that there are no other people in the world who love as they do, and that they will never be able to love so much any more. Yet, if they live as people may and should, this is only the beginning of a constant, widening, mighty current of love. It seems to me it is like a mountain stream which comes down the mountain side, laughing, sparkling, dancing, making a good deal of noise; after a while it gets more to a dead level, and the banks widen, the current deepens and broadens, and other streams flow in from right and left until, away down yonder, the little mountain brooklet that leaped out of the mountain gorge has become a great river, bearing on its majestic bosom the commerce of the nations. So married life, fresh, exuberant, a little noisy, a little showy at the start, deepens with the years, as it is tested and tried, and the one is close to the other through the long weary hours of sickness and when they stand together and weep over little coffins. Now they are gray-headed and old. Oh, the height and depth, the length and breadth of that love! Deep as the sea;—eternal as God, is love, for it is heavenly.

My brethren, it is a great pity if we who are old to-day, after thirty or forty years of experience, do not love more than we used to. If we have not increased the breadth of our Christian love, the depth and strength of it, then we have greatly neglected our privileges. If we are not better for the experiences through which we have passed, let us look again, just a moment, at the marvelous tokens of divine love that have come to us since our conversion.

Some of us have passed through deep waters; and as we went down into them and the great waves of affliction rolled over us, and the storm was upon the mighty deep, our hearts quaked. But there came to us through the waves and walking on the sea one who is Lord of land and sea, and he stilled the waves, and great peace came to us in our afflictions. This is not a passing dream or speculation, but the blessed experience of those who have attempted to walk with God. The old saint, scarred and weatherbeaten, who put to sea forty years ago, did not understand many things then that he understands now; he did not appreciate then the words, "I will never leave thee nor forsake thee," but now he knows it is all true. The heart is stronger now and fuller of love.

I will not forget this morning that I am talking in a city church. I have great concern for our city churches, for they need to be strong, surrounded as they are by the strongholds of worldliness. Oh, brethren and sisters, what we want back in our city churches to-day is the great heart and patience of Jesus Christ and of his love for men and women. We cannot fiddle people into the kingdom, and we cannot beguile them by worldly methods into the love of Jesus Christ. We want something you Methodists had—the zeal of John Wesley; and we Baptist people want the rugged earnestness of John the Baptist. We are compelled to live; we are compelled to fight; and ever-growing love, which is a part of experience, should feed itself day after day upon the ever-increasing number of divine blessings bestowed upon us, and so shall we be stronger to live aright and fight valiantly.

I was in a place somewhat north of this some years ago at a prayer meeting. I heard a great many things said that were not particularly edifying to my thinking—fanciful, flowery, and secular. After a while there was a lull, and a girl stood up and said, "I was converted a year ago, and from the day that I was converted I have made a practice of stopping quietly for a time every day, and thinking of what new blessing God has given me." And then she mentioned some new blessing or experience she had received that day. It was a good suggestion, this of stopping to think of the blessings that God gives us; for those blessings nourish our love, they broaden it and strengthen it.

I am not to dwell much longer on this point, but I cannot leave it without enforcing it. I wonder if there is here this morning somebody who is trying to serve God without love? There are such people in the world; they are all about us. Such service is perfunctory; it has a form of godliness, but it lacks power. If there are any such before me this morning, let me say that the idea is a mistaken one. Be done with it; be done with it! If you have never loved, seek now to love the Lord Jesus Christ. Men and women, throw yourselves down at the feet of the Christ until you are caught up by the great, swelling tide of Jesus' love; and don't try to serve God without love. I wonder if there is anybody here this morning who is trying to serve God under the old love—whose religious love is a recollection, a bright spot in the past? Let your love catch up with your years. You need it to help you to-day. I notice that people who are quick at cultivating a good many other things, and do not cultivate love, get into a bad state of mind. They are hard to please. The preacher cannot please them; nobody else can please them; not even God himself, not even the blessed adorable Christ can please them; and they never will get pleased until there comes back to them as a present experience the blessed love of Christ that passeth all understanding. Brother, sister, do not let this day go out until you have renewed your vows and come back into touch with the loving Christ.

But to the next point. This love is to be in knowledge. Love is a great force, comparable to a river sweeping on, blessing and making fruitful everything that it touches. Love that is thoughtless, indiscriminate, and degenerates into mere sentimentalism, wastes itself like a stream broken from its banks, burying itself in the sandy plain. There is a great deal of difference between the dignified and manly love of Jesus Christ and mere religious sentimentalism. I wish we could note the difference this morning. We have some in the world who go about with their mouths full of soft words. They love God and they love the devil; they love God's people and they love the devil's people, and they love them all the same way. They don't know any difference between right and wrong. They think God is so full of love that he would take the Apostle Paul to heaven, and the chariot would catch Judas in his downward descent and take him there too.

Let us understand that love does not necessarily make people foolish. Knowledge! knowledge! growing in knowledge! We ought to know the quality of the things we are going to love. There are some things to be loved, and there are some things not to be loved. A good thing is to be loved; a bad thing is not to be loved. I never was in a theatre but once; that was in the days of my ignorance. I went not knowing the guile in there; but I soon saw the difference between the theatre and the prayer meeting. I found things all about me which a church member had no business to love. There are many people who need to know things! And yet, they will not have knowledge. They will not let you talk to them. They go out on the streets and talk to infidels, and catch all sorts of loose notions; but they will not let God's people touch them—never.

Not a great many months ago a cultured woman came to me. Her face was the picture of intense suffering. She said, "I have come to consult with you about my boy." "Well," I said, "madame, tell me about your boy. How old is he?" "Twelve years old," she said. "What is the matter with him?" She said, "I cannot control my boy at all. He goes down town all the time, and he gets into all sorts of mischief, and now he is in the lockup. The mayor has just sent me a note that if I will be responsible for his punishment I may take him out. What am I to do with my boy?" I said to her, "Madame, you go down there and take your boy; and when you get him at home shut him in a room, and you go in there with him with a heart full of love and a bundle of switches, and stay with him a week if necessary; stay there with that boy until he is thoroughly conquered and thoroughly submissive to your will." She said, "I love my boy; I cannot whip him." "Oh," I said, "Madame, you don't love your boy with any common sense. Your love is not a love that has any knowledge of boy nature in it. You are raising your boy for the gallows. You had better stay with him in that room a week, and wear out on him all the switches you can get your hands on rather than let him go to ruin. Solomon was not the fool many modern people think he was on that subject." Yet, she did not do it.

Now, brethren, we want love, but we want love according to knowledge. This church needs to love the Lord Jesus Christ, and to love the souls of men, but you do not want to run about after all sorts of worldly ways. Think you that you can save men by encouraging them in their worldly lives? Oh, how we need sound knowledge! How much we need knowledge in our religious work and in our individual lives!

And then, not only abound in knowledge, but in judgment also. There is a great difference between knowledge and judgment. Judgment is that sense which enables us to make the right use of knowledge. A wise man, having all the facts before him, will know what to do. He will not know what to do unless he has the facts, for his judgment must have something to work on. He must have knowledge and then judgment to tell him what to do.

Now Christians ought to be wise people. We need to be harmless—as harmless as doves, but as wise as serpents. We want to be very wise in our church methods. We should so adjust our church methods as to reach out as far as we can to help people; but we want to be very wise, that when we reach out to take the world the world does not take us.

It ought to be a matter of profound study all the time how to be wise; how to be wise in the management of a definite case. The father wants to be wise with his boy. I have in the school where I am, a strong, resolute boy, at that critical period in his life when it is hard to say which way a boy is going. His father took hold of that boy with a strong grip, but with a grip that was flesh and blood, with warmth and tenderness. It saved the boy.

What I am insisting on now is wisdom—practical wisdom in our Christian lives. There are a great many people who seem to think that as soon as a man gets converted he must give up common sense entirely. We do not put into our religion the common sense we put anywhere else. Christianity is a monumental miracle because it has lived against the folly of people who have had it in hand. To illustrate: you have a congregation that wants to build a church house. They go to work to build the church, but don't know anything about the money. After a while they find themselves deeply in debt. Then they wonder how it all happened, and they go to praying for assistance, and try to pray the money out of somebody else's pocket to pay their church debt. If you intend to build a church you ought to know that you have to build it out of common material, out of wood and stone or bricks; and you want common sense in it; wisdom, practical judgment.

Now let us go back and come up these three steps rapidly. The prayer began with love, that it might abound more and more in knowledge and in all judgment—three great steps upward, landing us on a higher platform; a heart full of love, a mind well informed, a judgment well balanced. The result of it is most excellent—"That ye may approve things that are excellent."

The Bible is not given on the plan of telling us everything we must do and everything we must not do. There are great principles laid down, and we must have judgment to apply these principles. There are new tendencies coming up constantly that are new; and there is nothing specific about them in the Bible. But if a man's heart is right with God, and if his knowledge is as it ought to be, and his judgment is right, he will not have any great trouble to find out on which side of any common question of the day he ought to stand.

A great many of our people are greatly pestered by theatres and dancing and card-playing, and the like of that. They say in their confusion and in their anxiety, "Where is there anything in the Scriptures against these things?" Well, they are in a greatly unseasoned condition spiritually. Nobody doubts when he gets on the platform where Paul wrote this letter to the Philippian church. Nobody doubts which way the theatre is going: it is of the earth, earthy; and there is not a spiritually minded man or woman between the seas that doesn't know it. Nobody doubts where the ball room stands: it is of the earth, earthy; it is of the flesh, the world, and the devil. Every spiritually minded person knows where it stands and what stands for it. "That ye may approve things that are excellent." It is not excellent, is it?

I recall that some years ago I was interviewed by two ladies on this very subject. One of them was a church member; the other was not. They were both very elegant ladies. This very question of the ballroom was brought up, and my opinion asked. I can sum up what was said in a very few words. The church member said she did not feel that it was wrong. I said to her, "All right; but the next time you get dressed for a ball, while you are waiting for your escort, you open your Bible at the twelfth chap-

ter of Romans and read that chapter right through: 'I beseech you therefore, brethren, by the mercies of God, that ye present your bodies a living
sacrifice, holy, acceptable unto God, which is your reasonable service.
And be not conformed to this world: but be ye transformed,' and so on.
Then get on your knees and ask God to bless you and bless the ball, and
bless the ball to you, and to everybody there." The other lady, who was
not a member of the church, broke out laughing. She said afterward, "I
was not laughing at you; I was laughing at how ridiculous Cousin Dona
would look, on her knees, asking God to bless her and bless the ball."
They are things that do not go together, and will not hold fellowship with
each other.

Thousands of questions are coming up all the time, and a man ought
to be elevated enough in his spiritual life to discern the quality of things
and to approve the things that are excellent.

Then we are to be sincere. That is a very fine quality for the Christian.
To tell the truth; to be honest enough not to say, "I am not able to give"
when he is; not to say, "I cannot go to prayer meeting," when he just does
not want to go; not to say, "I cannot do this or that," when the real reason
is, he does not want to do it; but to be perfectly sincere and open before
God, being filled with the fruits of righteousness to the praise and glory of
God.

It was one of the first thoughts in my spiritual life that I should be saved.
Of course, we cannot help it—nobody can help thinking about that. I
think now I am going to be saved, and my heart is resting on that. I know
one thing for a certainty; I am not going to be saved because I am worthy
to be saved. But my feet are on the rock, and I expect to stand there. I am
not thinking now so much about being saved; I am thinking about
heaven. I feel that I am going to a city, now only a little way off. I can see
the spires yonder, I am so close; and I am not sorry it is close, not sorry at
all. Brethren, the thought in my mind now is, that I shall fill up all the
remaining days of my life with the fruits of righteousness, living the life of
service that God will help me to live, so that when I come into the presence of my divine Lord and Master, I may be like a transplanted tree
borne down with fruit, and not like a tree with leaves and no fruit.

I may not see you again until we meet before God's great throne. May
the Lord Jesus preserve your souls, and sanctify you, and help you, and
fill you with his Spirit. For Jesus's sake I ask it. Amen.

Virtus E. Gideon
The Infinity of the Little

Mark 12:41-44

The world is conscious only of the monumental things in life, forgetting the infinity of the little. We count nickels and noses, convictions and contacts, programs and personality, powers and politics.

> We are victimized by bigness. Our banks claim their millions in deposits. Our buildings, like the tower of Babel, must "reach unto heaven" and "make us a name." Every village not pathetically passé is eager to disfigure its beauty with factories. Every city not hopelessly moribund is ambitious to double its population. Meanwhile, in our crass chamber-of-commerce philosophies, we ignore the leading fact that a bigger city does not therefore breed better people. Even the Church brings forth "movements" which flourish for a day like a green bay tree and then die, having printer's ink for sap and being stricken by the blight of statistics.[1]

But in a time when these tendencies have never been more prominent, the world of science bids us consider the significance of the little things in life. The nuclear physicist points to the piece of uranium, golf-ball size, and observes, "There is contained potentially within this element the power to destroy a great city." Or the medical scientist isolates the drop of blood and says, "Two armies are contained within this drop of blood; the red struggles viciously with the white." Or the same medical scientist calls our attention to the drop of clear vaccine, which, he says, spells the difference between life and death. But generations before the first nuclear physicist lifted the piece of uranium, or the medical scientist isolated the armies contained within the drop of blood or called our attention to the drop of clear vaccine, Jesus indicated that there is an infinity of the little. He taught his disciples that the cup of cold water given in his name will not go unrewarded. He told the story of the man who had one hundred sheep. Ninety-nine were safe within the fold, but one was lost. This one was so important that the shepherd left the group within the fold to search for the sheep that was lost.

Jesus further illustrated this truth by the story of the woman who had ten coins. One was lost, and the missing coin was important enough to demand her best as she searched diligently for it. Once she had found the coin, she called her neighbors to join her in rejoicing. The Master also told the story of the prodigal son who returned to his home to find a glorious welcome from his father. A ring was placed on the prodigal's finger, shoes were provided for his feet, and a robe was placed about his body. This incident also reveals the infinity of the little. Although our society is captivated by the themes of majestic greatness and extreme magnitude, there is an infinite quality in the smallest imaginable thing in life. It is that quality that is usually overlooked but which must be emphasized in spiritual experience.

Jesus observed the people as they cast their gifts into one of thirteen trumpet-shaped receptacles placed in the Temple for that purpose. Some made rather large gifts, reflecting the financial self-sufficiency of which they were so proud. The self-styled religious man, drawing his robes close to his body as if to shut out all sin from his life, gave a large gift. He probably chose the largest coins, casting them against the sides of the container in order that the worshipers might determine the amount of his gift by the clanging of metal upon metal. But this woman, destitute though she was, gave all that she had—her living. In the language of the twentieth century, this widow gave less than a nickel. Although copper in the sight of the world, this gift became gold to the eyes of Jesus.

The infinity of the little is sometimes overlooked. In the experiences of life we find ourselves magnifying the great and overlooking seemingly insignificant things. Perhaps the most significant thing that we might do today is to speak a word of encouragement. The wise man of the Old Testament said, "A word fitly spoken is like apples of gold in pictures of silver" (Prov. 25:11). A Sunday school pupil or a neighbor may need a word of strength more than anything else which we could give.

It may be that we shall come under the condemnation of God by failing to tap the greatest resource of power. Roger Babson, a well-known news analyst, has been quoted as saying, "Prayer is the greatest unused power in America today." But we reply, "Words and prayers are insignificant."

Not so in the eyes of Jesus. Jesus has never seen a thing so little that it is unimportant. Mark says that prayer was so important to Jesus that he slipped away to a private place and there prayed (Mark 1:35). Jesus planned to pray because prayer was important to him. A contemporary judgment is that prayer is without urgency; however, a communion with God was so important that Jesus scheduled prayer. Therefore it could not be considered an insignificant experience.

But even in the matter of responsibility we are greatly tempted to overlook the little thing, for Jesus warned, "If any man would come after me, let him deny himself, and take up his cross, and follow me" (Matt. 16:24). And yet our world remarks, "Little things are unimportant. Someone else can perform the task; someone else can bear the burden; someone else can accomplish the deed. What is it to me that I should deny myself and take up a cross and follow a lowly carpenter! If I bear a cross, it must be an attractive cross, one which appeals to others." Attractiveness to the crowd becomes singularly important. Woe to the man who is determined to sacrifice only for that which appeals to human thought!

Likewise, in our attitude toward the Bible and its teaching we oftentimes overlook the tremendous, eternal verities which are found in small statements. Were it possible for one to take all the Bibles in the world, place them on a table before him, take one huge pair of scissors and begin to snip those precious words from the pages, without question many people would object to such an action. One might begin with the Old Testament, indicating that it is relatively unimportant in the light of the New and, turning to Psalm 23:1 begin to snip the words, "The Lord is my shepherd; I shall not want." But perhaps you would instantaneously object, "In the hour of my gravest physical need, this verse was precious to my soul!" So the culprit turns to John's Gospel, and there he begins to delete John 3:16, "For God so loved the world, that he gave his only begotten Son . . ." No doubt many would object upon the basis that this is the first biblical verse committed to memory.

Most deeds in life are of little consequence and are infinitesimal in nature. The man who lives only for the great deeds in life misses most of life's joy, for strangely enough life is not composed of great deeds but of multitudes of seemingly insignificant acts. Every spring throughout America thousands of young men are on the sandlots, participating in America's favorite pastime, baseball. But not many of those fellows will live to see the day that their names are listed on the roster of the New York Yankees or the Milwaukee Braves. Why do they play? Why do they discipline their bodies? Why do they spend innumerable hours in learning to throw, catch, hit, and run the bases? They do not do it out of a conviction that they shall become great stars. Neither do they play for the check which they are to receive; there is no check. They play because of the sheer pleasure that is derived from playing well the game which they appreciate. Thus shall we enjoy life—by performing well the little tasks of life.

The significance of the little thing is sometimes misinterpreted. Some people would look upon the little thing and say that it is unimportant, that life will be the same whether this act is performed or not, that regardless of one's intent or accomplishment, little things can contribute absolutely nothing to life or to its enjoyment. Many people who are disappointed in life and who are experiencing tragedy on every hand have committed, "Little things are unimportant." Some would look to the vocation, others to social approval, still others would look to ability, and say, "The little thing in life is unimportant. What I am, what I have achieved, counts, but not the little thing!" But you must not become the victim of such preposterous thought. The little thing in life is indispensable.

I was reared in west Texas, where it seemed that there were all kinds of surpluses. There was a surplus of cotton, a surplus of maize, a surplus of farmers, and a surplus of farmers, and a surplus of everything, with two possible exceptions—rain and money. But have you seen a surplus in God's kingdom? Have you seen a surplus of love, joy, forgiveness, dedication, or consecration? I have yet to see a surplus within the kingdom of God. These intangibles do not lend themselves to excesses.

But others would object, "The little thing is superficial within itself." No doubt the priests objected at this point to the widow's gift. Doubtlessly they said, "Why, this woman has not given anything! Look at our gifts. Our Temple is a wealthy institution, and she has given less than nickel. What can a nickel do for an institution as great as ours?" Oh, how tragic it is for one to make such accusations!

Jesus knows nothing that is superficial; rather, everything that he sees is important to him. Life, composed of a multiplicity of parts, many of them infinitesimal, is important to Jesus. I know Jesus to be interested in the little things of life. Therefore, I can take all of my problems to him. He made the butterfly's wings and the eyes of the insect; and he made it all beautiful. Jesus must be interested in the little things in life. He knows nothing that is valueless or insignificant. Jesus is cognizant of the sparrow's need; he clothes the lilies of the fields. Every person, then, must evaluate the little thing for himself. Once he has weighted the infinity of the little in its farthest outreaches and eternal consequences, he shall recognize that little things in life are important. Life is composed of a series of little acts, little deeds, little thoughts, but each important in its own way and in its own place.

Granting that there exists an infinity of the little, it only follows that lasting things in life are few. That is the reason Jesus said, "Lay up for yourselves treasures in heaven, where neither moth nor rust doth corrupt, and where thieves do not break through nor steal" (Matt. 6:20). Jesus' generation was guilty of laying up treasures on earth, as is twentieth-century America. Jesus indicated that there is a safe depository, the bank of heaven (Matt. 6:19). These lasting things of life are numbered, but the spiritual aspects of life may be deposited in a heavenly depository. If Christians realized that little things are important, the lamentable things of life would be decreased. There are broken hearts, broken homes, and sobbing souls all over the world today because some have failed to realize the significance of the little things in life. Life is composed of little things, and not one of these is unimportant in the eyes of Jesus.

A newspaper story which appeared several years ago told of a traveler who walked from the Golden Gate to New York State. Upon his arrival in New York State, a newspaper reporter interviewed him and asked, "What was your greatest obstacle? Was it the mountains you had to cross? Was it the lack of food? Was it the rivers you had to ford?"

"No, I could normally find a pass through the mountains; and by walking alongside the streams I could usually find a bridge; and, luckily, some farmer was willing to share his food if necessary."

"Then what was your greatest obstacle?"

"Mister, the thing that almost defeated me was the sand in my shoes."

And in the words of the text: "This poor widow hath cast more in, than all they which have cast into the treasury: for all they did cast in of their abundance; but she of her want did cast in all that she had, even all her living" (Mark. 12:43-44). Life becomes meaningful only when you acknowledge the infinity of the little.

NOTE

1. George A. Buttrick, *The Parables of Jesus* (Garden City: Doubleday, Doran & Company, Inc., 1928), p. 21.

J. D. Grey
A Christian in Spite of Everything

All the saints salute you, chiefly they that are of Caesar's household (Phil. 4:22).

At the close of Paul's letter to the Philippians he places a bright gem of Christian encouragement in a setting of pure gold. In the fourth chapter of this prison epistle and the twenty-second verse we hear Paul saying, "All the saints salute you, chiefly they that are of Caesar's household." A casual reading of this verse of Scripture does not mean anything to us, for we pass it over lightly and regard it as one of those usual, personal remarks that the apostle is making to his dear friends at Philippi. But when we look a little more closely and realize where Paul was when this word was written and from whom the greeting is coming, we understand then its deeper significance.

These words were written by Paul while he was in prison near the imperial palace in Rome. He wrote this epistle about A.D. 64, during the reign of Nero, which lasted from 54 to 68. Nero has been called the most despotically cruel of all the Roman emperors. In this very year, A.D. 64, Nero had a large portion of the city of Rome burned; and in order to turn suspicion away from himself, he accused the Christians of the crime. A most cruel persecution broke out. One biblical scholar described his act in the following words: "Nero lent his gardens for the purpose of exhibiting the tortures of the wretched victims and at night illuminated his grounds by the flames of the burning Christians." Now we hear Paul saying, the very year that this happened, while all this cruelty was going on, "All the saints salute you, chiefly they that are of Caesar's household."

And so we learn that actually there were Christians living in the palace of this cruel Roman emperor, Nero; and those Christians had asked brother Paul to send the message for them to their fellow Christians in

Philippi. If a person could be a Christian and live in the palace of this despotically cruel and inhuman ruler, Nero, one could be a Christian anywhere in the world.

In discussing this subject, let us center our attention on two lines of thought. Let us discuss, first of all, the matter of *being* a Christian in spite of everything, and secondly, the matter of *becoming* a Christian in spite of everything.

Now to begin with, in looking at the matter of *being* a Christian in spite of everything, let us remind ourselves over and over again that it is not now, it never has been, and it never will be an easy thing to be a Christian of the right sort. God has not promised us that we shall be "carried to the skies On flow'ry beds of ease, While others fought to win the prize And sailed thro' bloody seas." The Master well reminds us in the Sermon on the Mount, in Matthew 7:14, that "strait is the gate, and narrow is the way, which leadeth unto life, and few there be that find it." No, we are not going to have any easy time living the Christian life. The devil is going to see to it that our way is rough. A Christianity that is of the right sort—in other words, the sort that is genuine, the kind that is New Testament Christianity—will call upon us to bear crosses and to "endure hardness, as a good soldier of Jesus Christ." A person becomes sick and tired, as well as disgusted, with a modern-day, easygoing, luxury-loving religion that passes under the guise of Christianity and seeks to reach the masses by making the road easy. We see about us in this world in which we live a literal fulfilment of the words of Paul when he said, "The time will come when they will not endure sound doctrine; but . . . shall they heap to themselves teachers, having itching ears." A religion that does not call upon its followers to forsake sin, to be done with worldliness, to crucify self with selfish ambitions and lusts will be a religion that will be popular with the masses. But alas! alack! in the last day the Lord of life will stand before them and say, "Why call ye me, Lord, Lord, and do not the things which I say?" And what is more pitiful, he will say further, "I never knew you: depart from me."

The question often is asked me, "Can one, dare one, live the Christian life in this modern day, the year 1959?" My answer is always the same, "Yes, if you want to and if you are willing to pay the price."

First of all, we need Christians who will follow Christ regardless of the call and challenge of the world. The world, the flesh, and the devil are calling to people as never before. Satan is holding up the most attractive invitations and the most appealing challenges to people that man has ever heard. The call of the world is loud; the challenge of the world is appealing. But if you and I are to be Christians of the sort that were in Nero's palace, we will have to turn a deaf ear to the call and to the challenge of the world. I think constantly of our youth. My heart goes out in deepest sympathy for them. Temptations today come incessantly, and sin is made very alluring. The devil makes a great bid for the youth of today. But youth need to remember the great words of James Russell Lowell, so significantly uttered in "The Vision of Sir Launfal":

> At the Devil's booth are all things sold,
> Each ounce of dross counts its ounce of gold;
> For a cap and bells our lives we pay,
> Bubbles we buy for a whole soul's tasking,
> 'Tis Heaven alone that is given away,
> 'Tis only God may be had for the asking . . .

Furthermore, one can be a Christian in spite of comrades and the crowd. I am sure that these Christians who were friends of Paul in Nero's palace were taunted by their fellow servants and by the ones whom they served because they dared to be true to Christ. Constantly they were thrown with not only those who were different from them but those who were antagonistic to them. It is not an easy thing for one to go against the pleas, the appeals, and the calls of comrades and the crowd around him. These voices incessantly call out for one to forsake the Saviour; but even if it requires a definite break with bosom companions and with those with whom we live, we must face bravely the challenge and dare to be Christian in spite of everything.

To look further into the matter, we conclude that we must be Christian in spite of caustic criticisms that come. Ridicule is often the devil's most effective weapon. Those people about whom we read in Paul's Philippian letter undoubtedly were criticized from morning till night. The criticism which was leveled against them was harsh and unkind. Those with whom they labored and those for whom they slaved criticized them for following this defeated Galilean. I doubt not that they were told over and over again, "Why, this illiterate carpenter of Nazareth was nothing but a deceived maniac who had great obsessions of grandeur. He met death himself; many of his followers have been killed. This which he has started will soon play out; why waste your time with it?" And I can see those

Christians going on their way, smiling at their critics, but turning their tear-stained faces toward the risen Christ and pledging him anew their deepest loyalty and devotion. They evidently had as their motto the words of the wise poet who said, "Go on thy quiet way; God is thy Judge—not they; fear not! Be strong!"

Those Christians about whom we speak and Christians in this present day must, moreover, follow Christ regardless of conquests. Those Christians were a subdued people. Many of them had been brought from Roman provinces around the world to the imperial palace to become servants in various capacities. Some were perhaps secretaries and teachers. Others, perhaps, were personal attendants to the emperor. But they all had been vanquished in conquest. Yet they did not give up their faith in Christ when they had been brought into subjection to an earthly ruler. And today, regardless of who your superior may be in any of life's complex relationships, dare to be true to Jesus; dare to live the Christian life in spite of anything and everything that may come.

These Christians, furthermore, were serving Christ regardless of contrary conditions of every kind and description. I have often had people say to me, "Oh, I would be a Christian if my circumstances were more favorable, if I were in a better environment." But, beloved friend, the lily does not ask for white sand in which to grow. Put the lily in the blackest, most miasmatic soil and it will raise itself quickly, yet to give to the world its whitest blossom. Christians should be like the lily. They should learn to be Christian in spite of everything that is around them. The Spartan lad in leaving home for battle complained to his mother that his sword was not long enough for him to win in the struggle. That mother very wisely replied, "Then put another step to your sword!" When you and I are tempted to say, "I cannot live a Christian life where I am," let us say to ourselves, "Put more power, put more sacrifice into your faith."

Let us now briefly turn our attention to the matter of *becoming* a Christian in spite of everything.

You can become a Christian today in spite of other things that claim your attention. Satan always will see to it that appeals are made to you, that bids are made for your time, and that a multitude of things claim your attention. The matter of making a living is foremost in the consideration of many. But, dear unsaved friend, we urge you not to be so busy making a living for the few short years of this existence that you do not take time to make a life in Christ that shall abide for eternity.

Become a Christian in spite of hypocrisies and failures in lives that you see about you. I grant that there are many in all churches who make a miserable failure of living the Christian life. I do not defend them. I simply say to you, dear unsaved one, that their hypocrisies will not save your soul. Look to the perfect one, Jesus Christ the Lord, and not to some pitiful, shameful misrepresentation of him that you see about you in the world.

Moreover, I would have you know that you can become a Christian in spite of a past life of sin. Whatever your life may have been heretofore, whatever the sins you have committed, whatever the distance that you have gone from God, he will save you, and he will save you now if you will turn to him. Make your song a plea of confession and say:

> Just as I am, without one plea,
> But that Thy blood was shed for me,
> And that Thou bidd'st me come to Thee,
>   O Lamb of God, I come! I come!

You can today become a Christian in spite of loved ones and friends that hold you back. Many a person, many a child, is away from God today because someone who is dear to him is away from the Saviour, too. But in spite of this, I have known many Christians who have broken through the line of opposition that loved ones and friends put up and have come to the Savior in spite of them all.

In spite of all that the devil may say to you, in spite of the hindrances that he places in your way, in spite of his opposition to you, I pray you will say:

> Just as I am, and waiting not
> To rid my soul of one dark blot,
> To Thee whose blood can cleanse each spot,
>   O Lamb of God, I come! I come!

> Just as I am, Thou wilt receive,
> Wilt welcome, pardon, cleanse, relieve,
> Because Thy promise I believe,
>   O Lamb of God, I come! I come!
>   —CHARLOTTE ELLIOTT

Vance Havner
Look Who's Here!

When someone shows up unexpectedly, or when we suddenly encounter someone we have wanted to see or have not seen in a long time, we sometimes say, "Look who's here!" That expression could have been used often in the Bible. Think of the Israelites in the wilderness, often tempted to despair and even to rebel. But on many a night a Hebrew could pull back the flap of his tent, see the pillar of fire in the sky, and say to his companion, "Everything's all right. We're not alone. *Look who's here!*"

Or think of Elisha, the prophet of God and a one-man Central Intelligence System. When the Syrian king planned a move against Israel, Elisha learned about it through his hot line to heaven. The king sent horses, chariots, and a great host of soldiers to capture this troublesome prophet. When Elisha's servant started out next day he saw the soldiers everywhere and, overwhelmed, cried to his master, "(What) shall we do?" Elisha replied, "Fear not: for they that be with us are more than they that be with them." The servant must have thought, "But I don't see them!" Elisha prayed that God might open his servant's eyes and when He did, the servant saw that "the mountain was full of horses and chariots of fire round about Elisha" (2 Kings 5:17). *Look who's here!* "The angel of the Lord encampeth round about them that fear him, and delivereth them" (Ps. 34:7). We need to raise our sights these days to see who is on our side. We cannot be optimistic with a misty optic!

Then there was Isaiah who had a vision of God the same year that King Uzziah died. King Uzziah's passing was a national calamity. His death under sad circumstances overwhelmed the nation. People were saying, "If a good man like our king can end up like that, what hope is there for the rest of us?" Isaiah, too, was stunned, but for him there was a plus along with the minus. "In the year that king Uzziah died, I saw *also* the Lord . . ." [Isa. 6:1]. While everybody else saw disaster and despair, Isaiah saw the Lord, high and lifted up. Minus Uzziah but plus the Lord! *Look who's here!*

Do you remember the three Hebrew children in the fiery furnace? King Nebuchadnezzar looked in and said, "What's going on here? We threw three men into the furnace and I *see* four!" The three Hebrews might well have said, "We have company. *Look who's here!*" And they came out without even the smell of smoke! The fourth in the fire made the difference!

Consider Daniel in the lions' den. King Darius was a mighty ruler but he couldn't sleep. He lived in a palace but he couldn't sleep. His bed was covered with costly tapestries but he couldn't sleep. He arose early next morning and went, bleary-eyed, down to the lions' den to ask Daniel, "How are you doing?" The prophet might well have answered, "You might as well have had your sleep. God sent his angel. *Look who's here!*"

John the Baptist stood at the Jordan and said to his listeners, "There standeth one among you whom ye know not," and the next day he declared, "Behold the Lamb of God!" Every Sunday morning there stands among the churchgoers one whom many of them know not. It is the business of the preacher to present the Christ who is always there when we meet in His name and bid the congregation, *"Look who's here!"*

Jesus stopped at Jacob's well one day and began to talk to a wicked woman. He spoke to her of the Water of Life but she said, "Thou hast nothing to draw with and the well is deep." She was correct in her facts but wrong in her conclusion. What difference does it make if the well is deep and there is nothing to draw with when one is in the presence of Jesus Christ! *Look who's here!*

At the house of Jairus, Jesus stated that the daughter was not dead, but only asleep. "And they laughed him to scorn *knowing that she was dead.*" They were correct in their facts but wrong in their conclusion. That is as far as atheism, agnosticism, and unbelief ever get. "She is dead and that settles it." When you're dead, you're dead! They had already sent word to Jairus before he reached his home. "Thy daughter is dead, why trouble the Master any further?" It was all over, nothing could be done.

But when Jesus is present, death does not have the last word. When He is here, all considerations of mortal men fall short. *Look who's here!*

It is the same old argument of the scoffers Peter writes about who say, "Where is the promise of His coming? All things continue as they were from the beginning of the creation." In other words, there is nothing but natural law, cause and effect. Don't look for miracles. God is nowhere. But the Christian cuts that "nowhere" in two and says, God is *now here!*

But this very sense of God among us now, Jesus gathering where we meet in His name, the Holy Spirit consciously present, this is what we mean when we sing, "There's a sweet, sweet Spirit in this place." And the tragedy of our church life is that we produce everything else—and the occasional exception sadly reminds us of what should be the rule. How many church meetings have you attended that could be described best by saying, *God was here?*

At Bethany Martha said, "I know my brother will rise in the resurrection at the last day." She was right in her facts but wrong in her conclusion. She was a good fundamentalist but she didn't have to wait until the resurrection to see Lazarus live again. In front of her stood the Resurrection and the Life. *Look who was there!*

When Jesus said, "Roll away the stone from the sepulcher," Martha objected that Lazarus had been dead for four days and there would be a foul odor. She was right in her facts, wrong in her conclusion. What difference did it make if Jesus Christ was present? All other considerations don't matter in the fact of that! *Look who's here!*

Our Lord was taking a nap in a boat on the Sea of Galilee. A storm arose and the frantic disciples aroused Him, crying, "Carest Thou not that we perish?" They forgot that the *Son of God was there* in the boat with them. God gave Adam dominion over the birds of the air, the beasts of the earth, and the fish of the sea, but not over the wind and the waves. But when Jesus stood and said, "Be still!" that storm subsided and the amazed disciples said, "What manner of man is this that even the winds and the sea obey him?" He had what Adam never had—He is the new Adam! So the Christian can stand in any storm and say, *"So what! Look who's here!"*

After the resurrection our Lord stood on the shore of Tiberias. The disciples, who had fished in vain all night, did not recognize Him. He said, "Cast your net on the right side" and when they did they gathered more fish than they were able to haul in. John said to Peter, "It is the Lord!" *Look who's here!*

The Emmaus disciples were trudging along homeward from Jerusalem. They were bemoaning the fact that it was the third day since Calvary. That was exactly the reason why they should have gone down the road with one foot saying, "Amen" and the other "Hallelujah!" because He had said He would rise on that day and they might meet Him at any turn of the road! They were right about it being the third day but wrong in their conclusion. One feels like saying to them, "It *is* the third day and look who is walking beside you. *Look who's here!*"

But we live in glass houses and cannot throw stones. Our Lord has said that where two or three gather in His name, He is there. What would happen if the average prayer meeting at church should ever take that seriously and believe it? Instead, we pray, "Lord, be with us" when He is already with us! Instead, we ought to shout, *"Look who's here!"*

Evan Roberts, God's spokesman in the Welsh revival, was fearful that the people might look to him instead of to the Lord. On one occasion he arrived late to where a throng had been waiting, as though he had to be present before anything much could happen. He asked the crowd, "Do you believe God is here as He promised when we gather in His name?" They shouted their agreement whereupon he put on his hat and coat and left! It was a dramatic way of saying that what matters is the presence of the Lord. In that great revival they had no advance publicity, no choirs, no song books, no order of service or offerings, no famous preacher (great preachers attended but they sat in the congregation). All they had in this revival was God. Maybe we'll get around to that some day again. Maybe sometime heaven will come down without our "packing the pew," pin-the-tail-on-the-donkey, talking horses, karate experts, and theatrical personalities. "Where my people gather in my name, there am I . . ."—that is not just a promise but a fact! It shouts, *"Look who's here!"*

What would happen if just for once we gathered believing that we were to experience the personal appearance of Jesus Christ? I have often been appalled by the careless and sometimes frivolous way church choirs often enter the sanctuary; they might as well be singing "Mary Had a Little Lamb." I have observed congregations that appear cold and casual, some more interested in who's wearing what than in the main event. And I have often been convicted in my own heart of the careless way I have sometimes entered the pulpit—taking for granted the fact that I am about to participate in the greatest kind of gathering possible to man. One should enter the pulpit as though it were the first time, as though it could be the best time, and as though it might be the last time!

God forgive us for gathering in His name, not expecting much to happen, praying for rain but not carrying our umbrellas. We pay church staffs to do church work and then assemble on Sunday to watch them do it! It is a performance, not an experience. When the preacher stands up to preach, the attitude is "All right, preacher, let's see what you've got." When he finishes we say in effect, "I move we accept this as information and be dismissed." No wonder we meet at eleven o'clock sharp and end at twelve o'clock dull.

In this day of standardized, systemized, and computerized business we Americans have become so proficient and efficient in our church work that we have only a small place left on the program for the supernatural and the miraculous. We seem not to need the Holy Spirit. We quote, "Not by might nor by power but by Thy Spirit," and sing, "Kindle a flame of sacred love in these cold hearts of ours," but like the Laodiceans, we are rich and increased with goods and have need of nothing. We are doing so well with our know-how, our expertise, that the good has become the enemy of the best and we are less and less open to divine invasion and intervention. We do not pray, "O that Thou wouldest rend the heavens and come down." We have little use for miracles. We begin to disbelieve them, even in the Bible. As a result, in our churches it is business as usual because we have no unusual business! We are doing much that could be done just as well in the civic club, the fraternal order, the political party. Ephesus may be sound in doctrine but has left her first love. Sardis may have a "name to be alive" but is dead (Rev. 3:1).

How are we going to regain that consciousness of God that makes the difference and is the evidence that we are the people of God who Moses prayed about long ago (Ex. 33:12-17)? Elijah demonstrated just that on Mount Carmel. He called for a confrontation—a confrontation must always precede divine visitation; he repaired the altar and prepared the sacrifice—it is useless to expect fire from heaven with an unprepared altar and an unprepared sacrifice; then he did something that has been given little attention—he poured twelve barrels of water on the sacrifice. There had been a three-year drought and water was the scarcest of commodities but Elijah poured out what was most precious to make it clear that if fire fell it must be from heaven. Today we try to warm up the altar as if to help matters and make it easier for God. It is the drenched altar that God sets on fire. When we are prepared to be called fools if nothing happens and venture everything in holy desperation the fire will fall and men will have to say, "The Lord, He is God. *Look who's here!*"

Our Lord has promised to be with us when we gather in His name (Matt. 18:20) and when we go with His gospel (Matt. 28:19-20). But some say, "I can't see Him." He said to Thomas, "Blessed are those who have not seen and yet have believed." Peter was there when he said it and later he wrote in his epistle, "Whom, having not seen ye love; in whom, though now ye see Him not, yet believing, ye rejoice with joy unspeakable and full of glory." It is that faith that shouts to this unbelieving world, *"Look who's here!"*

And one of these days, every eye shall see Him and all who are ready for that great day will go marching home, their troubles over, their questions answered, and their tears wiped away, caught up to meet the coming King. And it can all be summed up then in one mighty shout: *"Look who's here!"*

Brooks Hays
Presidential Message

For the fourth time in our 113 years the Convention assembles in the great city of Houston, yet the Southern Baptist Convention was nearly thirty years old before it conducted its first meeting in the Lone Star State in 1874, and the first west of the Mississippi River. There were only 222 messengers in attendance at that meeting which was held in the historic little town of Jefferson. In 1915, when Houston was experiencing growing pains this even more famous city was our host for the first time. Fourteen hundred and eight messengers were registered. The spirit of expansion was animating Southern Baptists, and eleven years later, when the second convention was held here, the registration was 4,268— three times that of the 1915 session.

In 1915 the Convention received gifts totaling $1,397,000, distributed as follows: The Foreign Mission Board, $537,000; the Home Mission Board, $459,000; and the Sunday School Board, $401,000. This year, the Cooperative Program alone will account for gifts and offerings in excess of $40 million for both state and SBC causes. In the eventful 43 years since Houston's first convention, Southern Baptists have experienced unprecedented growth and the assembling of a power and influence undreamed of by our founders in 1845.

Before sketching briefly some of my activities as your president, submitting some recommendations for you to consider, let me say a word of appreciation for the great honor you conferred upon me a year ago. To be president of this Convention is both an exciting adventure and an exalted privilege. I thank you from the bottom of my heart for this enriching experience and for the opportunity of Christian service which you have

Southern Baptist Preaching Yesterday

afforded me. I began attending Baptist conventions fifty years ago. In 1908 my mother took me to Fort Smith to the Arkansas State Convention and it made a lasting impression upon my boyish mind. I saw that great and stalwart Texas Baptist, Dr. J. B. Gambrell, on the platform and heard his pungent comments on Baptist service. Of course I never dreamed that one day my name would be listed a few lines below his among the Convention presidents. The first Southern Baptist Convention I ever attended was presided over by Dr. Gambrell in the city of Washington in 1920. As a Treasury Department clerk, attending law classes at night, I slipped away to one of the Convention meetings as an observer and was thrilled by what I saw and heard.

I wish to thank also our two vice-presidents, W. Douglas Hudgins and Noel M. Taylor, for their wonderful helpfulness during this busy year. You have been tolerant of my deficiencies during these twelve months. I have not been constantly aware of two things about my background that did not fit the usual pattern for the Convention presidency. I am a layman. Second, I am in the service of a government which is institutionally independent of all religious societies. In retrospect, I can say something with which I believe you will concur: To be a layman is not of itself a handicap. The rank and file of Baptist men in the South are conscious of the fact that the choice of a layman represented a drawing together of ministers and men—of the ordained and the unordained—and for this I am grateful. On occasions I have needed professional help, and always I have found it available in spontaneous and generous measure. I know that Baptist laymen would want me to say in their behalf that there is deep affection and admiration in their hearts for our dedicated ministers.

The Brotherhood which assembled 5,000 laymen in Oklahoma City last September will report upon that eventful meeting, but its significance should be noted also in this report. The influence for good which was generated there will continue through the years. I was pleased that the duties of Christian citizenship received attention there. Human government is making such an impact upon the daily life of every person, and has opened so many doors of opportunity for Christian service, as it supplies concurrently the test of moral fiber of men and nations, that there is a certain appropriateness in our reaching across the shadowy line that divides State and Church to proclaim in both forums, that all of life is subject to God's law and impressed with God's love.

The biggest event in our year, according to the Baptist editors, was the launching of our Jubilee program under the direction of my beloved predecessor, Dr. C. C. Warren, whose message you are eager to hear. I have tried to give full support to this great undertaking and to provide an accurate interpretation of it in my talks across the country. At one point I was able to devote a few minutes to the subject on a coast-to-coast TV program that would have cost us in excess of $30,000 had we been purchasing the time. I have not been timid is seizing publicity opportunities for our Baptist cause.

During the past twelve months, I have journeyed in the Convention's interest from Hamilton, Ontario, to Houston, and from Los Angeles to Moscow. I was able to attend five state conventions and innumerable local and district meetings. First in importance in the many tasks I have had was to participate in efforts to preserve our unity in a period of tension, to hold together our scattered congregations in this hour of the world's supreme need. A common faith continues to bind us together. Territorial expansion has, of course, produced interesting new diversities. The problems of California, for example, are quite different from those of our Georgia brethren. Social conditions surrounding Baptist workers in Louisiana vary greatly from those discovered by our representatives in the exciting new outpost in New York City. It is a great tribute to the skill of those who have fashioned this voluntary assembly called the Southern Baptist Convention and a confirmation of the soundness of the basic principles which underlie Baptist polity. Only in great flexibility can Christian fellowship be found in this complex Twentieth Century. Just as we have historically given allegiance to the idea that "at the frontier of the soul the power of every state must stop," so in the ecclesiastical world we insist that no Convention pronouncements bind the individual or the congregation. I do not imply, of course, that this relieves us of the necessity to seek and proclaim moral judgments produced by study, prayer and exchange of opinion, with the full utilization of modern facilities which this mighty organization has supplied. There should be no reluctance on our part to confront controversy, nor should Christians ever flee from the duty of examining differences. I have had some new exposures to this fact in my service as your president, and never before have I been so conscious of the need of seeking to do the will of God and discovering the mind of Christ. In a year of controversy I have been able to look up with deep gratitude to my brethren, both those who differ and those who agree with me, for having spoken the truth in love.

In the Houston convention of 1915 a committee known as the Efficiency Committee filed a report indicating that we mid-century Baptists are not the first to concern ourselves with the structure and organization of the convention. I commend to you the work of the Survey Committee. Without passing upon the merits of specific proposals, I do heartily express appreciation for the dedicated service of these men and women under the chairmanship of Douglas Branch. And whatever our final decision with regard to its recommendations, I trust that the report will be considered solely in the light of serving the total purposes of our Convention, and that local and personal interests will be secondary.

This activity of the Survey Committee is the kind of work that is never finished. It has to do with a job that, left undone, might finish us. It would be sinful for us to permit an unplanned, uncoordinated, sprawling organization to dissipate our energies and destroy our effectiveness. Consequently, I hope that continuing studies of our organizational arrangements may be authorized, preferably assigned to the reconstituted Executive Committee. We need to re-examine procedures by which convention policies are determined. It is difficult to achieve in an assembly of 10,000 or more the deliberative atmosphere and to follow democratic principles under rules devised for the smaller bodies which originated them.

I find in the minutes of the 1915 Houston convention a message from Negro Baptists, simultaneously holding their convention at Danville, Virginia. This message, coupled with a long and deeply moving report of our own 1915 convention's committee on work among Negroes, served to remind me that this task of helping the minority racial group is also a continuing one. Some of the tragic governmental conflicts involving race have obscured the fact that there are proven and accepted ways by which Southern Baptists may express their Christian concern for the minority's welfare and progress.

During my unforgettable evening with the Mississippi Baptists in their state convention, I heard reports of the work being done in that state in behalf of ministerial training for the Negroes. It was a splendid demonstration of what can be accomplished in that field. I am not suggesting, of course, that traditional methods will always suffice. It would be well for us to recognize that imagination must accompany our compassion.

One of my gratifying experiences was a visit to the American Baptist Theological Seminary in Nashville. The check for $500 which I handed to President Turner in behalf of an unnamed friend was a modest symbol of our interest in his institution.

It is not my purpose in this report to dwell upon the complexities of the problem of race or other social issues. I realize that we cannot have complete unanimity in these matters, but it would be tragic for us to assume that we can function as a Christian body without assigning to trusted representatives of the convention the task of pointing out our Christian duty with respect to social evils and current conflicts. The Christian Life Commission has a dual role to fill. It is authorized to speak for Southern Baptists where specific mandates are given, as in the case of legislation affecting advertising of alcoholic beverages and the suppression of obscene literature upon the newsstands of America. Equally important is its role of familarizing our people with problems of this nature, supplying counsel and advice on the subject as well as information on the scriptural teaching in specific areas, and to seek a sensitizing of the Christian conscience wherever evil, injustice and oppression exist anywhere in the world. The problems of environment must be considered—if for no other reason, because our institutional survival requires it. If Christian institutions are to be swallowed up in a pagan society, freedom will die and the opportunities for Christian service and the evangelization of the world will vanish. We shall continue to struggle for an incorruptible state and a Christian society—not to relieve ourselves of the obligations of Christian education, which equips the individual to meet the recurring temptations of life. We know that finally it will be not the absence of allurements in the world that redeems men, but the integrity that springs from transforming spiritual experiences. We owe it to our youth to improve their environment, but any young man is best fortified when, being nurtured by a powerful religious influence, he is able to purpose in his heart as Daniel did, not to defile himself. We seek not to dominate but to influence the state, and we will send our sons and daughters into the world with a sense of Christian vocation. The Christian and the patriot may dwell in the same heart, but only if the patriot acknowledges the universality of faith and love, and repels the chauvinist. The generosity with which we support our home and foreign mission programs testifies to our willingness to accept world responsibilities.

On Friday evening I shall have something to say about my trip to Moscow, a trip financed by the Foreign Mission Board—a sacred mission, perhaps the most solemn and important one I have ever undertaken. The promotion of peace presents a great challenge to Southern Baptists and we should officially and formally accept it. Consequently, I recommend that the convention authorize the appointment of a committee to report within a year on what Southern Baptists can do to promote peace and good will in the world.

I wish there were time to speak of many other things in which I have developed a great personal interest as I have pursued my duties as your president. I have visited every one of our great seminaries, and as my pride in these institutions has increased, the conviction has grown that ministerial education must have high priority in our activities. If time permitted, I would speak of the great significance of the new ministries of the church—of our ministry of healing, viewed with such warm approval by the medical profession; of the ministry of social service, building new techniques in a changing world; of the ministry of campus life, with spiritual adventures to match the intellectual requirements of our times; of the ministry in the prisons, where the need of man's compassion and God's grace is most poignantly exhibited.

One of the most inspiring experiences of the year was my visit to the grave of our beloved Dr. Truett. It was in the mood of rededication that I stood in silence, recalling some of the eloquent words I had heard him use. I learned first from him literature's most devotional lines outside the Bible, the moving words of St. Augustine, "Thou hast made me for thyself, and my soul will not rest until it rests, O God, in thee." I remembered how he warned against the pressures of materialism with a simple incident, the anonymous note handed to him: "Pray for a young man who is getting rich very fast." Prosperity is, comparatively, a new experience for Baptists. As we pray for a denomination that is getting rich very fast, may we determine to use our power with nobility and wisdom.

I recalled, too, the new resolutions that I had made as I heard him speak of our mission on this earth. God did not propose to detract, Dr. Truett said, from the critical importance of this earthly existence. In boyhood I had avoided confusion on this subject by assuming that when a minister said that I should despise the world he meant I should despise worldliness. The Bible told me that God loved the world, and I thrilled to the song "This Is My Father's World." So in Dr. Truett's words were confirmation of the idea that this world is a Christian's workshop.

I thought, finally, of the action in Chicago in the closing hours of the convention, when in response to the appeal of Dr. Paul Caudill we expressed the desire for a deepened spiritual life. Emphasis was given in that resolution to daily Christian living, to Bible reading, to the practice of prayer and spiritual growth. The qualities which are most essential to the Christian cannot be measured by statistics. They lie outside the domain of mathematics. But they may be felt, they may be expressed and they may be transmitted. Let us not tire of this pursuit, for finally the world's redemption rests upon it.

W. Douglas Hudgins
Look to the Rock

Look to the rock whence ye are hewn, and to the hole of the pit whence ye are digged" (Isa. 51:1).

We are entering upon a most significant year! This congregation will be recalling—I trust with significant meaning—the 125th year of its existence. On June 9 of this year the First Baptist Church of Jackson, Mississippi, will have been organized a century and a quarter. What spiritual potential can be marshalled if the anniversary year is utilized aright!

An anniversary observance can be a dry-as-dust formality or it can be a period in which our congregation can receive new enthusiasm, increased strength, deepened spiritual life, and invigoration for an enlarged program of responsibility for our God. Some people do not like to observe anniversaries—particularly birthday ones—because it is not especially pleasant to realize that time inexorably marches on. However, we miss many of the finer things of life if we are not willing to turn back the pages of history to see what may be revealed therein.

The Essayist Carlyle, in his "Latter Day Pamphlets," says: "All history . . . is an inarticulate Bible." The same writer, in his "Essays on History," says: "History is the essence of innumerable biographies." Schlegel, the German philosopher, says: "The historian is a prophet looking backward." Tacitus, writing long before either of them, said: "The principal office of history I take to be this: to prevent virtuous actions from being forgotten; and that evil words and deeds should fear an infamous reputation with posterity."

Approximately twenty-five centuries ago the Old Testament Prophet Isaiah urged upon captive Israel a contemplation of their history. Fearlessly exulting in the all-sustaining providence of the Almighty, he admonishes God's people to "Look to the rock whence ye are hewn, and to the hole of the pit whence ye are digged." He was calling on his hearers to look back—to reflect upon their heritage. Actually, Isaiah was urging his people to look back upon their history.

It is of the history of our Church we think today. It will be our heritage we will remember during this anniversary year. In some ways this history is "an inarticulate Bible." It is "the accumulation of innumerable biographies." It is "prophecy looking backwards." It is "to assure that virtuous actions shall not be forgotten." It is "that evil deeds, false words, and tragic mistakes may warn us in dangerous days ahead."

Our picturesque text for this morning is taken from the 51st chapter of Isaiah. In this section, most students believe, the stalwart prophet is talking to his people in the heartbreak of their national failure. God's people are defeated and enslaved. This tragic condition had been in the making for more than eighty years. It began when God was relegated to the background; when the supremacy of governmental control took precedence over individual responsibility; when materialism began its inroad against the spiritual faith of the people of God.

The nation's spiritual decay was accelerated when clashes arose between the priests and the people, tensions arose between groups, and when spiritual reality in God-fearing worship disappeared in the convenient compromise of a surface morality. At the time of our text dissolution had overcome Israel and the residue of a once great nation was cringing disconsolately in servile bondage. In such a crisis God's prophet cried: "Look to the rock whence ye are hewn, and to the hole of the pit whence ye are digged!"

We are beginning the fourth year in this "Decade of Destiny." I do not like to be classified as a pessimist or a prophet of doom, but the passing of these last three years has not dimmed in one whit my conviction that unless and until there is a stern turning upward of our moral integrity as a nation, we face, in the remaining seven years of this decade, the most difficult period in our national history. For—again let it be repeated—as it was stated three years ago at this time—the ten years of the sixties will determine—in this speaker's judgment—whether or not this beloved nation of ours will continue to afford freedom to its people and light to the confused of earth. This "Decade of Destiny" will demonstrate whether we will be a nation "whose God is the Lord," or a sensuous, self-indulgent, supercilious, satiated people, morally decadent and crumbling in moral character. We have not reached yet—and pray God we never shall—the depth of degradation and failure, the imprisonment and servitude, heartbreak and defeat that was Israel's; but I would observe with all the earnestness of my heart that if the spiritual trend in our nation continues as it has in the past, it is not beyond the realm of possibility that by the time 1970 comes we would be an enslaved and non-free people. We are deeply involved with adequate defenses against attack from without, but it appears to me that our nearly two hundred million people are not aware of the danger of decay from within!

We are thinking today of a Church, our Church! An institution individual in its democracy, indigenous in its organization, and subject in authority to no one save the Spirit of our God. It has existed here in our city for 125 years! On the 9th of this coming June we will celebrate the founding of the First Baptist Church in Jackson.

I shall not burden you with historical data today but we do recall that tradition says that early in the settlement of this community on LeFleur's Bluff, a square block was laid out for four Churches—one on each corner. These were, I am told, for the Methodist, Baptist, Presbyterian and Catholic congregations. Galloway Memorial Methodist Church still is located on the original site. By 1838 Baptists were able to organize a small congregation, the actual constituting of which is recorded to be in May of that year.

What a tremendous growth our city has had! For many years Jackson was not the largest city in Mississippi but in the last generation we have seen our capitol city outdistance all others in the State. In this year of 1963 a glance at our extended city limits, our many community centers, our public buildings, our office structures, our residential sections, our educational institutions, our churches, our industries, and our prosperous economy produces in all our hearts a deep sense of pride and gratitude to God for his blessings.

In this present moment of permissible pride in our city and Church, it seems to me that we would do well to "Look to the rock whence we are hewn, and the hole of the pit whence we are digged."

What was the picture in Isaiah's mind when he used this quaint expression hundreds of years ago? The "rock whence ye are hewn"—what did it describe? Very likely the prophet had in mind a stone quarry, one out of which a beautiful slab had been cut for the cornerstone of an imposing temple; or the feel of a chisel and mallet in the hand of a sculptor as he brought to life his concept of a great personality. This particular piece of stone would have been chosen out of all the rest—chosen by the purpose of the builder or artist that it might eventually serve his desire and plan. The complementary expression, "the whole of the pit whence ye are digged," carries the same idea. In the author's mind there is the ever-growing emptiness of the quarry. As the stone is mined, layer after layer reflects the shimmering sunlight of the changing seasons; and as its treasures yield to the labors of the workmen, the yawning chasm in the earth grows larger.

Thus, Isaiah admonishes Israel to look to the limitless reservoir of God's resources and remember that their father, Abraham, was the select stone chosen by God for the accomplishment of His purpose. Since the people were descendants of this chosen one they, too, were included in the Almighty's redemptive purpose for the world. They are reminded, also, that in the accumulating evidence of history they have been selected, mined, and utilized for a divine purpose. It is a quaint and picturesque figure of speech that the prophet uses but the meaning is unmistakable. "Look backward to your beginnings," he might have said, "and remember that you were chosen by the Eternal from all His treasured best to accomplish a divine purpose as the centuries since Abraham have unfolded." It was as if Isaiah were saying, "Remember your humble but God-directed beginnings. Reflect upon your past; consider your history; interpret your heritage; but let such strengthen you spiritually for the situation of the present."

Our beginnings as a Church were most humble and inauspicious but the charter members of that day in May, 1838, were, themselves, the stewards of a God-given heritage. Two hundred years of Christian responsibility and trusteeship lay behind them. God's purpose in the extension of the gospel story through a then adolescent nation could not be denied. They—and their fellow-Christians—could not escape it. For 125 years now we have continued what they began. But, God's purpose through the gospel remains the same—a vital witness to the saving power of His Son, the Lord Jesus Christ. Customs, costumes and conveniences have changed. Houses of worship have enlarged. Programs have been augmented. Organizations have been added. Personnel has been increased. But, the purpose of God is the same.

In Isaiah's day God's people miserably had failed him. Their sins were upon them but hope still flickered that the day might come when they could once more be instruments in God's redemption of mankind. Today we are lolling in comfort and convenience; we are monied and talented; we are casual and self-content. But, is it not more incumbent upon us in the wealth of our blessings to "look to the rock whence we are hewn"?

The prophet continues his admonition to Israel. "Jehovah shall be your comfort," he cries. Literally, "Jehovah shall speak to your hearts." Not to your minds, but to your hearts. O my brethren, we've had our heads spoken to long enough, we need our hearts to be touched! Somehow in our modern, scientific materialism our heads know more than our hearts have experienced! We need God once again to break through to our hearts!

A word of warning is uttered. "Attend unto me, O my people, and give me your ear, because I will establish my justice for a light to the nations." Then, in language more graphic than often realized, Isaiah says: "Remember, look upon the heavens, look upon the earth beneath; for the heavens shall vanish away like smoke, the earth shall grow old and wrinkled, and they that dwell therein shall die like flies."

It is almost unbelievable but Isaiah uses a word in this passage that strikes fear in every modern man's heart. When he says "the heavens shall vanish away like smoke," he uses a word which, if we translated it literally, would make him say, "the heavens shall be 'atomized' in a flash!"

Isaiah may have known nothing about the atom; he may have known nothing about nuclear fission; he may have known nothing about the missiles of the space age; but he did know about the purpose of God with men. As God had a purpose in selecting Abraham, as he had a purpose in the development of Israel, as he had a purpose in the gift of his Son, as he had a purpose in the establishment of the Church, as he had a purpose in the establishment of this congregation—so we have a conviction that he has a purpose with his people now.

This purposefulness involves us, in this day, and we cannot escape it. May we hear, on this first Sunday in our Anniversary Year, Isaiah say to us "Look to the rock whence ye are hewn, and to the hole of the pit whence ye are digged!"

E. S. James
The Invincible Gospel

Psalm 119:97-104; 1 Peter 1:24-25

How beautiful it is for the people of God to meet together in His house to sing so wonderfully and pray—to meditate about the eternal truth of the Scriptures. I want to read a word about them right out of the heart of the longest chapter of the Bible. Let us begin at the ninety-seventh verse of the 119th Psalm and read just a few verses:

"O how I love thy law! it is my meditation all the day. Thou through thy commandments hast made me wiser than mine enemies; for they are ever with me. I have more understanding than all my teachers: for thy testimonies are my meditation. I understand more than the ancients, because I keep thy precepts. I have refrained my feet from every evil way, that I might keep thy word. I have not departed from thy judgments; for thou hast taught me. How sweet are thy words unto my taste! yea sweeter than honey to my mouth! Through thy precepts I get understanding; therefore I hate every false way."

And then another from 1 Peter—the first chapter and the twenty-fourth and twenty-fifth verses:

"All the glory of man is as the flower of grass. The grass withereth, and the flower thereof falleth away: But the word of the Lord endureth forever. And this is the word which by the gospel is preached unto you."

It has been announced to you; and you know already that it was our hope today to talk with you about "The Invincible Gospel of Jesus Christ."

We talk a lot about invincibility, and maybe we need to remember just what it means. I understand that the term "invincible" means that which is not possible to defeat, that which could never possibly suffer failure. The gospel is simply the good news that through the death and resurrection of Jesus Christ it is possible for all who are dead in sin to rise and live forever with God and unto God.

So this morning I think it will help us to meditate upon the invincibility of that good news. In other words, this is the only thing that has ever come to the attention of man that is impossible of failure. We talk a great deal about the invincibility of things when they are not invincible at all.

Three hundred sixty-six years ago the world's greatest naval fleet of that hour sailed out of the ports of Spain. Protestants had taken over England. The Pope had spoken and commanded that Protestantism in England should be defeated forever. He called upon the government of Spain as he still does; and they built what they termed the "Invincible Armada." Three hundred ships left Spain on that morning, headed for the English Channel. They formed a crescent five miles long as they approached England. They called it "invincible," and it seemed invincible indeed; for no man had beheld a sight like that. But sometimes Providence interferes with man's plans and efforts at invincibility; and on that day the little British fleet under Drake and Forbisher met them out in the Channel and drove this "Invincible Armada" into the port of Calais—setting fire to the Spanish ships. Those that escaped made their way up the Channel into the North Sea where a terrible storm came upon them allowing only two or three of the ships to ever come back to Spain. Man's efforts at invincibility had become nothing but an idle dream.

A long time before that, in the days of the Persian monarchy, they talked about "The Law of the Medes and Persians that altereth not." Because he disobeyed the king's decree Daniel was cast into the lion's den, for the law had gone forth; and they said, "it cannot be altered." However, when the angel of God intercepted the unalterable decree of mortal man, then Daniel, who was to have been a prize for the lions, became the president of a world domain.

Just ten years ago now the German Wermacht was marching in every direction. They had come to the English Channel. France had been crushed. Their legions were marching across North Africa toward Alexandria, Egypt. Their mighty hordes were sweeping eastward across the western steppes of Russia; and the world said, "there has come at last an invincible military force that will never be stopped." However, when they were met by the courage of the Russians at Stalingrad, by the might of

Montgomery and the British in Africa, and by the intrepitude of Eisenhower and our boys in Normandy the mighty Wermacht of Germany was crushed completely and remains today only a memory of man's effort at invincibility.

Yes, the mighty hordes of communism have swept throughout the land of Asia—being stopped only at the thirty-eighth parallel in Korea and possibly at the eighteenth in Indochina. Millions of people are wondering if the hordes of communism are invincible and if this be something that just never can be stopped. I would encourage you to remember, young friends and older ones, that there is only one invincible thing in this world—that is the Word of God, "and this is the Word which by the gospel is preached unto you." "For all flesh is as grass, and all the glory of man as the flower of grass. The grass withereth, and the flower thereof falleth away: But the word of the Lord endureth forever. And this is the word which by the gospel is preached unto you."

I wish I might be able to say a word that would leave in the hearts of our young people and children a new realization that the Word of God never fails—that the cause of Christ is a victorious cause. Those of us who march under the banners of Calvary are headed for definite and certain victory; and in the Bible we have in our hands the only thing the world has ever known that will never suffer defeat. I wanted to make a few observations about this Bible.

The first one is that: *It has for its authority inspiration from God the Father.* The second thought is: *It has for its message salvation through God the Son.* The third thought is: *It has for its power, transformation through God, the Holy Spirit.* And the fourth: *It has for its promise victory through the churches and the kingdom of our Lord upon the earth.* Let us examine them one by one.

IT HAS FOR ITS AUTHORITY, INSPIRATION FROM GOD, THE FATHER. That's what it claims. "The Word of the Lord that cometh unto me." More than twenty-four hundred times it is said in the Bible, "This is the Word of the Lord," or "the Word of the Lord which came unto me." Quoting from Paul now, "I did not receive it; neither was I taught it but by the revelation of God," "All scripture is given by inspiration of God and is profitable." Peter wrote, "For the prophecy came not in old time by the will of man: but holy men of God spake as they were moved by the Holy Ghost."

But that isn't all. Its historical assertions are correct. For a long time the world has been saying, "You can't depend upon the historicity of the Bible." They say, "It may be correct in the historical assertions, or it may be wrong." I remind you that there is not an error historically within the covers of the Bible—not one. That's been proved anew. According to the *Reader's Digest* of a few months ago, the premier of present Israel is rebuilding the land of Palestine on the historical assertions of the Old Testament. In the Books of Kings and Chronicles we have the historical records of the Jews of old. There is found in those and in 1 and 2 Samuel all about Solomon's mines thousands of years ago; but those mines have been lost. During the past twelve months the engineers have gone back according to the location related in the Bible, and they have found the mines of Solomon. They have today access to enough tin to meet the needs of a new nation in Palestine. They have gone back to the historical assertions of the Old Testament relative to the portions of soil in Palestine that would grow and produce certain crops; and in the last few years they have found it to be exactly according to the statements in the Bible.

In 1917 General Allenby with his army was encamped at Michmash in Palestine to do battle with the Arabs and Turks. On the morrow there would be a great and decisive battle. The old Christian general that night sat in his tent. That word *Michmash* nearby came to his memory. He called for his Bible and found that near Michmash, long, long ago Jonathan and his armorbearer found a little mountain with a half-acre clearing on top, and there were two jutting rocks with a narrow passage. Jonathan and his armorbearer went through that passage and defeated the enemy. That same night the British Army found that mountain with a half-acre clearing and two jutting rocks with the narrow passage. They made their way through it, and the next day Palestine was won again to Christendom after more than a thousand years under the iron heel of the Muhammadans. There are so many similar illustrations in the Bible, but that one illustrates the fact that it must be the Word of God.

Not only that, but its scientific indications are evident. The Bible does not claim to be a treatise on scientific subjects, but there is no scientific error in it. A long time ago some men thought that maybe the world was round. Copernicus was one of them. Then Galileo invented the telescope and gazing out into space he said, "I know it is." In 1492 Columbus sailed westward and proved that it is. However, they hadn't discovered anything. Eight hundred years before Christ Isaiah, the prophet, said the world is round. He said, "[The Lord] sitteth upon the circle of the earth."

Less than twenty-five years ago those two men, that doctor and his son in Italy, went up fourteen miles into the stratosphere and came back to say: "It is dark out there. All space is filled with darkness." That wasn't any news. Even before Moses lived Job said, "The Lord hath swaddled the earth in darkness." When Jesus came He said of the unsaved, "[They] shall be cast into outer darkness: where there shall be weeping [and wailing] and gnashing of teeth."

We know now that through wind and rain and erosion by glaciers and by other acts of nature layer after layer of soil and rock have been carried into certain valleys and areas of the world. Men dig down so far and find the remains of mortal man. They dig deeper and find the remains of mammals and below that reptiles and fowls. Finally, below that they find the remains of life in the sea. They cry out, "Eureka, we have found the order of life upon the earth." They have not found anything. Thirty-five hundred years ago Moses sat on Mount Horeb and wrote those truths into the Book of Genesis. He told us that in the beginning God created life and put it in the water and that then He created the fowls of the air, the reptiles, the mammals, and finally man. Men are just discovering today fresh confirmation of the scientific criteria that are laid down in the Bible. They are there to remind you and me in this later day that this Bible is the Word of God—that it is the only invincible thing in all the world.

IT HAS FOR ITS MESSAGE, SALVATION THROUGH GOD, THE SON. The Bible tells us everything we need to know—not everything we want to know. The Bible is dealing expressly with one thing; and that is salvation for men through Jesus Christ, the Son of God. I spent a year on this to be sure I was correct in the statement that, salvation through Jesus is the theme of every book in the Bible; and I found that He was promised in its Genesis, provoked by its law, prefigured in its history, praised in its poetry, promised in its prophecy, provided in its Gospels, provided in its Acts, preeminent in its Epistles, and prevailing in its Revelation. I found to my own satisfaction that salvation through Him is the only message of the Bible. Book by book I searched and found that:

In Genesis He is the Prepared Sacrifice. In Exodus He is the Fountain of Life. In Leviticus He is the Bleeding Lamb. In Numbers He is the Brazen Serpent. In Deuteronomy Jesus is the Great Rock. In Joshua He is the Bridge Over Jordan. In Judges He is the Delivering Savior; and in Ruth He is the Faithful Bridegroom.

In 1 Samuel Jesus is the Great Judge. In 2 Samuel He is the Princely

King. In 1 Kings He is David's Choice. In 2 Kings He is the Holiest of All. In 2 Chronicles Jesus is King by Birth. In 1 Chronicles He is King of Punishment. In Ezra, Jesus is the Authenticated Writer. In Nehemiah He is the Builder. In Esther He is the Avenger. In Job He is the Daysman. In Psalms He is the Good Shepherd. In Proverbs Jesus is the Epitome of Wisdom. In Ecclesiastes He is the Great Preacher. In the Song of Solomon He is the Great Church Lover.

In Isaiah He is the Suffering Savior. In Jeremiah He is the Redeemer of Israel. In Lamentations He is the Weeping Son of Man. In Ezekiel Jesus is the Glorious God. In Daniel He is the Reigning Prince. In Hosea He is the Mislaid Christ. In Joel He is the Judging Christ. In Amos, Jesus is the Eternal Christ, and in Obadiah He is the Forgiving Christ.

In Jonah He is the Controlling Christ; in Micah the Authoritative Christ; in Nahum the jealous Christ; and in Habakkuk the Spiritual Christ. In Zephaniah He is the Merciful Christ; in Haggai the Resting Christ; in Zechariah the Returning Christ; and in Malachi the Humiliated Christ.

In Matthew Jesus is the Fulfillment of Prophecy: in Mark the Militant Leader; in Luke the Universal Teacher; and in John He is Love Incarnate. In Acts He is the Impelling Force; and in Romans He is the Reconciler. In 1 Corinthians He is the Resurrection. In 2 Corinthians He is the Comforter. In Galatians Jesus is the Indwelling Savior. In Ephesians He is the Head of the Church. In Philippians He is the Believers' Pattern, and in Colossians He is the Exalted Prince. In 1 Thessalonians He is the Believer's Hope. In 2 Thessalonians Jesus is the Victorious Lord. In 1 Timothy He is the Preacher's Friend, and in 2 Timothy He is the Lord of All Life.

In Titus He is the Cleansing Lamb, in Philemon the Great Liberator, in Hebrews the Great High Priest, and in James the Brother of Man. In 1 Peter He is the Vicarious Sufferer, and in 2 Peter He is the Long-suffering Savior. In 1 John He is Man's Advocate, in 2 John He is the Truth of God, in 3 John the Stranger's Friend, in Jude the True Teacher, and in the Revelation He is the Final Consummation of Every Thing. That's the message of the Bible—salvation through Jesus, The Son of God.

THEN IT HAS FOR ITS POWER, TRANSFORMATION THROUGH THE HOLY SPIRIT. This Bible transforms continents. They talk of the fact that South America is behind North America because they thought the colonists of North America were looking for God while in South America they were looking for gold. I think that is an error. They were looking for God and gold in both Americas. The difference is that in South America the priests of Rome came with the Bible closed; and in North America Protestant ministers came with the Bible open. Today South America is just as rich in mineral. Its soil is just as productive. Its people are just as intellectual as we; but it is far, far behind our North America; and the difference lies in the place given to the Bible, for the open Bible will transform continents.

About one hundred and seventy years ago Voltaire, the philosopher, said to France: "We do not need the Bible. I give you a new philosophy of atheism." France swallowed it. Russia borrowed it through the office of Catherine the Second, their Queen. From that moment onward the French walked the downward trail until the scaffold of Louis was erected. The guillotine took the place of human judgment, and for 100 years even unto now France has been reaping from her folly. Those seeds of atheism lay buried in Russia until 1917 when they burst in all of their fury in the Red Revolution that has led to the communist state in most of Asia today.

At that very time, during Voltaire's influence in France, a few brave colonial fathers met in Independence Hall and declared the independence of a new nation. Thirteen years later they laid the framework of a constitutional government. They built a government upon the principles of an open Bible. America is not perfect. We are far from perfect; but America is the hope of the ideals of Western democracy today simply because of the influence of the Bible upon her life.

It will transform a country or continent or a city. I remember when Borger advertised for a preacher. They said, "This oil field community has gone wild, and we can not live here." In response a preacher with a Bible under one arm and hymnal under the other went. Some fine laymen, one of whom sits in our presence, went with their money to help build some churches. They opened the Bible; and Borger, Texas, today is a community of which its citizens are justly proud. The Bible has made it over.

The Bible will transform your home. The Invincible Word and the Holy Spirit will solve your home problems; and this Invincible Word will solve the problems of an individual life.

A little girl stood on a street corner playing a battered old violin. She couldn't play. She was begging for help, and passersby would drop in a little coin and hurry on. One day a stranger came and picked up the battered and marred and worn violin. He tuned it, tightened the bow, and as he drew it across the strings, the people stopped in wonderment. They had never heard such music on that corner before. It was the same old violin and the same old bow, but it was in the hands of a master now. Paganini now held the violin. There is many a battered, marred, disfigured life—almost ruined. The Word of God can change that life into a thing of beauty forever. When the Master takes hold of you and the Word of God finds entrance into your heart it will change you under the power of the Holy Spirit.

The last thought relative to its invincibility is that: IT HAS FOR ITS PROMISE, VICTORY FOR THE PEOPLE OF GOD. Christians talk too much about defeat. Jesus did not. He never used terms that indicated He expected to be defeated or that He thought maybe the day would come when righteousness would cease and His churches would fail. He didn't talk like that, and neither should we.

The battle is long, and it is hard. It's been going all these centuries between God and Satan, between right and wrong, between goodness and evil. It's a long, hard battle. Sometimes the sign of victory is bedimmed by the clouds of evil, error, sin, and trouble. However, Jesus Christ is carrying the banner. Jesus is the Victor, and He has promised victory unto His own; for the Bible says the hour will come when, "Every knee [shall] bow; . . . and every tongue [shall] confess that Jesus Christ is Lord, to the glory of God, the Father." So, we shall not fail.

There are so many enemies against us; but despite the fighting legions on the outside, fifth columnists on the inside, filthy fortunes on the top-side, and foolish fanaticism on the bottom side we are still a victorious army. This Sword of the Spirit is invincible. It can never suffer defeat.

Around us we see the picture, and it looks dark. Atheism is advertised. Wickedness is publicized. Government is subsidized. Armies are mobilized. Education is secularized. Liquor is legalized. Prostitution is publicized. Immorality is glamourized, and hell is oversized to take care of them; but the victory is ours yet. This is an invincible gospel. It will never know defeat. "The Word of the Lord endureth forever, And this is the word which by the gospel is preached unto you."

Outside the realm of Christendom—outside the Christian camp—are armies of nationalism, the curse of communism, the wiles of Romanism, and the vultures of expansionism; but we are not defeated yet.

Even inside our camp there are compromisers, unionizers, moderniz-
ers; and there are demonizers. Some of our people hesitate and some
vacillate, while some stagnate. We haven't lost the battle. This Word of
the Lord endureth forever and it will never know defeat.

The climax of the battle has already been reached. There has always
been a battle between right and wrong, and it will continue to the end; but
the climax was reached when Jesus went to the cross. There in a single
day the storms of the ages rolled in upon Him. Ah, there was a little while
when heaven and earth seemed a long, long way apart. Suspended on a
cross between them was the lifeless form of the Son of God. There for
three days hope seemed buried and victory an idle dream. Jesus Christ
lay buried in a human grave. However, He came out of that grave. He
stood alive upon the earth and gave this message to His people. He said,
"Go out with it and win the whole world unto me. I'll be right by your side
to the end of the conflict."

We have had some great statesmen but probably no greater than Woodrow Wilson. After the first war, he stood in the National Capitol on Armistice Day and made this speech. He said, "History grows weary as it
endeavors to pen the lives of those who have dashed themselves to
pieces in opposition to the inevitable. It required centuries of incessant
fighting to wring the Magna Charta from the hands of kings. Despite the
efforts of the Bourbons to keep the French in the dust the scaffold of
Louis was erected, and all France was swept into the whirlwind of red
terror. Despite the efforts of the Hanovers to hold the American colonies
in thrall and check the onsweep of freedom, this great American republic
today attests to the fatuous dreaming of George III. For more than a thousand years the kings of the earth outfaced destiny in their opposition to
Jesus Christ. Every onward step of Christianity has been marked by the
blood of martyrdom; but in spite of the wild beasts of the arena, in spite of
rack and faggot, in spite of unexampled massacre the cross looks up today everywhere; and a hundred million voices are lifted in praises that
reverberate around the world."

Evil and error do hold within themselves the seed of their own undo-
ing. Someday they will die; but all the powers ever possessed by man can
never check nor kill the onsweep of God's Own Eternal Truth. One might
more easily put a halter upon the wind or check the tide of the dashing
ocean than stay the progress of the Word of God.

"All flesh is as grass, and all the glory of man as the flower of grass. The grass withereth, and the flower thereof falleth away; but the word of the Lord endureth forever; and this is the Word which by the gospel is preached unto you." Amen.

Jesus Christ, the Message of Each Book in the Bible

[These are the Scripture references mentioned in the statement that "Salvation through Jesus is the theme of every book in the Bible." Dr. James said, "I spent a year to be sure I was correct."]

Book	Christ Presented	Chap.-Verse	Confirmed By
Genesis	Prepared Sacrifice	22:8	John 1:36
Exodus	Fountain of Life	17:6	1 Cor. 10:4
Leviticus	Bleeding Lamb	16:15-16	Rev. 13:8
Numbers	Brazen Serpent	21:8	John 3:14
Deuteronomy	Great Rock	32:31	1 Pet. 2:7-8
Joshua	Bridge Over Jordan	3:17	John 8:51
Judges	Delivering Savior	2:18	1 Thess. 1:10
Ruth	Faithful Bridegroom	4:10	Matt. 25:10
1 Samuel	Great Judge	2:25	Acts 10:42
2 Samuel	Princely King	5:3	Acts 13:22-23
1 Kings	David's Choice	1:29-30	Matt. 22:44
2 Kings	Holiest of All	19:22	Luke 1:35
1 Chron.	King by Birth	29:20	Matt. 2:2
2 Chron.	King of Punishment	18:19-21	2 Thess. 1:8-9
Ezra	Authenticated Writer	7:25-26	Luke 22:37
Nehemiah	The Builder	6:16	Matt. 16:18
Esther	The Avenger	9:12-19	2 Thess. 1:8
Job	The Daysman	9:33	2 Tim. 2:5
Psalms	The Good Shepherd	23:1	John 10:11
Proverbs	Epitome of Wisdom	4:7	Col. 2:3
Eccl.	The Great Preacher	1:1	Matt. 4:17
Song of Sol.	Church Lover	2:2	Eph. 5:25
Isaiah	Suffering Savior	53:3-9	Mark 15:24-37
Jeremiah	Redeemer of Israel	3:14	Rom. 11:26
Lam.	Weeping Son of Man	3:48	Luke 19:41
Ezekiel	The Glorious God	1:26	Rev. 19:16
Daniel	Reigning Prince	9:24	Rev. 20:4

Hosea	Mislaid Christ	8:14	Matt. 15:6
Joel	Judging Christ	1:15	John 5:22
Amos	Eternal Christ	4:13	John 1:1
Obadiah	Forgiving Christ	1:17	1 John 1:9
Jonah	Controlling Christ	2:1-10	Matt. 8:27
Micah	Authoritative Christ	4:1-3	Matt. 28:18
Nahum	Jealous Christ	1:2	1 Cor. 10:22
Habakkuk	Spiritual Christ	3:4	2 Cor. 10:4
Zephaniah	Merciful Christ	3:17	Heb. 2:17
Haggai	Resting Christ	2:4	Heb. 4:10
Zechariah	Returning Christ	14:5	John 14:3
Malachi	Humiliated Christ	3:1	Mark 15:16-20
Matthew	Fulfillment of Prophecy	2:5	Gen. 3:15
Mark	Militant Leader	2:15	Rev. 19:14
Luke	Universal Teacher	19:47	2 Chron. 6:27
John	Love Incarnate	3:16	Titus 3:4
Acts	Impelling Force	1:8	Acts 8:39
Romans	The Reconciler	5:10	2 Cor. 5:20
1 Cor.	The Resurrection	15:22	Rev. 20:12
2 Cor.	The Comforter	1:4-5	John 14:18
Galatians	Indwelling Savior	4:6	1 John 4:12
Ephesians	Head of the Church	5:23	1 Cor. 11:3
Philippians	Believer's Pattern	2:5	John 13:15
Colossians	Exalted Prince	1:17-19	Heb. 1:3-4
1 Thess.	Believer's Hope	1:10	Col. 1:27
2 Thess.	Heavenly Victor	1:8	Rev. 20:10
1 Timothy	Preacher's Friend	1:11	John 3:29
2 Timothy.	Faithful Lord	4:8	Rev. 19:11
Titus	Cleansing Lamb	3:5	1 John 1:7
Philemon	Great Liberator	1:8-10	John 8:36
Hebrews	Great High Priest	6:20	Heb. 7:24
James	Brother of Man	1:9	Heb. 2:17
1 Peter	Vicarious Sufferer	3:18	1 Tim. 3:16
2 Peter	Long-suffering Savior	3:9	Rom. 2:4
1 John	Man's Advocate	2:1	Heb. 7:25
2 John	Truth of God	1:1-4	John 14:6
3 John	Stranger's Friend	1:5-8	Prov. 18:24
Jude	True Teacher	1:3	Matt. 28:20
Revelation	Final Consummation	1:4-8	1 Cor. 15:24-26

C. Oscar Johnson
A Light in the Valley

Even though I walk through the valley of the shadow of death, I will fear no evil; for thou art with me (Ps. 23:4, RSV).

Even the darkness is not dark to thee, the night is bright as the day (Ps. 139:12, RSV).

But the path of the righteous is like the light of dawn, which shines brighter and brighter until full day (Prov. 4:18, RSV).

It is amazing to me as I consider how brief is the memory we have of those who yesterday seemed so absolutely necessary to the life that we live and the work that we carry on. The newspaper tells us the story of the serious illness of someone; it announces his death and the hour of the funeral, then reports a few remarks at the service. How amazing it is that all of this quickly fades out of the type in the newspaper and out of the memory of most people.

That is true as you observe it in connection with the people you know, and to be perfectly honest, it will be true of us. I suppose that it is good that it is that way. If we spent our time and energy in bringing up the memories of the past, weeping over them, and neglecting to do our work while we yet live, we would not be honoring our beloved dead. The way to honor them is to remember them but be busy about the worthy things to which they gave their lives.

Many years ago people used to ask funny little riddles. Some young chap came up to me and said, "Do you know something God can't do?" You had better be careful of these youngsters, for you have no idea what they are going to say or do. I said, "I can't think right now. Is there something God can't do?"

He said, "Yes."

I asked, "What is it?"

He said, "Make two mountains without a valley."

I do not know any life that has always been lived on the mountaintop, do you? Has yours? I sometimes think that most of the people I know spend most of their time in the valley. Just once in a while do they ever get up on a mountaintop. They are down in the fog somewhere, groping their way along the misty flats covered with clouds.

A doctor told me just this past week that a woman came to him with her troubles. Whatever the trouble was, the doctor said she was terribly upset, and she said, "I don't know what I am going to do. I am in deep trouble."

The doctor saw that the woman was very tense, so he said, "Let's just hold hands and jump out of this window together." That was a good way to answer that lady, as he found out later.

She laughed and said, "That would be silly, wouldn't it?"

He said, "The truth is, I think I know what to do."

Many times people can't find any light in the valley, and they do not find any strength to get up where they can see a little better. So much of our lives are spent in the valley. And if that is the way it is going to be, does it mean that he who made the mountains has forgotten the valley and is going to leave it dark and dismal because a lot of people are traveling there? Mountain climbing isn't easy, and there comes a time when we all will make our little journey down into the valley.

One of the first male quartets I ever heard sang that old song, "We Are Going Down the Valley One by One." That has a rather sad implication— "going down the valley one by one . . . going toward the setting of the sun." Billy Sunday said, "Don't throw away your ticket when the train goes into a tunnel; it will come out on the other side." We have people who delight in living in the valley. I am glad I don't have to think about my parents and sister and all those who have gone on before and weep about them. Paul said we should not weep as those who have no hope.

A Light in the Valley

I don't deny the valley. It is cloudy and dark down there, but, thank God, there is a light in the valley. We need a light when it gets foggy and dark. We feel somehow that these valleys are filled with ghosts, and there is fear lurking because we can't see very well. The farther we get in the valley, the more tense and anxious we become.

How many times have you read the twenty-third Psalm? I have read and recited it so many times. I love it, as you do. Not until last week did I read it slowly enough to get that which I hadn't seen in it before. That is the wonderful thing about this Book. You can read it over and over, and each time some new facet of truth comes which you didn't see before.

Here is the verse I read to you a moment ago. "Even though I walk through the valley . . ." Now, a lot of people stay there. There was a valley of dry bones in the Old Testament, but we go through this valley. "Even though I walk through the valley of the *shadow* of death . . ." I had never noticed particularly that word "shadow." We say death is the real thing; it is a monster; it is real. However, David said, "I walk through the valley of the *shadow* of death."

I said, "That is good. To a child of God death is only a fleeting shadow." I watched the shadow of the fast-moving plane as we were landing recently. How rapidly we moved, and suddenly we were in a cloud, and the shadow of the plane was gone. But the plane was still there, and I was on it. The shadow of death! I can tell you that there is a light in the valley, and David said, "I will fear no evil, for thou art with me."

One of the most evil things I know about some Christians is their conception of what they have the right to claim as children of God. When some loved one, like your mother or mine, is called home, we must face it like Christians, not as those who have no hope. Fear seems to lurk in this valley, even for Christian people. All of my ministry I have been trying to eliminate that from the minds of people.

"I will fear no evil." I think we are coming to a time when we are going to be more Christian. I have been in lands beyond the sea and have seen funeral services conducted there. If there was enough money, the relatives would hire mourners, and the louder they mourned, the more pay they received. At one funeral service I saw on Okinawa someone with considerable means was being buried and fifty mourners had been hired. However, in our own so-called Christian land I have seen almost as much of a demonstration of the lack of faith.

I do not understand the coming of Jesus if, when he told the disciples not to let their hearts be troubled, he did not mean to let them know that he was taking that fear away from them. I understand that he went into that tomb, which was a valley of darkness, and there seemed to be no light in it. The soldiers sealed it up, but they didn't keep out the light, because the light of God came down and filled the place and drove out the darkness forever for those who believe in Christ. "Let not your heart be troubled: ye believe in God, believe also in me. In my Father's house are many rooms: if it were not so, I would have told you. I go to prepare a place for you. And if I go and prepare a place for you, I will come again, and receive you unto myself; that where I am, there ye may be also" (John 14:1-3).

The Light Within

The light in the valley is within us. Jesus said, "I am the water of life," but he also said, "I am the light of the world." In John we read, "There is that light that lights every man as he is coming into the world." Jesus also said that if we would open the door, he would come in and sup with us.

If Jesus is the light of the world, when he comes into a human heart, that heart has a light within. When you walk into that valley of darkness, if Jesus, the Light of the world, has been received into your heart, then the radiance from within drives the darkness out. I don't see why we get so discouraged and linger so long and hopelessly in the valley. There is a light within if we have Christ. He is the Light of the world, and if we have him, we have Christ and God, his Father—our Father. Therefore, when we go through this valley, we go through with him who is the Light.

He is the Light of life. He said that he will light our pathway. He lights us along the journey, and when we come to the valley, we go through it, following along with the light that is within us and around us as our guide.

The Light of His Presence

When Jesus was here on earth, he could be with the disciples personally. They could see him and understand him. When they had a trial, they could talk to him. You will recall that there were some of his disciples down at the foot of the mountain trying to heal a sick boy, but they couldn't do it. When Jesus came down from the mountaintop, the man ran to him to say of his son, "I brought him to your disciples, and they could not heal him" (Matt. 17:16, RSV). These disciples later asked Jesus why they could not perform this miracle. His answer was, "This thing cometh forth only by prayer and fasting."

What became of the Light after the ascension? Where did the Light go? Some people act as if they thought the Light never appeared again. I would invite you to tarry a while in the upper room at Jerusalem. Ten days after the promise had been made, there came in that room a sound as of a rushing, mighty wind. It was not a rushing, mighty wind; it sounded like one. "And there appeared unto them cloven tongues like as of fire, and it sat upon each of them. And they were all filled with the

Holy Ghost" (Acts 2:3-4). To everyone who received him there came the light that God had promised. That day the Holy Spirit came to represent Christ, and he is now the oil in your lamp when you go through the valley. This Light lighteth every man, not only as he comes into the world but through his life, through the valley, and on to where Jesus said, "I go to prepare a place for you."

How very wonderful is that place he has prepared for those that love him and have accepted him. An Italian Christian lad was selling papers in New York, and when a gentleman bought a paper, he said, "My, but it is a bitter cold day!" As the Italian lad made change, he said, "Yes, but by-and-by, think of that."

A newsboy in Boston, selling his papers, addressed a man, saying, "Paper, mister?" Phillips Brooks had just passed by and purchased a paper from the boy. The man said, "Mighty cold day, isn't it?" The boy said, "Yes it *was* until Mr. Brooks came by." A light that God has put in us—the light of the Holy Spirit who is the oil in our lamps, the never-exhausted supply which God gives to light us on our way—burns brightly until the end of the perfect day. Yes, there is a light around us in the person of the Holy Spirit. We need to be assured of his presence today.

Some years ago a motorist was going through a valley out west, and the roads were rough and narrow, and there were detours. Finally, the man came to a homestead and asked the owner how he might get to the good road. He gave this very strange answer.

He said, "Go right down here to the end of the lane, turn to the left, and you will come to the cemetery. Pass right through the cemetery, turn to the right, and in a few yards you will find the highway, which is as smooth as glass, and your troubles will be over."

Good instructions! Go right through the cemetery. Some people say that Jesus went into the grave and came out of the grave. I like to think that he passed through the grave. He passed *through* death. He was journeying, and this little tunnel was merely along the way, and he went through it. "Yea, though I walk through the valley of the shadow of death, I will fear no evil."

The preparation we make if we want a light in the valley is to receive that Light into our own hearts. Without that, I doubt if you can see the path, even though there are bright lights burning. We must have the light within if we are prepared to go through the valley to the other side. This

Light in the valley is for us, and it is for all of those who want at last to come out on the other side to the place which the Lord has prepared.

How I thank God for the ability of my father and mother to say long years ago, "Our children are all in." That is a great joy as you enter the valley. There is a Light in the valley for those who are approaching that opening that leads through the valley to the hills of God. Do you have that Light?

Leon Mobley Latimer
Divinely Commissioned

It is fitting in this opening session of our annual convention that we pause to remind ourselves why we are here. The constitution of this body, in the second section of the first paragraph, declares that, "The object of this convention shall be to furnish a medium of cooperation for the Baptist churches of Georgia in their *Divinely Commissioned* work of missions, education, and benevolence." It is not my intention tonight to discuss these three comprehensive types of work carried on by this body, our order of business for two days will be devoted to that, but it is my purpose to focus attention upon the supremely important statement in this declaration of object that we have a divinely commissioned task.

Surely nothing could so solemnize us for the serious business of this convention and nothing could send us back to our work with a more compelling urge to greater achievement for our blessed Lord than a quickening of our sense of divine mission. It was precisely this conviction that was the great dynamic of the early disciples and the great Christian leaders throughout the centuries. Certainly no one has more clearly and forcefully declared this mighty truth than did Paul in his inspiring word to the Ephesians which is our text tonight:

"For we are His workmanship, created in Christ Jesus for good works, which God afore prepared that we should walk in them" (Eph. 2:10). This text raises four vital questions about our subject.

Created in Christ Jesus

First, who are Divinely Commissioned? Those who are created anew in Christ Jesus, the redeemed. *"For we are His workmanship, created in*

250

Christ Jesus." Paul makes it clear in the first verse of this epistle to the Ephesians that the message of this letter is not directed to the world, but to the regenerated: "To the saints (consecrated to God) who are at Ephesus, and to the faithful in Christ Jesus."

The Apostle is ever zealous to safeguard and keep clear fundamental truth, so here in the text he reiterates first of all, the essential preparation for the Divine Commission: "We are His workmanship," not mere products of human culture, not merely reformed men, not merely self-cleansed by new resolutions but, "created in Christ Jesus," made new by the Grace of God. Such are the Divinely Commissioned.

The Bible recognizes that God sometimes uses unregenerate man to accomplish His holy purpose, and even makes the wrath of man to praise Him, but it also makes clear that to bring in His Kingdom, Christ is counting on His Divinely Commissioned, redeemed children. It was to His own disciples in the upper room that He said: "As the Father hath sent me, even so send I you." And again it was to the disciples that He gave the great commission: "Go ye into all the world, and preach the gospel to every creature."

It is not strange that the Master thus committed His message to His disciples rather than to the world, or, even to the angels in Heaven for who could so bear witness to a redemptive gospel as redeemed man? And it is ours to declare everywhere that Heaven's supreme plan, and the only adequate remedy for the healing of the nations is the making of new creatures in Christ Jesus.

I confess that I have not always had the deep unclouded conviction on this truth that is mine tonight. I began my ministry with a passion for the social gospel and I preached it with great ardor. I still believe it and preach it, because I am convinced that applied Christianity is one of the needed points of emphasis in all of our Christian teaching. However, my early passion for the social gospel led me to devote most of my time to exploiting social and economic problems of the day and I was primarily concerned with applying the principles of Christianity to the evils of our social order. But my emphasis on abstract principles and general problems did not satisfy my own heart nor meet the deepest needs of my people. It was then that it became clear to me that the New Testament solution of every problem is the bringing of the sinning soul face to face with the sufficient Saviour.

No prophetic voice can ignore the social sins which broke the hearts and loosened the tongues of the prophets of ancient Israel. Those social sins are present, in changing garb, in every age, and will ever need to be pointed out and condemned. No man ever attacked the hypocrisy and wrongs of his day more fearlessly and relentlessly than did our Lord. We thank God that He has been the inspiration and His words have been the two-edged swords of the great reformers for two thousand years, and yet the center of Christ's attack was not the evils of His day, but the hearts of the evil doers.

This was the mighty truth which Nathaniel Hawthorne made vivid seventy-five years ago in his graphic parable of the "Earth's Holocaust." With daring imagination, Hawthorne pictures the blotting out of all of the evils of the world by the combined work of all the reformers and Utopian dreamers of the ages. On a vast plain they assemble in one gigantic bonfire everything to be found in the world which is evil, or, has been used for evil purpose. They bring the crowns and scepters of the tyrants, all the instruments of oppression and cruelty ever used, all the alcoholic liquors which have cursed mankind, all the weapons and munitions of war, all the gew-gaws of fashion, and everything else which would mar a perfect world. And as the flames of the mighty bonfire reach their height, the devil laughs to scorn the whole enterprise.

"There's one thing," he said, "that these wiseacres have forgotten to throw into the fire, and without which all of the rest of the conflagration is just nothing at all; yes, though they had burned the earth itself to a cinder."

"And what may that be?" eagerly demanded the last murderer.

"What but the human heart itself?" declared the devil.

Though all the evils of the world were blotted out, the unchanged human heart would bring them all back again. So Jesus went immediately to the center of things and to the solution of every problem of evil when He said, "Ye must be born again." We go nowhere if we do not start here.

Therefore, in our text, Paul begins with the fundamental fact of the new birth: "For we are His workmanship, created in Christ Jesus." This redemption through Christ constitutes not only the ground of our hope but lays upon us the obligation to accept unreservedly the Divine Mission which He laid as definitely upon us as upon the disciples who heard Him, when He said: "As the Father hath sent me, so send I you." Therefore, the Georgia Baptist Convention, affirming its faith in the New Testament principle of a regenerate church membership, takes its authority from the

Master Himself when it declares that we are a Divinely Commissioned people. If any have no sense of mission, they may well question whether they have the prerequisite for it, the new life in Christ Jesus.

For Good Works

Second, why are we Divinely Commissioned? "For we are His workmanship, created in Christ Jesus *for good works*."

When Paul says that we are "created in Christ Jesus for good works" he is not speaking of the price of our redemption, but the fruitage of it. The Apostle to the Gentiles has been so recently rescued from the bondage of the law with its endless rounds of petty performances that he takes extra precaution to make clear the place of works in the new life in Christ Jesus. Therefore, in the two verses preceding our text, Paul declares, "By grace are ye saved, through faith: and that not of yourselves, it is the gift of God: not of works lest any man should boast."

If any man ever had ground for confidence in his ancestry, training, and conformity to the demands of the law, Paul says, "I more." But all these things he counted but refuse when he found Christ. He had found through bitter, disappointing experience, the emptiness and futility of "the righteousness which is of the law." No man ever condemned the works of the law, its endless ceremonies, its petty rules for cleansing, fasting and Sabbath observance, as did Paul. And likewise no man ever preached more emphatically the duty of the redeemed to bear fruit, nor laid out his life, full length, in more consecrated service to Christ than did the great Apostle to the Gentiles.

In our repudiation of the false doctrine of salvation by works, whether they be ceremonies, sacraments, or a mere endless round of activities, let us be as guarded as Paul that we do not encourage the paralyzing heresy of indifference and do-nothingism. The Apostle was keenly aware of the peril here, so when he warns that salvation is "by grace," "not of works," he hastens in the next sentence to declare that the divine purpose of our recreation in Christ Jesus is "for good works," the fruitage of the regenerated life.

And what are these good works which God is expecting of His Divinely Commissioned Georgia Baptists? Our constitution declares that it is cooperation together in carrying forward the work of missions, education, and benevolence. I said in the beginning that I would leave it to the convention to discuss these specific fields of service but I cannot pass this point without just a word of endorsement of this great cooperative program of our Lord.

First there is the task of missions. We thank God tonight for Christ's missionary commission, which beginning in every church of the convention extends out through the local field, the association, the state, the homeland, to earth's remotest bounds; embracing every lost man, woman, and child in all the world. We accept Christ's mandate, "The field is the world," but we need the passion that Paul had when he said to the Ephesians, "Remember that for the space of three years I ceased not to warn every one night and day with tears."

Then there is education. A program which not only takes in our seminaries and training schools, but also embraces junior and senior colleges, schools with the Christian perspective. May they never be like some institutions of our materialistic age which well might emblazon on their coat of arms the motto of the old Roman coin which bore a picture of the "Pillars of Hercules" and carried underneath the inscription, "Ne plus ultra," no more beyond. We want teachers and education that mould life and character in the light of the "more beyond." An education so Christian that it will stamp indelibly upon the youth of our churches whom we commit to them for a season, the profound conviction that whatever their calling, be it medicine, law, business, mechanics, farming, teaching, preaching, or what not, they are to enter it with a sense of divine mission. "For we are His workmanship, created in Christ Jesus for good works which God afore prepared that we should walk in them." I am happy to believe that Georgia Baptists have such schools, worthy of such support as we have never given them.

Then there are our benevolences, whose loving ministries are like those in the daily life of our Lord. As we think of our orphans at Hapeville, we think of Him who said, "Suffer the little children to come unto me for of such is the Kingdom of Heaven." As we think of our hospital we are reminded of the Master's own story of the good Samaritan and of His own long days of tireless, compassionate ministry to sick and suffering humanity. As we think of relief for the aged, dependent soldiers of the cross, we think of the ministry of the ascended Lord through the consecrated church at Philippi to the necessities of the aged and imprisoned Paul at Rome. We have hardly begun to meet our obligations and responsibilities in these great fields of benevolence.

In addition to fostering these great interests of our comprehensive cooperative program, we are also Divinely Commissioned to bring forth abundant fruitage of good works in the manifold local ministries of our churches, and in short, to make Christ preeminent in every civic, social, and business relationship of life.

Afore Prepared

Third, what will it mean for Georgia Baptists to be really mastered by the conviction that we are a Divinely Commissioned people? It will mean setting our faces steadfastly forward with the determination and high purpose that is possessed only by those who know that they walk in a divinely prepared pathway. "For we are His workmanship, created in Christ Jesus unto good works, *which God afore prepared (before ordained) that we should walk in them.*"

It will mean the sharing of the conviction and high spirit of the great achievers of religious history, who, under the urge of a mighty sense of mission, have often walked in strange paths with God. See them as they pass before us tonight; Abraham, "Going out not knowing whither he went," except that God had prepared the way; witness the sense of mission which gripped Joseph in his dreaming boyhood, and sustained him through betrayal by his brethren and persecutions in Egypt until he could say with the kiss of forgiveness to his unworthy brothers, "So now it was not you that sent me hither, but God"; see Moses at the burning bush divinely commissioned to deliver a nation from Egyptian bondage; see this dominant conviction in the life of Jesus Himself. How surprised He was as a boy of twelve that it had taken His parents so long to comprehend that He was mastered by a sense of Divine Mission. "Wist ye not that I must be about my Father's business?" And how like the dominant theme of a great oratorio does this keynote of Divine Mission run through His whole ministry until we hear it in a grand climax on that crucifixion day, when in answer to Pilate's challenge "Art thou a king?" He declared, "To this end was I born, and for this cause came I into the world, that I should bear witness unto the truth." And what shall I more say? For the time would fail me to tell of the mighty urge of the sense of Divine Mission which inspired David, Nehemiah, all the fearless prophets, John the Baptist, the disciples, Paul, the martyrs, the great reformers, the missionaries, and all of the great souls who through the centuries have lived close to God.

I shall never forget the very hour in which this compelling truth first gripped my mind and heart, twenty years ago. I was sitting on a mountain side at old Farm School, North Carolina, with several hundred other college students from all parts of the south gathered in a Y.M.C.A. summer conference. Dr. Robert E. Speer, of New York, was delivering the sunset address on life work and in the midst of it he quoted from that great sermon by Horace Bushnell, "Every man's life a plan of God." He pictured how the stars, the hills, the mountains, the plains, all function after a divine plan and fulfill a beneficent purpose. Then he raised the question, "Is it conceivable that God should have such a plan for inanimate creation and have no high mission for man, the very crown of creation?" To ask the question was to answer it, and yet there arose in my mind the challenge, if God has a divine plan for man, why all of the sin in the world, even among His people? The question arises even tonight why the lame, halting progress of missions, education, and benevolence which we have declared is our Divinely Commissioned work, if it be God's plan?

To answer these questions we must remind ourselves of the distinct difference between the outworking of God's plan in inanimate creation and in man. The hills, the mountains, the valleys, the plains, must function exactly as designed of God, they have no choice; but man, endowed with free will, may accept or reject God's best plan for his life. The very first pair in the garden exercised that freedom and fell from their high estate. So the sin of our lives and the failure of our people to carry out the Divinely Commissioned tasks are not to be charged against God, nor His plan, but against us. This tragic truth calls us to confession and repentance before Him in this hour.

We are grateful tonight that "The Lord is merciful and gracious, slow to anger, and plenteous in mercy. He will not always chide; neither will He keep His anger forever. He hath not dealt with us after our sin; nor rewarded us according to our iniquities." While we have fallen far short, and may not have carried out His best plan for our lives, we may rejoice tonight that God does not reject utterly His children, but ever offers them the next best thing available when they have rejected His best.

> "God has His best things for the few
> Who dare to stand the test,
> God has His second choice for those
> Who will not have His best."

How tragically does Moses illustrate this arresting truth. Divinely Commissioned at the burning bush, he returns to Egypt to deliver Israel. Through many trying ordeals with stubborn Pharaoh, he passes, but always leaning upon God. It is with a sense of utter dependence upon the Lord that he leads Israel out, and on through the Red Sea into the wilderness. But, with the passing of time, Moses waxes self-sufficient and at the rock in an outburst of arrogant presumption he said, "Hear now, ye rebels; shall we bring you forth water out of this rock?" And he struck the rock to which he had been commanded to speak in the Lord's name. In his pride and self-sufficiency, Moses had failed to exalt God and it was no longer possible for him to carry out the Lord's best plan for his life. God therefore said to Moses, because of this disobedience, "Ye shall not bring this congregation into the land which I have given them."

However, God does not cast Moses utterly aside because he has rejected His best through disobedience, but graciously gives to him the next best thing which was now possible for him. He leads Moses to Nebo's lofty height and, from that mountain top, shows to him the Promised Land, which now he could never enter with the chosen people. No man knows tonight where in lonely Moab the angels made the unknown grave of Moses, but all the Christian world knows that Mt. Nebo stands as an immortal monument to a great Divinely Commissioned leader who through presumptuous sin died with a second best. My friends, where do we stand tonight in the plan of God? Have we accepted His best; or, have we, through indifference, sin, and failure, dropped to the second, third, or far down His scale of choices for us?

But some may ask, "Preacher, where does that line of thought lead us?" Ah, it leads us face to face with the kind of service which we have rendered. It leads us to the third chapter of 1 Corinthians and reminds every one of us that, "We are laborers together with God," building for eternity. He honors us by giving us the privilege of selecting the building material which is made up of the kind of service we render to Him. If we are faithful and consecrated, giving Him our best, our materials are gold, silver and precious stones; if we are indifferent, half-hearted, and inconsistent, our materials are the perishable wood, hay, stubble. The tragedy of so many who really do love the Lord is that after building well with the gold, silver, and precious stones of consecrated service, they lapse into the wood, hay, and stubble of indifference and disobedience which will not stand the test of the last day. Paul declares that at that time "Every man's work shall be made manifest; for the day shall declare it, because it shall be revealed by fire; and the fire shall try every man's work of what sort it is. If any man's work abide, which he hath built thereupon (Christ the foundation), he shall receive a reward. If any man's work shall be burned, he shall suffer loss: but, he himself shall be saved; yet so as by fire." All of the Lord's people saved at last, but these concluding words picture one saved as from a burning building without so much as a change of clothing. A bare entrance into Heaven, with no trophies of service to throw at His feet.

> "Must I go—and empty-handed?
>   Must I meet my Savior so?
> Not one soul with which to greet Him?
>   Must I empty-handed go?

> "Oh ye saints arouse, be earnest:
>   Up and work while yet 'tis day;
> Ere the night of death o'ertake you,
>   Strive for souls while yet you may."

We are told that these troubled words of the song were written by one who was dying in youth without ever having brought one soul to Christ.

We sometimes hear the statement, "I will be satisfied if I just get inside the pearly gates." This is false modesty, or, the spirit of the time-serving hireling, and is utterly unworthy of any redeemed soul. "We are laborers together with God," and if we had no higher aspiration for ourselves than "bare entrance" we should have higher regard for our holy partner.

Christ's ambition for us is that we may dedicate our best to Him that He may give His best to us. He yearns to give to every one of His redeemed ones that welcome plaudit: "Well done, thou good and faithful servant, thou hast been faithful over a few things, I will make thee ruler over many things; enter thou into the joys of thy Lord."

We said that God permits His children to accept or reject His Divine Commission. That is true, yet it is just half of the truth. We must not forget the other half which recognizes God's sovereignty, running like a parallel track alongside man's free agency through the centuries. How could we meet life's adversities if it were not for this eternal truth which draws back the curtain and reveals "God standing in the shadows, keeping watch above His own"?

How gracious are His loving disciplines to arrest our willful careers, to bring us to richer fruitfulness and greater power for Him! God's yearning for fruit, more fruit, better fruit, is the secret of what many times seem strange Providences to us. "Every branch in me that beareth not fruit, He taketh it away: and every branch that beareth fruit, He purgeth it that it may bring forth more fruit." What to man is a tragic disappointment or overwhelming sorrow may be in God's plan a merciful pruning hook preparing His child for larger and better service.

Isaiah thus interprets the meaning to him, of the death of his best friend, when he tells how it led him to God and a full surrender of his life to the call of the Lord. "In the year that King Uzziah died, I saw the Lord." Many like Isaiah have seen God, and themselves, in the time of trouble and have repented of their sin and yielded their lives to His will.

We are not saying tonight that every trouble and sorrow that touches our lives is disciplinary in purpose but that if we are mastered by a sense of divine mission, we will seek in every experience of life to see His hand and to learn the lesson that He has in it for us.

Again, to be dominated by the conviction that we are Divinely Commissioned means strength to carry on through apparent failure. Many are keenly conscious that the visible fruitage of their service has been very meager and they who have been so eager to accomplish much, have seemingly achieved so little. Let us not be discouraged. Nothing could be further from the Master's purpose than to imply that the fruit of the spiritual life like that of the vineyard must always be apparent.

What a seeming colossal failure was the very climax of Christ's own work, the cross. "To the Jews it was a stumbling block, to the Greeks foolishness," and to the Romans insanity, but all the Christian world has come to know that it is indeed "the power of God unto salvation, to every one that believeth." In the cross, Jesus exemplified the mighty truth which He declared to His disciples, "Except a corn of wheat fall into the ground and die it abideth alone: but if it die, it bringeth forth much fruit."

This process of living by dying is one of the profoundest teachings of Jesus and we approach it only in the measure in which we appropriate the Master's sense of mission. Our first American Baptist foreign missionary, Adoniram Judson, is a typical example of how our heroic missionaries have been sustained in the midst of indescribable hardships and apparent failure by this dominating conviction that they are Divinely Commissioned. After seven years of seeming fruitless toil and terrible persecution, without winning a single convert; and with his half-hearted supporters in America urging him to give up, Judson sent back this ringing word: "If they ask what promise of ultimate success is here, tell them as much as there is an Almighty God who will fulfill His promises, that and no more. If they are unwilling to risk their bread on such a forlorn hope as has nothing but the Word of God to sustain it, beg them at least not to prevent others from giving us bread, and if we remain some twenty or thirty years, you will hear from us again." He did fight on for thirty-seven years and God privileged him to see more than sixty churches established in Burma, many workers trained and over seven thousand souls won to Jesus Christ. The work of Adoniram Judson has always been one of my greatest inspirations, but I never really caught the keynote of his life until I heard his honored son, Dr. Edward Judson, tell of how he had written it on a photograph of his sainted father and placed it over his study desk in the Judson Memorial Church, of New York. And here is that immortal motto of Adoniram Judson's life: "If we succeed without suffering, it means that someone suffered before us; if we suffer without success, it means that someone will succeed after us."

Ah, my friends, it was this same sense of mission which wrote that thrilling chapter in the history of our beloved Southern Baptist Theological Seminary, in the crucial days of 1865. In that darkest hour there was little prospect for students and every circumstance, and many people, said that the Seminary must die. When it seemed that the end was inevitably at hand, those four great teachers, Broadus, Boyce, Williams and Manly, came together and Broadus said: "Suppose we quietly agree that the Seminary may die, but we'll die first." Thank God the four professors held steadfast. Through those Divinely Commissioned heroes who were not disobedient unto the heavenly vision, God has given Southern Baptists the greatest Seminary in the world.

The university preacher was right when in answer to the student who said that he would like to give his life to missions or the ministry but such work was too intangible and unreal, declared "What could be more real, more tangible, more actual, than the laying away of one's life in the lives of his fellowmen?" That was indeed the high privilege of Judson, Carey, Livingstone, Morrison, Emmett Stephens; of Broadus, Carroll, Willingham, Gambrell, McDaniel, and a host no man could number, of heroic souls in high place and in low place, who, dominated by a sense of mission, have carried on for God.

Two Suggestions

Fourth, how, then, may we be gripped anew with the conviction that we are a Divinely Commissioned people?

Many suggestions might be made in answer to that question, but I will mention only two tonight.

First of all, if we are really to be gripped and mastered by this mighty sense of mission, we must make sure of our full surrender to His will. No mere passive curiosity to know, nor lukewarm, reluctant willingness to accept His plan will avail. There must be unreserved committal of life and all to Him and His mission for us, if it is really to get hold of us. "He that willeth to do His will shall know."

Such was Paul's complete surrender on the road to Damascus when he cried out, "Lord, what wilt thou have me to do?" It was not difficult for the Holy Spirit, through the years, to keep a life so yielded from the false detours, as He did when the Asian province beckoned to the south and Bithynia called to the north, but God said, on to the west, and on to the west Paul went to win a new continent for Christ.

There must be no reservation in our surrender, for when Christ said to the rich young ruler, "One thing thou lackest," that one thing meant everything. But why should we hesitate to yield ourselves completely as instruments to the great Master who made us and who can bring forth from our lives music undreamed of? "For we are His workmanship, created in Christ Jesus for good works, which God afore prepared that we should walk in them."

And then finally, if we are to be really mastered and directed as a Divinely Commissioned people, we must go to Him continually in prayer. Not as we go to our friends for approval and commendation of plans already formulated, but with surrendered minds and hearts seeking His plans and ready to do His will.

We Baptist people have spent much time in recent years tampering with machinery, formulating denominational policies and projecting doctrinal statements. Might I humbly suggest that this Augusta Convention return again to the Lord's route to unity of purpose and action, the route which leads through the upper room to the throne of grace and to His plan and His will? This was the route which led to the first Pentecost and to every Pentecost since. It is marvelous indeed how Christians are of one accord and win mighty victories when they pray themselves together.

May we at this convention stand with Christ as did the disciples in the ninth chapter of Matthew. You remember how the Master was moved with compassion when He saw the multitude "scattered abroad as sheep having no shepherd." Then He said, "The harvest truly is plenteous, but the laborers are few; pray ye therefore the Lord of the harvest, that He will send forth laborers into His harvest." Then the disciples went apart to pray, each in his own place. We can imagine Simon Peter saying: "Father, I saw today, through the eyes of the Master, a lost world and it broke my heart. The Master told us to pray to the Lord of the harvest for laborers and now I beg Thee to send them. O, send them, Lord, the fields are white," and on, and on, into the night Simon prayed until in the wee hours of the morning there dawned upon Peter that he knew one man who could help, and that man was Simon Peter himself. Then there came over him that gripping sense of mission and he said, "I see it, Lord; here am I, send me." And the other disciples apart, each in his own place, prayed themselves to the same conclusion and to the same surrender. Then, whatever may have been the varying opinions among the twelve the day before, as to the work to be done and how to do it, a night of prayer had brought them to complete unity in the Master's own plan. The next chapter tells how Christ sent them out Divinely Commissioned into the great harvest field.

May we likewise stand with the Master at Augusta and catch His vision of a lost world and the crying needs of our own local churches, and go out from this city with such a mastering sense of mission as Georgia Baptists have never known before, to apprehend that for which we were apprehended of Christ Jesus.

And to meet this challenge I commend to you the personal prayer and watchword of Eula Hensley, who spent one brief year in China and God took her home. A motto sacred to me, for I have kept it long years above my desk, on my study wall:

"Put any burden on me, only sustain me,
Send me anywhere, only go with me,
Sever any tie that binds, save this tie
Which binds me to Thy heart and to Thy Service."

"For we are His workmanship, created in Christ Jesus for good works, which God afore prepared that we should walk in them."

J. B. Lawrence
The Secret of Christian Living

Work out your own salvation with fear and trembling (Phil. 2:12).

One of the dangers of a sacramental system of religion is that it substitutes external observances for spiritual experience and Christlike living. The sacramentarian says, do these things and you will be saved. The whole process is external and mechanical. The Christian believes the teachings of Christ and is drawn naturally into the fellowship of the church, but the Christian life is more than church membership. One becomes a Christian by personal faith in Christ and not through sacraments. Salvation is of God, but it is not without faith in Christ, nor is it without struggle in life. To put sacraments in the place of the delivery of the whole personality to Christ through faith is to build the Christian life on a foundation of sand. There is a warfare to be waged against the wicked world outside of us, and we are to struggle against the tendencies to wrongdoing inside of us. The chanting of the Apostles' Creed as a substitute for sacrificial living makes Christianity too easy.

"I protest," says Huxley, "that if some power would agree to make me always think what is true and do what is right, on the condition of being turned into a kind of clock and wound up every morning, that I would close immediately with the offer." This is the word of a serious-minded man who is voicing the infinite desirability, the infinite difficulty of being good.

Down deep in the heart of every redeemed individual there is the desire to become good, and if on earth there is not some plan whereby Christian character can be developed, then God's supreme gift to the world has been overlooked. But there is a way. Under right conditions it is as natural for the believer to grow a beautiful character as it is for a flower

263

to unfold its petals. In the redemptive work of Christ provision has been made for the disciples of Christ to become good. In the light of the provisions of grace we can say with Browning, "Man was made to grow, not stop"; or in the language of the divine philosopher, "Whom he did foreknow, he also did predestinate to be conformed to the image of his Son."

I

The text gives us a twofold view of the Christian life. At first it seems a paradox. We are told that God is working in the believer to will and to do, and then we are told that the believer is to work out his own salvation with fear and trembling. But it is not a paradox at all. The two truths stated here, when kept together, give us the whole truth on Christian living. When separated they furnish the war cry of contending groups who have kept up an age-long theological controversy over the question of faith and works. One faction in this controversy contends that salvation is in part if not in whole the result of man's efforts who works it out; the other group contends that man's salvation is wholly in God's hands who worketh in man to will and to do.

Neither position is correct. God works in us and we work. Christian character is not made to order. Christianity, as a way to the highest, is planned in heaven, nevertheless as an experience in life it is worked out on earth. To the individual believer it is another word for character. In the world it is the way to a Christlike social order. To both the believer and the world it is the kingdom of God. As believers in Christ we are to work our salvation out into conduct and character. We are to give expression to our faith in words and deeds.

Many honest believers are bewildered by false opinions, false ideas, and false conceptions. They have not come to a true understanding of the Christian life and the means and methods by which the Christian is to succeed in living it. Not understanding the demands made in the Scriptures upon believers and not knowing how to meet these demands, they settle down in religious inactivity convinced that there is no use to try to meet such a high standard of living. They fail because they failed to discover the secret of Christian living.

There are others who think that the Christian life is wrought out by Christ for the believer, and that all one has to do is to receive it. Those who hold this idea live in idleness. "If the Christian life is wrought out by Christ," they say, "why work it out?" If the Christian character is a matter of divine manufacture, made in heaven like a coat at a tailor's shop and placed upon the individual by the divine hand—a coat of righteousness which one can put on for religious occasions and off when selfish interests demand a rougher garment—if this is the nature of the Christian life, why should anyone worry or work?

These are mistaken ideas growing out of a misconception of the Christian life. Salvation is simply another word for character. It differs from other character developments, not so much by its processes, as by the high sphere in which it is taking place. As believers in Christ, we are to work our salvation out into life. Our religion must be wrought into character and translated into the fabric of human affairs. No man lives to himself alone. Christian character, while it is personal, is also a community and world asset. God working in us "to will and to do" is setting to work the spiritual forces which feed the power lines that furnish the life-giving currents of redeeming grace to the world.

II

The salvation we are to work out is not our justification nor our recommendation to God. It is the translation of an experience of grace, which has taken place in our hearts, into the terms of everyday living, glorified by the highest motives and the most exalted ends. The "fear and the trembling" is not a bondage of fear, not a fear of the loss of divine love, for the adoption of children prevents such apprehensions and the covenant promises of God in Christ give assurance that no such thing should happen. But it is the fear of any unholy weariness in the tasks of love and a dread lest we should fail of success in living for Christ.

God is working in us to live victoriously, creatively, for Christ. Salvation in its full meaning is the attainment of this high ideal. It is the unfolding, the coming to maturity of the spiritual life. When a child is born he is a human being, but his birth is the beginning and not the end of his existence. So with a Christian. When he is born from above he is saved, but this is the beginning and not the end of the Christian life. He is to work out to its full consummation the life he has in Christ. He is to give himself to the growing of a soul as he gives himself to the growing of a body.

In this work of growing a soul the Christian is not left to his own religious impulses. God works in him to will and to do. This is a gracious provision of grace, for if God did not work, the motives and impulses to Christian living would come only from one's own inner self and would vary in objective with every individual. But with God motivating the soul, every believer is directed along the same great highway of creative living. We thus can have unity in God's world program of redemption. There are tasks of supreme importance for every believer in this program. The social order is to be made Christlike. The world of mankind is to become one brotherhood living together in peace and working together for the common good. God working in all believers unifies the kingdom forces and gives one divine objective for Christian service.

In growing a Christian life there are two parts: the working in and the working out of God's will. The working in is the divine part. The working out is the human part. We find these same two parts in nature. Take the beehive, what of its mystery? It is not the making of the hive; it is the conceiving of it. If you can tell me how the bee got the idea I will tell you how he worked it out. The thing which wakes my wonder is the instinct— the process within the bee. God worketh in the bee both to will and to do. So is it with the soul of man. Every Christian is building a character which is Christlike. How is he to get the idea? Where is he to get the impulse? The impulse comes from God. God worketh in him both to will and to do.

This is something peculiar to the Christian religion. The great religions of the world—Hinduism, Buddhism, Mohammedanism, and all the great ethnic faiths—stress the human will. The keynote of these religions is, work for your salvation. They teach that the power that saves you is yourself, the chains that bind you are of your own forging, the virtue that delivers you is of your own manufacture, and the grace that redeems you is your own merit. The Christian religion is different. The Christian's God loves the sinner and goes out to seek and to save him. The human will is acted upon directly by the Holy Spirit, who, after regenerating the soul, comes into the life to inspire and guide. The regenerated heart is the homing place of the Spirit of God. Like the sun which warms the earth and kindles the living germ in the seed, causing them to sprout and grow, so does the Holy Spirit warm the heart, kindle to activity the will, and cause the Christian to produce in his life the rich fruits of righteousness.

III

It is encouraging to know that salvation is of God. From him comes the desire by which we long for it, the grace by which we attain it, and the power by which we live it. All is of grace. He gives grace for grace, not grace for good works. Consider the strength which this truth bestows. The one in whom we trust and to whom we look is not a guide outside of us, but a God within us. He is not one who can teach us when we are willing to hear, but one who works within us creating righteous desires and impulses in the soul. We do not have to persuade him to help us; but it is his good pleasure to work in us both to will and to do. But let no one think that because salvation is of God the believer has nothing to do. There is work, severe work, work so great that the worker needs and must have the power of the Holy Spirit. We are to work out the whole of our salvation to its complete and full consummation.

With the new birth Christian living begins. The soul that is born from above is to be "transformed, by the renewing of the mind, so as to prove what is the good and acceptable and perfect will of God." This transformation is produced in a twofold way: by growth in grace, in which the mind is renewed and made like unto the mind of Christ; and by obedience to the commands of Christ, in which the will becomes subject to the will of God. These two processes are simultaneous. They are closely related and yet separate. The one, growth in grace, is the spontaneous unfolding of the Christ life received in the new birth; the other, obedience to Christ, is the response of the human will to the divine impulse as God works within the soul to will and to do. These two spiritual processes, properly understood and properly related, will give the secret of Christian living.

Growth in grace can be hindered or helped by the individual as he co-operates with or fails to co-operate with the means of grace, but the impulse to grow is one of the things nature holds in her own keeping; it is mysterious and effortless. The act of growing is automatic, spontaneous, without fretting, and without thinking. This is true in all spheres; applied to plants, to animals, to the body, or to the soul, this is the law. A doctor may tell us how growth may be stunted or helped, but the impulse to grow is not affected, only the results. The physician of souls, in like manner, may prescribe more earnestness, more prayer, more Bible reading, more Christian work; these things will create conditions favorable to growth, but the soul grows because of the spiritual life within it and the act of growing is without trying, without fretting, without thinking. Manuals of devotion with complicated rules for growing in grace would do well to return to the simplicity of nature; and earnest souls who are attempting spiritual development by struggle instead of by faith, would be spared much unnecessary effort if they would simply trust implicitly in Christ and leave the soul to grow by its own inherent spiritual impulse.

Some may raise an objection to this on the ground that it takes away all conflict from the Christian life. But those who raise this objection confuse growth in grace with working out one's salvation. The two things are different, and the differences lies in the balance between faith and works.

In the physical life we never think of connecting the growth of a boy with the work he does. Work, in fact, is one thing and growth is another. If it is asked, Is the Christian wrong in agonizing efforts after growth? The answer is, Let him agonize to live right, and growth will take care of itself. When a boy runs a race or does a piece of work, he does not say, "This will help me to grow." It may or it may not, but if he is doing these things in order to grow he has quite a mistaken idea of growth. His anxiety here is altogether misplaced. What he should be anxious about is the quality of his work and his faithfulness in it; nature will take care of growth.

In the spiritual life the same law holds. We are to work with all our might, but not to force nor to secure spiritual growth; growth is spiritual and spontaneous. We do not work as a necessary means to growth; we are taken in hand. We do not plan; we are "God's workmanship, created in Christ Jesus unto good works which God hath before ordained that we should walk in them." Let us live right, think right, act right, study the Word, keep our hearts attuned to prayer, rest in perfect trust and forget about our spiritual growth; the newborn life will do its own growing.

IV

The question may be asked, if God works in us, why should we work? Is there no such thing as inspiration? When the child is working and the mother stands in the door and says, "Bravely done, my child," is there no new light in the eye? Is there no alacrity added to the hand? Is there no ambition stirred to do better? Does not the mother work in the child to will and to do, and does not the child co-operate with the mother's will by carrying out her wishes?

In the midst of battle, men who have unflinchingly fought until they are well-nigh cut off and are thinking of retreat, are nerved to renewed effort by the voice of their commander crying out to them and sending a shout of victory through the air as did the Confederate commander when he shouted to his men, "Look, there stands Jackson like a stone wall!" Inspired by that voice, they are nerved with fresh energy, and with a new surge of effort they go on to victory. That success is the result of another mighty soul working in them, inspiring them to will and to do.

A wandering, weary, spent, hungry traveler sits down, benumbed, to give up in despair. He is met by a hunter. Is his weariness cured? Is the cold dissipated? Is his hunger satisfied? No. But the hunter says to him: "Arise, my man. Pull yourself together. Follow me. And now you shall not wander in circles, and in vain. I know the way; and if you will make another effort you will be safe." The hunter works in the man to will and to do. He brings him out of danger.

These are imperfect illustrations, for the ones who work to bring new life and enthusiasm cannot get on the inside of the ones they are influencing. But blessed be God, there is a Spirit who works within the believer, who develops a power within the soul and who guides to successful living. This is the gracious provision of divine grace. They who fall back into indifference and selfishness are without this comfort; but those who realize their privileges and avail themselves of this divine help are under the administration of a Father who loves them better than they love themselves, and who is working intelligence and inspiration and purpose in them, who will by and by complete in them the glorious work of emancipation from sin, bring them into his power and love and give to them the joy and victory of the upper kingdom.

This does not in any way supercede or violate man's freedom. God respects our integrity as rational and responsible creatures. He works within us the impulse to righteousness, but any action to be wrought into character must have the stamp of the will upon it. Aspirations may come up in the soul, righteous desires may clamor for recognition, and holy impulses may tug at the door of your will and mine, but these will have no currency in your life and mine unless they are caught up by the will and wrought into deeds. Take obedience, for instance. How do we come to obey the law of love? It is by practicing submission to the will of Christ. So is it with sympathy, humility, gentleness, kindness, generosity. No one, just because he is converted, has all the graces of the Christian life. These things are worked out in obedience to the inner impulses which come from God. If we ever come to love our neighbor as we love ourselves, to do unto others as we would have them to do unto us, to have the spirit of benevolence, to give of our substance as the Lord has prospered us for the ongoing of his kingdom, to develop in our individual character the Christian graces, it will be because we have practiced these things in the actual experiences of life. God is working in us to will and to do these things, but they will become actual elements of character only when the stamp of our will is put upon them and they are made our own habits of conduct.

Let us suppose that we have an organ which is a conscious thing with a will of its own. Here are all the keys with their possibilities of matchless and almost unlimited combinations of harmony. At the keyboard sits a master. He touches its keys. The organ feels the impulse to wonderful harmony but it closes its mouth. It says: "I will not respond to the touch of the master. He is working in me to will and to do of his own good pleasure. His purpose is exalted. Matchless harmony will result if I obey the impulse he has created, but I will not." Under such conditions music would be impossible. The organ must respond to the will of the master at the keyboard.

At the keyboard of your life and mine sits a Master—Christ, the Son of the living God—and he is touching the keys of your life and mine as it pleases him, working in us both to will and to do of his own good pleasure. But unless you and I respond to that touch, harmony is impossible. The matchless combinations of tone can only be secured in your life and mine when we work together with God.

V

The development of Christian character is little by little. As the individual obeys the higher laws and works in response to the inner divine impulse in the development of permanent habits of living, he is changed into the likeness of Christ. We do not spring full-fledged into maturity with all the elements of righteousness full-formed. But day by day, week by week the elements of strength and righteousness are built up. This is the process by which God works in nature. An orchard does not spring full-fledged into fruitage the day of its planting. It takes time. The trees are cultivated and they grow. When the springtime comes they bloom and then the fruit matures and ripens. So it is with character. We put off the old man with his deeds; we put on the new man with his habits. Unbelief is replaced by faith, disobedience by obedience, and sin and unrighteousness by right doing. Those who fail in the Christian life are those who fail to recognize this law of spiritual development. They either fail to obey the inner impulses, or else grow weary and fall by the wayside, because the Christian character cannot be formed in a day.

In working out our personal salvation we work out also the salvation of the social order in which we live. While every man's life is a private affair, it also belongs to the community and to the world. No one lives to himself alone. As Tennyson says, "I am a part of all that I have met." It is as men come in contact with their fellows, as soul touches soul, and life reacts upon life that the social order is estabished and civilization is given its character. How shall this order be changed? Christian living by individuals alone can change it. The social order will become Christlike when the men who compose the social order live Christly lives. This Christ knew; hence he did not give instruction for the reorganization of the state. He set himself to make men over. Changed men will change the world. Christian living by Christian people is the only hope of changing the social order of the world.

Roland Q. Leavell
Evangelism Is Essential in Kingdom Building and Christian Living

From that time Jesus began to preach, and to say, Repent: for the kingdom of heaven is at hand (Matt. 4:17).

Does the average church member know what it means to become a Christian? Exactly what is it to which a soul-winner invites a lost person when asking him to be a Christian?

A woman who had been a church member for some years was much perplexed and concerned about her spiritual life. She had accepted her denomination's form of baptism, had completed a course of doctrinal instruction, had regularly observed the ordinances, and had been told that she was a Christian. But she could not feel the assurance of salvation. One day a friend asked her if she could speak in unknown tongues. No! Forthwith she was forcefully told that she was in nowise a Christian. Back to her pastor she went. He told her that her spiritual needs were all cared for in her faithful performance of church duties. However, she found no peace. In a conference with another Christian worker she boldly asserted that she did not dance, play cards, drink liquor, nor swear. She recited her many negative virtues. Then she asked if that did not assure her that she was a Christian.

In this experience three beliefs about how to become a Christian were set forth. First, there was a ritualistic, ecclesiastical plan. The minister believed that punctilious performance of church duties and observance of ritualistic ceremonies made her a Christian. Second, there was the emotional plan. The friend believed that ecstatic, emotional upheavals, leading to rapturous excesses, were necessary for one to become a Christian. Third, there was the legalistic or moral plan. She herself believed that to become a Christian was equivalent to submitting to a series of taboos and

272

"thou shalt not" restrictions. Christianity to her was an organized system of negative self-denials. Who was right?

The Christian worker gave her another plan altogether. From the Bible he showed her that she must repent of her sins. He pointed her to the Lord Jesus Christ. He reminded her that no one of the other three plans ever mentioned Jesus Christ as Saviour. No one mentioned a trust in Christ's atoning blood to cleanse her heart from sin. No one mentioned taking Jesus Christ as the Lord and Master of her life. No one mentioned the indwelling spiritual life which must come from God to give a soul peace and power.

Those who would help others to become Christians should seek to know to *whom* and to *what* they are inviting lost people. Soul-winners must try to state clearly and intelligently what it means to *become* a Christian, and then what it means to *be* a Christian. Every Christian should know the way to the door of the kingdom of heaven, should be able to handle the key aright, and should have a soul-gripping conception of the plan, power, and purpose of the life of a citizen of the kingdom.

1. Understanding the Meaning of the Kingdom of God

"Repent: for the kingdom of heaven is at hand" (Matt. 4:17) was the first clarion call of Christ. "Except a man be born again, he cannot see the kingdom of God" (John 3:3) was the straightforward statement of our Lord. But what and where is the kingdom of heaven?

"It is all foolish to point upward when referring to heaven, because Jesus said that the kingdom of heaven is within," said an uninstructed teacher to her class. The unfortunate teacher did not know the difference between the place heaven and the kingdom of heaven. There is a tremendous difference. There is a vast difference between the place Great Britain and the kingdom of Great Britain. The kingdom of Great Britain is in the hearts of all those who are loyal to the king. A loyal subject to the king, residing in America, is yet a part of the kingdom of Great Britain. Just so, the kingdom of heaven is composed of all people who are loyal to God through faith in Jesus Christ as their Lord and King. The soul-winner seeks to lead his lost friend to enter the kingdom of heaven here on earth, assuring him that he will enter the place heaven in the hereafter.

1. The People of the Kingdom

(1) *A personal relation.*—The people who are in the kingdom of heaven are those who have entered into the right relationship with Jesus Christ. The test of whether or not one is in the kingdom is whether or not in his heart he has accepted the Lord Jesus Christ. Lost men must be brought to see the King in his beauty. The crucial questions to ask a lost person are these: "What think ye of Christ? What relationship is there between your soul and the Saviour?"

(2) *A permanent transaction.*—The experience which brings one into the right relationship with Jesus is a permanent one. When a sinner puts his trust in the crucified and risen Christ, the Spirit of God works a change in that heart which is *eternal* and *everlasting*.

(3) *A process of development.*—To become a citizen of the kingdom of God is a moment's experience; to develop into a better citizen of that kingdom is a continual process throughout life. There are many areas in a Christian's life in which Christ would rule more and more perfectly. The Lord's Prayer teaches the Christian to pray for this more perfect rule of Christ in these areas.

The Lord's Prayer indicates that the way to glorify the name of our Father in heaven is to bring in the kingdom: "Thy kingdom come." His kingdom rule is perfected in four areas of living, namely: (1) the human will: "Thy will be done"; (2) the economic life: "Give us this day our daily bread"; (3) the social realm: "Forgive us our debts, as we forgive our debtors"; and (4) the relation to Satan's program of sin: "Lead us not into temptation, but deliver us from evil." Let the unsaved man know that if he chooses Christ as his King, the choice implies a definite break with the old life under the kingship of self or Satan.

2. The Program of the Kingdom

Christ the King has a definite program for the kingdom of God on earth. To invite one to become a Christian is to introduce him to this heavenly program and to ask him to accept his responsibility in its promotion.

(1) *The ideal.*—The ideal of the kingdom of heaven is summed up in this: "Thy will be done in earth, as it is in heaven." That would mean that the world would be motivated by love. That would mean a life which is victorious over such enemies as sin, ignorance, poverty, and death. That

would mean the elimination of prejudice, injustice, dishonesty, and impurity among men. That would mean the destruction of fear, unbelief, disobedience, and rebellion toward God. That would mean the absolute exaltation of Jesus Christ to the throne in the heart of every man. This is a glorious prospect for sin-cursed, defeated, distressed, despairing, and doomed men.

(2) *The unit.*—The unit of the kingdom of heaven is an individual who is a new man in Christ. Such a man has turned his back upon the life of selfishness, sin, and satanic control. He has been lifted up into higher life by those hands which were nailed to a cross. God the Father has forgiven this kingdom man. God the Son has redeemed him. God the Holy Spirit has regenerated him. Of such the kingdom of heaven is built. Surely this is a glorious possibility to which lost men may be directed.

(3) *The organization.*—The organization which Christ formed as the promotional agency of his kingdom is his church. When a man accepts Christ as Saviour and Lord, his love for Christ leads him to enter the church. Through the church he gives his life in spreading the kingdom. No other institution except the church can or will do very much to bring others into the kingdom of heaven. Without churches the program of soul-winning would soon cease to be.

3. The Primacy of the Kingdom

Jesus commands his kingdom subjects: "Seek ye first the kingdom of God, and his righteousness" (Matt. 6:33). Therefore it should be made clear to one who is about to become a Christian that to do so means to give the Lord Jesus Christ the very first place in his life. Being a Christian is not just a part of life; it is life itself. In truth Christ must be "Lord of all or else he is not Lord at all." All authority is his. If one does not mean to renounce his own selfish will and gladly accept the sovereign will of his sovereign Lord, he has no right to profess to be a Christian.

II. Becoming a Child of God

The soul-winner should make it clear to the one whom he would win to Christ that to become a Christian is to become a child of God. That definitely means that one must have a radical change from the old life. Jesus says that this change must be through regeneration or a new birth (John 3:3,5), through his Holy Spirit.

1. Born a Child of God

(1) *Inherent need for new birth.*—The sinful nature of fallen humanity cannot inherit the kingdom of God. The base metal of the human heart needs a heavenly alchemy to transform it into gold. Like the crab apple tree, the old flesh will continue to bear its bitter fruit until a new nature is grafted in.

> Where is one that, born of woman,
> Altogether can escape
> From the lower world within him,
> Moods of tiger and of ape?
> —TENNYSON

(2) *Partakers of the divine nature.*—The philosopher William James made an exhaustive study of the change that is wrought in men when they believe on the Lord Jesus Christ. He studied the difference that faith in Christ wrought in men like Saul the persecutor, Augustine the profligate, Bunyan the profane, Gough the drunkard, John Newton the slave trader, and Torrey the skeptic. He discovered that names which were dirty in dishonor became resplendent in glory. He saw the stench of sensuality replaced by the perfume of spirituality. He saw enslaved men turned into conquerors. Menials became kings. He was compelled to admit that the Christian experience brings into human hearts some new attributes and new attitudes which no mere psychological experience can explain. Such changes are explained only by saying that God the Holy Spirit implants the divine nature in the heart of every one who believes on the Lord Jesus Christ.

(3) *Not reformation only, but regeneration.*—To become a child of God is a deeper matter than simply reforming from one's evil ways. There is a world of difference between man's fitful desire reaching up for a better life and the omnipotent hand of God reaching down to loose him from his sins and to lift him into heavenly habitations. There is a vast contrast between a soul lingering in the barren plains of man's sin-weakened will power and a soul moving in the fulness of God's changeless grace. Reformation is good only so long as man can maintain his good behavior. Regeneration is an eternal metamorphosis of the soul.

A man can reform himself at times, but no man can "born himself again." To believe on the Lord Jesus Christ is the responsibility of man, but regeneration is the responsibility of God. The Scripture uses the passive voice to describe the change. Examine such passages as: "until Christ be formed in you"; "we are changed into the same image"; "begotten of God"; "be ye transformed"; and "to them gave he power to become the sons of God, even to them that believe on his name."

2. Bearing the Name of God

"If my people, which are called by my name" is one of the most arresting phrases in the Word of God. No one should fail to appreciate the high privilege that is implied in those words, nor should the serious responsibility therein be underestimated.

(1) *Privilege.*—"Wherefore God also hath highly exalted him, and given him a name which is above every name" (Phil. 2:9). What words of men or angels can describe the high privilege of being called by the name "Christian"? It should move every Christian to a consciousness of unworthiness and to a sense of gratitude.

(2) *Responsibility.*—Every great privilege carries with it a great responsibility. To be a child of the King demands a higher life than that which is expected of non-Christians. There is a story about a king's son who was incorrigible. His instructors made every effort to induce him to walk worthily as a king's son should. Finally they fell upon the plan of dressing him in royal purple. After that, whenever the temptation allured him to deeds unworthy of his noble birth, the purple reminded him of his responsibility to live worthily as one of royal blood. It is no little responsibility to be known as a child of God.

III. Presenting the One Plan of God

Any soul-winner should be able to state in intelligent and unmistakable terms what a sinner must do to become a Christian. Paul's statement in Acts 20:21 about how to become a Christian is an irreducible minimum. He sums it up in two words, repentance and faith. It is sufficient both for Jews and for Gentiles. So the soul-winner may confidently declare to every lost man that, in order to be saved, he must experience "repentance toward God, and faith toward our Lord Jesus Christ."

1. God's Word Teaches But One Plan

It is agreed that there is no salvation possible except by the plain way taught in the Bible. God's Word reveals but one plan. Clearly it is said: "Neither is there salvation in any other: for there is none other name under heaven given among men, whereby we must be saved" (Acts 4:12). Every sinner who has ever been saved was saved through repentance toward God and faith in the Lord Jesus Christ as Saviour.

(1) *One plan for atonement.*—The day of atonement, described in the sixteenth chapter of Leviticus, reveals how men were saved before Jesus Christ was born on earth. The high priest offered a goat for a sin offering. While the congregation knelt and beat upon their breasts, they confessed their sins in true repentance toward God, and they pointed to the blood upon the altar. The only saving grace in the blood of a sacrifice was in that it typified and pointed to the blood of Christ on the cross. Therefore, the people exercised "repentance toward God, and faith toward the Lord Jesus Christ."

(2) *One plan in experience.*—If Adam was saved, he was saved just as men must be saved today. Through his sacrifice his faith looked forward to Jesus Christ, even as our faith must look back to him.

> Not all the blood of beasts,
> On Jewish altars slain,
> Could give the guilty conscience peace,
> Or wash away the stain.
> . . . .
> But Christ, the heavenly Lamb
> Takes all our sins away—
> A sacrifice of nobler name
> And richer blood than they.

2. God's Holiness Demands Repentance

Repentance is the most reasonable thing that God ever required of a sinner. His holiness cannot allow him to ignore or to condone sin.

(1) *The preaching of repentance.*—All the great soul-winners of the ages have preached and taught the necessity of repentance toward God. The mighty men of Old Testament times proclaimed this righteous requirement of God. John the Baptist came demanding that men should "bring forth . . . fruits meet for repentance" (Matt. 3:8). Our Lord took up the same message, crying, "Repent: for the kingdom of heaven is at hand" (Matt. 4:17). Simon Peter preached repentance on the day of Pentecost. Paul preached it at Athens, Ephesus, and wherever else he went. Our Lord vigorously reiterated the truth: "Except ye repent, ye shall all likewise perish" (Luke 13:3,5). Surely every one who would win others

to Christ should know that the lost man must repent of his sins against God.

(2) *The practice of repentance.*—Furthermore, a soul-winner should know exactly what the experience of repentance means. Repentance means a change of mind, or a change of attitude. True repentance is more than shame for sin, or fear of sin's consequences, or quitting one's meanness. Repentance is a reversal of one's thinking and one's entire attitude.

Hear Jesus, as he said, in substance: "Change your attitude toward God, for the kingdom of heaven is at hand!" He who loves sin hates God. Love for God will make anyone hate sin.

True repentance does not come except by the conviction of the Holy Spirit. "He will reprove the world of sin, and of righteousness, and of judgment: of sin, because they believe not on me" (John 16:8-9). Soul-winner, if you will lovingly point men to the beauty and holiness of Jesus Christ, then the Holy Spirit will convince them of the emptiness and ugliness of a life of sin.

(3) *The permanence of repentance.*—Genuine repentance is a complete and final reversal of one's direction in life. Some have been so foolish as to say, "If I should be saved, and saved once for all, then I could sin all I want to, without being lost." If one feels that way, he has never repented. The very meaning of repentance is that one has changed his mind about wanting to sin.

3. God's Son Merits Faith

He who repents toward God earnestly desires to trust Jesus as Saviour. Those who could help others to become Christians should be alert to the privilege of pointing men to the Lamb of God. The whole matter of salvation depends upon the sinner's relation to him.

(1) *Saved by his death.*—"Christ died for our sins" (1 Cor. 15:3). Nothing else avails. Morality is of no avail. Charity does not save. Culture is a failure. A sinner must see and accept Christ as dying in his stead. Barabbas, the murderous thief, was pardoned by Pilate on the day that Christ was crucified. Possibly they crucified Jesus upon the very cross which was prepared for Barabbas. Imagine what Barabbas thought if he went out to Calvary. There he saw the Son of God dying in his place. Just so, the sinner must see Jesus dying in his place, for his sins, according to the Scripture.

(2) *Saved through faith, not feelings.*—Men are prone to trust in their feelings rather than consider their faith. Salvation depends on him whom the sinner trusts rather than upon how the sinner feels about it.

A passenger crossing the ocean was terrified by a storm at sea. In fear he asked the sailor if the boat would sink. The sailor laughed hilariously at the idea. Which of the two was safer? Neither! They were both the same. Their safety did not depend on their feelings but upon the boat in which they had put their faith. Salvation does not depend upon so fickle a thing as human feelings. The sinner is safe indeed when his faith is fixed upon the Son of God.

Let the plan of salvation as taught in God's Word be taught to every seeking sinner.

"Except ye repent, ye shall all likewise perish" (Luke 13:3).

"Believe on the Lord Jesus Christ, and thou shalt be saved" (Acts 16:31).

IV. Living the Life from God

As it has been said already, to become a Christian is the experience of a moment. To be a Christian is the experience of a lifetime. To be a good Christian is to exercise the fine art of superior, victorious daily living. Jesus, "the pioneer of life" (Acts 3:15, Moffatt), promises to push back the narrow horizons of ordinary existence, giving new qualities and new powers for a godly life. Jesus promises to build a superior type of character. He insures victory in superior battles. He is the *way* of life. He is *the* life. The personal winner of souls should present to the lost men the great alternative of life, "Christ or chaos."

Paul describes superior Christian living as having three aspects: "We should live soberly, righteously, and godly, in this present world" (Titus 2:12).

1. Living Soberly in Self-control

The sober life is a life of self-control. Christ in a Christian's heart supplies the power for self-control, self-discipline, and self-direction. To be a good Christian demands a self-controlled separation from the sinful things which appeal to the old nature. It means separation unto the holier, higher, happier things of the life in Christ. The acceptance of the lordship of Christ means absolute renunciation of the lordship of selfish desires.

The body of a Christian should be sober because it is sacred. It has been purchased with a price. It is the property of King Immanuel. It is not for hire to worldliness, carnality, or the devil. To become a Christian is to say what Bunyan's Christian in *Pilgrim's Progress* said to Apollyon: "I have let myself to another." Like the saints in Caesar's household (Phil. 4:22), a Christian may be kept pure by the power of God amid a sordid, sensual, sinful environment. Let every unsaved soul know that Christ is able to save unto the uttermost.

2. Living Righteously Toward Others

Living as a Christian means living according to superior social standards. To live righteously means to live rightly toward others. "Love thy neighbour as thyself" is the startling social standard which Christ held up for his followers. It was uniquely superior to any standard which the people of his day had accepted. To love the unlovely requires a God-given grace, but Christ can supply it. To love one's enemies is not natural but divine. To love others lavishly will constantly constrain a Christian to deal honestly, think purely, speak kindly, and serve humbly in all relations with his fellow man. This standard for right conduct toward others is the solution for all the social ills of the present day.

3. Living a Godly Life

A godly life is a superior life because it is one in which all areas of living—physical, social, mental, and moral—are under God's spiritual sovereignty.

Ungodly men are not necessarily wicked men, guilty of murder, swearing, lying, or theft. The ungodly are those who ignore God, leaving him entirely out of consideration in their lives. They do not pray to God. They do not walk with God. They do not read God's Word. They do not worship God, either in God's house or at the family altar. They have no concern for helping others to come into God's kingdom.

Ungodly men lack the divine assurance of victorious, abundant living. They need God. All conquering Christian characters draw on divine resources as they fight the battles of daily life. Washington needed God at Valley Forge. Gladstone needed God in Parliament. Victoria needed God to help her rule. Woodrow Wilson needed God in government affairs. Ministers and missionaries need God in their responsibilities. Merchants and professional men need God in their business matters. Parents need God in the home. Young people need God in their choices of the courses of life. To be a Christian is to take God as the controlling factor in life. The world sorely needs characters who live soberly and righteously in this present world. The world's biggest problems are problems of the way people live. The great international problem is one of how nations can live together in peace. The race problem is how to live in love instead of with prejudice. The domestic problem is a matter of unlovely living in the home. In the final analysis all the problems of individuals or groups are problems of how to live the victorious life. Let every heart in all the world hear the heavenly words of the Lord Jesus: "I am come that they might have life, and that they might have it more abundantly" (John 10:10).

Robert G. Lee
The Constant Call of Christ's Cross

And when she had so said, she went her way, and called Mary her sister secretly, saying The Master is come, and calleth for thee (John 11:28).

Mrs. Browning, the woman Shakespeare of England and of the world, taught that our ears and hearts are besieged and assaulted by calls. She said, "World-voices east, world-voices west."

We live in a world of calls.

There are bird calls—some as raucous as the crow's voice and some as sweet as the lyrics of the lark, the Mendelssohns of the meadows, and as melodious as the many-voiced mockingbird, the Beethoven of the boughs.

There are fire calls—with loud alarms, when fire, man's good servant, is master.

There are factory calls—with shrieking whistles that summon to work or rest.

There is the call of the wild—when men prefer the wolf's howl to human voices.

There are the calls to arms—to which men respond, willing to choose garments of flame and blood for garments of service.

There are political calls—when many fingers point many eyes to ballot boxes.

There are love calls—which were old when the Pyramids were new and which are as young as the flowers that blossomed this morning and as multitudinous as the stars.

There are calls of distress—as when the *Titanic* went down.

But I would ask you today to pitch your mental tent in the councils of eternity, in Egypt, in Palestine, at Calvary—and consider the call of Christ's cross.

283

It is a

I. Call to Thought About the Preparation of the Cross

The cross, where the history of human guilt culminates, was conceived in the councils of eternity, where Father, Son, and Holy Ghost knew infinite rejoicing without interruption or diminution.

The cross, where the purposes of divine love are made intelligible, was made ready while Jesus had glory with God before the world was, while he was loved by the Father before the foundation of the world—for then the cross was conceived in the mind of God.

The cross, where the majesty of the law is vindicated, where the problem of human redemption is solved, where the fountain of salvation is unsealed, was a reality in heaven before ever there was an earth.

The cross, where Satan is crushed, where our sorrows hide in Emmanuel's wounds, where our death sentence is revoked, was a goal in the heart of God from all eternity.

The cross was prepared in heaven before creation—and, amidst the angels of heaven who worshiped Christ. Jesus *felt* the weight of the cross ages before he *fell* beneath its weight in the midst of men who despised him and women who wept over him.

Though it is a tremendous subject and as far beyond and above our mental capacity to comprehend as a teaspoon lacks capacity to hold a ton of sand, still God would be pleased and we will be profited to give thought to the preparation of the cross.

Give thought to the majesty of it.

Give thought to the mystery of it.

Give thought to the eternity of it.

Give thought to the wisdom that conceived it.

Give thought to the love that prepared it.

Give thought to the tragedy that necessitated it.

Give thought to the Christ who validated it.

The song writer, gazing at the starry heavens, said:

Thoughts of wonder! O how mighty!
How stupendous! How profound!
All the stars that sparkle yonder
Roll in orbs of vastness round.

But the cross of Christ is more impressive than that—to him who really gazes at it and stops long enough to perceive what it means!

It is a

II. Call to Thankfulness Through Perception of the Cross

Can one, knowing of many to be fed, fail to be thankful for fruitful fields?

Can one, knowing how dreadful would be continuous darkness, fail to be thankful for light and eyesight?

Can one, knowing the tragedy of being crazy, refuse to give thanks for a functioning mind?

Can one, knowing the handicap of a maimed body, fail to be thankful for eyes that can see, for ears that can hear, and feet that can walk, and a tongue that can talk, and a body rich and strong with health?

Can one, knowing the danger of voyaging in unknown waters, when fierce storms rage, fail to be thankful for lighthouses that guide and bell buoys that warn?—and for the harbor when the voyage is over?

Can one, knowing the wasting of disease, fail to be thankful for medicines that restore?

No! Then let me ask—can anyone, surveying the cross, having perception of its stark cruelty and shame, considering the Christ who died thereon, fail to be thankful for all it makes possible?

If we look at the cross and see only two pieces of wood on which a good Jew died—we do not have the key that unlocks the gate to the palace of truth.

From God's side the cross *was* a divine necessity.

From God's side the cross *is* a divine necessity.

From man's side the cross *was* a divine necessity.

From man's side the cross *is* a divine necessity.

From the time when man sinned, he has known that there was something wrong between him and God.

And he tried in many ways to right that wrong—to bridge the chasm between him and God.

Athens, though drunk with the wine of intellectual skepticism, had so many altars and idols adorning her streets that she was laughed at by a satirist who said she had more gods on her streets than men.

286 Southern Baptist Preaching Yesterday

In Pompeii, excavators found marble steps before a heathen altar—steps worn down so hard as to make them almost a smooth ramp.

Behind that altar, after the ashes of Vesuvius had buried them for one thousand years, were found the forms of thirty people who fled there for refuge at the great eruption—when thousands found nothing to breathe but flame, and nothing to walk in but hot ashes, and no cover but steaming lava.

In Persia, many mothers tried to get right with God by laying the babies that had nursed their breasts ever and anon by day and night, in the arms of red-hot Moloch in the morning. In India the mothers heard the cries of their babies drowned by the greedy gulpings of the crocodiles—hoping to get smiles of approval rather than frowns of displeasure from God.

And the Jews slew a million lambs on the rock of the Mosque of Omar. But—

> Not all the blood of beasts,
> On Jewish altars slain,
> Could give the guilty conscience peace
> Or wash away the stain.

Nothing man *could* do, or *can* do, will make things right between him and God—because all man *could* or *can* do sprang and springs from and partook of the nature of bankrupt, diseased, and wrecked humanity.

Can a bankrupt pay his debts?

Can a sick man cure himself?

Can a ditched engine put itself on the track?

Can a man on crutches outrun an athlete who has no lameness?

Can an eagle with both wings broken, and featherless, soar to the clouds?

Can a sick man's moan reach farther than the shriek of a locomotive whistle?

Toplady answers these questions in these words:

> Could my tears forever flow,
> Could my zeal no languor know,
> These for sin could not atone;
> Thou must save, and Thou alone.

God's nature and the nature of sin are eternally opposite in eternal and antagonistic antithesis.

Thus we see the necessity of the cross.

God hates sin so greatly that under his providence the wages of sin is death.

But, while he hates sin, he loves the sinner—even though, as the Word declares, "God is angry with the sinner every day."

If he were to make the sinner pay for his sin by death, he would destroy sinners.

Only one thing, therefore, is left—and that is to have one pay who could not be destroyed by death.

That is what took place at the cross where Jesus died—"the just for the unjust that he might bring us to God."

Perceiving the cross, Wesley wrote:

> When I survey the wondrous cross,
> On which the Prince of glory died,
> My richest gain I count but loss,
> And pour contempt on all my pride.

The call of Christ's cross is a

III. Call to Tribulation Through Participation with the Cross

Paul sets this truth before us in these words:

I am crucified with Christ: nevertheless I live; yet not I, but Christ liveth in me: and the life which I now live in the flesh I live by the faith of the Son of God, who loved me, and gave himself for me (Gal. 2:20).

Knowing this, that our old man is crucified with him, that the body of sin might be destroyed, that henceforth we should not serve sin (Rom. 6:6).

And that he died for all, that they which live should not henceforth live unto themselves, but unto him which died for them, and rose again (2 Cor. 5:15).

Jesus did not turn a hand to save himself from the cross: "I lay down my life. No man taketh it from me. I have power to lay it down. I have power to take it up again."

He set his face like a flint toward Jerusalem and defied and resisted all who tried to thwart him.

He is the only One in human history who went to death as he died.

And if we hear and respond to the call of the cross, we will share his crucifixion.

And:

> We are troubled on every side, yet not distressed; we are perplexed, but not in despair; persecuted, but not forsaken; cast down, but not destroyed; always bearing about in the body the dying of the Lord Jesus, that the life also of Jesus might be made manifest in our body. For we which live are always delivered unto death for Jesus' sake, that the life also of Jesus might be made manifest in our mortal flesh (2 Cor. 4:8-11).

He paid the price for our redemption—to bring us back to God.

A greater price God paid to bring us back to him.

And we ought to be willing to pay the price to live for him—to say to him:

> Not for ease or worldly pleasure,
> Nor for fame my prayer shall be;
> Gladly will I toil and suffer,
> Only let me live for Thee.
> My life, my love I give to Thee,
> Thou Lamb of God who died for me.

Dr. Rutherford said: "Men want a cheap Christ, but the price will not come down."

If you cannot say, "I am crucified with Christ," you cannot say, "Jesus is mine."

A crucified Christ and a cushioned disciple do not go together.

An agonizing Christ and an ease-seeking disciple have little fellowship.

We do not have nails driven through hands and feet anymore. We need them driven through our pocketbooks to have here what we ought to have here to honor God.

We can avoid that if we wish, but we cannot avoid nails in our pocketbooks and self-will and belong to Christ; and do not delude yourselves with the idea that nickels and dimes are *nails*.

Making a manifestation of Christianity a mere convenience or a sulking in the tent is not giving our hands to the nails.

But, again, the call of Christ's cross is a

IV. Call to Trust Through Permanent Protection of the Cross

Culture offers no protection for man from the penalties of sin.

Education is a roofless house for protection.

Good behavior is a wall which falls when you lean on it.

Rituals and observances of days are a leaking boat for a long and dangerous voyage.

Dependence on good works to save from sins is a silk thread, not a chain to anchor the ship in time of storm.

Human goodness and kindness is a house built upon shifting sands.

> Other refuge have I none;
> Hangs my helpless soul on Thee.
>
> In my hand no price I bring,
> Simply to Thy cross I cling.
>
> Cover my defenseless head
> With the shadow of thy wing.

The only place the first-born was safe when the death angel passed through Egypt was in the house where the blood was on the doorposts—placed in obedience to God's commands. No portals were protective that had not the blood.

The only place where Rahab found refuge for her and her loved ones, when Joshua's army captured Jericho, was in her house, on the wall, with the red rope tied in the window—placed there in obedience to the instruction of the spies.

The only place where the unwitting slayer found refuge from the pursuing avenger was in the City of Refuge—prepared by Joshua in obedience to the protective commands of God.

So only in Christ's cross can we find safety.

But again, the call of Christ's cross is a

V. Call to Triumph Through the Power of the Cross

Many times through the centuries gone forever into the tomb of time has man sought power to make himself master of the forces of the universe.

And he has mastered many forces in his search for power.

One day I took a fast train up the Hudson to Albany.

I thought of Fulton's little teakettle of a steamboat that struggled up the Hudson to Albany in three days—despite its nickname, "Fulton's Folly," despite the dire prophecies to the contrary.

And on another day, over that same route, right up the Hudson, a man flew the distance in sixteen minutes in a jet plane.

Power that masters gravitation, winds, and distance!

But what about the cross and the power thereof?

Is it still an ornament worn about a lady's neck or on a preacher's vest?

Is it still a thing that crowns only a church steeple?

Does it still mean no more to many than an adornment for a church altar?

As a power, is it still not utilized—not appropriated?

As a power, is it still only something mentioned in anthems and hymns?

The *cross* is the *way* to *spiritual power*.

How foolish man is not to use the cross for spiritual power!

The cross is the way home;

The cross is the way home to purity,

The cross is the way home to peace,

The cross is the way home to joy,

The cross is the way home to power,

The cross is the way home for you,

The cross is the way home for me,

The cross is the way home for the world.

The power of the cross works—

Just as electricity in a motor works;

Just as steam in a locomotive works;

Just as gravitation works in the universe.

Those who make it an experience do the most in the spiritual world.

Christ gave the cross its meaning.

His triumph thereon is shown in that five hundred millions of souls who call him Lord today.

The cross was an experience with Paul who said, "I die daily";—and there are ten thousand churches bearing his name.

The confessors and martyrs upset the Roman Empire and snuffed the altar fires of Diana with no weapon except the cross.

Did not the potent cross meet Judaism in the first century—and conquer Judaism?

Did not the cross meet pagan philosophy in the third century, in the fourth century, in the fifth century—and conquer pagan philosophy?

Did not the cross meet English deism in the last century and conquer English deism?

Did not the cross meet French skepticism in the seventeenth century—and conquer French skepticism?

Did not the pages of ancient history become replete—not only with adoration and worship of Christ as the Son of God, but with evidences of triumphs of his cross?

Did not the medieval war lord who lifted up a cross and said, "In this sign I conquer," pay tribute to the power of the cross?

Does not modern history cry out for the power of the cross?

Notwithstanding that many present educators seek to play his deity down to the level of human divinity, notwithstanding numerous organized efforts which seek to revile and discredit him, notwithstanding many present-day functionaries are arrayed against his Saviourhood and Lordship, no personality so grips the human thought, so dominates, so controls, so consumes the human soul as the personality of Jesus.

But, *would* this be—*could* this be—without the cross?

Would, and could the witness of literature, and of art, and of civilization testify that Jesus is the central, supreme, and superlative fact of the ages were the cross left out?

Where but in the cross can we hope for power to stem the tides of materialism today?

Moody knew the cross as something more than an ornament. He gave his all to Christ. And he is still drawing thousands to Chicago and thousands to Northfield almost fifty years after his death. Northfield has a grove of trees at the foot of the hill where he and his wife lie sleeping—with the name of a missionary on every tree, inspired to go by the cross-loving Moody and those who have perpetuated his spirit.

There is power in the cross—wonder-working power.

The cross lifts men buried in sin and brings them up into the light of a new day.

Utilize the power of the cross.

Without it, we are weaklings.

But, lastly, the call of Christ's cross is a

VI. Call for Trepidation If We Pass the Cross

There is no hope to take the place of despair,
There is no heaven to take the place of hell,
There is no cleanliness to take the place of dirt,

There is no justification to take the place of condemnation,

There is no devotion to take the place of devilment,

There is no virtue to take the place of vice,

There is no salvation to take the place of sinfulness, if we pass the cross by—if we "highhat" the cross, if we have only a passing glance for the cross.

You may blame the Jews for crucifying Christ if you want to; and there is no denying the fact that he died at the hands of the Jews.

But your sins and my sins drove him to the cross—and you were there when they crucified my Lord.

The question of the old heart-stirring spiritual can be changed from a question to a positive statement.

What were the sins that crucified Christ?

> Hatred,
> Jealousy,
> Self-satisfaction,
> Self-will,
> Self-righteousness,
> Greed,
> Pride,
> Congealed religion,
> Concealed hypocrisy,
> Pomp.

His simple faith rebuked their parades.

His simple needs condemned their greed.

His love of people punctured their love of praise.

His forgiving spirit made their censorious spirit look like a blot of ink. And they crucified him!

But the sins are all your sins and my sins. So don't say you had no part in that crime.

He died for the sins of the world—yours, mine, everybody's.

They all together nailed him to the cross.

This being so, the cross calls us to *come* penitently to the cross—not stand afar off as a mere beholder of mere historical fact.

The cross calls us to *stop* with repentance at the cross.

The cross calls us to refuse to pass the cross by. One of the two thieves who died with him answered that call.

The Roman centurion who said, "Truly, this was the Son of God," probably answered it.

Maybe some of those who beat upon their bosoms beholding it answered it.

And the three thousand who were converted on the day of Pentecost, when accused by Peter of crucifying Christ, answered it.

What does that call mean to you?

Is that call as a whisper or as a strong voice in your ears?

Is that call as a soft-speaking stammerer or as a trumpet tone?

Is that call a feeble brook or a forceful river?

Is that call as a sparrow's twitter or an eagle's scream?

Is that call a jest or as a judicial summons

Is that call as a zephyr or cyclonic wind in force?

Is that call the light laughter of a stranger or the passionate plea of a love call?

Are you answering that call by repenting in humiliation?

Or, are you saying, "At some more convenient season"?

Are you just "almost persuaded now to believe"?

Are you just "almost persuaded Christ to receive"?

View such an attitude of passing the cross by with trepidation.

There is great peril, for "almost is but to fail."

A plane came all the way from the Orient some months ago, bound for Chicago—

Crossing the biggest ocean,

Flying above mountain ranges,

Flying over hundreds of islands, and was dashed to pieces in a wreck—almost home.

"Almost" is a tragic word—terribly tragic.

Some years ago a cruising vessel made a journey around the world, and cast anchor in the home harbor of England, only to be wrecked the night before she was going to discharge her passengers.

To the pastor of the captain fell the sad lot of informing his wife and children, as they were spreading the table for his coming, of the truth that the ship had sunk and their loved one with it.

Much of that sad visit remains untold—too sacred for the world to know. But one sentence, wrung in anguish from the mother's lips, has been given to us: "Lost, and so near home!"

Almost home, but lost!

Repent! Repent! Repent! rings like fire bells all through the Bible.

Today that Book urges you to *repent*.

"Now is the accepted time."

"Today is the day of salvation."

Will you answer that call with humiliation and trepidation—lest you pass the cross by?

No man will strut through the gate of heaven swinging a gold-headed cane. No man will go in on his Masonic badge, no man will go in on his political achievements, no man will go in on his stars and bars and silver medals, no man will go in on his college diplomas, no man will go in on his record as a soldier or statesman. No man will go in on his ordination paper. No man will go in on his pile of money, no man will go in on his scientific discoveries.

We will all go in, if we go at all, just as we are, without one plea—except the plea of the riven hands and the pierced side.

The cross calls!

I relay the call to you!

Answer not as the fool answereth!

C. E. Matthews
Heaven

Let not your heart be troubled: ye believe in God, believe also in me. In my Father's house are many mansions: if it were not so, I would have told you. I go to prepare a place for you. And if I go and prepare a place for you, I will come again and receive you unto myself; that where I am, there ye may be also. And whither I go ye know, and the way ye know. Thomas saith unto him, Lord, we know not whither thou goest; and how can we know the way? Jesus saith unto him, I am the way, and the truth, and the life: no man cometh unto the Father, but by me (John 14:1-6).

Our subject for this sermon is one that delights the soul more than any other known to human conversation. Because of the fact that a great sorrow in our home has led the writer to search the Scriptures for everything the Bible has to say on this subject, and because of gratitude to Him for the great privilege of having her sweet fellowship for eleven years, this sermon is dedicated to the blessed memory of our daughter, Kathryn Louise Matthews.

The Old Testament is filled with references to the land beyond called heaven. There is little or no information however as to what heaven really is until we find recorded in the fourteenth chapter of John's Gospel its description given to His disciples by our Lord and Savior Jesus Christ.

The occasion was brought about by a near collapse of hope on the part of the apostles when they understood for the first time that the Messiah was to be crucified by His enemies. These disciples knew that Jesus was God, and as such, they did not believe that God could die. They were well acquainted with Old Testament history. They had read of the translation of Enoch and the prophet Elijah. Three of them had witnessed the transfiguration of Jesus, and they undoubtedly believed that Christ would not and could not taste of death. They believed that He would be translated when He had succeeded in establishing the earthly throne of David. This was their ambition and belief concerning Jesus, and words could not express the awful despair that gripped their hearts when they learned definitely that Jesus must die a death of humiliation on the cross. In order to comfort them by reviving hope, our Lord told them about heaven.

What Is Heaven?

In this message we shall attempt to answer the queries of the human mind about the future home of the redeemed. One of the first questions asked by those who are seeking light is, what is heaven?

According to our text, heaven is a place. Jesus said, "I go to prepare a place for you" (John 14:2b). It is just as definitely a place for human beings as is this world.

Heaven is a beautiful place. It is indescribably beautiful. I used to wonder why John failed to have words and understandable descriptive phrases of the world beyond which he saw with the prophetic eye as he wrote the account in Revelation. I could never figure it out until a few years ago when I visited the famous Carlsbad Caverns of New Mexico.

On that day, four hundred and fifty-six people went down a huge hole in the earth to a depth of seven hundred and fifty feet. I shall never forget what my eyes beheld, but to save my life I can't describe it.

Behind my wife and me there was a man and a lady. The lady had been through the cavern before, but her companion had not. He kept saying, "Isn't this wonderful?"

The farther we went, the more beautiful was the scenery. Finally, our friend seemed to grow irritated because his wife had not told him of the marvelous place.

He asked in a tone of disappointment as we reached the matchless King's Palace. "Why haven't you told me about this?"

She answered, "I couldn't. I could find no words to describe it."

That is exactly the case of John when he saw the Pearly White City. In the twenty-first and twenty-second chapters of Revelation he tried to describe the portion of heaven which he saw, and in those chapters we learn more of its celestial beauty than can be found anywhere else in the world. Paul had a glimpse of it, and heard some of its language when he was miraculously saved, and he came back to say, "Eye hath not seen, nor ear heard, neither have entered into the heart of man, the things which God hath prepared for them that love him" (1 Cor. 2:9).

Where Is Heaven?

The next question we would discuss is the location of heaven. Where is it? Heaven is up above this earth somewhere. Of this we can be certain, for Elijah ascended up in a chariot of fire when he was translated, and Jesus was taken up from the earth when He went back to the Father.

When Do We Go to Heaven?

Another, and a very vital question is, when do we go to heaven? Is it at the second coming of Christ or is it at death? Does the soul sleep in the body until the morning of the resurrection? Thank God, the Scriptures are plain on this matter in spite of much false teaching concerning it today. Let us turn to the Bible for our information.

In the story of Lazarus and the rich man, we read, "And it came to pass that the beggar died and was carried by the angels into Abraham's bosom" (Luke 16:22).

Here we see the spirit of the humble believer delivered into the home of the redeemed at death.

When the dying thief on his cross felt the quaking of the earth, saw midnight darkness at midday, and heard divine words fall from the lips of Jesus, he was convicted of his guilt in the sight of God. With a penitent heart, he turned to the One whom he suddenly recognized as the Son of God, and humbly begged, "Lord, remember me when thou comest into thy kingdom."

"And Jesus said unto him, Verily I say unto thee, Today shalt thou be with me in paradise" (Luke 23:42-43).

Some may ask, where is paradise? Is it an intermediate state of the dead? Not the paradise spoken of in the Bible, for that paradise is synonymous with heaven. Paul, relating his conversion, says that he was "Caught up into paradise and heard unspeakable words, which it is not lawful for a man to utter" (2 Cor. 12:4).

Preceding this statement, he calls the place where he was caught up to "The third heaven" (2 Cor. 12:2).

That is where Jesus is, and in order to be sure that no one should misunderstand this great comforting truth, Paul tells us again, "To be absent from the body and to be present with the Lord" (2 Cor. 5:8).

This removes every doubt concerning the question, and assures us that the soul of the child of God goes to heaven at the moment physical death takes place.

Shall We Know Each Other in Heaven?

Another important and comforting truth concerning heaven is in this question, "Shall we know each other when we get there?"

We should be thankful again that concerning this, we can be certain, and we do not have to base our belief on speculation. The Bible is full of information on this point. When we touch anything concerning the future life, we must come to Christ and upon Him build our structure of belief.

John said, "Beloved, now are we the sons of God, and it doth not yet appear what we shall be: but we know that, when he shall appear, we shall be like him; for we shall see him as he is" (1 John 3:2).

From this scripture some may contend that because we shall be like Jesus that all will be exactly alike after the resurrection. This is not John's idea at all. He means that we shall have a glorified body like our Lord, but that we shall retain our identity.

The following examples are some which we find concerning this truth.

Jesus was identified by Thomas after His resurrection because He retained not only His earthly appearance in His glorified state, but His resurrected body even had the print of the nails in His hands, and the scar left by the Roman spear was still in His side.

"Then saith he to Thomas, Reach hither thy finger, and behold my hands; and reach hither thy hand, and thrust it into my side and be not faithless, but believing. And Thomas answered and said unto him, My Lord and my God" (John 20:27,28).

When Lazarus, the beggar, was in Abraham's bosom, he was recognized by the rich man in hell.

At the Mount of Transfiguration, Moses and Elijah came down from heaven to talk to Jesus about His crucifixion. Elijah had been translated nine hundred years and Moses' disembodied spirit had been in heaven nearly fifteen hundred years, but they both retained their identity and were still Moses and Elijah.

For a concrete statement on this great truth we must look again to Paul. Thank God for the apostle Paul. In his great discourse on the resurrection, he settles the matter once and for all. Here it is: "For one star differeth from another star in glory. So also is the resurrection of the dead" (1 Cor. 15:41,42).

Any astronomer will tell you that no two stars in the heavens are alike. Of all miracles, the greatest is the human family. There are over one billion people living today (when this sermon was preached), and no two of them are exactly alike physically. Neither, Paul says, will they be alike in heaven. We retain our identity.

What Conditions Prevail Up Yonder?

To me the most interesting thing about heaven is the conditions which prevail in the mansions above. John describes them in his prophetic book of Revelation, chapters twenty-one and twenty-two. The description he makes of conditions up there are the most unique in all literature. He describes the state of the redeemed of the future Kingdom of God by taking up the curses that sin has wrought on the earth and saying these will be "no more" in heaven. More than any other prophetic promise in the Bible, his "no mores" in heaven stimulate in the believer jubilant hope.

He says there will be no more sea. John knew the terror of the sea; its storms and fathomless depths formed a prison wall about him that shut him off from his beloved land and people and held him a prisoner in exile when he wrote the book. Physical waters will never jeopardize the life of a saint in glory.

There will be no more tears, for God shall wipe away all tears from their eyes. It is not that the redeemed will be incapable of weeping, but all causes for a sorrowing heart will be removed.

There will be no more poverty in heaven, for there they neither hunger nor thirst anymore. Oh, for that land that will put an end to the starving of men, women and little children. I doubt if there is anything that moves the heart of a human being to compassion and genuine sympathy like the sight of one starving to death. Heaven will end that.

There will be no more darkness, spiritual or physical. Up yonder they need no sun, neither light of a candle, for the Lord God is the light thereof. They have no clouds to darken the day.

> O they tell me of a home far beyond the skies,
>   O they tell me of a home far away.
> O they tell me of a home where no storm clouds rise;
>   O they tell me of an unclouded day.

There will be no more death. Of all the curses wrought by Adam's sin, there is none so universal as death. "It is appointed unto men once to die" (Heb. 9:27).

We know when our children are given to us that some day they shall die. We look at mother when we leave her to go for a day, a week, or a year, with the knowledge that perchance we shall never see her again in this world. We lie down at night to sleep, never knowing if we shall awake. Everywhere we are stalked by death, but heaven will end it all.

There will be no more nations, and only one language in heaven, for we shall be like Adam and Eve were before the fall. It was sin that caused more than one language to be spoken. Man committed that sin at the building of the tower of Babel. All nations will truly be of one blood and one color up there.

"In the midst of the street of it, and on either side of the river, was there the tree of life, which bare twelve manner of fruits, and yielded her fruit every month: and the leaves of the tree were for the healing of the nations.

"And there shall be no more curse."

Every curse known to the human race is removed in heaven by the power of God, and the redeemed will all be true brothers and sisters together, and God shall be our Father and Christ our elder Brother and King.

How Does One Get to Heaven?

We close with the most vital of all things concerning heaven. If we could sum up its glory, its music, its beauty, its magnitude, and all of its nameless wonders together, they could not amount to so much in their importance as this one great fact. Miss it and you miss it all. What is this fact? It is the fact that there is only one way into heaven. Somehow I feel that there is not one person living now, or who ever lived, who is in his right mind but who does not want to go to heaven when he dies. That was the longing of Thomas when Jesus told him of His Father's house of many mansions.

"Thomas said unto him, Lord, we know not whither thou goest; and how can we know the way?"

"Jesus saith unto him, I am the way, and the truth, and the life: no man cometh unto the Father but by me" (John 14:5,6).

My dear lost friend, don't forget these words; Jesus is the way into heaven. "If thou shalt confess with thy mouth the Lord Jesus, and shalt believe in thine heart that God hath raised him from the dead, thou shalt be saved" (Rom. 10:9).

May the desire to point the lost soul to Christ be the hunger, the longing, the ambition and the aching throb of every Christian heart who reads these lines.

George W. McDaniel
An Analogy on Prayer

> How much more shall your heavenly Father give the Holy Spirit
> to them that ask? (Luke 11:13).

Jesus often reasoned from the human to the divine and argued that if men would not accept the human they could not understand the divine. In the passage before us the Saviour illustrates his doctrine of prayer. The context contains a disciple's request to be taught to pray, an allusion to the prayer life of John the Baptist, Jesus' model prayer for the Christian, a forceful example of the power of importunity, an earnest exhortation to ask, seek and knock, a sure promise of answered petition, and a beautiful analogy of the blessing received through prayer.

A father will not give his son a stone for bread, or a serpent for a fish, or a scorpion for an egg. If an earthly father, with all his imperfections, gives good gifts unto his children, how much more, Jesus argues, will God, who is holy in nature, give the best—the Holy Spirit—to them that *ask him?*

This analogy makes prayer not only very intelligible, but perfectly natural. Familiar relations are used to simplify the mysterious. It is Jesus' method of explaining the abstract by the concrete, and thus clarifying the most abstruse doctrines. How marvelously did he present those profound and difficult subjects over which philosophers have puzzled their brains and scientists wearied and confused their pupils! To Jesus, prayer was like breathing his native air, like a child talking with a parent, and the acceptance of his words dissolves our doubts.

The existence of a personal God is assumed in the text. Elsewhere are arguments for the existence and personality of God, but we cannot enter upon that field just here. The point at issue in the text is the willingness, readiness and ability of God to do what his children request him to do. It is safe to assume that the reader believes in an all-powerful Being, who made all things and whom we call God. Only one among the thousands doubts this teaching. The problem appears when we enter the realm of prayer, and it would be going too far to assume that those who think have no difficulties in understanding how God answers prayer. Perhaps you deny that prayer is answered and assert that the only benefit is reflexive. Docile and unprejudiced attention to the words of Jesus will dissolve doubt and induce to the constant exercise of prayer. Trace the analogy for yourselves.

1. Like an earthly father, God gives his children many blessings *without the asking*. Before the child is able to ask, the father provides food, clothing and all creature comforts. The watchful eye is above the innocent cradle and guides and trains the inexperienced steps. All though infancy and throughout youth the parent bestows unsought gifts upon the child.

Just so does God give much without being asked. Sunshine, water, fuel, friends, loved ones, guardian angels, blessings, temporal and spiritual, beginning before birth and continuing through life, and crowning all our days.

2. Like an earthly father God often *awaits the request* before bestowing the blessing. The wise father delays certain gifts until the child is thoughtful and anxious enough to ask. They are in the father's purposes and plans, but are withheld until the child is ready to receive. How foolish it would be to give a riding pony to an infant in the cradle. When the boy arrives at the proper age and desires to use a pony for exercise, or attending the distant school, then the father may permit him to select the one of his choice from the pasture.

The second Psalm, verses 7-9, presents this thought clearly: Jehovah has accepted the King as his Son: and now the King takes up Jehovah's declaration and appeals to the divine decree of sonship and the promise of worldwide dominion. Inheritance is the natural right of sonship. Even the son must plead the promise and grant its fulfillment: "Ask of me and I shall give the heathen for thine inheritance, and the uttermost parts of the earth for thy possession."

The Holy Spirit is for all Christians, but his coming upon the individual waits for the asking. Read the Acts of the Apostles to see how the disciples waited and prayed for the fulfillment of the promise. In twenty-eight chapters of the Acts prayer is mentioned twenty-nine times, and the Holy Spirit sixty times.

3. Like an earthly father God sometimes grants the petition *in a manner to develop the child.* The judicious father does not lavish countless gifts upon the unprepared child. Such a method would create discontent and corrupt character. Rather does he place responsibility upon the growing son and develops him by partnership in the father's business. God is no less wise. Prayer is not merely words. It is the output of vital energy, and the answered prayer is the bestowal of responsibility, the association of the believer with God in a vast enterprise. God desires the cooperation of his people with himself, and waits until that spirit is manifested before executing his plans. As Bishop Brent says: "He enfolds us in himself with a tightening embrace, as by loyalty to his laws and repeated acts of faith, we expose new portions of our nature for him to lay hold on."

4. Like an earthly father God has sufficient reasons for sometimes *denying the requests of his children.* How foolish we sometimes are in the things we want to do. A Virginia father sent his son to V.M.I. The boy chafed under military discipline, and appealed in letters to be allowed to leave. The father tactfully replied from time to time, declining to give permission. One day the boy wired that he would start home the next day. The father wired that he was on his way to Lexington, and the boy was kept at school. He is now a substantial business man and influential public citizen, and a useful member of a church. He says: "I largely owe what I am to my father's firm refusal to my foolish request."

The analogy holds in the life of prayer and explains many an unanswered petition. The aged saint, looking back upon life, thanks an all-wise God for the requests that were withheld, as well as for those granted.

5. Like an earthly father God desires *confidential and intimate relations* with his children. The successful parent is he who cultivates the companionship and holds the confidence of his children. He finds no higher pleasure than to be with them, and the door to his heart is ever open. It is a blessed hour when the child comes for no other purpose than to be with father, when he cares less for what he may receive and more for the father himself.

Just so is God longing for confidential relations with his children. It is well pleasing to him when they come for communion. This, I suppose, is more acceptable to God than any other attitude one may assume. In these busy, stressful days the soul is impoverished by neglecting the trysting place with the Divine. As we grow in years and grace we think more of the "secret place" with the Lord.

Paul, communing in the desert of Arabia, had his life stored with the power of God, and Tennyson said that "solitude is the mother country of the strong."

These analogies being true, and they are, though I fear they are so simple that the worldly-wise stumble over their simplicity and miss their preciousness, certain conclusions follow.

(1) The execution of God's will waits upon prayer. The great unused dynamic of the church is prayer. It releases vital energy and puts at the command of the Christian divine resources. As Dr. Forsyth says in the *Power of Prayer:* "Prayer is for the religious life what original research is for science,—by it we get direct contact with reality."

The most practical writer of the New Testament makes the unqualified statement, "the supplication of a righteous man availeth much in its working." The idea is that prayer puts power at the disposal of God. It does not change the will of God, but enables God to change the wills of men. We do not persuade God, but put ourselves in the attitude where God can bring power to bear to persuade men. The reason so little is accomplished with this dynamo of power is because it is so little used. "Ye have not because ye ask not."

In that critical battle recorded in Exodus 17, the issue turned on prayer. Joshua's sword was ineffective when intercession ceased, but while Moses and Aaron and Hur, on the mountain, interceded with God, victory crowned the army of Israel. The lesson is patent and impressive for Christianity to-day. The efforts of our missionaries on foreign fields will be unavailing if they are not supported by spiritually minded members and praying churches on the home field.

(2) The prayer spirit is the most needful force in modern missions. It puts feelings in the hearts of those who should go and thoughts in the minds of those who direct the activities. We are in the habit of saying that we need two things supremely,—more men and more money; but back of these is the need of that spiritual atmosphere which is created by prayer.

Robert McCheyne was oppressed by the dearth of volunteers in his congregation. He made it a subject of prayer and in a short time seven missionaries had gone out from his church in Scotland.

At a meeting of the Northamptonshire Association of Baptist ministers in 1784, John Ryland's appeal to the churches was adopted, which contained a plea that "the spread of the Gospel to the more distant parts of the habitable globe be the object of your most fervent requests." On that occasion Andrew Fuller preached his first written sermon on "Working by Faith." Two years later William Carey was baptized by the same John Ryland and ordained by Andrew Fuller. Carey and the whole modern missionary enterprise which began with him are explained by the prayers of Baptist preachers at an association. Earnest prayer will enlist sufficient volunteers to cover every mission field on the globe.

The money problem is fundamentally a spiritual problem. We make it too much a financial problem. An emergency arose in a mission in China and $1,000 was imperatively needed. A telegram was sent to the Secretary in America. He betook himself to prayer that God might provide the means. That afternoon a plainly clad old gentleman called upon the Secretary. He asked if there was any special need for money and was shown the cablegram. Tears came in his eyes and he confided that he and his wife, while engaged in family prayers that morning, had been impressed that they ought to be more generous with the Lord's work, and under that conviction he called at the Mission Board. Taking a roll of bills from the inside pocket of the worn overcoat, he handed them to the Secretary and withdrew, while a heavenly light was upon his face and a supreme joy in his soul. When the roll was counted the amount totaled $1,000. Prayer in China, supplemented by prayer around an altar of an humble home, supplied the funds for pressing needs.

(3) The *highest exercise* of the soul is communion with God. Prayer is a reaching up of the heart to God in complete surrender, and taking whatever he has to give. It is not dreaming, but intelligent action, and was the holiest experience in the life of Jesus. He has put it first in the lives of his people. Preaching is of tremendous importance, and Paul aptly asks, "how shall they hear without a preacher?" But Jesus' first concern for his preachers was that they be men of prayer (Matt. 6:5-16).

Teaching and healing consumed not a little amount of the Master's time, and they are receiving a new emphasis among Christians; but prayer was more urgent with Jesus than either of these, for when the multitudes were thronging him to be taught and healed he retired to pray

(Luke 5:15,16). Rest and sleep are the gifts of God, and are essential to health, but Jesus forgot both and betook himself to prayer when crises arose (Mark 1:35; Luke 6:12). Workers are urgently needed in the world's whitening harvest field; but the only method suggested by Jesus for securing them is prayer (Matt. 9:38). Heaven has many activities: but the only revealed one of the ascended Lord is the holy activity of intercession. "He ever liveth to make intercession" (Heb. 6:28). That intercession makes possible the salvation of the world. "Wherefore he is able to save to the uttermost." While on earth Jesus provided a plan of salvation, which was complete in his death and resurrection, but that salvation is not applied effectively without intercession.

> The camel, at the close of day,
>   Kneels down upon the sandy plain,
> To have his burden lifted off
>   And rest to gain.
>
> My soul, thou, too, shouldst to thy knees,
>   When daylight draweth to a close,
> And let thy Master lift the load
>   And grant repose.
>
> Else how couldst thou to-morrow meet,
>   With all to-morrow's work to do,
> If thou thy burden all the night
>   Didst carry through?
>
> The camel kneels at break of day
>   To have his guide replace his load;
> Then rises up anew to take
>   The desert road.
>
> So thou shouldst kneel at morning's dawn,
>   That God may give thee daily care,
> Assured that He no load too great
>   Will make thee bear.

Paul A. Meigs
The Object of a New Testament Church

Ephesians 3

Someone said, "Is the church a holy place or is it a marketplace?" If it is a marketplace, about all that we have is a smile and handshake. But, if it is a holy place, then we have both a message and a mission. We are not here just to sell wares; we are here with a gospel to preach and a message to give.

Phillips translates verse 10 as follows:

All the angelic powers should now see the complex wisdom of God's plan being worked out through the Church, in conformity to that timeless purpose which he centered in Christ Jesus, our Lord.

From the King James Version we read:

To the intent that now unto the principalities and powers in heavenly places might be known by the church the manifold wisdom of God.

Weymouth translates the tenth verse like this:

It is the stewardship of the truth which from all the Ages lay concealed in the mind of God, the Creator of all things—concealed in order that the Church might now be used to display to the powers and authorities in the heavenly realms of innumerable aspects of God's wisdom.

In this marvelous passage, Paul is setting forth the tremendous responsibility of a New Testament church. It was the eternal purpose formed in Christ Jesus, our Lord, in whom we have bold and confident access to him (God) through faith in Christ, to the intent that may be made known the truth of God through his churches throughout the ages. That is the great truth he's talking about, the great redemptive plan of God, the great redemptive program of God.

The purpose stated in this passage is that through the church (your church, our local churches) shall be revealed not only to the people around us, but also to the principalities, the heavenly powers, and all of these powers, that God was wise in his great redemptive program.

Then in the last verse of this great chapter of Ephesians we read: "Unto him be glory in the church by Jesus Christ throughout all ages, world without end."

Stewards of Truth

In 1 Timothy 3:15, Paul speaks of the church as "the pillar and ground of the truth"—"pillar and foundation of the truth." Now, with that in mind, we might say that a New Testament church is a veritable stronghold of the truth. It is a bulwark of the truth. Therefore, every Christian, every New Testament church, is a steward of the truth. I believe that a New Testament church is, in one sense, a fellowship in truth—the truth about God, about the Bible, about sin, about the lostness of men, about Jesus Christ the Savior. A New Testament church, then, is a spiritual institution to deal with spiritual matters and must give a spiritual message and must be made up by spiritually born again men and women.

Somebody asked, "Can a man be a Christian and contain Christ— bottle him up in his heart?" Billy Graham says, "No, we have to share him." Can a church, in the sense of the New Testament meaning, be an introvert—disinterested in sharing the message? I don't think so, for in Acts 1:8 we read: "You shall receive power when the Holy Spirit has come upon you; and you shall be my witnesses" (RSV). This is a God-given imperative. Being a Christian witness is not optional. For a Christian this power was for witnessing—witnessing power if you please.

In the light of this passage, we have to go further. We can read a little more closely and find that the church is to be a spectacle to the angels and is to be "for the Glory of God." And that is what he is saying in this passage. It is a strong passage as to the meaning of a New Testament church.

All of the churches can truly be a spectacle and place of instruction for the glory of God, even to the powers of heaven, to the principalities of all the spheres. To realize that God is a God of wisdom and that we are to reveal the eternal purpose of God, which he purposed in his own heart, by coming to him through faith in Jesus Christ, is to understand the redemptive work of God. New Testament churches, therefore, are stewards of this truth. We dare not give stones for bread.

During a recent Christmas season, a close friend of our family attended a T.E.L. class Christmas party. As most groups do, they had drawn names to exchange token Christmas gifts. The teacher got the name of an unsaved woman who had been attending the class only a few weeks. She gave a deck of cards to the unsaved woman for her Christmas present. When the woman opened the package, she said: "I don't think I will ever go back to hear her teach again. If this is all that she knows, then she has no message for me." As the story came to me, I thought of the passage in the Scriptures where Jesus asked if man would give a stone for bread. I guess this would be just as appropriate.

Paul is setting forth the objective of a New Testament church with full force in the Ephesian passage. There are two immense facts that the churches must present: (1) the fact of the soul, and (2) the fact of eternity.

As we search further, we find that a New Testament church is a fellowship of experience, a kindred experience. We sing "Blest Be the Tie That Binds" and that is correct, for we are born of the Spirit, bound together, being committed to God by faith in Jesus Christ. This forms a society of witnesses to the grace of God.

A New Testament church, then, must be a herald of the truth, an interpreter of the kingdom. A New Testament church must be made up of evangelists for Jesus Christ. We cannot find a lesser meaning in the objective of a New Testament church than is stated in this. What a tremendous responsibility for a church!

Names Used Concerning the Church

Let me cite some names used concerning the church. First, the church is spoken of as *the body of Christ*. A body is for service. My body is a body for service. The church is a body for service. Believers must be incorporated in Christ, being added to this body through faith in Christ and baptized into Christ. The Bible goes on to say that the body must have a living, vital connection with the head, and Jesus Christ is the head of the church. The Bible has God as its author, truth as its subject matter, and salvation as its end. As a body of Christ, a New Testament church must have a vital connection with its head, and every member of that body must have a vital connection with each other. If there is a part of my body which is dead, then that part is a poison to the entire body. If I get a splinter in my finger and it causes an infection, it impairs the health of my entire body. A member of a church should not be a focal point of infection. The church is a body for service.

Paul in Philippians states that for the Christian to live is for Christ to live over again through him. "For to me to live is Christ." In 1 Corinthians, Paul makes strong reference to the fact that the church is the body of Christ and if one member offend it, that member affects the entire body. Or, in other words, the service and ministry of the body is limited by the offender.

Secondly, the church is referred to as a *temple*. I go back in my thinking to the Old Testament Temple. There were three great uses for a temple. It was (1) a place of prayer, (2) a place for praise, and (3) a place for prophetic utterance. The church today must be a place of prayer. Jesus said, "My house shall be a house of prayer for all the nations." The church is a place of praise when we sing to God. It is glorious when we can sing "All Hail the Power of Jesus Name," "Blessed Assurance," "Amazing Grace," "I Will Sing the Wondrous Story," and many more of the great hymns of faith and praise. The church is to be a place of praise. Our lips praise him because we have joy in our hearts as redeemed ones. The word "joy" comes from a word which has a root meaning of winsome, charming, or gracious. The Christian is a winsome person. One could go further and state that the most winsome Christian is the one who wins some. Then, as a place of prophetic utterance, every believer, every member, should give his testimony of Jesus. In Revelation 19:10 we read, "The testimony of Jesus is the spirit of prophecy." Thus, the spirit of prophecy lies in giving testimony of Jesus. And, in this connection, every child of God should be giving prophetic utterance.

Thirdly, the church is the *bride of Jesus*. When we think of a bride, we think of love, affection, faithfulness, purity, and fruitfulness.

Some years ago I fell in love with a certain young lady, and one night I proposed to her. I asked her to be my wife, and she consented. There was a wooing, a question, and an answer of yes. We became engaged. Some months later, we were married; she became my bride. In the course of the years, two lovely daughters and two fine sons were born into our home. There was motherhood. This was the normal home for us.

When I was a lad of thirteen, the Holy Spirit wooed my heart and I said yes to Jesus by faith in him. I became a part of the bride of Jesus. May I reverently say that if the church, the bride of Jesus, is true to him, sons and daughters will be born into the kingdom of God—"When Zion travails, sons and daughters will be born into the kingdom."

The Objective

The objective of a New Testament church is plainly set forth in this passage: "To him be glory in the church and in Christ Jesus [now] to all the generations [or through all generations], for ever and ever." Do you see the responsibility, as Paul is setting forth here for the New Testament church? To all churches today, to him be glory throughout all generations. Oh, what a responsibility!

There are some who go on with ordinary services or services as usual; they go on one year, five years, or more, and not a soul is won to the Savior—not a soul! I say to you that if we are not witnessing for Christ and winning men to Christ, somewhere down the line we are missing the objective that God has in mind for a New Testament church.

The object of the New Testament church is to evangelize the nations of the world with the glorious gospel, and to make the name of Christ known through the world. Jesus commanded, "Go ye into all the world, and preach the gospel to every creature." Someone has stated that the germ of regeneration is the genesis of missions. We need to recapture our sense of mission today. We have a charge to keep, a Lord to obey and glorify, a mission to carry out, and a task to perform.

In Acts (the Acts of the Holy Spirit), there are four tremendous passages in this area. First, we are told in Acts 2:1 that they (the Christians or believers) were all together when the day of Pentecost was fully come. They were together in purpose, in prayer, and in witnessing. In Acts 2:42 these believers were a studying group and they guarded the fellowship. In Acts 4:31 they are described as a praying group. Then, Acts 5:42 reads: "And daily in the temple, and in every house, they ceased not to teach and preach Jesus Christ." In the early church, the believers were together in study, in prayer, and in witness.

The Ephesians passage certainly teaches that the power is not in the externals, but in the power of God. In the prayer principles that Jesus taught us, he closed with this doxology:

For Thine is the Kingdom—(It must be first);
Thine is the Power—(Not in our strength, but in God's strength);
Thine is the Glory—(Every service should be for his glory).

We should not only know the truth but also should be grounded in love and concern. I hear people say, "as far as I am concerned." Well, how far are we concerned? Someone has said that our zeal will be in direct ratio to our conviction in a given situation. In other words, we do as we believe, the rest is more or less just religious talk. Saved people believe in the saving business.

How Can We Glorify God in the Church?

(1) We can glorify God through worship in the church. Whether we preach, teach, or sing, Paul states in Corinthians, we are "to do all" to give a message, the message of Christ.

(2) We can glorify God in the work of the church. Again, a saved person believes in the saving business. We get our mission from the Great Commission. Someone has said, "If we don't get our mission there, we don't have a mission, and therefore, should get out of the commission."

(3) Finally we can glorify God in the walk of the church. In Ephesians, Paul says, "Walk carefully, walk worthily, walk lovingly, and walk as sons of the light."

May we treasure the word of Paul in Ephesians 3:10 and 3:21. Keep in mind that Jesus said, "My church." May God help us to carry out this God-given objective. We have a message and a mission.

The object of your church and mine, my friend, made up of true believers in Jesus Christ, is to be a fellowship of the concerned. The angels of all the heavenly spheres are looking down upon you and me, upon our churches today. We are responsible to let it be known that God was wise in His great redemptive program and purpose. We are also responsible to conduct our ministry and service in such a manner as to bring conviction upon those about us.

There are some crosscurrents today, some head winds in evangelism. But, I say to you, that the power that Jesus promised was and is a witnessing power. We are His witnesses.

H. Guy Moore
Intruder in the Heavens

The heavens declare the glory of God . . . The law of the Lord
is perfect . . . enduring for ever . . . Keep back thy servant
also from presumptuous sins (Ps. 19:1,7,9,13).

There are so many things happening in our world today that fill my heart
with apprehension and resentment. It seems that there are so few places
left untouched by humans hands and unsoiled by human sin. How many
times we have found release from our troubled world by going out at
night, lifting our eyes to the starry heavens, and saying, "Here, at least, is
one place that man has not invaded. Here is the unspoiled handiwork of
our Creator, revealing in all of its majesty and mystery the glory of God.
Here is God's great masterpiece, bearing the unmistakable autograph of
his hand." We, too, could sing with the poet.

And now even that realm has been invaded. An intruder has hurled
himself on the stage of God's drama of the heavens. He bears only the
signature of man—and a man that disavows God at that! He does not
know the music of their beautiful harmonies and vast silences. His voice
is an unintelligible "beep"—like a crude "burp" in the company of celestial guests. In the heavens it sings not of the glory of God. In one nation it
inspired only pride in man's achievements; in another it inspires jealousy
that the glory was not theirs first.

Religion and the Intrusion of Science

It is that irreverent intrusion that I resent. And some will say, "That's
exactly what we expected from religion." For the past four hundred years
religion has been resenting the intrusions of science. It started back in
1543 when Copernicus published his great work, setting the sun at the
center of our universe and pushing the earth aside to a lesser if not an
insignificant role. For with this conclusion the neat little bandbox universe

314

with the earth as the main theater of operation and with man as the principal actor was swallowed up in the awful immensities of space, time, and motion of the vast universe then unrolled. The religionist complained that science was making God inaccessible.

Then it was Galileo who stepped in to demonstrate that the earth rotated on its axis. Immediately John Calvin, the great theologian of the Reformation, denounced him. He quoted the Bible as his authority to silence the scientist: "The world also is established that it cannot be moved!"

Later still came Isaac Newton with the intrusion of the law of gravity. Even though Newton was a most devout and saintly man, he did not escape the theological onslaught. They said, "He has dethroned Providence—substituting gravity for God."

No one, however, came in for more bitter denouncing than the intruder Darwin. With his theory of evolution he had man crawling over the primeval slime and by millenniums of slow development becoming what he now is. Cried the religious leaders, "You are making nonsense out of Genesis!"

So it has been. With every new advance in science there have been those who were sure their faith was going to be swept away. In the seventeenth century some were so afraid that science would destroy their religious faith that they wouldn't even look at the heavens through a telescope. Now it is our turn. *If man goes into the business of star-making, God is finished!*

Whither Goes Thou, Intruder?

No, it is not the intrusion of science per se that we resent. Even if we did, it would do no good because science is here to stay. Whatever else we may say about it, its facts are convincing. "I have not heard," writes Carlyle Marney, "any so-called *religieux* denying atomic theories, have you? Nagasaki and Hiroshima, whatever they were morally, were intellectually convincing."[1]

If science would stay with the facts so far as its revelation is concerned, it would add to rather than subtract from the wonder and greatness of God. A visitor to a famous observatory relates this experience.

I stood one night on the summit of Mt. Wilson, California, and looked through the most powerful telescope in the world. It was turned upon the constellation of Orion, which can be seen any winter night in the Southern sky. The telescope was directed at the star known as Betelgeuse. I was looking at that marvelous flaming body in the heavens, when the astronomer standing beside me said: "We measured Betelgeuse quite accurately in 1920 with the interfermometer, and we found that it is 260,000,000 miles in diameter." He continued: "Compare that with our earth, with its 8,000 miles in diameter, and it will give you an idea of its immensity." Then, pausing a moment, he said: "It is 32,500 times bigger than our world," and when I gasped with amazement, the astronomer added: "You see, science is compelling us to think great thoughts of God."[2]

As science gives to us a wider and deeper view into the mysteries of God's universe, we ought not to be afraid to think greater thoughts about God. Whether scientist or religionist, we should be able to say with reverence:

> As wider skies broke on his view
> God greatened in his growing mind
> Each year he dreamed his God anew
> And left his older God behind.[3]

If science could prove by the assembling of indisputable facts (though we cannot grant that it has) that creation of man started with a piece of one-celled protoplasm and produced a Moses or a Paul, a Lincoln or an Einstein, that would be some doing! Indeed, it could only be God's doing. If God can make a man that can make a star, then man has proved to be what the psalmist long ago declared him to be—"a little lower than the angels."

That does not in my mind disprove God. It only adds to his marvels of creation. It makes man his masterpiece. The important thing is not how or when, but that back of all creation is God. "In the beginning God created . . ." That is important!

Ah, but here lies the trouble. The creature forgets his Creator. He doesn't want to be an image of God; he wants to be God. He becomes intoxicated with a sense of his own importance. . . .

He forgets who made him. He defies him in whose image he is made. He ignores whose he is and whom he serves. He forgets to give God the glory.

The question, then, to science and to all of us who accept and use its marvelous gifts, is, "To what purpose?" "The heavens," God's creation, "declare the glory of God," but what do science's creations declare? The

Greek had a name for heaven; they called it *ouranos*. It is the same word from which we get our word "uranium." What a parable in words! Out of the same stuff—heavens or an atom, heaven or Hiroshima. We hold in our human hands the power to enrich the earth into a garden or to burn it into a cinder. It all depends on what purpose we choose to serve with the discoveries of science.

The record from Eden to Hiroshima is not at all encouraging. Read with shame the list that one writer has compiled for us, or compile your own.

> We learned to build airplanes and then turned them into "Hell-Cats." We made amazing discoveries in the world of the atom, and the first use we made of it was to turn it into a bomb. We created the movies and with it degraded our morals with sex and slapstick and the commercialization of the Sabbath. We invented machinery to lighten burdens in our factories and with the factories turned our cities into slums. We dreamed up the radio and filled the air with soap opera and with dreary hours of advertising bally-hoo about washing our socks in Sneeze and curing that run-down feeling with Dr. Snickelgruber's laxative. Tune in this mechanism some Sunday afternoon—this mechanism of technical perfection which has absorbed the genius of a million men—and ask yourself if it is worth the six hundred and thirty-two million dollars a year it costs to do that to our world. One woman after a long session of listening to the "Crime Doctor" and the series of mo-ronic shockers that followed that program asked, "Can't we find a nice pleasant morgue somewhere in which to spend the rest of the evening?" Harpo Marx says that television is the greatest educational influence in his life; everytime someone turns it on, he goes off to read a book in another room. Then there were the two monkeys who came out of their native world to view the haunts and ways of men. For two horrible hours they stood listening, then they took to their heels and raced back to the peace and quiet and contentment of their jungle. There is an awful disproportion between the magnificent possibilities of Man's inventions and the trivial, im-moral uses to which they have been put. God gave us bricks to build a New Jerusalem, and out of them we have made this Babylon.[4]

And what is the alternative? Why, we stand on the threshhold of the unlimited universe of space. Columbus' penetration of the New World is nothing compared with the possibilities now within the grasp of science. That which sounded like sheer space-man fiction for boys' imaginative minds suddenly looms into reality.

With the launching of the Russian satellite civilization enters a new era. Man's first space vehicle has been safely projected aloft.

Traveling at a speed of eighteen thousand miles an hour at an altitude of 560 miles, the launching required more power than is generated by the largest hydroelectric station in the world.

While the achievement implies untold significance for the present in advanced scientific information, the greatest implications concern the future. A leading scientist now says that perhaps within ten to twelve years a "space station" accommodating a crew of fifty or seventy-five technicians will be assembled at an altitude of about one thousand miles; and from this "space station" a "moon ship" will be designed within another three years which will carry man to the moon.

The trip around the moon from the "space platform" would take only a few days, and would involve speeds of at least twenty-five thousand miles per hour.[5]

To what purpose this fantastic achievement? A friend of mine expresses it in a letter she wrote on Monday morning after hearing a sermon on this subject on Sunday. "Only a short time before coming to church I tossed the morning paper down in disgust when I read: 'Destination: Moon! Reds May Be Ready. . . . The moon could, say some experts, become a valuable base for launching guided missiles.' And then I thought as you did of Psalms: 'When I consider thy heavens, the work of thy fingers, the moon and the stars, which thou hast ordained.' And yet we would try to use the moon as a base of destruction."[6]

That may well be the awful alternative. Give God the glory, and we find our place among the singing spheres or destroy ourselves!

Where Do We Lose Our Way?

With all of our marvels of science we have lost our way among the stars. "The intellectual life of modernity," writes William Ernest Hocking, "has largely lost the way to ripen the fruit of its own genius." Can we blame science for that? In fact, science has discovered that it needed two of the great words of religion in order to go on living in this world that it had discovered: *mystery* and *purpose*. For great scientists suspected from the outset that what we did not know was infinitely more important than what we did know about this world in which we live. Science needed the help of religion and needed it badly. The only escape from the nightmare of a universe of endless and pointless wheeling planets lay in religion's historic confidence in the reality of the mysterious and continuing purpose of God in creation. The individual scientist was far from through when he discovered and described this new universe: he had to live in it, he had to work in it, and he had to justify the importance of the work he was doing.

Rather than condemning science, those of us who know God, or at least claim to, should join hands with it and try to find our way.

If we are to find our way, two things in God's universe must be kept together. Immanuel Kant said it a long time ago: "Two things fill me with increasing awe, the starry heavens above and the moral law within." We lose our way when this created universe no longer speaks to us of the mystery, and the power, and the glory of God.

> The late H. G. Wells was one of the most gifted men of his generation: brilliant mind, tireless student, keen prophet and an excellent writer. But there was a puzzling despair and doubt hovering over all that he wrote. The longer he lived the gloomier he became until, in his last public interview, he gave up the cause of civilization as hopeless. Wells gives us the clue to his morbid outlook in this autobiographical note, "There was a time when my little soul shone and was uplifted at the starry enigma of the sky. That has gone absolutely. Now I can go out and look at the stars as I look at the pattern of wallpaper on a railway station waiting room."[7]

When we lose sight of the meaning and purpose of God in creation, we soon lose our sense of his meaning and purpose in life. If the starry heavens have no more meaning than the designs on the wallpaper of a railway station waiting room, then life has no more purpose than a round-trip ticket to the next town!

Again, we lose our way when we lose sight of the meaning of God's eternal law. For the psalmist these two belonged together, both speaking to him of God: "The heavens declare the glory of God . . . The law of the Lord is perfect . . . *enduring forever*."

How long can we endure and ignore God's moral law or, for that matter, any of his laws? The man-made satellite stays in its orbit around the earth only because it was made to function in the framework of God's laws. His moral laws are as unchanging and demanding. Forget them, ignore them, and life goes to pieces.

That is why Jesus summed up the purpose of man's living in these two great, eternal precepts: "Thou shalt love the Lord thy God with all thy heart, and with all thy soul, and with all thy mind. . . . Thou shalt love thy neighbor as thyself."

The purpose of life and the meaning of existence are found in loving God and loving one's neighbor. He that does this will live a life that counts. But the particular form that this neighbor love will take and the role that each will play in the general scheme of things—this we cannot tell them. Only the God who is the author of the play in which we are all actors, and who directs its course to its grand finale, can do that. And he can do that only when he is known well enough for it to be obeyed.

Who is able to do that? No wonder the psalmist, overwhelmed with the greatness of God who made the heavens and the holiness of God revealed in the moral law, cried out in his own inadequacy: "Who can understand his errors? cleanse thou me from secret faults. Keep back thy servant also from presumptuous sins; let them not have dominion over me."

His desire was that both his inward thoughts and outward acts might praise God. "Let the words of my mouth and the meditation of my heart be acceptable in thy sight, O Lord." But how could they except in him who has both "his strength and his redeemer"?

Nor can we praise God or keep his law save by the grace of his hand outstretched in Christ, in whom is revealed both the glory of God and the meaning of life?

> When I am with God
> I look deep down and high up,
> And all is changed. . . .
> When I enter into God,
> All life has a meaning. . . .
> My fever is gone
> In the great quiet of God.
> My troubles are but pebbles on the road,
> My joys are like the everlasting hills.[8]

NOTES

1. Carlyle Marney, *Faith in Conflict* (Nashville: Abingdon Press, 1957), 19.

2. John Sutherland Bonnell, *What Are You Living For?* (Nashville: Abingdon Press, 1950), 61.

3. Harold A. Bosley, *Preaching on Controversial Issues* (New York: Harper & Brothers, 1953), 67.

4. J. Wallace Hamilton, *Ride the Wild Horses* (Westwood, N.J.: Fleming H. Revell, 1952), 70-71.

5. *The Survey Bulletin,* October 21, 1957. Nashville: The Sunday School Board of the Southern Baptist Convention.

6. Edith Deen, November 4, 1957.

7. Harold A. Bosley, *Sermons on the Psalms* (New York: Harper & Brothers, 1956), 52.

8. Walter Rauschenbusch, "The Postern Gate," as quoted from D. R. Sharpe, *Walter Rauschenbusch* (New York: The Macmillan Co., 1942), 451-452.

Walter L. Moore
What I Have I Give

Then Peter said, Silver and gold have I none; but such as I
have give I thee; In the name of Jesus Christ of Nazareth rise
up and walk (Acts. 3:6).

To the cripple at the gate Beautiful, Peter said, "Such as I have give I."
What a motto to live by! What I have I give!

This seems to express the attitude of the early Christians on all occasions. At every opportunity they gave their witness. Without any appeal or every-member canvass, they sold their possessions and brought the money to give it to the Lord and to their brethren. Whenever need arose, they were ready to give their service. Almost every one of them finally gave his life for his faith.

Peter prefaced his statement by saying, "Silver and gold have I none." Judas, of course, could not have said this. He had money. He was the treasurer of the disciples' band, and John tells us that he had become a thief. For thirty pieces of silver he had sold his Lord and his own soul. He could not say, "Silver and gold have I none." Neither should he have said, "What I have I give." His motto was: "What I can, I get." There seemed to be far more people living by the motto of Judas than by the motto of Simon.

The man who addressed the cripple was on his way to a prayer meeting. Sometimes it is suggested that Christian experience is divided into two mutually exclusive realms. One man expresses his devotion to God by singing hymns, meeting in churches, praying, and engaging in church activities. The other expresses his devotion by service to his fellowmen.

Actually this division does not obtain. He who truly worships truly develops a spirit of giving. Charitable causes depend very largely upon active church people for their support.

In a sense Peter expressed an inescapable law of life. We cannot give what we do not have, and we cannot avoid giving what we do have. This applies to material possessions. Upon reading of large gifts given by a millionaire to religious and charitable causes, a man said, "How I wish I had a million dollars that I might do great things for my fellowman, too." The treasurer of his church, who happened to be listening, said nothing. He knew that this man who had a comfortable income, gave very little to anything. Our generosity is expressed not by what we would do if we had more, but by what we do with what we have.

However, we do give of our means, if not to the church, then to others. What we give our money for indicates what our real interest is. For some, life's prime objective is to leave a large estate, and they leave it. The same law applies to spiritual qualities. What we have we give. If we have faith, others will be moved to believe. If we have an optimistic spirit, we share it. If we have love for Christ, others will be influenced to love him, too.

But if we have bitterness or doubts or sin in our lives, someone else will be contaminated. We cannot give what we do not have, but we cannot keep from giving what we do have.

A man who was a heavy drinker and gambler came to his pastor and said, "I have two fine boys. I do not want them to be what I am. I want them to be like you and your deacons. Won't you do me the favor of taking up as much time as you can with my boys?" The pity was, however, that the older boy was already beginning to walk in his father's footsteps. What the father had he was giving.

Peter told the beggar, "Look on us." We do not have to tell people to do that. They will look, and they will take in what they see.

If, then, we would give to the world something noble and fine, we must have noble and fine characteristics within ourselves. That which we give unconsciously is our most precious contribution.

In another sense giving is the secret of all truly great living. The world is full of people who live to get what they can, but the great souls are those who live to give.

Marie and Pierre Curie, distinguished scientists, were the first to isolate radium, which was a great boon to mankind. They were quite poor and had very inadequate equipment with which to work. When success crowned their efforts, they were offered large sums of money by various commercial enterprises for the exclusive privilege of exploiting their discovery. They considered the matter seriously and reached the decision that it would be contrary to the scientific spirit for them to conceal their discoveries from the world and give one concern the privilege of exploiting them. The world needed what they had found, and the world should have it. So they published freely all of the results of their experiments. They were great scientists, but they were greater persons. Their concern was to give to mankind what they could and not to get for themselves all they could.

George Washington Carver was a great physicist. His discoveries for the use of peanuts, sweet potatoes, and clay have been of inestimable value for the South. He was also a deeply devoted Christian. For many years he taught a Bible class of young men. For him, scientific investigation and religious faith were closely related. He approached his experiments in a spirit of prayer and felt that success was God's gift in answer to his prayer. Therefore, he refused to sell his discoveries. He lived on the meager salary of a faculty member of Tuskegee Institute, making no effort to profit by the discoveries and refusing money offered to him for them. His one aim was to improve the lot of his race, not merely the colored race, but the human race. Dr. Carver was a great scientist, but he was a great person. He lived to give.

The kind of greatness possessed by Carver and the Curies does not always bring fame. Many a quiet little mother, a modest school teacher, an old family physician, or a humble minister of the gospel has shared the same spirit. But however obscure the life, the extent to which it is lived to give is the measure of its greatness.

Albert Schweitzer was one of the world's great organists, a distinguished theologian, and a well-trained physician. But his true greatness was seen only when he left everything behind to go to Lambaréné, the neediest spot he could find in the world, to give himself in service for his fellowman.

Getting in itself is not wrong. We can give only because we have first gotten. But there is all the difference in the world between the man who gives only a little in the hope of getting a lot more, and the man whose only motive for getting is that he may have to give.

Life can be transformed for one who comes into contact with a person such as Simon Peter. The beggar at the gate called Beautiful doubtless had not thought that his life would be greatly changed that day. His hope was to collect a few pennies to keep body and soul together. Surely he felt himself to be less fortunate and less happy than the people around him. His body was incapable of leaping, and his soul had nothing about which to leap. But there came his way that day a man who had something more precious than money and whose one desire was to share what he had. Peter lifted the man up, and together they went into the temple. There was a new song on the lips, a new spring in the legs, and a new joy in the heart of the man who had been a beggar.

A quiet little man who had served as pastor of a country church for more than fifty years died. At the funeral service a young minister said concerning his old pastor: "Having known this man, I have more faith in God and more faith in humanity. I know God is real, for he walked with him. And I know human nature can be refined by God's grace, for he was like Jesus." Fortunate is he whose life has been profoundly influenced by a great soul who has learned to give.

The true meaning of Christian living is found in Jesus, who Himself lived only to give. He came, not to be ministered to, but to minister, and to give His life. Calvary was the ultimate expression of this life purpose. He gave His all. We are His true disciples as we share this spirit.

A minister asked a businessman for help on a worthy project. The man complained, "Apparently all there is to Christianity is give, give, give." The minister replied, "I want to thank you for the best description of Christianity I have ever heard."

Those who have not the spirit of giving do not understand this. They think of giving as a painful process and feel that those who give generously must be under some kind of compulsion.

On the other hand, for him who has the Spirit of Christ, who gave His all, the only pain connected with giving is seeing needs which he has not the resources to supply. The measure of his generosity is one: "[What] I have I give."

He has learned the true meaning of life itself, who, looking out at the needs of others and then looking at the resources God has given him, says resolutely: "[What] I have I give."

E. Y. Mullins
The Irreducible Christ:
in Christian History

John 17:3

We must also glance at Christ's place in Christian history. There is no space for a full statement. But the task has been well performed. One can find an admirable account of what Christ has done for women and children, and slaves, for the sick, the oppressed and down-trodden, for improved laws, and for better relations between men in such a volume as *Gesta Christi,* by the late Loring Brace.

In Part IV of my *Why Is Christianity True?* the same theme has been developed in five chapters. So also there is a convincing chapter in Professor Glover's *The Jesus of History*. Dr. Glover portrays the elements of outward grandeur in the old religious life of the Roman Empire, its many gods, its stately ceremonial, its apparently imperishable strength. Then came the little group of obscure and despised Christians. One of them wrote an Apocalypse predicting the downfall of Rome, an absurdity to pagan contemporaries. "Yet," says Professor Glover, "the dream has come true, that church has triumphed. Where is the old religion? Christ has conquered, and all the gods have gone, utterly gone. They are memories now, and nothing more. Why did they go? The Christian Church refused to compromise." Again: "The Christian proclaimed a war of religion in which there shall be no compromise, no peace, till Christ is Lord of all; the thing shall be fought out to the bitter end. And it has been. He was resolved that the old gods should go; and they have gone. How was it done? Here we touch what I think one of the greatest wonders that history has to show. . . . If we may invent, or adapt three words, the Christian 'outlived' the pagan, 'out-died' him, and 'out-thought' him" (see pp. 212-213).

Do not forget that the power of Christianity as a regenerating moral and spiritual force has always depended upon keeping Christ central for faith, as in the New Testament preaching. A striking illustration is seen in the career of Savonarola as compared with that of Luther. Savonarola stands out as one of the moral heroes of Christian history. He preceded Luther a few years only. The same general conditions of a corrupt papacy, church and society existed for both. Both were men of tremendous personality and moral force and course. Both had a passion for truth and righteousness. And yet Savonarola was burned at the stake and his movement failed. Its influence was obliterated like the trail of an ocean liner in the sea after the great ship has passed on. Luther's movement, on the other hand, changed the course of history. It is a mighty factor in the world to-day. Why the difference? The answer is not difficult. Savonarola's was an effort for moral reform. Luther's was a religious movement. Savonarola attacked the current morals. He burned the Vanities in the streets of Florence. He wanted a civil government for the city with Christ as King. But he never sought to change or correct the religious foundations. Salvation through sacrament, priest and church, he accepted.

Martin Luther went forth and shook the world with a great religious principle: Justification by faith. He began with the fact of sin and man's need. He went to the New Testament for the remedy. He found there Christ as atoning Redeemer, risen and glorified. For him Christ was all in all as the Revealer of God. Trust in him brought divine forgiveness, and a new standing. The conscience was thus purged from dead works to serve the living God. Thus by restoring Christ to men seeking salvation and reaffirming the central truth of Paul's preaching he opened again the flood-gates of life eternal for mankind. The tide ebbed and flowed. There were many abuses. Many wars resulted. But to this day Protestantism has kept Christ central in its preaching and life.

The power of Christianity as a conquering force has always depended upon the centrality of Christ in the message. Where Christ grows dim in the vision of church or preacher, the Christian power wanes. Evangelism is vain and futile apart from Christ as religious Object and Redeemer of men. Says Professor Glover: "Wherever the Christian church, or a single Christian, has put upon Jesus Christ a higher emphasis—above all where everything has been centered in Jesus Christ—there has been an increase of power for church, or community, or man." John Wesley and Whitefield and all the great evangelists have found this to be true. The great foreign missionary enterprise of modern times, as is well known, took its rise out of motives and incentives supplied by the evangelical faith. And it is yet to be shown that modern liberalism has in it the spiritual resources for such a movement.

One phase of current liberalism is its emphasis upon the ethical and social aspects of the gospel. But the ethical and social fruits of the gospel can only come when the moral and spiritual life of man is renewed and sustained by the power of a redeeming Christ. From the beginning of the Reformation era the ethical and social fruits of the evangelical faith have been manifest. John Calvin's ideal and passion sought a perfect society at Geneva. Righteousness in all relations of life was implicit in his theology. Puritanism in the British Isles was a marvelous ethical and social manifestation of the new faith. The Puritan Revolution under Cromwell showed the dynamic power of the gospel for political reform and for a restoration of human rights. The conscience and will of John Knox became the vehicle of a divine purpose manifesting itself on a wide social scale. The Puritan and Pilgrim migration to America, and the new commonwealths established here, were direct social fruits of the evangelical faith. The abolition of slavery, and a hundred other reforms bear witness to the same truth. To-day there are two supreme questions seeking solution. One is the adjustment of industrial, the other the improvement of international relations. These are momentous problems which must be solved. The resources, moral and spiritual, for the solution are to be found only in the faith of the New Testament.

Many men are reckoning with new mechanical adjustments of human relations to cure these ills. Some imagine that material progress alone is sufficient. But we are seeing with increasing clearness that the supreme factor is the spiritual. Science may give us new engines of power. We may invent new political machinery for world peace. These may be good or bad. But they will not be good unless operated by good men. A circular saw is a marvel of efficiency. But it will cut a human body in twain as easily as a log of wood. Our improved social and scientific mechanisms may destroy society as well as improve it. The true prophet to-day knows that a regenerate heart is the key to social progress.

A most interesting phase of Christ's present power in the world is the way he is influencing modern thought. Directly or indirectly, consciously or unconsciously, men are gravitating to him for their ultimate ideas. In modern education the worth and value and rights of personality control the best thought. In political life the common man with his value and his rights is the underlying ideal. Christ taught these truths to men and enforced them as never before. "Ye are of more value than many sparrows." "What shall it profit a man if he gain the whole world and lose his own soul?" Professor Ely has declared that the teachings of Christ in the parable of the talents contain the key to the proper solution of the economic problems of our day. In the realm of philosophic and speculative thought it is striking to note how great thinkers borrow from Jesus and the gospel, even when they repudiate them. Modern Pragmatism insists that the will is an essential factor in the knowing process; that the test of a truth is its workableness. Jesus announced this principle in religion when he declared that he that willeth to do the will of God should know the doctrine. Knowledge comes through doing. Albrecht Ritschl founded a school of theology on the doctrine borrowed from Kant, that we cannot know things in themselves, but only in their manifestations. We know God in and through Christ, but cannot and need not know who or what Christ was in his essential nature. Thus Ritschl sought to protect himself from scientific attack by silence on the offensive phases of Christian truth. In the end this is a fatal proceeding, as history has shown. But he retained the New Testament truth that we know God only through Christ.

William James in a remarkable study of religious experience reaches the conclusion that there is a divine and genuinely miraculous power which regenerates men. But he remains agnostic as to whether Christ is the cause or not. He also defines the conditions under which the divine life flows into the human. It is self-renunciation and self-surrender on man's part, whereupon there supervenes the inflow of divine and spiritual power. Professor Eucken, while willing to dispense with Christ himself, nevertheless borrows a Christian idea as the central truth of his philosophy. Man can find no means of overcoming the conflicts and contradictions of this temporal life until he comes into contact with the transcendent life of God. Such contact resolves the contradictions and gives man victory. Thus Eucken constructs the spiritual foundations of his system upon Christ's doctrine of the new birth, while rejecting the Author of the doctrine. So also, modern idealism, in representatives like Professor Green and others, takes over the Christian conception of incarnation and atonement, while repudiating the historic incarnation and atonement in Christ. The life of God is an act of eternal sacrifice. The principle of incarnation, atonement, resurrection, ascension, is a true and sound thought of God's life and activity. But it is a universal principle. There was no special manifestation of it in the career of Jesus of Nazareth. Thus idealism cuts loose from history and fact and builds a structure high in the air, from materials borrowed from our historic faith. It goes to the very heart of Christianity for its formative principle, but leaves Christianity itself a vapor ready to vanish.

Professor Josiah Royce in his work, *The Problem of Christianity,* adopts as central in his philosophy of religion, the words of the creed: "I believe in the Holy Ghost, in the Holy Catholic Church, the communion of saints." Or as he expresses it elsewhere, it is the ideal of one of the Pauline Churches of the New Testament: The Holy Spirit in the blessed community (see p. 12). Out of this conception Professor Royce develops man's relations to God and to other men. In the ideal he finds the goal of history and the secret of the spiritual universe. But the Spirit is substituted for Christ. He makes this very rash statement: "The name of Christ has always been, for the Christian believers, the symbol for the Spirit in whom the faithful—that is to say the loyal—always are and have been one" (see p. 426). An idealist easily sublimates the facts of history into the rational principles with which he works. One can scarcely understand otherwise the statement that Christ has always been taken as a "Symbol for the Spirit." Professor Royce denies that we can know Christ. "The existing documents are too fragmentary. The historical hypotheses are too shifting and evanescent" (see p. 427). Now Professor Royce, although thus denying the historical Christ, says: "The literal and historical fact has always been this, that in some fashion and degree, those who have thus believed in the being whom they called Christ, were united in a community of the faithful, were in love with that ommunity, were hopefully and practically devoted to the cause of the still invisible, but perfectly real and divine Universal Community, and were saved by the faith and by the life which they thus expressed" (see p. 425).

Thus we obtain an idea of the wonder-working magic of a philosophical principle in the hands of a skillful thinker. Faith in Christ the unifying bond; the church itself the community; the blessed community expressing and manifesting the divine life, and foreshadowing the goal of the spiritual history of mankind. But, mark you, the central object of the faith, Jesus Christ, unknown and unknowable. When one recalls what was quoted on an earlier page from Professor Royce, that every philosophy is simply a new insight from a new angle, one wonders at the dogmatic confidence of his conclusions in the last chapter of his book. When one recalls the terrific assaults upon this and other idealistic systems by Professor James and the pluralists, one wonders how stable Professor Royce's conclusions are. And particularly when one observes how he plays fast and loose with history and the name of Christ, one is relieved of any dread that such a theory will long endure.

At the same time, Professor Royce's theory illustrates strikingly how "modern thought" borrows from Jesus. "The Holy Spirit in the Blessed Community" is indeed a blessed fact. But so is the Christ who is and has been and ever will be the center of the faith of the members of the blessed community.

Thus it appears that modern thought even among those who come short of full appreciation of Christ borrows freely from him. In ethics and economics his influence is most palpable. But so also Pragmatism with its doctrine of the will; Ritschlianism with its judgment of value; James with his doctrine of miraculous conversion; Eucken with his philosophy of the new birth; and Royce with his doctrine of incarnation and atonement and the church are all indebted to Jesus for the leading ideas of their systems. He cannot be evaded or escaped.

This volume has not dealt formerly with questions of doctrine. I have discussed Christian doctrine in my work, *The Christian Religion in Its Doctrinal Expression*. The purpose here has been to make clear the issue now before the religious world. Fundamentally it is an issue as to the facts of Christian history, and the facts of Christian experience. A doctrine of incarnation, of sin and atonement, of the deity of Christ, of regeneration and justification and so on through the great circle, is implicit in all that has been said. But the strength of the Christian position is the stability of the foundations in the New Testament records, the deeds of Christ in history, and the experience of redemption through his power. Doctrines are inevitable as arising out of these facts. Indeed a statement of many of the facts is virtually the statement of the doctrines. But for the purposes in view in the present discussion, formal doctrinal discussion has not been necessary.

The impregnable citadel of the evangelical faith is the Fact of Jesus Christ, with all that the name implies. Dr. Fairbairn has pointed out with great force that it is easy to adopt a premise which will enable us to disprove the evangelical position in two ways, by rational logic, and by analytical criticism. Rational logic may show to its own satisfaction the inconsistencies or absurdities of the early definitions of Christ's Person in the Nicene and Chalcedonian decisions. So also analytical criticism may theoretically reconstruct the New Testament records and change their import in a radical way. But even so, the real problem has not been faced. The facts concerning Christ, and the ideas to be construed are infinitely more complex than the premise in each of these instances was allowed to express. The argument seemed strong because the premise was narrow. Says Dr. Fairbairn in *The Philosophy of the Christian Religion*: "We have not solved, we have not even stated and defined the problem as to the person of Christ when we have written the life of Jesus, for that problem is raised even less by the Gospels than by Christ's place and function in the collective history of man; or, to be more correct, by the life described in the Gospels and the phenomena represented by universal history viewed in their reciprocal and interpretative interrelations. . . . The very essence of the matter is that the Gospels do not stand alone, but live, as it were, embosomed in universal history. And in that history Christ plays a part much more remarkable and much less compatible with common manhood than the part Jesus plays in the history of his own age and people. And we have not solved, or even apprehended, any one of the problems connected with this Person until we have resolved the mystery of the place he has filled and the things he has achieved in the collective life of man" (see pp. 12-14).

American Protestantism numbers between twenty-five and thirty millions of members. Each group is organized and militant. Innumerable enterprises, missionary, social, civic, philanthropic, are conducted by these bodies. They are the fountain of benevolence for all great appeals. They are the ethical and social centers of life and power. They are teachers of patriotism and also the love of humanity. They live to serve. There are qualifications, of course, shortcomings, inconsistencies, failures. But there is overwhelming proof of the main proposition. Now these great groups are founded on the evangelical faith. Christ is central. His deity and atonement are believed in. His relation to man's faith is recognized. In millions of lives it is being demonstrated every day that the gospel is the power of God unto salvation to every one that believeth.

Consider then the irreducible Christ. He is irreducible in the experience of saved men. He is irreducible in the New Testament records. He is irreducible in the centuries of Christian history. He is irreducible in his ministry to the larger spiritual life of the world. He is irreducible as the inspirer of a better social and economic system, and better international relations. He is irreducible as the goal and inspiration of the higher thought of the age. He is irreducible as the moral and spiritual dynamic enabling the world to realize its ideals. He is above all irreducible as the eternal Son of God and Saviour of men, sinless, crucified for our sins, risen from the dead, reigning in glory, and destined to come again in his own time.

Now if modern naturalism, or liberalism, imagines it can cut away the great features of this world-conquering faith and reduce it to proportions which will fit into the narrow cage of physical continuity, it is open to it to make the effort. If men believe they can sweep this ocean out of its bed, or remove this Matterhorn from its base, or turn back the current of this Gulf Stream in the ocean of man's religious life, let them try. But at the same time let them remember that they are primarily fighting not a system of doctrine, or any particular form of doctrinal propaganda. They are fighting life itself, at its deepest and most significant level; the life that is in Jesus Christ, whom men know as Redeemer and Lord, as the completion and realization of the religious ideal, who is made unto them wisdom, righteousness, sanctification and redemption.

Pat M. Neff
Christian Education

With knightly courtesy I salute you.

There are three scriptural institutions dedicated in service to mankind—the home, the church, and the Christian college. Through these institutions, from the morning of youth until manhood has reached its high noon, pass those who live the abundant life. Christian education is the one thing that gives to both the home and the church their growth and glory, and without which they would soon dry up and be gone with the wind.

The Bible places a very high value on education. It declares wisdom to be better than rubies, and understanding more valuable than choice gold. One of the sacred writers sums it all up in these significant words: "My people perish for lack of knowledge." Education has always measured the difference between barbarism and civilization. It is the barometer of growth. Education is an investment that builds up the state. Ignorance is a canker that destroys it. It is the verdict of the ages that a civilization cannot be carried upon the backs of the ignorant.

Mankind, in its march around the earth, has always recognized its relation to institutions of learning. The builders of governments have always been the founders of universities. With this thought in mind, some three hundred years ago our American forebears braved the unknown dangers of a chartless ocean to find somewhere a land where they could enjoy, unharmed and unhindered, civil and religious freedom undergirded by an educated citizenship. These adventurous souls, with their skyline of thought lifted high, sailed the surging seas in search of such a land. A divine hand guided them to Plymouth Rock, on the rugged New England

334

shore. Beneath these western skies, with hope and faith and courage sublime, they commenced to build a new civilization. These fearless, founding fathers of ours recognized for the first time in the march of man the power of combined religion and education in the building of a civilization. As the walls of Troy rose to the music of Apollo's harp, so in answer to the prayers of our pilgrim patriots the towers and steeples of our colleges and churches lifted high their heads in this wilderness of the West.

Pericles had built a civilization on the basis of a common culture. It failed. Caesar had built a civilization on the law. It failed. Alexander constructed his government on power. It failed. Our forefathers knew then, as we know now, that a civilization founded on any other basis than that of religion and education, the two greatest forces on earth, would necessarily be an artificial structure. Therefore, their first public buildings were churches and colleges, built side by side, thus saying to all the coming ages:

> Fear not the skeptic's puny hands
> While near the school the church spire stands;
> Fear not the blinded bigot's rule
> While near the church spire stands the school.

During those early days while America was in the making, our pioneering patriots, in the name of the Christian religion, founded Harvard, Yale, Dartmouth, William and Mary, Pennsylvania, and Brown Universities.

Before the first child born in America became twenty-one years of age, Harvard University opened its doors. Above its ancient archway to this day can be read the reason why it was built: "Erected that an educated ministry may not perish from the earth."

Sixty-five years later the foundation of Yale University was laid. In its charter the builders set forth their reason for its establishment—"That the youth of the land may be trained to serve both the church and the state." A little later Princeton, laying her foundation, declared that the institution should be a place where the minds of youth should be trained to serve the pulpit, the bench, and the senate.

Within the shadow of Brown University, the Baptists of that day erected their church building, declaring that in it they would worship God and hold commencement exercises. This Baptist church, the first in America, was also the first church in the world bravely and openly to proclaim religious, democratic freedom to all mankind. It was from this combined college and church that the democratic doctrine of civil and religious freedom spread throughout the colonies, giving to Thomas Jefferson in Virginia his first thought of a democratic government. Christian education gave birth to the American Republic. It has carried the blessings of civilization from the Atlantic seaboard to the Golden Gate.

As the years passed, to the colonial colleges founded in the name of the church, the Baptist Denomination added many institutions of higher learning. Baylor University, with its rich and romantic history of nearly one hundred years, is typical of the denominational universities now functioning throughout the nation. Twenty-three of the first twenty-four universities built in America were founded by religious denominations. Out of the first hundred and nineteen educational institutions located east of the Mississippi River, one hundred and four were founded and supported by church organizations.

Christian education is a fundamental function of the church. "Go teach" is its imperative command. There has always been a constant flow of life blood from the church to the college, and from the college back to the church. They have been linked together in a wholesome interdependence. They are partners promoting a great program. Sever the connection, and both suffer. A religious denomination must continue to cultivate the field of education, or go out of business as a denomination.

In America, for one hundred and fifty years, church organizations provided all the institutions of higher learning. The American way of life is largely the product of this college culture. From the scholastic halls of these church constructed colleges came the leaders of thought and the champions of liberty who made this Republic possible. Thomas Jefferson was an alumnus of William and Mary, James Madison of Princeton, and Alexander Hamilton of what is now Columbia University. All but eight of the fifty-five men who signed the Declaration of Independence, and most of those who wrote our Constitution, had breathed the atmosphere of church supported institutions of learning.

Out of these church built and supported colleges came the leaders of both church and state, founders of our early secular institutions of higher learning. Thomas Jefferson, who declared that if a people expect to be both ignorant and free, they expect what never was and never can be, counted the founding of the University of Virginia as the crowning achievement of his life. Benjamin Franklin, the oldest and wisest of the men who had part in the writing of our Constitution, rejoiced that he was the founder of the University of Pennsylvania. George Washington evidenced his belief in the importance of a university in the making of a civilization by bequeathing in his last will fifty thousand dollars for the building of a college. Washington and Lee University finally became the beneficiary of this bequest, and in this way George Washington continues to live and to serve.

No country ever did or ever will rise independent of her schools. The foundations of a government can be no broader than the foundations of knowledge extended by her institutions of learning. If a country must educate or perish, if a government cannot rise independent of her schools, how then can religion be expected to live without Christian education?

In keeping with the genius of our Government, religion cannot be taught in our state supported institutions. Wisely we keep separate church and state. The government should never enforce religion, and religion should never coerce the government. The state must not enter the domain of religion with a governmental system of education. Neither should religion prescribe the courses to be taught by the state.

He is not a good citizen who does not stand bravely, courageously for our public school system. The state must educate for self-preservation. The church must support her institutions of learning in order that both the church and the state may live. Every citizen should support our public schools as a patriotic duty and our denominational institutions as a moral obligation.

We Texans are happy for the world to know that we support here in our commonwealth a splendid, cooperative, dual system of higher education—one by the state that the state may live, and one by the church that Christianity may live. Our fighting forefathers, before the blood of San Jacinto had dried on their swords, were laying plans broad and deep, to build here beneath the light of the Lone Star this dual democratic system of education. In Texas, however, for fifty years religious organizations furnished all the institutions of higher learning.

Measured by accomplishments already achieved, by services already rendered,our church supported universities everywhere should command the support of every citizen who loves his country. They have been the depositories of orthodox Christianity and the bulwarks of good citizenship. Leaders in the affairs of both church and state who gave direction and destiny to the American Government, came largely out of these schools.

Sixteen of the first eighteen presidents of the United States who were college graduates came out of denominational universities. Seven of the first eight chief justices of the Supreme Court, who were college graduates held diplomas from church supported institutions. While only one-third of the college graduates of America now living attended church controlled schools, it is indeed a challenging thought that from this one-third is drawn 70 percent of all the college graduates whose names appear in *Who's Who in America*.

Christian education is the development of the threefold nature of man, the physical, the mental, and the spiritual. It is education "plus." Culture is not enough. Knowledge is not enough. To the academic curriculum must be added character. A short time ago Harvard University made a survey of four thousand persons who had lost their jobs. More than half of these were without work because of defects in traits of character. Character is the most valuable granite block in the enduring foundation of worthy manhood.

Christian education is not merely declaring the doctrines of a denomination; it is not merely proclaiming the code of some church, or making converts to some religious creed. A Christian college is a place where all the arts and sciences are taught:—music and mathematics, philosophy and psychology, biology and botany—measured by all the academic requirements of a standard university. In addition to this, it is also a place where students are taught these courses by Christian teachers, in a religious atmosphere, amid religious environments, where the temptations of life lead upward and onward.

The difference between Christian education and secular education is not in form but in spirit; not in technique but in traditions; not in curriculum but in character; not in property but in personality; not in cast but in culture; not in mechanics but in dynamics; not in information but in inspiration; not in minds trained but in destinies determined.

If our colleges are to remain Christian, those who teach therein should be Christians. At this point, those in authority should guard the gates with the watchfulness of the cherubims who guarded the ark of the covenant. The professor who teaches geology should not only know something about the age of the rocks, but he should also know something about the "Rock of Ages." If he teaches botany, he should not only know how to classify a Texas bluebonnet, but he should be able to "consider the lilies of the field." He should be a real human being with a warm, sympathetic heart, and not merely a stilted Ph.D. on some lofty Mount Olympus.

A Christian university does not consist merely of lands, libraries, and laboratories. The best part of a university is invisible. More important than brick and mortar is the spirit of an institution. No university can be great, whatever may be its endowment or its scholastic standards, that does not develop within its own life a pure, white, academic soul.

The thing of superlative importance about any institution, more important than the wealth of Croesus, is its atmosphere. The atmosphere of a college, like the atmosphere of the earth, should be a mixture of life-giving components. A university should be permeated and environed with an atmosphere that stimulates and inspires. It should be calm in culture and warm with human sympathy. It should pulsate with intellectual health and Christian thinking. This is true because at least 60 percent of all college culture is atmospheric. What is taught in a university is not as important as the atmosphere in which it is taught. The student who does not get anything out of his college career but the information he gets out of his books studies in vain.

Someone may ask why these Christian colleges produce leaders in so many of the worthy endeavors of life. It is because in these institutions, if they be worthy the name, a shift is made in the philosophy of life from property to personality, from money to manhood. They do not tag success with the dollar mark. They do not make the students believe that on life's final examination the ledger should be balanced with figures only. They are taught to see more possibilities in a red-faced boy than in a white-faced calf, and to believe that they should never hear the squeal of a pig above the cry of a child. Therefore, these graduates thus trained go from college halls as flaming evangels, declaring with Alfred Tennyson that

> He alone deserves to be great,
> Who either saves or serves the State.

Now in a world that is upside down and wrongside out, amid the falling of governments and the wreckage of empires, if we are to hold dear the "Faith of our Fathers—living still," and preserve inviolate our democratic way of life against enemies from within and enemies from without, whether armed with gold or steel, we must rise above the fog and bog of a world mobilized for war and say with Edwin Markham,

> Love and not hate must come to birth,
> Christ and not Cain must rule the earth.

During the first World War, in a futile effort to make the world safe for democracy, we sent the flower of American manhood three thousand miles across the ocean and flooded the gory fields of France with as fine a soldiery as ever followed a flag or fought beneath a plume. Now the sons and daughters of these brave boys who fought on a foreign soil to make the world safe for democracy are on land and sea and in the air around the world, fighting a greater battle—a battle not to make the world safe for democracy but to make democracy safe for the world.

This democracy for which we fight is today groping like a blind Cyclops around the walls of his darkened cave, trying to get a glimpse of the flickering light of civilization as it filters through the Stygian darkness of a chaotic world.

If we are to reconstruct the world's civilization on our shattered shrines of democracy so that law, order, and truth; so that life, light, and liberty shall be enthroned in the world of tomorrow, we must keep our church supported institutions of learning profoundly, fundamentally, and eternally Christian, with no touch of a diluted religion. We must continue to teach that truth is truth, and that God is God. Let no one now declare a moratorium on Christianity. Let no one now sound a dirge or beat a retreat. Rather let us beat a battle charge that will wake the patriotic dead from Bunker Hill to Pearl Harbor; and through them proclaim to all mankind that though spiritual ideals, like stocks and bonds, are tumbling down around the world, our denominational schools must forever remain what Woodrow Wilson declared them to be: "Light-houses to make plain the pathways of men."

Louie D. Newton
Southern Baptists—Yesterday, Today, and Tomorrow

The Committee on Order of Business for the 1947 session of the Southern Baptist Convention has stabbed us live awake in the suggestion of the theme: "Human Designs—God's Destiny." It is a fitting sequel to last year's memorable theme—"Widening Reach and Heightened Power," plucked from the fragrant garden of flower and fruit in the gracious ministry of Dr. John A. Broadus.

Look at the words for a moment—*design*, which stems from the Latin *designare*—to mark, to sign, to plan, to purpose, to outline; *destiny*, which stems from the Latin *destinare*—to stand, to fix or decree beforehand, as by Divine will or superhuman causes, to predetermine, to foreordain.

Strong words, sobering words, challenging words, timely words, we must agree.

Dr. Samuel Johnson would remind us that: "Many things difficult to design prove easy to performance" (ch. XVI, *Rasselas*).

Dante Gabriel Rossetti would caution us to remember that:

> If God in His wisdom has brought close
> The day when I must die,
> That day by water or fire or air
> My feet shall fall in the destined snare
> Wherever my road may lie.
> —*The King's Tragedy*

Man's *designs*—Southern Baptists' *designs*—may they purpose sincerely, clearly, intelligently, faithfully, courageously—to mark, to sign, to

341

plan, to fulfill, and that alone, the predetermined, foreordained will of God, remembering, against any fateful day of forgetfulness, that we "were born, not of blood, nor of the will of the flesh, nor of the will of man, but of God" (John 1:13); and, that, "Not everyone that saith unto me, Lord, Lord, shall enter into the kingdom of heaven, but he that doeth the will of my Father which is in heaven" (Matt. 7:21); until, with our blessed Lord, we shall today and evermore be able to say, "Not my will [not my *design*, O Lord] but thine [Thy *destiny*] be done" (Luke 22:42).

Southern Baptists Yesterday

I bid you come for a moment and stand with me in the golden twilight of yesterday, and glance with reverent, grateful hearts across the first century of Southern Baptist *design*—aye, beyond that century to glimpse the little band of valiant souls in Kittery, Maine, in 1682, who followed Pastor William Screven to the jail, where he had been sentenced for preaching the gospel, and from that jail to the settlement on the banks of Cooper's River to constitute the first Baptist church in the South, in 1683.

And from that first Baptist church in the South, now located in Charleston, I bid you scan the saga of Southern Baptist life across the generations until that blessed day of man's *design* and God's *destiny* when, in response to the call of the Virginia Board of Foreign Missions, some 328 messengers from eight states and the District of Columbia met at Augusta, Georgia, on May 8, 1845, and organized the Southern Baptist Convention, for the purpose—*the design*, if you please: "To elicit, combine, and direct the energies of the whole denomination for the propagation of the Gospel."

The March of Time

I bid you join me in salute to those pioneers, and their successors—Johnson and Howell and Fuller and Hartwell and Crane and Taylor and Jeter and Brantly and Broadus and Boyce and Williams and Manly and Mell and Mercer and Sherwood and Yates and Furman and Campbell and Sears and Burrows and Landrum and McCall and Jones and Curry and Frost and Carroll and Hawthorne and Gregory and Eaton and Hatcher and Eager and Kerfoot and Gambrell and Haralson and Northern and Eagle and Stephens and Levering and Dargan and Mullins and McDaniel and McGlothlin and Pitt and Cody and McConnell and Willingham and Tichenor and Robertson and Love and Scarborough and Truett and all that blessed host of men and women, preachers and laymen, too numerous to recite, but whose names are written in the Book of Everlasting Remembrance.

I bid you join me in quick review of the march of time as Southern Baptists, beginning at Augusta in 1845, set themselves to the task of evangelism and enlistment and stewardship and education and benevolence, expressed first and always in the ministry of the local churches in rural and urban communities, and then through united and cooperative effort through the district associations, the state conventions, the denominational papers, the Foreign Mission Board, the Home Mission Board, the Seminaries, Woman's Missionary Union, the Sunday School Board, the Brotherhood, the Relief and Annuity Board, the hospital, the Radio Commission, the Committee on Public Relations, and numerous other expressions of organized Christian testimony.

I bid you join me in acknowledgment of the constant witness which Southern Baptists have given to civic righteousness—insistence upon the observance and enforcement of the laws which guarantee freedom from the anarchy of every sort and fashion—emphasis upon the responsibility of the individual to express himself or herself at the ballot box, jury service, and every other form of Christian citizenship.

And from the little band of Baptists who organized the Convention in 1845 we behold a great and mighty host a century later, numbering more than half a million, with churches serving rural and urban life from ocean to ocean and with missionary, educational, and benevolent ministries encircling the globe. Southern Baptists, yesterday, served with "widening reach and heightened power," through *designs* that centered in the will and to the glory of the Father, Son, and Holy Spirit. "Hitherto hath the Lord helped us" (1 Sam. 7:12).

Southern Baptists Today

Turning into the second century of organized Southern Baptist life, what do we discover as we examine the *designs* of the 6 million people who compose the twenty state conventions, the 928 district associations and the 26,401 churches?

I do not have time in this brief address to detail the panorama of Southern Baptist life, beginning with the local church in its ministry to the newborn babies and extending through denominational ministries to the care of aged servants of the Lord, waiting at the gates. Such information is available, every week, through the denominational papers and in reports of this Convention, to which I fraternally urge the careful attention of our people.

Suffice it to say that Southern Baptists today present a picture that surely would make glad the hearts of the fathers and mothers, from the early settlement on the banks of Cooper's River even to this good hour.

Our people are united.—United in doctrine, united in purpose, united in effort. I have known something of the life of Southern Baptists for the past forty years. I attended my first Southern Baptist Convention in Louisville, Kentucky, in 1909. I have read our denominational papers, beginning with *The Christian Index,* from which my sainted mother taught me the alphabet, for the past fifty years. I have observed the ebb and flow of the tides in the life of Southern Baptists. And I venture to say that never, within the past half century, have Southern Baptists been so united in their doctrinal position, their cooperative work, their common purpose, and their glad and grateful commitment to the will of the Lord Jesus Christ.

May I pause to join you, my dear fellow Baptists of the South, in unceasing gratitude to God for this spirit of unity and understanding. It is precious beyond any words of any man to describe. And may we pray without ceasing that such fellowship shall ever more be our portion, for Christ's sake.

Our people are informed.—Informed, first and most importantly, in the Bible. I would not imply that we have yet attained such knowledge of and such commitment to the Scriptures as we need to have and make; but I rejoice to see the steadily increasing systematic, intelligently guided study of the Bible in the home, in the Sunday School, in the Training Union, in the Missionary Union, in the Student Union, in the pulpit, in the colleges and seminaries, in the denominational papers and in all the publications of our beloved denomination. Baptists will do well so long as they are a people of the Book—as broad and as narrow as its teachings. They will suffer defeat the day they cease to regard the Bible as the complete and final rule and guide for their faith and practice.

Our people are enlisted.—Enlisted as they have never before been enlisted in the great central tasks of evangelism, education, stewardship, benevolence, and rehabilitation. Well may we rejoice as we witness the sustained prayers of our people for a revival—a revival from above, based upon 2 Chronicles 7:14 and upon the call of the prophets and from Jesus Himself, "Repent: for the kingdom of heaven is at hand." Except ye repent, ye shall all likewise perish." Well may we rejoice as we witness our people, refreshed from on high, engaged in soul winning in their communities, throughout their district associations, throughout their state conventions, throughout the South—to the ends of the earth. Evangelism is, and I pray shall ever be, the first concern of Southern Baptists—evangelism that acknowledges all men as utterly lost and undone until they are convicted of sin by the Holy Spirit and, in godly sorrow, cry out, "What must I do to be saved?" May we go forth from this Convention, recharged with the power of the indwelling Spirit of God to call men everywhere to repentance from sin and faith towards the Lord Jesus Christ, claiming His promise that, "Whosoever believeth on the Lord Jesus Christ, shall be saved."

One million tithers!—I emphasize with all my heart the present effort of our people to enlist 1 million tithers. We must admit that there is a sad commentary implied in this goal, when it is recalled that there are 6 million members of Southern Baptist churches. Why should we be satisfied with less than 6 million tithers? Even so, it is an altogether significant and worthy goal which we have set for this year in seeking to enlist 1 million Southern Baptists as tithers. The effort is meeting with heartening response, and I earnestly and fraternally urge every messenger to this Convention to return to your church, highly resolved to enlist every member as a tither. The attainment of this goal will undergird every agency and institution of our denomination, state and Southwide, for greatly enlarged ministry and bless everyone who thus obeys God's command.

The Cooperative Program offers us today, as it has since the hour it was adopted, the surest method of eliciting, combining, and directing the energies of all our people in the propagation of the gospel. It is simple, practical, and scriptural. It has won its way into the confidence of our people. It deserves our complete support in our prayers, our gifts and our loyalty.

Evidences of Growth in the Lord's work are reflected in the constant increase of attendance in Sunday School, Training Union, Woman's Missionary Union, Brotherhood, hours of worship, and in encampments, assemblies, Bible institutes, evangelistic and stewardship conferences, association and convention meetings. Further evidence of growth is reflected in increased gifts in every area of the Convention. Our schools and colleges and seminaries are overflowing. We are caring for more orphaned children, more sick people, more aged ministers than ever before. New missionaries are going forth at home and abroad. Our denominational papers have more than trebled their circulation since 1940. Best evidence of God's favor upon our people is the report of more than a quarter of a million persons received into the churches the past year upon profession of faith.

Southern Baptist today!—It is a picture which lifts up before us blessed memory of those who have gone before—faithful souls who laid well the foundations in *designs* that centered in the *destiny* of God's good and perfect will. We give thanks unto Him for them, and for His favor upon their labors.

The Bell Tolls

Giving thanks for the past and the present, we pause at this juncture to pay tribute to all who have passed from our fellowship since last we met as a Convention. I mention but a few names—B. D. Gray, Rufus W. Weaver, Isaac J. Van Ness, Walter M. Gilmore, C. W. Pruitt, O. P. Gilbert, Henry Alford Porter, Moses N. McCall—with which cherished names will be linked every member of every Baptist church in all our fellowship for whom the bell has tolled. Will you please rise in a moment of silent prayer as we reverently acknowledge our sense of obligation and thanksgiving for each of them. (Silent prayer.) And with the loved ones of all who have "entered into life" within the past year, we humbly claim the promise, "Blessed are the dead which die in the Lord from henceforth: Yea, saith the Spirit, that they may rest from their labors; and their works do follow them" (Rev. 14:13).

Southern Baptists Tomorrow

Tomorrow! One's heart all but stops at the thrust of the thought of tomorrow in our troubled world, until, with Shakespeare, we are tempted to mutter:

> Tomorrow, and tomorrow, and tomorrow,
> Creeps in this petty pace from day to day,
> To the last syllable of recorded time;
> . . . .
> Life's but a walking shadow, a poor player
> . . . .
> . . . It is a tale

> Told by an idiot, full of sound and fury,
> Signifying nothing.

Ah, no, no! Rather, will we stand close beside Coleridge as he more correctly declares:

> Often do the spirits
> Of great events stride on before the events,
> And in today already walks tomorrow.

And with Cicero we would insist that, "Thus in the beginning the world was so made that certain signs come before certain events," and with Byron we prefer to sing:

> Be thou the rainbow to the storms of life,
> The evening beam that smiles the clouds away,
> And tints tomorrow with prophetic ray!

And finally, with our own American poet, Longfellow, we believe that, "Nothing that is can pause or stay." We are what we are becoming. God lives! Yes, tomorrow's world forebodes nothing good, but let us ever remember that, "The world passeth away, and the lust thereof: but he that doeth the will of God abideth forever" (1 John 2:17).

What, then, shall be our attitude as Southern Baptists toward tomorrow? Retreat, or advance? Cowardice, or courage? Fear, or faith?

Professor Toynbee, in his monumental *Study of History,* declares: "We cannot say for certain that our doom is at hand; and yet we have no warrant for assuming that it is not; for such would be to assume that we are not as other men are; and any such assumption would be at variance with everything that we know about human nature either by looking around us or by introspection . . . And, inasmuch as it cannot be supposed that God's nature is less constant than man's, we may and must pray that a reprieve which God has granted once will not be refused if we ask for it again in a contrite spirit and with a broken heart."

Unceasing prayer, then, is to be our first and last approach to the tasks at hand and ahead. We are to pray in confession of our sins—our sins of commission and our sins of omission. Moreover, we are to pray for wisdom. "If any of you lack wisdom, let him ask of God, that giveth to all men liberally, and upbraideth not; and it shall be given him. But let him ask in faith, nothing wavering" (Jas. 1:5-6). James goes on to remind us that we receive not because we ask not, and, further, that we too often ask amiss. One never really prays until he truly asks, "Not my will, but Thine be done." Prayer, I repeat, is our first need as we face tomorrow.

Danger of debt.—I presume to sound a word of caution as we face tomorrow in our Southern Baptist *designs*. I am thinking of the temptation to local churches, district associations and our state and Southwide agencies and institutions to incur debt at this juncture of instability in our general economy. Southern Baptists have suffered enough in the past from good intentions but unsound expansion. Neither peace nor prosperity are assured in tomorrow's world. Unwise obligations incurred in today's fictitious economy may levy hard burdens tomorrow.

Moral disintegration.—Southern Baptists face a society of moral disintegration. Government, local, state, and national, is making a fatal error of encouraging revenue from the vices of the citizenry. Crime, disease, poverty, anarchy, bankruptcy await such folly. The home is under attack as never before—one out of every three marriages ending in divorce. Juvenile delinquency increases in ever-alarming proportions. Drunkenness, prostitution, gambling, malfeasance, murder are everywhere rampant. Southern Baptists are largely responsible for the moral conditions in the South. We dare not retreat from this battleground, remembering, as we must not forget, that: "Except the Lord build the house, they labor in vain that build it: except the Lord keep the city, the watchman waketh but in vain" (Ps. 127:1).

Religious Liberty.—Baptists have, in every age, stood stoutly and fearlessly and, at times, sacrificially, for religious liberty and its inevitable corollary, the complete separation of church and state. And let us be well aware that we are today confronted by the most determined and adroit campaign to batter down the wall that separates church and state ever undertaken in our country. Time restrains me, but I cite two or three facts that should summon this Convention to uncompromising and unapologetic action in the crisis now confronting our nation. First, I cite the unauthorized and unfortunate and dangerous action of the President of the United States in December 1939 when he named Mr. Myron C. Taylor as his "personal" representative to the Vatican. Although interpreted at that time as a "temporary expedient," without cost to the taxpayers, Mr. Taylor is still accredited by the Vatican as ambassador, and the cost of the embassy to the taxpayers last year was approximately $40,000. President Truman promised me and other spokesmen of the evangelical churches of our country last June that Mr. Taylor's appointment would be terminated at an early date, certainly not later than the signing of the treaties. The treaties relating to countries immediately adjacent to Italy have been signed, but Mr. Taylor's appointment has not been terminated. Southern Baptists should, and I trust will, at this Convention, ask Mr. Truman why he has not called Mr. Taylor and the embassy at the Vatican home. I cite the decision of the U.S. Supreme Court on February 10, 1947, in the case of Iverson versus New Jersey as added evidence that the wall which separates church and state is being battered down, and I say here today what I said in Washington a few minutes after I sat and listened to the decision, namely, "This ominous decision casts a shadow, now no larger, it may appear, than a man's hand, but portending a cloud that may be drifting out over every hamlet and dale from Plymouth Rock to the Golden Gate to darken the torch of religious liberty in our beloved land." I close this urgent appeal for action by quoting the words of Mr. Justice Jackson in his supporting argument to the minority decision, when he said, "The Court, in the majority decision this day, has turned back the hands of the clock." I plead with Southern Baptists, in this Convention and out to the last church, to stand up and face this challenge to religious liberty in sleepless vigilance until once again Washington and every other center of government in our free land shall know beyond any question that we will not compromise with political ecclesiasticism and clerical fascism on any terms whatsoever and that we will resist such encroachments in the conviction that they endanger every freedom of every person and institution and sanctity for which our fathers suffered to win for us, even at the sacrifice of life.

Conflicting ideas.—Ideas rule the world—always have, and always will. Tomorrow's world is torn in the conflict of at least three contending ideas—ideas that momently seek our consideration and acceptance. They are (a) Communism, (b) political ecclesiasticism or clerical fascism, and, (c) Christian democracy. Communism, though stated by Marx in plausible words that declare, "From each according to his ability, to each according to his need," is, in its age-old manifestations, a philosophy which may be bluntly stated in these words, "What you have, I will take, if I can." The first example I find in history of Communism is the slaying of Abel by Cain, occasioned by the fact that Abel had something, (the favor of God), which Cain coveted, but for which he was not willing to pay the price. Political ecclesiasticism is that idea, ancient in its manifestations, which today, in our Western civilization, is represented in the Roman

Catholic hierarchy, stemming from its world-girdling base in Vatican City. Time does not permit discussion, but I have already alluded to at least two incidents which dramatically reveal the menacing pressure of this idea upon our own people. Christian democracy, the third idea dominant in tomorrow's world, is the message and the mission of Southern Baptists and all other children of God who gladly make their *designs* in accordance with His intended *destiny* for the many sons which He purposes to bring into glory. Jesus has stated the philosophy of Christian democracy once and for all, when He said, "A new commandment I give unto you, That ye love one another; even as I have loved you" (John 13:34), from which commandment and all His other teachings, we adduce this *design* as our answer to tomorrow's world, "What I have, I will share, as you have need." God condemned the basic idea of Communism in his curse upon Cain. Political ecclesiasticism has long ago written its own epitaph of failure. Christian democracy has not only the authorship and approval of God, but the guarantee of ultimate victory—"He shall see of the travail of his soul, and shall be satisfied" (Isa. 53:11). The one great concern for us is that we shall so *design* as to enter into His *destiny* with all who serve Him in sincerity and truth.

Other Tasks.—I would, if time permitted, speak of other tasks that await Southern Baptists in tomorrow's world—the Christian approach to race relations, management, and labor, the revolution in agricultural methods which will call for many adjustments on the part of those who will be left without employment as mechanization of farm work proceeds, conservation of our natural resources, these and many other situations we should regard not as problems but as opportunities. But my time is gone.

A final word.—Man's *designs*—God's *destiny!* Strong, sobering, challenging, timely words are these which the Committee on Order of Business has thrown up for this Convention's consideration. Grateful for the past, committed to the present, hopeful of the future, let us look again at the words, quoted by Luke in Acts 2:17, from the prophet Joel, "And it shall come to pass in the last days, saith God, I will pour out of my Spirit upon all flesh; and your sons and your daughters shall prophesy, and your young men shall see visions, and your old men shall dream dreams." The Lord grant unto us this day such vision of His coming kingdom here in our beloved nation and to the ends of the earth, until, with John Rippon, we shall be able to sing with perfect *design:*

Let ev'ry kindred, ev'ry tribe,
On this terrestrial ball,
To him all majesty ascribe,
   And crown him Lord of all.

J. Winston Pearce
"We Do Well to Conform"

Matthew 3:13-17; Mark 1:9-11; Luke 3:21-22

The hour had struck for Jesus. For thirty years he had been biding his time. For most of these thirty years, he had been "making things for God" in the carpenter shop at Nazareth; both he and his work had been pleasing to God, for it was his Father's business that he was doing. But now the summons was to a new and different task. As Francis Thompson said, there came a trumpet sound "from the hid battlements of Eternity." The Trumpeter he knew, and he knew what the trumpet said. How did the call come to him? What was the setting for it? What means, human or otherwise, did God use? What were its distinctive notes—notes that called for and received the full and complete commitment of Jesus?

The call came in connection with the preaching of a great man, John the Baptist. Crowds from Jerusalem had come to the Jordan as to a revival meeting. Many who "came to scoff, remained to pray." It was a scene of mass evangelism with no holds barred! There was much of the "hellfire and damnation" in the message that was preached. But the people heard, and the people heeded, for John was a *man*. No one who saw him, heard him, felt his influence, and observed his habits could doubt that. He was a man, but he was more: he was a *man of God*. Thomas Carlyle once said of a certain church and people that what was needed was a preacher who knew God other than secondhand. John was such a preacher. His hearers knew it. There had been no such preaching in Israel since the days of the great prophets. A man of God had come with *God's message*. John cared only for two things, his Master and his message. He was not concerned about personal preferment; he was content to decrease so long as his Master increased. No wonder the people heard, heeded, and were healed!

A Great Encounter

To this outdoor revival on the banks of the Jordan Jesus came and presented himself for baptism. John demurred; Jesus insisted; John baptized him. It was a strange scene. The incident not only troubled John, it has troubled Christians ever since! John felt that it was he who should be baptized by Jesus and not the other way around. And were it not our assurance of the superior wisdom of Jesus, we would most certainly vote with John. As we see it, there were several things that Jesus might have done. Any one of these things might be easier for us to understand than what Jesus actually did do.

He might have ignored the whole situation. Baptism, as such, was not new. The mystery religions practiced it; their initiations were largely based upon baptism. The Jews practiced baptism for proselytes as they came into the Jewish faith from paganism. This was to be expected for these proselytes had to be purged from the evil of their Gentile ways. But for someone to say that a Jew, a true son of Abraham, needed baptism was to say something that had never been said, certainly never practiced before. Jesus might have passed it up as some new and useless fad.

He might have openly criticized John and his whole revival effort. He could have pointed out that many of the decisions were being made under great emotional stress, that the chances were better than two to one that many of those who were making professions and were being baptized would become nonresident members. Two years from the date they were baptized, few would be even making a pretense at living up to their commitment. Too, he could have pointed out that John's preaching was negative; it was a sounding of don'ts and shall nots. John seemed more concerned about what man should not do than he was with what God was able to do. He was thundering against man's sin instead of pleading God's grace. The note of repentance that John sounded so emphatically was not neglected in the preaching of Jesus, but certainly the major emphasis in the preaching of Jesus was different. And *it* is the emphasis that we remember. Longfellow contrasted the men in these verses:

> A voice by Jordan's shore!
> A summons stern and clear;—

Reform! be just! and sin no more!
  God's judgment draweth near!

A voice by Galilee,
  A holier voice I hear;—
Love God! thy neighbour love! for see,
  God's mercy draweth near!

O voice of Duty! still
  Speak forth; I hear with awe;
In thee I own the sovereign will,
  Obey the sovereign law.

Thou higher voice of love,
  Yet speak Thy word in me;
Through duty let me upward move
  To thy pure liberty!

Consenting to Conform

There was a third approach that Jesus could have taken to John's preaching, to the revival, and to the baptizing. This was what he did. He went to John and said, "I wish to be baptized." What a strong and tender sight it must have been. Luke puts it this way: "Now when all the people were baptized, and when Jesus also had been baptized." Does this mean that Jesus at first stood unnoticed in the crowd, listened to the preaching, watched reactions of the people, and rejoiced in the results? Then after praying to the Father, just as John baptized the last candidate, did Jesus walk out to John, still standing in the Jordan, and request baptism? Why?

He did it as an act of renunciation—but not as a renunciation of sin. Christian faith finds it impossible to believe that in requesting John's baptism, Jesus was repenting of sin. His challenge, "Which one of you convicteth me of sin," has never been seriously questioned. We are able to believe that he was tempted in all points as we are tempted, but with the writer of Hebrews we go on to affirm, "yet, without sin." We respond warmly to the lines in John Oxenham's little poem:

He was a boy—like you—and you—,
  As full of jokes, as full of fun,
But always He was bravely true,
  And did no wrong to anyone.

And one thing I am sure about—
He never tumbled into sin,
But kept himself, within, without,
As God had made Him, sweet and clean.[1]

Christians have not denied the difficulty of this position; they have only recognized the greater difficulty in any other position. It is the view based on Scripture. Also, followers of Jesus have never claimed that this position could be maintained apart from Christian faith.

As Jesus was not renouncing sin, neither was he renouncing a life of waste and uselessness. Even as a carpenter he had been "about his Father's business," and when the voice from heaven said of him "I am well pleased," it must have referred to all he had done. Both he and his work were in the center of God's will; the work was helpful to man, and it honored God.

He was renouncing the quiet life, the family joys, the simple if arduous responsibilities of making plows and yokes in the shop. In the place of these, he was assuming the dreadful responsibility of making and remaking men out on the horizons of God's great world. It was Erasmus who said that by a Carpenter mankind was made, and only by a Carpenter could mankind be remade. In the baptismal experience, Jesus was renouncing the strong guidance of Joseph, the loving care of Mary, the simple comforts of home, the kind if sometimes dull teaching of the synagogues, the warm if uncultured greetings of neighbors in and around Nazareth, the haunts where he had observed the flowers of the fields and watched the birds of the heavens. He was going out as one who had not where to lay his head, going out to become one who would be despised and rejected of men, one acquainted with grief, even to one day hanging on a cross.

Both Good and Bad

This scene at the Jordan represented not only an act of renunciation, it also represented an act of involvement. And just here is one of the areas where modern man is so unlike the Master. Modern men—you and I—do not like to become involved. For example, in the predawn darkness in New York City, a young woman by the name of Kitty Genovese was being stalked by a killer. At last he stabbed her; then he left, returned, and stabbed her again and again. It took thirty-five minutes for him to kill her. Forty of her neighbors were roused by her screams; they saw her being stabbed, but no one helped, no one called the police. . . . On a bridge between San Pedro and Terminal Island in Los Angeles harbor, California, two highway patrolmen grappled with a man bent on suicide. They needed help. They called to passing motorists, but no one stopped. . . . In Riverside, California, a young woman on her way home from church was dragged into a field where she was choked and raped. Headlights from passing automobiles picked out the young woman and her attackers. No one stopped. . . . In a building in the Bronx, New York, an eighteen-year-old switchboard operator ran naked and hysterical down a stairway into a vestibule. She was in plain sight of a crowd gathered on the sidewalk. Olga Romero bled and screamed as her rapist tried to drag her back upstairs. No one helped; no one even called the police.

Witnesses to the two rapes and the murder told police later, "I didn't want to get involved." It was probably the same among those who saw the patrolmen struggling on the bridge. This extreme desire for noninvolvement is a symptom of life today. Dr. Edward Stainbrook, psychiatrist, says, "One no longer values other individuals. They don't know them, so they aren't concerned about them." Dr. Edward Walker, police inspector, says, "Thousands of persons can live in one building and not pay any attention to the next person. They just don't want to get involved with him." Dr. Svend Riemer, sociology professor, says, "Part of the personality of the big city is not wanting to be involved. There is little cohesion between people. They don't worry about the other guys."[2]

We do not want to get tied up, tied down; we do not want our liberty curtailed; we do not want to become involved in the corruption of city government and politics, with the race issue and the "poverty pockets." Middle-aged people are single and lonely because they are afraid of becoming involved; young, healthy, capable married couples are childless because they do not wish to become involved; multitudes live isolated lives in giant apartment buildings, not knowing the names of their neighbors even on the same floor because they do not wish to become involved. So we go on living our self-centered lives in our own little backwaters or eddies, refusing to step out into the muddy, rushing, whirling, confusing waters of the Jordan and become involved!

Not so the Master. He wished to identify himself with and to become involved in all of life. He said, "He who is not for me is against me." What if John's preaching and emphasis were different from his; what if it did sound a note that was more of the past than of the present and the future? John came neither eating nor drinking; Jesus came doing both. John lived his life in the desert wilds; Jesus lived his among the thronging multitudes. John was a voice crying in the wilderness; for a time, Jesus was the most popular dinner guest in all Palestine. But what of all this? John was a man who stood foursquare for God; he was a flaming witness; he had the eye and the ear of the people; he was emphasizing truths that had been neglected since the day of the prophet Amos; he had the courage of a lion and the passion of a red hot furnace!

Years later Paul would write to Philippi: "What then? notwithstanding, every way . . . Christ is preached; and I therein do rejoice, yea, and I will rejoice." By his words and his actions Jesus wanted to show that *he* rejoiced; he was grateful; he wanted John to know. Jesus wanted John to know that he expected to be a part of the remedy and not a part of the problem. He would become involved with John and in this work that John was doing.

It is fearfully easy to criticize. The words are chosen with care. It is easy to criticize, and it is a fearful thing to do. Because you do not like the cut of the captain's hair or the sound of his uncultured voice or his uncouth manners, you may refuse to serve in the army of the King. In so doing, you may give aid and comfort to the enemy while the captain may be giving all and the best that he has. A man once criticized Dwight L. Moody's evangelistic methods. Moody admitted that he was not altogether pleased with them himself and asked the man what methods he would suggest. "Well," hedged the man, "I do not have any methods to suggest." "Then," said Mr. Moody, "I like my methods better."

Dr. Leslie Weatherhead, the distinguished former minister of City Temple, London, once wrote:

> I well remember conducting a mission at the University of Leeds. After each session there was an opportunity for private conversations. A girl who was about to take her final degree examinations said something like this: "When I get back home, I know that the hardest thing in my religious life will be to stick with the services in our little village chapel. . . . So," she added, "I think I shall simply go up to the hills or into the woods. I shall more easily find God there . . ." Of course I told her that would never do as a rule. God ceases too soon to be real when we evade men, especially fellow-seekers, and seek Him selfishly for ourselves; and I reminded her of Him who was in the synagogue on the Sabbath day *"as His custom was."* I reminded her that

He must have had to listen to some pretty poor stuff from those old Rabbis; but that if others lifted their heads during the prayers and saw His face, they would come again; that in any case when He was there, it would be easier to pray; that she had something to give in a service as well as to get; and that her minister would break his heart if she deserted him instead of helping him to make the service what both wanted it to become. Since that date, the spiritual life of that little village church has been transformed and renewed, and it has overflowed to another village. The girl not only attended regularly but started a group which has become the spiritual powerhouse of the neighborhood.[3]

Jesus not only became identified with and involved in all that was good, he identified himself with and became concerned about all that was bad. After two thousand years the scene still shocks us! The sinless Christ wades out into the muddy waters of Jordan to be baptized at the hands of sinful (for he was only man) John.

Sinlessness approaches the sinful; strength goes out to weakness; the divine goes out to the human; God goes out to man! Here is an example, a thumbnail sketch, of what his entire life and his death would be. He was a friend of publicans and sinners; he was numbered with the transgressors; he bore the sins of many. He came to save not the righteous but the sinners; he did not come to minister to the well but to the sick. Augustine said that God had one son on earth without sin but never one without suffering. "It was fitting," wrote the author of Hebrews, "that he [God], for whom and by whom all things exist, in bringing many sons to glory, should make the pioneer of their salvation perfect through suffering" (2:10, RSV).

In his baptism Jesus became involved with the world's evil and suffering. Men and women need to know this truth. Listen to Jeanne D'Orge writing in the *New York Times:*

> I wish there were someone
> Who would hear my confession.
> Not a priest—I do not want to be told of my sins;
> Not a mother—I do not want to give sorrow;
> Not a friend—she would not know enough;
> Not a lover—he would be too partial;
> Not God—he is too far away;
> But someone who would be a friend, lover, mother, priest,
>   God, all in one,

And a stranger besides—who would not condemn or interfere;
Who, when everything is said from beginning to end,
Would show the reason of it all
And tell you to go ahead
And work it out your own way.[4]

As basic biblical theology, those lines may lack something; but as a cry of the human heart, it speaks to our condition. In its pervading tone, it points to One who involved himself with all that was bad.

Call to Consecration

Again, his baptism was an act of consecration. In some deep and significant way, he was doing here at the beginning of his active ministry what he did at the close of his human sojourn among men. In John 17 we hear him saying, "For their sake I consecrate myself." At his baptism we do not listen to these words; but by his life and actions, he was saying much the same thing—acting out his purpose.

He was consecrating himself to the service of men. He had been serving men as he worked in the carpenter shop in Nazareth. Yet, "life is more than meat, and the body is more than raiment." When God wants a man to make a plow, the man does not honor God by insisting that he be allowed to make a sermon. But this does not alter the fact that a sermon which is used of God to bring men into a saving relationship with him is more important than a plow that helps man to make more or better ears of corn, for life is more than bread. It was a new and a higher service to which Jesus was now dedicating himself. He would be preaching the gospel to the poor, proclaiming release to the captives, the recovery of sight to the blind; he would be setting at liberty those who were oppressed; and he would be proclaiming the acceptable year of the Lord. The Spirit of the Lord was coming upon him for that purpose.

One of the church fathers said, "The kingdom of Heaven, O man, requires no other price than yourself; the value of it is yourself; give yourself for it, and you shall have it." Let us say it reverently; this was true for Christ no less than for his followers. He could gain the kingdom of God on no other grounds. This, surely, should be enough to banish any pink-tea dreams that the kingdom can be gained in our day.

Gilbert K. Chesterton, that thorny thistle in the side of his own church as well as the churches of all persuasions, saw that many people feel the kingdom of God can be gained through criticism and complaint alone, that once a group has pronounced judgment upon other groups for what they have done or have not done, they have thereby qualified themselves for the kingdom. So Chesterton wrote,

> The Christian Social Union here
> Was very much annoyed;
> It seems there is some duty
> Which we never should avoid,
> And so they sing a lot of hymns
> To help the Unemployed.[5]

In the act of baptism, Christ was consecrating himself to conflict. There must have been irritations and conflicts in the carpenter shop. Probably human nature then and there was not very different from what it is here and now. G. A. Studdert-Kennedy has raised this question:

> I wonder what he charged for chairs at Nazareth
> And did men try to beat him down
> And boast about it in the town—
> "I bought it cheap, for half-a-crown
> From that mad Carpenter."[6]

What Christ consecrated himself to face in conflict, however, was something quite different. On the stage of history during that first century, the world saw a cosmic paradox. God himself had come to earth in the person of his Son to redeem men from their sins. In times past God had spoken through the prophets, but now he was ready to speak through his Son. It was like the famous pattern of a three-act play. Two acts had been played out. In the first act the characters were introduced and the circumstances were given. The second act showed the characters hopelessly entangled in sin and conflict. Then God was ready to lift the curtain on the third act; God's love and purpose were about to be revealed. Against the dark clouds of sin, he placed a rainbow in his sky; and men would marvel: "Behold, what manner of love the Father hath bestowed upon us, that we should be called the sons of God!"

But before the victorious climax, evil will struggle more viciously than ever; and before that conflict is over, history's darkest deed will be done. In that crime it will appear that God has forgotten man, but the very opposite will be true. That deed will be a sign that God has come in the person of his Son to reveal God's love for man, and all the forces of evil will recognize this and gird themselves for battle. They will cry out, "What have we to do with thee, thou Jesus of Nazareth? art thou come to destroy us? I know thee who thou art, the Holy One of God!" So evil and God's Son will stand toe to toe. On the first day of that mortal combat evil will seem to win, and God's Son will appear to be completely crushed. But never judge God's battles at the close of only the first day. With God there is always a third day! Christ was consecrating himself to and for this conflict.

Endless Enduement

His baptismal experience was also a time of enduement for Christ. Christian faith has always cherished the description that the Gospel writers give us of this event. Matthew, Mark, and Luke recorded it as an event to be remembered and cherished by all believers. Here it is in Luke's words: "Now when all the people were baptized, it came to pass, that Jesus also being baptized, and praying, the heaven was opened, and the Holy Ghost descended in a bodily shape like a dove upon him, and a voice came from heaven, which said, Thou art my beloved Son; in thee I am well pleased."

Here is new and additional enduement. In his farewell speech to the children of Israel, Moses had spoken for God the words, "As thy days, so shall thy strength be." Strength from God is like the manna in the wilderness in this: it has to be received fresh each morning, and each person may take as much as he can use. There is no limit to the supply, there is only a limit to the capacity and the need of the individual. God had given to his Son all the light and power needed in the carpenter shop. Now as he faced additional need, God was ready to supply more strength.

This great truth is seen in several phrases. First, God was giving new light to his Son. "The heaven was opened"—new truth, new understanding, new insight into the purpose of God was promised. Inscribed on the Eddystone lighthouse on the English coast are the words, "To give light is to give life." In order to be the *life* of the world, Christ had to be "the light of the world." That Light was the light from heaven. That is why it could not be put out. John came "as a burning and shining light," and men were willing to rejoice in the light that John gave them for a season. The light, the truth, the testimony that Christ brought was greater. He was the Light that the world could not put out.

It seemed a small light. One man, a working man, a carpenter by trade, one who had grown up among them, one whose brothers and sisters they knew, one who came from a town and community of no repute and a country that was held in bondage by military power, was in John's words "the true Light, which lighteth every man that cometh into the world." No man who followed him ever walked in darkness. Two men once went out one night; one took a torch and the other did not. When they returned, the latter reported that he found nothing but darkness; but the other said, "Everywhere I went I found the light."

In his biography of St. Francis of Assisi, Chesterton says, "While it was yet twilight a figure appeared silently and suddenly on a little hill above the city, dark against the fading darkness. For it was the end of a long and stern night, a night of vigil, not unvisited by stars. He stood with his hands lifted . . . and about him was a burst of birds singing; and behind him was the break of day."[7] So, to some lesser degree, it has been with every "St. Francis" who has followed the Light that lighteth every man. And, to a much greater degree and very different dimension, the light came to Jesus at his baptism.

He was also endued with fresh power. The Spirit of God descended like a dove upon him. Of course power had been given to make good yokes, but the baptism power was given to make good men, a much greater requirement. For this task nothing less was, or is, required than the presence and power of God. Writing about General Charles Gordon, a devout follower of Christ, one person said that the Sunday before the general left England for the Sudan, he "drove around to a number of churches to take communion as many times as possible, and thus start brimful of God." One may doubt that such was the purpose of the good general; witnesses must be God-filled, however, if good men are to be made.

> Did He call Lazarus back from death's abyss?
> Did He turn water into wine that wedding day?
> Yes, but His greatest miracle was this:
> To make a Christian from our common clay.[8]

We are told that there was also a "voice from heaven." Here is new communication, too. This is a distinct ministry of Christ. He knew the Father; he communicated with the Father. John called him the "Word": "In the beginning was the Word, and the Word was with God, and the

Word was God." Christ was the communications link between God and man.

To the Jew, a word was more than mere communication; it was something active, dynamic, creative; it did things; it had an existence of its own. The spoken word was something alive, charged with power. Sir George Adam Smith, the great Bible scholar, tells of meeting a group of Arabs on one occasion who greeted him with, "Peace be unto you," the regular salutation for one of their own. Later the Arabs discovered that Dr. Smith's party was made up of Christians. The Moslem Arabs then returned to Dr. Smith and begged for a recall of the blessing; they did not want those active, creative words to do their beneficent work in the lives of Christians.

Jesus said that no one knew the Father but the Son and no one knew the Son but the Father. The communication between the Father and the Son was of a nature the earth could not understand. It was the distinct work of Jesus to impart this understanding to men. To this undertaking he gave himself; to accomplish this task he died.

Another step was required. The word from heaven said, "This is my beloved Son, in whom I am well pleased." Here is approval, divine approval. It is approval for the past; what Jesus had done in Nazareth and the carpenter shop was good. The decision that Jesus had made to leave the carpenter shop and the pleasures of home was good. The decision of the Son to identify himself with all that was good and with all that was bad was good. God was well pleased.

In his book *Jesus Came Preaching* George Buttrick has called attention to the famous picture in the Boston library which shows the young Galahad approaching the throne seat that was said to rob a man of his life. Carved on the chair are the words, "He who sits herein shall lose himself." Galahad is shown moving forward; the knights of the Round Table watch his movements and stand in awe as they make the sign of the cross with their uplifted sword hilts. At the throne an angel has drawn back the red coverlet from the chair. You can almost hear the young knight saying, "If I lose myself, I save myself."

"This is my beloved Son," said the voice from heaven. "in whom I am well pleased." Christ had come for the purpose of losing himself; in losing himself he saved others.

NOTES

1. John Oxenham, "The Other Boys," *Christ and the Fine Arts*, Cynthia Pearl Maus, Comp. (New York: Harper & Bros., 1938), 109.

2. *San Francisco Chronicle*, May 31, 1964, 1B.

3. Leslie D. Weatherhead, *How Can I Find God?* (New York: Fleming H. Revell Co., 1934), 126.

4. *New York Times*, Books Section, July 7, 1940, 19.

5. G. K. Chesterton, *The Autobiography of G. K. Chesterton* (New York: Sheed and Ward, 1937), 167.

6. G. A. Studdert-Kennedy, "The Carpenter," *Quotable Poems I,* Comps., Thomas Curtis Clark and Esther A. Gillespie (Chicago: Willett, Clark and Co., 1931), 13.

7. G. K. Chesterton, *Saint Francis of Assisi* (New York: Doubleday & Co., 1962), 36-37.

8. Edwin Markham, "His Greatest Miracle," as quoted by William L. Stidger, *Planning Your Preaching* (New York: Harper & Bros., 1932), 71.

W. R. Pettigrew
The Rending of the Veil

And, behold, the veil of the temple was rent in twain from the top to the bottom (Matt. 27:51).

The Holy of Holies was a cubicle chamber in the Temple. Within its mysterious gloom dwelt God—God, greatly to be feared, distant and unapproachable by ordinary man.

A mighty veil hung before that shrine. The pattern of this magnificent tapestry was a revelation from God to Moses. It was "curiously wrought" in colors of blue, purple, and scarlet. It was sixty feet long, thirty feet wide, a hand's breadth in thickness, and required 300 priests to move it. It was supported by pillars overlaid with gold and hung from hooks of solid gold.

On the momentous moment when the crucified Christ had finished drinking the bitter cup of our redemption, and had dismissed His Spirit to the Father, and, as the earth quaked, and, as rocks were rent, and, as graves gave up their dead: "Behold, the veil of the temple was rent in twain from the top to the bottom."

What meaneth this sacred sign and this interpretive wonder? It meant: (1) That atonement had been made; (2) That a "new and living way" to God had been laid; (3) That all believers to the priesthood had been ordained.

The Rending of the Veil Meant That Atonement Had Been Made

The high priest dared not go beyond the veil and into the presence of God until first the life and blood of a bullock had been offered up for his, and the sins of his family. Furthermore, when he went beyond the veil he

365

bore in his hands the blood which had been shed for the sins of the people!

Before the veil was rent and the way was opened for all men to come to God, atoning blood for the sins of all men had to be shed. Witness that blood shedding!

Come with me to Gethsemane where the Lamb of God prays in agony. Unsandal your feet for if ever you stood on holy ground it's here! With the aid of a full-orbed moon, look and wonder at the ruby drops standing on His sacred brow. This is the beginning of the shedding of atoning blood, which had to be shed before the veil could be rent.

Isaiah had prophesied that the hair would be plucked from His cheeks and that His visage would be marred "more than any man." Before Caiaphas they spat upon Him, buffeted Him and smote Him with the palms of their hands. It must have been here also that they tangled vicious fingers in His beard and tore it from His face! If, if—your eyes can endure to behold the sight, look on His torn, swollen, and bleeding face and know that this, too, is atoning blood that had to be shed before there could be the rending of the veil!

Pilate has condemned Him to be scourged, and He is about to receive the chastisement of our peace and the stripes of our healing upon shoulders that have never bowed under any sins but ours. The rugged Roman with the cruel whip in his hand takes his stance. The metal-slugged thongs of leather zing through the air, cut into His quivering flesh, and blood streams down! This, too, is atoning blood that had to flow before the "new and living way . . . through the veil, that is to say, his flesh," could be opened for sinful men to come to God!

Harken ye to the coarse and scurrilous laughter echoing through the stone barracks of the legionnaires. The soldiers ridicule Him: "So this is the fellow who says he is a king! Give him a robe!" They drape His bleeding shoulders with an old toga! They force a reed in His hand and call it His sceptre. "A king must have a crown and here is one that will not fall off," and amid jeers and mockery they press a thorny crown down on the finely chiseled brow of the Son of God. From under the piercing points of each in-turned thorn there streams blood—atoning blood—that had to be shed to open the way for sinning men to come to God!

Atop gray, gruesome Golgotha two crosses already stand with their writhing victims. A third cross lies upon the ground and by it stands the

Lamb of God. The soldiers strip Him, visiting torturing humiliation upon Him. They stretch His already bleeding body upon the cross and drive spikes through His hands—hands that had blessed little children—and spikes through His feet—feet that had followed wandering mankind along the torturous path of their sin to their deepest hell.

The cross is lifted and dropped into its place with a sickening thud. The spikes tear His hands and feet. See, from His hands and feet, blood streaming, streaming, streaming down!—atoning blood that had to be shed before the veil between man and God could be rent!

"Father, forgive them; for they know not what they do." And the blood flows down!

"If thou be Christ, save thyself and us." "Dost not thou fear God? . . . Lord, remember me when thou comest into thy kingdom." "To day shalt thou be with me in paradise." And still the blood flows down!

"Woman, behold thy son! Behold thy mother!" And the blood streams down!

"My God, my God, why hast thou forsaken me?" And the blood trickles down!

"I thirst." And the blood drips, drips, drips, drips—drips down!

"It is finished. Father, into thy hands I commend my spirit." And the blood drips . . .drips . . .drips down!

"And, behold, the veil of the temple was rent in twain from the top to the bottom."

Atonement—full atonement—had been made! Christ had tasted death for every man and "whosoever" could now come to God. There was no veil between!

The Rending of the Veil Meant That a "New and Living Way" to God Had Been Laid

On that divinely dramatic day when the veil was rent, a "new and living way" was "consecrated" by which men could with "boldness . . . enter into the holiest"—into the presence of God.

This new way to God was "new" in that it was not by indirection. This way to God was not circuitous by ways of systems, rituals, ceremonies, ordinances, mysteries, symbols, or intermediaries.

Too often the souls of men are betrayed by our perverting the simple Gospel with pageantry, muddling it with magic, loading it down with litanies, or by ruining it with rituals. Coming to God for salvation by this new way is as simple and direct as was the Israelite's look to the brazen serpent for healing!

Spurgeon, under conviction of sin, sought salvation for five years among the many trappings of religion, not discerning the simple but glorious truth that "there was life in a look at the crucified One." While on his way elsewhere, a storm forced him to worship in a little, primitive Methodist Chapel. In the absence of the minister, a very unlearned layman spoke, using as his text "Look unto me, and be ye saved, all the ends of the earth." Said he:

My dear friends, this text says look. Now that does not take a great deal of effort. It ain't lifting your foot or your finger; it is just looking. Well, a man need not go to college to learn to look. You may be the biggest fool, and yet you can look. A man need not be worth a thousand pounds a year to look. Anyone can look; a child can look. But this is what the text says: "Look unto me." "Look unto me; I am sweating great drops of blood. Look unto me; I am hanging on a cross. Look unto me; I am dead and buried and arisen. Look unto me; I ascend. Look unto me; I am sitting on the Father's right hand."

Suddenly the humble man turned upon young Spurgeon and said: "Young man, you look very miserable, and you will always be miserable if you do not obey my text and look to Jesus for salvation."

The boy, who was to become one of the greatest preachers of all ages, looked—simply looked—and was born again!

Let it be our glory that we lift up Christ and cry to dying men: "Look to Jesus: simply, directly, look! There is life in a look at the crucified One!"

Before the veil was rent the people never came into the presence of God except by proxy. The priest represented them before God when he went within the veil. When the veil was rent the way to God was open, not only to the holiest priest, but also to the humblest peasant. An intermediary between God and man became superfluous.

A young father and mother, tortured with grief, came asking that I conduct funeral services for their child. They sobbed out their story:

They and their priest had become estranged. When the baby came the priest had withheld baptism until the parents met certain demands of the Church. This had further infuriated the parents and the baby had not been baptized. That had been three years ago; and last night the baby had died, and without the blessings of the Church. Believing their baby lost, their grief knew no bounds. The baby was to be buried in unconsecrated ground. Would I be kind enough to conduct some kind of a service over the little body?

In a quiet hill-top cemetery and at the appointed hour, I met them, their relatives and their friends, bearing the little white casket. Standing there by the open grave I told them of how Jesus had said His Kingdom was for little children, and how Jesus had told them who would interpose themselves between little children and Him to stand aside and to forbid not the little children to come to Him. I explained how "Indirection to Deity" had been done away and that the spirit of their child had been under no necessity to go to God by way of a priest, church, or sacraments. Their baby's spirit had gone directly to be with Jesus in a heavenly paradise and was not in a hopeless purgatory.

The moment for lowering the little casket had come. Asking that it be opened again, the father knelt down, encircled it with his arms and said: "Oh David, you are with Jesus. Thank God! Mother and I will see you again."

Five men and women who stood by that little grave, including the parents, forsook the devious, indirect, man-made ways to God, and began their walk in the "new and living way" to God. I baptized them upon their confession of simple, direct, personal faith in Christ as Saviour.

Let us ever be saying to this world that the veil has been rent; that the way to God is open and direct to all, and that no church or ecclesiastical group has the right to interpose themselves as essential media between God and His creatures—between the Saviour and sinners.

The Rending of the Veil Meant That All Believers to the Priesthood Had Been Ordained

Before the rending of the veil it was unthinkable that an ordinary man should go beyond the veil and into God's presence. That privilege belonged to the high priest and to him alone.

When Christ died and the veil was rent, the Holy of Holies came to include the vast domain of all believing hearts. Henceforth God was to dwell in the midst of His people and be directly approachable to all. It was to be true that

> They who seek the Throne of Grace
> Find that Throne in every place.

Henceforth the blessings of God were not to be distributed to men through a stratified ecclesiastical society. Henceforth the caste system in religion was to be done away with. The priest in his stately robes and the peasant in his scant rags could come alike into the presence of God. In the hour of the rending of the veil all believers became priests before their God.

The priesthood of believers is a doctrine of priceless privilege. The sinning one may go directly to the God of the rent-veil sanctuary, there confess his sins, and have God say to him, "I absolve thee; I forgive thee; go and sin no more." The nobody may boldly go to his God and God will make him somebody! The nameless may go to God and God will give him a name! The weak and faltering may go directly and boldly to God, and in His presence, be made strong! Thanks be unto God that there is no longer a veil between God and man; that an intermediary is superfluous and that God's people may do business with Him without the necessity of a middle man!

The priesthood of the believer is not merely an article of faith but also a challenge to action in faith. The high priest when he went into the presence of God offered an appropriate sacrifice to God. The word "priest" means "sacrificer," and we priests of the rent-veil sanctuary are to fulfill its meaning. What are we to sacrifice? Paul answers: "I beseech you, therefore, brethren, by the mercies of God, that ye present your bodies a living sacrifice, holy, acceptable unto God, which is your reasonable service" (Rom. 12:1).

We are to present ourselves to God in holy life and holy deed even unto death.

Henry Martin, honor student of Cambridge, scholar, and refined gentleman, so offered himself unto God when he went to India. There among people who smeared their bodies with revolting filth as an act of worship; there among people whose holy men sat in one position until their limbs became as rigid as stone, and their finger nails grew through the backs of their clenched hands; there among people whose men married little girls and wrecked their bodies with lust; there among people whose many revolting heathenisms must have sickened Henry Martin—yes, there among these people and for these people he said, "Now let me burn out for God."

Our pastorates, our pulpits, and our places of service must become veritable altars upon which we vicariously live and die for God. When

God's believer-priests so come to offer themselves in utter self abandonment, then and only then shall come the "revival in the midst of the years," and then and only then shall come the rebirth of a hope for a doomed age.

Accompanying the privilege of direct access to God is the responsibility of intercession for them who know not for themselves the God of the rent-veil sanctuary.

Would to God we felt the weight of this priestly duty as did John Welch, who kept a plaid that he might wrap himself when he arose to pray at night. His wife would upbraid him when she found him lying on the ground weeping. He would reply: "Oh woman, I have the souls of 3,000 to answer for and I know not how it is with many of them." There would be a real hope for lost humanity if God's believer-priests felt like that!

It is said that when the high priest emerged from the Holy of Holies, he brought to the people something of the glory of God in his face and something of the love of God in his heart. Peter says that believer-priests "are to show forth the praises" of God. The Christian, having access to God, has the staggering responsibility of abiding in that Presence, until, when he goes out among men he shall convey to them something of the love, light, and life of God.

Some years ago a minister arose in a gathering of ministers and asked to be permitted to relate a story. Said he: "God gave my wife and me a precious baby boy. He grew normally for three years and was our joy. Then a subtle disease reduced his little body to a thin emaciated form. No remedy seemed to help. One day our faithful physician sat by the little bed with his finger on the faint pulse. Suddenly he looked up and said, 'I'm sorry, but your baby is gone.'" The minister faltered and then continued: "I told my wife to heat all the blankets in the house. I tore open my clothes, pressed the little form to my heart and had my wife to wrap about us the blankets. I held him there for nine hours." There was a pause and then the minister said: "That was twenty-five years ago: my son is a minister of the Gospel, and this is his birthday."

Believer-priests, we should tarry in the presence of God until our own hearts are so filled with the love and compassion of God, that when we go forth from the Holy of Holies, we may gather the spiritually dead to our hearts and make them alive to God through Christ.

So shall we be worthy priests of the rent-veil sanctuary.

Ramsey Pollard
Undivided Heart

Galatians 2:20

In Galatians 2:20, Paul rises to sublime heights. He touches upon that intimate relationship which exists between the Redeemer and the redeemed. He (Paul) speaks of "I"—"Me"—"Himself." Paradoxes thrive:

"He is crucified, yet he lives. Yet, he doesn't live, but Christ lives in him. The life he lives in the flesh, he lives by faith."

Paul's letter to the Galatians is quite severe. But, it is the severity of a compassionate heart. He is making an impassioned protest against false teachers and their doctrine of heresy. The grand old preacher is amazed that in so short a time his beloved friends are standing on shaking ground.

Salvation Attacked

Judaizers have created havoc among the children of God in the churches of Galatia. Salvation by Grace was being attacked. False teachers were busy saying, "Surely, there is something in addition to faith. Salvation is by faith, they argued, plus what we can and must do to bring it about."

Paul's indignation against such false teaching was white hot. He did not sit back for fear someone might say, "Old Paul is intolerant; the old man is narrow-minded; he is a bigot." He let loose all the brilliance of his keen mind. He hammered untruth to pieces with keen and forceful logic.

Superstition, paganism, and half-truths were the enemies of God and of the souls of men. The very soul of Christianity was at stake, and Paul had no hesitancy in drawing his sword and making a frontal attack on such false teaching. In our day non-Christian cowardice would meekly bleat, "Do not forget we are all brothers and headed for the same place."

372

Paul's Godly intolerance made him condemn false teaching which allowed the eternal distinctions of right and wrong to be blurred. He didn't spend much time fearing that someone would label him as a "bigot." When God's truth and the eternal destiny of human souls were at stake, Paul spoke with all the fire, concern, and thunder at his command.

Much modern Christianity is so weak and lacking in conviction that the power of protest is gone. We are expected to swallow every kind of false teaching and heresy without blinking our spiritual eyes. Paul would not agree that anything was necessary to salvation but faith in Jesus Christ. He stood his ground. He was a herald, not an apologist. "For I determined not to know any thing among you, save Jesus Christ and Him crucified" (1 Cor. 2:2).

No Spiritual Showmen

We are not to be ecclesiastical showmen. But we are to contend for the faith once delivered to the saints.

The best contending we can do is not in debating or arguing these truths, but by faithfully and earnestly preaching God's word of love and redemption in Christ Jesus. When modern Judaizers preach salvation by works, by baptism, by church membership, by ritualism, by "doing the best you can," let the ambassador of God tell of Christ's atonement wrought out on Calvary.

Preach it! Tell it to men everywhere! Proclaim it in sermon and song; from pulpit and through the air! Send the message of God's Grace into every television set in all the land. God's Grace, wonderful grace, sustaining Grace, keeping Grace—Grace that is greater than all our sins.

Paul faced a battle, and we face the same today: The conflict between those who minimize God's Grace; those who would make salvation dependent, in the final analysis, on man's integrity and goodness, rather than on the Grace of God and the eternal and sufficient priesthood of Jesus Christ.

Paul declared that the law is our schoolmaster to lead us to Christ; Christ is the end of the law for righteousness to everyone that believeth.

Solitary High Priest

Christ on the cross was a solitary High Priest. Paul does not mean he shared in the sufferings of Christ when He died for our redemption. As a sacrifice for human sin, the crucified Saviour stands alone and solitary.

That aspect of the cross cannot be shared. Let no man, or set of men, dare enter the Holy of Holies. The atoning work of Christ was foreshadowed in Leviticus 16:17.

And there shall be no man in the tabernacle of the congregation when he goeth in to make an atonement in the holy place.

In Isaiah 63:3, we read: "I have trodden the winepress alone, and of the people there was none with me . . ."

Christ died alone—He was forsaken by God and man; forsaken of God because "He was made to become sin"; forsaken of man because of man's sin and treachery.

Have you ever considered the loneliness of Christ? He was surrounded by folks who misunderstood him, who misinterpreted His message and mission, and who forsook Him when the supreme trial came.

His solitary priesthood is vividly pointed out in Hebrews 7:25:

Wherefore, He is able also to save them to the uttermost that come unto God by Him, seeing He ever liveth to make intercession for them.

His priesthood is forever eternal because He arose from the grave. Death was conquered that day. Christ broke the bonds of sin and death. We have an eternal, solitary High Priest who offered up Himself, once for all. No one shared His suffering for our sins; not even Paul. Christ paid it all.

Christ-Mastered Men

But, there was a sense in which Paul entered into the sufferings of Christ. So far as the claims of DIVINE JUSTICE are concerned, Paul was crucified with Christ. Christ's crucifixion stands for his. By faith, Paul was so identified with Christ that the Saviour's death was Paul's death.

Knowing this, that our old man is crucified with Him, that the body of sin might be destroyed, that henceforth we should not serve sin. For he that is dead is freed from sin (Rom. 6:6-7).

Paul was free from the law—free from condemnation. In Romans 8:1, Paul with a jubilant spirit shouts:

There is therefore now no condemnation to them which are in Christ Jesus, who walk not after the flesh, but after the spirit.

"I am crucified with Christ," does mean in a very vivid way that Paul knew how to relate himself to Christ. The selfish, arrogant, overbearing, Christ-hating Saul was dead. He properly related himself to His Redeemer. Ambition, save to "glory in the Cross of Christ," was dead.

Another great herald, John the Baptist, put in these words: "He (Jesus) must increase, but I must decrease."

Both of these men were Christ-mastered. They were crucified to the world.

"But God forbid that I should glory, save in the cross of our Lord Jesus Christ, by whom the world is crucified unto me, and I unto the world."

Paul had experienced crucifixion:

And that he died for all, that they which live should not henceforth live unto themselves, but unto him which died for them, and rose again (2 Cor. 5:15).

He suffered for Christ and His Gospel. He agonized over lost souls. He wept over churches led astray. He sacrificed self so far as this world with all its allurements is concerned. This heroic preacher did not feel sorry for himself. He gloried in tribulations for Christ's sake. Paul longed to enter into the sufferings of Christ. In Philippians 3:10, he says: "That I may know Him and the power of His resurrection, and the fellowship of His sufferings . . ."

But after every experience, Paul wiped the blood from his eyes and began looking for lost souls.

Preacher's Union

Recently, I read of a man who wanted to start a "preachers' union." He advocated shorter hours, better pay, fewer telephone calls about nothing, no Sunday funerals. To these, I would add another suggestion—double time for wedding rehearsals and wedding receptions. Of course, in some cases, this double time would mean exactly nothing.

However, I doubt that Paul would have been interested in joining such a union. God's preachers are to be men of sacrifice; men who gladly suffer for Christ's sake. Power comes through suffering. Paul was proud of his battle scars. In the closing words of his letter to the Galatians, he cries out! "From henceforth let no man trouble me, for I bear in my body the marks of the Lord Jesus."

He vindicated his apostolic authority by bearing the marks of Christ in his body. By suffering, rejoicing suffering, victorious suffering, the Gospel has been carried and planted among all the nations of the earth.

Christ's Love

Paul greatly rejoiced in the love of Christ for him. The dynamic of his great life was the realization that Christ loved Paul; the wonder of it; he was overwhelmed; he was utterly amazed that the Lily of the Valley, God's Son, The Rose of Sharon, The Fairest of Ten Thousand, loved him.

Paul faced the fact that Christ loved him even when he was persecuting the saints of God. It dawned upon Paul that Christ loved him as though there were no others upon whom he might lavish His love. God help us that this majestic truth may burn itself into our every heart.

An old woman of the slums, gloriously converted, became the subject of taunts, persecution, and jeers. They ridiculed her zeal for Christ. Finally, one persecutor said, "I think you are the ugliest old woman I ever saw." Then answered the redeemed soul, "Isn't it wonderful that Christ could love an old ugly woman like me?"

For Paul, Jesus came into the world; took upon Himself Paul's sins; died on Calvary for Paul's salvation; arose from the grave for Paul's justification; and now, He is at the right hand of God making intercession for Paul. It was not Paul's love for Christ; but Christ's love for Paul that sent him out with a flaming heart to preach the unsearchable riches. That, and that alone, explains the greatest life of the Christian era.

John Wesley had such an experience. He had been a preacher, after a fashion; but one day, in great spiritual unrest, he went to a service in Aldersgate Street. Something happened. Hear his words:

"About a quarter before nine, I felt my heart strangely warmed. I felt I did trust in Christ alone for salvation, and an assurance was given me that He had taken away my sin." From that day on, John Wesley was a different preacher. There was a note of compassion never before evident in his ministry.

That is what Paul meant when he said, "I am constrained by the love of Christ."

Lack of Compassion

If you want to know the secret of Paul's zeal, of his compassion, of his power, of his earnestness, I believe you will find it in the fact that he was overwhelmed by the knowledge of Christ's love for him. The curse of modern-day preaching is the shameful lack of compassion. Too many preachers are calm expositors of truth rather than impassioned preachers of the gospel.

We have allowed intellectual pride to stifle heart power. We have allowed ourselves to be laughed out of our enthusiasm. We have let the devil convince us that if compassion and zeal are elements in our preaching, some "highbrow" will point the finger of scorn and contempt in our direction and pronounce that we are emotional, and therefore, lacking in intelligence.

There is no conflict between intelligence and emotion. Paul had both; and, if we are to be worthy witnesses for Christ, we must have something to say, and we must deliver our souls with compassionate zeal. A great revival will never come until preachers have the same spirit Paul had when he wept: "I have great heaviness and continual sorrow in my heart for I could wish that myself were accursed from Christ for my brethren."

He loved Christ, and he loved lost souls. The secret of his desire for others was the glorious reality of the love of Christ for him. He cried out: "For the love of Christ impels me . . ."

Let this fact grip you! Christ died for you! He loves you and intercedes for you! As this fact floods your soul, you will love Christ. Why do we fail to win souls? Why are we self-satisfied? Why the lack of evangelism in nearly 5,000 Southern Baptist churches reporting not one single soul baptized last year? The reason is evident. We do not love Jesus Christ. What is wrong with Sunday School teachers, Training Union leaders and sponsors, W.M.S. officers, deacons, Brotherhood leadership, when they fail to function in their places of responsibility? The reason is obvious— they do not love Jesus Christ!

When Jesus turned to Simon Peter and asked, "Lovest thou Me?" He asked a revealing question. God help us—we do not love our Lord like we should. Why have we not carried the Gospel to the ends of the earth? Why have we not taken the Southland for Christ?

He Gave Himself

Just one answer comes from the thoughtful and honest heart. We do not love Jesus. Paul did love him; therefore, he gave his life in service. He preached Christ crucified; he magnified the blood; he gloried in His resurrection; and with unspeakable joy, anticipated His second coming.

Paul lived a life of gratitude—gratitude to God—gratitude to Christ. No motive in all this world is so powerful as the motive of love. Because of Christ's love, Paul was a flaming evangelist—winning the folk Christ died to save. "Who loved me and gave Himself for me."

Paul had a worthy conception of the atoning work of Christ. Men who are not clear on this subject should not attempt to preach Christ. There is no place on our seminary faculties for teachers who "wobble on the axle" concerning the propitiatory work of our Saviour. If he is not crystal clear at this point, he should be dismissed—and that speedily.

Baptist people do not want their money used to pay the salaries of seminary and college professors who hedge on the fundamental and basic truths of Christianity. The forgiveness of sin, which is man's greatest need, is eternally bound to the death of Jesus Christ. We are redeemed with atoning blood. Peter says:

> "For as much as ye know that ye were not redeemed with corruptible things, as silver and gold, from your vain conversation received by tradition from your fathers; But with the precious blood of Christ, as of a lamb without blemish and without spot" (1 Pet. 1:18-19).

In Ephesians 1:7 Paul states: "In whom we have redemption through his blood, the forgiveness of sins, according to the riches of his grace;"

In Colossians 1:14, "In whom we have redemption through his blood, even the forgiveness of sin."

In Hebrews 9:12, "Neither by the blood of goats and calves, but by his own blood he entered in once the holy place, having obtained eternal redemption for us."

If a man rejects the atoning blood of Christ, he cannot be right with God. Paul never could get away from the fact that Christ died for his redemption. It broke his heart; it enabled him to endure; it fired his soul with compassion; it challenged his keen, intellectual powers; it produced an intense longing in his heart that all men might know his wonderful Redeemer.

It gave birth to an inexpressible longing in his heart to see Jesus in the new Jerusalem; it made him perfectly willing to stay below and continue his preaching of "Christ and Him crucified."

There are several theories of the atonement. Some of them confuse, rather than give light. The best theory I know is, "Jesus died for my sins."

All of us can understand that, and it is the greatest fact in all the world. No wonder Paul, in great joy, proclaimed:

> I am crucified with Christ; nevertheless I live; Yet not I but Christ liveth in me; and the life I now live in the flesh I live by the faith of the Son of God, who loved me and gave himself for me (Gal. 2:20).

W. F. Powell
Love Is the Answer

The general theme for the 1944 Baptist Hour messages is "Religious Foundations for Tomorrow's World." The first in the series, however, was "The Sermon on the Mount." Our Lord's climax and conclusion was to make the matter of an enduring foundation intensely personal and perilously imperative. It could be built only by translating his doctrines into deeds. "Everyone therefore that heareth these words of mine, and doeth them, shall be likened unto a wise man, who built his house upon the rock; and the rain descended, and the floods came, and the winds blew, and beat upon that house; and it fell not: for it was founded upon the rock."

> The strongest cities that men build will fall,
>   Their marble, bronze and brass will yield to rust,
> Their shrines, their mosques and temples, wall by wall,
>   Will someday be a portion of the dust;
> But, though their hands' hard labor turns to naught,
>   The saga of the spirit life of man
> Expressed through written word or uttered thought,
>   Will last—has lasted since the world began.
> Think deeply, scholars, and write well, ye scribes,
>   Dig deep within the present, search the past,
> Speak out for your own races, lands and tribes,
>   Shape well your odes, for this alone will last.
> The record of men's march across the sod
>   Toward the everlasting citadels of God.
>   —GRACE NOLL CROWELL

Jesus alone leads the world to an enduring foundation. The chief characteristic of Hinduism is mysticism; of Buddhism, asceticism; of Mohammedanism, fanaticism; but the genius of Christianity is love. Three men lived in Rome at the same time: Nero, the imperial butcher; Seneca, the Stoic, philosopher, and statesman; and Paul, the imprisoned apostle of his Lord. Today the world has become a slaughterhouse by the bloody business of imperial butchers who hold nothing so cheap as human life, and we have had little help from the Senecas in classrooms, in editorial columns, in legislative assemblies, and, all too often, in modern pulpits— exponents of a Christless culture, proponents of materialistic or socialistic philosophies without any program, passion, or power for the redemption of mankind.

Today, behold the chaos created by the world's Neros and Senecas! They have built their houses upon the sand, and crowns are crumbling, dynasties are dissolving, empires are passing, and peoples are perishing in a global war. A bleeding, blinded, broken world must yet hear the answer for an enduring foundation from that third man, Paul:

> If I speak with the tongues of men and of angels, but have not love, I am become sounding brass, or a clanging cymbal. And if I have the gift of prophecy, and know all mysteries and all knowledge; and if I have all faith, so as to remove mountains, but have not love, I am nothing. And if I bestow all my goods to feed the poor, and if I give my body to be burned, but have not love, it profiteth me nothing. Love suffereth long, and is kind; love envieth not; love vaunteth not itself, is not puffed up, doth not behave itself unseemly, seeketh not its own, is not provoked, taketh not account of evil; rejoiceth not in unrighteousness, but rejoiceth with the truth; beareth all things, believeth all things, . . . endureth all things . . . . But now abideth faith, hope, love, these three; and the greatest of these is love.

What a word for the world today! Love hopes where reason despairs. It is the medicine for moral evil. Love is the wave length of God. It is the lever by which he lifts the world. It has nailprints in its hands. It has a spear thrust in its side. A crown of thorns is on its brow. It conquered a cross and turned a tomb into a vestibule to glory. Love lights a candle in the sun. "God is love," is the only enduring foundation.

> When the last day is ended and the nights are through,
>   When the last sun is buried in its grave of blue,
> When the stars are snuffed like candles,
>   When the seas no longer fret,

When the winds unlearn their cunning,
  And the storms forget.
When the last lip is palsied,
  When the last prayer is said,
Love shall live forever
  When the world lies dead.

A Kingdom Built on a Cross

There have been only three foundations on which nations have been built: military power, commercial supremacy, and national righteousness. Rome's foundation was military power. Babylon built on commercial supremacy; Israel, the theocracy of the Old Testament; and our own United States, once the democracy of the New Testament, were born of spiritual motive, seeking the happiness possible only to that people whose God is the Lord. We who so bravely began our upward climb to the New Jerusalem are lost today in the jungle of greed and self-indulgence and strife, and in the reeking rot of moral and social disintegration—having abandoned, as did Israel of old, our first foundation—having left our first love, until to one generation, religion is a conviction; to the second, a tradition; but to the third generation it is often a nuisance.

History can point to no parallel to our country's composing only five and one-half percent of the world's population, but possessing fifty-eight and one-half percent of the world's wealth. We have turned our backs upon our spiritual heritage, despising our blood-bought birthright to deathless love for country and home and the Saviour of the world so completely that, being indifferent now to the spiritual salvation of other nations of the world, we are proceeding, by the lives we are living, to destroy our own. America cannot survive another fifty years the disintegration now being insidiously wrought among us by increasing dissipation, insanity, and debilitation from drink and social diseases, by adult indifference to home, church, and country, and by the rapidly increasing delinquency of youth.

Military power and commercial supremacy cannot save America, nor the nations of the world. The only pattern to be permanent now is the pattern of *A Kingdom Built on a Cross*.

Jesus and Alexander died at thirty-three,
  One lived and died for self; one died for you and me.

The Greek died on a throne; the Jew died on a cross;
   One's life a triumph seemed; the other but a loss.
One led vast armies forth; the other walked alone,
   One shed a whole world's blood; the other gave His own.
One won the world in life and lost it all in death;
   The other lost his life to win the whole world's faith.

Jesus and Alexander died at thirty-three,
   One died in Babylon, and one on Calvary.
One gained all for himself; and one himself He gave,
   One conquered every throne; the other every grave.
The one made himself God, the God made Himself less,
   The one lived but to blast, the other but to bless.
When died the Greek, forever fell his throne of swords;
   But Jesus died to live forever Lord of lords.

Jesus and Alexander died at thirty-three,
   The Greek made all men slaves; the Jew made all men
      free.
One built a throne on blood; the other built on love.
   The one was born of earth; the other from above.
One won all this earth, to lose all earth and heaven.
   The other gave up all, that all to Him be given.
The Greek forever died; the Jew forever lives.
   He loses all who gets, and wins all things who gives.
                              —CHARLES ROSS WEEDE

The Principle for Universal Peace

"The world must choose between Christ and chaos," said Lloyd
George at the close of World War I. The world did not choose Christ. We
who profess him did not choose him either for ourselves or for others.
Had we loved him as he loved us—had we loved the world as he loved
the world, then World War II had never been. Chaos is the high cost of
not loving him and the lost world for which he died. And when we have
disposed of Hitler and Hirohito, the problem, of which they are manifestations, must yet be solved. Science has made the world a neighborhood.
The world cannot survive as a neighborhood unless it becomes a brotherhood. The brotherhood of man must be found in the Fatherhood of
God. That is possible only through Jesus. Salvation, regeneration, and
redeeming love came by him to the world, and, working in human hearts
that love, bind men and nations to one another and to God.

The greatest menace to navigation in all maritime history has been that of icebergs—mountains of ice coming down from Arctic heights, glaciers gliding silently across sea lanes of seafare, colliding with and crushing ships and men. The navies of the nations have kept warships on guard to shell them out of their sea lanes. And how helpless science and force have been to solve this sinister peril of the sea! But God solves the problem. He sends the Gulf stream with its warmth to melt the icebergs, and the mountains of ice, centuries old, are melted into a liquid bed for ships safely to float upon in peace.

The icebergs of hatred and age-long antipathies between nations, groups, and races, have been battled by science, and all human, political, intellectual, and social techniques in vain. Nineteen hundred years ago Jesus launched the Gulf stream of everlasting love from Calvary. Only love can melt mountains of frozen hatred into love which begets love and deepens for tomorrow's world the enduring foundation of love. The greatest peace movement began on a mountainpeak in Galilee. The intent, extent, and content of Christ's Commission is to build the nations and races of this world into his kingdom of love.

In his redeeming love Jesus visions individual value. He begins where man's need is greatest—in the heart. For at the heart of all human problems is the problem of the human heart. Solve that problem and the world can be saved. Jesus solved that problem. "For God so loved the world, that he gave his only begotten Son, that whosoever believeth in him should not perish, but have everlasting life." The price of my life is his love for me. The principle of my life is my love for him. "And the life which I now live in the flesh I live by the faith of the Son of God, who loved me, and gave himself for me." And the life filled with his love accepts the supreme obligation: "Thou shalt love the Lord thy God with all thy heart, and with all thy soul, and with all thy strength, and with all thy mind; and thy neighbour as thyself."

All New Testament Scriptures on love only enlarge the foundation and develop the dynamic for a life of love. Peter was saved by believing in Jesus as the Son of God. But he was sent to serve by professing his great love for Christ. Service is from the heart. The size of every man's service is the size of his soul. Love measures my praying—my Bible reading—my meditation. Love measures my giving. Love measures my witnessing. Love measures my ministry as a winner of souls. The risen Lord reminds us, "As the Father hath loved me, so have I loved you." "As my

Father hath sent me, even so send I you." Sent to all the world! The dynamic of the individual is declared to that end. "But ye shall receive power, when the Holy Spirit is come upon you: and ye shall be my witnesses both in Jerusalem, and in all Judea and Samaria, and unto the uttermost part of the earth." The dynamic which makes an individual an uplifting force in all the world is that love by which a unit embraces a universe. Thus in the individual Christianity becomes incarnate love.

> O love that wilt not let me go,
>   I rest my weary soul in Thee;
> I give Thee back the life I owe,
>   That in Thine ocean depths its flow
> May richer, fuller be.

And cherubim shiver to the tips of their wings beholding the transforming power of Christ's love working in a life lived by love for him and the world for which he died until his love is perfected in life's perfection. And while one single sin defiles his child the crusade for Christlikeness continues until Christian character becomes a sea of glass mingled with fire, and man reflects the image of his God again.

> The amaranthine crown is Character.
> When the whole world breaks to ashes, this will stay,
> When punctual Death comes knocking at the door
> To lead the soul upon the unknown road,
> This is the only crown not flung aside
> By his fastidious hand. To the crowned soul
> The path of Death is but an upward way.
> Touched by this crown, a man is king, indeed,
> And carries fate and freedom in his breast;
> And when his house of clay falls ruining,
> The soul is out upon the path of stars!
> This is the crown God sees through all our shows,
> The one thing that is stronger than the years,
> That tear the kingdoms down. Imperious Time,
> Pressing a wasteful hand on mortal things,
> Reveals this fair eternity in man—
> A power that rises even from the tomb,
> And lays its austere scepter on Today.

> The beggar, he may earn it with the king,
> And tread an equal palace full of light,

Fleet Youth may seize this crown; slow-footed Age
May wear its immortality. Behold!
Its power can change bare rafters to a home
Sweetened with hopes and hushed with memories;
Can change a pit into a holy tomb
Where pilgrims keep the watches of the night;
Can change an earthly face until it shine,
Touched with unearthly beauty. It can turn
A prison to a temple of the soul,
A gallows to an altar. In its might
A reed did once become a scepter,—yea,
A cross became a throne; a crown of thorns,
A symbol of the Power above the world.

—EDWIN MARKHAM

Prayer

O thou wonderful Lord Jesus, Giver of Life, Conqueror of Death, Arbiter of Destiny, from thy pierced hands all the centuries have fallen like grains of sand. Thou art the same, yesterday, today, and tomorrow. Other foundation can no man lay than that which is laid in thee. Bring a peace victorious to thy cause back to a war-broken world and empower thy people to build tomorrow upon the sure foundation of thy everlasting love, we pray today. Amen.

Ray E. Roberts
The Unpaid Debt of Southern Baptists

Romans 1:14-16

When financial income is at an all-time high, it may seem out of place to call attention of Southern Baptists to unpaid debts. In speaking to a group of students on one occasion, a college president is reported to have given a warning on unwise budget planning and the accumulation of personal debts. He said, "If your *out*go exceeds your *in*come then your *over*head will be your *down*fall." Although there is much wisdom in this brief statement, the text found in Romans 1 indicates the debt referred to in this message is of a far different nature.

I. The Nature of the Debt

When the apostle Paul said, "I am debtor both to the Greeks and the barbarians, both to the wise and the unwise," he might have been giving one of the most concise and accurate definitions of stewardship anywhere to be found. He was expressing a sacred and inescapable obligation which had been thrust upon him due to an experience which had occurred on the road to Damascus. He had an encounter with Jesus Christ which had completely revolutionized his life. This experience had caused him to know firsthand that the gospel was "the power of God unto salvation." It had worked for him and for everyone else who had given Christ a chance in their lives. He knew it would work—he was not ashamed of it—it had never failed—he had never had to be embarrassed to recommend it to lost sinners. Without hesitation he could say in answer to the query of the Philippian jailer, "Believe on the Lord Jesus Christ, and thou shalt be saved" (Acts 16:31). Paul didn't need to worry about God's being

387

dead because he was spiritually alive himself and was in constant touch with the power of God as it transformed the lives of sinners.

As born-again children of God who are fortunate enough to be members of Southern Baptist churches, we are not just stewards of material possessions or time or talent. We are stewards of a wonderful, glorious experience that came to us through a personal encounter with Jesus Christ who saved us and transformed our lives. We have an obligation to share this experience with a lost world.

Statements of our Lord such as "ye shall be witnesses unto me" (Acts 1:8), "Go ye" (Matt. 28:19), and "As my Father hath sent me, even so send I you" (John 20:21), serve to remind us that this debt is of a divinely spiritual nature and that "every one of us shall give account of himself to God" (Rom. 14:12) in the light of how seriously we acknowledge this debt. When Lyman Beecher was on his deathbed, someone asked, "Dr. Beecher, will you please tell us the greatest work that man can do in this world?" "The greatest work," replied the dying theologian, "is not to rule a kingdom. It is not political or ecclesiastical power; neither is it scientific, philosophical, nor even theological knowledge. The greatest work that a person can do in this world is to lead a soul to Jesus Christ."

II. The Scope of the Debt

"Both to the Greek and the barbarian, to the wise and the unwise." It is said that a Greek philosopher who served as tutor for Alexander the Great when he was a young boy said to him one day, "There are only two kinds of people in the world, Greeks and barbarians." "If that be the case," he responded, "I will capture the world and make Greeks out of everyone." How near he came to succeeding is a matter of history and is reflected in Paul's statement here. "Greeks and barbarians, wise and unwise," points out to us that the debt is universal in its scope. This scope is magnified in the marching orders which Christ gave to the church in Matthew 28, "all nations." In Acts 1:8 "in Jerusalem, and in all Judea, and in Samaria, and unto the uttermost part of the earth." John 3:16 points up the scope in "God so loved the *world*" and "*whosoever* believeth in him."

None of God's people in any age have ever had such an opportunity to face up to the scope of this debt as Southern Baptists have today. With all of the resources available to us, we're responsible to God for doing everything we can in every way we can to preach the gospel to everybody we can as rapidly and as effectively as we can. There is no danger of oversimplication of our task. We must preach the gospel as it is to lost people where they are.

When Jesus commanded us to "preach the gospel to every nation," he was not assigning to us an impossible task. No generation that ever lived has had such opportunity as we to carry out his orders. Facilities of transportation, communication, and resources make it not only possible but also probable. The allies of Satan himself are getting their messages into the last home, in the furtherest corner of the world. They hawk their wares by *Telestar* around the world and deliver their products by jet so it will arrive fresh and at its best.

III. Status of the Account

Conditions such as those just mentioned caused us to realize that payment on our debt is long overdue. We add up all the contributions to our foreign mission effort last year and are tempted to boast about twenty-five million dollars when actually a little more than two dollars each for over ten million Southern Baptists was all that kept us from being a bunch of "nonmissionary hard shells." We say to the leaders of our Home Mission Board: Let's get down to business and win America to Christ. Then for a period of twelve long months in 1965, we back up our words of concern at the rate of about seventy-five cents each or one and one-half cents per week.

If Christ is worth listening to at all, he is worth taking seriously and surely, in prosperous America, we could not claim to be taking him seriously with that sort of financial support for our mission programs. For about one hundred years, our Convention was satisfied to concentrate its efforts in the South and West as far as America was concerned. During the same time, a great spiritual vacuum existed in the northeastern part of our land where three fourths of the population of our country lived. In this area, the ratio of unchurched people over those in churches is two to one, just the opposite of the ratio in the old traditional Southern Baptist territory.

We could go less than two hundred miles from this hall tonight in order to take in Chicago, make a two hundred mile trip to Cincinnati on the Ohio, then draw a line northeast to Baltimore and not only encircle about two thirds of the population of America but also include seven of the nine largest cities of our nation. This area controls *every* national election, houses the centers of national and world government, mass media, education, finance, commerce, and industry. Southern Baptists still have less than fifteen hundred churches in this entire area. We are late in coming; but thank God, even though the account is way past due, we are here and we are here to stay until Jesus comes.

IV. Some Payments on Account

Volumes could be written on the blessings of God in this area. Every one of the hundreds of new churches since 1950 is a thrilling story all of its own. Each of these would list a dedicated preacher and family, most of whom paid a tremendous price to go and stay by the work until it was on its feet. None of them could have gotten started without dedicated laymen. God has raised up a "new breed" of laymen in this area, many who have borne the burden in the heat of the day to get a church started when there was no preacher, or prevented one from falling apart when a pastor left. The ratio of baptisms in this territory is better than one to ten and the opportunity for winning adults to Christ is unlimited.

One pastor went to a little church in Cleveland, Ohio, with thirty-one members. He had just graduated from one of our seminaries. He had been trained in our schools, his full-time ministry was made possible by a supplement from our Home Mission Board. A site was secured with help from the Home Mission Board. With a loan from the Board, a modest building was erected the first year, mostly with volunteer labor although the pastor did much of the work on the building himself. A goal was set to win to Christ and baptize fifty-one people that year. They went over the goal and with less than one hundred members are running on schedule in an effort to baptize one hundred during this current year.

I was preaching for them the morning two of the fifty-one came. One was a teenager and the other a lady in her sixties who had never had anyone talk to her about Jesus until the pastor was in her home. Her husband had made his profession the Sunday before but she had fallen in the mud of the church lawn, walking across boards that had been placed in lieu of a concrete walk. I wouldn't say she was attracted to the church by what they had to offer in the way of beautiful and convenient facilities but that pastor and his people are thoroughly convinced that the gospel of Jesus Christ "is the power of God unto salvation" (Rom. 1:16). I would say this is an example of a valid payment on the past-due account. Such true stories could be repeated in varying degrees hundreds of times in this territory but not often enough to even make a dent on the population increase.

Jose Beltran, a native of Spain, product of our Southern Baptist mission work, left Madrid when our church there which he pastored was padlocked by the authorities. He went to the Canary Islands where he could work with fourteen people. He baptized forty-four people the first year (1956) and a total of three hundred since. His church is self-supporting, and he has started another one already. During my visit with him, he pled with me with tears streaming down his face, "Brother Roberts, Southern Baptists must win America for Christ, without that all the rest will be lost."

I believe this with all my heart but I know we can't do it with slow, conventional methods. If we ever make an impact on the masses in America, we are going to have to use every resource that is known to man in confronting them with the gospel. We have come to know that the gospel has power when it is preached in the unction of the Holy Spirit, whether it be on the street, under a tent, in a rented hall, or in a beautiful church building.

If one man can have faith to buy prime time and have an unadulterated evangelistic service on television on a nationwide hookup, where without apology he takes his Bible, preaches the gospel, and pleads with people to be saved, then eleven million Southern Baptists ought to be able to do it. We have scores of people in our state who were saved and hunted up our churches and were baptized into them because of Billy Graham's evangelistic telecast. God has given us wonderful leadership in our Radio and Television Commission but we are not facing our obligation to preach the gospel through the medium of television by telecasting religious soap opera that can be used on "free time." Let's put the means at their disposal whereby the gospel of Jesus Christ can be preached and his claim upon their lives can be presented.

We are going through a period in the life of our Convention when the subtle and indirect approach is being espoused by many. I believe in keeping up with the times and of experimenting with every new and effective way of approaching people. It may not be the best to start down the street with a Bible under our arm, as big as a Detroit telephone directory, buttonholing people to ask if they know Christ, but I would rather do that than to be so sophisticated and suave that people don't know what my business is. If I should look out my window and see fire belching from the upstairs window of my neighbor's house, I wouldn't calmly pick up the phone and invite him over for coffee in order to give him a lecture on the principles of spontaneous combustion.

We as Southern Baptists are far in arrears in our obligation to preach the gospel to the lost multitudes. The world is in a desperate condition. We are in no position to deal in abstractions, indirect approaches, and the low pressures sales method. It is time that we wake up to the perilous times in which we live and begin to act as though we mean business for God.

With the help of Texas Baptists and the Evangelism Division of our Home Mission Board, our churches in the Dayton area are launching an all-out effort next year to confront every one of the 1.5 million who live there with the gospel. Leaders of these two groups have agreed to ask their committees to help provide the resources in finance and man power to plan with us in the greatest all-out evangelistic effort this territory has ever known.

All the mass media will be employed to the fullest. The lost will be located through census and personally contacted. Large central meetings will be conducted, local simultaneous revivals will be held in every church and mission and even in places where new ones will be established. Some of the outstanding preachers of our Convention will come to preach in these meetings. Nothing will be spared in this all-out effort to face up to our obligation to tell people about the saving power of the gospel.

We pray that this will ignite a fire in the hearts of our people in this northern territory that will spread over the nation. Our prayer is to see a similar effort in every metropolitan area in the north. Already requests are coming from other cities in Ohio to do the same in 1968. By the end of the Crusade of the Americas in 1969, we believe that Southern Baptists will have conducted such an all-out effort in every city in the north. We believe that states other than Texas will want to help with man power and resources; we believe that every commission, Board, and agency will do their best to help us. This is an opportunity for Southern Baptists to prove that they mean business for God in facing up to our unpaid debt.

> But drops of grief can ne'er repay The debt of love I owe;
> Here, Lord, I give myself away, 'Tis all that I can do.

God has let us live in this glorious day of opportunity. May we not fail him now.

A. T. Robertson
Good Out of Ill

Philippians 1:12-20

The interpretation of Providence is not always easy if one looks at the whole problem. There are always glib interpreters, like Job's miserable comforters, who know how to fit the cap to others with complete satisfaction to themselves. Our problem is to be able to see the hand of God in a world of law and order when things go against us. Paul was able to get sweet out of bitter. It is easier to see the good after it has come out of the ill. But it would be a dreary world if one could not believe that God cares for his people and overrules the evils of life for the progress of man and of men.

Progress of the Gospel (v. 12)

It is possible that Epaphroditus brought to Paul a letter from the Philippian church which was full of concern for Paul's welfare. He had been a prisoner for some years now, two at Caesarea and one or two in Rome. At any rate, Paul was anxious for them to know the true state of the case about his affairs. Paul tells of his experiences in Rome, because only thus can he relieve their anxiety. There are two extremes in this matter. Some men talk too much about themselves, and some do it too little. The use of "rather" clearly implies that the Philippians had expected the worst for Paul. He hastens to tell them that he has good news, not bad news, about the progress of the gospel in Rome. The word for progress seems to mean cutting a way ahead, blazing a trail before an army to come afterward. The pioneers, like Daniel Boone in Kentucky, blazed the path for civilization and Christianity. In the Stoic philosophy the word is used for progress toward wisdom. Paul uses it for the progress of a young minister in culture and power (1 Tim. 4:15). So then the opposition to Paul in Rome had kicked the gospel upstairs. The Jews from Asia did not stop the onward march of the gospel when they raised their hue and cry in the Temple in Jerusalem. The hand of God was with Paul when he was at the mercy of the mob and before the Sanhedrin. Even Felix and Festus did not stay God's arm. In spite of shipwreck and delay on the part of Nero, work had gone on. Paul had not courted imprisonment, but he did not fret unduly because of his chain. This very chain was used of God to spread the gospel.

Sermons in Bonds (v. 13)

The precise way in which good has come out of ill Paul goes on to show in an explanatory clause of result. Paul's bonds were literal bonds, for he was constantly chained to a Roman soldier (Acts 28:20). He probably meant to say that his bonds had become manifest in Christ. It had become plain that he was a prisoner for no crime but solely for Christ's sake, so that Paul could properly call himself "the prisoner of Christ" (Eph. 3:1). This fact attracted attention to Christ and gave Paul a fresh opportunity to preach Christ to those interested. Paul was never ashamed of Christ. He was not ashamed of his bonds. They become a badge of honor, for they came to preach Christ to all who saw them and who knew why he had them. In particular Paul had a fresh opportunity each day with the guard to whom he was chained. The soldiers relieved each other. He not only talked to this guard about his armor (cf. Eph. 6:10-20) and his service, but he told him of Jesus. By this means alone the knowledge of Jesus would be conveyed to many.

But Paul insisted that the gospel by means of his bonds had become known "throughout the whole praetorian guard." The expression is ambiguous in the Greek and can be interpreted in four different ways. It may mean the ten thousand picked soldiers who formed this notable guard. It may be the barracks where the guard was stationed in Rome. It may refer to the imperial palace, as it is used of the governor's palace in the provinces (cf. Matt. 27:27; John 18:28,33). It may refer to the judicial authorities of the imperial court. There seems to be no way of determining the matter finally, for good arguments are adduced for each meaning. We know that there were converts in Caesar's household (Phil. 4:22), although this fact does not prove that Paul himself had access to the emperor's palace. There were Jews connected with the household of Nero (his wife Poppaea, for instance). The Christians there probably were slaves or other menials. It is possible that Paul was removed to the praetorian camp *(castra praetoriana)* and thus had ready access to the whole guard. But if not, he was still able slowly to spread the knowledge of Jesus through this famous band of soldiers. He would probably make visits to the camp with his guard, who went with him from his lodging. In a way, therefore, Paul became the friend and chaplain of these soldiers. Mithraism already was beginning to get a powerful hold upon the Roman soldiers, and Paul would not be slow to seize the opportunity to counteract this influence and to tell the men about Jesus. The Roman soldier probably took kindly to Paul (cf. the centurion Julius in Acts 27:3 who treated Paul kindly). Certainly Paul had a manly message to present. He was manifestly proud of the fact that he had set all the praetorian guard, almost the flower of the Roman army, to thinking and to talking about Jesus. Preaching to soldiers has always appealed to strong preachers. The shadow of death in the battle of tomorrow brings the message close home to strong men's hearts. One is able to preach as a "dying man to dying men." Whether Paul was able to address the soldiers in large companies in formal sermons we do not know, but he was able to make skilful use of conversation. These rough and ready men of affairs saw the steady joy of Paul the prisoner. They watched him day by day, and his buoyant optimism caught their fancy. Jesus is the secret of Paul's life of joy. Thus the contagion of Paul's love for Jesus spread to "all the rest," whether to soldiers or to people in Rome is not clear. He had spoken to the Jews, we know (Acts 28:17,23). There was much in the soldier's life that appealed to Paul's heroic nature, and he drew frequent illustrations from the life of the soldier.

Spurring Others to Action (v. 14)

This was the second result of Paul's imprisonment in Rome. There are always timid souls who lose heart in times of persecution. Some even go to the extent of apostasy when the cause seems lost. The early Christian centuries furnish examples of those who renounced Christ for Caesar under the pressure of the Roman state (cf. 1 Cor. 12:1-3). Paul had long foreseen the coming conflict between Christianity and the man of sin or lawlessness embodied in the Roman Empire (2 Thess. 2:3-12). Here in Rome itself that dark shadow loomed blacker than ever, in spite of the fact that Nero had not yet come out openly against Christianity. The faint-hearted in Rome knew the power of the state. Paul was a prisoner, and the outcome was uncertain. These fearful saints would take no chances. There was a minority of the brethren in Rome who exercised extra caution because of Paul's activity for Christ. They wished no responsibility for his conduct if things went against him. There are always these shirkers who practice absenteeism from church in times of struggle, these cowards in a crisis who slink away till danger is past. They come in for the shouting after victory is won. In case of disaster they are ready to say, "We told you so."

But in this case "the most of the brethren" constituted that inner circle of the brotherhood that does and dares things for Christ while the rest hang back. Paul was lucky to have won a majority to this scale of activity. It is usually the minority of Christians who put energy into the work while the majority drift along or criticize what the minority do. The papyri give plenty of examples of "brothers" in the sense of fellows in service or members of guilds or brotherhoods. Paul's courage and contagious enthusiasm had shamed many into action who had at first held back through fear of indifference. These gained confidence in the Lord; this is the probable translation rather than "brethren in the Lord." This confidence in the Lord was caused by Paul's bonds. Paul's chain rebuked their lethargy and cowardice and stirred the conscience so that they were "bold to speak the work of God without fear." Manifestly they had been afraid to open their mouths for a while till they saw how brave Paul was in spite of his bondage and impending trial. Some, never eloquent before, now found tongues of angels as they caught the spirit of Paul. The bolder spirits were rendered "more abundantly bold" than they were before. These cast caution to the winds and were overwhelmingly daring in their championship of Jesus. They spoke "the message of God," Paul's phrase here for preaching and telling the story of the gospel of grace. There are always in a crisis some choice spirits ready to die for Christ, like the ten thousand native Chinese Christians who at the time of the Boxer movement died rather than renounce Jesus. Fortitude is contagious. Paul's courage was like that of a brave general leading his troops. There is nothing that will quicken a dying church into life like courage on the part of the leaders. Prophets today have to call to the dry bones to live. Paul waked up the church in Rome by going ahead in spite of his limitations and doing his duty boldly as opportunity came to him. It is a great achievement to revive a dead church. There are plenty of them dead or dying or asleep. Much of the pastor's energy is required to keep his church awake or to wake it up. It is not enough to galvanize a corpse. Life must come back into the body. This is no artificial or mechanical process. Paul did his own part heroically. That is the way to wake up our churches. Let each one lay hold of his own task. That is better than conventions, conferences, or resolutions. Life is more contagious than death. Life can put death to flight if it is given a fair chance. "And he hath put a new song in my mouth, even praise unto our God; many shall see it, and fear, and shall trust in the Lord" (Ps. 40:3).

Preaching Christ from Envy of Paul (vv. 15a,17)

But Paul had no bed of roses in Rome. The minority furnished plenty of thorns for his side. Some of these were provoked by Paul's activity to preach Christ, it is true, but they did it "even of envy and strife"—pitiful enough motives for Christian zeal. Envy is a powerful motive in human life. It played its part in the trial and death of Jesus (Matt. 27:18). There was a personal side to this preaching which was as much against Paul as in favor of Christ. Kennedy pleads for "rivalry" rather than "strife" in this passage, and the word often has this sense. Envy and rivalry often lead to open strife.

We do not, indeed, know to what class of teachers Paul refers. It may be some of the old teachers of the church in Rome, who did not relish Paul's leadership since it displaced them—a form of jealousy that one sees only too often. In that case, their fresh activity would be with a view to regaining their former prestige and influence, partly by depreciating Paul. If it was not personal pique that stirred these men; they may have been Jewish Christians who disliked the note of universality in Paul's message and feared that he did not sufficiently guard the interests of Judaism. It may have been the Judaizers, Paul's old enemies who did him such harm in Jerusalem, Galatia, and Corinth. This is the usual view since Bengel, but it is open to the objection that Paul here apparently condoned their preaching. That, however, is not quite true, as we shall see. We do not, indeed, know that the Judaizers had reached Rome, although there is no inherent difficulty in that supposition. As a matter of fact, it is quite likely that all of these elements enter into the situation, for Paul expressly says that these men proclaimed Christ from mixed motives, "not sincerely." In fact, they preached from a partisan or selfish motive. It was primarily "labour for hire," and the word was applied to those in official position who looked after their own selfish interests rather than the common good. Kennedy argues for selfishness as the meaning here. But in any case, these selfish partisans cared as much for giving trouble to Paul as for preaching Christ. They thought that they were stirring up tribulation for Paul by making his chains gall him. They found added zest in the thought that the growth of their peculiar type of Christian doctrine would irritate ("annoy," Moffatt) Paul. One must confess that some Christians seem to enjoy sticking pins in the preacher. It is possible for one to be more of a denominationalist than a Christian, to care more for the progress of one's special views than to be concerned for the kingdom of God.

There are ministers with small jealousies who wreck churches like a tornado with their winds of doctrine. Paul's very success made these men in Rome jealous, resentful, and determined to nag him if they could not stop his onward march. These men felt that they were entitled to success as much as men less able who got ahead of them. So the destructive spirit ate its way into their hearts and lives. It was a pity that this spirit should burst forth against Paul in Rome at the time of the crisis in his imprisonment. But at such a time small men feel like taking advantage of such a situation, and they struck Paul when he was a prisoner. Wolves turn and rend one of their own pack who falls in the fight. It is a small thing to try to undermine another preacher's power. One may wonder that God should bless at all the message of men with such a spirit. But, after all, we should be glad that our own wrong motives do not wholly hinder the reception of whatever truth is preached to men. The power is from God and not from the preacher, in God's message and not in the preacher's heart.

Preaching Christ from Love of Paul (vv. 15b-16)

There is action and reaction in all things. The factious opposition of the minority stimulated the majority to increased efforts out of love for Paul. They did it out of good will as well as love. There was this good that comes out of a church dissension. Some sluggish souls woke up and began to take an interest in the affairs of the kingdom; they had not done so before the disagreement arose. There is this consolation to be found in the midst of the bitter strife of the ages among various Christian sects. We can excuse much even of rancor in theological debates and wranglings over minor points because of the obvious sincerity and conviction of the disputants. We may rejoice in the larger spirit of charity now in the world with the hope for its increase, provided the result is not a spineless uniformity without point or pith. Love calls for no sacrifice of principle. Love and good will moved the majority to stand valiantly by the side of Paul in his exposition of Christianity. One can be a conscientious denominationalist today and full of love and the spirit of cooperation in all wise and proper ways. These men were active because of good will to Paul, and their zeal sprang out of love. Some loved Paul for the enemies that he had made, even among Christians, but most loved him for his great achievements in Christ. When Paul was thus under attack in Rome, the faithful rallied round him, as the disciples did in a circle at Lystra (Acts 14:20). They recognized Paul as "set for the defence of the gospel." They rejoiced in his courage in chains and took his view of his situation. His defense was an apology in the original force of the word (1:7). Paul was a living apologetic for Christ, a typical example of the word in Jude 3. To desert Paul at this juncture was to desert Christ. The cause of Christ was here identified with the cause of Paul, its leading exponent. The cause was crystallized in the man. One cannot stand by Christ in theory and leave Paul in the lurch in practice. Too often church members fail to rally to the support of the pastor or of the denominational servants. They are willing to give up the preacher to save the cause, as Caiaphas proposed about Jesus in John 11:50, voluntary offering of someone else as a sacrifice. Sometimes, to be sure, the minister is at fault and has to go for the good of all concerned. Christianity is incarnated in men and women. This fact gives dignity to the Christian's task, but it makes it imperative that one shall be really doing the work of Christ if people are to suffer with him for Christ's sake. Otherwise the very love of the people for the man and minister may lead many into the pit. The words of Jesus here are final: "Inasmuch as ye did it unto one of the least of these my brethren, ye did it unto me. . . . Inasmuch as ye did it not unto one of these least, ye did it not unto me (Matt. 25:40,45).

Paul's Conquering Joy (v. 18)

Nowhere does Paul appear to better advantage than in this verse. He faced frankly the limitations of ministers and men in the service of Christ—limitations in preacher and hearer. What is to be the attitude of the preacher toward other preachers who do not see things as he does in all points of Christian doctrine? This is a practical question and one that men must answer today. People are often diligent to stir up jealousy between preachers. The effort was made to make John the Baptist jealous of Jesus, but it failed miserably (John 3:22-29). There is joy enough for all the workers in the kingdom, for the one who sows and the one who reaps (John 4:36-38). People criticize the preachers in the most inconsistent ways, and it is hopeless to try to please them all. They found fault with John and with Jesus for directly opposite things (Luke 7:31-34).

It has been objected here that Paul seems to condone the errors of the Judaizers which he had so severely criticized in 2 Corinthians 10—13 and in Galatians. But this estimate fails to understand Paul's spirit here. He speaks out in Rome with the same courage and clearness as heretofore. He abates no whit his own convictions. But the issue before Paul is simply whether or not he is to spend his time railing at preachers who have the same right to preach as he has and give ground for charges of pique and jealousy besides filling the ears of the Roman soldiers with stories of the shortcomings of these envious preachers. He could have done that, and angels would have wept and the ungodly would have sneered at this exhibition of so-called Christian love. Jealousy had found a place even in the ranks of the twelve apostles. Paul rose to the high plane of conquering joy in Christ. "What then?" The answer of Paul was "only that," "in every way" or in any event "Christ is preached." This is what matters most. One must learn to see things as they are and to find the consolation in the big truths of life in spite of the minor drawbacks.

The alternative here between pretense and truth is a very common one. Some men were using the name of Christ as a cover or mask for personal and selfish ends. We are shocked at that statement, and yet we may also thank God that he can use such poor preaching for his glory. God can even bless insincere preaching. Even hypocritical preaching can be blessed of God. Somehow God uses the grain of truth that is mixed in with error and bad motives. He places no premium upon error or upon pretense. But Paul's problem was one of personal adjustment. Was he to embitter his own heart because all preachers of Christ were not pure? Far from it. He the rather seized upon the salient point in the situation. Christ was preached. This is what matters most. Other things are important in varying degrees, but this is primal. Paul knew how to put first things first and to keep them there. So he took his stand. "And therein I rejoice, yea, and will rejoice." He did not rejoice in false preaching but in the fact that even in such preaching Christ is found by souls that hunger after him.

Surely we can all rejoice that God does bless indifferent preaching. Over and above all the clangor of contending voices in modern Christendom rises the fact of Christ. It is Jesus that saves men from their sins. This is the universal note in the eternal Christ. We look at him from different angles and with imperfect eyes, and we tell what we see in broken speech, sometimes incoherent and contradictory. But if by means of it men see Jesus, it is worthwhile.

Christ Magnified in Paul (vv. 19-20)

Paul turned to his own case and declared that it mattered little what happened to him in Rome. Already the imprisonment, as he has shown, has turned out for the progress of the gospel. He was grateful for their prayers ("your supplication") and for "the supply of the spirit of Jesus Christ" (both source and gift). Paul's attitude is measured by the earnest expectation and hope that Christ shall be magnified now as always in his body. Whether this is by life or death is not material. If Christ is made great in the hearts and eyes of men, it is a small matter what happens to Paul. Then he shall not be put to shame in anything. Hence Paul knew that his present troubles would turn out at last for his eternal salvation, not merely rescue from imprisonment, for the situation applied (v. 20) both to death and life. He would get the spiritual development that God meant for him to receive from his imprisonment and from the personal antagonisms in Rome. What the future held in store for him on earth was all one to Paul. He was sure of the prayers of the Philippians and of the presence of the Spirit of Jesus and the triumph of Jesus in his work, whether by life or death. So he faced the future with calmness, whatever doubt as to the course of events may have existed. As to that, Paul was not sure of his own mind, as he then proceeded to show.

John R. Sampey
Where Are the Righteous Dead?

With me in paradise (Luke 23:43); Lord Jesus, receive my spirit
(Acts 7:59); With the Lord (1 Thess. 4:17).

Would you like to know where the spirits of the righteous dead are? I
can only answer in the words of Jesus and his apostles. Science can give
no answer. Profane history has no answer. Spiritualism gives no satisfactory answer. The apostle Paul claims to have been caught up into paradise, but what he heard were "unspeakable words, which it is not lawful
for a man to utter" (2 Cor. 12:4). We cannot share with Paul this mystic
visit in vision to paradise. He carried it to the grave as a secret he could
not discuss with others. He did not even know whether his body went
with him to paradise or not. He felt sure that he was there in his spirit.
The vision was real; of that he was sure, and he could never forget the
wonderful things he saw and heard. From that hour paradise with all its
glories was as real to Paul as Rio de Janeiro is to me after repeated visits
to that beautiful city in South America.

The teaching of the Bible is quite plain that the final abode of the righteous will be a haven of rich rewards and unspeakable joy, while the
wicked are banished to the place prepared for the devil and his angels.
The Lord Jesus himself closes his account of the final judgment with the
words, "And these shall go away into eternal punishment: but the righteous into eternal life."

Now between the present and the final abode in heaven or hell must
come physical death, the intermediate state, the second coming of
Christ, the resurrection of the body, the final judgment. Where is Paul?
Where is Chrysostom, the most eloquent preacher of the early centuries
after Christ? Where is St. Francis of Assisi? Where is Spurgeon, the greatest preacher of the nineteenth century? Where is John A. Broadus, my

great teacher in the Seminary? Each of us just now has in mind dear ones whom we have loved long since, and lost awhile. Where are they? We must not presume to affirm confidently, unless we have some clear word from our Lord or his apostles. I think we have enough to guide us to some conclusions that are well grounded, and we can comfort one another with these words.

What can we learn from the language of our Saviour to the penitent robber on the cross? You will recall that two robbers were delivered up to the Roman centurion to be crucified with Jesus. Both of them heard Jesus praying for the soldiers as they drove the nails into his hands and feet. No doubt the robbers cursed the soldiers. At first both of the robbers seem to have reproached Jesus: "If thou art the King of the Jews, save thyself," and us; and one of the robbers kept railing at Jesus. The other robber was deeply impressed with the patience and forgiving spirit of Jesus. He began to say to himself that Jesus was all that he claimed to be, a *King.* Turning his face toward his comrade in sin, he rebuked him, "Dost thou not even fear God, seeing thou art in the same condemnation? And we indeed justly; for we receive the due reward of our deeds: but this man hath done nothing amiss." And then words follow that make us think of this robber as a man of remarkable insight. Looking into the face of the innocent sufferer beside him, he said, "Jesus, remember me when thou comest into thy kingdom." He was not thinking of an earthly kingdom that he might share with Jesus, but of a heavenly kingdom. The reply of Jesus to the robber's plea throws a world of light on the problem we are facing this morning. How it must have thrilled the soul of the penitent robber: "To-day shalt thou be with me in paradise." Their bodies would be taken down from their crosses and buried, but their spirits would meet that day in paradise, the home of the blest. In paradise Jesus would be King and the robber would be a member of his kingdom. I stand amazed at the faith of a man who believed that the good man dying beside him was really a King who would yet preside over his kingdom. He longed to have part in that kingdom. The first sinner saved by the blood of the Saviour was this penitent and believing malefactor.

Consider, my friends, what rich teaching is wrapped up in our Saviour's promise to the penitent robber. The bodies of both Jesus and the two malefactors would presently be buried, but the spirit of the penitent robber would at once enter paradise. There he would see Jesus welcomed as King. There he would share in that kingdom. It would not be necessary to wait for the resurrection and the final judgment before he could enter into the joys of the world to come. His spirit would at once enter paradise. There he would be in the company of the righteous dead. That very day he would see Jesus in the glory land.

The second text to which I invite your closest attention is the story of the stoning of Stephen. Perhaps no man in all the tides of time has preached Christ with greater eloquence than Stephen. He was a man full of faith, full of grace and power, full of the Holy Spirit. He was a radiant Christian, his face shining like the face of an angel. When put on trial for his life he boldly charged the Sanhedrin as the betrayers and murderers of the Righteous One. When the council turned on him with anger, gnashing on him with their teeth, the historian says, "But he, being full of the Holy Spirit, looked up stedfastly into heaven, and saw the glory of God, and Jesus standing on the right hand of God, and said, Behold, I see the heavens opened, and the Son of man standing on the right hand of God." No wonder the enraged council became an angry mob thirsting for his blood! They thrust him out of the city and stoned him to death. As they began to stone him, he cried aloud, "Lord Jesus, receive my spirit." He knew that his body would be broken under the shower of stones, but his spirit would be welcomed by Jesus to his immediate presence in the world above. His last act was worthy of his Lord. "He kneeled down, and cried with a loud voice, Lord, lay not this sin to their charge." Saul of Tarsus, who was guarding the garments of the men who stoned Stephen, could never forget the scene nor the prayer for the forgiveness of his murderers.

When Stephen saw the heavens opened, it was not a mere hallucination. The historian says that he was full of the Holy Spirit. It was a divine revelation and not mere fanaticism. Evidently Stephen expected that his spirit would presently be in the presence of the Lord Jesus in glory.

We do well to remember that Jesus after his crucifixion was raised from the dead. Early on Sunday morning he came out of Joseph's tomb. He bore in his hands and feet the print of nails. As he expired on the cross, he said, "Father, into thy hands I commend my spirit." Three days later spirit and body were reunited as he came out alive from Joseph's tomb. When he ascended to heaven forty days later he took with him his glorified body. Jesus our Saviour has location in God's universe. By virtue of his deity he can be present with his followers everywhere at the same moment. His glorified humanity makes it possible for him to manifest himself to all his followers when they pass through the gates of death. Paul expected at death to pass into the presence of the Lord Jesus. Thus he writes to the Christians in Philippi, "For to me to live is Christ, and to die is gain." If he might still have profitable work here on earth, he hardly knew how to choose and he says, "But I am in a strait betwixt the two, having the desire to depart and be with Christ; for it is very far better."

Evidently Paul looked forward to an immediate entrance after death into the presence of Christ. Can we doubt that our loved ones have been admitted to the very presence of the Lord Jesus? Could we wish any higher privilege than this for our sainted dead? Could one of us on the eve of our departure from this world have any more joyous prospect than the privilege of coming at once into the presence of our Saviour and the redeemed souls who worship him?

The apostle Paul compares the Christian in the body as away from Christ. Hear him compare the experience of the Christian now and after death: "Being therefore always of good courage, and knowing that, whilst we are at home in the body, we are absent from the Lord (for we walk by faith, not by sight); we are of good courage, I say, and are willing rather to be absent from the body, and to be at home with the Lord." Here in this world we have opportunities to work for our Master, and we must stick to our task until he calls us home.

In the first of his letters the apostle Paul comforts the church at Thessalonica with the thought that their loved ones who had fallen asleep would be raised from the dead at the return of the Lord Jesus. Hence they ought not to sorrow like the heathen, who have no hope. What a difference in the attitude of the Christian and the agnostic when death visits the home! Oh, the difference between merely giving our ashes to fertilize a tree, and passing into paradise to be with our Saviour and those who have loved him! Paul sums up the happy lot of all who love and obey Jesus Christ in that great day when he shall come again: "and so shall we ever be with the Lord" (1 Thess. 4:17).

Christians in all ages have enjoyed personal fellowship with the Lord Jesus Christ. We do not say of him that he lived in the days of Tiberius Caesar, but that he *lives*. He rose from the dead; he ascended on high; he manifests himself to those who are making disciples throughout the world. The founders of other religions lived and died, but their followers cannot claim their presence and aid.

Dr. E. Y. Mullins says: "Call Buddha, and Buddha does not come. Call

Mohammed, and Mohammed does not come. But call Jesus, and he comes." The apostle John enjoyed the most intimate fellowship with Jesus during the years of his earthly ministry, leaning back on his bosom at the Last Supper. Long years after Jesus ascended to heaven John could still say, "Our fellowship is with the Father, and with his Son Jesus Christ." Time and again Paul felt the immediate presence of Jesus, but never did he need him more than in the dungeon in Rome just prior to his martyrdom. Hear his testimony: "At my first defence no one took my part, but all forsook me: may it not be laid to their account. But the Lord stood by me, and strengthened me." When all Paul's friends forsook him except Luke the beloved physician, Jesus was with him in the death cell.

David Livingstone had a saying concerning the Lord Jesus that he is a gentleman of his word, and we learn that in his farewell address to his disciples in the upper room Jesus said, "He that hath my commandments, and keepeth them, he it is that loveth me: and he that loveth me shall be loved of my Father, and I will love him, and will manifest myself unto him." Jesus delights in personal fellowship with all who love and obey him.

Sometimes the Saviour manifests himself to a soul in the crisis of conversion, when the soul surrenders itself to the Lord Jesus for all time. Well do I recall the hour when, at the age of thirteen, I committed myself to Jesus Christ as my only hope. For months I had labored under deep conviction for sin. I felt the burden resting on my soul. I was well-nigh desperate. I lay on the trundle bed beside my younger brother, who had fallen asleep; but I could not sleep. At last I said: "Lord Jesus, I do not know what to do. I have prayed but I get no relief. I have read the Bible, but my sins are still a burden on my soul. I have listened to preaching, but find no help. I do not know what to do except to turn it all over to you, and if I am lost, I will go down trusting you." Then something happened. It seemed that a great Presence filled the room and said to me almost in audible words: "My boy, I have been waiting for you to do what you have just done. You can count on me to save you. I will not fail you." The tears that dropped on my pillow were not tears of fear but of gratitude and joy that Christ Jesus was now my Saviour. I looked up to the old family clock on the mantel and it was five minutes to eight on the evening of March 3, 1877, the day before Rutherford B. Hayes was inaugurated as President of the United States. On March 3, 1945, I celebrated my sixty-eighth birthday as a Christian.

The next notable interview with the Lord Jesus occurred during my first year in college, when it was my privilege to win one of my schoolmates to Christ. A revival broke out in the Christian school I was attending and the Christian boys agreed to select each one some fellow student for special prayer, after which he would invite him to become a Christian. I chose a fine fellow by the name of Hayes, who was of a Methodist family. I made bold to knock on his door and when he rose to greet me, I said to him: "Hayes, old fellow, I just came in to ask you if you would give your heart to the Lord Jesus." It was the first time I had ever asked anyone such a personal question, and my heart was in my throat. I turned and quietly withdrew. The next Monday I passed his open door and he beckoned for me to come in. As he stood behind his study table, he said: "Sampey, I just invited you in to thank you for the good word you spoke to me last week. I have given my heart to the Lord Jesus, and yesterday I joined the Methodist church." I was so happy that I could not answer him a word. I quietly climbed the steps to the second floor and walked to the other end of the dormitory to my own room. I was supposed to be alone, but I had company, the best possible. The same Presence that spoke to me on the trundle bed was again with me. I sat in quiet for half an hour as he seemed to say to me: "This is the great work to which I have called you, to win men to faith in me."

As the years have come and gone the Lord Jesus has let me feel his presence in great crises, and I never speak to him in prayer that I do not have the feeling that he is listening. Perhaps if I had spoken to our friend and neighbor, Irvin Cobb, in this strain he might have taken me for a religious enthusiast. I would remind his many friends that the man whom he justly described as "the greatest gentleman that ever lived" taught more about heaven and hell than any other person in the Bible. In the parable of the rich man and Lazarus, Jesus brings out clearly the happy state of the poor beggar as the angels carried him to recline in Abraham's bosom and the painful experience of the selfish rich man as he was tormented in Hades. When a man dies *in* his sins, Jesus, the kindest and best man that ever lived, offers no hope for him either in the intermediate state or in the final judgment when the righteous and the wicked are judged according to their works.

Let us lift up our hearts in praise to God that no man need spend eternity in the place prepared for the devil and his angels. Jesus Christ suffered on the cross for the sins of men and offers himself as our Saviour. My friend, do not be content to stand on the side lines and cheer Jesus and his followers, but take up your cross and follow him in the Way. Then at death he will receive you into paradise, and when human history closes in the final judgment, he will say, "Come, ye blessed of my Father, inherit the kingdom prepared for you from the foundation of the world."

L. R. Scarborough
The Tears of Jesus

John 11:35; Luke 19:41; Hebrews 5:7

I read three passages of scripture:

Jesus wept (John 11:35).

And when he was come near, he beheld the city, and wept over it (Luke 19:41).

Who in the days of his flesh, when he had offered up prayers and supplications with strong crying and tears unto him that was able to save him from death, and was heard in that he feared (Heb. 5:7).

We find in this first scripture Jesus weeping at the grave of Lazarus. In this second scripture we find Him weeping over a city which being doomed had rejected His message. And in the last scripture we find Him shedding tears and offering prayers in the days of His flesh over a ruined world for which He was to die.

We find in this second scripture that He was coming to Jerusalem for the last time. He had been out among the people for three and a half years, preaching, teaching, healing and performing many miracles. The blind could see when he touched their eyes; the lame could walk, the dumb could speak, and the dead came forth out of the grave at His word of authority and power. But He had come now to Jerusalem for the last time. Just a few days afterwards he was crucified in the city he had come to save; and coming in that morning from the east side, with a great crowd meeting Him and following Him, praising God in accordance with the promises concerning Him, as He came up over the crest of Mount Olivet He saw that beautiful city with a wonderful history. I am sure, since He knew all things, there was present in His mind the past history of triumphs, of defeat, of prosperity and adversity. I am sure that He saw with His historic mind the things that had transpired in that city—there where a great people had builded a great city, the center of the religious life of the world, where He had trained a race to be His chosen people. And as He looked upon that city the scriptures say "He wept." This Son of God, this Son of man, seeing that city wept bitter, briny tears over what He saw. This is one of the three times in the scriptures where it speaks of the tears of Jesus. On one occasion before this He stood at the grave of one of His friends, the grave of Lazarus, and wept, joined in the sorrow of the loved ones for the man who had been hospitable to Him, a man He loved. And there the Son of Man at the gate of death shed tears. And the other time where it speaks of His tears is where I read you from the 5th chapter of Hebrews. It says that "in the days of His flesh with strong supplication and tears he prayed unto Him Who was able to save Him from death." There in that case Jesus Christ not only wept over a lost city, but he wept over a lost world.

Now I want us to think for a little while of the weeping Savior—the tears of Jesus Christ.

Whose Are These Tears?

Who is this strange person who has filled all history and yet who standing on the crest of the mountain we see weeping? His heart is torn and there comes from His eyes and from His heart tears that represent the attitude of His soul toward a lost city and toward the lost world. Who is He? Why, He is the author of our Bible, the founder of our churches, a refuge to our souls, the hope of our resurrection, the builder of our heaven, and the source, the provider of all our spiritual blessings. The Scriptures call Him our advocate, the alpha and omega of our spiritual life, the ancient of days, the anointed one, the balm in Gilead for our souls, the bread of life for our strength, the day-spring and morning star of our hopes, the corner stone and the foundation of our lives, the commander of God's army which is to conquer all sin, the counsellor and wisdom and guide for our feet. He is the founder and the fountain on which we build and from which we drink. He is the hiding place for our tempest-tossed souls, the high priest of our communion with God; He is the Immanuel, the very presence of the Most High. He is King over kings and Lord over lords. He was the Lamb of God slain from before the foundation of the world as a sacrifice and atonement for our sins. He is the leader of God's mightiest hosts, the Lion of the Tribe of Judah. He was the Man of Sorrows and who was acquainted with grief. He is the conqueror over sin and the enemies of God, the mediator between man and God, the messenger of God's covenant to a lost world, the Messiah of hope for a coming day of full redemption. He is the Prince of Life and the Prince of Peace, the redeemer, the rock of ages, the rose of Sharon, the scepter of Israel, the shepherd of God's sheep. He is God's only begotten and most beloved son; and here on the mount overlooking Jerusalem He weeps with a heart full of compassion and love for a lost world and establishes here again the doctrine of the chief and central and supreme passion of the gospel wrought out in His ministry and death and intercession for a sin-cursed world. He is the mightiest among the mighty and loveliest among ten thousand, the maker and preserver of our lives and the Savior of our souls; He weeps over our sin and doom and destiny. In His hands the reins of the universe are held. This man is the Son of God, is very God Himself. He controls all the things of our lives; and yet yonder in the city where He had taught and preached and was soon to be crucified, we see Him shedding the bitterest of tears. He is not some conqueror come to destroy, but a Savior come to save. He will not call down the wrath of the clouds and gather the powers of the storms to destroy those people. He has come to weep over them and die for them and save them. He is weeping today over a lost world.

I raise another question.

Why These Tears?

Why is it that this Son of Man, this Son of God, is weeping over the city of Jerusalem, and was constantly during the days of His flesh appealing unto God with strong supplications and tears? I say to you He is not weeping for Himself, though He sees the shadow of the cross just ahead of Him, He sees the dark, unspeakable sorrow of Gethsemane through which He is to go, the cruel crown of thorns which is to be pressed on His head, and though already doubtless the pierce of the nails is in His hand and the sword in His side. Yet He was not weeping over Himself. He was not weeping like a defeated conqueror. He was not weeping over a life of defeat, though in the eyes of the world He was living a life of defeat. He was not weeping because of His own failure or because of any discontent in His heart. Jesus was not weeping for Himself; but He was weeping because He saw some things from the Mount of Olivet. He was not weeping over that city which through the centuries had been builded by the sacrifices and labors of His people. He was not weeping for its reputation, though He saw the ruin of that city about which He here prophesied. He was not weeping for the falling walls and the ruins of the Temple. Why was He weeping that day? What was it He saw that caused the tears to come from His eyes?

I want if I can to bring you this day into a sympathetic attitude with Jesus Christ, as He stood on Mount Olivet. What was it that brought the tears from His eyes and broke His heart? It lies in three directions. In the first place, he wept because He saw the spiritual *condition* of men; He saw men in their sins; He saw them in the darkness of their unbelief, in the night of their unfaith in Him, sinners, dead in trespasses and sins; He saw the wrath of God on them if the love of God was not in their hearts; He saw them rejecting the only light come to them. He saw them without hope and without God in the world. As He looked upon the soul of an unbeliever no wonder it brought tears to His eyes, no wonder it brought a desire to be crucified for the life and salvation of that individual. The condition of men today ought to bring tears and burdens to the hearts of God's people.

I stood the other day by the side of a wife as she looked upon the pale, emaciated face of her loving and affectionate husband. The doctors had just operated on him and said he had typhoid fever. At that time he was suffering from a hemorrhage which it looked like he could not stand. His face was white and his finger tips and toe tips seemed to be drained of blood. I stood by her side as we went into another room to pray. Oh, there was such a wringing of the wife's heart as she said, "He cannot stand the loss of blood! He cannot stand the battle of the germs of disease in his body!" She realized the condition of her husband.

I stood by the side of a mother as she looked into the face of, as she thought, her dying baby. Her heart was wrung. The doctors had said, "He must die." She was torn by the realization of the condition of her child.

I will tell you, my friends, we need today to look into the lives of the unsaved men all about us and see their peril and condition before Almighty God. Every man and woman and young person in this community without Jesus Christ in their hearts by faith, is lost and dead in trespasses and in sins, is away from God and has no hope. The immoral decay of sin is in every particle of their spirit. Shall we look on them unmoved while the Son of God seeing a lost and ruined city shed tears over its condition? I trust that God's people seeing the unsaved about them today and during this meeting will join the Savior in weeping over a lost world.

I shall never forget when my first child, just five years of age, a little boy (one Sunday afternoon, after I had preached in the morning), as I was lying on my bed was sitting astride my body. Suddenly he changed the subject from what we had been talking about and looking into my face he said with a trembling voice, "Daddy, I am lost. I want you to show me the way to Christ." I do not explain it. I only tell you the story. It was the first time I realized the spiritual condition of my child. It was the first time he had appealed to me from his own lost soul. From that time until he was saved I kept the prayers hot up to God. I carried him to the Savior day by day. I believe it was because of the concern created in my heart that day that I kept the prayers hot. I want us in these days to remember the spiritual condition of every man that does not know Jesus Christ.

I think another thing that stirred the heart of Jesus was not only the condition of men, but the *destiny* of men He saw, the place to which these people were going when they were carried to the cemeteries. He was thinking of their destiny. He was thinking of their destiny, not their power. He the Son of God was thinking of where those people were going after death. And it is a matter that should stir our hearts—not what we possess here. Not a question of how much education or how little we have, but the question of destiny, of where you are going, should be the important question. It matters not that we die. How little value there is to the bodies of men, how little value! But, my friends, it is the eternal destiny of the soul that is the important question. I want us to know in the battle that we are going to fight here within the next few days that we are fighting a battle for the destinies of men. Every unsaved man in your community is going to hell. I do not know how you feel over here. I bless God I know there is a heaven for those who believe in Christ and a hell for those who do not believe in Christ. I am going to preach the gospel on this point. I want us to see the destinies of men and be moved like our Savior was moved.

There was another thing that stirred the heart of our Savior and that was *their refusal to hear Him and their rejection of Him*. Oh, the saddest thing that can come to the heart of Jesus Christ is for Him to be rejected! I wonder what will be the attitude of the people of this community. Jesus there looked upon that sinning, wicked city. He had wrought among them and yet they had rejected Him. I tell you, there is a demonstration on every hand that Jesus Christ is the Son of God and the Savior of the world. I wonder what we will do with this demonstration the next few days.

This incident in the life of the Savior but illustrates the care Jesus has for men.

The Savior's Care

He has shown, not only in His earthly life and sacrificial death, but in His heavenly ministry for these twenty centuries how much He cares for men. Even the hairs of our heads are numbered and not a sparrow falls without His loving care. Every detail of our lives is of interest to the Savior and all those things that make for our salvation and spiritual strength and service for Him are of the deepest concern to our Savior's heart. Does He not show in His attitude at Lazarus' grave that He loves and cares for the suffering loved ones at every grave? Does He not show by the many examples of healing, of raising the dead, of straightening the limbs of the crippled, opening the eyes of the blind and the ears of the deaf, that He cares for our bodies and our souls? Never a tear falls from the heart of a sorrowing widow nor from the penitent soul of the sick sinner that misses the loving care of our Savior. He has shown it in giving us the Bible with its many promises. He has assured us of it by His multiplied providences of loving care. That is the beauty of that great picture on Mount Olivet. Jesus loves men and has a concern for their salvation. He has shown it in His creative power, in His preserving, providential power, in His earthly ministry and in His death on Calvary.

You and I should take up the work of Jesus Christ and care for lost men. This is the message that I bring you this morning. This is the message—do you care for the lost men and women of this city? I wonder how many of you do. Will you stand with Jesus on Mount Olivet today and say, "We, too, will weep for our loved ones and join our Savior in caring for their souls"?

Some time ago I was in a great convention. I spoke to that convention on compassion for the lost. It was some years ago when our boys were gathering in the army camps all over our country. In that crowd was a rather old, plainly dressed woman. She and her husband were messengers to that convention evidently from some inland church. When the service was over she and her husband came down the aisle to shake hands with me. She took me by the hand and said, "Do you live at Fort Worth?" I said, "I do." Then she started to say, "My boy is in Camp Bowie near Fort Worth." She stopped and wept. Seeing her weeping her husband came up and putting his arm around her, he said, "Mary, what's the matter?" She said, "I was thinking of our baby boy yonder in Camp Bowie. You know he isn't saved. We have written letters to him about it; we have prayed for him and others have prayed for him." She said, "Here's a preacher that lives near where our soldier boy is and I was trying to put our boy, our baby boy, on the heart of this preacher." Then she turned to me in a way and with a question I shall never forget. I thought I loved lost men. For twenty-five years I have given strength without reservation to the winning of lost men to Christ. I thought I loved lost men. But this dear old mother looked up with all the love of a mother and said *"Preacher, do you love lost men?"* Oh, that question rings in my heart today!

You have made great preparation for this meeting and I bless God for it. The great question now is, Do we love lost men? If we do, God help us to join Jesus Christ in soul-agony for them that we may win them to Him. I wonder how many of you can say, "Deep down in my heart I do have a tender affectionate concern for the unsaved of this community and I can join with my Savior in a deep compassion for their salvation."

Listen to what God says, "They that sow in tears shall reap in joy. He that goeth forth and weepeth, bearing precious seed, shall doubtless come again with rejoicing, bringing his sheaves with him." God help us to be stirred in our souls for the lost of this community.

Franklin M. Segler
Grace Abounding

Romans 5:1-2,8,19-21, ASV

John Bunyan, author of the immortal allegory *The Pilgrim's Progress,* wrote another significant little book which is not quite so well known. Bunyan was a very wicked young man. After a long struggle, in repentance and faith he became a Christian. In intensely interesting fashion he told the story of his conversion under the title *Grace Abounding to the Chief of Sinners.* These words remind us of Paul's testimony, "Christ Jesus came into the world to save sinners; of whom I am chief" (1 Tim. 1:15). After Paul's experience on the Damascus road, he could never again forget the contrast between sin and grace. As a matter of fact, the entire letter to the church at Rome deals with this theme: the contrast between sin and grace—the depths of sin, the power of grace, and the results of God's redemptive love in the life of the believer.

In a paean of praise in the fifth chapter of Romans, Paul proclaimed the abounding grace of God against the dark background of abounding sin. He declared, "Where sin abounded, grace did much more abound: that as sin hath reigned in death, even so might grace reign through righteousness unto eternal life by Jesus Christ our Lord." Paul affirmed two facts in this statement: sin abounded and grace abounded. The gospel is epitomized in this concept: the tragedy of sin and the triumph of grace. The gospel is eternally effective. Therefore, if Paul were speaking today, he would say, "Sin abounds, and grace abounds more exceedingly."

Sin is a stark reality in the experience of man. It continually multiplies and grows until the offense is so great that it is unbearable. The word used for sin here is *hamartia.* This word appropriately expresses "the sum total of evil." Later, by repeated acts of disobedience to the law, sin

416

"bulked larger as offence was added to offence." Sin is man's personal offense to a personal God. The essence of sin is self-centeredness. It is an attitude, a disposition. The form which sin takes is not the most significant thing. The important thing is the attitude. Drunkenness, idolatry, impurity of life, vile language, lying, cheating, slander—these are but the fruits of sin. The essence of sin is invisible except to God. Sin is selfish, wilful rebellion against the loving will of God.

Sin abounds in its scope. Sin is universal. The universality of sin does not mean that everything in the life of man is bad and that he can do no good thing, but it does mean that sin affects all mankind. No one is exempt from its power. It means also that the actions of life are affected by a sinful motive. Sin steals in to ruin that which is noble and good.

All of the world's great religions recognize the problem of evil in the life of man, and although they define sin variously, they still are aware of the power of evil. All the governments of history have set up laws meant to restrain the evil acts of man. All great literature includes this tragic element. Read again the tragedies of Shakespeare—*Hamlet, Othello, King Lear, Julius Caesar*—and observe the scarlet thread of evil as it entwines itself about the life of man. Sin is no respecter of persons. It enters into the lives of people of all classes of society and into every home.

Sin abounds in its consequences. First, it affects the personality of the individual. Sin is a perversion of the good. That which is meant for righteousness is turned to selfish and evil ends. Ambition is a good thing until it becomes an obsession with the individual and leads him through progressive stages of self-exaltation of his own destruction. The acquisition of wealth is not evil until the spirit of possessiveness dominates the motivations of the heart. There seems to be no end to the creative power of the imagination in the mind of man, but when the imagination is perverted, it becomes a creative force for evil ends. Over two decades ago two brilliant university students allowed their imaginations to become perverted. Pursuing the study of science, the two students began to imagine how a human being would react when he was tortured and murdered. Their unrestrained demonic curiosity led to the slaying of little Bobby Franks.

Sin affects not only the individual but society as well. "For none of us liveth to himself, and no man dieth to himself" (Rom. 14:7). Isaiah saw himself a sinful man living in the midst of a society of sinful men. The sins of a man are multiplied in his neighbors as they join him in his transgression. The idea that it is nobody else's business what the individual does is absurd, for one's every act affects the life of his neighbor. A certain man who lived in a little Texas village many years ago was known as an avowed skeptic and critic of the church. Because of his invectives against the church and righteous living, the lives of many persons were affected over a period of years. His sins multiplied and abounded in the lives of others who followed his example. When the army of Israel invaded the city of Ai, Achan disobeyed God's orders by hiding certain objects of material value among his possessions. For this sin not only was Achan punished, but his entire family was stoned with him.

Sin abounds in its effect upon man's relationship to God. God is holy, and to him sin is serious. "The wages of sin is death" (Rom. 6:23). A man's sin separates him from God and places him under the judgment of outraged holy love. Man is conscious of the separation which is the very essence of his misery.

In the play *The Entertainer* the eminent British actor Laurence Olivier portrayed the practices of the cheap entertainer as he attempted to make people laugh. There seemed no end to the things the entertainer would do or say in order to provide entertainment for the crowd. As he sank lower and lower in his own ideas and practices, others were affected by his sinfulness. His own family was led into the dark depths of perverted thinking and living. Toward the climax of the play the entertainer's daughter appeals to her father to get a grip on himself, to live up to life's noble idealisms, to follow his God-given conscience. In the spirit of hopeless dejection and with deep pathos the actor exclaims, as he shrugs his shoulders, "You know, I just don't feel a thing." Perhaps the greatest consequence of sin is that it gradually leads one down a deceitful path, constantly dulling his sensitivity concerning life's spiritual values until, finally, he exclaims, "I just don't feel a thing."

To Paul the gospel was both the setting and the jewel. Although the setting is sin, abounding sin, the jewel is abounding grace. It shines the more gloriously because it is in contrast to its setting. Abounding sin demands abounding grace. The God of unlimited love meets the needs of abounding sin. "Though sin has multiplied, yet God's favor has surpassed it and overflowed, so that just as sin had reigned by death, so His favor too might reign in right standing with God which issues in eternal life through Jesus Christ our Lord" (Rom. 5:20-21, Williams).

Grace abounds in the love of God. "God commendeth his love toward us, in that, while we were yet sinners, Christ died for us" (Rom. 5:8). The grace of God is the favor of God bestowed to man who does not deserve this favor but who comes to it by means of faith in him who bore the penalty for man's sins. A missionary was once seeking for the word in the native language which would translate the word "grace" from the English Scriptures. After awhile a native came to his aid as he exclaimed, "I have it; it means too much love!"

During World War II a little girl was walking with her father along the street when she noticed blue stars in the windows of the houses. She asked her father the meaning of them, and he explained to her that the stars represented fathers or sons who had gone out from the homes to war. A little later she noticed a gold star in the window. "Daddy, what does this star mean?" "It means," he replied, "that this home gave a son in the war." She was silent for a while as they walked along the street, and then, lifting her face toward the heavens, she saw a bright gold star in the west. "Oh, Daddy, look. Yonder's a gold star in heaven!" Then she asked, "Did God also give a son?" "Yes," he replied, "God also gave a Son." Indeed, the beloved apostle John wrote that God so loved that he gave his only Son.

Grace abounded in the life of Jesus Christ. The Gospels tell us that Jesus went about doing good—preaching, teaching, and healing. He healed the blind man. He cleansed the leper. He called little children unto him and blessed them. He forgave sinners, sinners like the woman at the well, Simon Peter, Zacchaeus the publican, and Mary Magdalene. As Jesus saw the needs of humanity, as he looked upon the multitudes and saw them lying about bruised and bleeding like the sheep without a shepherd, he had compassion upon them and ministered to every need as he had opportunity. The greatest compliment ever paid Jesus was paid him by his critics, the Pharisees, who accused him of loving sinners, of being concerned about outcasts, and of answering to the cries of broken humanity in its misery. Little wonder that the poet exclaimed,

> No mortal can with Him compare,
> Among the sons of men;
> Fairer is He than all the fair
> Who fill the heav'nly train.

The grace of God overflowed and multiplied exceedingly in the death of Jesus. The gospel of suffering love was manifest in the death of Christ. This message was predicted by Isaiah as he declared, "Surely he hath borne our griefs, and carried our sorrows: yet we did esteem him stricken, smitten of God, and afflicted. But he was wounded for our transgressions, he was bruised for our iniquities: the chastisement of our peace was upon him; and with his stripes we are healed. All we like sheep have gone astray; we have turned every one to his own way; and the Lord hath laid on him the iniquity of us all" (Isa. 53:4-6).

Paul caught up the message of redeeming grace as he exclaimed, "We preach Christ crucified" (1 Cor. 1:23), and again, "For when we were yet without strength, in due time Christ died for the ungodly" (Rom. 5:6).

> There is a green hill far away, without a city wall,
> Where the dear Lord was crucified, who died to save us all.
> Oh, dearly, dearly has He loved, and we must love Him, too,
> And trust in His redeeming blood, and try His works to do.

Grace abounds and overflows in the life of every man who will open his heart to receive it. Abounding grace does not ask how great is the sin, but how needy is the sinner. Not only does the gospel of grace manifest the love of God, but it also affects man's total relation to God. Forsyth said, "God in Christ's Cross not only manifests His love but gives effect to it in human history. He enters that stream, and rides on its rage, and rules its flood, and bends its course. He reseats His love in command upon the active centre of human reality. He does the thing which is crucial for human destiny."[1]

God's grace changes the lives of men. The gospel invites every man, regardless of his condition, to accept the grace of God and thereby experience a dynamic change in his own character and way of life. Jesus Christ is not only the reconciler but also the bringer of eternal life, as Angus Dun reminds us. George Burnham, the newspaper man from Chattanooga, Tennessee, who has for several years traveled with Billy Graham, writing news stories concerning Graham's campaigns, gave this testimony. Said he, "George Burnham was just a washed-up alcoholic newspaper reporter. He heard a preacher proclaim the gospel, promising that when a man accepts Christ he becomes a new creature. George Burnham accepted that Christ, and it has made all the difference in his life. Now it is his delight to travel over the world telling the good news of the gospel of Christ's love."

God's love is extended to all men everywhere. "For the grace of God hath appeared, bringing salvation to all men, instructing us, to the intent that, denying ungodliness and worldly lusts, we should live soberly and righteously and godly in this present world; looking for the blessed hope and appearing of the glory of the great God and our Saviour Jesus Christ; who gave himself for us, that he might redeem us from all iniquity, and purify unto himself a people for his own possession, zealous of good works" (Titus 2:11-14, ASV).

In an art museum in Brussels, Belgium, named for the artist Wiertz, there is one picture more impressive than all the others. About twelve by sixteen feet in size, it occupies one entire end of a display room. It portrays Christ on the cross. From the cross powerful beams of light are radiated in every direction. In the background is the Garden of Eden. Guilty Adam and Eve are attempting to hide themselves. The old serpent draws back in fear. At the bottom of the picture is the appropriate title selected by the artist, "Christus Victor!" Indeed, Christ is triumphant, and although "sin abounded, grace did much more abound: that as sin hath reigned unto death, even so might grace reign through righteousness unto eternal life by Jesus Christ our Lord" (Rom. 5:20-21).

NOTE

1. P. T. Forsyth, *Positive Preaching and Modern Man* (London: Hodder & Stoughton, n.d.), 346.

James Wilson Storer
A New Heaven and a New Earth

And God saw everything that he had made, and, behold, it was very good. And there was evening and there was morning, the sixth day (Gen. 1:31, ASV).

For we know that the whole creation groaneth and travaileth in pain together until now (Rom. 8:22, ASV).

And I saw a new heaven and a new earth: for the first heaven and the first earth are passed away; and the sea is no more. And I saw the holy city, new Jerusalem, coming down out of heaven from God, made ready as a bride adorned for her husband. And I heard a great voice out of the throne saying, Behold the tabernacle of God is with men, and he shall dwell with them, and they shall be his peoples, and God himself shall be with them, and be their God: and he shall wipe away every tear from their eyes and death shall be no more; neither shall there be mourning, nor crying, nor pain, any more: the first things are passed away. And he that sitteth on the throne said, Behold, I make all things new. And he saith, Write: for these words are faithful and true (Rev. 21:1-5, ASV).

It was not a Christian but a skeptic who said, "There is nothing new under the sun." If new objects had no attraction, we should go on living a squirrel-in-a-cage existence until apathy and cynicism consumed us.

New things have a charm which is felt by us all. But that charm need not destroy within us the stability which a priceless gift of the accustomed way of doing things ensures.

New things form a familiar theme in the Bible. The Bible tells of a new covenant, of a new commandment, and assures us that there is a new song on the lips of the redeemed.

One day a poet was sight-seeing in heaven and, looking about him, began a stanza thus:

I saw a new heaven and a new earth: for the first heaven and the first earth are passed away; and the sea is no more. And I saw the holy city, new Jerusalem, coming down out of heaven from God, made ready as a bride adorned for her husband. And I heard a great voice out of the throne saying, Behold the tabernacle of God is with men, and he shall dwell with them, and they shall be his people, and God himself will be with them, and be their God (Rev. 21:1-3).

I am so glad that sightseer was a poet and that what he saw he used his poet's perception to describe—this man who could always touch the sky with his finger. It would have been so flat and drear if a statistician had described it—or a psychologist or a preacher! Any of the three would have become cluttered up with what he thought was logic. Not that the poet is illogical, not that at all; simply that it takes more than the two-plus-two-makes-four formula to be logical about the greatest things in life—love, for example.

But this poet John, grown old now but not weary, looked about him and saw much. His eyesight was so keen. And the poet John not only saw, he heard. His hearing was so good. The key to his life is found in "I saw" and "I heard" and "I loved."

Now you can always be sure the real poet will see and hear the striking things; he is never impressed with the multiplicity on display. His soul dwells on the essentials. In private (that is why most of us have so much trouble with the Book of Revelation) we say about this closing book of the Bible, "It is so meaningless," because we each wish to construct a calendar and a code whereby we can unravel all the threads of its discourse and then say, "This all means this."

I know that the very title of the book means not a concealing but a revealing. But remember it is a revealing of the length and breadth and height and depth of the love of God and of His purpose for mankind.

People who are not baffled by the thinking of God are not the great thinkers. "Without controversy great is the mystery of godliness," declares Paul in 1 Timothy 3:16.

God is the climax of all mystery. No one's intelligence is to be envied who, when he looks at the works and words of an omnipotent God, is not baffled by them. And I am afraid many of us tell best what we don't know.

In the opening words of the book is stated its theme, "The Revelation of Jesus Christ"—or the unveiling—or taking away the mystery concerning Jesus Christ.

In chapter 1 we have an unveiling of the person of Jesus Christ, in the second and third an unveiling of Jesus Christ in relation to the church, and in chapters 4 through 22 the unveiling of the processes of God's kingdom. As Campbell Morgan outlines the passage:

1. Jesus in His glory.
2. Jesus in His grace.
3. Jesus in His government.

The Bible opens with the sentence, "In the beginning God created the heavens and the earth" (Gen. 1:1). It closes with, "I saw a new heaven and a new earth" (Rev. 21:1). Likewise, the Bible is an account of processes which stretch across centuries unaccountable. It does not ever indicate the timeless hour when the present world began nor the date of the coming of a new heaven and a new earth. Only men with finite minds do that, and how they vary in their verdict! What a difference there is in the way the exiles of time whiled away their sentences!

Napoleon on Saint Helena, fretting and fuming, an eagle chained in a cage, consumed with tragic betrayal, saw no bright visions nor beauty of celestial design. Quite the opposite, he was constantly shrouded in gloom. Shortly before he died on the wild May night in 1821, his close companion, Bertrand, came to tell him there was a comet to be seen very clearly. To this Napoleon replied, "Before the death of Julius Caesar there was also a comet," and sank down on the sofa. That was your man of blood and iron, the epitome of glory in war and ashes in defeat.

But our poet John, our exiled poet John on Patmos, saw a new world of marvelous creation, of inexhaustible loveliness. He saw a world which man had blotched and ruined, perverted all out of resemblance to the world which God had made, and of which he had said it was "very good."

There are three texts that should be taken together: (1) "God saw everything that he had made, and, behold, it was very good" (Gen. 1:31); (2) "We know that the whole creation groaneth and travaileth in pain together until now" (Rom. 8:22); (3) "He that sat upon the throne said, behold, I make all things new" (Rev. 21:5).

God's World as It Was

God's world would not be improved upon; there was no unseemly thing to mar it. Nothing was out of order in it either in a material or a moral sense. There was no sin in the world when God made it. God's own report about it was that it was very good—a moral as well as an artistic world.

God's World as It Is

Ichabod was written across the face of it—its clear glory has departed. Not that chaos has engulfed it. God is still in His heaven and maketh the wrath of man to praise Him.

Between Strasbourg and Basel on one of the main transcontinental railway lines is an Alsatian town named Clomar. When you drop into the local museum, you will find a famous picture by Matthias Grünewald. It is of the crucifixion. There hangs the Christ, stretched out in the agony of the cross with all its grim reality. There is no attempt at the beautiful. The flesh is torn and rough; the muscles are contorted. When you look at it, you know you are in the presence of an actual grieving event of history and that it is an extreme experience of pain rather than an aesthetic portrayal of some ineffable mystic rite.

On the right of the cross there is a curious figure. Clad in a rough cloak, with an open book in his hand, he puts out an unnaturally long finger and points straight at the wounded heart of Christ. "Behold the Lamb of God, that taketh away the sin of the world!" (John 1:29).

As one looks at the pointing finger of another John (this one the Baptist), he is reminded of the primary function of our churches. Anything else is limp inadequacy.

Whenever his hand is not thrust from the tiller, the ship will stay on course. And the blitz flowers do their best to cover with beauty the shambles men made of London—that for the natural world of material things.

But it is in the moral realm that men have with deliberate intent substituted their wills for the will of God. As John wrote when he was a young poet with fire and thunder as his garment:

> In the beginning was the Word, and the Word was with God, and the Word was God. . . . All things were made through him; and without him was not anything made that hath been made. In him was life; and the life was the light of men. And the light shineth in the darkness; and the darkness apprehended it not. There came a man, sent from God, whose name was John. The same came for witness, that he might bear witness of the light, that all might believe through him. He was not the light, but came that he might bear witness of the light. There was the true light, even the light

which lighteth every man, coming into the world. He was in the world, and the world was made through him, and the world knew him not. He came unto his own, and they that were his own received him not. But as many as received him, to them gave he the right to become children of God, even to them that believe on his name: who were born, not of blood, nor of the will of the flesh, nor of the will of man, but of God. And the Word became flesh, and dwelt among us (and we beheld his glory, glory as of the only begotten from the Father), full of grace and truth (John 1:1-14, ASV).

This is what is wrong with this word of ours—sin entered it and with sin came death. Jeremiah 9:1 declares, "Oh that my head were waters, and mine eyes a fountain of tears, that I might weep day and night for the slain of the daughters of my people!" (ASV).

God's World as It Will Be

"I saw a new heaven and a new earth," sang out the poet John. The hope of renewal and restitution of all things was not new. Long had it been cherished. Such prophets as Isaiah and Ezekiel had voiced it, though once Ezekiel sadly had lamented, "The days are prolonged, and every vision faileth" (Ezek. 12:22).

It was to be "new heavens and a new earth, wherein dwelleth righteousness," declared Peter (2 Pet. 3:13).

There are two words which are translated *new* in our English version. One is *neos* which relates to time; the other is *kainos* which relates to quality. It is this latter word which is used throughout this chapter and throughout the Book of Revelation.

The newness which is pictured is the newness of freshness. The old, decaying, corrupting elements are swept away. All things will be new, full of fresh and fair beauty, but all things will not be strange except that it will be strange to find only purity and peace pervading.

Who will live in this new city? "He that overcometh shall inherit all things; and I will be his God, and he shall be my son" (Rev. 21:7).

And how do they overcome? Our poet John tells us in chapter 5 that the four living creatures and four and twenty-elders sang a new song to the Lamb:

> Worthy art thou to take the book, and to open the seals thereof: for thou wast slain, and didst purchase unto God with thy blood men of every tribe, and tongue, and people, and nation; and madest them to be unto our God a kingdom of priests; and they reign upon the earth (vv. 9-10, ASV).

May we now turn to consider the thought that God makes all things new by the uprising of personal faith. Speaking of Christ in Ephesians 2:14-15, Paul wrote:

> He is our peace, who made both one, and brake down the middle wall of partition, having abolished in his flesh the enmity, even the law of commandments contained in ordinances; that he might create in himself of the two one new man, so making peace (ASV).

When we fix our faith on Christ as our personal Savior, all things become new. Do you remember this story of John Wesley? He tells us how on the evening of May 24, 1738, he went most unwillingly to a little gathering in London. Someone read aloud from Luther and "about a quarter before nine," he relates in his journal, "while he was describing the change which God works in the heart through faith in Christ, I felt my heart strangely warmed. I felt I did trust in Christ, Christ alone, for salvation; and an assurance was given me that He had taken away all my sins." Thus, God made all things new for one man as he has for millions.

Sin makes old, but God alone makes new. He abundantly pardons; He saves to the uttermost; He casts out sins as far as the east is from the west and remembers them against us no more.

Ask Him to do this for you. Put your soul into your prayer. He will hear you and make you a new creature in Christ Jesus.

F. B. Thorn
True Greatness

For he shall be great in the sight of the Lord (Luke 1:15).

A song is more impressive, a noise more startling, and a declaration of truth more challenging when preceded by a period of silence. For four hundred years there had been no direct message from heaven. The priests had ministered without the direction of a prophet. A dozen generations had lived, listened, and died with something of a sense of disappointment. Out of the patience of God there had grown the impatience of man. The religious thinking of the people had divided into camps. There were the Pharisees, the formalists, whose religion had degenerated into a slumbering habit of bowing heads, mumbling prayers, urging fasts, and quoting laws the essence of which had been forgotten. There were the Sadducees, the rationalists, who emphasized the intellect to the neglect of the heart until they had become critical and sneering, denying immortality. There were the Essenes, the mystics, who, tired of the formalism of the Pharisees and the skepticism of the Sadducees, cried out for a life of self-denial. They had sent many into seclusion to live simple, calm, self-sacrificing lives. There were the Herodians, social gospelites, who wanted to make Herod king and produce an ideal economic and social state in the world. The best that can be said for these cults is that they unhappily tolerated each other. All missed the mark. Inherent weaknesses inhibited the production of a single great character or leader. Deliverance must come from an outside source.

Not as they had planned, but as God willed, an announcement was made by an angel to an obscure priest, Zechariah, that an unusual character was soon to be born into his home, one who would be *great in the sight of the Lord*. Is not this God's way of saying that men would appraise

428

him differently? They would not see in him the elements that make for greatness, according to their own petty standards. He would cross swords with their religious gladiators, for his mission was higher and his message different. His heroism was to be of a new kind—the heroism of the commonplace. "John did no miracle," worked no wonders. He was only a voice borne on the desert air, calling men to repentance, that they might be ready for the coming of the Lord.

In selecting her great, the world often passes over the gold that will stand the fire. She selects her heroes from the battlefield, the gridiron, the rescue guard, the stage, and the realm of philanthropy. She forgets that glamor and greatness are not synonymous. The greatest struggles of earth have been without beating drums and newspaper headlines. Real greatness is found in the training camp as often as at the battlefront. David's heroism was not his fight with the Goliath but his fight for recovery. Jesus' illustration of greatness was not the emperor of the nation nor the president of the Sanhedrin, but a little child from the market-place. It has been said, "The launching of a boy or girl to live for Christ is greater than the launching of a battleship." The truly great are those who do what God wants them to do, when and where He wants it done.

By accepted standards, John the Baptist was not great. He would not rank as a philosopher. God gave him a simple message. He delivered it. He left no book for future generations to read; no poem to stir and inspire; no painting to hang in the art gallery. He was a stranger to social circles; took little stock in political movements; financially a failure. This single-handed preacher had no house in which to deliver his message, no organization to support him, no publicity department, and no advance agent. His ministry was short—less than a year, yet God called him great—great because he was faithful to his charge.

1. *John was great as a preacher.*—For thirty years, in preparation, he had lived in the wilderness. This gave him time to think, mature, and be disciplined. From this seclusion, he weighed the conflicting notions against the spiritual gropings of the people. His spirit burned within him, as he longed, not for a better civil government, but for the kingdom of God on earth. His love for humanity was consuming. Its popular vices and shallow convictions called loudly for a remedy. Others had failed in this charge, not John.

The preacher's message bore the unfailing marks of eloquence. Men heard him and did what he said. Fluency is not to be confused with eloquence. John was not a fluent speaker. His messages were brief, attended by few words of description, with no effort to make them poetic. He never resorted to tricks of oratory, but with simple words and brief sentences, like the blows of a trip-hammer, he broke men's hearts. One of the highest moments of eloquence I have ever witnessed was a period of silence. One of the most eloquent men to whom I have ever listened, stammered his words and broke his sentences into ungrammatical bits; but there was conviction that amounted to passion, earnestness that was contagious, and persuasion that could come only from one who has lived and breathed his message. John's beautiful consistency of life-message and lip-message made him a pulpit power. His words were relatively few, but they were not fruitless.

"Repent ye" was the opening note of his message. This same note sounded until the "amen." Repentance was the first necessity and preliminary to everything that was to follow. It was the first step in preparing the way of the Lord and making the paths straight. Sin was everywhere. There could be no kingdom of God until men turned their backs upon sin. The ground must be leveled, the high places brought down, and the low places built up. The Jews must learn that it meant nothing to be a member of Abraham's family without Abraham's faith. The Pharisee must learn that he was no better than his fellows. The beggar must learn that there was hope for him. All must learn that God is no respecter of persons. "Except ye repent, ye shall all likewise perish." We wonder if the greatest need of the world and the churches today is not a *voice* crying, "Repent! Repent! for the kingdom of God is at hand."

The multitude swarmed from everywhere to hear this strange Elijah-type preacher. They were not attracted because he commanded them to repent. Men by nature do not want to repent. In part, they were drawn by his strange garb, his plain manner of life, his fearlessness, and his fiery energy. But most of all, they came because he sounded a rousing proclamation that the kingdom of God was at hand. The sunlight was about to break and banish the long night of spiritual darkness. To men's hearts and souls he brought God's message without fear or favor. The transparent sincerity of his soul and message made him great as a preacher.

2. *John was great in conviction and courage.*—Conviction, that he cherished more than life, and courage, that set a standard for all generations, soon landed him in the fortress of Machaerus. There was nothing unusual about that. The kingdom has advanced that way from the begin-

ning. The front-rank soldiers die first; forward the next rank over their dead bodies!

When Jesus heard of John's death, He said to His disciples, "What went ye out into the wilderness to see, a reed shaken by the wind? A man clothed in soft raiment? Nay, a prophet of God." Prophets are born to die for the cause. This is the essence of moral greatness—that a man have a grip on truth, a conviction as deep as the marrow of the bones, that criticism cannot weaken, that persecution cannot faze, that martyr's fires cannot break.

Nor must we forget that such moral courage is not reached in a day. Skyscrapers have deep foundations. Good soldiers are of long training. Great courage reaches far beneath the surface. Who can ever know the battles John fought with fear, hesitation, and doubt ere he reached the place where he could face the proud Pharisee crowd and say, "Ye generation of vipers"?

Present-day Christianity in America knows nothing of such courage. To find it now, you must go to the far-flung picket lines with the missionaries in China, Africa, and South America. But for them, the world would lose this mighty example of courage. Here we are soft and cowardly. The least criticism, even a lack of compliment from associates, and we are willing to quit. Did not Jesus say, "Some seed fell on shallow soil"? There is much shallow soil in our church fields. Go read the story of John and let conviction grip you. Read of Paul's last journey to Jerusalem, and hear him say, "None of these things move me, yea, I count not my life dear unto me that I may finish my ministry which I have received of the Lord Jesus." Oh, for an army of young men and women to come forward and take the place of men like John and Paul and Bunyan!

3. *John was great because he had a high standard for his life.*—The height of one's standard of life is in exact inverted ratio to his self-denial. All efforts, both of threat and flattery, could not move him one inch from his firm conviction that Christ is all, and he, himself, but a voice to introduce Christ. His humble submission and feeling of utter dependence, as always, gave him that boldness and courage that placed him in the top rank. Only men of the highest plane submerge themselves out of sight and hide themselves in the background, that they may not detract from the glory of the Christ. When his followers were inclined to honor him, he quickly said, "One mightier than I cometh, the latchet of whose shoes I am not worthy to unloose; he shall baptize you with the Holy Ghost."

Like many another man, John found himself, temporarily, the most popular man in the land. Popularity has its perils. Many believed he was the Messiah. Had he assumed that role, he would have found no lack of followers. A rather impressive committee came and asked him if he were the Christ. He quickly replied, "I am not the Christ." Then they asked, "Who art thou? What sayest thou of thyself?" He answered, "I am the voice of one crying in the wilderness, make straight the way of the Lord." His recognition of the Lamb of God shattered every dream of his own importance. Many a man has become weak and useless because he stepped beyond the line of his limitations. Uzziah was stricken with leprosy and died because he presumed upon God and assumed the function of the priest. The moment a man usurps that which does not belong to him, he becomes powerless. The moment a church claims for herself that which belongs to Christ, she writes "Ichabod" over her portals. John cared little what men thought of him. He cared what Christ thought. He lived on that high plane.

4. *John was great in his contention for truth.*—He has been referred to as "this man of iron." Certainly he had a clear conviction of his duty and a keen sense of wrong. He has been called radical and dogmatic. His declarations were brief and sharp. Every one of them was a battle-cry, introducing a contest between Christ and Satan, the final score of which would be settled upon the cross—"Behold the Lamb of God, that taketh away the sins of the world."

Repent, prepare, purge, and burn are the strange words from the lips of the forerunner of Jesus. But a new crowd had come asking baptism. They were not sincere, knew no repentance. He flashed a soul-mirror before them. Some looking, saw themselves as vipers, some as a tree with the axe at the root, some as chaff already blown from the wheat. John was contending for truth. They were not ready for baptism. "Bring forth fruits meet for repentance." Who can measure the inestimable harm that has come to Christianity by receiving and baptizing unsaved persons? How greater could one curse a friend than by placing him inside the fold, a stranger to the shepherd—no love for the sheep? He would be of all men most miserable.

On this truth John staked his life; that the permanency of grace depends upon the depth of repentance; that private righteousness must precede public reformation; that self-denial must be found before self-sacrifice can be made; that all the virtues and graces worth while must root deep in the sacrifice of the Lamb of God.

5. *John was great in his stand against the popular sins of his day.*—A man may condemn the sins of the past and the anticipated sins of the future with little to fear from his contemporaries; but when a man looks sin and the sinner squarely in the face and speaks the blistering truth, he may expect trouble. John shared the common knowledge of Herod's sin. How he came to preach in his presence is not revealed. Perhaps the King was, by nature, friendly and tolerant, and possessed a desire to hear this strange voice. At any rate, the day came and the Baptist stood in his presence. How tempting to turn from his straightforward duty and glory in the honor! How much harder to speak his message in royal atmosphere than in the unhampered spaces of the wilderness! How much easier to rebuke a congregation than an individual! This may have been the supreme test of his character and ministry. He measured up to the occasion. The voice that cried, "Repent," on Jordan's banks, cried, "Repent," in the King's court. Without apology, he shot straight at the mark. "It is not lawful for you to have your brother's wife." It would have been easier to have employed modern-day tact, which is another name for cowardice, and with complimentary phrases offered a gentle rebuke. By this, he might have saved his life, but with the same stroke he would have murdered truth.

The sledge-hammer blow of that rebuke did not cease with the one who delivered it. It still stands to rebuke the Christian world for its compromising attitude toward popular sins. How faltering our stand! How gentle our challenge, if indeed, we challenge at all! Leniency is justified on the ground that in the long run it will pay. In truth, we are trying to save our skins, at heart we are cowards. To our commission, we are traitors. Under the guise of pose, sensibleness, and respectability, we permit sin in high places to go uncondemned. God, pity us when we stand in the judgment!

6. *John was great in his death.*—That day when the sermon was finished, it bore the marks of failure. Not a hand was raised for prayer. No one came forward seeking a better life. There was no weeping on account of sin. Strange terror seized the King, but it did not lead to repentance. Herodias swore vengeance. The preacher was thrown in prison. He had preached his last sermon.

After a time Herod made a great feast on his birthday. Amid the gala celebration, Herodias sent her daughter in to dance in the presence of the King and his lords. Perhaps she was too young to know the perils of the dance floor. What chance had a young life in such a sty of royal filth, directed by a depraved mother? The half-drunken King was elated with her beauty and offered her up to the half of his kingdom. At the behest of her mother, she asked for the head of John the Baptist. Terror seized the King, but he kept his vow and the ghastly scene took place. The shaggy head of him who feared not life nor death was delivered to Herodias; and his weeping followers buried his body.

The end of the story is disappointing. We like to see the slave boy become the ruler. But not every Joseph can become a king. Not every David can rise to prominence. Not everyone cast into the furnace can come out without the "smell of fire on him." Not every Bunyan can write a *Pilgrim's Progress*. Not every blind Milton can write a *Paradise Lost*. Truth, often, is clothed in apparent failure. Success is marked by scars and blood stains. So it was with John. But he was great in the sight of the Lord. What else matters?

George W. Truett
Baptists and Religious Liberty

Southern Baptists count it a high privilege to hold their Annual Convention this year in the national capital, and they count it one of life's highest privileges to be citizens of our one great, united country.

> Grand in her rivers and her rills,
> Grand in her woods and templed hills;
> Grand in the wealth that glory yields,
> Illustrious dead, historic fields;
> Grand in her past, her present grand,
> In sunlit skies, in fruitful land;
> Grand in her strength on land and sea,
> Grand in religious liberty.

It behooves us often to look backward as well as forward. We should be stronger and braver if we thought oftener of the epic days and deeds of our beloved and immortal dead. The occasional backward look would give us poise and patience and courage and fearlessness and faith. The ancient Hebrew teachers and leaders had a genius for looking backward to the days and deeds of their mighty dead. They never wearied of chanting the praises of Abraham and Isaac and Jacob, of Moses and Joshua and Samuel; and thus did they bring to bear upon the living the inspiring memories of the noble actors and deeds of bygone days. Often such a cry as this rang in their ears: "Look unto the rock whence ye were hewn, and to the hole of the pit whence ye were digged. Look unto Abraham, your father, and unto Sarah that bare you; for when he was but one I called him, and I blessed him, and made him many."

435

The Doctrine of Religious Liberty

We shall do well, both as citizens and as Christians, if we hark back to the chief actors and lessons in the early and epoch-making struggles of this great Western democracy, for the full establishment of civil and religious liberty—back to the days of Washington and Jefferson and Madison, and back to the days of our Baptist fathers, who paid such a great price, through the long generations, that liberty, both religious and civil, might have free course and be glorified everywhere.

Years ago, at a notable dinner in London, that world-famed statesman, John Bright, asked an American statesman, himself a Baptist, the noble Dr. J. L. M. Curry, "What distinct contribution has your America made to the science of government?" To that question Dr. Curry replied: "The doctrine of religious liberty." After a moment's reflection, Mr. Bright made the worthy reply: "It was a tremendous contribution."

Supreme Contribution of New World

Indeed, the supreme contribution of the new world to the old is the contribution of religious liberty. This is the chiefest contribution that America has thus far made to civilization. And historic justice compels us to say that it was pre-eminently a Baptist contribution. The impartial historian, whether in the past, present or future, will ever agree with our American historian, Mr. Bancroft, when he says: "Freedom of conscience, unlimited freedom of mind, was from the first the trophy of the Baptists." And such historian will concur with the noble John Locke who said: "The Baptists were the first propounders of absolute liberty, just and true liberty, equal and impartial liberty." Ringing testimonies like these might be multiplied indefinitely.

Not Toleration, but Right

Baptists have one consistent record concerning liberty throughout all their long and eventful history. They have never been party to oppression of conscience. They have ever been the unwavering champions of liberty, both religious and civil. Their contention now is, and has been, and, please God, must ever be, that it is the natural and fundamental and indefeasible right of every human being to worship God or not, according to the dictates of his conscience, and, as long as he does not infringe upon the rights of others, he is to be held accountable alone to God for all religious beliefs and practices. Our contention is not for mere toleration, but for absolute liberty. There is a wide difference between toleration and liberty. Toleration implies that somebody falsely claims the right to tolerate. Toleration is a concession, while liberty is a right. Toleration is a matter of expediency, while liberty is a matter of principle. Toleration is a gift from man, while liberty is a gift from God. It is the consistent and insistent contention of our Baptist people, always and everywhere, that religion must be forever voluntary and uncoerced, and that it is not the prerogative of any power, whether civil or ecclesiastical, to compel men to conform to any religious creed or form of worship, or to pay taxes for the support of a religious organization to which they do not belong and in whose creed they do not believe. God wants free worshippers and no other kind.

What is the explanation of this consistent and notably praiseworthy record of our plain Baptist people in the realm of religious liberty? The answer is at hand. It is not because Baptists are inherently better than their neighbours—we would make no such arrogant claim. Happy are our Baptist people to live side by side with their neighbours of other Christian faiths and to have fellowship with such neighbours, and to honor such servants of God for their inspiring lives and their noble deeds. From our deepest hearts we pray: "Grace be with all them that love our Lord Jesus Christ in sincerity." The spiritual union of all true believers in Christ is now and ever will be a blessed reality, and such union is deeper and higher and more enduring than any and all forms and rituals and organizations. Whoever believes in Christ as his personal Saviour is our brother in the common salvation, whether he be a member of one communion or of another, or of no communion at all.

How is it, then, that Baptists, more than any other people in the world, have forever been the protagonists of religious liberty, and its compatriot, civil liberty? They did not stumble upon this principle. Their uniform, unyielding and sacrificial advocacy of such principle was not and is not an accident. It is, in a word, because of our essential and fundamental principles. Ideas rule the world. A denomination is moulded by its ruling principles, just as a nation is thus moulded and just as individual life is thus moulded. Our fundamental essential principles have made our Baptist people, of all ages and countries, to be the unyielding protagonists of religious liberty, not only for themselves, but as well for everybody else.

Such fact at once provokes the inquiry: What are these fundamental

Baptist principles which compel Baptists in Europe, in America, in some far-off seagirt island, to be forever contending for unrestricted religious liberty? First of all, and explaining all the rest, is the doctrine of absolute Lordship of Jesus Christ. That doctrine is for Baptists the dominant fact in all their Christian experience, the nerve center of all their Christian life, the bedrock of all their church polity, the sheet anchor of all their hopes, the climax and crown of all their rejoicings. They say with Paul: "For to this end Christ both died and rose again, that he might be Lord both of the dead and the living."

From that germinal conception of the absolute Lordship of Christ, all our Baptist principles emerge. Just as yonder oak came from the acorn, so our many-branched Baptist life came from the cardinal principle of the absolute Lordship of Christ. The Christianity of our Baptist people, from Alpha to Omega, lives and moves and has its whole being in the realm of the doctrine of the Lordship of Christ. "One is your Master, even Christ, and all ye are brethren." Christ is the one head of the church. All authority has been committed unto Him, in heaven and on earth, and He must be given the absolute pre-eminence in all things. One clear note is ever to be sounded concerning Him, even this, "Whatsoever He saith unto you, do it."

The Bible Our Rule of Faith and Practice

How shall we find out Christ's will for us? He has revealed it in His Holy Word. The Bible and the Bible alone is the rule of faith and practice for Baptists. To them the one standard by which all creeds and conduct and character must be tried is the Word of God. They ask only one question concerning all religious faith and practice, and that question is, "What saith the Word of God?" Not traditions, nor customs, nor councils, nor confessions, nor ecclesiastical formularies, however venerable and pretentious, guide Baptists, but simply and solely the will of Christ as they find it revealed in the New Testament. The immortal B. H. Carroll has thus stated it for us: "The New Testament is the law of Christianity. All the New Testament is the law of Christianity. The New Testament is all the law of Christianity. The New Testament always will be all the law of Christianity."

Baptists hold that this law of Christianity, the Word of God, is the unchangeable and only law of Christ's reign, and that whatever is not found in the law cannot be bound on the consciences of men, and that this law is a sacred deposit, an inviolable trust, which Christ's friends are commissioned to guard and perpetuate wherever it may lead and whatever may be the cost of such trusteeship.

Exact Opposite of Catholicism

The Baptist message and the Roman Catholic message are the very antipodes of each other. The Roman Catholic message is sacerdotal, sacramentarian and ecclesiastical. In its scheme of salvation it magnifies the church, the priest, and the sacraments. The Baptist message is non-sacerdotal, non-sacramentarian, and non-ecclesiastical. Its teaching is that the one High Priest for sinful humanity has entered into the holy place for all, that the veil is forever rent in twain, that the mercy seat is uncovered and open to all, and that the humblest soul in all the world if only he be penitent, may enter with all boldness and cast himself upon God. The Catholic doctrine of baptismal regeneration and transubstantiation are to the Baptist mind fundamentally subversive of the spiritual realities of the gospel of Christ. Likewise, the Catholic conception of the church, thrusting all its complex and cumbrous machinery between the soul and God, prescribing beliefs, claiming to exercise the power of the keys, and to control the channels of grace—all such lording it over the consciences of men is to the Baptist mind a ghastly tyranny in the realm of the soul and tends to frustrate the grace of God, to destroy freedom of conscience and terribly to hinder the coming of the Kingdom of God.

Papal Infallibility or the New Testament

That was a memorable hour in the Vatican Council, in 1870, when the dogma of papal infallibility was passed by a majority vote. You recall that in the midst of all the tenseness and tumult of that excited assemblage, Cardinal Manning stood on an elevated platform, and in the midst of that assemblage, and holding in his hand the paper just passed, declaring for the infallibility of the Pope, said: "Let all the world go to bits and we will reconstruct it on this paper." A Baptist smiles at such an announcement as that, but not in derision and scorn. Although the Baptist is the very antithesis of his Catholic neighbour in religious conceptions and contentions, yet the Baptist will whole-heartedly contend that his Catholic neighbour shall have his candles and incense and sanctus bell and rosary, and whatever else he wishes in the expression of his worship. A Baptist would rise at midnight to plead for absolute religious liberty for his Catholic neighbour, and for his Jewish neighbour, and for everybody else. But what is the answer of a Baptist to the contention made by the Catholic for papal infallibility? Holding aloft a little book, the name of which is the New Testament, and without any hesitation or doubt, the Baptist shouts his battle cry: "Let all the world go to bits and we will reconstruct it on the New Testament."

Direct Individual Approach to God

When we turn to this New Testament, which is Christ's guidebook and law for His people, we find that supreme emphasis is everywhere put upon the individual. The individual is segregated from family, from church, from state, and from society, from dearest earthly friends or institution, and brought into direct, personal dealings with God. Every one must give account of himself to God. There can be no sponsors or deputies or proxies in such a vital matter. Each one must repent for himself, and believe for himself, and be baptized for himself, and answer to God for himself, both in time and in eternity. One man can no more repent and believe and obey Christ for another than he can take the other's place at God's judgment bar. Neither persons nor institutions, however dear and powerful, may dare to come between the individual soul and God. "There is one mediator between God and men, the man Christ Jesus." Let the state and the church, let the institution, however dear, and the person, however near, stand aside, and let the individual soul make its own direct and immediate response to God. One is our pontiff, and his name is Jesus. The undelegated sovereignty of Christ makes it forever impossible for His saving grace to be manipulated by any system of human mediation whatsoever.

The right of private judgment is the crown jewel of humanity, and for any person or institution to dare to come between the soul and God is a blasphemous impertinence and a defamation of the crown rights of the Son of God.

Out of these two fundamental principles, the supreme authority of the Scriptures and the right of private judgment, have come all the historic protests in Europe and England and America against unscriptural creeds, polity and rites, and against the unwarranted and impertinent assumption of religious authority over men's consciences, whether by church or by state. Baptists regard as an enormity any attempt to force the conscience, or to constrain men, by outward penalties, to this or that form of religious belief. Persecution may make men hypocrites, but it will not make them Christians.

Infant Baptism Unthinkable

It follows, inevitably, that Baptists are unalterably opposed to every form of sponsorial religion. If I have fellow Christians in this presence today who are the protagonists of infant baptism, they will allow me frankly to say, and certainly I would say it in the most fraternal, Christian spirit, that to Baptists infant baptism is unthinkable from every viewpoint. First of all, Baptists do not find the slightest sanction for infant baptism in the Word of God. That fact, to Baptists, makes infant baptism a most serious question for the consideration of the whole Christian world. Nor is that all. As Baptists see it, infant baptism tends to ritualize Christianity and reduce it to lifeless forms. It tends also and inevitably, as Baptists see it, to the secularizing of the church and to the blurring and blotting out of the line of demarcation between the church and the unsaved world.

And since I have thus spoken with unreserved frankness, my honored Pedo-baptist friends in the audience will allow me to say that Baptists solemnly believe that infant baptism, with its implications, has flooded the world and floods it now with untold evils.

They believe also that it perverts the Scriptural symbolism of baptism; that it attempts the impossible task of performing an act of religious obedience by proxy, and that since it forestalls the individual initiative of the child, it carries within it the germ of persecution, and lays the predicate for the union of church and state, and that it is a Romish tradition and a corner stone for the whole system of popery throughout the world.

I will speak yet another frank word for my beloved Baptist people, to our cherished fellow Christians who are not Baptists, and that word is that our Baptist people believe that if all the Protestant denominations would once for all put away infant baptism, and come to the full acceptance and faithful practice of New Testament baptism, the unity of all the non-Catholic Christians in the world quickly would be consummated.

Surely, in the face of these frank statements, our non-Baptist neighbours may apprehend something of the difficulties compelling Baptists when they are asked to enter into official alliances with those who hold such fundamentally different views from those just indicated. We call God to witness that our Baptist people have an unutterable longing for Christian union, and believe Christian union will come, but we are compelled to insist that if this union is to be real and effective, it must be based upon a clear understanding of the Word of God and a complete loyalty to the will of Christ as revealed in his Word.

The Ordinances Are Symbols

Again, to Baptists, the New Testament teaches that salvation through Christ must precede membership in His church, and must precede the observance of the two ordinances in His church, namely, baptism and the Lord's Supper. These ordinances are for the saved and only for the saved. These two ordinances are not sacramental, but symbolic. They are teaching ordinances, portraying in symbol truths of immeasurable and everlasting moment to humanity. To trifle with these symbols, to pervert their forms and at the same time to pervert the truths they are designed to symbolize, is indeed a most serious matter. Without ceasing and without wavering, Baptists are, in conscience, compelled to contend that these two teaching ordinances shall be maintained in the churches just as they were placed there in the wisdom and authority of Christ. To change these two meaningful symbols is to change their Scriptural intent and content, and thus pervert them, and we solemnly believe, to be the carriers of the most deadly heresies. By our loyalty to Christ, which we hold to be the supreme test of our friendship for Him, we must unyieldingly contend for these two ordinances as they were originally given to Christ's churches.

To Baptists, the New Testament also clearly teaches that Christ's church is not only a spiritual body but it is also a pure democracy, all its members being equal, a local congregation, and cannot subject itself to any outside control. Such terms, therefore, as "The American Church," or "The bishop of this city or state," sound strangely incongruous to Baptist ears. In the very nature of the case, also, there must be no union between church and state, because their nature and functions are utterly different. Jesus stated the principle in the two sayings, "My kingdom is not of this world," and "Render unto Caesar the things that are Caesar's, and unto God the things that are God's." Never, anywhere, in any clime, has a true Baptist been willing, for one minute, for the union of church and state, never for a moment.

A Free Church in a Free State

Every state church on the earth is a spiritual tyranny. The utterance of Jesus, "Render unto Caesar the things that are Caesar's, and unto God the things that are God's," is one of the most revolutionary and history-making utterances that ever fell from those lips divine. That utterance, once for all, marked the divorcement of church and state. It marked a new era for the creeds and deeds of men. It was the sunrise gun of a new day, the echoes of which are to go on and on until in every land, whether great or small, the doctrine shall have absolute supremacy everywhere of a free church in a free state.

In behalf of our Baptist people I am compelled to say that forgetfulness of the principles that I have just enumerated, in our judgment, explains many of the religious ills that now afflict the world. All went well with the early churches in their earlier days. They were incomparably triumphant days for the Christian faith. Those early disciples of Jesus, without prestige and worldly power, yet aflame with the love of God and the passion of Christ, went out and shook the pagan Roman Empire from centre to circumference, in an amazingly brief time.

An Incomparable Apostasy

Presently there came an incomparable apostasy in the realm of religion, which shrouded the world in spiritual night through long hundreds of years. Constantine, the Emperor, saw something in the religion of Christ's people which awakened his interest, and now we see him uniting religion to the state and marching up the marble steps of the Emperor's palace, with the church robed in purple. Then and there was begun the most baneful misalliance that ever fettered and cursed a suffering world. For long centuries, even from Constantine to Pope Gregory VII, the conflict between church and state waxed stronger and stronger, and the encroachments and usurpations became more deadly and devastating. When Christianity first found its way into the city of the Caesars it lived in cellars and alleys, but when Constantine crowned the union of church and state, the church was stamped with the impress of the Roman idea and fanned with the spirit of the Caesars. Soon we see a Pope emerging, who himself became a Caesar, and soon a group of councillors may be seen gathered around this Pope, and the supreme power of the church is assumed by the Pope and his councillors.

The long, blighting record of the medieval ages is simply the working out of that idea. The Pope ere long assumed to be the monarch of the world, making the astounding claim that all kings and potentates were subject unto him. By and by when Pope Gregory VII, better known as Hildebrand, appears, his assumptions are still more astounding. In him the spirit of the Roman church became incarnate and triumphant. He lorded it over parliaments and council chambers, having statesmen to do his bidding, and creating and deposing kings at his will. For example, when the Emperor Henry offended Hildebrand, the latter pronounced against Henry a sentence not only of excommunication but of deposition as Emperor, releasing all Christians from allegiance to him. He made the Emperor do penance by standing in the snow with his bare feet at Canossa, and he wrote his famous letter to William the Conqueror to the effect that the state was subordinate to the church, that the power of the state as compared to the church was as the moon compared to the sun.

This explains the famous saying of Bismarck when Chancellor of Germany, to the German Parliament: "We will never go to Canossa again." Whoever favours the authority of the church over the state favours the way of Canossa.

When, in the fulness of time, Columbus discovered America, the Pope calmly announced that he would divide the New World into two parts, giving one part to the King of Spain and the other to the King of Portugal. And not only did this great consolidated ecclesiasticism assume to lord it over men's earthly treasures, but they lorded it over men's minds, prescribing what men should think and read and write. Nor did such assumption stop with the things of this world, but it laid its hand on the next world, and claimed to have in its possession the keys of the kingdom of heaven and the kingdom of purgatory so that it could shut men out of heaven or lift them out of purgatory, thus surpassing in the sweep of its power and in the pride of its autocracy the boldest and most presumptuous ruler that ever sat on a civil throne.

Absolutism vs. Individualism

The student of history cannot fail to observe that through the long years two ideas have been in endless antagonism—the idea of absolutism and the idea of individualism, the idea of autocracy and the idea of democracy. The idea of autocracy is that supreme power is vested in the few, who, in turn, delegate this power to the many. That was the dominant idea of the Roman Empire, and upon that idea the Caesars built their throne. That idea has found world-wide expression in the realms both civil and ecclesiastical. Often have the two ideas, absolutism versus individualism, autocracy versus democracy, met in battle. Autocracy dared, in the morning of the twentieth century, to crawl out of its ugly lair and to propose to substitute the law of the jungle for the law of human brotherhood. For all time to come the hearts of men will stand aghast upon every thought of this incomparable death drama, and at the same time they will renew the vow that the few shall not presumptuously tyrannize over the many; that the law of human brotherhood and not the law of the jungle shall be given supremacy in all human affairs. And until the principle of democracy, rather than the principle of autocracy, shall be regnant in the realm of religion, our mission shall be commanding and unending.

The Reformation Incomplete

The coming of the sixteenth century was the dawning of a new hope for the world. With that century came the Protestant Reformation. Yonder goes Luther with his theses, which he nails over the old church door in Wittenberg, and the echoes of the mighty deed shake the Papacy, shake Europe, shake the whole world. Luther was joined by Melancthon and Calvin and Zwingli and other mighty leaders. Just at this point emerges one of the most outstanding anomalies of all history. Although Luther and his compeers protested vigorously against the errors of Rome, yet when these mighty men came out of Rome, and mighty men they were, they brought with them some of the grievous errors of Rome. The Protestant Reformation of the sixteenth century was sadly incomplete—it was a case of arrested development. Although Luther and his compeers grandly sounded out the battle cry of justification by faith alone, yet they retained the doctrine of infant baptism and a state church. They shrank from the logical conclusions of their own theses.

In Zurich there stands a statue in honour of Zwingli, in which he is represented with a Bible in one hand and a sword in the other. That statue was the symbol of the union between church and state. The same statue might have been reared to Luther and his fellow reformers. Luther and Melancthon fastened a state church upon Germany, and Zwingli fastened it upon Switzerland. Knox and his associates fastened it upon Scotland. Henry VIII bound it upon England, where it remains even till this very hour.

These mighty reformers turned out to be persecutors like the Papacy before them. Luther unloosed the dogs of persecution against the struggling and faithful Anabaptists. Calvin burned Servetus, and to such awful deed Melancthon gave his approval. Louis XIV revoked the Edict of

Nantes, shut the doors of all the Protestant churches, and outlawed the Huguenots, Germany put to death that mighty Baptist leader, Balthasar Hubmaier, while Holland killed her noblest statesman, John of Barneveldt, and condemned to life imprisonment her ablest historian, Hugo Grotius, for conscience's sake. In England, John Bunyan was kept in jail for twelve long, weary years because of his religion, and when we cross the mighty ocean separating the Old World and the New, we find the early pages of American history crimsoned with the stories of religious persecutions. The early colonies of America were the forum of the working out of the most epochal battles that earth ever knew for the triumph of religious and civil liberty.

America and Religious and Civil Liberty

Just a brief glance at the struggle in those early colonies must now suffice us. Yonder in Massachusetts, Henry Dunster, the first president of Harvard, was removed from the presidency because he objected to infant baptism. Roger Williams was banished, John Clarke was put in prison, and they publicly whipped Obadiah Holmes on Boston Common. In Connecticut the lands of our Baptist fathers were confiscated and their goods sold to build a meeting house and support a preacher of another denomination. In old Virginia, "mother of states and statesmen," the battle for religious and civil liberty was waged all over her nobly historic territory, and the final triumph recorded there was such as to write imperishable glory upon the name of Virginia until the last syllable of recorded time. Fines and imprisonments and persecutions were everywhere in evidence in Virginia for conscience's sake. If you would see a record incomparably interesting, go read the early statutes in Virginia concerning the Established Church and religion, and trace the epic story of the history-making struggles of that early day. If the historic records are to be accredited, those clergymen of the Established Church in Virginia made terrible inroads in collecting fines in Baptist tobacco in that early day. It is quite evident, however, that they did not get all the tobacco.

On and on was the struggle waged by our Baptist fathers for religious liberty in Virginia, in the Carolinas, in Georgia, in Rhode Island, and Massachusetts, and Connecticut, and elsewhere, with one unyielding contention for unrestricted religious liberty for all men, and with never one wavering note. They dared to be odd, to stand alone, to refuse to conform, though it cost them suffering and even life itself. They dared to defy traditions and customs, and deliberately chose the way of non-conformity, even though in many a case it meant persecutions and punishments. They pleaded and suffered, they offered their protests and remonstrances and memorials; and, thank God, mighty statesmen were won to their contention, Washington and Jefferson and Madison and Patrick Henry, and many others, until at last it was written into our country's Constitution that church and state must in this land be forever separate and free, that neither must ever trespass upon the distinctive functions of the other. It was pre-eminently a Baptist achievement.

Glad are our Baptist people to pay their grateful tribute to their fellow Christians of other religious communions for all their sympathy and help in this sublime achievement. Candor compels me to repeat that much of the sympathy of other religious leaders in that early struggle was on the side of legalized, ecclesiastical privilege. Much of the time were Baptists pitiably lonely in their age-long struggle. We would now and always make our most grateful acknowledgement to any and all who came to the side of our Baptist fathers, whether early or late, in this destiny-determining struggle. But I take it that every informed man on the subject, whatever his religious faith, will be willing to pay tribute to our Baptist people as being the chief instrumentality in God's hands in winning the battle in America for religious liberty. Do you recall Tennyson's poem, in which he sets out the history of the seed of freedom? Catch its philosophy:

> Once in a golden hour,
>   I cast to earth a seed,
> Up there came a flower,
>   The people said, a weed.
>
> To and fro they went,
>   Through my garden bower,
> And muttering discontent,
>   Cursed me and my flower.
>
> Then it grew so tall,
>   It wore a crown of light,
> But thieves from o'er the wall,
>   Stole the seed by night.
>
> Sowed it far and wide,
>   By every town and tower,

> Till all the people cried,
>   "Splendid is the flower."
>
> Read my little fable:
>   He who runs may read,
> Most can grow the flowers now,
>   For all have got the seed.

Very well, we are very happy for all our fellow religionists of every denomination and creed to have this splendid flower of religious liberty, but you will allow us to remind you that you got the seed in our Baptist garden. We are very happy for you to have it; now let us all make the best of it and the most of it.

The Present Call

And now, my fellow Christians, and fellow citizens, what is the present call to us in connection with the priceless principle of religious liberty? That principle, with all the history and heritage accompanying it, imposes upon us obligations to the last degree meaningful and responsible. Let us today and forever be highly resolved that the principle of religious liberty shall, please God, be preserved inviolate through all our days and the days of those who come after us. Liberty has both its perils and its obligations. We are to see to it that our attitude toward Liberty, both religious and civil, both as Christians and as citizens, is an attitude consistent and constructive and worthy. We are to "Render unto Caesar the things that are Caesar's, and unto God the things that are God's:" We are members of the two realms, the civil and the religious, and are faithfully to render unto each all that each should receive at our hands; we are to be alertly watchful, day and night, that liberty, both religious and civil, shall be nowhere prostituted and mistreated. Every pervasion and misuse of liberty tends by that much to jeopardize both church and state.

There comes now the clarion call to us to be the right kind of citizens. Happily, the record of our Baptist people toward civil government has been a record of unfading honour. Their love and loyalty to country have not been put to shame in any land. In the long list of published Tories in connection with the Revolutionary War there was not one Baptist name.

Liberty Not Abused

It behooves us now and ever to see to it that liberty is not abused. Well may we listen to the call of Paul, that mightiest Christian of the long centuries, as he says: "Brethren, ye have been called unto liberty; only use not liberty for an occasion to the flesh, but by love serve one another." This ringing declaration should be heard and heeded by every class and condition of people throughout all our wide-stretching nation.

It is the word to be heeded by religious teachers, and by editors, and by legislators, and by everybody else. Nowhere is liberty to be used "for an occasion to the flesh." We will take free speech and a free press, with all their excrescences and perils, because of the high meaning of freedom, but we are to set ourselves with all diligence not to use these great privileges in the shaming of liberty. A free press—how often does it pervert its high privilege! Again and again, it may be seen dragging itself through all the sewers of the social order, bringing to light the moral cancers and leprosies of our poor world and glaringly exhibiting them to the gaze even of responsive youth and childhood. The editor's task, whether in the realm of church or state, is an immeasurably responsible one. These editors, side by side with the moral and religious teachers of the country, are so to magnify the ballot box, a free press, free schools, the courts, the majesty of law and reverence for all properly accredited authority that our civilization may not be built on the shifting sands, but on the secure and enduring foundations of righteousness.

Let us remember that lawlessness, wherever found and whatever its form, is as the pestilence that walketh in darkness and the destruction that wasteth at noon day. Let us remember that he who is willing for law to be violated is an offender against the majesty of law as really as he who actually violates law. The spirit of law is the spirit of civilization. Liberty without law is anarchy. Liberty against law is rebellion. Liberty limited by law is the formula of civilization.

Humane and Righteous Laws

Challenging to the highest degree is the call that comes to legislators. They are to see to it continually, in all their legislative efforts, that their supreme concern is for the highest welfare of the people. Laws humane and righteous are to be fashioned and then to be faithfully enforced. Men are playing with fire if they lightly fashion their country's laws and then trifle in their obedience to such laws. Indeed, all citizens, the humblest and the most prominent alike, are called to give their best thought to the maintenance of righteousness everywhere. Much truth is there in the widely quoted saying: "Our country is afflicted with the bad citizenship of good men." The saying points its own clear lesson. "When the righteous are in authority, the people rejoice, but when the wicked bear rule, the people mourn." The people, all the people, are inexorably responsible for the laws, the ideals, and the spirit that are necessary for the making of a great and enduring civilization. Every man of us is to remember that it is righteousness that exalteth a nation, and that it is sin that reproaches and destroys a nation.

God does not raise up a nation to go selfishly strutting and forgetful of the high interests of humanity. National selfishness leads to destruction as truly as does individual selfishness. Nations can no more live to themselves than can individuals. Humanity is bound up together in the big bundle of life. The world is now one big neighbourhood. There are no longer any hermit nations. National isolation is no longer possible in the earth. The markets of the world instantly register every commercial change. An earthquake in Asia is at once registered in Washington City. The people on one side of the world may not dare to be indifferent to the people on the other side. Every man of us is called to be a world citizen, and to think and act in world terms. The nation that insists upon asking that old murderous question of Cain, "Am I my brother's keeper?"—the question of the profiteer and the question of the slacker—is a nation marked for decay and doom and death. The parable of the good Samaritan is heaven's law for nations as well as for individuals. Some things are worth dying for, and if they are worth dying for they are worth living for. The poet was right when he sang:

> Though love repine and reason chafe,
>   There comes a voice without reply,
> 'Tis man's perdition to be safe,
>   When for the truth he ought to die.

Things Worth Dying For

When this nation went into the world war a little while ago, after her long and patient and fruitless effort to find another way of conserving righteousness, the note was sounded in every nook and corner of our country that some things in this world are worth dying for, and if they are worth dying for they are worth living for. What are some of the things worth dying for? The sanctity of womanhood is worth dying for. The safety of childhood is worth dying for, and when Germany put to death that first helpless Belgian child she was marked for defeat and doom. The integrity of one's country is worth dying for. And, please God, the freedom and honour of the United States of America are worth dying for. If the great things of life are worth dying for, they are surely worth living for. Our great country may not dare to isolate herself from the rest of the world, and selfishly say: "We propose to live and to die to ourselves, leaving all the other nations with their weaknesses and burdens and sufferings to go their ways without our help." This nation cannot pursue any such policy and expect the favour of God. Myriads of voices, both from the living and the dead, summon us to a higher and better way. Happy am I to believe that God has his prophets not only in the pulpits of the churches but also in the school room, in the editor's chair, in the halls of legislation, in the marts of commerce, in the realms of literature. Tennyson was a prophet, when in "Locksley Hall," he sang:

> For I dipped into the future, far as human eye could see,
> Saw the vision of the world, and all the wonder that would be;
>
> Saw the heavens filled with commerce, argosies of magic sails,
> Pilots of the purple twilight, dropping down with costly bales;
>
> Heard the heavens filled with shouting, and there rained a ghastly dew
> From the nation's airy navies, grappling in the central blue;
>
> Far along the world-wide whisper of the south wind rushing warm,
> With the standards of the people plunging through the thunder storm.
>
> Till the war drums throbbed no longer, and the battleflags were furled,
> In the Parliament of Man, the Federation of the World.

A League of Nations

Tennyson believed in a league of nations, and well might he so believe, because God is on his righteous throne, and inflexible are his purposes touching righteousness and peace for a weary, sinning, suffering, dying world. Standing here today on the steps of our Nation's capitol, hard by the chamber of the Senate of the United States, I dare to say as a citizen and as a Christian teacher, that the moral forces of the United States of America, without regard to political parties, will never rest until there is a worthy League of Nations. I dare to express also the unhesitating belief that the unquestioned majorities of both great political parties in this country regard the delay in the working out of a League of Nations as a national and world-wide tragedy.

I can certify the men of all political parties, without any reference to partisan politics, that the same moral and religious forces of this country, because of the inexorable moral issues involved, cannot be silent and will not be silent until there is put forth a League of Nations that will strive with all its might to put an end to the diabolism and measureless horrors of war. I thank God that the stricken man yonder in the White House has pleaded long and is pleading yet that our nation will take her full part with the others for the bringing in of that blessed day when wars shall cease to the ends of the earth.

The recent World War calls to us with a voice surpassingly appealing and responsible. Surely Alfred Noyes voices the true desire for us:

> Make firm, O God, the peace our dead have won,
>   For folly shakes the tinsel on its head,
> And points us back to darkness and to hell,
>   Cackling, "Beware of visions," while our dead
> Still cry, "It was for visions that we fell."
>
> They never knew the secret game of power,
>   All that this earth can give they thrust aside,
> They crowded all their youth into an hour,
>   And for fleeting dream of right, they died.
>
> Oh, if we fail them in that awful trust,
>   How should we bear those voices from the dust?

The Right Kind of Christians

This noble doctrine and heritage of religious liberty calls to us imperiously to be the right kind of Christians. Let us never forget that a democracy, whether civil or religious, has not only its perils, but has also its unescapable obligations. A democracy calls for intelligence. The sure foundations of states must be laid, not in ignorance, but in knowledge. It is of first importance that those who rule shall be properly trained. In a democracy, a government of the people, for the people, and by the people, the people are the rulers, and the people, all the people, are to be informed and trained.

My fellow Christians, we must hark back to our Christian schools, and see to it that these schools are put on worthy and enduring foundations. A democracy needs more than intelligence; it needs Christ. He is the light of the world, nor is there any other sufficient light for the world. He is the solution of the world's complex questions, the one adequate helper for its dire needs, the one only sufficient Saviour for our sinning race. Our schools are afresh to take note of this supreme fact, and they are to be fundamentally and aggressively Christian. Wrong education brought on the recent World War. Such education will always lead to disaster.

Pungent were the recent words of Mr. Lloyd George: "The most formidable foe that we had to fight in Germany was not the arsenals of Krupp, but the schools of Germany." The educational center of the world will no longer be in the Old World, but because of the great War, such a center will henceforth be in this New World of America. We must build here institutions of learning that will be shot through and through with the principles and motives of Christ, the one Master over all mankind.

The Christian School

The time has come when, as never before, our beloved denomination should worthily go out to its world task as a teaching denomination. That means that there should be a crusade throughout all our borders for the vitalizing and strengthening of our Christian schools. The only complete education, in the nature of the case, is Christian education, because man is a tripartite being. By the very genius of our government, education by the state cannot be complete. Wisdom has fled from us if we fail to magnify, and magnify now, our Christian schools. These schools go to the foundation of all the life of the people. They are indispensable to the highest efficiency of the churches. Their inspirational influences are of untold value to the schools conducted by the state, to which schools also we must ever give our best support. It matters very much, do you not agree, who shall be the leaders, and what the standards in the affairs of civil government and in the realm of business life? One recalls the pithy saying of Napoleon to Marshal Ney: "An army of deer led by a lion is better than an army of lions led by a deer." Our Christian schools are to train not only our religious leaders but hosts of our leaders in the civil and business realms as well.

The one transcending, inspiring influence in civilization is the Christian religion. By all means, let the teachers and trustees and student bodies of all our Christian schools remember this important fact, that civilization without Christianity is doomed. Let there be no pagan ideals in our Christian schools, and no hesitation or apology for the insistence that the one hope for the individual, the one hope for society, for civilization, is in the Christian religion. If ever the drumbeat of duty sounded clearly, it is calling to us now to strengthen and magnify our Christian schools.

The Task of Evangelism

Preceding and accompanying the task of building our Christian schools, we must keep faithfully and practically in mind the primary task of evangelism, the work of winning souls from sin unto salvation, from Satan unto God. This work takes precedence of all other work in the Christian program. Salvation for sinners is through Jesus Christ alone, nor is there any other name or way under heaven whereby they may be saved. Our churches, our schools, our religious papers, our hospitals, every organization and agency of the churches should be kept aflame with the passion of New Testament evangelism. Our cities and towns and villages and country places are to echo continually with the sermons and songs of the gospel evangel. The people, high and low, rich and poor, the foreigners, all the people are to be faithfully told of Jesus and his great salvation, and entreated to come unto him to be saved by him and to become his fellow workers. The only sufficient solvent for all the questions in America, individual, social, economic, industrial, financial, political, educational, moral, and religious, is to be found in the Saviourhood and Lordship of Jesus Christ.

Give us a watchword for the hour,
A thrilling word, a word of power;
A battle cry, a flaming breath,
That calls to conquest or to death;
A word to rouse the church from rest,
To heed its Master's high behest,
The call is given, Ye hosts, arise;
Our watchword is Evangelize!

The glad Evangel now proclaim,
Through all the earth in Jesus' name,
This word is ringing through the skies,
Evangelize! Evangelize!
To dying men, a fallen race,
Make known the gift of gospel grace;
The world that now in darkness lies,
Evangelize! Evangelize!

While thus caring for the homeland, we are at the same time to see to it that our program is co-extensive with Christ's program for the whole world. The whole world is our field, nor may we, with impunity, dare to be indifferent to any section, however remote, not a whit less than that, and with our plans sweeping the whole earth, we are to go forth with believing faith and obedient service, seeking to bring all humanity, both near and far, to the faith and service of him who came to be the propitiation of our sins, and not for ours only, but also for the sins of the whole world.

His commission covers the whole world and reaches to every human being. Souls in China, and India, and Japan, and Europe, and Africa, and the islands of the sea, are as precious to him as souls in the United States. By the love we bear our Saviour, by the love we bear our fellows, by the greatness and preciousness of the trust committed to us, we are bound to take all the world upon our hearts and to consecrate our utmost strength to bring all humanity under the sway of Christ's redeeming love. Let us go to such task, saying with the immortal Wesley, "The world is my parish," and with him may we also be able to say, "And best of all, God is with us."

Let us look again to the strange passion and power of the early Christians. They paid the price for spiritual power. Mark well this record: "And they overcame him by the blood of the Lamb, and by the word of their testimony; and they loved not their lives unto the death." O my fellow Christians, if we are to be in the true succession of the mighty days and deeds of the early Christian era, or of those mighty days and deeds of our Baptist fathers in later days, then selfish ease must be utterly renounced for Christ and his cause, and our every gift and grace and power must be utterly dominated by the dynamic of his cross. Standing here in the shadow of our country's capitol, compassed about as we are with so great a cloud of witnesses, let us today renew our pledge to God, and to one another, that we will give our best to church and state, to God and to humanity, by his grace and power, until we fall on the last sleep.

If in such spirit we give ourselves to all the duties that await us, then we may go our ways, singing more vehemently than our fathers sang them, those lines of Whittier:

> Our fathers to their graves have gone,
> Their strife is passed, their triumphs won;
> But greater tasks await the race
> Which comes to take their honoured place,
> A moral warfare with the crime
> And folly of an evil time.

456 Southern Baptist Preaching Yesterday

So let it be, in God's own sight,
We gird us for the coming fight;
And strong in him whose cause is ours,
In conflict with unholy powers,
We grasp the weapons he has given,
The light and truth and love of heaven.

W. O. Vaught, Jr.
Passing Through the Midst of Them

But he passing through the midst of them went his way (Luke 4:30).

For many months now a great text has been burning its way into my mind and heart. I do not know why this text has lingered for so long. Perchance through it God is trying to say something to me and to you about the great opportunity which is now ours. It is entirely possible that those who come after us may sit amid the chaos of what is now our Western civilization and vainly wish to have back again the opportunities which are now ours.

I sat only recently in a great congregation of at least five thousand of our Southern Baptist preachers. In this group were preachers from the city and preachers from the country, preachers with little or no formal theological education, and preachers with the best training our schools can afford. As I surveyed the faces of these earnest men and thought of the tremendous task with which they are burdened in our modern world, our text again flashed upon my mind and heart—"But he passing through the midst of them went his way" (Luke 4:30).

I began to ask myself the question, "Why is this text haunting my mind and thoughts?" Certainly, as I survey the church and the work of the ministry among our Southern Baptist denomination, I have no reason to believe that we are headed for failure. Indeed, this is a day of successful church programs, bigger and better church buildings, mounting church budgets, and more efficient and effective church organizations. But somehow this text keeps coming back and I ask myself this question, "Is it possible for us to succeed and yet find that in the midst of our success Christ has passed through our midst and has gone on his way to establish his kingdom?"

It Happened in Nazareth

I am sure you recall that arresting Scripture passage in the fourth chapter of Luke where we read:

> He came to Nazareth, where he had been brought up: and, as his custom was, he went into the synagogue on the sabbath day, and stood up for to read. . . . there was delivered unto him the book of the prophet Esaias. . . . when he had opened the book, he found the place where it was written, The Spirit of the Lord is upon me, because he hath anointed me to preach the gospel to the poor; he hath sent me to heal the brokenhearted, to preach deliverance to the captives, and recovering of sight to the blind, to set at liberty them that are bruised, to preach the acceptable year of the Lord. . . . he closed the book, and he gave it again to the minister, and sat down. . . . the eyes of all them that were in the synagogue were fastened on him. . . . he began to say unto them, This day is this scripture fulfilled in your ears (vv. 16-21).

That day in the Nazareth synagogue Jesus announced his program of world conquest. What he said that day was so far-reaching, so breathtaking, and so all-inclusive that the provincial minds of Nazareth were not prepared to accept him. They had never seen beyond the limits of their city and their nation. Their sympathy was confined to the narrow limits of clan and kin. Their minds had never comprehended any extensive salvation. The kingdom of God on earth had no part in their limited thinking. But that day in the Nazareth synagogue, Jesus presented them with a high order founded on giving, love, brotherhood, and good will. Here was a gospel which confronted their complacency, their greed, their selfishness, their exploitation, and their unbrotherliness.

I do not believe that I am exaggerating the point when I say that Christ's program, announced in the Nazareth synagogue, stunned his listeners. They would certainly ask the question, "Can any good thing come out of Nazareth?" In their own words they said, "Is not this Joseph's son?" No one who had worked in their city and had grown up in their community would be able to teach them. Their ears were stopped, and their eyes were closed. Rebelling quickly against such a breath-taking program, they led Jesus to the brow of the hill on which their city was built and were bent on casting him down headlong. But his hour had not yet come.

When I was a lad, I remember hearing a preacher describe this incident. He told how Christ hid himself and slipped away from them before they were able to throw him down the steep cliff. For many years I thought that this was an accurate explanation of what really happened, but such is far from the truth. That day in Nazareth, on the hillside of his city, Jesus did not hide himself. Neither did he slip away out of their midst. He simply turned and looked at them. As he gazed into their eyes, they saw something in him that they had never seen in the life of another man. Within his soul was the determination and the power to accomplish the program which he had announced. The power that was with him was greater than the power that was with them. And as they reached out their hands to destroy him, they found that their hands were powerless. As they were intent on his destruction, he passed through the midst of them and went his way—went his way to establish his kingdom in the hearts of men.

Far removed from that Nazareth synagogue, we stand facing our modern world of the twentieth century. Many in our day have sought to bow Jesus off the stage. They say, "Surely nothing he announced in the Nazareth synagogue could have any bearing on the needs of our modern world." Yet, the Christ of the Nazareth synagogue is back again, confronting us. His program as announced that day in Nazareth faces us still. Will we be big enough to accept his program and establish his kingdom, or will he pass through the midst of us and go his way?

The Fire of His Judgment

Seeking to find perspective in this event in Nazareth, let us look at that last memorable week that Jesus spent on the earth before his crucifixion. On that never-to-be-forgotten Sunday before the crucifixion, we read that Jesus entered Jerusalem in triumph. He had come to Jerusalem quite often unnoticed and without pretense. In fact, in the past he had hidden himself often, shunning publicity among the multitudes. On this occasion, however, he entered the city in majestic triumph. In this triumphal entry we see him drawing attention to himself, compelling the whole city to gaze upon him as the King. Riding on a colt brought to him, Jesus entered the city as the meek King. Mark tells us:

> Many spread their garments in the way: and others cut down branches off the trees, and strawed them in the way. . . . they that went before, and they that followed, cried, saying, Hosanna; Blessed is he that cometh in the

name of the Lord: Blessed be the kingdom of our father David, that cometh in the name of the Lord: Hosanna in the highest (11:8-10).

And when someone suggested that such a demonstration should not have been given to his entry, Jesus replied, "I tell you that, if these should hold their peace, the stones would immediately cry out" (Luke 19:40).

That day of the triumphal entry into Jerusalem, we read that all the city was stirred until they said, "Who is this?" We are justified in concluding that Jesus thrust himself openly and publicly out before the whole city so that they should see him enter as King. In the midst of his teaching in the Temple that day, we also read, "He looked round about on all things." It was the look of investigation; it was the look of inquisition. He was looking as one who had the right to look, one with supreme and final authority. I am also quite sure that there were tears in his eyes as he looked, for it was a look of infinite compassion.

As the next day dawned, Jesus found himself entering Jerusalem again with his disciples. As they journeyed near the city they saw a fig tree covered with leaves. Though the fig tree was prematurely covered with leaves, there was no indication of fruit. It was a barren tree. The tree was a celebrated failure. As Jesus saw the fig tree with leaves but no fruit, he cursed the fig tree that day, saying, "No man eat fruit of thee hereafter forever."

As they entered the city of Jerusalem that day, Jesus went into the Temple and cleansed it. As a result of his investigation, he cleansed it because he had found it to be a den of robbers. He opened the cages of the doves and let them fly away. He opened the pens of the sheep and the oxen and drove them from the Temple. He turned over the tables used by the money changers and warned them to flee from his Father's house. With majestic dignity he announced to the people that this was his Father's house. His Father's house was to be a place of prayer, but they had made it a den of thieves.

On the following day, Jesus and his disciples entered Jerusalem again, and they found that the fig tree which had received his curse had withered from the roots. What Jesus had seen in a fruitless tree, he had seen in a fruitless nation. Like the fig tree which had failed to produce any fruit, so the nation had failed to produce any faith. When his disciples asked Jesus for an explanation of his actions, he exclaimed, "Have faith in God." The answer to failure is faith. Christ found faith missing in the Temple and in the men who had made his Temple a den of robbers.

These money changers, some contemporary writers tell us, were so nefarious in their practices that their witness was refused in a court of law.
All of this they were doing in the name of religion, and Christ cleansed
their Temple and condemned them because their lives were fruitless
lives—faithless lives.

We go back to Nazareth to the synagogue when he officially began his
public ministry, and we connect what happened in the synagogue at Nazareth with what happened in the Temple in Jerusalem five days before his
crucifixion. He passed through their midst at Nazareth, for their little
molds would not hold the breadth of his soul and the compassion of his
heart. Three years later in Jerusalem he continued to pass through their
midst, going on his way to establish his kingdom.

Big Questions

The question keeps coming back, haunting my mind. Will he pass
through the midst of us as he passed through their midst at Nazareth? I
wonder! I simply ask the question—I ask your heart to answer it. I remember again that our churches are bigger than ever before, our programs apparently more successful, money given adds up to larger sums,
church membership in the United States is at an all-time high, more missionaries have gone afield than ever before, the gospel is being preached
in the whole world. There are many indications of the coming of the
kingdom, but with all this advancement there is a paralysis gripping the
church beyond anything we have known before. Could it be that so-
called human success might be divine failure? If Christ were to come to
look round about on all things in our churches today, would he pass
through out midst and go on his way to establish his kingdom?

Realizing that a venture to answer such a question may call forth such
labels as pious, pessimistic, superficial, I dare venture an answer to these
questions. In the first place, Christ may pass through our midst because
of a lack of our personal dedication. Is it possible that we have allowed
the promotion of our programs to so consume our effort and energy that
we no longer keep the fires burning at the place of prayer? If I could
engrave one motto upon the desk of every preacher, I know it would be
this:

> Every morning lean thine arms awhile
> Upon the window-sill of heaven
> And gaze upon thy God,

Then, with the vision in thy heart,
Turn strong to meet the day.

There is no substitute for prayer. Program building, sermon preparation, and persistent promotion can never replace prayer. What would happen in our churches if every servant of the Lord rebuilt the altar of prayer? Years ago I heard a great student speaker say: "If I cannot be great myself, then let me live in the shadow of great people." Following her exhortation, I have made it a rule to get close to great people to discover the secret of their power. I have asked world Christian leaders of all denominations to tell me the secret of their spiritual power, and every one has answered in essence: "I have a quiet hour with God every day." Could it be that Christ will pass through the midst of us because we have forgotten the altar of power, the place of prayer?

In the second place, could it be that Christ will pass through our midst because of our dependence upon human ingenuity? The know-how of church promotion surpasses anything we have known in the history of the world, and yet in this very fact we may find our failure. Becoming adequate and self-sufficient in the discharge of our program, we may have forgotten our absolute dependence upon the power of God. When men become personally adequate and self-sufficient, they come to rely less and less upon the strong arm of a mighty God.

In the third place, conformity to the world around us may cause Christ to pass through our midst. "Everybody's doing it" applies to the preacher as well as to the layman. Living as the world lives, talking as the world talks, walking as the crowd walks may be the chief temptation of the modern preacher. Has it not been true that often the modern preacher, in order to tickle the fancy of some modern congregation, has spoken messages which have contained words other than the powerful word of God? The prophet of God must be different from the world.

In the fourth place, it may be that Christ will pass through our midst because of our lack of sacrifice and our lack of faith. Living in a secure world with comforts and luxuries provided by the technical know-how of our day, is it possible that we have forgotten what it means for a man to make a sacrifice for Jesus Christ? In my observation of the ministry today, I have concluded that the majority of preachers and religious workers do not have any real compassion for the salvation of others. What would happen in our churches today if every born-again Christian would take the responsibility of his stewardship seriously and would honestly attempt every week to lead some unsaved soul to Jesus Christ? Is it true that 95 percent of the work in the church is done by 5 percent of the membership? Is it true that 95 percent of the soul-winning is done by 5 percent of the people? I will allow you to answer.

Would you let me tell you about the most amazing conversion I have ever witnessed? In my city there lived a desperately wicked man. His influence had gone very far in leading many astray. He was recognized in the whole community as one of the evil influences, degrading and down-dragging. I recall one day that his daughter came to my office and said to me, "Sir, you have been in our city for fourteen years, but you have never spoken to my father about Christ." I remember how I thought, "No, I have never spoken to your father because your father is a very wicked man, and I am quite sure he would not respond to the call of Christ." But how wrong I was!

As the days passed, this man became a distinct burden on my soul. One day I remember that I called him for an appointment, but I must admit with much shame that I did not have enough faith to believe that he would be saved. I remember as though it were yesterday how I spoke to him about Christ. I reminded him that if he were to die in his condition, he would go to the depths of hell. With my Bible I read verse by verse, and then I handed the little Testament to him, and he read verse by verse.

The mighty power of God began to work in his heart. Before the hour was done, God's great Holy Spirit had done his mighty work. For two evenings in a revival meeting, I saw this man literally wrestle with God as he fought from the bitterness of his sin to find his way into the forgiving arms of God. When he walked down the aisle of our church to make his profession of faith in Christ, our whole congregation was stunned and surprised. Could this man be saved? When the news spread across the city, many said, "It can't be true; it won't last."

I remember how I warned this man about the importance of a genuine decision, and how I suggested that because of his wicked past that it might be wise for us to spend some weeks in the study of the Word of God before he made his public stand for Christ. I suggested also that it might be wise for him to make a close study of the Bible for a number of weeks before his baptism.

Again I must admit that I am ashamed of my lack of faith. Only a few days had elapsed after he had made his public stand for Christ when I called on the telephone to talk with him. He exclaimed, "Preacher, I believe you've led me wrong. I have been reading my New Testament, and I find that the New Testament teaches that a man should be baptized immediately after he has been saved." "In fact," he said, "I have been reading where a man was converted at midnight and baptized immediately. Preacher, when can I be baptized?" You may be sure that he was baptized that following Wednesday night and was received joyously and happily into the membership and fellowship of our church.

What has happened since? Several months have passed, and today this man is probably the outstanding evangelist of this city. In his business establishment every morning, he begins the day with a few verses of Scripture and a word of prayer. Hundreds of his friends who once knew him as a sinful man have heard testimony from his lips concerning the glory and the power of God. Evil habits that once formed the daily pattern of his life have slipped away until today his body and his mind and soul are pure. If there is any tragedy connected with this story, it is simply this—I lived in this city fourteen years before I had enough courage to speak to this man about his salvation. Unless the church and the ministry can return to a powerful pattern of personal witnessing, I am persuaded that Christ will pass through our midst and go on his way to establish his kingdom.

Could I close with a question? A burning question? It is simply this: Where is Christ in your life? Are you committed? Have you crossed the line? Are you his, all his? Yes, David Lloyd George was right when he exclaimed, "It is Christ or chaos for the world." Yes, M. E. Dodd was right when he placed that little motto on his pulpit—words he had to see every time he preached to his congregation in Shreveport. Those words were these: "We would see Jesus." A complete dedication and surrender must be ours if we are to meet the challenge of this day, unless it be said to us also: "He passing through the midst of them went his way."

Perry F. Webb, Sr.
The Sin of Tolerance

But though we, or an angel from heaven, preach any other
gospel unto you than that which we have preached unto you,
let him be accursed (Gal. 1:8).

Perhaps there are some who will think the subject is wrongly stated, that
it should be "The Sin of Intolerance." Of course, there is such a sin, and it
is a very wicked one. It means the unwillingness to bear with or endure
people who may have a contrary opinion. Impatience, prejudice,
bigotry—all of these are synonyms of intolerance, or at least they accompany it; and they are an evil-looking, evil-acting, and evil-smelling brood.
In a certain meeting a few years ago, one man boasted he was "a 100
percent American." But another arose and declared, "I am a 200 percent
American—I hate *everybody!*"

But, even so, my subject is correctly stated, for I am speaking of a sin
that is very general and prevalent and dangerous—dangerous because it
is so seldom recognized as sin. It is the sin of tolerance. Today, speakers
and writers, preachers and columnists, glibly and pompously, and sometimes piously, profess they have a tolerant spirit. This is supposed to
make them big and grand and worthy. One is sometimes led to wonder
how much of such profession is unthinking, parrot-like repetition of some
catch phrases, how much is pure hokum, and how much springs from
knowledge and a good spirit.

Much has been said lately about religious persecution, but it is a fair
question, Who is persecuting whom for his religion today? Let each
group speak for itself. I can speak for the Baptists, and confidently affirm
that Baptists are not persecuting anyone. We are *taking* persecution in
Spain and elsewhere. According to the *Philadelphia Ledger*, a law was
recently passed in Spain that non-Catholics may "exercise their religion
privately." One can readily see the spirit of bigotry and persecution behind

465

this decree. But we may thank God that, from the days of Christ, Baptists have a clean record in the matter of religious persecution. In fact, it is a simple matter of history that everywhere we have been the champions of complete religious freedom.

We may suggest several reasons that have prompted all this present-day talk of tolerance. First, there are those who have a sincere desire to cultivate good will among all men. May God bless them and increase their number! Certainly, it is good and right that every man should be respected, provided, of course, that he is respectable. Second, there are those who feel their much talk of tolerance will increase their popularity in certain minority groups, or will make friends for them among the intellectual dilettante, or will give them more votes in case they are running for office! Third, there are others who have an ulterior purpose, a hidden motive. They speak of tolerance because they wish to silence all opposition to their schemes and plans. They do not wish anyone to speak up or to speak out against their practices, and so they try to label anyone who does so as "intolerant."

All of which reminds us of two little boys playing in the back of a shanty. Occasionally one would let out a fearful cry, until presently the mother called, "What's going on out there?" The reply was, "Make Benny stop yelling every time I hit him over the head with this hammer!" Similarly, there are those who would bludgeon or intimidate us into silence and acquiescence and surrender with *this* "hammer": "You are intolerant if you say anything about this or that." In other words, they would have us remain silent in the presence of religious, social, and political forces we believe to be inimical to righteousness and freedom. Such people, whether preachers or priests or writers or politicians, who go around with a bundle of labels trying to paste their opinion of "intolerance" on everybody who refuses to agree with their selfish plans and schemes, are nothing better than pests, and it is time for all of us to work on them with the "flit gun" of truth.

In the fourth place, there are those who constantly prate of their tolerance who are really only advertising their lack of basic principles and convictions. They are broad but equally shallow, like the river which is supposedly three miles wide and three inches deep. They have a passion for the middle of the road. They advocate that strange doctrine, "peace at any price; religious union, no matter what the sacrifice." When a Modernist preacher resigned his pastorate (I wish all of them would resign), one of his members expressed regret that he was leaving. "When you came," he said, "I didn't care for God, man, or the devil; but under your fine ministry I have learned to love all three."

It is time for somebody to extol the blessings and delineate the virtues of *intolerance*. There would still be human slavery in America if somebody hadn't been intolerant. We would still be afflicted by the curse of child labor, with little ones toiling and weeping in the playtime of others had not somebody been intolerant. We would be ruled today by autocrats and dictators if someone had not been intolerant enough to say, "God is tired of kings."

As we read the Scriptures, we are impressed first with the tender, compassionate love of Christ for all people. "A bruised reed shall he not break, and smoking flax shall he not quench" (Matt. 12:20). Our hearts are warmed as we see his gentleness with little children and penitent supplicants. He was genial and merciful, and it is our delight to dwell upon these cordial qualities of his life and ministry.

But no survey of Christ's matchless life is complete that does not take knowledge also of his noble severity and regal austerity. We cannot but be impressed by his inflexible adherence to the principle of righteousness and by his corresponding revulsion with respect to all sham, pretense, hypocrisy, and ungodliness. While he was tender, he was also firm. His meekness was not weakness, it was a thousand miles from that idle and amiable Laodiceanism that so often marks the lives of his liberal followers today. The sweetness of Jesus was not insipid; his patience was not indifference, nor did it arise from a lack of concern. He refused to compromise with error or to violate truth in order to gain popularity. While his overtures of grace were broad, his requisitions of righteousness were exact and unyielding.

Consider the question of sin. How indifferent to sin, careless and tolerant of it people are today. The most popular indoor or outdoor sport is to leer, jeer, and sneer about sin. It has become a huge joke, and any comedian or speaker at a luncheon club, or a sophisticated columnist who touches the subject in a cynical or satirical way, is sure to be greeted with a round of applause.

It has been said that some doctors are trying to find a cure for blushing. It has been claimed that when one is unable to blush, it is a sure sign of a crime having been committed. This reminds us of Jeremiah 8:12, "Were they ashamed when they had committed abomination? Nay, they were not at all ashamed, neither could they blush." Here was brazen sin, bold and arrogant and unashamed.

But, although people may joke about it, sin is not a joke. "The wages of sin is death." "The soul that sinneth, it shall die." Jesus said, "I go my way, and ye shall seek me, and shall die in your sins: whither I go, ye cannot come" (John 8:21). No, everybody isn't going to the same place. Nothing could be further from the truth. Jesus plainly spoke of a "broad" way that leads to destruction, and a "narrow" way that leads to life.

It was sin that forced the closing of Eden, that destroyed Sodom and Gomorrah, that brought in the flood during Noah's day, that turned the Jews into captivity, that crucified the Lord Jesus Christ; and its terrible and desolating influence is among us today. It will steal the bloom from the fairest cheek, dull the luster of the brightest eye, destroy the happiness of the finest home, and turn the heart into a witch's cauldron of unspeakable corruption, sending immortal souls into an endless eternity, without God or hope. For the difference between heaven and hell is simply the difference between sins repented of, and therefore cleansed and forgiven, and sins loved and practiced. Surely, only a fool would make light of sin or be tolerant toward it.

The late Dr. Adolf Lorenz, a famous Austrian surgeon, was called some years ago from Austria to Chicago to treat the child of a wealthy meat packer. I do not know what was wrong with the child, but I do know it must have been extremely serious because of what the parents did about it. Likewise, I cannot answer all the questions about sin, but I do know it is a terrible thing because of what God did about it. "For God so loved the world, that he gave his only begotten Son, that whosoever believeth in him should not perish, but have everlasting life" (John 3:16). Oh, what a solemn accounting preachers and religious leaders must give who seek to flatter sinners and promise them spiritual blessings except on the basis of genuine repentance of sin!

Consider the matter of worldly and wicked practices. How intolerant of them was Jesus! In the twenty-third chapter of Matthew, for illustration, it is our glorious Saviour who uses such terms as fools, hypocrites, whited sepulchers, serpents, generation of vipers, and the damnation of hell. These perfumed "Christianettes," with their soft and easygoing philosophy of religion and their lazy nonchalance in the presence of social, moral, and political corruption, can never find any comfort for their attitude in the teachings and example of Jesus. "Ye cannot serve God and mammon" said the Master. And Christ's greatest missionary, the apostle

Paul, boldly said, "Have no fellowship with the unfruitful works of darkness, but rather reprove them" (Eph. 5:11). We are to reprove evil things, not only by word of mouth, but by abstaining from them.

Further, consider the matter of divorce. The sin of tolerance in this particular is just about wrecking the American home. How tolerant was Jesus about divorce? Listen carefully to what he said: "What therefore, God hath joined together, let not man put asunder" (Mark 10:9). "It hath been said, Whosoever shall put away his wife, let him give her a writing of divorcement: but I say unto you, That whosoever shall put away his wife, saving for the cause of fornication, causeth her to commit adultery: and whosoever shall marry her that is divorced committeth adultery" (Matt. 5:31-32). How utterly plain and heart-searching are these statements from the Son of God!

Once again, think of salvation. Is there more than one way in which a man may be saved? Dear friends, let us not make any mistake at this point! Broadness and tolerance certainly are not to be considered when one's eternal salvation is at stake. There is only one way from earth to heaven, from death to life, from condemnation to salvation, and that way is Jesus Christ, the Lord. "I am the way, the truth, and the life: no man cometh unto the Father, but by me" (John 14:6). "Neither is there salvation in any other: for there is none other name under heaven given among men, whereby we must be saved" (Acts 4:12). "For there is one God, and one mediator between God and men, the man Christ Jesus" (1 Tim. 2:5). "But though we, or an angel from heaven, preach any other gospel unto you than that which we have preached unto you, let him be accursed" (Gal. 1:8).

Dr. H. A. Ironside told once of a ritualistic preacher who was called to the bedside of a woman thought to be dying in a hospital. He said, "Confess your sins, and I will absolve you." She didn't know what he meant, and he sought to explain. "Just confess your sins to me, and I will forgive you." The woman opened her eyes slowly and said, "Let me see your hands!" Willing to humor what seemed to be a childish request, the minister showed her his hands. She then said, "The one who forgives my sins must have the print of the nails in his hands!"

Yes, there is only one Saviour and one way, but it is a sure way, a safe say, and a blessed way. And that way is open now for every penitent heart. Will you turn from your sins and receive Christ as your Saviour today?

K. Owen White
The Great Door and the Many Adversaries

For many weeks now our messages in the Sunday morning services have been based on the book of 1 Corinthians. We come today to the last chapter and the closing message in this series. If you believe that this sort of preaching would be helpful, if you would like to follow a similar course in the study of some other books in the Bible, I wish you would let me know, individually and personally. I think there is a great need today for greater knowledge of God's Word, and I believe there is a blessing for us in making a consistent and thorough study of it. I would be interested to know how you feel about it in your own heart.

In the 16th chapter, a number of topics are discussed. Paul is gathering together the loose ends and on the basis of the great Christian doctrines previously discussed he is making several practical applications.

1. Concerning the Collection (vv. 1,2)

"Now concerning the collection for the saints, as I have given order to the churches of Galatia, even so do ye. Upon the first day of the week let every one of you lay by him in store, as God hath prospered him, that there be no gatherings when I come."

Here in the first verse, in outline form, is God's way for financing His work! It is so simple, it is so plain, yet we wonder why through the years the churches have blundered along dishonoring the Lord, hurting their own reputation, struggling along with one-half of a program when they could have a whole program, with ice cream suppers, cake sales, candy sales, rummage sales and all sorts of efforts to raise funds, even going from door to door to beg from unbelievers for the support of the church!

470

How dishonoring to the Lord it has been! But here is God's way of financing His work:

"Upon the first day of the week," that is

(1) *Regularly!*—Some people, some Christians give to the Lord nothing at all, others give Him an occasional gift, still others are spasmodic in their giving, with no plan or purpose in their hearts, but giving occasionally. Some give when they are present at the services of the church, and of course, give nothing when they are not present. Oh, but there are some, and we thank God for them, who give to the Lord regularly "upon the first day of the week"! Whether in the services or not, they lay aside a certain amount. They mail that amount to the church or the next time they come they bring it with them. The work goes forward because of their love and their gifts.

"Upon the first day of the week, let every one of you," that is

(2) *Individually.*—What a fine thing it is when a family, for example, tithes the income and the father, mother, boy and girl each give something. It leads them to establish the custom of giving. It may be but a penny in the little hand of the baby in the Cradle Roll, it may be but the three or four pennies in the hands of the child in the Beginners Department, it may be the ten cents in the hands of that boy or girl in the Junior Department, but regularly upon the first day of the week they bring an offering to the Lord! As they grow to young manhood and womanhood they never lose that habit! "Upon the first day of the week, let every one of you." No church should be supported by one millionaire. No church should be supported by a small group who give all the money and dictate all the policies, but every church ought to carry on its work by the unanimous support of every member, great and small.

"Upon the first day of the week, let every one of you (individually) lay by him in store," that is

(3) *Wisely!*—It is not the money you have laid by in the bank, it is not the money you have put in those stocks and bonds, it is not the money you have invested in real estate or other business affairs, which is laid by in store, but the money which you have laid aside for the service of God in the Lord's church to be used for world-wide activities and which will be literally "treasure laid up in heaven"!

"Upon the first day of the week, let every one of you lay by him in store as God hath prospered him," that is

(4) *Proportionately!*—If the Lord has given you much, He has a right

to expect much from you. If God has given to you a moderate amount, He will not expect more than a moderate amount. If the Lord has given you very little, He will not expect from you more than you are able to give, but He will expect and has a right to expect that which you are able to do. "Let every one of you lay by him in store as God hath prospered him"! I care not whether the church be great or small. I care not whether it be a country church or a city church up on the hill in the best residential section, or whether it be across the tracks, whether it be a church filled with college graduates or whether its members be those who work in the mill, every church can carry on a great program if all the members will come in this way, upon the first day of the week and lay by them in store as the Lord has prospered them! Oh, then the Lord's work will go forward and will never suffer need. I wonder why, when the way is so simple, when the way is so plain, we have carried on the work in such an unsatisfactory and disobedient way!

The second thing in the chapter is

2. A Great Effectual Open Door (v. 9)

"For a great door and effectual is opened unto me, and there are many adversaries."

A great effectual open door! To Metropolitan, in the heart of Washington, there is opened a great effectual door, for

(1) *The preaching of the Gospel!*—Oh, how my heart burns within me when I recall that there are in this city men and women by the thousands from all parts of the world. How I long to have the opportunity and privilege of preaching the Gospel to those in the embassies and legations and in various other political positions in Washington. Many come from other lands, never hearing the Gospel at all. Others have heard only a part of it or a perverted gospel. Many are religious, but even though they may be religious they are lost because they know not Him "whom to know is life eternal." Paul preached the Gospel, "how that Christ died for our sins according to the scriptures, and that He was buried, and that He rose again the third day according to the scriptures"! Oh, pray that the radio ministry may reach the hearts and homes of some of these who have come from foreign lands to our great city. God forbid that they should go from Washington with the only recollection that of cocktail parties, social functions, entertainments and musicals, and no knowledge

of Him who loved us and died for us! Oh, a great open door is given to us for the preaching of the Gospel!

A great effectual open door is given to us

(2) *For witnessing for Christ.*—Friday night at Wabanna at the Baptist Training Union Summer Assembly, I had the privilege of speaking on "Individual Responsibility" and I reminded my own heart and those present that Christian witnessing is more than speaking an occasional word to men and women. It is more than speaking a frequent word. It should be much more than that. There must be loyal, consecrated, consistent Christian living to reinforce every spoken word! Many a sermon has been rendered powerless because the life of the preacher did not bear out the message. Many a Sunday School lesson has been taught, yet the lesson has been nullified by the life of the teacher. Many an active Christian worker has been set aside because the life did not correspond with his work at all. Oh, listen, Christian people, the eyes of the world are upon us! What about that habit, that seemingly insignificant thing, that thing about which the Spirit of the Lord has been speaking to you? It is just a little thing, yet it is standing between you and the Lord; that unworthy and contemptible thing in your life has been standing for years between another man and the Lord. There is a great effectual door opened to us for sincere, consecrated witnessing for our Lord!

There is a great effectual open door given to us

(3) *For building for time and eternity!*—A few weeks ago I mentioned a vision that burns within my own heart. I said at that time that there is room in Washington for a great New Testament church with a membership of not less than 5,000, which should have not less than 2,000 in its Sunday School summer and winter and not less than 750 every Sunday evening in its Baptist Training Union, filling the auditorium at the midweek Hour of Power, where there should be baptized on profession of faith at least 365 every year, one for every day in the year. I say that there is a place in Washington for just such a church with an adequate building to provide for such a program when the people come! I say that there is no reason at all why we should not have just such a church here at Metropolitan. The answer to the vision then is the loyal, consecrated support of every single member. We can have such a church if we want it and pray for it and work for it. Yes, a great door and effectual is open unto us!

3. There Are Many Adversaries

"For a great door and effectual is opened unto me, and there are many adversaries."

I know that if I had been writing this verse, I would have said, "For a great door and effectual is opened unto me, but there are many adversaries." Paul knew that the many adversaries were inevitable, they always accompany the wide open door. What then shall we do, shall we shrink from them, shall we retreat, shall we allow the door to close?

I might talk with you this morning about the great adversary, the devil, about the mighty power of Satan and sin, or about the sinfulness of sin! There are many adversaries but we will mention only three or four.

(1) *Childishness of believers!*—Many there are who have never been anything but babes in Christ. They have never grown in their Christian lives. They have never gone beyond "the milk of the Word." They have never desired the meat which is for strong Christians. They are babes! They talk the baby language, they toddle, they stumble, and act like babies! They cannot help themselves and they cannot help others. Why? Because they never have put themselves in the place where God could strengthen and help them! If you want to be a growing Christian, ask Mrs. Nash here, how it can be done. She will tell you to join the Training Union, get with other Christians, learn to pray in public, learn to talk in public, learn to do something rather than sit at home nine-tenths of the time! The childishness of believers! So easily hurt, so quick to criticize, yet unable to do anything constructive!

(2) *Jealousy!*—I have seen it among deacons. I have seen it among pastors in associations. I have seen it among workers in denominational affairs. I have seen it among teachers in the Sunday School, among members of the choir! But I care not where you find it, it is a miserable, unworthy, contemptible thing! It grows out of pride, that foolish personal pride! It means that we have forgotten Paul's word, "In lowliness of mind let each esteem other better than themselves."

(3) *Worldliness on the part of many!*—I am speaking to you this morning from experience when I say it is not the atheism, the infidelity, agnosticism, or skepticism, it is not the contemptible unbelief of those who are unregenerate that burdens the heart of the preacher, that fills his heart with grief, for he knows he must ever face these. But it is the miserable, selfish worldliness of the members of the church! There are those

who sit and listen to the message time after time, as from a broken heart the messenger brings "the whole counsel of God." They are unmoved and untouched, yet they come and say, "Great sermon, preacher!" Yet, they have not the slightest inclination to do anything about it, to give up some of the habits that are crippling their testimony! They can listen to a sermon on soul winning and witnessing and go out and live in such a way that the people the preacher is trying to win to the Lord are repelled and driven away as they say, "If this is a sample of the Christian life, I want nothing of it!"

Oh, tell me, did you come this morning with a feeling in your heart that even today you might make some decision, that even today you might decide to give up something that might be standing between you and the Lord? If I should call upon you to "come out from among them and be ye separate and touch not the unclean thing," what would your answer be? I am not calling upon you to sacrifice anything, but I am calling you to a great and high privilege!

(4) *Pessimism and lack of faith!*—I have seen it in the deacons' meeting. I have seen it in the Sunday School Workers' Council. I have seen it in the church conference. The leader or leaders have caught the vision and after the possibilities have been presented, some shake their heads and say, "No, that is too big for us. That program is just too great for us at this time. No, it isn't wise!" When the time comes for the enthusiastic support of the members, the program dies because of pessimism and lack of faith! Do you believe that we could have on Capitol Hill the kind of church I was talking about? Do you believe it is possible? The only thing that will keep us from having such a church, will be pessimism and lack of faith!

Another thing in the chapter is

4. A Call to Christian Manhood (v. 13)

"Watch ye, stand fast in the faith, quit you like men, be strong."

I thank God for the fine work the women are doing in our church. Their influence is great! But I am saying this morning that I would not be content to be a pastor of a church that did not have a great group of strong Christian laymen who are willing to spend some time in the Lord's work. The call to Christian manhood! Paul says, "watch out, wake up, be alert, be alive to the possibilities, but be alert to the dangers also." Look to the open door and with confidence step through it in the face of many adversaries. "Stand fast in the faith." I do not ask that you be marvelous organizers, or that you be brilliant leaders, or generous far beyond the average, but simply that you will stand fast in the faith, standing for the mighty New Testament doctrines which we have been emphasizing during these days, regarding them as the essential things that undergird your Christian life. "Stand fast in the faith, acquit yourselves, equip yourselves like men, be strong," not "willy-nilly, namby-pamby, or goody-goody," but plain, wholesome, cleancut, whole-hearted Christian men! Oh, how our churches need these kinds of men today!

Now the closing word.

5. The Centrality of Christ (v. 23,24)

"The grace of our Lord Jesus Christ be with you. My love be with you all in Christ Jesus."

This great book opens and closes with the centrality of Christ! Oh, all that we have been talking about for the past sixteen weeks is "in Christ." Our spiritual gifts, our hope, our victory, our influence, our work, it is all "in Christ," and the "grace of our Lord Jesus Christ" comes only to those who find Him at Calvary's Cross in repentance and faith and confession of their sins and make Him Lord of their lives. So we come again at the close of the book to Calvary, to ask, are you a Christian, have you been saved by grace through faith, have you committed yourself to Him for time and eternity? Let me review the things that are in this last chapter. There is the matter of the collection, God's way of financing His work. There is a great effectual door open to every one of us! There are many adversaries that accompany the wide open door. There is the call to Christian manhood, and then an earnest reminder of the centrality of Christ!

Will you trust Him now as Savior and commit yourself to Him as Lord of your life?

W. R. White
Around the Corner

Men's hearts failing them for fear, and for looking after those things which are coming on the earth; for the powers of heaven shall be shaken (Luke 21:26).

The world trembles with possibilities. Our Saviour predicts a time in this passage before us in which the hearts of men will be filled with anxious fear concerning world conditions. The atmosphere will be regnant with nervous anticipation; an upheaval of worldwide proportions is described. The psychology depicted by the Master is quite similar to the state of mind upon the earth today. Society is characterized by paradoxes.

We have an increase of knowledge with a corresponding decrease of wisdom. Men never knew so many different facts, but the leaders never knew so little as to what they should do. There is a groping in the midst of a wilderness of knowledge. Confusion and dismay fill the atmosphere. The inspired writer fittingly describes our times when he says, "ever learning and never coming to the knowledge of the truth." The world is a whispering gallery in which peoples of the earth talk to one another daily, but seem to have little wisdom as to the right course to pursue. Wisdom has been defined as "the right use of knowledge." This confusion in the midst of great learning is due to the fact that man has ignored the basic reality of the universe—God. "Therefore is judgment far from us, neither doth justice overtake us; we wait for light, but behold obscurity; for brightness, but we walk in darkness. We grope for the wall like the blind, and we grope as if we had no eyes: we stumble at noonday as in the night; we are in desolate places as dead men" (Isa. 59:9,10).

There is an ever-increasing need in the world's life, while man deliberately decreases supply. There has been an artificial reduction of production in order to stimulate the price level. Millions of people are hungry and improperly clad; great food supplies and raw materials are destroyed. It is entirely possible that we will face a famine of necessities in the face of deepest need.

We have more houses and fewer good homes than perhaps history has ever witnessed. There was a time in our history in which the houses were quite modest, but the homes were powerfully influential in building noble characters and fine citizens. Before the depression came, the American people had more beautiful homes than any people in the world, far surpassing those of any previous generation or face. But the increase of good houses was offset by a tragic decrease of happy homes. There is no substitute for the things of the Spirit.

We have more peace pacts and peace alliances, and at the same time more preparation for war. With the exception of the period that preceded the World War, mankind has never made such gigantic preparations for conflict. The cries of "peace, peace," seem to be a smokescreen behind which the god of war whets his sword. Why is it that the people of the world want peace, while the leaders are preparing for war? Selfishness and greed are prominent; fear is regnant. The Prince of Peace is being left out of the calculations of men, hence the futility of man's feverish efforts. Yet the nations continue in their former folly.

It is singular to note that with the increase of respectability there is a corresponding decrease of real decency. The popularity of membership in churches and lodges and clubs and civic organizations makes it quite attractive to assume a cloak of respectability regardless of what may be the conditions of the heart or life. Beautiful phrases and high-sounding terms seem to provide a convenient cover for rotten lives. Men are willing to assume a form of godliness while denying the power thereof.

It is interesting to observe the contrast between the increase of comforts and the loss of happiness. We never had quite so many conveniences and material comforts as today. When did we have as little contentment and as much restlessness? Man has found that he cannot rest and relax while depending upon mere things. Much of the drudgery and the monotony of living has been removed. But happiness must come from within. Man continues to pursue "some other way."

We have more emphasis upon human values and less regard for them than in any previous generation. There is hardly an address to any group but that there is some emphasis placed upon human values. Our reckless automobile driving takes almost as large a toll annually as the total loss to the American Army in the World War. Almost every institution that preys upon human weakness and exploits the baser side of human nature is being released and clothed with the garments of legal respectability. One parasite after another is being turned loose to suck the blood out of legitimate business and to exploit the frailties of human nature. Yet, service clubs are growing in number each day, which proclaim, as principles, the supremacy of spiritual values above the material. Man continues to stimulate cross-currents.

There are some bright aspects to world conditions. In many cases great losses have been replaced by superior gains. Many people have suffered severe economic losses but have come to a greater appreciation of their family, friends, and the noble simplicities of life.

A mother who had grieved several days over the loss of a home with a number of cherished relics, refused to be comforted. Her little son sought in vain to get her attention. Finally, one night in the wee hours he obtained her attention and said, "Mother, I am so glad the fire didn't burn up you and Daddy." After waiting a few minutes he began to get restless and said, "Mother, aren't you a little bit glad the fire didn't burn me up?" The light broke upon the mother's heart as she realized that the most precious possessions she had ever had were still hers. She turned to a new conception of life.

Graduates of Yale and Harvard are now turning to a simple life of wholesome contentment and cultured simplicity instead of being slaves to the passion for economic supremacy.

There is a widespread disillusionment that has come to many revealing a new sense of values. Millions have been laboring under a misconception of the real significance of life. The brilliant light of material things has faded, while the golden glow of worth-while things has come into view. They no longer see things in a false light but in the revealing exposure of a clear illumination.

In spite of the feverish efforts of leaders who largely ignore God, we have a growing conviction on the part of the people that God must be recognized. Now and then leaders pay a tribute to the Supreme Being, but most of their efforts seem to carry too much emphasis on the human side. God is largely and politely bowed out of their program. Too many of our leaders seem to think a passing courtesy is all that God deserves. The great masses are coming to feel more and more that God alone can extricate us from our present predicament. This is one bright spot amidst the world's gloom.

There are three possibilities for the future. Many would like to peer around the corner and see what is coming. We have been talking much about turning the corner. To some it seems as if we are living in a round-house in which there are no corners. The corner is somewhere ahead; sooner or later we are going to come to it and make our turn. What are we expecting to greet our eyes?

If a man makes only a superficial restitution, if he makes only a partial return to God, if his repentance is not thorough and deep enough, he may be able by artificial means, to bring about an impressive but temporary recovery. It will be somewhat like a desperate operation on a cancer which brings immediate and seemingly sound relief, only to be succeeded, after a brief period, by a worse condition. There are many factors available whereby human beings by manipulation may produce a measure of stimulation. Men must dig down to foundations and relay with great principles the whole structure of life, otherwise, our recovery will be like the man who cast out the devil by his own power, swept and garnished himself, but into whom, after a period, the devil returned. The last state of that man was worse than the first. May God save us from this possibility!

It is possible for a man to give himself to a thorough-going and genuine repentance. God brings two kinds of judgments: First, there is a judgment of mercy. In this God comes to shock us, to arouse us, and to stop us. Often the peoples of America and England have been awakened by some visitation of judgment and have come back to God in the form of a great spiritual revival. Thus our nations and civilizations have been preserved. Great and glorious things have issued. Some people say the Sermon on the Mount will not work, but the time has come when its principles must work or nothing else will work. Many must surrender the rule of gold for the Golden Rule. This possibility is described in 2 Chronicles 7:14, "If my people, which are called by my name, shall humble themselves, and pray, and seek my face, and turn from their wicked ways; then will I hear from heaven, and will forgive their sin, and will heal their land." If man will not heed the judgment of mercy, then there will inevitably come to him a judgment of doom.

There is this other very plausible possibility—namely: the second coming of Christ. Sooner or later we know our King will come in glory. It may be necessary for him to come in order to establish order in our present chaos. It is entirely possible that this age has been weighed in the balances and found wanting. The fall of Babylon illustrates the possibilities of this hour. Doctor Haldeman gives us a description of that tragedy. We reproduce it in substance:

> There was an immense wall around the city of ancient Babylon something like 150 feet high. It was wide enough for four chariots to pass one another without jostling. There was a ditch around the walls something like 75 feet deep. The water could be rushed into it by mechanical devices similar to modern equipment. There were 100 brazen gates, each guarded by 1,000 soldiers. The river flowed through the city, bound by marble banks; beautiful boats floated upon its bosom; artistic bridges arched its waters. There was an upper and lower city. The buildings were the same height and flat at the top. They were connected by walks. The paved streets and the walks of the lower city crossed each other at right angles. The famous Hanging Gardens, constructed of terrace rising above terrace, fronded at the top with palms, constituted scenes of unfading interest. High above everything else, coming at the top of a spiral stairway, was the famous image of the god Belus, worth its weight in gold. In the heart of the city was the palace of Nebuchadnezzar, larger and more glorious than Nero's golden palace. Within this palace was an incomparable banquet room. Within this banquet hall was Belshazzar, a thousand of his lords and their wives and concubines. This was a gala feast. From secret places in the walls sweet perfumes pervaded the atmosphere. The walls and the floor represented the finest work of ancient art. The ceiling was an imitation of the star-fretted sky. The richest and rarest foods of the earth were before them, drinks of every kind were available. Entertainers representing the fertile creation of the oriental mind were presented.
>
> The sensual indulgences of the king and his lords reached blasphemous depths. The golden vessels of the Temple of the living God were ordered. Out of them they drank their mixed wines in sacrilegious defiance. A solemn hush came over the banquet, a sleeveless, armless hand wrote upon the wall. The drunken conglomeration was suddenly sobered into indescribable terror. The king was shaken to the depths, his blurred and astonished eyes read the doom of his kingdom and the end of his boasted civilization.

The coming of Christ will produce two different reactions. First, is that of the lost. Revelation 6:12-17, —"And I beheld when he had opened the sixth seal, and, lo, there was a great earthquake; and the sun became black as sackcloth of hair, and the moon became as blood; and the stars of heaven fell unto the earth, even as a fig tree casteth her untimely figs when she is shaken of a mighty wind. And the heaven departed as a scroll when it is rolled together; and every mountain and island were moved out of their places. And the kings of the earth, and the great men, and the rich men, and the chief captains, and the mighty men, and every bondman, and every free man, hid themselves in the dens and in the rocks of the mountains; and said to the mountains and rocks, Fall on us, and hide us from the face of him that sitteth on the throne, and from the wrath of the Lamb: for the great day of his wrath is come; and who shall be able to stand?"

The other reaction is well described in Luke 21:27,28,—"And then shall they see the Son of man coming in a cloud with power and great glory. And when these things begin to come to pass, then look up, and lift up your heads; for your redemption draweth nigh."

To which crowd do you belong? The Christian, the real child of God, is ready for any eventuality. When some tragic, deceptive, temporary prosperity comes, followed by chaos, the genuine Christian will shine as a light into its darkness and will witness against it. Christ will see him through. If repentance and a new and more glorious day issue, the real child of God will be the dominant influence and shall rejoice in it. He will be the salt of the earth and the light of the world, If his Lord should come, the disciple of Christ will smilingly welcome his appearance and cry out, "Even so, come quickly Lord Jesus." If we are hid with Christ in God, we are ready for any eventuality. If we are hid in the Rock of Ages, we will not have need to cry for the rocks and the mountains to fall upon us and hide us from the presence of his glory. Are you ready?

J. Howard Williams
Love in Action

And from Jesus Christ, who is the faithful witness, and the first begotten of the dead, and the prince of the kings of the earth. Unto him that loved us, and washed us from our sins in his own blood (Rev. 1:5).

John was the apostle of love. It was he who gave us that "gospel in one verse," John 3:16. It was he who caught the "eleventh commandment" as it fell from the lips of the Master: "A new commandment I give unto you. That ye love one another; as I have loved you, that ye also love one another" (John 13:34). It was John who gave us the briefest of all the definitions of God, for he said, "God is love" (1 John 4:8).

Of the five books which are attributed to John's authorship, the Revelation is the last. In it he had progressed no further than the fifth verse until again he was playing on his golden string of love, for he said, "Unto him that loved us, and washed us from our sins in his own blood, and hath made us kings and priests unto God and his Father; to him be glory and dominion for ever and ever. Amen."

This verse actually is a burst of praise. One cannot appreciate it fully without being aware of its context. John was thought to have been at least ninety-five years old when he wrote the Revelation. He was an exile on the bleak and lonely penal Isle of Patmos. It is thought that he was the youngest of the apostles whom Jesus called and that he lived the longest. He had given approximately seventy-five years of life in direct and personal service to his Lord and to the new cause ushered in by the Saviour. He had seen it grow in numbers and in power until leaders of the great Roman Empire had become concerned about it. Local persecutions had spread into a witch hunt throughout the empire. The disciples, first scattered from Jerusalem, had become the pitiful victims of imperial wrath. Tens of thousands of them had died rather than recant. As it is recorded in Hebrews 11:36-38:

483

And others had trial of cruel mockings and scourgings, yea, moreover of bonds and imprisonment: they were stoned, they were sawn asunder, were tempted, were slain with the sword: they wandered about in sheepskins and goatskins; being destitute, afflicted, tormented; (of whom the world was not worthy:) they wandered in deserts, and in mountains, and in dens and caves of the earth.

Perhaps John's life had been spared only because of his great age.

The grand old apostle might have folded his hands and spent his time in weeping. He might have thought of his life's ministry as having come to nought. Frustration, defeat, and even the destruction of the movement to which he had given himself would have been the logical response of worldlings. Instead, however, John burst forth in the paean of praise: "Unto him that loved us, and washed us from our sins in his own blood, and hath made us kings and priests unto God and his Father; to him be glory and dominion for ever and ever. Amen." This was possible only because he realized that what God had done for him and his fellow Christians was so much more significant than anything Rome could do to them that they had ample room for rejoicing. In the midst of the debris of defeat he had within the deepest recesses of his heart the confidence that God was on his throne and that the cause for which Christ died would move on to triumph.

This verse indicates that John saw love in action, and he could join with the apostle Paul, who wrote, "Love never faileth." We, therefore, center our thinking around three words: liberation, elevation, and adoration.

Liberation

A careful study of the words of the text is most interesting. The first verb, "loved us," is translated in the King James Version in the past tense. Actually, most ancient manuscripts give it in the present tense and, therefore, instead of "loved" it would be "loveth." The context indicates that it was no one act of love but rather a continuous flow of love. Like a river, fed by mountain springs, which flows through a valley and is lost in a cavern, so the love of God flows out of eternity through time and into eternity. The word "washed" also may be translated "loosed." It is in the aorist tense in the Greek, which indicates specific and completed action in past time. The word can be translated either "washed" or "loosed,"— "washed" in the sense that it frees us from our guilt, "loosed" in the sense that it has liberated us from sin. Freely translated, therefore, this would read: "Unto our Lord and Saviour, who out of his unfailing, unchanging, continuing love hath freed us, liberated us, emancipated us from our sins in his own blood, be glory and dominion for ever and ever."

The language indicates something of John's conception of the price of our liberation, for he freed us from our sins "in or by his own blood." The measure of God's love is indicated by the extent of his sacrifice. John in his Gospel perhaps recognized that he could not describe the love of God nor define its limits. Therefore, he said, "God so loved the world." Worlds of love are implied in the little word "so."

It is the nature of love to act. Love can no more fail to act than light can fail to shine or fire can fail to burn. Love finds a way in every realm of life, and there is no other explanation of God's concern for the lost than that he so loved the world. Nor can we claim to love the Lord or one another if we fail to express that devotion. On one occasion Jesus said, "Not every one that saith unto me, Lord, Lord, shall enter into the kingdom of heaven; but he that doeth the will of my Father." One who says he loves the Lord and yet makes no sacrifice of time or money deceives no one but himself. A real love for God cannot help but find expression.

Elevation

John said, "Unto him that loveth us, . . . and hath made us kings and priests unto God, and his Father; to him be glory and dominion for ever and ever."

One can read this verse and think of another subject: "From the chains of slavery to the robes of royalty." The love of God not only liberates us from our sins; it elevates us to kingship. A king is one who rules. His subjects may be many or few. His domain may be small or large. A king is one who rightly is master of that domain. If there are to be kings of the earth, they, under the plan of God, are to rule in benevolence and as the ministers of God in service for the people. The people themselves become the subjects. It was in the plan of God, however, that each of us should be a king or a queen, that each of us should be master of his circumstances, ruling passion and pride, having dominion over self and substance. No better demonstration of that royalty can be found than in John himself, who, instead of weeping from the top of Patmos, shouted for joy. Paul the apostle, shivering in his prison cell, calling for a cloak he had left elsewhere, wrote to the Philippians: "Rejoice in the Lord alway:

and again I say, Rejoice." Paul rejoiced because he could see more through the bars of his prison cell than Caesar from the height of his throne. Paul was bigger than his circumstances. He was the master of himself.

It is difficult to understand how men and women made in the image of God, capable of thinking the thoughts of God, privileged to become co-laborers with God in a program of world redemption, can permit themselves to become the victims of the incidentals of life. "A man's life consisteth not in the abundance of the things which he possesseth" (Luke 12:15). The farmer must be bigger than his farm, the banker than his bank. The professional man must see in his profession a tool which he is to use for the service of God and men. John rejoiced that God had so honored him and his fellow Christians as to make them kings.

The ascension from slavery was even to a higher level than that of kingship. It was to that of the priesthood. Actually, the concept of John's mind may have been that "he hath elevated us to be a kingdom of priests," a kingdom in which all are kings and all are priests. A priest is a go-between. In times long gone Job, in the misery of his terrible affliction, cried out, "Neither is there any daysman betwixt us, that might lay his hand upon us both." Job did not understand God and God's dealings with him. He felt at the same time that God did not understand him. Therefore, he cried for a priest who would interpret God to him and him to God.

We know, of course, that every man is his own priest. Since that day when the veil of the Temple was rent in twain, the mercy seat has been exposed to all. Each man may enter for himself the holy of holies and plead his own case before the Lord. There is a sense, however, in which each of us as a Christian becomes a priest, not only for his own soul but for others about him. This is true in a pre-eminent sense for the husband and father of a household. Since the home is the greatest institution on this earth, the head of that institution holds the highest office attainable by man. What a blessed thing when a man, as the spiritual head of his house, interprets its needs at the throne of grace and also assumes that sacred role and responsibility to interpret God to his own household. In an even wider ministry we as Christians stand between God and a needy world. Is it our holy privilege to seek to interpret God to a lost world and at the same time to bear up a stricken world on the wings of prayer to the very throne of our Lord. It is any wonder that John exulted in the exalted privilege which was his to be both a king and a priest?

Adoration

Since God's love for man issued in his liberating and elevating him, man's love for God inevitably expresses itself in adoration and service. Man's love, too, must and will go into action. Mindful of all that God had done, John said, "Unto him . . . be glory and dominion for ever and ever. Amen." How normal it is to glorify God in songs or praise and with lips that have been touched with coals from off the altar. On that historic occasion of the Lord's birth the angel said, ". . . Behold, I bring you good tidings of great joy, which shall be to all people. For unto you is born this day in the city of David a Saviour, which is Christ the Lord. . . . And suddenly there was with the angel a multitude of the heavenly host praising God, and saying, Glory to God in the highest, and on earth peace, good will toward men" (Luke 2:10-14). Much will never be known by the angels who have not been redeemed by the blood, but the heavenly hosts seemed to have been aware that the event about which the prophets had spoken and the Old Testament poets had sung, and the hearts of people through centuries of time had yearned, had arrived at last. Mindful of what that meant to the world, they burst forth in praise. This may be but a slight glimpse of that larger chorus, when ten thousand times ten thousand, and thousands of thousands, shall raise their voices in the land beyond as they sing the song of Moses and of the Lamb, the song of deliverance and of redemption.

John, however, seemed as if he wanted to come back to earth from such elevated thoughts and acts of praise to say, "Unto him . . . be dominion." The climax of this season of elation was not shouting and praise but humility in service. "Unto him . . . be dominion for ever and ever." Having been liberated from the slavery of sin, John willingly became the bondslave of his Lord. The exaltation that came with the realization of redemption was to be translated into a glorified service so long as he remained on the earth. John may have been mindful of that prayer of our Lord: "Thy kingdom come, Thy will be done on earth as it is in heaven."

Any one of us should be willing to pray, "Have dominion." Mindful of the tragedies we bring to our own lives under the dictates of our own wisdom, we can pray not only "Thy will be done in our lives" but "Take charge, have dominion forever and ever." In like manner, let us pray that somehow the peoples of the nations of the earth shall voice this prayer. With the terrible record of one war for each year of recorded history, with the confusion, frustration, and fearful days through which we are passing as evidence that we are inadequate for our needs, let us join with fellow Christians everywhere in the prayer that the leaders of the nations of the earth shall welcome the leadership of the Lord and pray with all sincerity: "Have dominion; take charge; thy will be done."

Kyle M. Yates
From Doubt to Certainty

Psalm 73

Surely God is good to Israel, even to such as are of a clean heart. But as for me, my feet were almost gone; my steps had well-nigh slipped. For I was envious at the foolish, when I saw the prosperity of the wicked. For there are no bands in their death; they are not in trouble as other men. Their eyes stand out with fatness; they have more than heart could wish. And they say, How doth God know? And is there knowledge in the Most High? Behold, these are the ungodly, who prosper in the world; they increase in riches. . . . Surely I have cleansed my heart in vain, and washed my hands in innocency. For all the day long have I been plagued, and chastened every morning. . . . When I thought to know this, it was too painful for me, until I went into the sanctuary of God; then understood I their end. Surely thou didst set them in slippery places; thou didst cast them down into destruction. How are they brought into desolation, as in a moment! They are utterly consumed with terrors. . . . Nevertheless I am continually with thee; thou dost hold me by my right hand. Thou shalt guide me with thy counsel, and afterward receive me to glory. Whom have I in heaven but thee? There is none upon earth that I desire besides thee (vv. 1-5,7,11-14,16-19, 23-25).

Would you look with me upon the face of a man who is radiantly happy in the certainty that God is good and that life is filled to the brim with good things? His face beams with a strange radiance. There is a light in his eyes. He has found God and has felt a rich blessing flooding his

489

soul. Doubt and fear and confusion have gone out the window. There is something contagious about his enthusiastic confidence. It will help us to find out from him the secret. We need to know how to be so certain of vital matters.

We find him quite willing to share with us the spiritual biography. It is a thrilling story of experiences that involved temptation, pitfalls, self-pity, disappointment, envy, doubt, and near disaster. He tells of the moment when he was on the very verge of an unspeakable calamity. He felt his feet going out from under him and the foundations on which he had depended crumbling. His faith was almost gone. Perhaps no one of us is able to realize the tragedy contained in that description. You would be alarmed to find that you were on the point of losing your hearing or your sight or your health. If the physician announced such disastrous news to you it would be almost more than you could bear. What about the realization that your faith is slipping away, that the grip on God is about gone, that you are losing the assurance of God's mercy and love and saving power? How would you react? Is it a matter of concern?

The psalmist, with unusual daring, pulls back the curtain and shows us the soul struggle that almost took him over the brink of the falls. We can watch him as he suffers under the cruel grip of doubt and envy and then see him as he turns to the one solution of his problem. At the end he lifts us up to the plane where we can not only rejoice with him but find the source of light and joy and assurance. The wreck into which he almost plunged is a disaster that all of us need to shun. The pitfalls are yawning before us. The confidence and certainty and joy which he found are possible for all of us. How may we become the possessors of such a faith? How may we avoid the perils that he missed? What is the secret? We shall look first at his problems (1-14) and then at the solution (15-28).

In this gripping story we see God sitting by, quietly listening to the wild, unfair, angry talk of one who insisted on giving utterance to the deep envy of his hot soul. God, knowing that he would be ashamed of himself, let him talk on until he had poured forth all the perilous stuff that had produced his malady. How patient God is! We would be up and about the task of answering such charges. The psalmist prattled on about his neighbors and their prosperity, their wickedness, their false pride, their open blasphemy, their health and immunity from either sickness or sorrow or disappointment. He quit going to church and nursed his grievances day by day as his soul became soured. His morbid brooding gave envy an opportunity to get firm root in his mind. As he saw it life was filled with inequalities. While he and his family endured illnesses and poverty and loneliness his wicked neighbors enjoyed luxury and excellent health. These men who gave no thought to God prospered amazingly. No want of theirs was unsatisfied. They grew richer and richer. They were strong and healthy. Their characters were warped. Pride and selfishness ruled in all their behavior. Every time the psalmist thought of these men he was swept a step nearer apostasy. He became more certain that God was failing in His task of ordering the affairs of men. God was either asleep or uninterested or lacking in the proper regard for righteous standards or was unwilling to rule His creatures as justice demanded. Faith could not hope to stand in such an atmosphere. Self-pity came in and took possession. Envy grew by leaps and bounds. Bitterness had its inning. It goes without saying that the psalmist was miserable. His family must have suffered with him for he could not help make the home atmosphere what it needed to be. When one is out of tune with God he is not in position to bring happiness and contentment to others. We shudder to think of the unhappy situation in his home as he writhed in the throes of envy and self-pity.

As envy grew it was quite natural for him to ask, "Why be good? What is the use of the kind of loyalty that I used to have? Have I cleansed my heart in vain?" He was not in position to answer such questions. His perspective was bad. His conclusions must be wrong. He was on the very point of surrendering his faith. The foundations for his faith were giving way. No one would want to worship a God who was undependable. Something must have happened to show the miserable man the danger of his position. He realized that his faith was almost gone and that soon he would be a godless creature without hope or stay or anchor or God. Fortunately he became aware of the necessity for a decision. How could he solve his problem? What was he to do? Should he renounce God, peddle his doubts, go the way of the cynic, or go into the sanctuary to give God a chance to reclaim him? What would you do? Do you think you are as wise as this psalmist proved to be?

The psalmist tells us that he ran into the sanctuary for the solution. He put himself where God could deal with him. Realizing his own helplessness he turned to the holy place where the Great Physician could be found for diagnosis and healing. He found himself strangely steadied by the mysterious power of the holy place. Memories of other days flooded his mind. How near God had been in those days! What joys he had known! How rich had been the fellowship in this sacred place! Strangely enough he felt that God knew he was there and was making His way to him. It warmed his heart to know that his God was singling him out for a special revelation. He tells us nothing of the furnishings, the choir, the sermon, or the program of worship. Do you think a seeking stranger could be as conscious of God's presence if he came to your church next Sunday? This poor fellow found God and knew that God was vitally interested in him and his problem. He realized that God was working out a special demonstration that would solve his problem. How easy it would be for many of our distraught people to find the solution to their problems in the sanctuary!

As he sat reverently in the place of worship a new panorama was unfolded before his eyes. In some mysterious way he was enabled to see his wicked neighbors in their true light. These men who had seemed to be so prosperous, so carefree, so happy, were now pictured in dangerous waters. Fears, disquietude, hidden yearnings, unsatisfied desires, and cankering sores showed up in glaring reality as God's picture opened before him. Their triumphs and their prosperity are temporary. Their outward manifestations of contentment but cover a heart filled with unsatisfied longings. Terrifying perils surround them. Feverish fears and anxieties paralyze them. Thirsts and hungers that hitherto had been unobserved are clearly evident in their hearts and lives.

Suddenly the psalmist catches his breath as he looks upon the certain destruction that awaits them down the road. They are rushing blindly and madly toward a fearful end. Prosperity at best is but a passing and temporary thing. The strong hand of a righteous God is in full control and will bring about the certain destruction for those who have left Him out of their hearts. Why be envious of wicked men? Why begrudge them the fleeting pleasures that come their way in life's brief stay? Why lose faith in God because of the passing prosperity of men who are about to be plunged into miseries unspeakable? In a moment he saw his own folly, his own foolish heart, his own shallow conception of what is really important in life. He saw that he had greatly exaggerated the things that these godless men had enjoyed. They had no inner wealth. They knew no genuine joys. They possessed nothing that would last. They had no anchor for the approaching storm. They had no God. Sudden destruction was near. The inevitable crash must engulf them. It is a stupid man who envies the godless man the little that his poor mind enjoys. Let us remember that it was in the sanctuary that the poor stumbling man found this divinely-given truth.

Suddenly and without warning the worshiper saw himself on the screen before him. He was rather startled for he had not contemplated such an opportunity. He found to his amazement that he was in possession of great wealth. He realized that he was constantly in the very presence of his God. No one could estimate what a treasure he had. *I am continually with thee.* What a store of riches that line uncovers! All through his days of misery and envy and doubt he has had the eternal God near him. He has been near to protect him, to sustain and nourish and keep him, to point the way at every crossroad, to drive fear away when danger and uncertainty sought to overwhelm him, to bind up and heal and restore him in hours of pain and distress and exhaustion, to fill all the days and all the nights with a calm assurance and a steady faith, to give sweet fellowship when loneliness threatened, to set the joybells ringing in his heart when it seemed all music had fled, to provide the needed courage and strength to undertake the impossible in the realization that underneath are the everlasting arms. In shadow, in sunshine; in work, in play; in tears, in joy; in youth, in old age; in life, in the hour of death, the poet realizes that he has the continual touch of a loving God as the source of uncounted, unfailing wealth. He has been with him all the way and he did not realize it.

No sense of the full meaning of the divine presence had ever entered his mind. He now sees that all the money, all the prosperity, all the success and popularity, could never bring such blessings to godless men. He now knows that God is near to help, ready to hold his right hand, willing to guide every step, able to supply every need of the journey, anxious to satisfy every thirst and every hunger of his soul. One day He will welcome him into the beautiful home at the end of the way. No wonder he says, *Whom have I in heaven but thee? There is none upon the earth that I desire besides thee. . . . God is the strength of my heart, and my portion forever. . . . It is good for me to draw near to God. I have put my trust in the Lord God, that I may declare all thy works.* He is overwhelmed with a tremendous conviction of God's marvelous goodness. He is still just as poor, just as far from earthly prosperity and popularity, but he is going back into life with a new inward possession. He has God! God's gracious nearness, His supporting grasp, His unfailing counsel, His directing finger, His royal welcome into the heavenly home, are opened up to the mind of the worshiper as he lets God teach him. Confidence has broken in on his soul. He is no longer envious. Instead of ugly self-pity he has genuine compassion for the poor godless ones who stumble on without such matchless treasures; instead of doubt he has a faith that is clear as the sunlight; instead of gloom and sadness he has ringing joy-bells in his heart; instead of complaint he has jubilant praise and unrestrained thanksgiving. Faith has climbed through struggle to higher ground as the soul has been open before the wooing call of a loving Father. He has a firm hold on the reality out of which the doctrine of the resurrection can easily grow. He knows that he will be in God's hand. Knowing Him as he has now come to know Him, he is certain that he will be safe in this world and forever. Such assurance is born in the crucible of God's own presence. Surely he was created to walk with God and to continue in God's presence throughout eternity. It was the victory of religious experience. He realized that he was in the shadow of God's love and care. We can almost hear him say with Whittier:

> I know not where His islands lift
> Their fronded palms in air;
> I only know I cannot drift
> Beyond His love and care.

Nothing can now separate him from the love of God. We wish we might give him a copy of Paul's triumphant message in the eighth chapter of Romans. The love that refused to let go will keep him in the intimacy of God's presence. He knows God's message for a troubled heart. Confusion and frustration cannot bring distress to his soul. He has arrived at a settled faith that will prove an anchor through all the days ahead.

Is your soul torn with confusion? Have you lost your grip on God? Has your soul become embittered by pain, discouragement, loneliness, fear, or doubt? Are you in danger of losing your footing, your faith, your courage in the slippery way? Would you seek a remedy? Would you welcome the individual treatment that God stands ready to give to those who seek Him? Why not turn to the sanctuary? Have you lost your touch with His holy place? Why not come back and put yourself in the atmosphere where God can give you a clear picture of His loving heart?

You may be certain that an answer awaits you in the sanctuary. Something happens there. If life is demanding more than your weary soul can bear; if you feel yourself crushed under life's cruel blows; if self-pity, bitterness, envy, and cynicism reach for the controls of your better self, run eagerly to some sanctuary of God. You will find Him there. You will be thrilled to know that He has an individual welcome for you. His voice will speak to your heart. Your problem can be spread out before One who is a loving Father. You will be blessed by His words: *My grace is sufficient for thee.* What a blessed assurance! In the house dedicated to the worship of God, weary hearts have found a strength, a solace, a blessing that no words can describe.

Eddie Cantor tells of an experience in one of our largest cities. Without warning a terrific wind swept through the city, accompanied by a blinding rain. Along with many others Mr. Cantor found himself crouching in the huge, sheltering doorway of a church. His words to us carry a much needed lesson: "The world today is going through something far more threatening than a windstorm. Every single one of us needs refuge of one kind or another. I know of no better place to go for it than a church. The greatest calamity that can befall a people is the loss of religion. Don't let it happen here. Go to church."

In His sanctuary you will find God. You will be conscious of His deep interest in you and your problems and your faith. You will be thrilled by the thought that you have the constant presence of God in every moment of your life. *Lo, I am with you always.* You will be lifted out of fear and doubt and discouragement and despair by the undergirding arms about you, keeping you in all your journey. You will be strengthened by the assurance that you are to enjoy true guidance as your feet reach out into the unknown way.

In the darkest hour you can feel the strong hand of the Guide directing your steps. How can you fear? How can you miss the way? The keenest realization of all will come to your soul in the knowledge that He is directing your steps into the eternal home already prepared for you at the end of the journey. No joy could ever be richer than yours when you see and understand the full import of that assurance. He has gone to prepare a place for you. He is coming again to receive you unto Himself and into that eternal home where joys unspeakable will be yours throughout the endless ages of eternity.

Are not these the very assurances that your heart craves? Can you compare these treasures with all the things the world can offer? A loving Father wants to give you the golden certainty of these riches. Will you surrender your will to Him, and let the sunlight of certainty flood your soul? You will find Him in the sanctuary.

PART II
How They Preached and Prepared

Theodore F. Adams

Each summer I review the preaching of the year gone by and plan a general program of preaching for the year ahead. I prepare a folder for each month and put down each Sunday of the month with space for subjects for morning and evening services. I put into each folder anything that seems to be suitable for that month—Thanksgiving in November, Christmas in December, and so on. I also put in the appropriate folders materials dealing with stewardship, tithing, missions, evangelism, and so on. And I include materials in observance of Mother's Day, Father's Day, Baptist World Alliance Sunday, and other special days.

I then plan a general preaching program, indicating when I want to have a special series. The series of sermons may be for homemakers on Sunday evenings in January, a doctrinal series for Sunday mornings in January, an expository series on some book of the Bible, or other series as they seem to fit in best with the over-all program.

Everything that I read which I feel can be used goes into the proper folder. Within each monthly folder I place other folders for special sermons or special days or events. When I have an idea for an individual sermon, find a good text in my Bible study, or discover helpful material on some special theme such as prayer or immortality, it goes into the appropriate monthly folder. I also have some extra folders for special themes and occasions so that the monthly folders do not get too bulky.

Each month I organize the material for the coming weeks and give my church secretary and music director a preaching program for the month ahead. This makes it possible to plan appropriate music and to announce to the congregation in advance any sermon series or sermons connected with special events.

When I come to the actual preparation of the sermon, I take the material that has accumulated in the folder, go through it carefully, and set down a tentative outline for the sermon if that has not already been done. This, of course, calls for a study of the text and Scripture passages that have been jotted down as helpful material or as a basis for the sermon. After careful study of the Scriptures, text, and illustrative materials, I read other things that may be helpful from books, magazines, and commen-

499

taries. I try to have in mind sermons for some weeks ahead but concentrate each week on messages for the coming Sunday.

In preparation I make a rough outline and note illustrations and added material from which I may want to quote. Then I prepare a finished outline that I take into the pulpit with me. I do not preach from a manuscript but from these notes. They are full enough that I can give the message again almost as it was given originally. I take these notes into the pulpit with me, but I am not confined to them except for quoting something. I feel more at ease preaching without a manuscript, although each man must do it his own way.

Always in the preparation of a sermon I ask myself the purpose of the message. I find that this helps me to prepare the outline and to keep my objectives in mind. Always, too, there is a prayer for the leading of the Holy Spirit, that I may really be God's messenger to my congregation and may give to them the Word of life.[1]

1. H. C. Brown, Jr., *Southern Baptist Preaching* (Nashville: Broadman Press, 1959), 11-12.

R. Earl Allen

Like Vance Havner and many others, Earl Allen accepted the call to preach as a boy. He was licensed at the age of twelve. Upon his death he had preached the gospel for fifty-six years.

When Allen in 1956 moved from First Baptist Church, Floydada, Texas, to Rosen Heights Baptist Church, Forth Worth, Texas, this tribute came from the Floydada Church:

> . . . like a good shepherd, he seeks the lost. He does not wait for the erring to come to him or to the church, but he seeks them. I have never seen a young minister with a greater passion for the lost. . . . Our pastor has a consuming fervor for his work and he is diligent in study. For he spends hours of preparation in his large library, filling his mind with abundant resources of thought that he may obey the admonition of Jesus, "Feed my sheep."[1]

Leon McBeth noted:

> Earl Allen is primarily a preacher. Because of his personality and promotional ability many encouraged him to go into denominational work. However, he said "I determined to be a preacher." The pulpit has always been the focal point of his entire ministry. He spends hours of study on a single sermon, seeking not only to understand the Bible but also to understand people and their needs, and to present timeless truths in the most timely terms. . . .
>
> Allen's pulpit ministry is remarkably well-planned, sometimes for months in advance. His sermons are not served up haphazardly from week to week. . . . this planning does not grow out of an ivory tower, but from meeting head-on the crucial spiritual needs of his people. . . .
>
> Occasionally Allen stresses continuity in his preaching by preaching several sermons from different aspects of a larger theme. The larger theme may deal with Baptist doctrines, nurture for the Christian life, or moral guidance from the Bible for specific life situations . . .[2]

Most of Allen's preaching has been expository or textual. If the occasion called for it, he would preach topically. . . .

Allen is also a doctrinal preacher in the better sense of that word. He often emphasizes that beliefs are important, and in his preaching seeks to explain what the Bible teaches. His doctrinal sermons are models of clarity, however, and do not have the murky quality that beclouds so many sermons of this type.

Blessed with a remarkably clear and resonant voice, Allen's sermon delivery helps communicate the message. His voice has a good range allowing his various shades of emphasis. Allen never preaches long sermons, but he makes even a brief sermon seem complete by making every sentence contribute to the overall objective.[3]

1. Leon McBeth, *Victory Through Prayer: A History of Rosen Heights Baptist Church 1906-1966* (Fort Worth, TX: Rosen Heights Baptist Church, 1966), 141.

2. Ibid., 181,182.

3. Ibid., 182,183.

C. Roy Angell

My method of sermon preparation may not be worth a thing to anyone else. Even to me it seems to be most unorthodox. Through the years I have read many, many books on how to prepare a sermon and also many statements from the pens of great preachers on their particular methods. Mine is out of step with all of them.

Getting started.—There are numberless ways to find a starter for a sermon. Many times I read a good story or an incident, and it immediately suggests to me a thought, a theme, a text, or maybe all three. For instance, I read a one-page article about a diamond cutter who was working in the big display window of a jewelry shop. He was using diamond dust to cut and polish the ugly, uncouth stones to make them so beautiful that any woman in the world would love them. It brought to mind what Paul said about the sufferings of this day and the glory revealed in us. The beautiful theme of God's using the diamond dust of suffering, self-sacrifice, stewardship, and so forth, to shape our lives and make them adorn the gospel was written all over that story.

A sermon might get started in my devotional readings by some verse that suddenly blazes up or by some Old Testament story that so deeply interests me that I know the message in it will be helpful to others. Again, in my counsel room or in a visit in the hospital or the sickroom I find some need and the answer to it in God's Word.

In my study at home I keep a clip board on which I write down at the top of a blank page one of these texts, incidents, or sermon topics that is suggested to me. At times there will be fifty such pages on the clip board. I spend a while with them each week and prayerfully wait for guidance in selecting the sermons for the immediate future.

Securing material.—I have been asked literally hundreds of times, "Where do you find your illustrations?" My answer is the same, "Everywhere," for I am always on the alert for a human-interest story. Every good story written or told illustrates something. I find them in the periodicals that come to my desk or, as Roy Smith said, "The sidewalks are full of sermons." The artist with his trained eye sees pictures of beautiful scenes that I miss completely. The woodsman with his trained ears and eyes sees things to which I am deaf and blind. You can train yourself to watch for the sermons that go walking around you in your experiences in the ministry. You can train yourself to find them in your personal reading.

Since I love a good story and use so many of them, my friends clip the interesting and unusual and mail them to me. The newspapers of today, the histories of yesterday, and the biographies of great men abound in sermon illustrations.

Somewhere along here I should put in parentheses and say this: "No matter how full of grand truths your sermon is, *if it is not interesting enough to catch and hold the attention of your listeners, it will not do them any good*." Many of our preachers are able to do this without the use of illustrations. I envy them, but I have not copied their methods because I have found that to me the best and most effective way is to use a story that the audience will remember and thus nail down the truth more concretely.

I have no intricate filing system but keep a number of folders in one big file with such subjects as Christmas, Easter, Stewardship, and Missions.

Every Sunday both sermons are transcribed on a tape recorder, and my secretary types, dates, and files them for future reference. The notes for all sermons also are dated and filed in another alphabetical file.

Arranging time for work. — Practically all of my sermon preparation is done between five o'clock and eight o'clock in the morning. Around five-thirty in the morning I can pick up my Bible and preach from almost any verse in it. At five o'clock in the evening I can pick up the same Bible and can't see a sermon in any text in it. I guess you will laugh at me, but you will be laughing with me too, because I can't understand it. I love it; I am thrilled by it. There is nothing I would rather do at five o'clock in the morning than to work on a sermon.

No later than Monday morning I select from my topic board the two sermons for next Sunday. Then for about two hours I jot down notes, thoughts, and Bible references that come to mind, without trying at all to organize them or to outline the sermon. The last thing I do at night is to read over the notes I have made, along with some of the Scriptures, and lay them aside. I find my subconscious works on it through the night.

Many times I have read the statement by some preacher that four hours is sufficient time for preparing a sermon. Once more I am offside, for it takes me much longer.

If the outline and most of the material are not in shape by Thursday night, I often have a terrible dream. I think I am in the pulpit without my tie, my coat, or even without my shoes, or that I can't remember my sermon subject; or maybe I left my Bible at home, or I can't find the text. In short, it's a nightmare if the sermon is not well on the way.

Lastly, I lock myself up on Saturday morning and put the final touches on the Sunday morning sermon. Sunday afternoon I go to bed and sleep for an hour or so. It's the best way to forget the morning sermon. I seldom come out of my study until five o'clock on Sunday afternoon.

Delivering the sermon.—I never write my sermons out but outline them fully. Sometimes an outline will cover four or five pages. Then I boil the outline down to one or two pages which I photograph with my mind. I leave the outline in the prayer room and take nothing into the pulpit with me except my Bible and an occasional poem that I want to read.

Practically all of my sermons are like Gaul—divided into three parts. I try to make these points so definite that they will be remembered easily. I use as few words as possible to express these points and quite often repeat them for special emphasis. I try to build every sermon to a climax, with an evangelistic appeal and an invitation to accept Christ as Lord and Saviour.[1]

1. Brown, Ibid., 21-22.

Wallace Bassett

Bassett was a combination of a strong body and a brilliant mind, a preacher's preacher.

He kept his materials up-to-date and relevant because of an extensive library and wide reading of newspapers, magazines, and journals. His library volumes numbered into the thousands, and books were carefully indexed.

He spent at least twenty-five hours every week in sermon preparation. He developed a "sermon sprout" book.

He explained his methodology in *The Baptist Standard* (August 17, 1960):

> This loose leaf book has two or three hundred texts or subjects. Of course many of these will never be used. I read them several times each year so they are kept fresh in my mind. I am constantly adding to them. My subjects are selected several weeks in advance, and some of these "sprouts," when they are large enough, are removed to another loose leaf book. Then I concentrate on the special texts, or subjects, and study them more carefully. I write everything I can think of on a subject and read everything I can find on it, and write it out without regard to form. Then I block out the outline on scratch paper. When the outline is finished I dictate to my secretary the sermons, often thinking of other things I want to say as I dictate. Of course I keep a complete file of sermons preached, and often go through these sermons and find valuable materials used years before which I had forgotten. Well, if I have forgotten it, no doubt the people have forgotten it too. By following this method I have more material than can be used. ("Preaching to the Same People Year after Year," August 17, 1960, 8.)

In the pulpit Bassett preached extemporaneously. During the actual delivery of the sermon, Bassett stood erect with both hands lying on the pulpit. Eye contact, a forceful voice, and good content held the listener's attention. His gestures and movements were kept to a minimum.[1]

---

1. From E. E. Lacy, "A History of Representative Southern Baptist Preaching from 1895 to the First World War," Unpublished Thesis, Th.D., Southwestern Baptist Theological Seminary, 1960, 69-71.

James Petigru Boyce

James Petigru Boyce was the founder and first president of The Southern Baptist Theological Seminary. He served nine terms as president of the Southern Baptist Convention. "His vision for theological education and his commitment to the great principles of historic Christian orthodoxy still stand as much-needed guideposts for all who continue to 'press toward the mark for the prize of the high calling of God in Christ Jesus.'"[1]

Boyce was known as a powerful preacher, a scholar on fire. He had a high view of the Scriptures. He emphasized the fundamentals of the Christian faith. Consider his statements concerning biblical preaching:

> I have heard sermons objected to because they contained too much Scripture quotation. It is a good fault, if fault it be, and a very rare one. An objection might much more frequently be drawn from the absence of Scripture. How abundantly Christ did use it. . . .
>
> Lastly, our preaching must be uncompromising. It is God's Word and not ours. It is His message which He has sent us to deliver. And we dare not vary that message from the instructions we have received. Our message may be unpalatable, but it is God's message of mercy and of warning. . . .
>
> There is special need in our day for this uncompromising spirit in speaking for God. . . .
>
> So also it is painful to utter threatenings and denunciation and woe, and I fear so painful that the threatenings of God's Word are not often uttered. . . . Some have learned to believe it best always to speak of a Savior's love, and many regular attendants upon the sanctuary have begun to despise, as rude and unpolished and impolite, and low, and vulgar, and unfashionable, and nauseous, and disgusting, and still others as unwise, and fitted to drive men from the house of God, mere allusions to the hell to which thousands around us are daily hastening. My brethren, to what are we drifting in these compromises of the truth of God? . . .[2]

John A. Broadus himself, the Baptist master of homiletics, wrote the *Memoir of James Petigru Boyce.*

> He [Boyce] usually prepared by making a rather extended sketch—what lawyers call a "brief,"—which he kept before him when speaking. Most of these were allowed to perish in the course of years. At the outset we find him grasping with decided vigor the thought of several thoughts of the text,

explaining and strongly indicating the great doctrines of Scripture, applying the truth to hearers with direct and fervid exhortation. There is still not much of illustration, but now and then an expanded figure that shows imaginative powers worthy to be oftener employed.[3]

Boyce was a blending of the theoretical and practical. He had a knack for appealing to all ages. He was a gentleman who emphasized politeness and the social graces, humor and seriousness—a preacher-scholar-administrator who captivated people for the cause of Christ and Christian education.

Eight of his most popular sermons were collected by Timothy George: "In the Beginning God" (Gen. 1:1), "Thus Saith the Lord" (Ezek. 2:4), Christ Receiving and Eating with Sinners (Luke 15:2), The Place and Power of Prayer (1 John 5:14-15), The Prayers of Christ (Mark 1:35) [perhaps his most famous message], A Christmas Sermon to Children (1 Kings 3:5), The Uses and Doctrine of the Sanctuary, Making Sacred Our Houses of Worship (Ps. 26:8), and Life and Death the Christian's Portion (1 Cor. 3:21-22).[4]

1. Timothy George, *James Petigru Boyce: Selected Writings* (Nashville: Broadman Press, 1989), v.

2. Ibid., "Thus Saith the Lord," sermon by Boyce, 74-75.

3. John A. Broadus, *Memoir of James Petigru Boyce* (Nashville: Broadman Press, 1927), 119-120.

4. George, Ibid., 62-141.

John Albert Broadus

When Southern Seminary opened in 1859 at Greenville, South Carolina, John A. Broadus was "Professor of the Preparation and Delivery of Sermons, in connection with his other chair of New Testament Interpretation." His plan for Homiletics as quoted by his biographer—Dr. A. T. Robertson—was as follows:

> Homiletics, or Preparation and Delivery of Sermons; Ripley's Sacred Rhetoric; Vinet's Homiletics; numerous lectures; ample exercises in formation of skeletons [outlines], criticism of printed sermons, general composition, and discussion; opportunities for students to preach, but no preaching merely for practice.[1]

To this day Broadus is to homiletics what Toscanini was to symphonic conducting. His monumental Preparation and Delivery of Sermons has been a classic in the literature. Broadus set the tone for future homileticians. He discussed preparation and delivery in five parts—the materials of preaching, arrangement, style, delivery, and public worship. The materials studied were the text, subjects, particular occasions, and the general materials—explanation, argument, illustration, and application.

The arrangement part dealt with its importance, its several parts, and different types of sermons. Thirdly, Broadus spoke of style, including perspective, energy, and elegance. He also touched on imagination. The fourth part, the delivery of sermons, espoused the "free speech" or extemporaneous method, after painstaking preparation. Then he wrote of voice and action—at the time called elocution.

And from all accounts we learn that Broadus tried to follow his methods. In 1888 he gave the Yale Lectures on Preaching extemporaneously with notes! He did it to prove such could be done not only in preaching but lectures as well.[2]

By following his own principles he created a following of those eager to hear him. He could not abide froth and pomposity which was often considered in vogue during the 1880s. Neither did he want to be chained to a manuscript. Rather, he desired eye contact with the congregation which sufficient preparation and minimal (or no) notes would allow.

In 1854, seventeen years before he published The Preparation and

Delivery of Sermons, twenty-eight-year-old Broadus published an essay in the *Religious Herald.* He had already begun putting together his approach to preaching:

> The modes of preparation and delivery, commonly employed, are: to write and read; to write and repeat from memory; and to speak extemporaneously. (We use this last term because it is comprehensive, although aware of its great ambiguity. . . .)
>
> We come now to the third method, to speak extemporaneously. This does not mean to extemporize the thinking, nor even that the choice of language shall of necessity be left to the moment of delivery. . . . We include under this head all those methods which do not involve writing out just what it is proposed to read or say, whether the preparation be made with or without writing down thoughts and whether the delivery be with or without notes.
>
> Among the numerous advantages of this method we may name the following: It accustoms a man to think rapidly and trains the mind to work for itself, without such entire dependence upon outward helps. It enables him to spend his strength chiefly upon the most difficult parts of the subject. . . . Indeed, the general question between this and the former methods would seem to be, which deserves greater attention, power of thought or precision and prettiness of expression? . . . In delivery, the advantages of speaking extemporaneously are not only numerous and great, but so obvious as to need no detail.
>
> This, then, is the plan we recommend: to think over the subject with all possible thoroughness, arranging the topics in the most natural order; to fix it in the mind, running over the arrangement till the whole is familiar; then going without paper into the pulpit to stand up and speak. [Later Broadus advised either going with a few brief notes or none at all.][3]

1. Edwin Charles Dargan, *The Art of Preaching* (Nashville: Sunday School Board of the Southern Baptist Convention, 1922), 218.

2. Dargan, Ibid., 230,231-232.

3. Archibald Thomas Robertson, *Life and Letters of John Albert Broadus* (Philadelphia: American Baptist Publication Society, 1910), 123-125.

Benajah Harvey Carroll

B. H. Carroll, pastor, professor, and founder of Southwestern Baptist Theological Seminary, was considered one of Southern Baptists' preeminent preachers of the late 1800s and early 1900s. He was a large man in body, mind, and soul.

His love for preacher brethren was enormous, and indeed many endeavored to imitate his style of preaching. In spite of his many accomplishments, his forte was his power as a preacher of the Word of God. Carroll was so unique that he could not be boxed and labeled as to his preaching methodology.

Like many successful preachers, he was dynamic in personality and presentation, and his keen intellect was brought into play.

His mastery of the pulpit would leave his listeners breathless and praising God. Many of his sermons could be classified as lectures and addresses to inform, not necessarily to inspire. J. B. Cranfill noted that Carroll read an average of 1,000 pages a day for more than fifty years and that he had a photographic memory. J. B. Gambrell called him "an intellectual Colossus."

Carroll usually began his messages deliberately and unemotionally and then warmed to his theme. Carroll's fire was stoked and then sprang into flame. Carroll rose higher and higher in enthusiasm and power as he forged ahead toward the climax of his message.

It seems that Carroll never had a particular homiletical formula in mind. As it should be, the Bible was the core of his preaching. Carroll "magnified the office." He exulted, "Lord God, I am glad that I am a preacher, that I am a preacher of the glorious gospel of Jesus Christ."

In *Christ and His Church* (Broadman, 1940, Foreword), J. B. Cranfill wrote of Carroll:

> As an interpreter of the Bible, he has had no superior in any land or any age. As a preacher he combined the eloquence and power of the greatest men of this and former times. . . . While it is impossible that any one great preacher or teacher can combine all the high qualities of all his contemporaries or predecessors, I do not hesitate or declare that B. H. Carroll came nearer to this ideal than any man I have ever known or studied."

A wealth of his sermons were left behind. There are found powerful statements of his theology and ethical thought. His written sermons were well organized and seemed to have complete thought. One of his strong points was preaching for total commitment. He referred to a sermon as "the exposition of the thought of God in a given passage of Scripture." Seldom did he preach on specific sins, but when he did he was bold in attacking them.[1]

---

1. Gathered from Lacy, Ibid., 94-101, and from J. Dee Cates, "B. H. Carroll: The Man and His Ethics," unpublished thesis, Th.D., Southwestern Baptist Theological Seminary, 1962, 2,31,71.

Baker James Cauthen

"As [Cauthen's wife] Eloise found out, however, Baker's preparation for preaching was a solo matter between him and the Lord. Having traveled from place to place with denominational workers and having heard them give the same message over and over again, she was immediately impressed that Baker always 'preached fresh.'

"Cauthen's preparation was not traditional. It didn't include the manuscript recommended by the preaching professors; nor did it include a year's planning of projected titles. Each week he went to the Lord to find the Scripture through which God would speak to His congregation. Then he worked long and hard over that passage, developing a detailed outline that he half printed, half wrote on any convenient piece of paper he could tuck in his Bible."[1]

Throughout his ministry as pastor, missionary, and FMB chief executive, he preached the whole counsel of God with spiritual passion. Perhaps no one could make a more stirring appeal to receive Christ and/or to accept the call to missions.

"But ultimately, Baker James Cauthen's life-style can only be understood in terms of his preaching. Since he's preaching all the time, preparation for preaching dominates any time not committed to his administrative tasks.

"Frank Means calls him a preaching administrator. . . . 'But you don't really know the man till you see him as a preacher' . . .

"Cauthen himself says: 'I see myself as a Chinese coolie carrying a heavy load on a pole. If I put office work on one end and preaching on the other, they can balance each other' . . .

"If he's on his way to preach, that's all he thinks about." Unlike most preacher-administrators, Cauthen seldom preaches the same sermon twice. He kept a notebook on texts and ideas and was constantly making notes in it. His devotional life led to many sermons.

"Observers feel that Cauthen comes as inspired to the pulpit as any preacher in Southern Baptist life. As he preaches he is a dynamo of action. He leans into the pulpit with his left hand on one side and his right hand on the other, his left foot forward. He lets his voice carry most of the emphasis, but every now and then he backs away and a stabbing right finger adds emphasis. He does not shout, but his voice gets louder and louder, rising on crescendos. Then it settles again to begin a new round of rising. At times he and the audience can get caught up in an interaction that is absolutely magnetic."²

1. Jesse C. Fletcher, *Baker James Cauthen: A Man for All Nations* (Nashville: Broadman Press, 1977), 76.

2. Ibid., 259,260,261.

H. Gordon Clinard

. . . Sermon construction begins when an idea is born. For me this idea may come from any one of multiple sources. Often sermon ideas have come from the needs of the people to whom I have preached. Indeed, the best sermons are always preached with a specific audience objective in mind. Most of my sermon ideas have come from the biblical study I have sought to pursue without reference to specific sermon preparation. Others have come from assigned or special occasions, from general and religious reading, from observation, and from other sermons heard or read. If an idea and objective are in mind, the search for the completed sermon is a thrilling adventure.

Once the idea has captured me, the formulation of the sermon formally begins. I like to have time for a sermon to mature. Thus, I have a seedbed of sermon ideas on which I am gathering material in advance of specific preaching occasions. If the minister so works, there is new purpose in his reading and study.

Formal preparation begins with the exegesis of the text. No matter whether the idea or the text occurs first, they must be brought together. Biblical exegesis and exposition may be already in hand from daily study. If so, the text should still be studied and new material added. When I am satisfied that I have found what the text says and when I have in hand the fruit of lexical and commentary study, I place textual material in a file folder, and I am ready to gather other material for the sermon. Such material is necessary if sermons are to be other than lectures. The most biblical sermon is enhanced by the spice of illustrative and supportive material. If the heart of the sermon is the text, such material can be woven into the text so as to make the biblical truth live for the contemporary hearer.

Much of my supporting sermon material comes from my current reading. Some comes from former reading which has been preserved in a filing system. Every minister must file material according to his own personality. I have never cared for an extensive filing system, such as some men use fruitfully. My system is a self-made topical system, much like the one suggested by Dr. L. R. Elliot in his book, *The Efficiency Filing System* (rev. ed.; Nashville: Broadman Press, 1959). Most of the material in this

516 Southern Baptist Preaching Yesterday

file, however, has been used in sermons before being filed. If one has his idea for a sermon in mind and time to mature it, it is surprising how much of his current reading in books, journals, magazines, and dailies will fit perfectly into the sermon. I like the freshness of material found in this way. Aside from classic and biblical illustrations and quotations, most of my supporting sermon content comes from these current sources. Notes from these sources are added to the sermon folder.

I then read sermons in my library on the text and subject. My own sermon and the sermons of others are filed by text and are readily available for such study. From this source other material may be added to the folder.

Now I am ready to organize the sermon. Under ideal circumstances all the work to this point has been done well in advance of the preaching appointment. But the organization and maturing of the sermon occurs a few days before its delivery. This guarantees that the sermon will "come alive" just prior to its delivery, which for me is vital.

Having all of the previously gathered material and exposition before me, I begin a free association of ideas. From this the formulation of a proposition, title, and an outline follows. Although I have used various kinds of outlines, a study of my preaching reveals that I have had a preference for phrase and sentence outlines which more frequently number the traditional three major points. These points are selected with unity and order in mind, so that they progressively present the idea of the sermon. The nature of the outline is determined by the text and the approach, ranging from biblical to topical-biblical and using the various options therein. At the completion of the outline I write the introduction and conclusion. I seek arresting material for the opening sentences of the introduction. My purpose is to "raise the issue" in a contemporary sense and to involve the audience in it in the first moments of the sermon. Once the introduction has accomplished this, the text is introduced and the biblical journey is begun. Because my final point is often in the climax of the sermon, my conclusion is usually based upon it, although I seek to conclude the entire sermon idea and to make an appeal for decision based on the sermon objective.

For many years I have written most of my sermons in full. At times the sermon is born "full grown," and the outlining and writing steps are combined so that I can write the sermon from beginning to end in one sitting. More often, the writing is an additional step after the outline has been formed and the introduction and conclusion composed. I have found writing to be my most demanding discipline, but it is rewarding in the development of style. It does not make the sermon wooden for me. Instead, next to the actual delivery of the sermon, this is the moment of my greatest joy in preaching.

After I have written and corrected the manuscript, I am ready to prepare it for actual delivery. I usually complete the manuscript a few days prior to preaching it, and there is time to put it aside for some hours. To return to the manuscript after your mind has rested from laboring with it gives you a new identity with it. Gradually, by reading, concentration, and memorizing biblical references and other quotations, I become familiar with the manuscript. When the time comes to preach, I deliver the sermon without notes. Such free-style delivery has given me greater freedom than I ever knew when I preached with notes. I make no deliberate effort to deliver what I have written word for word, except in the case of quotations, but I have been surprised to discover that I usually repeat about 60 percent exactly as it was written. I do not feel every minister should preach without notes. Rather, he should choose the method of delivery which affords him the greatest liberty. It has been my observation, however, that the free-style delivery affords new vitality in the pulpit for a majority of those who try it. It is demanding in time, but the extra preparation is well worth the effort.

The foregoing has concerned human preparation altogether. Certainly every step of sermon preparation must be saturated with prayer and the leadership of God's Spirit. The minister should prepare as if preaching depended totally on him and rely on God as if it all depended on him. Only God can adequately inspire the preacher to select the sermon which will most effectively speak to the people; only God can rightly guide the mind of his preacher in the interpretation of the text and the use of material; only God can make the delivery of the sermon a true encounter with the living Lord for those who hear. But if the minister comes from his study and from his knees, the pulpit becomes his throne, and God speaks through him. Surely no task in the kingdom of God is more rewarding and more humbling!

---

1. H. C. Brown, Jr., *More Southern Baptist Preaching* (Nashville: Broadman Press, 1964), 1-4.

James Britton Cranfill

J. B. Cranfill never "tooted his horn." Rather, he compiled and edited many books of sermons by B. H. Carroll and at least two volumes by George W. Truett. Through his efforts in papers he edited, he was known as a strong supporter of Prohibition. He founded *The Baptist Standard*, the Southern Baptist newspaper of Texas.

As with many preachers of the past, unfortunately not much information is available concerning his preparation and preaching. Most accounts speak of his versatility as a writer and speaker. He was licensed as a medical doctor (M.D.) by Texas and received the LL.D. from Simmons College and Baylor University.

President S. P. Brooks of Baylor declared in 1920:

James Britton Cranfill, I have no academic formula to recite over you . . . soon a teacher in the public schools of Texas, yet quite soon a medical doctor by virtue of a medical examination before the State Medical Board of Texas . . . you, sir, are versatile—contributor to magazines, preacher, politician, nominated for Vice-President of the United States on the Prohibition ticket in 1892; I know of no place where you put your hands that you fail . . .[1]

1. *Baptist Biography*, Ed. by B. J. W. Graham (Atlanta: Index Printing Company, Publishers, 1925), 95-98.

Edwin Charles Dargan

E. C. Dargan was a professor of homiletics who preached what he taught and practiced. He was renowned for his pulpit craft.

While professor at Southern Seminary he wrote the monumental two-volume *A History of Preaching.*

Dargan left the seminary for the pastorate of the First Baptist Church, Macon, Georgia, having longed for the pastorate. *The Christian Index* of Georgia exulted:

> Dr. Dargan is a brilliant preacher, and now that he has for the pastorate thrown off the repressive conditions under which a theological lecturer labors in his class room, we can understand how he just revels in his freedom and inspiration of pulpit utterance (May 7, 1908, 1).

Dargan was called to the Sunday School Board in 1917 where he became editorial secretary. He retired there in 1927.

Because of his preaching he was often called "golden mouthed." His sermons were vividly outlined and had balance between the text, theme, and sermon body.

Dargan believed in writing sermons as we would telegrams, leaving out all excess verbiage. He also emphasized having no more than three main points and having three minor divisions under each main point.

Basically Dargan was a textual preacher. His major source of illustrations was the Bible. He often used word pictures and figures of speech. Most of his emphases were inspirational, calling for consecration and devotion.[1]

1. Lacy, Ibid., 171-174.

Amzi Clarence Dixon

A. C. Dixon was a pastor, fundamentalist apologist, lecturer, teacher, missionary, and author. His biographer wrote of his energetic ministry in *A. C. Dixon: A Romance of Preaching.*[1] A native of North Carolina, Dixon would later become known around the world, even as one of Charles Haddon Spurgeon's successors at the Metropolitan Tabernacle in London and D. L. Moody's successor at Moody Church in Chicago.

In his early ministry Amzi led a boy to Christ and baptized him. Later the fellow became a preacher and won George W. Truett. "'So Truett is my grandson in the Gospel,' A. C. Dixon used to say, when illustrating the far-reaching effects of personal soul-winning. 'The Lord helped me to win to Christ the man who won him'" (74).

Dixon was cosmopolitan, preaching to mobs in open-air meetings and fashionable parishioners in some of the outstanding pulpits of the world. He became a friend of men like J. M. Gray; C. I. Scofield; W. B. Riley; Thomas Spurgeon, C. H.'s brother; F. B. Meyer, Len G. Broughton, General Booth of the Salvation Army, R. A. Torrey, J. Wilbur Chapman, D. W. H. Griffith Thomas, and G. Campbell Morgan.

His messages were a mixture of low-key talk along with rising cadences to triumphant shouts.

The chairman of the deacons at the Metropolitan Tabernacle wrote:

> He took our hearts by storm . . . No one who has ever seen his smile could forget it. But the principal impression made upon his English audiences was his faithfulness to the Word of God. His ordinary preaching was evangelistic in tone. In fact he was too much of an evangelist to make a preeminently successful pastor. His great heart was too big to be confined to the limited circle of a single congregation (265).

Dixon disliked levity and irreverence. He wrote: "In order to do the most good we must reach the largest number. But let not the small congregation discourage if it cannot make it larger by legitimate means. Better preach to half a dozen the pure Gospel with freshness, than draw ten thousand by the clap-trap of sensational methods" (270).

Upon his death *The Baltimore Sun,* which had thoroughly criticized him, wrote:

Internationally he was as broad as the map of the world. He was one of the most aggressive leaders of the church militant. The dictionary contained for him no such word as compromise. He asked and gave no quarter to those whom he considered the enemies of Christianity or of morality, in whatever guise they came, as modernists, evolutionists, spiritualists, or emissaries of alcohol.

A curious complex of breadth and narrowness, of pacifism and belligerency, he had a magnificent courage that nothing could appall or weaken, a splendid sincerity that even devils must have respected. As he passes from us, we stand uncovered in reverent admiration of his brave and unfaltering faith (319).

1. Helen C. A. Dixon, *A. C. Dixon: A Romance of Preaching* (New York & London: G. P. Putnam's Sons, 1931), 74,265,270,319.

Monroe Elmon Dodd

The Western Recorder (March 14, 1912) reported: "Dr. Dodd is a preacher of unusual power, zeal, consecration, and genuine scholarship." He was renowned for his missionary emphases, evangelistic heart, and stewardship promotion.

His sermons were heavily proof texted. Many verses were quoted or referred to without explanation or interpretation. His sermons ranged from simple to complex. The title was developed first and the text, second. Sometimes his main points sprang directly from the text either as textual or expository.

In sermons where the title was primarily developed the structure became involved. Numerous major points were introduced with no certain direction. In some cases no more than one major point was directly related to the text.[1]

Except for expository series, Dodd usually began with the subject rather than the text. Some of his sermons were developed completely without settling on a specific Scripture reference to govern the content. Because of this inclination, it was easier for him to preach in series.

His second step in preparation was general study rather than biblical exegesis. He often asked seminary professors for recommendations concerning appropriate resources. When he had finished the second stage, he had put together text and topic. He decided on these many weeks ahead of time.

On Sunday night Dodd started intensive preparation for the sermons planned for the next Sunday. He read the Scripture passages then and all during the week.

Dodd used the *King James Version* in his study. Seldom did he employ a modern translation. His notes were filled with Greek word studies. He seemed to find the most assistance in expository works by G. Campbell Morgan and Ian Maclaren.

Then came the outlining. He kept a scratch pad nearby at all times. Toward the end of the week, he made an outline for the sermons. Then he took all kinds of material, putting it where fitting in the structure.

The final action was making pulpit notes. He wrote out the final notes on from three to six pages of small loose-leaf note paper, which he carried to the pulpit. He wrote out the introduction in more detail than the rest of the sermon.

Dodd maintained a subject file, arranged in alphabetical order by topics. The regular filing cabinet suited him best.[2]

1. Lacy, Ibid., 87-88.
2. Austin B. Tucker, "Monroe Elmon Dodd and His Preaching," Unpublished Thesis, Th.D., Southwestern Baptist Theological Seminary, 1971, 67ff.

Thomas Treadwell Eaton

M. E. Dodd in 1907 described T. T. Eaton as the "truest, best, and greatest." In the latter part of his ministry, Eaton was known as a "controversialist," but he was also recognized as a contender for time-honored Baptist tenets.

Eaton was a preacher, lecturer, and debater. "It was his nature to fight for what he believed in," wrote W. E. Hatcher in *The Baptist Argus* (July 11, 1907, 16). Because of his outspokenness, Eaton could also incur the wrath of the brethren.

Eaton was a strong evangelistic preacher. He did far more than "edify the saints."[1] As early as 1879, nine years after he started preaching, he was in constant demand for conventions, associational meetings, baccalaureate addresses, and other occasions.

C. Ferris Jordan examined over 200 of Eaton's sermons and concluded:

> In his choice of texts, Eaton favored neither Testament in the Bible above the other and often chose less frequently used passages without proper regard for their contents. Definitely biblical in their content, Eaton's sermons were almost exclusively topical or textual in their construction. An introduction, three divisions, and a conclusion was the pattern most often followed in the development of the outline. His messages were frequently written in full, but one of Eaton's contemporaries commented that he "seldom or never" read the sermons from the pulpit.

Eaton was so fired up that his delivery was rapid, gaining the nickname "Talking Tom."[2]

---

1. Lacy, Ibid., 148-150.
2. From C. Ferris Jordan, "Thomas Treadwell Eaton: Pastor, Editor, Controversialist," Unpublished Thesis, Th.D., New Orleans Baptist Theological Seminary, 1965.

Richard Fuller

Richard Fuller was a leader in the Triennial Convention, helped in the organization of the Southern Baptist Convention, and in the pre-Civil War era was an outstanding preacher-debater.

He at first was accepted at the legal bar as a lawyer and joined the Episcopal Church. In 1832 he became a Baptist and was immersed. Fuller entered the gospel ministry at the age of twenty-eight.

He was by many considered one of the outstanding pulpiteers of the nineteenth century. He preached (1846) the first annual Southern Baptist Convention sermon in Richmond. For thirty years thereafter it was understood that he would preach sometime during the annual Convention.

Fuller is best known for publishing his opinions on the crucial issues of the day. He was also recognized as a debater for the Southern cause. He favored the work of the American Colonization Society and the peaceful abolition of slavery.

His ideas on preaching were discussed under these headings: The Call of the Preacher, The Central Theme for Preaching, Reciprocal Relations, Ideas on Style, and Extemporaneous Preaching.[1]

Fuller emphasized the importance of the divine call and insisted that the preacher preach and live in the light of divinity. Preaching was to be Christocentric, which is the case of any genuine God-called minister.

He believed the preacher should talk easily and naturally. He stressed brevity and simplicity in preaching and eschewed the inordinate use of metaphors and embellishment, scraps of poetry to fill the gaps.

Fuller firmly espoused extemporaneous preaching. He would refer to it as "free preaching." Early on he used notes but later dispensed with them.[2]

1. Joe Madison King, *A History of South Carolina Baptists* (Columbia, SC: South Carolina Baptist Convention, 196), 210-212.

2. From George Alexander Jones, "Richard Fuller and His Preaching," Unpublished Thesis, Ph.D., Southern Baptist Theological Seminary, 1953, 77-84.

James Bruton Gambrell

J. B. Gambrell was known as a "commoner," that is, the rank and file happily listened to him preach and lecture and avidly read his prose which was filled with down-to-earth expressions. He served as pastor, state paper editor, and denominational leader in Mississippi, Georgia, and Texas. Because of his erudite ability as a writer and administrator, his preaching powers were often bypassed.

Livingston Johnson of North Carolina wrote: "I had heard Dr. Gambrell speak often and knew that he was a master of assemblies on the platform, but had never heard him preach. I am forced to confess that I did not expect such a sermon as he gave us. It was full of pathos, power, and practical suggestion, in regard to Christian work."[1]

B. H. Carroll noted that "Gambrell's inimitable way of putting things—his easy, lucid, off-hand style, his quaint humor and power of apt illustration in homely things the people can understand," enlivened his preaching style.[2]

"Many of Gambrell's published sermons did not have a formal text, although he used the Bible freely for illustrations. Generally Gambrell's sermons were devoted to contemporary and practical subjects or themes, making his preaching primarily topical."[3]

Gambrell wrote about preachers:

> In the Kingdom he is the elect of the elect, a chosen vessel for the highest possible use in the King's service. On the minister's faithfulness depends not only the salvation of souls, but all the highest interests of the home, the church, and the state. The faithful minister is far away the most important man in any community. . . . I believe the greatest weakness in the ministry today is lack of a proper purpose. . . . Place-hunting, a desire to get up in the ministry, has kept many a man down in the ministry all his life. Commit yourself fully to the Lord and remember that it is absolutely safe to do so. . . . The best preaching and teaching is that which brings the sinner, by the shortest road, to look upon Jesus by faith, that keeps all thoughts of mere process out of the way. . . . The preacher who makes service second to position is spoiled.[4]

1. Livingston Johnson, "Dr. J. B. Gambrell in North Carolina," *The Baptist Standard*, January 22, 1914, 11.

2. Quoted in "J. B. Gambrell: Ten Years in Texas," *The Baptist Standard,* 1909, 8.

3. Johnson, Ibid., 29ff.

4. George W. McDaniel, *A Memorial Wreath* (Dallas: Baptist Standard Publishing Company, 1921), 92-93.

J. D. Grey

Dr. B. A. Copass, my professor at Southwestern, used to say to us young preachers, "Preach out of the overflow." I appreciate his point of view, but have not always been able to do this. I understood this grand old man to mean that the studying a preacher does should not be simply in preparation for one specific sermon but that he should, out of his constant study, be getting materials to be used.

The sermon, Scripture, and idea for a sermon must grip the heart of the preacher if he expects it ever to grip the hearts of his listeners. This is axiomatic, and unless these first grip his own soul, he will know it as he tries to preach, and his people will know it also.

In reading various periodicals, books of sermons, and the Bible, when an idea for a sermon "hits" me, I make a note of it and indicate the source. If it has come from periodicals, I clip these and file them systematically. When I hear other ministers preach, I make notes and file these. I call all of these thoughts that I have filed "sermon seeds." Frequently a point will be made that is not too germane to the subject being discussed, but this will spark my own thinking, and a sermon will be developed from it.

When the text for a particular sermon has been selected, I put that text and its context under the microscope for close examination. I study it in the various translations. I study it in the *Expositor's Greek Testament*. In doing this I make notes that would clarify the meaning. I then turn to my sets of general commentaries, making notes of illuminating and inspiring thoughts as I run across them. I also makes notes of illustrations that fit into the sermon. I then turn to my file of clipped material for added help, such as illustrations, examples, etc. If the sermon is doctrinal, I turn to the standard works of theology by Strong, Mullins, and Connor. I study the text further in my cross-reference Bibles to see what other parts of the Bible say on the subject.

After all these random notes have been made, I study them carefully and prayerfully, asking God to guide as I begin to build a logical outline. Sometimes the three to five main headings come easily; at other times I may write out as many as twenty-five different points that need to be brought out, then arrange these under logical headings, naming the headings as I do. I make rather full notes, even putting in a gist of the illustrations. I do not write out sermons except those for radio and television use, where split-second timing is a factor, or sermons that are to be delivered at conferences, conventions, etc., or when a manuscript is requested. The sermon "A Christian in Spite of Everything," included in this volume, was delivered on radio in a fourteen-minute time limit.

In delivering my sermon from notes, I usually (though not always) have the outline before me. But I try to familiarize myself with it so that my reference to the outline will be such that I am not a slave to it. I try to develop the outline in my sermon in such a way that the life and meat of the sermon will be discernible rather than the skeleton upon which the meat hangs. The preacher must take care lest he duplicate the experience of Ezekiel and nothing but dry bones will be seen!

In my ministry I have done many things wrong. However, under the guidance of my pastor who helped me prepare my first sermon, I started out and have continued to do one thing that I think was wise—I have kept an outline of every sermon I have ever preached. I have these classified by subjects and keep the sermons under one subject in separate envelopes. I also have written on the back of each sermon the place and date it has been preached.

If it is true, as we said at the beginning, that a sermon must first grip the heart and soul of the preacher, then his heart and soul must be under the direction of the Holy Spirit, both while the sermon is being prepared and while it is being preached. The sermon must be believed and felt by the preacher or he will never be able to get his hearers to believe it and feel it! When he preaches the sermon, his hearers must know that he believes it. His hearers must feel, as a wise man said, that he has something to say and not simply that he has to say something.

1. H. C. Brown, *Southern Baptist Preaching*, Ibid., 75-77.

Vance Havner

"If ever a man was born for the pulpit, it was Vance Havner."[1] Havner spent about half of his life as a preacher to preachers, encouraging them in conferences and conventions. He was also a prolific writer of sermon books, many intended for the pastor.

Havner did not necessarily consider himself an evangelist but rather a prophet. The number-one characteristic of his preaching was plainness, although his quips and "Havnerisms" injected verve into his messages. At the age of twelve, he was preaching to crowds of 2,000 or more. Throughout his ministry, he pulled no punches. Early on he was criticized for the pungency of his declaration. One of his major aims was "to lead God's people to 'Get right with God' in a full surrender of themselves and their lives to the will of Christ, their Savior and Lord . . ."[2]

Havner filled his life with solitude, meditation and prayer, and intensive study of God's Word. In spite of his vast influence, he never talked about his methodology of preparing a sermon. No doubt he thought through his messages step by step, or he could not have come up with his now-famous quips and memorable quotes.

Havner urged preachers to bow their necks and preach the unvarnished truth, regardless of the consequences. "But he [the preacher] must not only be quiet enough to get a message from God, he must be brave enough to give it."[3] "Primarily a sermon is not a work of art but of heart."[4]

Preaching, noted Havner, must be *apostolic, anointed, authoritative, absolute, affectionate, and apocalyptic.*

Dr. Havner seldom raised his voice, hardly ever shouted. He didn't have to. Listeners hung on his every word from God.[5]

---

1. Douglas M. White, *Vance Havner: Journey from Jugtown* (Old Tappan, NJ, 1977), 21.
2. Ibid., 98.
3. Vance Havner, *On This Rock I Stand & Other Messages* (Grand Rapids, MI: Baker Book House, 1981), 103.
4. Ibid., 105.
5. Ibid., 109ff.

W. Douglas Hudgins

Elegance is the word best describing the preaching of W. Douglas Hudgins. He maintained a balance between informality and formality. He often coined words, and when he did, his listeners understood their meaning.

In his sermons he would at times employ "big" words, but for the sake of commonality could turn around and deliberately say "ain't." He was adept at keeping his congregation's attention because of his careful speech, his uncomplicated outlines, and his virtually perfect diction.

Hudgins was a preacher who could appeal to the "silk stocking" crowd as well as listeners from the country. Most of his sermons were textual or topical. Sometimes he would skillfully blend methodologies. He was not afraid to preach on controversial issues and often did.

His messages contained choice illustrations, but he did not use them merely for the sake of taking time. Although his ministry was not widely publicized, many felt he was perhaps the most articulate preacher in the SBC.

As most successful pulpiteers, he read hungrily—God's Word first—then magazines, journals, newspapers, and books.[1]

1. From the editors.

Ewing Stanford James

E. S. James was distinguished as a pastor and as the plain-spoken editor of the *Baptist Standard*.

"James refused to think of himself as a denominational leader or as a great editor. He summed it up in a 1963 interview: 'I have never thought of myself as being particularly influential as a person in any way. If I have exercised any influence for good through the paper, it has been because of the mercy of the Lord through the work of my predecessor.

"'I have never presented myself to the world as anything but a country preacher. I try to write pretty much in the same vein. I am not particularly courageous, but I am not afraid to speak what I believe . . .

"'If I have therein been of some influence for good, I shall always be grateful. But I think of myself as just a country preacher who came to town to edit the *Baptist Standard*.'"

He had served thirty-four years in the pastorate before going to the *Standard*. He was gifted with words from the pulpit and with the type-writer.

He always asked the question, "What impact will a message or editorial have?" He preached in different frameworks, mostly topical and textual. He endeavored to preach "the whole counsel of God." He was sensitive to issues and was a prophet-pastor, a person difficult to find today. He was considered, in the words of Glenn L. Archer, "a graceful, eloquent pulpiteer, for few men could unfold the Holy Word with such perception and clarity."[1]

---

1. "E. S. James: Editor of Strong Convictions," *Baptist Standard*, May 5, 1976 12-15.

C. Oscar Johnson

In preparing my sermons I perhaps pursue a very unorthodox method. This is partly necessary because of the many engagements which claim much of my time, both in my office and on the road. I spend a great deal of time thinking and praying about my messages for several Sundays ahead. Unfortunately, too many of my sermons must be colored by the necessity of special emphases. However, I secure my general idea and as soon as possible select my text. Then, with some reading and clippings from here and there and references from the Bible bearing upon the topic, I proceed to outline my sermon. First, I secure the three main headings or more if necessary. Then, beginning to enlarge upon each one, I give thought, study, and prayer to the preparation. Much of this must be done as I travel. Then in my study I fit the reference reading into the message. The type of sermon depends somewhat upon the occasion.

The outline of the sermon is used either in an expository or topical way. This outline is important, especially if the sermon is to be topical. The naming of the sermon for publicity purposes is also very important. The title of the sermon should cause people to want to hear what my message will be.

I do not write my sermons out, but I dictate four pages of outline from the handwritten notes which I have made at various times and places. This outline is on sheets the same size as the Bible which I hold in my hand in the pulpit. These notes are typed, and I seldom refer to them, but there are often paragraphs which I like to quote verbatim. I deliver my messages without a manuscript and as seldom as possible refer to my notes. I think it is far better to speak freely and without being tied to a manuscript. Of course, there are few preachers who are able to read a sermon effectively. For that reason I believe most of our congregations appreciate our speaking the sermon to them without giving the appearance of reading. Will Rogers once said, "I do not like to hear a preacher read his sermon. I always think if he can't remember it, how does he expect me to."

The beginning of a sermon is a very important item. It is well, if possible, to make the first sentence and the introductory paragraph one that will at once capture the attention of the audience. This may be done by a quotation, by reference to some recent event, or by an appropriate story or illustration. The preacher must use caution not to make this too effective or too long, because he is in danger of making the rest of the sermon an anticlimax.

Nothing else can take the place of prayer in preparing a sermon. The preacher needs to pray when he lies down to sleep, even on Sunday night when the service is over. Even then he might begin praying about the sermons for next Sunday. He will pray as he travels, as he reads. He will allow time for quiet meditation and prayer; he will allow God to speak the message which he wants the minister to give when the hour of preaching arrives.

Illustrations are a very important part of every sermon. They are difficult to secure. Of course, those that are really personal happenings are the best. There is danger of taking someone else's experience and making it the preacher's own, which is not the proper thing to do. But each sermon must have windows in it if people are to stay awake and get the message. Many books of illustrations are published, but my experience has been that one book of hundreds of illustrations may have only a dozen in it that will serve my purpose.

All of these things, plus a leadership of the Holy Spirit, should enable a preacher to bring God's message to the people. To sum up then—plan, study, pray, and deliver. This would be a simple way for the young preacher, or any other preacher, to preach.

1. Brown, *Southern Baptist Preaching,* Ibid., 104-106.

Roland Quinche Leavell

The heart of Roland Q. Leavell and his ministry was evangelism, whether as pastor, director of evangelism of the Home Mission Board, seminary president, author, or professor of evangelism. His preaching therefore would be called evangelistic preaching, prophetic preaching as in both the Old and New Testament. He proclaimed the Word of God and called people to repentance and faith in Jesus Christ with a sense of urgency in the power of the Spirit.

The content of his preaching was centered in the Bible, emphasizing the gospel of Christ: the death, burial, and resurrection of Jesus Christ. It was Christ centered and built around the doctrines of the grace of God and the salvation of persons; namely a righteous but forgiving God, repentance, faith, regeneration, and the work of the Holy Spirit. His sermons were primarily topical but filled with quotations from Scripture.

His objectives were to create conviction, to lead to conversion and commitment to Christ, and to build character in the believer. Thus, his sermons include an educational content with a strong doctrinal base, a devotional content, stressing a complete dedication to Christ, and an emotional content, stirring the hearts of hearers to turn from sin and to respond to the love of God as revealed in Christ. His messages included biblical materials blended with descriptions, narratives, illustrations, including personal illustrations, poetry, and some humor. He avoided sentimentality and overemotionalism. He applied his message throughout the sermon, but also made a persuasive appeal in the conclusion. His sermons were well organized generally with three or four points. His introductions were usually appropriate, sometimes long, and usually interesting, often based on the text or other biblical material. His conclusions were somewhat brief and led into the invitation to respond to the Word of God.

Dr. Leavell gave thorough preparation to his sermons. He first of all prepared his heart for the message and urged his students to prepare themselves thoroughly through prayer and the study of Scripture. He often rehearsed his message aloud as he passed down the hallway or across the room. His sermons were typed across the narrow width of a half sheet of letter-size paper. They were not full sermon manuscripts but full sermon outlines, with the main headings stated in full and with subdivisions written in phrases. The introductions and conclusions were briefly sketched and illustrations indicated by a one-idea sentence. The sermon filled the front and back of the sheets and sometimes had handwritten notes made on the typescript, indicating new materials or changes in the outline.

In delivering his message, Dr. Leavell conducted himself with dignity in the pulpit. His delivery was marked by sincerity and pathos and with a sense of urgency. He used an abundance of illustrative material narrated appropriately and quoted poetry often. He spoke with clarity, easily understood, and his speech was marked by a Southern accent. It was varied in rate and pitch, sometimes gruff, but with a certain elegance. He was quick to analyze his audience and spoke to their needs.

Dr. Leavell was exemplary as an evangelistic preacher, for he practiced what he preached. He taught students to be personal soul-winners and to preach evangelistically. He wrote that men called of God should preach prophetically, as they did in Bible times and as they should now in our present day. Preaching should be biblical in content and relevant to the lives of the listeners. It should be a call to repentance from sin and faith in Jesus Christ and to dedicated service for Him.

References:
John N. Langlois, "A Study of Roland Q. Leavell's Concept of Evangelism," Th.D. dissertation, New Orleans Baptist Theological Seminary, 1972.
Roland Q. Leavell, *Prophetic Preaching: Then and Now* (Grand Rapids, MI, Baker, 1963).
Submitted by Paul Gericke, New Orleans Baptist Theological Seminary.

Robert G. Lee

I read the Bible with prayer in my heart that God will direct me to the choice of a subject and a text upon which to pitch my mental tent. Having chosen a subject and a text, I see what sort of outline would be most attractive and helpful to me in preparation and in preaching the message. I try to get a full outline first. I don't pay much attention to homiletic regulations. I do not have much friendship for firstlies, secondlies, thirdlies, or fourthlies. Sometimes my outline has ten or fifteen divisions.

After I do the best thinking I can on the passage, I search the Bible for substantiating statements of God's truth. Then I take time to see what some other men, preachers preferably, have to say on the subject, though I am not a slave to commentaries. Then I get what truths I can from any realm—history, biography, poetry, philosophy. I then try to put my thoughts into the best words I know or can find. Sometimes I pause in preparation and do some praying. I try often to find some statements by others that are contrary to my convictions, and I prepare rebuke for these statements and for the people who make statements in antithesis to Bible truth.

I always try to minister with blood in the bowl, knowing that "without the shedding of blood there is no remission of sins." I try in my sermon preparation to remember that some lost people will hear me—and brokenhearted people, people in despair, complacent people, and people who dance to the music of self-indulgence and chase the short-lived butterflies of pleasure. And I try to prepare something that will help me to "speak and exhort and rebuke with all authority," as is urged by the apostle Paul. In my sermon preparation I try to keep Jesus as the central theme, since he is the theme of the Bible from first to last. I anchor myself to the truth that if there is not much of Christ in a sermon, it is like having no salt in bread, no melody in music, no heat in fire, no fact in history, no fiction in literature, and no blood in the body.

I oftentimes ask myself the question: What does Jesus think of this? What would he say about my pulpit assertions were he incarnately present in the audience and came and said something to me after the benediction?

I never dictate a sermon through a dictaphone or to my secretary. I think best through the point of my pen, and I write all my sermons out with my own hand. I give them to my secretary, who types them. When the sermons are typed, I read them over several times, picturing the words, and deliver the messages—usually without notes. Sometimes when I have finished, I feel like praying the prayer which Mr. Spurgeon said he sometimes prayed when he had finished preaching: "Lord, thou canst make something out of nothing. Bless my sermon."

And always as I preach I remember my need for the Holy Spirit's help, acknowledging, too, the truth that moonlight ripens no harvest.[1]

1. Brown, *Southern Baptist Preaching*, Ibid., 112-114.

Charles Everett Matthews

"Charley Matthews was associated with L. R. Scarborough for twenty-five years; as a student in Dr. Scarborough's class in evangelism two years, always as a close friend, and as a member of the seminary board of trustees for 16 years."

Dr. Jeff D. Ray, professor of homiletics, recognized Charley's inquisitive mind but also his deficient background for preaching. Dr. Ray suggested, "'Charley, you learn fast, but you started your career in religious work late in life. If you will write your sermons before you deliver them, it will broaden your vocabulary, it will make you study, you will learn logic and you can be a great preacher in spite of your handicaps.' Little did the teacher think that his pupil would grow a church larger than Charles Spurgeon did!"

Matthews himself testified: "I was pastor of churches for twenty-five years. During that period I doubt if I ever preached a sermon that I had not written beforehand. Writing sermons was the most practical thing in the way of spiritual growth in preparation for preaching that I ever engaged in."[1]

C. E. Matthews's number-one emphasis was soul-winning. By his example he was able to inspire hundreds, and later thousands, of preachers and laypersons to become soul-winners. C. E. Wilbanks wrote: "His close observation through an analytical mind drove home that a soul-winning church could not exist without a soul-winning pastor."

His sermons were sprinkled with personal experiences from his personal visitation.[2]

1. C. E. Wilbanks, *What God Hath Wrought Through C. E. Matthews* (Atlanta: Home Mission Board, Southern Baptist Convention, 1957), 52-53.
2. Ibid., 76.

George White McDaniel

George White McDaniel was considered during his day one of the ablest presidents in the history of the Southern Baptist convention. Mc-Daniel became a brilliant preacher but was not considered a student in the strictest sense of the word.

The Baptist Standard (June 2, 1904, 5) wrote of him: "His manner was deliberate, his gestures graceful and his words chaste and elegant."

Clarity was a hallmark of his preaching. He was straightforward with his themes. His preaching was also referred to as simple, practical, apt, and effective. He got through to his listeners, and isn't that the point? McDaniel was like the preacher who commented, "I tell 'em what I'm gonna tell 'em, then I tell 'em and then I turn around and tell 'em what I done told them."

To him the Bible was "the Books of books." Even though books were important, there was no substitute for the Book. McDaniel thoroughly prepared for every sermon. In writing the sermon, though, every resource but the Bible would be discarded. Then he would outline the sermon aided by an amazing memory. At his death 5,000 of his sermon outlines were prepared and preserved among his papers.

McDaniel used all kinds of illustrations in his sermons. He gathered illustrations from his reading, his study of people, and from poems he loved to memorize. An outdoorsman, he used many experiences about dogs, horses, and the hunt.[1]

1. Lacy, Ibid., 119-125.

H. Guy Moore

It is difficult to set a definite time for the preparation of any given sermon because it is difficult to know actually when and how a sermon has its beginning. It often comes out of the awareness of the need of the people to whom one is preaching, or again it may come out of reading of the Scriptures or out of reading in general. Suddenly the idea strikes fire in the mind, and it seems that this is God's message and that it must be preached.

I have, therefore, as I am sure all ministers have, a central drawer where ideas are placed. It is the "seed plot" of future sermons. Sometimes they are individual sermons, sometimes part of a series, but with this beginning the sermon begins to grow and take shape.

I usually plan at least two series of sermons during the year. A great deal of time is spent both in the searching for a general theme and then the subject for each sermon. These series are kept close at hand so that as I read, notations can be made of material applicable for each sermon and the sources.

So far as weekly sermons are concerned, I must know at least by the early part of the week what sermons I will be using the following Sunday. Having decided upon the sermon to be preached, I begin the accumulation of the material. Some years ago my library was catalogued, and a text catalog was set up so that each book or periodical that has to do with a given passage of Scripture could be easily found. This, I have discovered, saves a great deal of time and makes my entire library more usable.

Three days a week are set aside for definite preparation. Wednesday is given to the preparation of the Wednesday evening message. Friday and Saturday are set aside for the final preparation of the Sunday sermons. When I come to my desk with the Scripture passage in mind, I look in the Scripture catalog and bring all the material to the desk that has to do with that particular passage. The first preparation is to understand the Scripture through use of the exegetical works: *The Expositor's Greek Testament, Word Pictures in the New Testament,* etc. I also use the various translations in order to get the exact meaning of the Scripture. As I read, I keep before me blank sheets of paper on which I jot down ideas and notations of material which will possibly be used.

Having accumulated material, I begin to outline the sermon. While I do not write it out in full, the notes are very complete with quotations and illustrations copied in full. When a sermon is to be printed, I like to prepare the manuscript after I have outlined and often after I have preached it.

I have found that the preparation of my own mind and spirit is as important as the preparation of the sermon. Unless it is absolutely necessary, I accept no Saturday evening engagements. Several times during the evening I turn to the sermon and let it become a part of my own mind and heart. Often much is added that is not in the original sermon—ideas that come as a result of quiet meditation. Sunday morning is given to going over the sermon again and in reading of prayers, not necessarily to be repeated but to give direction to my own mind in leading pastoral prayers in the worship service.

No matter how well one prepares the sermon, always a post-mortem on any given experience reveals it should have been done ever so much better. The challenge is always to endeavor to do a better job next time. One is always conscious that the unsearchable riches of the gospel of Christ are inexhaustible.[1]

1. Brown, *Southern Baptist Preaching*, Ibid., 139-141.

Walter L. Moore

When a preacher writes of his study habits, he may forget the exceptions that almost become the rule and tell what he thinks he should do rather than what he does. Matters of pastoral care and church administration constantly demand rearrangement of schedules.

Sermon preparation is of two kinds. One is long-range and general; the other is immediate and specific. The general preparation includes systematic Bible study, reading current magazines, both religious and secular, and books, both religious and secular.

I buy books on the basis of reviews, authors, and titles. Even so, I find that perhaps half the books I buy are not of sufficient interest to me to be read straight through. I underline and write in the margins. When I find material of sufficient interest, I make note of the reference.

As far as possible, I try to look over the magazines when they come, clipping material that I want to save and filing the few magazines that are of sufficient interest to keep.

I use 6 by 9 inch Manila envelopes, kept in a metal file, for gathering material for sermons. On each envelope I type the title, text, classification, and bibliography as it accumulates. Inside I put clippings and typed notes. These envelopes are arranged by texts according to the books of the Bible. After the sermons are preached, they are filed the same way.

Most of my preaching is expository, with a number of successive sermons from the same book of the Bible. I try to have a general plan at least three months in advance, but specific texts and subjects may not be chosen until the beginning of the week in which they are to be preached. Usually I have from twenty-five to fifty sermons in the process of accumulating material at any particular time.

I usually begin with the Bible study, then type out the related ideas that occur to me, accumulate illustrations, and prepare the outline. Sometimes I write the manuscript in full but usually not. I carry the outline into the pulpit but try to have it well in mind. The sermons are recorded on tape as delivered, and my secretary types them out afterward.

Considerations determining the selection of material for sermons include: spiritual needs discovered in pastoral contacts with my people, the program of the church, community social issues, world affairs that are on the minds of the people, and my own intellectual and spiritual growth. As truths become clear to me I try to share them with my people.[1]

1. Brown, *More Southern Baptist Preaching,* Ibid., 71-72.

Edgar Young Mullins

E. Y. Mullins, recognized as one of Southern Baptists' greatest theologian-educator-preachers, distinguished His Lord as long-time president of The Southern Baptist Theological Seminary where he began to teach theology in 1899 and also served as president of the institution until his death in 1928.

In addition to his lecturing and preaching, he wrote widely in theology and other related Christian fields. Some of his outstanding books were *Why Is Christianity True?* (1905), *The Axioms of Religion* (1908), *Baptist Believers* (1912), *Freedom and Authority in Religion* (1913), *The Christian Religion in Its Doctrinal Expression* (1920), and *Christianity at the Cross-Roads* (1924).[1]

He spoke widely as a preacher and lecturer and was so versatile he could appeal to any type of audience from a rural church to a university or seminary. He had a simplicity and aptness for illustration which carried his points.

He applied the gospel in his living, teaching, and preaching, and related Christ to every aspect of life—social, spiritual and material.

Mullins was an expository preacher par excellence. At times he deviated from exposition as the occasion demanded it. In his preaching he magnified the Christ of the Bible.[2]

In the pastorate he established study hours from eight to twelve noon. His wife Isla May was also literary, and they often read and studied the Bible and other literature together. She was a homiletical helper, especially in the early years.[3]

"He read widely in preparation, he concentrated intensely in thinking through and through his subjects, he wrote with unremitting care."[4]

Relevance was key in his preaching. His sermons concerning the burning issues of the day were such as: "The Freedom of Faith," "Faith and Science," "The Response of Jesus Christ to Modern Thought," "Are We Sitting at the Deathbed of Christianity?", "Meeting the Present-Day Challenge," and "Social Problems of Today."[5]

---

1. From *Edgar Young Mullins, A Study in Christian Character, A Memorial by the Faculty of the Southern Baptist Theological Seminary*, "The Beeches," Louisville, KY, 1929.

2. Isla May Mullins, *Edgar Young Mullins: An Intimate Biography* (Nashville: Sunday School Board of the Southern Baptist Convention, 1929), 89-90.

3. Ibid., 29-31.

4. Ibid., 152.

5. *Edgar Young Mullins, Faith in the Modern World* (Nashville: Sunday School Board of the Southern Baptist Convention, 1930), see 11-171.

Louie D. Newton

Addressing a group of seminarians, a professor of homiletics suggested, "It's good to have at least one point to a sermon." Dr. Louie D. Newton was consistently a three-point preacher.

While a great writer, journalist, and editor whose typewriter poured forth reams of noteworthy articles, he put few sermons in print. He left no sermon outlines; never took notes to the pulpit. What he wanted to say was etched in his mind. His memory of faces, Scripture, literature, and history was phenomenal, and it remained with him without demission until his death at the age of ninety-four.

Dr. Newton's sermons seemed to have evolved from his keen observation of life. He moved in and out of experiences with ease and great concern for each particular event whether it surfaced in his garden with a plant pushing its head through a crack in the ground or an emergency arising from a hospital bed calling for the most profound prayer reaching for God's help and comfort. His notice and comprehension of God's creation, from the bleating of his flock of sheep to the down-and-out people of the city, was amazing. Few things escaped his eye.

Not only was his life identified with humanity in general but due to his own personal stature he was invited into the ranks of royalty and nobility and into the halls of intellectuals. His association with all walks of life provided illustrations for sermons. He was a master storyteller always holding the audience captive until the main thrust of the message was understood.

When a need, situation, or topic surfaced he referred it to the Bible finding answers in the teachings of Jesus, the theology of Paul, or from the richness of the pages of the Old Testament.

With the Scripture for the sermon in hand, he would expose it to exhaustive textual study, being sure it was in proper context. Then he would refer to the great scholars of the church, many whom he knew personally from A. T. Robinson to Karl Barth. And then from his vast knowledge of history and literature he could lift events and characters and weave them skillfully into the sermon illuminating the Scripture.[1]

---

1. Submitted by E. Moss Robertson, Dr. Newton's son-in-law.

Archibald Thomas Robertson

A. T. Robertson is still considered one of the outstanding Greek and New Testament scholars in the world. His most outstanding work was *A Grammar of the Greek New Testament in the Light of Historical Research*.

His method of lecturing and preaching was inimitable. "Most of his books are samplings of his hermeneutics as he took the original text and exegeted the Scriptures for the edification of congregations. *The Glory of the Ministry* (1911) is an example of this. Here is Paul's Exultation in Preaching, an exegetical and expository treatise of 2 Corinthians 2:12—6:10. If every pastor could do this with Roberston's skill, what preaching would result! Geared to human needs, the interpretation and application came from a professor whose heart was warm and whose aim was to let the truth speak for itself. Thus, the scholar and professor claimed the whole counsel of God with acceptance. Robertson points the way to become an expository preacher of the New Testament order, and demonstrates it with simplicity and sincerity."[1]

Robertson always considered himself primarily a preacher of the gospel. In spite of his brilliant intellect and profound understanding of the Greek New Testament, he wanted to be known as a preacher.

During his college days he had fought a serious speech impediment which he worked to overcome. He spent hours in elocution and improvement of his speech, memorizing not only huge portions of the Scriptures but also voluminous literary works. He was considered the scholar-preacher of Southern Seminary. His thoroughness of coverage was amazing and yet, when he preached, he put it in "people talk."

Early in his ministry Robertson preached more on subjects or topics. He would select a theme, make an outline, and then put the sermon together. As he grew in his knowledge of the original language, he became perhaps the greatest expository preacher of his day.

John R. Sampey recalled that Roberston's sense of humor enlivened his sermons. His slight stammer often added to the wit in his messages.

Robertson did not resort to oratory. He used no special voice effects, affectations, or contrived cadences. He was simple, incisive, clear of diction, sincere, earnest, honest, and humorous, explained Everett Gill.[2]

1. Ralph G. Turnbull, *A History of Preaching: Volume III* (Baker Book House: Grand Rapids, MI, 1974), 194.
2. From Lacy, Ibid., 186-189.

John Richard Sampey

John R. Sampey served as president of The Southern Baptist Theological Seminary from 1928 until 1942, but he is also remembered as a preacher. James M. Frost of the Sunday School Board commented of Sampey: "What a preacher is John R. Sampey. In him God turned upon the earth a rare bird. He is a rare minister of God's Word."[1]

Upon graduation from Southern in 1885, Sampey joined the seminary faculty and spent over fifty years on the staff of that institution. At first Sampey taught Greek, Hebrew, and Old Testament. When A. T. Robertson joined the faculty, Sampey switched solely to Hebrew and Old Testament.

Sampey, as did several other professors, pastored small churches in the Louisville area. "I am persuaded that my experience as a pastor made my teaching of young preachers in the seminary more practical and vital."[2]

In his role of leadership, not only in the SBC but also in the Baptist World Alliance, Sampey was swamped with requests for speaking engagements.

One of Sampey's outstanding traits was his ability to make Old Testament characters come alive. His students nicknamed him "Tiglathpileser," and he was affectionately known as "Old Tig." But he did not neglect the New Testament. Sampey often published his sermons for magazines and Baptist papers.[3]

1. "Personal and Editorial," *The Baptist Courier,* July 6, 1899, 5.
2. Gaines S. Dobbins, "John Richard Sampey," *Encyclopedia of Southern Baptists* (Nashville: Broadman Press, 1958), II, 1182-83.
3. Ibid.

Lee Rutland Scarborough

L. R. Scarborough, even as president of Southwestern Seminary, was most recognized as an evangelist J. M. Dawson, pastor of First Church, Waco, Texas, many decades ago, wrote:

> He [Scarborough] is certainly among the foremost evangelists in Baptist ranks. . . . He has conducted revivals from the smallest country church up to the largest in the country. His revivals are revivals; they are not distinguished by super-organization and sensation. He preaches the gospel soulfully, fervently, believingly, successfully. His faith is daring and his personal work is bold yet tactful. . . .[1]

Strangely enough, as with most of these preachers of long ago, very little has been written about his preparation and pulpit decorum. Yet, much can be learned from his books. To this day *With Christ After the Lost* (1919) is still in print. It is no doubt one of the outstanding books on evangelism in modern history. Another most revealing book is *My Conception of the Gospel Ministry.*[2]

A few quotes will give more insight into the ministry of man.

Concerning Prophetic Preaching . . .

> Their (the prophet's) characteristics should be largely the characteristics of preachers today. They found the will of God and interpreted it to them. So should we. They lived lives of separation and dedication — separation from sin and dedication to and union with God" (13).

Concerning "The Preacher on His Throne" . . .

> A preacher is called to preach. It is God's orders. He is ordained to preach — it is his church's wishes. He is educated to preach — his teachers expect it . . . The gospel pulpit is the preacher's throne. His home is his throne room, but the pulpit is his throne . . . Paul says the Cross is central, essential, dynamic, climactic. His deep-laid purpose was to preach, and to preach the Cross, Christ crucified. It was his major joy and glory. . . . It should be the living, flaming ambition of every God-called preacher, his deepest prayer, his most impassioned longing, his daily purpose, and his consistently pushed plan to be a preacher of the glorious gospel; not a lecturer, not a pyrotechnic star-scraper, not a flamboyant elocutionist, not an eloquent after-dinner speaker, but a gospel preacher, . . . (56-57).

Concerning Ministerial Danger Signs
(This was published in 1935, but how contemporary!)

Exaggeration, Self-Promotion, Commercialization, Sensationalism, Social Border Lines (namely, sexual sin), Studylessness, Prayerlessness, . . . (67-74).

Scarborough influenced thousands to be compassionate, caring soulwinners and proclaimers of the gospel.

1. H. E. Dana, *Lee Rutland Scarborough: A Life of Service* (Nashville: Broadman Press, 1942), 79.
2. Lee Rutland Scarborough, *My Conception of the Gospel Ministry* (Nashville: The Sunday School Board of the Southern Baptist Convention, 1935).

James Wilson Storer

It is a moot question among many brethren whether there is more value in the preparation or in the delivery of sermons. Unworthiness in either will bring failure to both, and it has been my sad experience to discover that one cannot possibly deliver what he does not have.

Through the forty-five years of my pastorates, I have majored on expository sermons rather than topical. A different approach is necessary for each.

In the case of expository sermons, I have followed the path of what I call the "book" approach. That is, I take the book of Ephesians, for example, and lay out its main thesis. Under this I set up my outline, and though the time element permissible to each theme must be kept in mind, I proceed to treat each in the light of the main thesis. Then I seek to support each theme in the outline by other and corollary Scriptures.

For example, following the introduction (vv. 1-2) of chapter 1, there is a long sentence—verses 3-14 (Paul's longest)—which merits an expository study of at least two Sundays and which is preliminary to the first of the two prayers in Ephesians.

As one proceeds, facets of the great truth regarding the grace of our Lord literally leap at the preacher and call for his attention and treatment. This is the beauty of expository preaching; there is always something to preach, and it is the Scriptures that do it. The mind is never exhausted.

As a stimulant to thought, try this as a preaching outline of Ephesians:

Introduction—1:1-2
The calling of the church—1:3 to 3:21
The conduct of the church—4:1 to 6:9
The conflict of the church—6:10 to 6:18
Conclusion—6:19 to 6:24

The purpose of the church, using that word in its specific connotation, such as the First Baptist Church of Tulsa, gives the preacher both freedom and limitation, and will supply him with such an abundance of material as will embarrass him with riches.

The same will apply to the theme of "conduct"—both of the church as an entity and as to that of the individuals who form it: walk worthily and worship sincerely. Note those words "put away" and "put on" and see how the spiritual life affects the social life. When a man is in right relationship with God, he is in right relationship with man, and not until then. This will give an inkling, at least, as to how I go about preparing for expository preaching.

My experience has been that for the long and wearing run of preaching to the same congregation through a quarter of a century, nothing feeds the flock like expository preaching. And remember that what the Bible says is much more important than what the preacher says about it.

There is, to be sure, a place—a very vital place—for topical preaching, but an addiction to this type of preaching is dangerous. It quite naturally tends to bring what the preacher thinks into more prominence than what the Bible says.

Newell Dwight Hillis and T. DeWitt Talmadge were striking examples of this tendency. With their passing, also passed their churches. Charles Haddon Spurgeon's preaching, on the other hand, was a wonderful example of a happy wedding of the Word of God and compelling attractiveness in its presentation. To sum it all up, major on the Book, and let all your reading, your constant careful observation, and your thinking line up your sights on the great themes of God's Word.

Doing this, you will never be at a loss for something to preach. You will never be caught between Sundays with your tank empty.[1]

1. Brown, *More Southern Baptist Preaching*, Ibid., 113-114.

George Washington Truett

George Washington Truett, predecessor to W. A. Criswell as pastor of the First Baptist Church, Dallas, Texas, "was considered, not only by Southern Baptists but by many other Christians, to be the 'Prince of Preachers.'" Although Truett was a gifted pastor and Christian statesman, he is best remembered as a titan of the pulpit.

Truett was a diligent student in preparing his sermons, reading and studying in depth, coupled with seasons of anointed prayer.

Even though Truett spent many hours in preparation for his preaching, Sunday morning's sermon was distilled to notes the Saturday afternoon or night before. He did not write out his sermons and addresses but spoke from very brief notes and outlines.

He often made his notes on the back of envelopes with his own system of abbreviations which only he could decipher. During the sermon he rarely ever glanced at his notes. Truett often depended on spur-of-the-moment thoughts given by the Holy Spirit.

His delivery was aided by his impressive appearance and forcefulness of his personality. As with many preachers, he began in a low, slow voice, and his momentum picked up during the sermon. He often moved into a staccato cadence.

His sermons were filled with biblical truth and many illustrations which helped his hearers deal with life situations. His was a sermonic balance—teaching, how to cope, and evangelism. Truett never deliberately spelled out his objective, but it became plain as his message progressed.

Truett was not renowned as an expositor, but he did preach Bible-saturated sermons. Truett used the Word of God to buttress his points.

As to development, Truett used four methods: subject development, expository, textual, and a combination in which he unfurled the subject and the text. Seldom were his sermons of one type. He was strong with the closing invitation for decisions.

Truett was an illustrator par excellence, averaging thirty-five illustrations a sermon. His illustrations were biblical, biographical, personal, figures of speech, poetry, analysis, familiar quotations, news items, rhetorical devices, and stories.

His number-one strength? He magnified Jesus Christ.[1]

1. Lacy, Ibid., 88-94.

Perry F. Webb, Sr.

In all sermon preparation there are several requirements. These may not be consciously followed on every occasion, but they are all involved. The formal routine may vary, but the end results are generally reached by the same essentials or techniques.

First, I try to prepare myself. This is done by a quiet time with the Lord, which includes prayer and devotional Bible reading. One needs to "stand" upon his watch to see what the Lord will say to him (Hab. 2:1). As one thus meditates and communes, the mind is cleared and the Spirit makes contact. It will be of small purpose to prepare a sermon until and unless one prepares himself. Further, this self-preparation involves a careful mental and spiritual survey and consideration of the particular needs of the people, the church, and the community. It is a constant temptation to the preacher to deal in glittering generalities, pleasing platitudes, scattering sophistries, religious redundancies, and fanciful flights into the verbal stratosphere. Such spiritual gymnastics and pulpit extravaganzas will fall a thousand miles short of bringing men to God, which after all is the primary purpose of preaching.

Having arrived at a conclusion as to what is needed for a particular occasion, I select the text. This may include a single verse or an entire section, or it may include several texts, each throwing some light upon the theme by way of parallel or contrast, illustration or connotation.

In all true exposition of a text, it is necessary to ask such questions as: Who said it? When and under what circumstances was it said? To whom was it said? Just exactly what was said? What were the results? How does it all apply today? To answer these questions correctly requires familiarity with the context, the historical, biographical, and geographical background, as well as the social, civil, and religious antiquities. You can thus readily see that full preparation requires considerable research and thus takes time. Facts are the fuel of faith, and they give a preacher confidence and conviction in his message. But the preparation is not yet complete. Words are to be analyzed, linguistic understanding is to be clarified, and the exposition is to be organized. More study and more time. Bible dictionaries, commentaries, and various other expositions and studies will serve to feed the flame of truth that should by this time be burning in the soul. (It may be helpful to add that I keep quite a supply of sermon ideas "in soak" all the time.)

After I have traveled these avenues of study and research, it is altogether likely that some sort of an outline will have suggested itself, along with appropriate biblical, historical, literary, or contemporary illustrations. I always preach a sermon to myself before I preach it to my people! I do not write out my sermons, and only on rare occasions do I take any notes with me into the pulpit. No, I do not memorize my sermons, but I try to be so familiar with the truth I wish to declare that I preach out of the "overflow." The outlines I make for study and filing are generally fairly full and contain the essential points I wish to make, along with enough of the illustrations to easily call them to memory for future occasions. I try to memorize the Scripture references I use in the course of the sermon, although I have found it very effective on occasions to read them, if they can be readily found by paper clip and marking on the pages desired. My method of delivery is therefore largely "eye to eye."

A preacher should feel that every sermon he delivers is *the* sermon God wants the people to hear for that particular occasion.[1]

1. Brown, *Southern Baptist Preaching,* Ibid., 209-211.

W. R. White

I prepare my sermons in various ways. I shall discuss what I consider to be my best method. Other methods may be much better, but I like the one I am describing.

Finding my subject or theme is very important. When I discover a subject which grips me, I am on my way. My subject usually comes out of my study or some living situation. I study on planes, trains, and in my bedroom. An administrator has little opportunity to work in his study or office. In the pastorate it is different.

I read much in secular and religious magazines. I read many books, I study my Bible. I read very few sermons today. Those I do read are largely from men who think. Subjects grip me while I read and study.

Great issues and living situations confront me. I like to grapple with them. They cause me, as well as other people, to ask questions. I am eager for answers. Out of all this will come a subject.

After a subject arrests me, I search for more material both in and out of the Bible. The subject determines the quest and precipitates the general outline of development.

Then I begin to organize the material into a clear, homiletical outline. As a rule I see three main points, rarely ever more than four. My introduction usually has two purposes: (1) to introduce properly the heart of the discussion, and (2) to get immediate attention. Sometimes it is a single striking statement; at other times, it is composed of several strong statements. If it is a purely expository sermon, I use a sentence that will throw the essence of the Scripture into immediate focus, or I make several analytical observations.

To each of the main points I may add several subpoints. Sometimes I write out a paragraph on each. These developments tend to be brief and sketchy. They spark my mind.

I seek to move into the climax with increasing intensity and action. Sincerity with imagination and spiritual passion is fundamental here.

The conclusion is usually a practical application in the form of a resumé and apt illustration. I try to move into my illustration logically without alerting my audience too much toward the illustration.

I memorize the substance of the outline and key sentences. I then deliver my message extemporaneously, or at least without notes before me. A period of quiet meditation and prayer before the sermon is ever desirable.[1]

1. Brown, *More Southern Baptist Preaching,* Ibid., 141-142.

W. O. Vaught, Jr.

I consider sermon preparation my most important task. I do not mean to convey the thought that I believe sermon preparation is more important than prayer, soul-winning, or everyday Christian service. I do mean to say that sermon preparation is my most important task; and if sermon preparation is given adequate time and thought, I believe it will stimulate prayer, soul-winning, and Christian service. For many years I would classify my preaching to have been topical preaching—simply selecting a subject and developing the subject in the best possible way.

A number of years ago I decided that I would preach through the New Testament, beginning at the first verse and going through the New Testament verse by verse and chapter by chapter. This has been the most gratifying and satisfying experience I have had since I have been a preacher. Let me illustrate. For the calendar year of 1959, I preached from the Gospel of Mark. This seemed to fit well into the program of our Southern Baptist life since the Gospel of Mark was the subject of the Bible study book for the month of January. Preaching through a book like the Gospel of Mark makes it possible for the preacher to touch on practically all subjects related to the Christian life.

In the course of such a study the preacher has an opportunity to deal with subjects that are definitely related to the spiritual needs of the people. Looking over the sermons that have been preached from the Gospel of Mark, I find these subjects:

Mark 1:1-13—"Jesus Came from Nazareth"
Mark 1:14—"The Authority of Jesus"
Mark 1:38—"For Therefore Came I Forth"
Mark 3:2—"They Watched Him"
Mark 3:35—"No Turning Back"
Mark 4:2—"He Taught Them Many Things in Parables"
Mark 4:41—"Who Then Is This?"
Mark 5:1-20—"What Is Thy Name?"
Mark 5:28—"When We Touch Christ"
Mark 6:1-6—"What Christ Could Not Do"
Mark 6:30—"What Happens When We Obey Christ"

Mark 7:8-9—"Tradition or Christ?"
Mark 7:37—"He Hath Done All Things Well"
Mark 9:1—"The Coming of The Kingdom of God"
Mark 9:19—"A Faithless Generation"
Mark 9:50—"The Price We Pay for Peace"
Mark 10:9—"What God Hath Joined Together"
Mark 10:45—"For the Son of Man Also Came"
Mark 11:12-14—"Nothing But Leaves"
Mark 12:43—"When We Give All"
Mark 13:37—"Watch"
Mark 14:10-21,43-47—"Forgetting to Remember"
Mark 14:27-52—"In The Shadows with Jesus"
Mark 15:24-28—"There They Crucified Him"
Mark 16:1-8—"The Stone Was Rolled Away"

This indicates that such a series of sermons preached from one of the Gospels helps the preacher cover a wide range of subjects applying to almost all types of people and all major spiritual needs.

Believing that it is necessary for me to have my subjects not later than Monday afternoon, on Monday morning I begin to study the Scripture for the following Sunday's sermons. I study the scriptural background of the message first, trying to discover through the language of the text exactly what the writer meant to convey. I do my best to call to my assistance all the aids that are available so that I will know the meaning of the Hebrew and Greek language of the text.

After this preliminary preparation has been done, I begin to read the commentaries which have meant the most to me in sermon preparation. I refer mainly to three: Maclaren, Spurgeon, and G. Campbell Morgan. After I have thoroughly studied what some of these great writers have said about the text, the subject matter begins to take form in my mind. Calling on many sources of material for illustrations that will give color and life to the subject, I use Thursdays and Fridays to write down in full both the Sunday morning and Sunday evening sermons.

After the sermons have been written down in full, I begin to study and preach them, quite often preaching them aloud. On Saturday I put these sermons in short outline form, laying aside the written copies of the sermons and turning to the outline which I try to photograph in my mind. When I go to the pulpit on Sunday, I lay aside both the written sermon and the outline, for I have discovered that I have more freedom and am more alert in presenting the subject when I have no notes.

Heart preparation.—Sermon preparation, however, is not primarily preparing material, as important as this may be. Unless a preacher's heart and soul are prepared and unless the subject glows in his own mind and heart, he is not prepared to preach. Through visitation, soul-winning, and prayer throughout the week, quite often it is possible for me to use these great spiritual experiences to fire my soul for preaching. As one of our greatest preachers said, "Quite often I can make one visit and witness the power of the gospel and come back to my pulpit as brave as a lion to preach the gospel of Christ." I am quite sure that this heart preparation is of major importance.

Topical sermons on occasions.—There are certain occasions on which I deem it wise to turn from the regular order of preaching and present a special subject which may be related to some event of major importance in the life of the congregation, the community, or the nation. Sometimes when great issues are facing the people, it is quite wise for the preacher to relate his sermon to the specific needs of the congregation. Let me illustrate what I mean. One of our enterprising preachers in the state of Florida used an experience on one occasion to bring a tremendous blessing to many people and to pave the way for the conversion of a great sinner. A great fish, one of the largest ever seen on that coast, had been washed up on the coast of Florida. Almost everybody, not only in Florida but in all the nation, talked about this unusual event. Pictures of the big fish were in all the papers. Since this occurrence had been in popular discussion throughout the week, the preacher preached his Sunday morning sermon on the subject, "Running from God," taking the story of Jonah and his experience as the basis for his sermon. He took advantage of this opportunity to talk to his people about obeying the will and the voice of God.

In the congregation that day was one of America's notorious sinners. He had been an alcoholic for many years, but through that sermon he heard the voice of God and made his commitment to Jesus Christ. As he came to the altar that day, he fell on his knees and prayed that God would forgive him of his sins. Relating that experience later, this man said, "I had been running from God for twenty-five years; but that day, after I had walked into the auditorium and heard that message, I knew that my running was over." Quite often I believe we can use such local events to a great advantage as we bring spiritual truths to the minds of people.[1]

1. Brown, *More Southern Baptist Preaching,* Ibid., 121-124.

J. Howard Williams

Sermon preparation may take on various methods. An exact routine is not necessarily desirable, if at all possible.

The first thing that concerns me is the selection of a theme, a passage, or a subject. Sometimes one and then another will come first. A subject may be suggested by an occasion or by a program of preaching. One can set for himself a long-range program of preaching, during one year of which he may wish to magnify certain phases of the gospel. Within the given phase or series certain subjects logically should present themselves. One may wish to preach on the books of the Bible, or questions raised in the Bible, or direct questions asked in the Bible, or questions which have been asked him during his ministry.

Normally a pastor should think in terms of a "balanced diet" for his people, in which case he would need to outline in general fashion a program of preaching. Frequently, however, an event or a Scripture will come to the forefront and demand attention in a more or less isolated case or situation.

Having decided what to preach, one would need to examine thoroughly a particular Scripture or a series of Scriptures relating to the subject. The context of the Scripture chosen is of supreme importance. The text as related to the general trend of scriptural teaching within that field of thought must be considered. Having studied the Scripture passage and its context, one can give attention to a word study within the text or passage selected. This can be one of the most fruitful of all studies.

I have found deep satisfaction in studying the Scripture itself first and following that study with a review of what commentators may have said about it. It is well to add to such studies what may have been written on the subject recently. The use of appropriate poetry and illustrations, when timely and unstrained, is highly desirable. Furthermore, one needs to think of the theme or text and the Scripture selected in the light of the experience of the audience which he is to address. Theoretical preaching may have its place, but practical application also is important and even indispensable if the people are to go away with a sense of having been fed.

Sermon preparation calls for personal preparation of both mind and heart. Devotional life properly cultivated results in a sensitivity both to the Spirit's leadership and to the needs of the people. A sermon well born is far toward completion.

A joy in preparation is usually followed by liberty in delivery. Writing a sermon in full is sometimes difficult but is excellent discipline. Francis Bacon said, "Reading maketh a full man . . . and writing an exact man." But woe betide the man who depends upon reading his messages to the people! Reasonably full notes in the pulpit can be helpful but should never become a crutch. One is fortunate who has so prepared that his sermon is well in mind and his delivery is free of frequent glances at his notes. Spontaneity in delivery that grows out of adequate preparation is more likely to be well received and long remembered by the people.[1]

1. Brown, *Southern Baptist Preaching*, Ibid., 219-221.

PART III
Biographical Sketches

ADAMS, THEODORE FLOYD

Dr. Theodore Floyd Adams was born in Palmyra, NY, September 26, 1898, and died February 27, 1980. He was ordained in 1924. His Baptist pastorates included Cleveland, OH, 1924-27; Toledo, OH, 1927-36; and First Church, Richmond, VA, 1936-68 (pastor emeritus, 1968-80).

On February 26, 1925, Adams married Esther Josephine Jillson. They had three children; Theodore F., Jr., John Jillson, and Betsy Ann.

His educational background included public schools in Oregon and Indiana, and he was a graduate of Denison University (B.A., 1921) and Colgate Rochester Divinity School (B.D., 1924). He received ten honorary doctorates from universities in the United States and Canada and was a member of Phi Beta Kappa, Beta Theta Pi, Phi Mu Alpha, and Omicron Delta Kappa.

Adams served on the executive committee, Baptist World Alliance, 1934-80. He was vice-president of the Alliance, 1947-50, and president, 1955-60. He assisted in the organization of the World Council of Churches, a member of the Foreign Mission Board, SBC, trustee of Virginia Union University, Denison University, the University of Richmond, Southern Baptist Hospital, Virginia Baptist Children's Home, and Virginia Institute of Pastoral Care. Adams was also an organizer of CARE, serving as vice-president and board member.

Dr. Adams was instrumental in founding Richmond Memorial Hospital and served as chairman of its board. For twenty-two years he conducted a daily radio broadcast in Richmond and did extensive work in television. Upon his retirement he was visiting professor of preaching at Southeastern Seminary, 1968-78. Honors bestowed upon Dr. Adams included the Freedom Foundation Award in 1960, the E. Y. Mullins Denomination Award in 1967, the National Brotherhood Citation, and the *Upper Room* Citation for outstanding leadership in the World Christian Fellowship.

His books included: *Making Your Marriage Succeed, Making the Most of What Life Brings,* and *Baptists Around the World.* He is buried in Westhampton Memorial Park, Richmond, VA.

ALLEN, R. EARL

R. Earl Allen was born May 26, 1922, at Benbrook, TX, the son of James Roy and Mary Ellen Allen. He was called away on September 11, 1990.

Growing up in North Fort Worth, he attended Sam Rosen school and later graduated from Northside High. It is amazing that many years later his mother's church, Rosen Heights, would call him as pastor. Earl had joined the Azle Avenue church as a boy. The Fostepco Heights Church licensed him to preach when he was twelve. On September 9, 1940, the Azle Avenue church ordained him to the ministry.

Earl was educated at Howard Payne College, where he met his wife, Norma Joyce Lovelace of Santa Ana, TX. They were married on December 25, 1941, while students at Howard Payne. They had three children: Norma, who died tragically at age ten, James Todd, and Joy Earline.

Allen pastored rural churches while in college. He served First, Archer City (1945-47); First, Seagraves (1947-50); and First, Floydada, all in Texas (1950-56).

On October 1, 1956, Allen was called to Rosen Heights where he had a phenomenal ministry, serving until his death.

His education included the B.A., B.S., and M.A. from Howard Payne University, Linda Vista Baptist College, and Midwestern University. He attended Southwestern Seminary, where he later served as adjunct professor.

He was given five honorary degrees: D.D. from Howard Payne; LL.D. from Atlanta School of Law; Litt.D. from John Brown University, DH.L. from Linda Vista College, and D.ST. from Southwest Baptist University.

He authored close to thirty books, including other writing contributions. He received three George Washington Freedom Foundations awards. Allen is widely known for his books, including these from Broadman—*Memorial Messages, Christian Comfort, Strength from Shadows, Sign of the Star, The Personal Jesus, Persons of the Passion, Prayers That Changed History, For Those Who Grieve, Jesus Loves Me, Let It Begin in Me, Southern Baptist Preaching Today* (co-compiler with Joel Gregory), and this present book (also with Gregory) on which he did considerable research and work before his death.

He served in denominational life in the association, state, and SBC. He was a trustee of Howard Payne and a trustee at Valley Baptist Academy and Wayland Baptist University. Allen served a total of twenty-four years as a member of the Sunday School Board of the Southern Baptist Convention, Home Mission Board, and SBC Executive Committee.

ANGELL, CHARLES ROY

Dr. Charles Roy Angell was born in Boone Mill, VA, October 8, 1889, and died in Miami, FL, September 11, 1971.

He was a graduate of Richmond University (B.A.), Penn University (M.A.), Crozier Theological Seminary (B.D.), and Johns Hopkins University (Ph.D.).

Stetson University awarded him an honorary D.D. degree, June 1, 1942.
Angell married Ilma Meade of Elizabeth City, NC, on October 8, 1915.
Their children were Charles Roy, Jr., Pattye Kathryn, and Ilma Louise.

His pastorates included Elizabeth City, NC; First, Charlottesville, VA;
Fulton Avenue, Baltimore, MD; First, Baton Rouge, LA; First, San Antonio,
TX; and Central, Miami, FL, where he served from 1936 until his retirement
in 1962.

He was a frequent speaker at campfire services at Ridgecrest, especially
during Student Week and Training Union Week from 1937 to 1960. He was
the author of several sermon books noted for their apt illustrations. Included
are: *Iron Shoes* (1953), *The Price Tags of Life* (1959), *God's Gold on Great
Days* (1968). All were published by Broadman Press. Angell served as vice-
president of the SBC, 1945-46; president of the Florida Baptist Convention,
1949; and as trustee of Baptist Hospital of Miami and of Stetson University.
In 1951 he delivered the annual sermon at the SBC in San Francisco.

BASSETT, WALLACE

Dr. Wallace Bassett was born in Middle Grove, MO, December 31, 1884
and died in Dallas, TX, October 8, 1968.

Pastor and denomination leader, son of a Missouri farmer, he attended
school at William Jewell Academy, Newton Theological Seminary, and Kansas City Theological Seminary. Degrees were conferred by LaGrange College, Ph.B., 1909; D.D. 1916; and Baylor University, D.D., 1920. He
married Lottie Bounds in December 1906 and had four children: Margaret
(Travis) Johnson, Elaine (William) Mayfield, Verona (John) Olson, and Wallace H. Bassett.

Dr. Bassett was pastor of two First Baptist Churches in Texas, Sulphur
Springs and Amarillo. In 1918 he went to Cliff Temple Baptist Church, Dallas, TX. His first wife died in 1938, and in 1940 he married Hassie Mayfield.
He spent 48 years at Cliff Temple, served 44 years as president of the Annuity Board of the SBC, 39 years on the Texas Baptist Executive Board, and 41
years on the Baylor University board. He was president of the Baptist General Convention of Texas, 1947-48.

He published two books, *Beatific Verities* and *A Star at Midnight*.

BOYCE, JAMES PETIGRU

Dr. James Petigru Boyce was born on January 11, 1827, in Charleston, South Carolina. He died December 28, 1888, in Paris, France. He married Elizabeth Ficklen. They had three daughters.

Boyce was founder and first president of The Southern Baptist Theological Seminary. He served nine terms and as president of the Southern Baptist Convention and a member of the Board of the Slater Fund for the education of freed-men.

Boyce was educated at Charleston College, Brown University, and Princeton Theological Seminary. He was pastor of the First Baptist Church in Columbia, South Carolina; editor of *The Southern Baptist;* professor of theology at Furman University, and professor of systematic and polemic theology at The Southern Baptist Theological Seminary.

His published works include *Abstract of Systematic Theology* and *A Brief Catechism of Bible Doctrine*.

BROADUS, JOHN ALBERT

Dr. John A. Broadus was born in Culpeper County, VA, on January 24, 1827, and died on March 16, 1895.

In 1871, Broadus published *A Treatise on the Preparation and Delivery of Sermons.* This became the standard preaching textbook and still has its influence today. His aim was to make it impossible for someone not to understand the proclamation of the Word of God.

Broadus graduated from the University of Virginia and began a struggle between the pastorate and the classroom. After trying both, then each, he made a definite move toward the classroom as a part of commitment to plan the organization of The Southern Baptist Theological Seminary. He was one of the original faculty members of the seminary.

Broadus mastered ten languages and gained wide recognition as a teacher. He authored several works including: *Lectures on the History of Preaching* (1876), *Commentary on the Gospel of Matthew* (1886), *Jesus of Nazareth* (1893), and *A Memoir of James Petigru Boyce* (1893).

BROWN, FRED FERNANDO

Dr. Fred Fernando Brown was born in Glenville, Jackson County, NC, November 27, 1882, and died August 9, 1960, in Knoxville, TN. He was ordained in 1913, and his pastorates were in Harrodsburg and Frankfort, KY; First Baptist Church, Sherman, TX, 1916-21; and First Baptist Church, Knoxville, TN, 1921-46. He served as special chaplain with the American Expeditionary Force and Army of Occupation, World War I, at the request of President Woodrow Wilson. He led the devotional service for dedication of Great Smoky Mountains National Park at request of President Franklin Roosevelt, 1930.

He married Nona Lee Dover, April 12, 1914. Their children are Nona Lee (Mrs. John A. Kaserman), Ailene (Mrs. W. J. Card), Imogene (Mrs. Hugh Ed Kaserman), Fred F., Jr., and Mary Elizabeth (Mrs. Christian Goedbloed).

Dr. Brown earned the B.A. (1908) and M.A. (1909) from Wake Forest College; Th.M. (1912) and Th.D. (1913) from Southern Baptist Theological Seminary. He was awarded a D.D., Wake Forest College, 1925; an LL.D., Carson-Newman College, 1951, and an H.H.D., Lincoln Memorial University, 1951. He authored *This is My Church* in 1929.

He was executive secretary of the promotion committee of the Southern Baptist Convention, 1931-33; was a leader in SBC debt-paying campaigns, including the Crucible Service Campaign, 1932-33; and was president of the Convention, 1933, although he never presided over a session because of his illness. He served as trustee for Carson-Newman College, Southeastern Baptist Theological Seminary, and East Tennessee Baptist Hospital; was director of Tennessee Baptist Orphanage, and member of executive board, Tennessee Baptist Convention.

BROWN, HENRY CLIFTON, JR.

Dr. Henry Clifton Brown, Jr., was born in Bossier City, LA, September 16, 1921, and died in Fort Worth, TX, June 10, 1973. He was ordained August 4, 1946. During college days he was pastor of Mora, LA, Baptist Church, 1943-44; president of the Baptist Student Union council, 1944-46; state BSU president, 1946; and associate pastor of the Pollock, LA, Baptist Church, 1945-46. The Pollock Church ordained him, August 4, 1946. He was pastor of Pigeon Fork Baptist Church, Waddy, KY, 1947-49.

On May 25, 1945, he married Dorothy Ruth Ware. They had two children, Mary Kathryn and Clifton Scott. Brown married Velma Lynn Darbo, November 17, 1967, following his first wife's death, November 6, 1966. He graduated from Louisiana College (B.A., 1946), The Southern Baptist Theological Seminary (Th.M., 1949), and Southwestern Baptist Theological Seminary (Th.D., 1954). In August, 1949, he became an instructor of preaching at Southwestern Seminary. He was named professor of preaching in 1954. He wrote, edited, or contributed to twenty-seven books. Prominent among them was his coauthorship of *Steps to the Sermon* (1963). Other preaching-related books of note were *Southern Baptist Preaching* (1959), *Southwestern Sermons* (1960), *More Southern Baptist Preaching* (1964), and *A Quest for Reformation in Preaching* (1968). Two of his books, *A Search for Strength* (1967) and *Walking Toward Your Fear* (1972) were biographical. The former dealt with his grief upon the loss of his first wife; the latter, with his life as a heart patient.

CAMPBELL, ROBERT CLIFFORD

Dr. Robert Clifford Campbell was born in Cleveland County, NC, July 2, 1988, and died in Galax, VA, March 25, 1954.

Campbell attended Wake Forest College, 1911-12, and graduated from Carson-Newman College in 1915. In 1921 Campbell attended Southwestern Seminary. Ordained in 1910, he married Ella Myra McCurry on May 24, 1911.

Campbell served ten different churches as pastor: Clifton, SC; Second Baptist Church, Shelby, NC; First Baptist Churches in Canton, Scotland Neck, and Hickory, NC; in Belton and Lubbock, TX; in Columbia, SC; and in Little Rock, AR; and Popular Springs Church, NC. His published works included fourteen books: *Heaven or Hell, Which?; Modern Evils; Universal Message; Youth and Yokes; The Coming Revival; Militant Christianity; A Quest for God; Around the Cross; Rocks of the Ages; The Christ of the Centuries; The Right Way; God's Plan;* and *How Firm a Foundation*.

Campbell, elected vice-president of the SBC in 1953, served as executive secretary of the Baptist General Convention of Texas from 1936-41. He had a major role in starting two of Southern Baptists' greatest movements, one of which was stewardship and tithing. His booklet on stewardship entitled *God's Plan*, widely read and adopted by many churches, sold approximately 500,000 copies. Campbell was also the originator of the annual statewide evangelistic conference which spread to other states in the SBC.

CARROLL, BENAJAH HARVEY

B. H. Carroll was born on December 27, 1843; died November 11, 1914 in Carroll County, Mississippi. The son of a minister, Carroll was moved to Drew County, Arkansas when he was four years old. In December of 1858, the Carroll family relocated to Burleson County, Texas. In 1866, B. H. Carroll married Ellen Bell; they had nine children. In 1897 Ellen Bell Carroll died. Fifteen months later, Carroll married Hallie Harrison.

Carroll entered Baylor University at age sixteen. In 1861, during the Civil War, Carroll enlisted as a ranger to guard the Texas frontier. Baylor University later granted him his degree.

According to Carroll, preaching was the greatest task in the world. In 1869, Carroll was called to pastor the New Hope Baptist Church in Burleson County, Texas. In 1807 Carroll and Rufus Burleson co-pastored the First Baptist Church in Waco, Texas. At the end of that year, Carroll was called to pastor the church full-time. He pastored the church for the next twenty-eight years.

In 1905, Carroll founded the Baylor Theological Seminary. Twenty-five trustees applied to the state of Texas for a charter for the school on March 14, 1908. The name was changed to Southwestern Baptist Theological Seminary. He served as president until his death.

CAUTHEN, BAKER JAMES

He was born on December 20, 1909, in Huntsville, Texas, and died on April 15, 1985 at Richmond, VA.

His last position held was as Executive Secretary of the Foreign Mission Board; he held the post for twenty-six years.

He was acting professor of missions at Southwestern Seminary (1935-39), missionary to China (1940-45), and Foreign Mission Board secretary for the Orient (1945-53).

Baker James Cauthen received the B.A. from Stephen F. Austin State College; the M.A. from Baylor University, and the Th.M. and Th.D. from Southwestern Baptist Theological Seminary.

Between 1933-39, Cauthen pastored the Polytechnic Baptist Church, Fort Worth, Texas. During his student years Cauthen served in several student pastorates in Texas, 1926-32.

Cauthen married Eloise Glass in 1934. They had two children: Carolyn (Mrs. Bill R. Mathews, Jr.,), 1937, and Ralph B., 1938.

CLINARD, HAROLD GORDON

Harold Gordon Clinard was Distinguished Professor of Bible at Hardin-Simmons University, Abilene, TX. He was born April 14, 1922, and was killed in a traffic accident in December 1973.

Clinard served two terms as president of the Baptist General Convention of Texas. He was the author of *The Gospel We Proclaim*, co-author of *Steps to the Sermon*, and a former editor of the *Southwestern Journal of Theology*. Clinard was a graduate of Union University (B.A.) and Southwestern Baptist Theological Seminary (B.D., Th.D.).

He served as pastor of Mount Olive, Union City, TN; Bethel, Yorkville, TN; Spring Hill, Trenton, TN; First, Rutherford, TN; Joshua, Joshua, TX; First, Burleson, TX; First, Huntsville, TX; First, San Angelo, TX; and was professor of preaching at Southwestern Seminary and held the Billy Graham Chair of Evangelism at Southern Seminary. Clinard was married to the former Christine Browder and had two children, Patricia and Truett.

COOPER, OWEN

Owen Cooper was widely recognized as a lay president of the Southern Baptist Convention, following in the steps of Pat Neff and Brooks Hays. He was born near Vicksburg, MS, on April 19, 1908, and died at Yazoo City, MS, on November 8, 1986.

He was educated at Mississippi State University (then Agricultural and Mechanical College), receiving a B.S. in agriculture (1929), and an M.A. in political science and economics from the University of Mississippi ("Ole Miss," 1936).

Cooper had been a school teacher before becoming executive director of the Mississippi Farm Bureau Federation. He was president of the Mississippi Chemical Corporation, Yazoo City, until his death. Cooper was a deacon, Sunday School superintendent, Training Union director in his church—First Baptist, Yazoo City—and was moderator of the Yazoo County Baptist Association.

Other state positions held were: chairman of the Mississippi Baptist Convention Board, chairman of the Education Commission, and president and trustee of the Mississippi Baptist Seminary.

In the Southern Baptist Convention, Cooper was member and chairman of the Board of Trustees of New Orleans Seminary and member and chairman of the SBC Executive Committee. In the Baptist World Alliance he was member of the General Council and secretary of the Men's Department.

CRAIG, W. MARSHALL

W. Marshall Craig was born on May 28, 1889 (Anderson, SC); died September 15, 1970.

He was one of three sons of Sam M. Craig, a druggist, and Mamie Partlow Craig. At Furman University, he met Loulie Ann Cullum, who later became his wife.

Craig attended Hiawassee High School, Hiawassee, GA, and Piedmont College in Demorest, GA. He graduated from Furman University (B.A., 1913). He would later be honored by Furman and Baylor University with the D.D.

He entered the ministry as assistant pastor of the First Baptist Church of Wilmington, NC; in this church, he was ordained to the gospel ministry. After serving this church for three years, Craig moved to the position of pastor at the Winter Park Baptist Church near the city of Wilmington. At the First Baptist Church of Kinston, NC, Craig became full-time pastor; he remained at Kinston for four years. Craig accepted the call to the First Baptist Church of Petersburg, VA. He served this church for seven years. Dr. Craig accepted the call to Gaston Avenue Baptist Church in Dallas in 1927. He preached at Gaston Avenue twenty-six years. Then, in 1953, he retired to begin full-time evangelistic work. He preached in every state of the union.

During his career, he devoted himself to many denominational offices. He served colleges, seminaries, and hospitals in various capacities. At various times, he served as trustee of Southeastern Seminary, New Orleans Seminary, the *Baptist Standard*, and Baylor University. He was elected one term as vice-president of the Southern Baptist Convention.

CRANFILL, J. B.

J. B. Cranfill was born in Parker County, TX, on September 12, 1858, and died in 1942. He married Ollie Allen at Crawford, TX, in 1878.

He practiced medicine for about three years after his marriage until he began the publication of the *Gatesville Advance*, a weekly paper distinguished for advocacy of prohibition. He was licensed to preach in 1886 and ordained in 1890 at the First Baptist Church, Waco, TX.

Cranfill was superintendent of Texas Baptist mission work from 1889 to 1892. He was editor of the Texas *Baptist Standard* and proprietor of the Kentucky *Baptist Standard* and the *Indian Baptist Standard*. He was Prohibition candidate for vice-president of the United States (1892).

Cranfill compiled and edited several books for B. H. Carroll and at least two for George W. Truett.

DARGAN, EDWIN CHARLES

Edwin Charles Dargan was born in Darlington County, SC, November 17, 1852, and died in Chicago, IL, October 26, 1930.

He was educated at Furman (M.A.) and at Southern Seminary. Honorary degrees came from Washington and Lee (1888 and 1920) and Baylor (1904).

Ordained in 1876, he pastored churches in North Carolina and Virginia. Then he served at First Baptist, Petersburg, VA; Dixon, CA; and Citadel Square, Charleston, SC, before becoming professor of homiletics at Southern Seminary. His two-volume set, the *History of Preaching*, was widely acclaimed.

He left the seminary to pastor First Baptist Church, Macon, GA, from 1907 to 1917. He then became editorial secretary of the Sunday School Board, where he worked until 1927.

His books include *History of Preaching, Notes on Colossians, Ecclesiology, Doctrines of Our Faith, Harmony Hall, Recollections of an Old Southern Home, Exposition of the Epistle to the Romans, The Changeless Christ and Other Sermons, The Art of Preaching in the Light of History,* and *The Bible, Our Heritage.*

DIXON, AMZI CLARENCE

A. C. Dixon was born in Shelby, NC, on July 6, 1854, and died in Baltimore, MD, on June 14, 1925.

He was educated at Shelby Academy and Wake Forest College (1874). He attended Southern Seminary. He became pastor of the Baptist church at Chapel Hill, NC, and then pastor of the Baptist church at Asheville, NC. In July of 1880 he married Susan Mary Faison of Warsaw, NC.

In 1882 he was invited to become president of Wake Forest College. Instead he accepted the pastorate of Immanuel Baptist Church, Baltimore,

MD. In 1890 he went to the Hanson Place Baptist Church, Brooklyn, NY, where he served until 1901.

In 1893 he worked one month with D. L. Moody, preaching to the crowds at the World's Fair. Dixon then pastored Ruggles Street Baptist Church, Boston, MA, until 1906, when he became pastor of the Moody Church, Chicago, IL. From Chicago, Dixon crossed the Atlantic to accept the pastorate of Spurgeon's Tabernacle, London, England (1911 to 1919).

For several months following his London ministry, he was engaged in Bible conferences, in evangelistic meetings, and in writing and preaching in support of the Fundamentalist movement. While attending a missionary conference in China in 1922, his wife died following a brief illness. Returning to America, he accepted the pastorate of the University Baptist church of Baltimore. He served this church from 1921 to 1925. In 1924 he married Helen C. Alexander, widow of Charles M. Alexander, widely known evangelistic singer.

DODD, MONROE ELMON

M. E. Dodd was born September 8, 1878, in Brazil, TN, and died in Long Beach, CA, on August 6, 1952. He married Emma Savage in 1904, and they had five children: Mrs. Clarence H. Webb, Mrs. Clayton Dupre, Mrs. J. A. Sporl, Monroe Elmon Dodd, Jr., and Mrs. Patrick Lewis Pellerin.

In 1898, he enlisted as a volunteer in the Spanish-American War. Dodd graduated from Union University in 1904 and was later given the D.D. and LL.D. from his alma mater and the D.D. from Baylor.

His pastorates included: First Church, Fulton, KY, for three years; First Church, Paducah, KY, two years; Twenty-second and Walnut Streets Church, Louisville, two years; and the First Church, Shreveport, LA.

Dodd held many positions of leadership among Southern Baptists. He served on the Home Mission Board, the Board of Trustees of Southern Seminary and the Board of Trustees of Southwestern Seminary. He was a member of the $75 Million Campaign Commission, chairman of the committee on founding the Baptist Bible Institute (later New Orleans Seminary), and led the debate in the Southern Baptist Convention for the establishment of the Baptist Hospital in New Orleans. Dodd was also chairman of the committee which formed and presented the Cooperative Program of the SBC, was president of the SBC in 1933-34, a member of the Baptist World Alliance Executive Committee, and president of the Louisiana Baptist Convention.

Dodd had a radio ministry and was the author of several books and many tracts.

DRUMWRIGHT, HUBER L., JR.

Huber L. Drumwright, Jr. was executive secretary of the Arkansas Baptist State Convention. He was born in 1924 in Walters, OK, and died in 1981 in Little Rock, AR.

Drumwright was the author of several books and articles, including *An Introduction to New Testament Greek* and *Prayer Rediscovered*. He was also a translator of *The New King James Version*. A graduate of Baylor (B.A.) and Southwestern Seminary (B.D., Th.D.), he did additional study at Princeton and the American School of Classical Studies in Athens, Greece.

Drumwright served as pastor of First Baptist, Allen, TX; Wilshire, Dallas, TX; Oak Grove, Fort Worth, TX; and First, Ada, Oklahoma. He was professor of New Testament at Southwestern, where he served as dean of the School of Theology (1973-80). Drumwright was married to the former Minette Williams and had two daughters, Minette Evalyn and Debra Kay.

EATON, THOMAS TREADWELL

Thomas Treadwell Eaton was born November 16, 1845, in Murfreesboro, TN. He died June 29, 1907, in Louisville, KY. He studied in Murfreesboro until 1859, then attended Madison (now Colgate) University.

In 1861, he enlisted in the Seventh Tennessee Calvary, C.S.A., and served under General Nathan Bedford Forrest. After the war he graduated from Washington and Lee University in 1867. In 1880 he received an honorary D.D. from Washington and Lee and an LL.D. from Southwestern Baptist University in 1886.

Eaton's pastorates included First Baptist Church, Chattanooga, TN; First Church, Petersburg, VA; and the Walnut Street Church, Louisville, KY.

He was known for his role in debates over evolution and the inspiration of the Scriptures, adhering to a fundamental stance. He was also editor of the *Western Recorder (Kentucky)*. He was highly evangelistic throughout his ministry.

FORD, WILLIAM HERSCHEL

W. Herschel Ford was born November 21, 1900, in Monroe, GA and the date of his death is not known.

Ford served the first vice-president of the Texas Baptist Convention in 1949-50, as a Board member of the Home Mission Board in Florida and Texas from 1942-45 and 1955-58. Between the years 1948-57 he was on the Board of the Texas Baptist Convention. Paisano Baptist Assembly was his first board position—as vice-president in 1948-58.

He is probably best known for his twelve books of *Simple Sermons*. These books have been used by preachers and laymen all over the world.

He received the B.A. degree from Wake Forest, NC, in 1932. He attended Southwestern. He received the D.D. from Carson-Newman College in 1936.

Ford served as pastor in many places: First, Andrews, NC; First, Henderson, NC; Broadway, Knoxville, TN; Kirkwood, Atlanta, GA; and First, El Paso, TX.

FULLER, RICHARD

Richard Fuller was born in Beaufort, SC, April 22, 1804, and died in 1876. He entered Harvard University at the age of 16 and graduated with his law class in 1824. Years later, in 1853, Harvard awarded him the D.D.

Fuller was admitted to the bar at the age of 23 and was successful. Becoming dissatisfied with law, he entered the ministry at the age of 28. He accepted the pastorate at the Baptist church of Beaufort where he remained until 1847, when he left for the Seventh Baptist Church in Baltimore. In 1871, Fuller became the pastor of the Eutaw Place Church which had grown out of the Seventh Baptist Church and led there until his death in 1876.

Fuller held a place of leadership in the Triennial Convention and later led in motions made toward the organization of the Southern Baptist Convention, serving as chairman of the committee which wrote the constitution for the new convention. Fuller preached the first annual Southern Baptist Convention sermon on June 10, 1846, in Richmond and preached during the annual Convention for the following 30 years! He was president of the SBC during 1859-61, a trustee of Furman University, and served on the Foreign and Home Mission boards. Fuller was renowned for his published opinions on live issues of the day, including slavery.

GAMBRELL, JAMES BRUTON

James Bruton Gambrell was born in Anderson County, SC, on August 21, 1841. He died on June 10, 1921, in Dallas, Texas. He served as a scout for General Robert E. Lee in the Confederate Army and was commissioned as a captain. He married Mary T. Corbell on January 13, 1864.

Gambrell attended the University of Mississippi and served as pastor of Oxford (now First) Baptist Church for five years. In 1877, he became editor of the *Baptist Record*. He was elected president of Mercer University, where he served from 1893-96.

Gambrell served as superintendent of missions in Texas, December, 1896, through February, 1910, when he resigned to become editor of the *Baptist Standard*. He was elected to the faculty of Southwestern Seminary, continuing as editor-in-chief of the *Standard* until December, 1914. Gambrell resigned both those positions when he was elected executive secretary of the Consolidated Board (mission and education) of the Baptist General Convention of Texas. He served in this position for six years, followed by four years as president of the Southern Baptist Convention.

GIDEON, VIRTUS EVANS

Virtus Evans Gideon was born on December 29, 1926, in Winters, TX, and died December 17, 1988, in Mansfield, TX.

Gideon was educated at Hardin-Simmons University (B.A., 1949; D.D., 1975); and Southwestern Seminary (B.D., 1952; Th.D., 1956; M.Div., 1973). His additional studies included work at the University of Saint Andrews, Saint Andrews, Scotland, 1964; Brite Divinity School of Texas Christian University, 1970-71; and North Texas State University, 1979.

Gideon served as pastor of Vickery Baptist Church, Dallas, TX, 1952-54, and assistant professor of Bible and Greek, Hardin-Simmons University, 1954-57. In 1957 he became a professor of New Testament at Southwestern, serving as vice-chairman of the Ph.D. Committee (1979-81) and chairman of the New Testament Department beginning in 1983.

The writing contributions of Gideon include: *Luke: A Study Guide Commentary; A Greek Grammar of the New Testament: A Workbook Approach;* co-author of *The New Smith's Bible Dictionary;* and many other articles. The following are translations published: the Translation of Mark, *New King James Version; The Word: The New Century Bible;* the adult version of *International Children's Version;* and *The Everyday Bible.*

GREY, J. D.

J. D. Grey was born in Princeton, KY, on December 18, 1906. He died on July 26, 1985, in New Orleans, LA. He married Lillian Tooke, and they were parents of twin daughters, Mary Beth and Martha Ann.

Grey earned the B.A. from Union University, and the Th.M. from Southern Seminary. He received several honorary degrees including the D.D. from Union University, LL.D., Louisiana College, and D.D., Baylor University.

Grey held pastorates at Vickery Church, Dallas, TX; Tabernacle Church, Ennis, TX; and First Church, Denton, TX. His last pastorate was First Baptist Church, New Orleans, LA.

Grey was president of the Louisiana Baptist Convention, 1948-50, and president of the Southern Baptist Convention, 1951-53. He served as a member of the executive committees of the Southern Baptist Convention and the Baptist World Alliance.

He wrote the hilarious *Epitaphs for Eager Preachers*.

HAVNER, VANCE

Vance Havner was born in Jugtown (now Vale), NC, on October 17, 1901, and died in August of 1986.

Vance Havner authored thirty-eight books, including *By the Way, That I May Know Him, Jesus Only, Pleasant Paths, It is Time, By the Still Waters, Peace Like a River, Consider Him, Rest Awhile, Road to Revival,* and *The Secret of Christian Joy*.

Havner held degrees from Catawba College, Wake Forest University, Moody Bible Institute, and Gardner-Webb College.

Havner's first pastorate was at Salem church in Weeksville, near Elizabeth City, NC. In the 1930s he entered full-time evangelism; he served the ministry of preaching the gospel for seventy-two years.

He was married to Sara Allred; they had no children.

HAYS, BROOKS

Brooks Hays was born in August of 1898, near Russellville, AR, and died October 12, 1981, in Washington, D.C. He married Marian Prather. They had two children, Steele and Betty.

Hays received a law degree from George Washington University. He was assistant attorney general of Arkansas, a member of the Democratic National Committee, a congressman from Arkansas to the House of Representatives, and a special assistant to President John F. Kennedy. Hays also conducted lectures at Rutgers University, the University of Massachusetts, and North Carolina State University.

Brooks Hays served as president of the Southern Baptist Convention. His published works include: *Hotbed of Tranquility: My Life in Five Worlds; Politics: An Autobiography; A Southern Moderate Speaks; This World: A Christian's Workshop;* and co-author of *Baptist Way of Life.*

HUDGINS, W. DOUGLAS

W. Douglas Hudgins was born May 4, 1905, in Estill Springs, TN, and died March 23, 1983, in Jackson, MS. He married the former Blanche Jones. They had three sons: Doug, Jr., Bob, and Jimmy.

Hudgins received the B.A. from Carson-Newman, the Th.M. from Southern Seminary, and a D.D. from Mississippi College.

Hudgins's pastorates included: New Providence, Lenoir City; Pleasant Hill, Lenoir City; Smyrna (now First), Smyrna, all in Tennessee. He was also pastor of First, La Follette, TN; Radnor, Nashville, TN; Broadway, Fort Worth, TX; and the First Baptist churches of Houston, TX, and Jackson, MS. In his early ministry he had also served as assistant pastor and educational director of Fifth Avenue church, Knoxville, TN.

Hudgins was a member of the Foreign Mission Board, the Southwestern Seminary Board of Trustees, the Executive Board of the Baptist General Convention of Texas. He closed out his career as executive secretary-treasurer of the Mississippi Baptist Convention Board.

JAMES, E. S.

E. S. James was editor of the *Baptist Standard* of Texas from 1954 to 1966. He pastored during the years preceding this editorship beginning in Oklahoma in 1923.

Born in Butler, OK, on March 1, 1900, James attended Oklahoma Baptist University and earned the B.A. from Southwestern Technological College in Weatherford, OK, in 1926. While he did not attend seminary, he was granted two D.D. degrees by Texas Baptist institutions, Howard Payne College, and Hardin-Simmons University. During his ministry, James committed himself to a self-study program making assignments for himself and often studying late into the night to meet his self-imposed goals.

E. S. James married Opal Clark at Leedy, OK, in 1925. They had two daughters and a son. James pastored churches at Leedy, OK, and Liberal, KS, as well as at Cisco and Vernon, TX. During those early years, he was school principal at Butler, OK, and superintendent of schools at Cheyenne and Hammon, OK.

Some of his credits include being chairman of the Texas Baptist Executive Committee and vice-president of the Southern Baptist Convention. In 1941 he preached the annual sermon at the Texas Baptist Convention.

James received several awards of merit. Among these awards was the 1960 POAU Annual Award. In 1963 he was presented the "Texas Baptist Elder Statesman Award" and in 1966 "The Good Citizen Award" from Texas Alcohol-Narcotics Education. The Christian Life Commission, SBC, presented him the Christian Life Commission Award in 1973.

"No one, including the president of the Southern Baptist Convention, wields as much influence with the . . . SBC as the *Standard's* balding, bespectacled editor, Ewing S. James," *Newsweek* magazine stated in its October 25, 1965, issue.

James was popular as speaker for conferences, revivals, and conventions. The 1952 *Texas Baptist Annual* was dedicated to him, highlighting his role as preacher, pastor, and denominational leader. He died April 26, 1976.

JOHNSON, C. OSCAR

C. Oscar Johnson was born in Anderson County, TN on September 23, 1886. He died in November, 1965. He was married to Rose L. Long. They had three children: Ralph, Frank, and Ruth.

Johnson earned the B.A. degree from Carson-Newman College and the Th.M. from Southern Seminary. He also studied at the University of Chicago. Many honorary degrees were given to him, including: D.D., Linfield College; D.D., Franklin College; D.D. Carson-Newman College; and LL.D., William Jewell College.

Johnson held pastorates at Newport Beach Church, Newport Beach, CA; South Park Church, Los Angeles, CA; Third Baptist Church, St. Louis, MO; and the First Baptist churches in Campbellsburg, KY, and Tacoma, WA.

Johnson held various offices. He was vice-president of the Southern Baptist Convention, 1948; president of the American Baptist Convention, 1932-33; president of the Baptist World Alliance, 1957-50; professor at Berkely Baptist Divinity School. He had numerous positions on the SBC and ABC boards.

LATIMER, LEON MOBLEY

Leon Mobley Latimer was born in Belton, SC on October 2, 1886. He died in Greenville, SC, July 17, 1958. He was the youngest of three sons of William Clement Latimer and Susan Josephine Mobley Latimer, both of whom were school teachers. Before the time of the public school system, individual communities financed their own schools and employed their own teachers. It was a precarious system, and teachers moved often. Thus Leon grew up in about a dozen small towns in South Carolina and Georgia. After working his way through Mercer University as mess hall manager, football team manager, and week-end preacher at a country church, he was graduated in 1908 (B.A.). From Mercer he went to Southern Seminary (1908-09) and Rochester Theological Seminary (1909-11, B.D.). Mercer conferred a D.D. degree in 1931 and Atlanta Law School the LL.D. in 1952. He received the Algernon Sydney Sullivan Award from Furman University and was elected honorary alumnus in 1953.

Latimer served as moderator of Flint River Association in Georgia (1925), trustee of Southern Seminary (1925-47), member of the Home Mission Board (1928-30), vice-president of Texas Baptist Convention (1932-34), president of Southern Seminary Alumni Association (1939-40), a member of the general board in Alabama, Texas, and South Carolina, and president of the South Carolina Baptist Convention (1951).

His pastorates included: First, Salem, OH (1911-13); First, Sylacauga, AL (1913-16); Parker Memorial, Anniston, AL (1916-21); First, Griffin, GA (1921-30); First, Austin, TX (1930-34); First, Greenville, SC (1934-52 and emeritus 1952-58).

On May 24, 1911, he married Mary Greer of Lafayette, AL. They had two daughters: Loulie (Mrs. Ollin J. Owens, after his death, William Robert Pettigrew): and Mary Sue (Mrs. James P. Wesberry). After the death of his first wife, Latimer married Emma Lenora Cooper of Laurens, SC, July 17, 1947.

In addition to his daughter, Loulie, he is survived by one granddaughter, Greer Owens Clayton, and one great-granddaughter, Susan Clayton.

LAWRENCE, JOHN BENJAMIN

John Benjamin Lawrence was born on July 10, 1873, in Rankin County, MS. He died September 5, 1968, in Atlanta, GA. He married Helen Alford. They had six children: John Hewit, Meriam Hoy, Katherine Alford, Elizabeth M., John B., Jr., and Helen Rebecca. His second was Helen Hurton.

Lawrence earned the B.A. and M.A. from Mississippi College. He was granted honorary degrees: D.D., Louisiana College, and LL.D., Oklahoma Baptist University.

Lawrence pastored churches in Greenwood, MS; Brownsville, TN; Humboldt, TN; Coliseum Place, New Orleans, LA; and First churches in New Orleans, LA, and Shawnee, OK. He served as editor of *Baptist Chronicle* and *Baptist Record*. He was president of Oklahoma Baptist University, vice-president of the Southern Baptist Convention (1916-17), a member of the SBC Public Relations Commission, a trustee at Oklahoma Baptist University, and secretary of the Home Mission Board of the SBC (1929-53).

Lawrence wrote a number of books including: *The Bible a Missionary Book; Biology of the Crow; Co-operating Southern Baptists; Hard Facts: A Christian Looks at the World; History of the Home Mission Board; Holy Spirit in Evangelism; Holy Spirit in Missions; Home Missions in the New World; Kindling for Revival Fires; Missions in the Bible;* and *Power for Service*.

LEAVELL, ROLAND QUINCHE

Roland Quinche Leavell was born in Oxford, MS, on December 21, 1891, and died while conducting a series of studies in the Gospel of Matthew at the First Baptist Church of Chattanooga, TN, on January 15, 1963. He married Lilian Forbes Yarborough on June 26, 1923. They had three children: Mary Delia (Bowman), Lilian Landrum (Fountain), and Dorothea Yarborough (Hudson).

Leavell received both the B.A. and the M.A. degrees from the University of Mississippi (1914) and the Th.M. (1917) and the Th.D. (1925) from Southern Seminary.

Leavell taught mathematics in the high school at Oxford (1911-13). From 1917-19, he served as secretary to the Overseas Young Men's Christian Association in France. He was ordained by Oxford First Baptist Church in 1913 and served as minister in the following churches: Oxford, MS, 1919-23; Picayune, MS, 1925-27; Gainesville, GA, 1927-36; and Tampa, FL, 1942-46.

In 1927 Leavell was Mississippi's member of the Foreign Mission Board. This was only the first of several positions in the Southern Baptist Convention. In 1929-30 he was vice-president of the Georgia Baptist Convention, and in 1929-36 he served as a member of the Home Mission Board, SBC, from Georgia, followed by superintendent of evangelism, HMB, 1939-42. As a member of the Committee on Evangelism of the Baptist World Alliance, he served as secretary, 1939-55, and as chairman, 1955-60.

Leavell was president of the New Orleans Baptist Theological Seminary from July 1, 1946, to May 1, 1958, when he was named president emeritus following a serious illness that forced his retirement.

Leavell's fifteen published books include the following: *An Unashamed Workman; Landrum Pinson Leavell* (1932); *Winning Others to Christ* (1936); *A Handbook for the Southwide Baptist Revival of 1939* (1939); *Helping Others to Become Christians* (1939); *Preaching the Doctrines of Grace* (ed.) (1939); *Saving America to Save the World* (1940); *The Romance of Evangelism* (1942); *Christianity Our Citadel* (1943); *Evangelism, Christ's Imperative Commission* (1951); *Corra Berry Leavell, A Christian Mother* (1952); *The Sheer Joy of Living* (1961); *Studies in Matthew: The King and the Kingdom* (1962); *Prophetic Preaching Then and Now* (1963); *The Apostle Paul, Christ's Supreme Trophy* (1963); and *The Christian's Business Being a Witness* (1964), published posthumously.

LEE, ROBERT GREENE

Robert Greene Lee was born in Fort Mill, SC, on November 11, 1886, and died in Memphis, TN, on July 20, 1978. He was married to Bula Gentry on November 26, 1913, in Greenville, SC. They had one daughter, Bula Gentry Lee King.

After working on the Panama Canal construction project to earn school money, Lee attended Furman University (B.A., 1913). He was awarded eleven honorary doctorates. He served as pastor of Red Bank Church, Saluda, SC, 1917; First, Edgefield, SC, 1918-20; First, Chester, SC, 1920-21; First, New Orleans, LA, 1922-25; Citadel Square, Charleston, SC, 1925-27; and Bellevue, Memphis, TN, 1927-60.

Lee was in great demand as a preacher and speaker. He traveled in every state of the US and to many foreign countries. He prepared fifty books of sermons and delivered his famous sermon, "Payday Someday," 1,275 times. It was also filmed and made into a sacred opera.

Lee was elected president of the Tennessee Baptist Convention four times in the 1930s, served as president of the SBC for three terms, 1948-51, and has had several memorials erected in his honor. These include the Lee Auditorium and the Lee Memorial Garden and Memento House at Bellevue Baptist Church, Memphis; Lee Chapel, Baptist Bible Institute, Graceland, FL; and Lee Memorial Library Room, New Orleans, LA. Two biographies were written about him, and he finally wrote his own memoirs, *Payday Everyday*, in 1974.

MATTHEWS, C. E.

C. E. Matthews was born March 23, 1887; died October 5, 1956. He was married to Nanan Mae Smith on December 24, 1910. Matthews lacked formal training for the ministry. He did not have a high school diploma or college training. Halfway through a seminary program (at Southwestern), he dropped out. He was granted an LL.D. by Baylor University. He did attend Hill's Business College in Sedalia, Missouri.

It is important to mention briefly his conversion experience. Neither he nor his wife were Christians when they married. His conversion occurred while reading the Bible with his wife when he was twenty-seven years old.

Matthews served the First Baptist Church of Fort Worth as their financial secretary. Soon after taking this position, he became education director. At that time, First Baptist of Fort Worth had the largest Sunday School program in the world. He was ordained at the First Baptist Church of Breckenridge in 1921. In the years that followed, Matthews pastored simultaneously the First Baptist Church of Birdwell and the First Baptist Church of Hurst. He became the pastor of Travis Avenue Baptist Church, Fort Worth, in September 1922.

Matthews served as a trustee for Southwestern Seminary for sixteen years; he was vice-president ten years, and president of the Board of Trustees for two years. Matthews originated the Southern Baptist "Simultaneous Revivals." There were many great revivals under his ministry. In the mid-1930s, Matthews led the state of Texas in massive programs for revival. He was committed to soul-winning. He was elected to the Home Mission board in 1947; he served as secretary of evangelism at the Board until 1956.

McDANIEL, GEORGE WHITE

George W. McDaniel was born in Grimes County, TX, on November 30, 1875. He married Martha Douglass Scarborough. They had a son, John, and a daughter, Mary. McDaniel died in 1927.

McDaniel attended a business college before entering Baylor in the fall of 1894. He graduated at the head of his class in 1898. Then he attended Southern Seminary, receiving the Th.B. while serving as supply pastor of the Central City Baptist Church, Louisville.

McDaniel served as pastor at Temple, TX, gaining state-wide recognition through a joint debate with the leading anti-prohibitionist of Texas. In 1902, he accepted a call to Gaston Avenue church, Dallas, serving there until 1905, when he went to First Baptist Church, Richmond, Virginia.

McDaniel was given a D.D. by Richmond College in 1905 and the LL.D. by Baylor in 1920. He wrote several books, including: *Our Boys in France; The People Called Baptist; The Churches of the New Testament; A Memorial Wreath;* and *Seeing the Best.*

MEIGS, PAUL AVERY

Paul A. Meigs was born in Brent, AL, on December 16, 1906, the son of Thomas Marvin and Hattie Avery Meigs. He died on July 17, 1987, in Jacksonville, FL. He married Margaret Beall on August 16, 1928. They had four children: Jane Adelaide (Mrs. J. W. Schaaf), Mary Paul (Mrs. Otis C. Wise, Jr.), James Thomas Meigs, and Joseph Avery Meigs.

Dr. Meigs was the first director of the evangelism department of the Florida Baptist Convention, where he labored for the Lord from 1957 until his retirement in 1970. At first he was director of evangelism and mission education and then became director of evangelism.

His churches included: County Line, Turkey Creek, LA; Vernon, Vernon, AL; Brownville, Heflin, AL; Commiskey, Commiskey, IN; Woodsonville, Munfordville, KY; Central, Atlanta, GA; Jefferson Avenue, East Point, GA; and Calvary, Berkeley, CA.

Educated at the University of Alabama (B.A. and M.A.), Southern Seminary (Th.B., Th.M.), and Golden Gate Seminary (Th.D.), he held many prominent denominational posts—member of the SBC Home Mission Board, member of the SBC Executive Committee, member of California Board of Directors and chairman of the Executive Committee (CA), and more.

He was honored with the D.D. by Howard College (now Samford University) and with the "Meritorious Service" award by Florida Normal and Industrial College. He wrote several doctrinal booklets for the Florida Convention, the Sunday School Board, and the Home Mission Board.

MOORE, H. GUY

H. Guy Moore was born in DuQuoin, IL, in 1909 and died on September 8, 1985. He was married to Myron O'Dell. They had four children.

Moore earned the B.A. from William Jewell College, the Th.M. from Southern Seminary, and was granted a D.D. from William Jewell.

Moore pastored three churches in Missouri: Leeds, Kansas City; Maplewood, St. Louis, and Wornall Road, Kansas City. He also served as pastor at Broadway Baptist Church, Fort Worth, TX, and Plymouth Haven Church, Alexandria, TX.

Moore was a member of the Board of Trustees at William Jewell and later served as president. He was chairman of the Committee of World Evangelization, SBC, a member of the Foreign Mission Board, a member of the Executive Board of the Baptist General Convention of Texas, moderator of the Tarrant Baptist Association, and president of the Fort Worth Minister's Alliance and General Pastor's Conference. He also served on the Board of Trustees of Mary-Hardin Baylor College and Texas Children's Home.

Moore contributed to the Baptist World Alliance Report, 1955. His other published works include *Christian Faith in Action* and *Magnifying His Church*.

MOORE, WALTER L.

Walter L. Moore was born near Quitman, LA, June 22, 1905. He died in Macon, GA, on January 6, 1978. He married Miriam McCall, and they had three children: Carol, Martha, and Walter L., Jr.

Moore earned the B.S. from Louisiana Polytechnic Institute. He also attended Southern Seminary and received a D.D. from Mercer University.

Moore served as pastor at the First Baptist churches in Waynesboro, GA; Cedartown, GA; Waycross, GA; and Meridian, MS. He was a missionary to Havana, Cuba, for four years.

He held several elected offices. He was vice-president of the Georgia Baptist Convention; a member of the Executive Committee of the Georgia Baptist Convention; Executive Committee member of the Southern Baptist Convention; and on the Board of Trustees at Mercer University.

Moore's published works included: *Courage and Confidence from the Bible* and *Outlines for Preaching*. For years *The Quarterly Review* published his sermon outlines.

MULLINS, EDGAR YOUNG

Edgar Young Mullins was born January 5, 1860, in Franklin County, MS. He died at noon on November 23, 1928, in Louisville, Kentucky. Mullins studied telegraphy at Texas A. and M. After pursuing this a couple of years, he decided to study law, but was shortly called into the ministry, and entered Southern Seminary in September of 1881. Later he took lectures in the Johns Hopkins University and the Newton Theological Institution. He spent a semester in lectures at the University of Berlin.

Mullins began to teach theology at Southern Seminary in 1899. He became president of the seminary and president of the Baptist World Alliance in 1923. He also served as president of the Southern Baptist Convention.

Mullins wrote a number of books. These are some of his most outstanding works: *Why Is Christianity True?* (1905); *The Axioms of Religion* (1908); *Baptist Belief* (1912); *Freedom and Authority in Religion* (1913); *The Christian Religion in Its Doctrinal Expression* (1920); and *Christianity at the Cross-Roads* (1924).

NEFF, PAT MORRIS

Pat Morris Neff was born near McGregor, TX, November 26, 1871, and died January 20, 1952, in Waco. In the last months of his life, he gave Baylor University his collection of papers and associated items integrating them as the Pat Neff Division of the Texas Collection.

Neff received B.A. and M.A. degrees in 1894 and 1898 from Baylor. The years between these degrees were spent teaching school in Arkansas and studying law at the University of Texas, where he received the LL.B. in 1897.

Neff practiced law nearly thirty-five years in Waco. He was county attorney of McLennan County, TX, 1906-12, a member of the Texas House of Representatives, 1901-05, and speaker of the house during the last two years, as well as leader of prohibition forces and state chairman of the League to Enforce Peace. In 1920, he was elected governor of Texas and served two terms. Neff led in the foundation of both the Texas College of Arts and Industries and Texas Technological College.

After his retirement from the governor's office, Neff returned to private law practice. In 1932, he became president of Baylor University. Neff was church clerk to his home church, First Baptist, Waco, from 1909 to 1918. He was president of the Texas Baptist General Convention from 1927 to 1928 and president of the SBC from 1942-46. His published works include: *The Battles of Peace, Making Texans,* and *Twenty-three Addresses.*

NEWTON, LOUIE D.

Louie D. Newton was born in Screven County, GA, on April 27, 1892. He died in Atlanta on June 3, 1986, at the age of ninety-four. He was married to Julia Winn Carstarphen on April 30, 1915, in Macon, GA.

After attending McPhaul Institute in Sylvester, Newton was accepted as a sophomore at Mercer University in 1910. He graduated in 1913 and became a history professor there. Newton earned a master's degree in journalism from Columbia University.

In 1919, Newton became publicity director for the $75 Million Campaign, the national crusade to retire debts of Southern Baptist Convention institutions. He became editor of *The Christian Index* in 1920. In 1929, he became the pastor of Druid Hills Baptist Church in Atlanta, continuing there as pastor until retiring on October 1, 1968.

Newton was president of the Georgia Baptist Convention and Southern Baptist Convention; vice-president of the Baptist World Alliance, president of the Atlanta Baptist Pastors' Conference and moderator of the Atlanta Baptist Association. He led in organization of Americans United for Separation of Church and State; he was named "America's Clergyman of the Year" in 1953; and he chaired the Southern Baptist Convention Finance Committee for twenty-five years.

Newton was a prolific writer and speaker. He wrote four books and penned weekly columns for *The Christian Index*. He had a weekly radio show.

PEARCE, J. WINSTON

J. Winston Pearce was born on September 2, 1907, and died on November 28, 1985, at Buies Creek, NC, where he was "Writer in Residence" at Campbell University.

Before his retirement he had been professor of preaching at Golden Gate Baptist Theological Seminary, Mill Valley, CA. He was educated at Wake Forest University (B.A.) and had attended Southwestern Seminary. He had done additional study at Yale and was recipient of a D.D. from Wake Forest.

He was married to the former Winnie Rickett. They had two daughters, Mrs. Patricia Dutton and Mrs. Paula Hinton, and one son, Perry Pearce. "Miss Winnie" followed him in death on June 21, 1987.

Pearce's pastorates included: First, Nevada, MO; First, Durham, NC; Seventh, Baltimore, MD; and First, DeLand, FL. He pastored for twenty-five years before beginning his teaching ministry.

He was a prolific writer of books, articles, and devotional materials. He was the writer for *Broadman Comments* from 1960-65. His books were: *A Window on the Mountain, The Window Sill of Heaven, I Believe, The Light on the Lord's Face, Say It with Letters, Paul and His Letters, Seven First Words of Jesus, God Calls Me, We Covenant Together, Come, Let Us Worship, Campbell College: Big Miracle on Buies Creek, Ten Good Things I Know About Retirement,* and *To Brighten Each Day,* a daily devotional book based on his previous writings.

He often spoke to writers' conferences, pastors' meetings, and at Baptist conference centers like Ridgecrest and Glorieta. He also wrote several articles for *Reader's Digest* and *Home Life* and many devotions for *Open Windows,* among other writings.

PETTIGREW, WILLIAM ROBERT

W. R. Pettigrew was born in Humboldt, TN, on June 30, 1900, and died at Louisville, KY, December 12, 1965. He married Mary Moody Yancey on September 4, 1920. They had two daughters: Mary Elizabeth (Mrs. Joe Madison King) and Ruth (Mrs. Lawrence Dillard).

His pastorates included Hazelwood, Louisville, 1924-27; First, Springfield, TN, 1927-36; Citadel Square, Charleston, SC, 1936-46; and Walnut Street, Louisville, 1946-65.

He received the B.A. at Union University and the Th.M. at Southern Seminary. Union later honored him with the D.D.

Pettigrew was highly evangelistic. In his pastorates, seldom did a Sunday pass without at least one person making a public commitment for Christ.

POLLARD, WILLIAM RAMSEY

W. Ramsey Pollard was born on February 15, 1903, and died on April 19, 1984. He had retired from the pastorate of the Bellevue Baptist Church, Memphis, TN.

Pollard attended Southwestern Seminary and received honorary degrees from Carson-Newman College (D.D.) and the Atlanta School of Law (LL.D.).

Before going to Bellevue, Pollard had been pastor of the Broadway Baptist Church, Knoxville, TN, for many years.

He was president of the Southern Baptist Convention for two terms, president of the SBC Pastor's Conference, a member of the Home Mission Board, the Radio and Television Commission, and the Executive Committee, SBC. He had also served as president of the Tennessee Baptist Convention.

POWELL, W. F.

W. F. Powell was born near Raleigh, NC, in 1878; he died in Nashville, TN, on June 5, 1959. He graduated from Wake Forest College in 1899 and attended Southern Baptist Seminary in Louisville, graduating in 1906.

Powell was pastor in Morgantown, NC; Roanoke, VA; Chattanooga First; Asheville, NC, First; and Nashville, First.

Powell served thirty-two years as president of the trustees of the Baptist Sunday School Board. Because of his special interest in young people he helped develop an outstanding program for college and university students. He was trustee of Peabody College and served on the boards of Belmont College and Baptist Hospital. He was a member of the Tennessee Historical Society and a Rotarian for thirty years.

ROBERTS, RAY E.

Ray E. Roberts died April 25, 1988, in Asheville, NC, and was born seventy-two years earlier about fifty miles from Asheville. Roberts was recognized for his ministry as executive secretary of the State Convention of Baptists in Ohio where he served from 1952 (as pioneer missionary for the first two years) until his retirement in 1980.

He and his wife, Margaret, had a daughter, Becky, and three preacher sons, Buddy, Roger, and Phillip.

When he arrived in Ohio from the First Baptist Church of Danville, Kentucky, there were only ten SBC churches in the state with a combined membership of less than 1,000 members. Under his leadership 500 churches were founded there, plus a number of congregations in New York, Pennsylvania, and West Virginia.

A gifted preacher, administrator, and organizer, he recruited preachers, promoted a pioneer area for Southern Baptists among denominational agencies, launched churches, led revivals, and preached all over the nation.

He preached the Convention Sermon in 1966, "The Unpaid Debt of

Southern Baptists" (included in this book). He served as president of the State Executive Secretaries' Fellowship on occasion; he was director of the North Central Mission Thrust in 1979, second vice-president of the SBC in 1966, and a member of the SBC Peace Committee.

Roberts was educated at Wake Forest University and Southern Seminary. He was awarded a D.D. from Georgetown College (KY). Early in his ministry, he had been pastor of South Ford Church, Winston-Salem, NC.

ROBERTSON, ARCHIBALD THOMAS

Archibald Thomas Robertson was born near Chatham, Pittsylvania County, VA, November 6, 1863, and died in Louisville, KY, on September 24, 1934. On November 27, 1894, Robertson married Ella Broadus, daughter of John A. Broadus. They had three sons: John Albert, Cary, and Archibald Thomas, and two daughters: Eleanor and Charlotte.

Robertson attended Boone Preparatory School in Statesville, NC until he was almost sixteen. He attended Wake Forest College from 1879 to 1885 and earned the M.A. degree. At Wake Forest, Robertson made 95 to 100 percent in every course and won medals in French and Latin, placing second in Greek.

Robertson was licensed to preach at age sixteen and preached his first sermon to a black congregation in North Carolina. He attended Southern Seminary from 1885 to 1888, receiving the Th.M. degree in May, 1888 and becoming assistant to John Albert Broadus, professor of New Testament and homiletics. He succeeded Broadus and continued in that position until his death.

Robertson began writing books at the age of 38 and ended at 70, including five grammars, fourteen commentaries and studies, six word pictures of the New Testament, eleven histories, and ten character studies.

SAMPEY, JOHN R.

John R. Sampey was born September 27, 1863, near Fort Deposit, AL; died August 18, 1946. He married Annie Renfroe on September 16, 1886, and after her death married Ellen Wood in 1926.

The president of Howard College, J. T. Murphee, visited the Sampey home on several occasions seeking John as a student; he entered Howard College on October 1, 1879. He obtained his B.A. in three years instead of

four. September 1, 1882, Sampey entered Southern Seminary. He graduated from Southern in 1885. In June 1887, Washington and Lee University
awarded him the D.D.; Sampey was twenty-three years old.

Basil Manly, Jr., taught him Old Testament interpretation; John A.
Broadus taught him New Testament interpretation and preparation and delivery of sermons; George W. Riggan taught Sampey Hebrew and Greek;
James P. Boyce taught him systematic theology, Latin, theology, and church
government and pastoral duties; William H. Whitsitt taught him church history and polemic theology.

Sampey served as a lesson writer for the International Lesson Committee
for forty-six years. During the years 1921-24, Sampey was absorbed in evangelistic meetings: he was in much demand in the United States and abroad as
a revival speaker. He was named president of Southern in May 1929. Sampey was elected president of the Southern Baptist Convention in the years
1935 and 1936: he narrowly defeated R. G. Lee. He served as a preacher for
sixty-seven years, professor of Old Testament Interpretation at Southern for
sixty years, and the president of Southern for thirteen years.

SCARBOROUGH, LEE RUTLAND

Lee Rutland Scarborough was born on July 4, 1870; died April 10, 1945.

Scarborough was born into the family of a Baptist preacher: his father was
George Washington Scarborough. His mother's name was Martha Elizabeth
Rutland. He had five brothers and four sisters; one brother and three sisters
died in infancy. He was married to Neppie Warren (born 1872). She was an
educated and gifted young woman. They were blessed with six children:
George Warren, 1901; Euna Lee, 1903; Lawrence Rutland, 1905; Neppie,
1908; Ada Beth, 1910; William Byron, 1912. All the children survived
childhood and made professions of faith at an early age.

Scarborough graduated from Baylor University and pursued further training at Yale University. At Baylor, he graduated with the B.A. degree in 1892.
The following year, he taught English in the preparatory department of Baylor. Moving from there to Yale, Scarborough received the B.A. in pre-law
studies in 1895. There Scarborough surrendered to the preaching ministry.
Entering Southwestern Seminary in 1899, Scarborough answered the fear
that he had long held—being called into the ministry. Later, he studied at
Southern Seminary.

He was licensed to the gospel ministry by the First Church Abilene, TX, on
June 26, 1886. His first pastorate was in Cameron, TX; he left this church
when his father died. After a time of study at Southern, Scarborough re-

turned to Cameron, then a married man. One year later he was called to the First Baptist Church of Abilene. Living on the plains gave Lee an opportunity to become an expert cowboy. He served five years in Cameron and seven years in Abilene.

In February 1908, Scarborough was led to begin the department of evangelism at Southwestern Seminary. For forty years, he engaged in one evangelistic meeting per month while maintaining his job as pastor and seminary president. Dr. Scarborough became president of Southwestern Seminary in 1915.

His books were: *Recruits for World Conquest, With Christ After the Lost, Endued to Win, Marvels of Divine Leadership, Tears of Jesus, Christ's Militant Kingdom, Holy Places and Precious Promises, A Search for Souls, How Jesus Won Men, Ten Spiritual Ships, Products of Pentecost, My Conception of the Gospel Ministry, A Blaze of Evangelism Across the Equator,* and *A Modern School of the Prophets.*

SEGLER, FRANKLIN M.

Franklin M. Segler was born in Ardmore, OK, on April 11, 1907, and his date of death is not known.

He was professor of Pastoral Ministry at Southwestern Seminary from 1951 until his retirement.

He was a graduate of Oklahoma Baptist University (B.A., 1930) and Southwestern Seminary (Th.M., 1938; Th.D., 1945).

He served as associate pastor of Polytechnic Church, Fort Worth, TX (1936-37); pastor of Carlisle Church, Henderson, TX (1938-40); pastor of First, Garland, TX (1940-45); and Emmanuel Baptist Church, Alexandria, LA, from 1945-51.

He authored a number of books, including syllabi on pastoral ministries and pastoral duties. One of his sermons was featured in *More Southwestern Sermons.* He wrote *Alive! and Past 65!, The Broadman Minister's Manual, Christian Worship: Its Theology and Practice, A Pailful of Stars,* and *A Theology of Church and Ministry.*

STORER, JAMES WILSON

James Wilson Storer was born in Burlington, KS, in 1884. He died in 1970.

Storer earned a B.S. from William Jewell College and received a D.D. from Union University, LL.D. from Oklahoma Baptist University, and D.D. from William Jewell College.

He served as pastor at the First Baptist churches in Pauls, OK; Ripley, TN; Paris, TN; Greenwood, MS; and Grover Avenue, Richmond, VA.

Serving in a number of elected offices Storer was a member of the Board of Trustees of Hillcrest Memorial Hospital, and president of the Board of Trustees, Oklahoma Baptist University. He was also vice-president of both the Tennessee Baptist Convention and the Oklahoma Baptist Convention. Later he served as president of the Oklahoma Baptist Convention and the SBC. He was also a member of the Foreign Mission Board of the SBC, Relief and Annuity Board, SBC, and Committee of Theological Education, SBC.

The published works of Storer include *Truth Enters Lowly Doors, By-Ways to Highways, Major Messages of the Minor Prophets, These Historic Scriptures,* and *The Preacher: His Belief and Behavior.*

THORN, FLOYD BRANTLEY

F. B. Thorn was born on August 13, 1895, in Mountain Home, AR. (The date of his death is not known.)

He was born to William Henry and Hannah (McPherson) Thorn. He was educated at Baylor (B.A.). Ten years later his alma mater bestowed the D.D. on him. He married Irma Rose Roller on September 9, 1918. He was ordained to the ministry in 1912.

He pastored First, Marlin, TX (1920-23); First, McAlester, OK (1923-27); Columbus Avenue, Waco, TX (1927-32); and Second, Houston. He was vice-president of the Baptist General Convention of Texas. He was a trustee of Mary Hardin-Baylor College and Memorial Hospital, Houston. He authored a book *The Higher Faith.* He was also a member of the Executive Board, Baptist General Convention of Texas.

TRUETT, GEORGE W.

George W. Truett was born May 6, 1867; died, July 7, 1944.

Truett was born in Hayesville, NC. His parents were Charles L. and Mary R. Truett. George was the seventh of eight children. Truett married Josephine Jenkins on June 28, 1894.

Truett spent ten years at Hayesville Academy and then began teaching in Georgia. He entered Grayson College at Whitewright wanting to become a lawyer; however, the church there asked him to speak to the congregation in the absence of the pastor—the church was then convinced he was called to preach. Without consulting him, the church called together the deacons to ordain him into the ministry. Truett attended Baylor in 1893-97.

Truett preached his first sermon at First Church, Sherman, Texas. As a student at Baylor, Truett also pastored the East Waco Church. Upon his graduation from Baylor, Truett received the call to pastor the First Baptist Church of Dallas Texas.

Truett was elected to many denominational offices. He was president of the Southern Baptist Convention in 1927, 1928, and 1929. He served as president of the Baptist World Alliance in 1934, after having delivered messages there in the 1911 and 1923 gatherings. He also served as a trustee for Baylor University; Southwestern Seminary, chairman, 1931-44; and Baylor Hospital in Dallas.

VAUGHT, W. O., JR.

Vaught was born in Versailles, KY, on January 16, 1911, and died in 1989 at Little Rock, AR. He married the former Mary Frances Bostick. They had one son, Carl.

Vaught earned the B.A. from Mississippi College, the Th.M. from the SBTS, and received a D.D. from Ouachita Baptist College.

Vaught was pastor of Bethany Baptist Church, Kansas City, MO; University Baptist Church, Abilene, TX; and Immanuel Baptist Church, Little Rock, AR.

He was a member of the Relief and Annuity Board, SBC; president of the Arkansas State Convention; member of the SBC Foreign Mission Board; president of the SBC Pastor's Conference; and first vice-president, SBC.

WEBB, PERRY F., SR.

Perry F. Webb was born in Ozark, AR, in 1897. His date of death is unknown.

He graduated from Ouachita Baptist College (B.A., 1919) and from Southern Seminary (Th.B., 1922). Honorary degrees were bestowed on him from Ouachita (D.D., 1934); Baylor University (D.D., 1945); and Howard Payne College (LL.D., 1958).

He was pastor of First, Malvern, AR (1922-25); First, Blytheville, AR

(1925-30); First, Pine Bluff, AR (1930-37); and First, San Antonio, TX, from 1937 until his retirement.

He was a member of the Mary Hardin-Baylor Board of Trustees; a director of the *Baptist Standard;* a chairman of the Board for San Marcos Academy; a member of the Executive Committee, SBC; president of the Executive Board of the Baptist General Convention of Texas; member of the Board of the Association for Blind and Texas Cradle Society, San Antonio. He also served on the mayor's Urban Renewal Committee, San Antonio.

He was the author of *Doves in the Dust.*

WHITE, K. OWEN

A native of London, England, K. Owen White was born on August 29, 1902, and died on July 12, 1985, in Tucson, AZ. He and his wife, the former Pearl Woodworth, and two children, Stanley Owen and Ruth Sampey.

In his early ministry he received a diploma from BIOLA University, Los Angeles, CA. Then he earned a B.A. from the University of Louisville and a Th.M. from Southern Seminary in the same year, 1932. In 1934, he earned the Ph.D. from Southern.

His pastorates in chronological order were: First, Santa Monica, CA; New Salem, Nelson County, KY; Central, Gainesville, FL; Kirkwood, Atlanta, GA; Metropolitan, Washington, D.C.; First, Little Rock, AR; and First Houston, TX, until his retirement. Then he worked as Metropolitan Missions Coordinator for Greater Los Angeles.

He served as president of the Southern Baptist Convention and also the Baptist General Convention of Texas. He held many other posts in the denomination: member of the Radio and Television Commission and chairman of the Executive Board of Texas Baptists, among others. His term as president of the SBC and the Baptist General Convention of Texas overlapped.

He wrote books and periodicals for the Baptist Sunday School Board for twenty-five years. His books included *Studies in Hosea* and *The Book of Jeremiah*.

WHITE, W. R.

W. R. White was born near Brownsboro, TX, on December 2, 1892. He died March 24, 1977, in Waco, TX. He was married to Edna Woods. His second wife was Catherine Tarwater. He later married Odera Mohr.

White received the B.A. degree from Howard Payne College and the Th.M. and Th.D. from Southern Seminary. He was granted a number of honorary degrees including: D.D., Howard Payne College; D.D., Baylor University; Litt.D., Hardin-Simmons University; L.H.D., University of Alabama; LL.D., Bishop College; and LL.D., Baylor University.

White served in pastorates at First Baptist churches in Goldthwaite, TX; Royse City, TX; Greenville, TX; Lubbock, TX; Oklahoma City, OK; and Austin, TX. He also served as pastor of the Broadway Baptist Church, Fort Worth, Texas. Moore was professor of missions at Southwestern Seminary, executive secretary of the Baptist General Convention of Texas, president of Hardin-Simmons University, editorial secretary of the SBC Sunday School Board, president, chancellor, and president emeritus of Baylor University.

White's published works include *Baptist Distinctives, Manifesto of Faith, Royal Road to Life,* and *That the World May Know*.

WILLIAMS, J. HOWARD

J. Howard Williams was born in Dallas, TX, in 1894. He died in 1958. He graduated from Baylor University, B.A., 1918; Southwestern Seminary, Th.M., 1922; and did graduate study from 1921-23 at Southern Seminary.

Williams was pastor of Trinity Baptist Church, Dallas, TX, 1914-18; chaplain, U.S. Army, World War I; and served overseas with the First Army Corps, 1918-19. Among other pastorates were Venus, TX, 1920-21; Middleton, KY, 1921-23; First, Sulphur Springs, TX, 1923-26; First, Corsicana, TX, 1926-31; First, Amarillo, TX, 1936-40; First, Oklahoma City, OK, 1940-46.

William served as executive secretary, Baptist General Convention of Texas, 1931-36 and 1946-53. He also was president of Southwestern Seminary, 1953-58; president of the Baptist General Convention of Texas, 1938-39; president, Board of Trustees of Oklahoma Baptist University, 1944-45; member, Executive Committee, Southern Baptist Convention for five years. He was a member of the Executive Committee of the Baptist World Alliance at the time of his death in 1958.

His published works include *The Importance of the Church to the Child* (1946) and *Stewardship in Action* (1948).

YATES, KYLE MONROE

Kyle Monroe Yates was born in Apex, NC, on February 7, 1895, and died on February 15, 1975, in Waco, TX. He married Margaret Webb Sharp on August 24, 1922. They had three children: Kyle, Jr., Jean, and Ellen.

Yates graduated from Wake Forest (B.A., 1916; M.A., 1917); Southern Seminary (Th.M., 1920; Th.D., 1922); and the University of Edinburgh (Ph.D., 1932). He was professor of Old Testament at Southern Seminary, 1922-24; distinguished professor at Baylor University, 1956-71; second vice-president of the SBC, 1955; one of the major translators of the *Revised Standard Version,* and a prolific writer.

He was ordained in 1916 and served as pastor in North Carolina and Kentucky, 1917-28; Walnut Street Church in Louisville, KY, 1942-46; and Second Church in Houston, TX, 1946-56.

Among his best-remembered books are the following: *The Essentials of Biblical Hebrew* (1938), *Preaching from the Prophets* (1942), *Preaching from the Psalms* (1948), *Studies in Psalms* (1953); *Preaching from Great Bible Chapters* (1957), and *Preaching from John's Gospel* (1964).

Bibliography

BOOKS

Allen, R. Earl, and Gregory, Joel. *Southern Baptist Preaching Today.* Nashville, TN: Broadman Press, 1987.

Angell, C. Roy. *Baskets of Silver.* Nashville: Broadman, 1955.

Bassett, Wallace. *A Star at Midnight.* Nashville: Broadman, 1942.

Bisagno, John; Chafin, Ken; and Others. *How to Win Them.* Nashville: Broadman, 1970.

Broadus, John A. *"Follow Thou Me."* Nashville: The Sunday School Board of the Southern Baptist Convention, 1919.

_____. *Memoir of James Petigru Boyce.* Nashville: Sunday School Board, 1927.

Campbell, R. C. *Keeping the Foundation.* Nashville: Broadman, 1946.

Carroll, B. H. *The River of Life.* Nashville: Sunday School Board, 1928.

Cauthen, Baker James. *Beyond Call.* Nashville: Broadman, 1973.

Clinard, H. Gordon. *Planting Trees You Will Never Sit Under.* Abilene, TX: Hardin Simmons U., 1977. Used by permission.

Dana, H. E. *Lee Rutland Scarborough.* Nashville: Broadman, 1942.

Dargan, E. C. *The Art of Preaching.* Nashville: Sunday School Board, 1922.

_____. *The Changeless Christ.* Nashville: Sunday School Board, 1918.

Dixon, A. C. *Through Night to Morning.* Grand Rapids, MI: Baker Book House, 1969. Used by permission.

Dixon, Helen A. C. *A Romance of Preaching.* New York & London: G. P. Putnam's and Sons, 1918.

Dobbins, Gaines S. *Encyclopedia of Southern Baptists,* Vol. I. 1958.

Eaton, T. T. *Conscience in Missions.* Louisville, KY: Baptist Book Concern, 1893.

Ford, W. Herschel. *Simple Sermons on the Great Christian Doctrines.* Nashville: Broadman, 1951.

Fletcher, Jesse C. *Baker James Cauthen: A Man for All Nations.* Nashville: Broadman, 1977.

Fuller, Richard. *Personal Religion: Its Aids and Hindrances.* Baltimore, MD: Innes & Co., 1873.

605

George, Timothy. *James Petigru Boyce: Selected Writings.* Nashville: Broadman, 1989.

Graham, B. J. W. *Baptist Biography,* Vol. III. Atlanta, GA. 1925.

Havner, Vance. *On This Rock I Stand & Other Messages.* Grand Rapids, MI: Baker, 1981.

Hill, John L., Ed. *Faith of Our Fathers.* Nashville: Broadman, 1942.

James, Powhatan W., Comp. *Truett Memorial Series: The Inspiration of Ideals.* Nashville: Sunday School Board, 1926.

King, Joe Madison. *A History of South Carolina Baptists.* Columbia, SC: South Carolina Baptist Convention, 1964.

Lawrence, J. B. *The Peril of Bread.* Nashville: Broadman, 1945.

Leavell, Roland Q. *Evangelism: Christ's Imperative Commission.* Nashville: Broadman, 1951.

_____. *Prophetic Preaching: Then and Now.* Grand Rapids, MI: Baker, 1963.

Lee, Robert G. *Pulpit Pleadings.* Nashville: Broadman, 1945.

Lowe, J. F., Ed. *The Southern Baptist Pulpit.* Philadelphia: The American Baptist Publication Society, 1895.

Matthews, C. E. *Life's Supreme Decision.* Grand Rapids, MI: Zondervan Publishing House, 1942. Used by permission.

McBeth, Leon. *Victory Through Prayer.* Fort Worth, TX: Rosen Heights Baptist Church, 1966.

McDaniel, George W. *A Memorial Wreath.* Dallas, TX: *Baptist Standard* Publishing Co., 1921.

_____. *Seeing the Best.* New York: Doran, 1923.

Mullins, E. Y. *Christianity at the Cross Roads.* Nashville: Sunday School Board, 1924.

_____. *Faith in the Modern World.* Nashville: Sunday School Board, 1930.

Mullins, Isla Mae. *Edgar Young Mullins: An Intimate Biography.* Nashville: Sunday School Board, 1929.

Pearce, J. Winston. *Seven First Words of Jesus.* Nashville: Broadman, 1966.

Robertson, A. T. *Life and Letters of John Albert Broadus.* Philadelphia: The American Baptist Publication Society, 1910.

_____. *Paul's Joy in Christ.* Nashville: Broadman, 1959.

Routh, Porter W. *Waiting in the Wings.* Nashville: Broadman, 1978.

Scarborough, Lee R. *The Tears of Jesus.* New York: Doran, 1922.

_____. *My Conception of the Gospel Ministry*. Nashville: Sunday School Board, 1935.

Thorn, F. B. *The Higher Path*. Grand Rapids, MI: Zondervan, 1937. Used by permission.

Turnbull, Ralph A. *A History of Preaching*, Vol. III. Grand Rapids, MI: Baker, 1974.

White, Douglas M. *Journey from Jugtown*. Grand Rapids, MI: Baker, 1977. Used by permission.

White, W. R. *The Royal Road to Life*. Nashville: Broadman, 1938.

Wilbanks, C. E. *What God Hath Wrought Through C. E. Matthews*. Atlanta, GA: Home Mission Board of the Southern Baptist Convention, 1957.

Yates, Kyle M. *Preaching from the Psalms*. Nashville: Broadman, 1948.

NEWSPAPERS

The Baptist Standard, Wallace Bassett, "Preaching to the Same People Year After Year," August 17, 1960, 8.

The Baptist Standard, Livingston Johnson, "Dr. J. B. Gambrell in North Carolina," January 22, 1914, 11.

The Baptist Standard, "E. S. James: Editor of Strong Convictions," May 5, 1976, 12-15.

The Baptist Courier, "Personal and Editorial," July 6, 1899, 5.

UNPUBLISHED THESES

(See acknowledgments in front of book.)